The Comple...

**PETER HENNESSY** is the author of a postwar trilogy: *Never Again: Britain 1945–51*; *Having It So Good: Britain in the Fifties*; and *Winds of Change: Britain in the Early Sixties*.

**ROBERT SHEPHERD** is a producer for radio and television. His documentary about the Foreign Office for Channel 4's *Dispatches* won Europe's Prix Stendhal.

# The Complete Reflections

*Conversations with Politicians*

Peter Hennessy and Robert Shepherd

Foreword by Melvyn Bragg

First published as two volumes in 2016 and 2019 by
Haus Publishing Ltd
4 Cinnamon Row
London SW11 3TW
*www.hauspublishing.com*

This first updated and expanded paperback edition published in 2020

A CIP catalogue record for this book is available from the British Library

These interviews were first broadcast on BBC Radio 4

ISBN: 978-1-912208-98-2
eISBN: 978-1-912208-99-9

Typeset in Garamond by MacGuru Ltd

Printed in the United Kingdom by Clays Elcograf S.p.A.

# Contents

# Acknowledgements

The authors would like to thank: Gwyneth Williams, former controller of BBC Radio 4; Mohit Bakaya, controller and former commissioning editor, BBC Radio 4; Martin Rosenbaum, executive producer of Reflections; our copy editors Paul and Polly Coupar-Hennessy; Barbara Schwepcke, founder of Haus Publishing; and Harry Hall, its managing director.

# Foreword

**Melvyn Bragg, on *Reflections, Volume II*, published in 2019**

Peter Hennessy has pulled off the triple! He is a distinguished academic in the crowded field of political commentary; in the House of Lords he is acknowledged, from his seat on the cross bench, as the gold standard in debates concerning constitutional matters – his views listened to almost reverently and widely discussed afterwards in the corridors and tea rooms; and here, in this book, he shows himself to have become a superlative interviewer of Those Who Rule Over Us!

From these compliments he may reel back in horror, but they are heartfelt and I've no doubt shared by all who know him. He is someone we attend to carefully, especially in our current constitutional turbulence.

This book consists of twelve interviews selected from his Radio 4 series, *Reflections*. The range is catholic, from Michael Heseltine to Margaret Hodge, Tony Blair, Sayeeda Warsi, Kenneth Baker, Harriet Harman, Michael Howard, Paddy Ashdown, Iain Duncan Smith, David Blunkett, William Hague and Vince Cable.

At first sight, the range can seem rather limited in that seven of the twelve are Members of the House of Lords. But none of them inherited the position. I would argue that, in the current disposition of Parliament, being in the Lords can be seen as not a limitation but an asset, above all a chance to speak freely and without constraint.

They have all had careers inside and outside politics which, as we can see in the interviews, have greatly enriched their views.

It is widely argued now that the perceived weakness, even mediocrity, of the House of Commons is directly related to the fact that so many of its Members have been professional politicians one way or another for most of their early adult lives – from student politics to political research to a safe seat, often parachuted in, largely untainted by contact with the outside world of hard knocks.

The Lords has a far broader span, and, despite its baggage of tradition, it conducts what to outsiders often seem to be more intensely informed and democratically driven debates than those of their masters in the other House.

Peter Hennessy is pitch perfect for the job he has set himself as an interviewer here. When the dust settles, what will be our enduring chronicles? It used to be the stories of kings and saints; it became the multi-volume hagiographies of the great and famous, men almost exclusively; now I would suggest the interview might prove to be the most enduring of all. It is vigorously various: snappy interviews; urgent interviews; hectoring, bludgeoning, interruptive interviews; sycophantic interviews; under-researched interviews... but at its best, as demonstrated in these pages, an interview can give, on television, but perhaps more especially on radio, here transferred to print, a portrait of its subject in a way which carries greater authority than anything previously attempted. The subject is not an object but an equal, and that brings a unique veracity. In the right hands, it can be the new First Draft of History.

Television seems to have the advantage. The human face, we are told by psychologists and film directors, can in itself without words transmit a cluster of impressions – is the face we see being honest or fake? Is it pretending to be modest? But what about that boastful imminent smirk? Is anger being held in, is passion being faked? There's no doubt that, as Ingmar Bergman said of his films, the greatest shots were always those of the human face, because it expressed so much more than anything else.

I suggest that radio at its finest can match and even surpass this. Partly because the paraphernalia of television, the cameras and the clutter in the making of a programme, is undeniably distracting, and vanity is teased and gets in the way. Few sane people enjoy being photographed for public consumption, and those who do strike a pose. Radio is a voice from outer space. The set-up is as simple as a sitting room. Peter Hennessy is there with one person, one microphone, a couple of chairs in a small and usually windowless studio, a table between himself and the politician – near perfect as an environment for trust. It is also an invitation to honesty.

But the trust has to be earned and the honesty has to be available. These interviews earn the trust of the interviewee and of the audience through the indisputable knowledge of the interviewer and his steady high purpose, his persistence to seek out the core. His questions are put with a gentle but steely persistence, and his subjects respond to that.

They know that they are with someone who respects their calling without needing to flatter their egos. Hennessy's method both reassures and spurs on his subjects. They know that what they say will be as good as they can hope to say in any public forum. They give a feeling to me that they are aware that they are on the record and they have to tell the truth.

I would be very surprised if most or all of them would fail to choose their *Reflections* interview as their most truthful chronicle.

And so we get Michael Heseltine scrupulously telling us the minutiae of his sometimes very lucky steps up the ladder. Hennessy allows Heseltine to be both playful and profound. There is a strong feeling of nothing being hidden. Without provoking self-congratulation, he is steered through the successful career which gave him such a formidable moral and financial reach. He is also endearingly rueful about why he did not finally make the top slot.

With Margaret Hodge, Hennessy is determined to track the difficult career she had and is full of admiration for it, but does not hesitate to take on the mistakes she made when, on Islington

Council, she did not by any means satisfy her own standards on the subject of child abuse: 'I was wrong. I was wrong.' I wish he could return to her for another interview now and we could hear her passionate, informed and despairing views on the Labour Party's anti-semitism.

Then there is Sayeeda Warsi. Her extraordinary life in a rigorous Muslim household, which included an arranged marriage for which she was taken to Pakistan, somehow through her own remarkable talents and drive took her to be Chairman of the Conservative Party. I feel in this interview that Hennessy's gentleness brings out a darker and more difficult side to her career than she usually wants to admit in public. The clues are there, and perhaps it is the fate of the pathfinder to meet the toughest opposition.

And on it goes.

For me, Paddy Ashdown was as revealing as I've ever heard him. His constant fear of seeming to claim too much for himself, his sense of duty – and, yes, neither of the men duck the transgression which briefly threatened to blemish his career.

With Tony Blair it was rather like a joust, but with both men in such prepared positions that, although blows were struck and well aimed, they were defended with the experience which has come from Blair's besieged life since the Iraq invasion.

# Preface

**Peter Hennessy and Robert Shepherd**

The series is over. Twenty-seven politicians interviewed over seven years between 2013 and 2019 on that choicest of mediums for thinking aloud, BBC Radio 4. What are our reflections on *Reflections?*

Firstly, that there is a touch of bravery about everyone who agreed to be interviewed; to allow us to eavesdrop on their lives even though, by becoming politicians in the first instance, they had placed themselves in the public sphere. A 45-minute conversation can be, we suspect, more daunting an undertaking than padding up for five minutes of choreographed combat on the question of the hour.

Why? Because it ranges from the formative early influences – family, place, schooling, the acquisition of values – through the tempest and dazzle of front-line politics to recollections in relative tranquillity about what it amounted to, what it was all for. There can be sadness for what might have been as well as satisfaction for what was accomplished, though several of our participants were still politically active and had good things to come.

Secondly, that there is something in what Disraeli declared: 'Read no history, nothing but biography, for that is life without theory.'[1] (What an interviewee he would have been, flitting from one aphorism to the next.) Both of us are historians, one of us is a political biographer, so reading history is a must for us. Yet biography can be the best way in – the door to past eras of British political life most

1 Benjamin Disraeli, *Contarini Fleming*, (Longmans, Green and Co, 1845), p113

easily opened for the young and the curious to enter. That is why we are so pleased that this Haus volume combines all the *Reflections* conversations in a lasting form. And our approach to shaping the interviews was to treat them as interim or mini biographies.

In making the programmes, we were conscious, too, of the rich tradition of interviewing largely, though not wholly, on the BBC-gold standards to which we could aspire but not attain. Above all, John Freeman's *Face to Face* series on BBC Television in the late 1950s and early 1960s[2] and Anthony Clare's *In the Psychiatrist's Chair* interviews on BBC Radio 4 in the 1980s and 90s.[3] These were shining examples of what that great BBC figure, Huw Wheldon, described as its mission to 'make the good popular and the popular good'.[4]

The *Reflections* interviews were conducted against the backdrop of a disturbed contemporary scene, generating political jet streams and storms that buffeted the shores of the country. These were aroused mainly but not exclusively by the 'European Question', which felled Prime Ministers, tore at the roots of our party political structures and placed a question mark over the very durability of the United Kingdom.

It was not an easy time for the BBC either. Times of political inflammation never are, as its pursuit of political impartiality often comes at the price of infuriating all sides (which is to the BBC's credit).

But if there exists a Valhalla to which old British politicians retire to refight long gone political battles, we hope that somewhere, tucked away in a corner, is a BBC studio with an interviewer and a producer waiting for anyone who wishes to pop in and reflect.

2 *Face to Face with John Freeman,* (BBC Books, 1989)
3 Anthony Clare, *In the Psychiatrist's Chair,* (Heinemann, 1992)
4 Quoted in Charlotte Higgins, *This New Noise: The Extraordinary Birth and Troubled Life of the BBC*, (Guardian Faber Publishing, 2015) p52

In the meantime, we owe a great deal to those who did come in and reflect for us. Each of them, in the philosopher/biologist Helena Cronin's phrase, was a walking archive.[5] It was fascinating, and it was fun.

5 Helena Cronin, *The Ant and the Peacock: Altruism and Sexual Selection from Darwin to Today*, (Cambridge University Press, 1991), p3

# Shirley Williams (Baroness Williams of Crosby)

Series 1, Episode 1, first broadcast 11 July 2013

**Born** 27 July 1930; **Educated** St Paul's School
for Girls; Somerville College, Oxford

MP (Labour) Hitchin 1964–79; Hertford and
Stevenage 1974–79; (SDP) Crosby 1981–83

Parliamentary Secretary, Ministry of Labour 1966–67; Minister
of State, Department of Education and Science 1967–69; Minister
of State, Home Office 1969–70; Secretary of State for Prices and
Consumer Protection, 1974–76; Secretary of State for Education and
Science, 1976–79. Deputy Leader, Liberal Democrats, House of Lords,
1999–2001; Leader, Liberal Democrats, House of Lords, 2001–2004

**Autobiography** *Climbing the Bookshelves,* 2009

### HENNESSY

With me today is that rarity: a politician with a gift for inspiring considerable respect across the parties, and a high degree of affection among the public, even when she espouses policies that do not inspire universal hosannas of approval. She's also a collector's item for being, over the span of her career, a powerful player in no less than three political parties: Labour, the SDP, and now the Liberal Democrats. Shirley Williams, welcome.

WILLIAMS

Thank you.

### HENNESSY

Shirley, you belong to a generation whose opinions were powerfully shaped by the Second World War and the events that led up to it, the slump and so on. When you went up to Oxford in 1948, do you think you were pretty well formed, as both a character and a political character, by then?

### WILLIAMS

Yes, I was born into a world where dreams were possible. It was a wonderful world. The war had been rough and tough, but at least it had broken down a lot of the old social class barriers, so that in the air-raid shelters or on the Tube you met a lot of people you wouldn't have met normally if it was the old middle-class structures of the 1920s and the 1930s, which were awful. That was the first thing that made me feel that I was somehow involved with people as a whole; I was one of them and they were part of me.

The second thing was an extraordinary sense of possibility. That was partly the nature of the Attlee government, which was absolutely full of stars, and what was brilliant about Attlee was he was a great cosmologist who could organise all these stars and get them to more or less work together. Most of them were driven by a really genuine wish to build a new society, they weren't there to get the odd sort of lobby position or anything of that kind, those things were rather rare at that time. So that was also very exciting: if you were a young person you could feel real commitment to your government, a real feeling of identification with it.

And the third thing I think was that we were plunged into a world which was no longer imperial but was very international. So great moments, like the sudden independence of India – and my family, which had been much involved in India, knew Pandit Nehru, knew some of the great figures like that – you suddenly realised you were entering into a completely new world, and a wonderful one.

So for all those reasons I remember having a feeling of almost total joy, and almost total compatibility when I got to Oxford, and that drove me through my three years in Oxford, which I found immensely satisfying, and very joyous. One of the reasons for that, I should add, is that of course about two-thirds of the men at Oxford – and there were very many men and very few women, one in eight were women – had gone through part of the war or all of the war, they were people who had been matured by their experiences and by the challenges they experienced. So it was to go to a very grown-up university, it wasn't a university which felt like an extension of school, as I'm afraid often they did, and do still, it was a university which was addressing the problems it was going to have to confront as it got out into the world outside the military forces, and that was also wonderful.

**HENNESSY**

I think you once said that the Attlee revolution was about the only revolution you could think of that hadn't devoured its own children.

**WILLIAMS**

[*Laughing*] Yes, that's correct! Indeed, far from devouring them, it actually gave them orange juice and various kinds of vitamin oils.

**HENNESSY**

I know you're a very optimistic person, but do you think you've been trying to replicate that glorious moment ever since? In many ways, because of the duress of Hitler, and the shared privations of the Home Front – an enormously well-organised Home Front for public purposes and warfare purposes – and the Beveridge Report, a new welfare system, and all the rest of it coming through, it's been downhill for one of nature's social democrats like you? You've had to live with many disappointments on the road from 1945 ...

**WILLIAMS**

That's true. I'm not somebody who spends a lot of time looking backwards; I hardly reminisce at all. I find when I wake up I think about what's going to happen this week, next week, years from now, but not much about where I was then. However, having said that, yes, there's something in what you say. I think in a sense, social democracy – which was a wonderful political movement – has probably almost reached the end of its potential. Why? Mainly because of globalisation. I was talking at a breakfast for doctors and medical people, and one of the things we discussed was whether the fashion for equality – equality of attitude and of status, very much part of a lot of legislation today – was no longer being applied to wealth and income. It was as if the feeling was that you couldn't do that, you couldn't get there. So we're looking at hugely growing inequalities, which I find extraordinarily painful to think about, and I suspect they're there as long as we don't come up with international answers. One example: I'm very strongly in favour of people dealing with things like tax avoidance, and all the rest of it; the trouble is, if you only have six tiny tax havens, you have the means of escaping from what democratic national governments can do. And I think it's taken me some time to think through how one could actually bring back social democracy, but it would have to be an international and no longer a national movement.

**HENNESSY**

Going back to the high water of those times, the 'never again' impulse, 'never again slump and war', the powerful motivation for your generation ... What about the politicians who you got to know through your remarkable mother, Vera Brittain, and your wonderful father, George Catlin? I mean you had a household in which the Herbert Morrisons of this world would quite naturally come through. You had great figures from the Labour movement who you knew from being a young girl, and who talked to you.

**WILLIAMS**

[*Laughing*] I think they felt it as an obligation to be nice to the child, the way you do, or did in those days. But I certainly remember meeting people like George Lansbury, who was a marvellously ideal figure, I mean somebody who was completely wrapped up in equality and peace and tolerance, and every good thing you could think about – but was not, perhaps for that very reason, a completely effective politician. I remember people like Herbert Morrison and Ernest Bevin being very dismissive of George Lansbury, who was the leader of their own party. The second thing, I think, was that we met a large range of people from what was still called the empire. It was just stopping being the empire, so they were people like Chief Lutuli from South Africa, and of course Nehru as I earlier mentioned, his sister, Mrs Pandit, and so forth – we met them all, and I think therefore that I imbibed from a very early age the feeling that the human race comes in rainbow colours, and that was terribly important. I didn't even have to think about it. The other thing I didn't have to think about as a result of my childhood was what I learned later, rather painfully, which was that, like it or not, women had for a very long time been seen as the second sex, and still to a great extent are. And I find as I get older, I get more and more irritated, when I try to take part in the conversation and I'm simply not there, and it's still true.

**HENNESSY**

Even now? Even for you?

**WILLIAMS**

Even now, even for me. But it's certainly diminished; it's not quite as universal as it used to be. But it's still there, sometimes.

**HENNESSY**

There was one side effect of this which you were very candid about in your memoir. You had a tendency to defer to men, right through, to some degree, not just these handsome young men back from the forces and so on, but Roy Jenkins your great friend, and perhaps Jim Callaghan and Harold Wilson too. You criticised yourself for being rather prone to thinking that the men are the big ones …

**WILLIAMS**

I think it was actually more manipulative than that. I learned early on that it was very difficult to get men to pay any serious attention to a woman who was a great deal younger than themselves. I learned therefore that the way to get their attention, and that didn't mean their physical or sexual attention, their intellectual attention, was in effect to be rather polite to them. Even sometimes a bit grovelling, you might say, when I was very young. And I found that there were very few men who were prepared to accept one's equality right away. One of those very few was Harold Wilson. I've always held Harold Wilson in quite high esteem because he was almost, I think, the only Prime Minister I've ever met for whom gender, religion and colour were totally irrelevant. He only minded about whether you were a decent politician, an able minister, and of course he wanted you to be a supporter of *him*, that's understandable, that's universal – but not on the grounds of race, colour or religion. He really didn't take any notice of them. And I think that was remarkable.

**HENNESSY**

You once came up with a wonderful piece of anthropology about the place of women in politics. I think you said that the men are only happy if they can categorise you into the dragon, the sexpot, the carer, or the chum.

**WILLIAMS**

That's correct. And I chose 'the chum' because that's the safest.

**HENNESSY**

And you were the chum, deliberately the chum.

**WILLIAMS**

I was deliberately the chum. I saw one or two of my colleagues fall on their swords in the pursuit of being sexpots, that's absolutely hopeless, no future in being a sexpot at all; for one thing you're going to get older, and you'll be an unsuccessful and unsatisfactory sexpot once you pass the age of about 45 or 50, which is exactly when you're likely to get positions of responsibility in politics, in the Cabinet or wherever. The chum thing was the easiest; for one thing it gave me a sort of non-sexual relationship to men, so I could be part of a group, which I often was. I remember being part of the Hattersley-Walden group very early on, after I first got into Parliament. The other thing I didn't much fancy was of course the sort of maternal roles, which was also part of what one might be. I think it was mostly the media that tended to see one in this light.

**HENNESSY**

The Education ministry, Social Security, those were the sort of jobs for senior women politicians?

**WILLIAMS**

Well, of course, and health.

**HENNESSY**

And health.

**WILLIAMS**

And what I longed for was something that was not typecast as a woman's job. Because I had a job at the *Financial Times* when I came into Parliament, I remember my maiden speech was about international financial relations. That's because I didn't want to be typecast as a 'woman's job' woman, and although I tried very hard to struggle away from that, of course I did actually end up with two almost archetypal women's jobs: Prices, and Education and Science, less so. Those two.

**HENNESSY**

They were your Cabinet-rank jobs.

**WILLIAMS**

They were my Cabinet-rank jobs, and they were what one might see as being the outstanding women's jobs.

**HENNESSY**

It could be an advantage though, Shirley, this chum side. I remember – leaping ahead a bit, to the mid-70s when Labour comes back with no majority in '74 – I was on *The Times* and my friend Ronald Butt, who was the conservative commentator on *The Times*, wrote a piece about you saying that it's not a particularly exciting government and the country's ill-at-ease with itself; but Mrs Williams is exempt from this, because she gives impressions to a wide swathe of people – and this is her appeal – that politics isn't the be-all and end-all for her, and she comes to a political meeting as if it were in-between bottling the fruit. That's what he said; it's always stuck with me. And it's sort of faintly patronising, but at the same time, he's on to something isn't he? That 'Shirley the Chum' meant Shirley who could embrace a large chunk of the political spectrum, albeit from left of centre.

**WILLIAMS**

Well, it's nice of him; I don't think it's quite accurate. First of all, I can't bottle fruit, I've never even tried. I'm not a bad cook, but bottling fruit, no, and for that matter, tapestry, no. Secondly, we should always add another bit to me, which of course relates to the theatre. I tried to be an actress at one time – I was an actress at one time – and I love reading poetry, and I love reading literature. And of course, because of my mother, I had a lot of links to authors. So I don't think it's quite right.

**HENNESSY**

But you were within an inch of becoming a world-famous Hollywood star, weren't you? Because when you were in America, evacuated in Minnesota for the first few years of the war, you were very close to becoming *National Velvet*, weren't you? The Elizabeth Taylor slot, that made Elizabeth Taylor the starlet she was and look what that led to.

**WILLIAMS**

Not just a starlet, but then the star! Well indeed, well what did it lead to: it led to seven husbands, which I think would have been very tiring; it led to a lot of jewellery, which I feel I would certainly lose, and not be able to find again; and I always thank God I didn't get the job!

**HENNESSY**

Going back to those big figures in the Labour party after the War; Clem Attlee was very hard to get to know; as Douglas Jay famously said, he never used one syllable where none would do. Very hard to chat with, Clem Attlee, I would imagine. But I think on one occasion you got him out of a hole, didn't you? Wasn't it some grand eastern district Labour Party conference in the 50s when you were a young candidate?

**WILLIAMS**

Yes, he was being terribly boring about China. I think he'd decided to be sort of semi-academic, so he was talking for something like 50 minutes about China, which was not really very high in the salience of most British voters at that time, so the chairman slipped me a note which simply said, 'For God's sake, do something', because by this time, the East Anglian ladies were doing something which you always did when you weren't listening to the speaker, which was to start knitting. And there was a front row which consisted of East Anglian ladies, all knitting.

**HENNESSY**

Clackety clacking!

**WILLIAMS**

Quite loud, yes. So I thought, well I've got to do something. Luckily, I had a friend, Val Arnold-Forster ... she was an intern in Parliament, she spent her time digging out people's waste-paper baskets, and she'd found in one waste-paper basket, in Attlee's office, a poem, which she handed me, and I thought, in desperation, I'll read that poem out. And I remember, it went like this: *In Limehouse, in Limehouse, before the break of day, I hear the feet of many men that go upon the way, That wander through the city, The grey and cruel city, Through streets that have no pity, Through streets where men decay.* It was a tribute to his time at Toynbee Hall, and of course what it said suddenly was, this is a man of very strong emotions, who isn't going to express them to you, who's going to keep them to himself, who's an officer and a gentlemen, and therefore very short in what he said. But underneath all that is this deep socialist heart, beating away, and the audience went up in rapture. They were so thrilled that afterwards the Chairman said, would you like to meet Mr Attlee? And I said, 'That would be wonderful'. So we went down. And I'd said that the poem was written in 1912. And all Attlee did was look at me and say, '1911, actually'. [*Hennessy laughs*]

**WILLIAMS**

And that's all he said.

**HENNESSY**

But you'd silenced the knitters ...

**WILLIAMS**

I'd silenced the knitters, but not aroused Mr Attlee.

**HENNESSY**

Harold Wilson brought you on very quickly. You win Hitchin in 1964, and Labour comes back with a very small majority. But Harold, within a few years, makes you a junior minister, and also obviously rated you very highly because you were one of the most rapidly promoted of the new intake, weren't you?

**WILLIAMS**

That's true; but it's also true that he wanted to make a point, that 'I'm open to young people of ability regardless of their sex'. And that was quite an important part of it. I think he would have probably promoted me somewhat slower if I hadn't been a woman. It was an advantage, not a disadvantage.

**HENNESSY**

I think too, you've very nearly resigned quite early on, didn't you, over the Kenyan Asians.

**WILLIAMS**

Harold Wilson once said to me that one of his backbench colleagues came to him and said, 'Shirley Williams will probably resign on this issue'. He said, 'That's all right, I've got a wardrobe full of resignation letters.'

**HENNESSY**

From you? You'd actually sent him a lot of resignation letters?

**WILLIAMS**

Not lots, but about four. One of the big ones was as you rightly say the East African Asians. I just couldn't stomach that. I thought it was completely absurd to break the promise that had been made to them quite openly by Duncan Sandys, who was Commonwealth Secretary, and by Iain Macleod, who was the Colonial Secretary, and both these men had gone out at the time of Kenyan Independence, and made an absolute pledge that anyone – probably a Kenyan Asian, presumably a Kenyan white also – who wanted to come to Britain, had the right of abode here. And that meant they couldn't be stopped by the Home Office, who like stopping people coming anywhere. So they then broke it. At least Macleod did not break it, but Duncan Sandys openly broke it and said, 'We can't possibly consider these people'. And I remember Jim –

**HENNESSY**

Jim Callaghan was Home Secretary.

**WILLIAMS**

Yes, and I think he felt two things, really. One was – it was the immediate aftermath of Powell making his 'Rivers of Blood' speeches – so he certainly feared the possibilities of a really major racial clash in the main towns of England, particularly the north of England. And secondly he thought it was bad politics. I was very angry with him. I thought, we have made an obligation, we have a promise, we've got to make it to these people. But I then said to Jim, look, you won't agree to having a whole lot right away; may I suggest we ask people to queue a bit, and I will go to India, and see the Foreign Secretary, and ask him if he will allow people to queue in India, who would then move in a year or two, when things had calmed down, to England. And he said, well you can do what you like. So I went to India, and I saw the Foreign Secretary, Swaran Singh, and I always remember he said, 'Oh, that's quite all right, my dear. We're such a big country we'll hardly notice them, but you have to keep your promise over the next few years'. And I came back triumphant, with the feeling that at least I'd made some difference. And I think over the next three or four years almost all the East Africans who wanted to come, particularly those from Uganda, managed to get here, and ever since then I felt terribly pleased about that particular aspect of my career.

**HENNESSY**

I think you liked being a Minister. Most of the senior civil servants always enjoyed working with you. And you enjoyed working with them.

**WILLIAMS**

I did, I like civil servants. I'm passionately against Francis Maude's mad idea of letting ministers appoint their own civil servants, because frankly I've seen America and although there are many things about America I admire, one of the worst things is the appointment of the first two or three layers down, because it means you begin to lose any sense of what it is to be part of a national community, and you don't get the right advice. Because you've appointed them you get advice which you want to hear.

**HENNESSY**

So it would end speaking truth under power, which is the great tradition of British Crown Service.

**WILLIAMS**

Well, it's not always unmitigated truth, but it's a sort of ... civil-service truth, which is not quite the same thing. But it does mean they will actually say to you, 'Excuse me, minister, this won't go down well, or this will not work, or we can't bring this about, or we can't deliver it', and I respect that. I think they are very good, and frankly I'm very sad to see the way in which special advisers are beginning to replace civil servants at the top, because I think special advisers, with a few exceptions where there is a great technical issue, such as with nuclear weapons, are basically not a good idea. I'm sorry, I'm very old-fashioned about that. I think, experts, yes, and I think, advisers maybe; but special advisers whose full-time job is advising, and then taking over from the minister – not much democracy, in my view.

**HENNESSY**

Can we talk a little bit about personal life, because by the time the Labour government fell in 1970, you'd risen rapidly through the ranks with a tremendous workload, and yet you were a young mother, and you were married to the brilliant philosopher Bernard Williams, who I only met once or twice but who was the most captivating, mercurial man.

**WILLIAMS**

Yes.

**HENNESSY**

Riveting to talk to.

**WILLIAMS**

He was like an intellectual dragonfly, every colour you can imagine, and he hovered around ideas, picking them up beautifully. He was an astonishing man.

**HENNESSY**

But I think you described in your memoir how 1970 was your year of catastrophe, the government fell and your marriage broke up. The price politicians pay in terms of family life can be immensely high and that year is searing on the page in your memoir.

**WILLIAMS**

It's still searing in my life. I was devoted to Bernard, he was a sort of tremendously colourful personality, tremendously attractive to women, and he didn't always find that resistible. I couldn't really blame him, he fell in love with somebody else, and he genuinely fell in love with them. But it was very tough. I remember it was very tough on my child, and it was very tough on me. And of course if you're a woman, you are particularly exposed. The media are fascinated, to this day, by women politicians and particularly by women politicians' private lives. You would see journalists sitting in trees when you drove home, and you'd see them poking about your garden when you tried to go into your house. And in some cases, which was worse, sitting at the school wall, asking teachers how my child was getting on, and how she was reacting to all this and so forth. So, no, it is very tough, there's no doubt about it, and it's not getting easier – it's probably getting worse.

**HENNESSY**

The 70s become increasingly tough politically for you, too. The European virus begins to eat deeply into the Labour party. It's been the Conservative party recently that's been three yards away from nervous breakdown on Europe, but in the 70s it was your party. And Roy Jenkins resigned over the referendum question and so on … it was all very tough. And at the very moment we went into the Community in 1973 … it's been one of the great motivators for you in life, in your political life –

**WILLIAMS**

Oh yes. Absolutely.

**HENNESSY**

I remember seeing the old film of Harold Macmillan on your arm, on the very day we entered the Community in January '73, going across Parliament Square with young people there celebrating.

### WILLIAMS

With bonfires. It was just like the First World War. Bonfires all over Parliament Square, made by the young people with screwed-up newspapers and things of that kind. And I remember Harold Macmillan sniffing the air which smelled unusually of bonfires, of burning wood, and I could see him literally move from my eyes back to Arras and Mons and away from Parliament Square, and you could suddenly see how the whole story of his life had culminated in this moment: when at long last the First World War and the Second were going to be put for ever behind us all. And it was, for him, a kind of renaissance almost, a sort of rebirth.

### HENNESSY

I think he said, 'Never again, never again' to you, didn't he, as he walked across the square.

### WILLIAMS

He did, he did. Not as a question. As a statement.

### HENNESSY

No more war – Europe's cracked it in that sense. Looking back, Shirley, your generation did sing a song of Europe. You always have sung a song of Europe. And yet, here we are, deeply scratching at ourselves, the emotional deficit with Europe is absolutely palpable. I mean, who knows how a referendum will turn out, if indeed we have one in the next few years. But that song of Europe, it isn't the dominant strain any more, is it, within the national family. It just isn't. That must be a real pain for you.

### WILLIAMS

I think it's a pain both ways. First of all, one has to say that the Europe we were talking about is not quite the same Europe we have now. The coming in – in a way a wonderful achievement – of the whole of Eastern Europe into the European Union was the culmination of the whole idea of a united Europe. On the other hand it brought with it people who had rather shaky ideas of what democracy means, not very strong senses of accountability – look at Hungary, and look at, for example, Bulgaria. It became almost entirely an economically centred community; that was partly, I'm afraid, Mrs Thatcher, who was only prepared to go ahead on the single market, and really never saw the point of political union, and that undermined any move towards democracy. And I have to be honest and say also that the Commission no longer has as its stars – rather like what you were saying about the Attlee government of 1945 – men and women who are capable of reaching out across the whole of the continent, and giving people a sense of belonging to that continent. Whereas I think when you look back to people like Brandt, or Schmidt, or for that matter Delors, you're looking at great men, and I would say one or two great women too, who have passed from the scene, who had a really huge vision.

For me, I think the other side of that is the United Kingdom itself. It's always had a lasting sickness about no longer being the head of the empire, which has been brilliantly handled by the Commonwealth concept and the Queen and all the rest of it ... brilliantly handled. But because it's been so brilliantly handled, we've never really quite faced up to the fact that we're no longer a great power, and we *are* no longer a great power – we can only be an influential power if we are part of a bigger unit than ourselves.

**HENNESSY**

So you think there's an emotional overhang from the imperial days, the great-power days, indeed superpower days, in some people's memory.

**WILLIAMS**

I do. It does mean that people still, particularly older people, find it hard to adjust to Britain's actual position, and to recognise, to put it bluntly, that if we actually walk out of the European Union, in my view we will count for almost nothing. We will go to the edges of the football ground, and be watching and shouting and no doubt barracking, but we won't be part of the match. I think that's terribly dangerous, because I think there are real contributions that Britain can make, and I think Britain as a country will eat its heart out if it has no international role any more. It's a country like France, which has an international sense. But if we go out of it, we're going to be a bad-tempered, small, deeply disappointed country.

And one other thing to say: I travel a lot, as you know, and when I've gone to places like China, South Africa, the United States – all three are totally puzzled about why we should think of getting out of the European Union. They understand the Euro-zone was badly handled. It was a foolish ideal; it might have worked if they had laid down conditions at the beginning, but they never did, so they have the Greeces and the Spains coming in without beginning by saying, 'These are the things you have to achieve before you can come in'. All that was a big mistake, but it's not a reason to get out of the Union. The Union still stands there, and I think it's absolutely critical. And I think therefore that the attitude of quite a lot of people, particularly the right-wing of my sister party over there, in the Coalition, really have got it terribly wrong, and I wouldn't even say any more – which really is painful – that the idea of any kind of conflict within the European Union itself is completely unthinkable. And that was certainly true for 50 years, a good long time to not have any wars in the Union part of Europe.

#### HENNESSY

Going back to Labour in the 1970s. You become Secretary of State for Education. Labour has very strong views on comprehensive schools, and you've been a great supporter of comprehensive schools. Do you not think they should have been more of an experiment, rather than the single model? Some of them became very big, certainly in urban areas, with the ending of streaming for example in many of them, and the ladder of opportunity for working-class kids, grammar-school kids, was considerably diminished. That's the criticism of what you did as Education Secretary, as you know.

#### WILLIAMS

Yes, OK, well first of all, I promoted the idea of a core curriculum, but not the complete curriculum, which Mr Gove has today. In other words about 50 per cent of the comprehensive school would be devoted to key subjects like Maths, English Literature and English Language and so forth. But the other 50 per cent – which is *much* more than today, much more – would be a matter for the school to promote and put forward what they thought was a proper curriculum for the kinds of kids that went to their school, for the kind of areas in which they lived, and so forth. In other words it retained a certain element of closeness to local authority. I didn't and don't agree with the idea of flinging the local authorities out altogether; I think it means you have, in the end, much more uniform kinds of schools than you would have had if you'd retained them, and I deeply disagreed with Ken Baker, in the 1988 Act.

#### HENNESSY

With his great Education Reform Act.

#### WILLIAMS

The great Education Reform Act, which booted the local authorities virtually out completely. I think that was a big mistake, and oddly enough, it doesn't fit very well with 'localism' as a concept. I secondly thought – apart from the idea of only a core curriculum, not a total curriculum – I also retained and fought for the right of schools to choose to be single-sex rather than co-educational, thinking partly of the arrival of our friends, the Muslims from East Africa. Most of them would not have sent a girl to a co-educational school at that time.

### HENNESSY

And Asia too, not just East African Muslims.

### WILLIAMS

No, of course not, so that's just one example. I very strongly believe therefore that people should be able to opt for single-sex. I believe that we should retain the church schools, the faith schools, as another alternative, including, if they want it, Muslim and Jewish schools. I believe there should be a good deal of autonomy for the schools, but not the kind of autonomy we've got today. I have to say I'm very, very dubious about the academy experiment, partly because I think it will almost inevitably lead back to selection in some form or other, not necessarily exam selection, but other kinds of selection. And on the third point: yes, of course it's true that there were some brilliant direct-grant schools, and one or two very good grammar schools, which is why places like Durham didn't want to go to comprehensive very much.

### HENNESSY

Which is a Labour authority …

### WILLIAMS

It's a Labour authority, yes. But the sheer number of youngsters today who went to comprehensive schools and who have come up to me at opera houses and choral schools and technical laboratories and so on, and said, 'I went to comprehensive school and now I *am* X, Y, Z', always makes me feel that it was right, because people tend to forget two things. One was that in most counties or shire education authorities, not more than about one child in eight or 10 ever went to grammar school.

### HENNESSY

Some were higher: a quarter.

## WILLIAMS

Some were. But some were even lower. I mean if you look at some of the Midland schools, you'd be lucky to get nine or 10 per cent going to a grammar school. None of them I think exceeded 25 per cent. And the other critical statistical point to make is that the transfer of youngsters who emerged from their primary school and began to blossom to grammar schools was tiny. One and half, 1 per cent a year. So, really, an awful lot of youngsters simply didn't have an opportunity, and I thought they should have, and I think they've actually made a great deal out of that opportunity.

Now, add two things to that: one is, we've never gone for the kinds of really advanced forms of training of teachers like that, for example, in a totally comprehensive country like Finland, now the best in the whole of the OECD world, by quite a wide margin over all other countries: totally comprehensive. But what they've done is to put their money into getting their teachers up to an MA or even a DEd status. Being a teacher in Finland is a very impressive thing to be. We've squabbled, we've fought, we've had divisions between unions and the executive – but we've never really given teachers the status that they ought to have. And even now, with Mr Gove, the status goes to the headteacher, but it doesn't really go to the teacher. And that's where you really need to have in-service training and all the rest of it, to make the teacher a very special person.

### HENNESSY

The Labour government, in which you were a very senior Cabinet minister by the end, you chaired all sorts of Cabinet committees as well as doing the Education job, ended in the wreckage of the Winter of Discontent and a Labour civil war that was already under way before the government fell, and Mrs Thatcher came in. In the civil war again you were in the epicentre, because you were on the national executive committee of the Labour Party, where it was fought out in brutal terms.

**WILLIAMS**

Correct!

**HENNESSY**

It must have been absolutely frightful.

**WILLIAMS**

It was perfectly horrid. Quite a lot of the time the national executive was directed primarily against poor old Jim Callaghan, who I actually think was quite a good Prime Minister, and quite a popular Prime Minister, and actually ran miles ahead of the party in the 1979 general election, a fact that the far left didn't take too much notice of. But he was put up almost as a cockshy; a lot of the executive motions were directed against the previous Labour government, almost as if it would have been better not to have had it. The other thing that was very central, and I think completely crazy, was the concept of the Trade Union Advisory Committee. I would say exactly the same thing, by the by, about big banks today. I don't think that major groupings in a society should have the ability to dictate to government what it should do. Of course they get to try to influence it.

**HENNESSY**

Trade Union power was excessive by the end of '79, you think?

**WILLIAMS**

Oh yes, much earlier than that, because you had the Trade Union Advisory Committee, which actually looked at every piece of legislation that was about to be put forward.

**HENNESSY**

That was 1974, yes.

**WILLIAMS**

And that was Wilson's attempt to try and keep them on board. But it was constitutionally, I think, very bad. And I would say exactly the same thing the other way round: you've got the influence of banks and big manufacturing and so on. And I could see that Labour was destroying its electoral base, and beginning to actually open the door to attitudes which had very little to do with democracy.

**HENNESSY**

But it tore into you, leaving the Labour party, because you loved it, didn't you. I think you said it was like drawing your own teeth.

**WILLIAMS**

It was, yes.

**HENNESSY**

I think you and Bill Rodgers of the four (with David Owen and Roy Jenkins) were the ones who felt that most powerfully.

**WILLIAMS**

Oh yes, we felt it much more strongly.

**HENNESSY**

You were flesh of the Labour movement's flesh, Shirley, really, weren't you?

**WILLIAMS**

That's right. And family of the family. Oh, absolutely. And I think both David and Roy, for other reasons, had shifted away from it some years earlier. I mean still quite a lot of me is still a social democrat, I can't deny it.

**HENNESSY**

I'd have thought every particle of you was, to be honest. [*Williams laughs*]

**WILLIAMS**

Yes, but there are things that my dear coalition does that I find quite hard to swallow down.

**HENNESSY**

We'll come back to that in a minute. But you make the break with the Gang of Four; the dear, sweet Michael Foot, who you loved dearly, was leader by this stage and begged you to stay, but you couldn't – you had to go in the end, didn't you …

**WILLIAMS**

Michael was a wonderful advocate and a wonderful writer; I don't think he was actually a natural political leader. He was a lovely man, no doubt. But as a political leader he probably didn't have the capacity for coming to terms with power in the way that, for example, Jim and also Harold had. So I don't think he would have ever actually managed to pull Labour out of this terrifying downward spiral it was going through. No, we had made our mind up by that time, so we had to stick with it. Though I should add to that, as you probably know Peter, that our last hope was Denis Healey – so many people's last hope. If he had won the election for leader, I think I would certainly have stayed for a bit longer, and then tried to back him and turn the Labour party back to what I regarded as its major job.

**HENNESSY**

You gave up in effect – when you went off with the so-called Gang of Four – your chance of becoming a Prime Minister, Shirley, because you were talked of as a Prime Minister. For a while, you were ahead of Mrs Thatcher in people's betting on who would be the first woman prime minister in the UK.

**WILLIAMS**

[*Laughing*] Well, two things. First one, you're quite right: I did give it up, and I realised that it would never happen. But also, I never had the simple targeting of purpose that she had. That's very important. She knew exactly what she wanted to be, and what she wanted to do, and she stood on a lot of people on her way. I think I was always more comfortable as a member of a team than as the single leader, whereas in her case she was much more happy being the single leader than being a member of the team. So it's partly psychological. I don't blame anybody for my not being prime minister except myself.

**HENNESSY**

You said of Michael Foot that he didn't have the necessary brutality to be prime minister.

**WILLIAMS**

Yes.

**HENNESSY**

Just simply not tough enough. Do you think that applies to you as well?

**WILLIAMS**

Probably.

**HENNESSY**

So no regrets?

**WILLIAMS**

[*Pause*] No –

**HENNESSY**

Not making it to Number 10?

No, no regrets.

There's a conventional wisdom about the impact of the SDP-Alliance, what became the Liberal Democrats, through the various mutations. One is, that by splitting the centre-left vote, you handed the bulk of the '80s to the Conservative Party, and indeed the early '90s. And the other is that you paved the way for Tony Blair, you so shocked the Labour Party that it was forced to modernise. That you were a catalyst, though you never actually got the commanding height, or even got anywhere near sharing the commanding heights with the two big parties. Now those are the conventional wisdoms, as you know, about the impact of what you and Bill Rodgers and David Owen and Roy Jenkins and the others did. Now what's your reading of all that?

OK, the second one is quite right, your second proposition which is that we, unknowingly, if you like paved the way for Tony Blair. That's true. The Labour party got in total despair about its inability, after three elections, all lost, to get back to government again. They were prepared to swallow down – in a way, I never thought they would – a wine bottle with a quite different wine inside it. It still had the name, 'the Labour party', but it was a totally different kind of Labour Party. It wasn't even social democrat, it was sort of half way to being Christian Democratic, it wasn't a party of the far left of centre or even the middle left of centre; it was the centre, really.

I think in the case of the first proposition, it's not true. If you look at the way in which voting broke down, a substantial number of people in the income groups that normally vote Conservative – a substantial number, not a majority, but a substantial minority – moved away from the Conservative party, partly because these were people who were anti-Thatcherite. They tended therefore to move to the SDP, because the idea of going to what was a very left-wing Labour party was unthinkable to them. So I reject that one. The second one I think is fair, and people like me have to live with that consequence – which wasn't all bad in some ways.

**HENNESSY**

Why didn't you rejoin the Labour Party?

**WILLIAMS**

Oh, really, I mean partly because ... [*laughing*]. First of all, I didn't think it was a social democratic party, in a funny way. Let me take one example, there's no time for many. It had a very bad record on civil liberties, in my view; it was over-run by the Home Office; it was not particularly good on prisons, and I had been a prison minister for a while; it was not very good on civil liberties – it was quite good on race, but it wasn't good on the basic freedoms that I believe are part of what the social democrats were all about. So that was a very central reason why I didn't rejoin it.

**HENNESSY**

Coming to the Coalition, where we now are. Watching you in the House of Lords, as I do quite a bit, because I sit opposite you pretty well, it seemed to me, on the Health and Social Care bill that it was a real strain for you, because you're a child of 1945, believe in the '48 version of it, free at the point of delivery, which we all sign up to, but in that Health and Social Care bill – which you spent hours on, Shirley –

**WILLIAMS**

Hours.

**HENNESSY**

It seemed to me that the two great weather systems of post-war British politics were fighting it out in every other clause: there's the

Clem Attlee, Nye Bevan, free at the point of delivery, we're all in it together, social solidarity for ever, all that; and the more market impulses of Mrs Thatcher's era. And it was a terrible strain for you, Shirley, because you had to try and be loyal to the Coalition, and yet we all knew your heart wasn't in it.

### WILLIAMS

Well I think I sounded quite as if my whole heart wasn't much in it. Behind the scenes, I was pushing as hard as I could. And we did come out against some of the obvious things. For example, the most key thing, I think, which nobody ever notices was that we managed to get the Secretary of State for Health back into the position of being responsible, albeit at one remove, for the health service. What that meant was, to put it very crudely, that the NHS survived.

Under the previous Secretary of State for Health, Andrew Lansley, you remember that the bill as it started said in very clear terms that the Secretary of State for Health would no longer have any direct responsibility for any part of the NHS; it would all be the responsibility of GPs, now turned into so-called CCGs[1]. That was the crucial constitutional change. And by getting Margaret Jay and, possibly even more importantly, the great Lord Mackay of Clashfern on board to say that this was not constitutionally acceptable that such huge sums of public money should have no minister who is ultimately responsible for the way it was spent and what it was spent on, by doing that I think we did take a key step towards what I've always believed in with the NHS – that you have to build up, in the end, a cross-party consensus behind it. I don't think it can survive if it's tossed to and fro between parties, and between private and public, so that there's never any time for the poor thing to settle down and stop being endlessly reorganised. I don't know how far we achieved that – there's some hope we may.

1 Clinical Commissioning Groups

But I'm proud that it's still something called the NHS; it still is the major supplier of health in this country. And we did take very strong views on such things as, for example, the role of competition policy, the responsibility of Monitor to ensure that patients' interests came before competition, and various other things of that kind. And a lot of that was behind the scenes, not noticed by some of the big pressure groups of the country, who got across the idea that the Liberal Democrats were somehow very keen on privatising the health service. That was never true. We had managed, in my view, to save the NHS – though it's not quite exactly as I would like it to be.

### HENNESSY

Shirley, you've always had a twin-track life, in the sense that you were a natural academic, and always interested in the political-science literature, as well as actually doing the political science life. And through that, you met your second husband, Dick Neustadt, the great Harvard figure, the greatest scholar of US presidency. He must have made a great difference to you.

### WILLIAMS

Yes, he did, but not in the ways you'd expect. Not by being a grand man. But because he'd already achieved so much he didn't have any resentment at all about what I did. He found it amusing, and entertaining, and challenging, and exciting. He was also a wonderful man to be married to, because his previous wife, who was a great friend of mine, died of multiple sclerosis some years of course before we got married – and in that I began to see in him his total belief in the idea of marriage, which goes through every weather, every climate, but you're still there – I mean, it's Shakespeare, really. And that was wonderful because I always knew I could rely on him, not to praise me, but to tell me exactly the way things were as he saw them, but to do that with such love that you had to accept that they were almost certainly not only well-intentioned but true.

**HENNESSY**

Shirley, what kind of trace do you think you'll leave on history?

**WILLIAMS**

[*Pause*] Not a lot.

**HENNESSY**

Are you sure?

**WILLIAMS**

Well, I'll tell you where I will leave a trace – I find myself more of a model of what women can be than perhaps would have been the case before I started battling on these things. I'm a bit of a model to young people, and I have quite an influence – which will not last, it never does – through television and broadcasting, and that's essentially a rather short-lived thing. I hope that at the end of the day, some of the things that I have stood for – Europe, comprehensive schools etc – will survive and last in some form. But I have to say, quite honestly, that the area where I would have loved to have had some impact, but haven't, is on the nature of companies and the involvement of people in them. We haven't got away in Britain from the sharp divisions between shareholders, managers, workers. We haven't completely destroyed the class system, though I think we've gone some way towards it. The area where we have done well I think, and I really applaud this, is we are generally a multicultural and multiracial society, not totally but we've gone a long way in that direction. And that's something I'm very pleased about.

**HENNESSY**

Regrets?

**WILLIAMS**

Not really.

**HENNESSY**

You don't do regrets, Shirley.

**WILLIAMS**

[*Laughing*] Don't do regrets! Do tiredness, but don't do regrets.

**HENNESSY**

Shirley Williams, thank you very much.

**WILLIAMS**

Thank you.

# Jack Straw

Series 1, Episode 2, first broadcast 18 July 2013

**Born** 3 August 1946; **Educated** Brentwood School; University of Leeds; President, National Union of Students, 1969–71

MP (Labour) Blackburn 1979–2015

Home Secretary, 1997–2001; Foreign and Commonwealth Secretary, 2001–06; Lord Privy Seal and Leader of the House of Commons, 2006–07; Lord Chancellor and Secretary of State for Justice, 2007–10

**Autobiography** *Last Man Standing*, 2012

### HENNESSY

With me today is a classic 'man of government', a politician far more at home in Whitehall than opposing from Westminster. The title of his autobiography, *Last Man Standing*, makes a virtue of him being the great survivor of the Blair and Brown Cabinets. He is also, by his own admission, a man who could – had he so chosen – have kept Britain out of a scarring and controversial war in Iraq. Jack Straw, welcome. Jack, it's a long way from a council house on the north-east rim of London to the marbled floors of the Foreign Office. You really are the incarnation of the post-war baby boomer: August '46 you came into this world, 12 months after the end of the war. You're one of Attlee's children, and I think you carry that with you, right through.

### STRAW

Yes, I think I do. My mother recently died, and in her papers I found this extraordinary letter that she had written to the *News Chronicle* – then a major newspaper on the left – just after the war, in which she had pleaded for German prisoners of war to be sent home to their families, rather than just punished further for having lost the war. And with that letter was a letter from the editor of the *News Chronicle*, written in hand, thanking her for this. Scores of letters had been sent to her about how sensible she had been. And what came through this was the extraordinary optimism of the Attlee period, and the sense that people like my mother – who was a teacher, but who came from a completely working-class background – their sense that at last, they owned the future. And that was a very powerful force that was conveyed to my siblings and to me, throughout our childhood.

### HENNESSY

Your political formation … I think you were quite precocious really because I think you started keeping a personal archive of notes and papers when you were a teenager, just a teenager at school. Does this suggest you had a cunning plan of a nice pathway eventually to the Premiership, or were you just a precocious, unusually self-aware youth?

### STRAW

I started earlier than that, actually, because I started when I was about nine. The only thing really that my parents agreed about was their politics and at that stage their pacifism. My father had been a pacifist during the war. And so we were members of the Peace Pledge Union. And my sister and I wrote to the man running the Peace Pledge Union, and we were then put on the subscription list for *War Resisters' International*, and so I kept all of those, and the correspondence. I was just a squirrel. But also, because of the breakdown of my parents' marriage, I think I became quite a solitary child as well. So retreating into records and newspaper cuttings and a life outside was a way of defending myself against what was a pretty bloody awful situation going on downstairs in the kitchen.

### HENNESSY

Was there a spark of political ambition though as well? You knew you were a man of the left.

### STRAW

No, it was when I went away to school – went to Brentwood – and found myself as somebody from very different circumstances from most of my peers in the boarding house, and needed to survive, and I became a kind of house socialist. I liked argument, which was just as well; it was one way of surviving in a very difficult environment. And in September 1959 a general election had been called by Harold Macmillan. I'd been sent out dishing out leaflets round the council estate we lived on, for the hapless Labour candidate for Chigwell and Ongar division. I read one of these leaflets of our candidate and thought it sounded a much better idea to become a member of Parliament for the Labour Party, far more productive, than dishing out leaflets on wet Wednesday afternoons. And then the local Labour Party decided on what I later learned was a gimmick, which was to have me make the opening speech at the formal adoption meeting for the Labour candidate. The speech went down rather well, and the local paper wanted a photograph of me, and the only photograph we had was of me wearing my school boater. So there is this young socialist, standing in his granny's back garden, wearing a boater. I think the paradox of this might not have been lost on the readers of the *West Essex Gazette*.

### HENNESSY

A singular beginning of a political career. It was a tough time you had at home, your parents not getting on, and there was the unbelievable trauma of your father having tried to gas himself. I mean, utterly searing, Jack.

**STRAW**

Well, it's extraordinary what children put up with, and plenty of other children in that period, and today in other countries, put up with much worse. But it was awful. Because on the Friday I had happened to see two of my uncles put my father against the wall of my grandmother's house and knock his teeth out. This was because he'd been unpleasant, as he had been, to my mother. And then the next day we were playing outside and I went into the kitchen of our maisonette, up the stairs, smelled gas and found my father making what was rather a half-hearted attempt to gas himself, although he could easily have blown up the whole house. And then hearing my mother get very impatient with him; she said to him, 'If you want to kill yourself, that's all right, but please don't do it in front of the children'. So there was a kind of brutality in their relationship.

**HENNESSY**

Your mother was a remarkable woman.

**STRAW**

She was, she was.

**HENNESSY**

Formidable in every way. I never met her, but she had a great reputation, Jack, and obviously you carry the particles of your mother's formation with you.

**STRAW**

She was the most important influence on me by a long way. She'd had to put up with very great adversity. She was a sort of classic Attlee socialist, because she had a very strong belief in helping people who needed help, but she had very, very powerful social aspirations for herself, and she wanted to break out of the working-class, lower-middle-class environment in which she'd been brought up, and become more middle-class, and saw nothing wrong with that, no contradiction between that and her values. So she was very taken with people who were sort of socialist toffs, a lot of people involved in an organisation called Forest School Camps, who lived in Hampstead and Highgate. That kind of group, the people who were around AS Neill in the progressive-school movement. A really, really interesting woman with a passion for nursery education, which was there the whole of her life; she became a headteacher in the dockland area of Newham for quite a long time, and did great work for children there. But she pushed her kids. And I wanted to go to boarding school anyway – it seemed like a good way of getting away from the rumpus of what was going on. But she essentially got her satisfaction through the achievements of her children.

#### HENNESSY

Do you think, Jack, there may be a pattern in your life? You've always relied on the kindness of strong ladies: Barbara Castle, your great friend and patron, and Alice, your wife. Do you think that Joan implanted that in you, because she was the rock of the family?

#### STRAW

I've never thought of that before, but I think there's a lot in that; the patronage of strong ladies. I like to think my relationship with my wife is more than about patronage, but anyway! [*Laughs*] She's certainly robust in coming forward with advice.

#### HENNESSY

One of the most surprising and also candid sections in your memoir is about what you call the 'impostor syndrome' that's broken out throughout bits of your life, that feeling that 'Surely I'm going to be exposed', and all the rest of it. Now that's very surprising, Jack, for those who only know you from the external Jack, holding all these great offices of state, a presence in political life for an extraordinarily long time. But where do you think that comes from? Do you think it comes from the uncertainty of that fragile childhood?

### STRAW

Oh, I'm not in any doubt it comes from that. And the sense that if you came from that kind of background, you didn't really deserve the success that you were achieving. The old sort of Groucho Marx observation, 'How could I become a member of a club that was willing to take me as a member of the club?'

### HENNESSY

Do you still feel that, at times?

### STRAW

No, I don't. I've got over that: years of therapy and a recognition that actually my career wasn't too bad at all. No, I don't feel that, but it was a very powerful sense for me, particularly through the '70s and '80s. I'd had a great time at university, I'd become President of the National Union of Students; I didn't have the impostor syndrome there at all, I was absolutely on top of the job. I did my bar finals very well, got a pupillage. But then all sorts of set-backs took place, not least in my private life, because of the difficulty in my relationship with my first wife: she got anorexia, she then got pregnant, and then we had this very wanted child, who was declared fit and healthy, and then died six days later. And that was awful. And then I get the nomination for Blackburn, it's a safe seat, I think, thank God for that; I get elected, pretty straight-forwardly; and then 18 months later, the Labour Party starts to fall apart.

**HENNESSY**

This is '79 and the aftermath of Labour's defeat.

**STRAW**

Yes, the aftermath of Labour's defeat. Benn and Co were trying to wreck the party, as it were, from the left; you had the Social Democratic Party, the people on the right of the party, trying to destroy the party from that wing. And it was a nightmare, literally a nightmare. Terrible. And then suddenly the Boundary Commission announced that 20,000 new voters are being added to my seat, and all the predictions are I'm going to lose. And on top of all of that the thing that triggered me to go and have psychoanalysis, was that one weekend I started to feel funny noises in my right ear, and over the space of the weekend I'd lost my hearing entirely in my right ear. It had been replaced with tinnitus, and there was a danger I'd lose it in my left ear. So if you add all that up together, I ended up really severely depressed. That's why my mother-in-law did me a great favour by recommending I see a psychoanalyst, which I did very intensively for about eight years.

**HENNESSY**

And it worked, Jack.

**STRAW**

And it worked, yeah. And I thought, well, you know, this is part of my story, I need to share this with people, so that I show to people that you can succeed while having this kind of background and while having these kind of monsters and impostors in your head. And the way I put it is this: these days, everybody accepts that you need to keep yourself physically fit, and there will be a period in your life when that fitness in challenged in one way or another, and you do something about it. You may break your leg, you may have an internal operation, well fine, you can get over it, and you can talk about it perfectly naturally. I think we're moving to a situation where we can talk about keeping ourselves psycho-logically fit. And our psychological state is partly dependent on us, but it's also dependent on where we've come from and on our childhood. So let's be open about this. It's been really interesting, the letters I've received. I had one the other day, actually from somebody who'd worked for me in the Civil Service, who said that reading my book had led her to seek help for her severe depression. And I said to my wife, I said to Alice, 'It was worth writing the book, just to save that one soul.'

### HENNESSY

We've mentioned Barbara Castle; she was the most remarkable woman. I'm sure she's still remembered, in our generation she most certainly is, but I'm not sure if the flavour, the very distinc-tive flavour of Barbara has carried through to the younger genera-tions. Encapsulate her for me.

### STRAW

Barbara Castle was the Labour Party's Margaret Thatcher. They were two peas in the same pod; quite remarkable similarities. And had Barbara not screwed up *before* a leadership election, rather than in Mrs Thatcher's case, 10 or 11 years after she'd become Prime Minister, Barbara could easily have been Labour leader, and probably Labour Prime Minister.

### HENNESSY

And she screwed up over 'In Place of Strife', which tried to curb trade-union power in the late '60s.

### STRAW

Yes, she screwed up over 'In Place of Strife', the right policy, but she pursued it in entirely the wrong way. So the Cabinet found out about this policy, which she and Harold Wilson had cooked up, from the pages of the *Financial Times*, and this apparent ambush by Barbara and Harold Wilson led to retaliation by Jim Callaghan – Callaghan, the Home Secretary, used his membership of the National Executive Committee to move a resolution to over-rule the Cabinet. Absolutely extraordinary. But Callaghan succeeded, and she was wounded, and she was only going to be there, after that, as long as Harold Wilson was there. Like Margaret Thatcher, she had an extraordinary sense of herself as a woman in a male world. She was contemptuous of women who wanted special treatment. She was very feminine, but she knew how to operate in masculine ways. She was totally competitive with her peers, again, as Margaret Thatcher was, and contemptuous of them. She was a nightmare to work with, but she was brilliant to work for.

#### HENNESSY

She brought you in as her special adviser, in '74, when Labour returned to power, because, she said later, of your guile and low cunning. Is that a compliment entirely, Jack?

#### STRAW

It was meant as a compliment – but I also think it was accurate. What happened was this: Barbara Castle had to see some senior visiting foreign dignitary. I think to help the meeting, both her special advisers were invited as well: one was Professor Brian Abel-Smith, professor of Social Administration at the LSE, very distinguished individual, and the other was me, J. Straw, aged 28. And the visiting dignitary asked Barbara what we two did, so quick as a flash, she said that she'd hired Brian for his brains, and J. Straw for guile and low cunning. And it sort of stuck, and I've used it against myself ever since. It says something, I suppose, about what I have to offer, though I'd like to think I have other things to offer as well.

#### HENNESSY

After Jim Callaghan becomes Prime Minister and sacks Barbara Castle – to her fury – you worked for Peter Shore. Very different man. Very interesting man. Again, not remembered to the degree that he should be, I think. What did you learn from Peter Shore?

### STRAW

Peter Shore shared with Barbara the most important thing you need in politics, which is a strong sense of conviction. What you're doing with your life, what you believe in. Beyond that, they were very different characters. He was much more cerebral, much more the gentleman. Where Barbara often over-reached herself, Peter often held back too much. He could have become leader of the party had Michael Foot not intervened disastrously and at the last minute when candidates were lining up to succeed Jim Callaghan. And I was with Peter on a Friday when Michael Foot came into Peter's room and said, 'On Monday, I, Michael Foot, will announce my backing for you, Peter Shore, to be leader of the Labour party,' and I was also there on the Monday, when Michael Foot came in, scratched everything there was to scratch on his person, shifted from foot to foot, as well he might, and said to Peter, 'As you know, I did say I was making a statement about the leadership today, and that's true, but the statement is going to be that I'm going to be the leader, and I'm standing for leadership.' Peter, to his great credit, asked all his supporters, including me, to vote for Michael if he, Peter, lost the first ballot, which he was bound to. So we did. I also have to say that at that stage, Michael Foot and Denis Healey were much more evenly balanced. Denis had made himself so unpopular in so many ways that it was quite easy to vote for Michael with a clear conscience.

### HENNESSY

Is your conscience clear now? This is 1980, and the Labour Party is really going into a civil war, which you hated every minute of. That you, Jack Straw, man of government, by voting for Michael seriously increased the chance of you, Jack Straw, never having a chance to be a minister, of any kind – it was very odd, paradoxically, looking back, that you should do that.

### STRAW

It was a bad decision. In a way, although one shouldn't push the parallel too far, it was a bit like actively supporting Gordon Brown in 2007. The problem is, you can only measure people's propensity for a future job on the way they've performed their jobs up to then.

### HENNESSY

But – I don't want to rub it in, Jack – but you compounded in the early '80s this strange misjudgement of yours, as I would see it, by voting for Tony Benn for the deputy leadership, and not for Denis Healey.

### STRAW

Well look, the two are different. My vote for Michael Foot was rational at the time; my vote for Tony Benn was really out of cowardice, and I was ashamed of it. I still am. But my world was falling apart. I was under huge pressure in Blackburn, they were trying to deselect me …

### HENNESSY

This Militant Tendency stuff …

### STRAW

Militant Tendency, and others. And Benn was ruthless. Underneath this upper-middle-class veneer – utterly ruthless in pursuit of his own ambition. So we had people in the constituency party who weren't in Militant interestingly but in the softer end of the hard left, who were intimidating me and saying I'd lose my seat and all the rest of it. And in the end I'd convinced myself that the best thing to do was to get this damn man Benn elected as deputy leader and let him see what he could do with it, with his position.

**HENNESSY**

Looking back, aren't you relieved that Labour lost the 1983 election in a way, because if that manifesto had been carried through, famously the longest suicide note in political history as Gerald Kaufman called it, we might well have come out of Europe, and we would have given up the nuclear weapon, or Michael would have tried to; and in many ways some would argue that would have made you, a) unelectable ever again, at least for the foreseeable future, and, b) given the SDP the propellant it needed to become the party of the centre-left.

**STRAW**

We were never going to win the '83 election. But the issue in the '83 election was whether we stayed in business. And we only just beat the share of the vote of the SDP-Liberal Alliance by one percentage point. We got many more seats than them, because of the first-past-the-post system, but it was a damn close-run thing. And it then took another nine years before the Labour Party ridded itself of this poison, this apostasy that had taken it over.

**HENNESSY**

Can we linger on the nuclear question for a minute? Because you came from a Peace Pledge Union home, you were campaigning for nuclear disarmament until, I think, a Communist member of CND said, 'The Russians must have their bomb because it's the Workers' Bomb, everybody else must give up theirs' [*laughing*], and that's when I think scales fell from your eyes ...

**STRAW**

They did. I still remember. I think we were marching on the Aldermaston march between Reading and Slough. Drizzle. There'd been the usual songs which kept us going, 'Down by the Riverside' and all those other things, and then I got talking to this guy from Loughton CND. What people forget these days is that CND was completely penetrated by the Communist Party. And I was saying – wide-eyed, aged 14 – that we needed unilaterally to disarm, because then the Americans would, and then the Soviet Union would.

**HENNESSY**

This is 1960. Height of the Cold War.

**STRAW**

Height of the Cold War. So this man said, 'Yes son, you're absolutely right about the United Kingdom abandoning its bomb, and you're right about the United States' – as it were the great Satan – 'but you're wrong about the Soviet Union.' So I said, 'Why?' And he said, 'Well, it's a Workers' Bomb.' So we had a brief conversation about the Workers' Bomb. And then I could almost feel the scales falling from my eyes, and I'm thinking, hang on, this is a load of nonsense. So it led to the beginnings of a high level of scepticism about CND.

**HENNESSY**

It's a long trail from that Aldermaston march to you being Foreign Secretary, and being one of Tony Blair's alternative nuclear decision takers. If he'd been wiped out by a pre-emptive nuclear strike, and you'd been in a protected place and survived, it would have fallen to you to decide whether one of our Royal Navy missiles – Polaris or Trident in those days – would have been launched against the person who'd attacked the UK. Now that's a most extraordinary transformation. I think you're the only ex-CND person who's been in that position ... [*Straw laughs*]

**STRAW**

Well, I was CND as a teenager. You go through a transition in your life. I, fairly quickly, by my early 20s, had completely abandoned any idea of pacifism and unilateralism. But if you take these jobs, you've got to take the responsibilities that go with them; and one of the things I discovered about myself quite early on was that I was capable of responsibility, and capable of making decisions. Thinking about them very carefully, making the decisions, then getting on with the next one. Which is a fundamental characteristic that you need if you're going to be a minister. So of course I took those responsibilities very seriously, though it was slightly abstract because we were unlikely to launch a nuclear attack on anybody, or have one launched on us. The less than abstract responsibility was the responsibility for deciding whether to send fighter planes up to intercept a passenger plane that had been hijacked.

**HENNESSY**

A British 9/11 …

**STRAW**

A British 9/11. And I had lots and lots of training for this, and I carried on that responsibility right until the end of the government in 2010. There was one terrifying Boxing Day when we were having lunch with friends in the Cotswolds, as we usually do on Boxing Day, and Downing Street got hold of me. I was put through to the control and told that they couldn't find the Prime Minister, but they'd got this aeroplane, a passenger plane, coming in to land. They'd lost all contact with it, and did we scramble the planes? So for about 20 minutes, I was the man who was having to decide whether to send the fighters up, and I got them ready, then Tony took over and by that stage, after a lot of signals to this aeroplane, the pilots had woken up out of their stupor and got back in contact with the control tower. But we could have taken that plane down.

**HENNESSY**

A very stretching 20 minutes.

**STRAW**

Oh, I can still remember every second of it.

**HENNESSY**

If the amazingly remote but absolutely cataclysmic contingency of a nuclear attack on this country had occurred, and it fell to you to decide, what would you have decided, Jack?

**STRAW**

It would have depended on the circumstances, and whether I felt that by launching a nuclear attack on the other country that would have made this country more or less safe. That's the issue.

**HENNESSY**

So, in certain circumstances you might have authorised it.

**STRAW**

Yes. I mean, very reluctantly – but you can't possibly agree to take on that responsibility, and then at the last moment say, oh, by the way, I'm a closet pacifist.

**HENNESSY**

One of the questions that's come right through our lifetime – those of us who were born post-war – is immigration, and the attempts to integrate people from the Commonwealth into British society, and the problems that that has caused. And you as Home Secretary were at the epicentre when the dreadful case of Stephen Lawrence, the murder of Stephen Lawrence[1], erupted into our consciousness. And it's run on ever since, as a kind of talismanic touchstone question, the Lawrence affair. How significant do you think all that was, and when it first broke into your domain as Home Secretary did you quite realise that it was going to have this percussive effect?

---

1 The black teenager Stephen Lawrence was murdered in south-east London in 1993. Difficulties in convicting his killers led to a public inquiry, which in 1999 concluded that the Metropolitan Police was 'institutionally racist'

### STRAW

[*Pause*] I knew it was profoundly important, and I'd spotted that in opposition. It took me three months to get agreement about the terms of reference for the inquiry, but the Home Office and the Met were in for any inquiry provided it was not a forensic inquiry into the death of Stephen Lawrence and the failure of the murder investigation. So I knew that it was important. Frankly, I never anticipated that it would be as important, or as long-running. But one of the things that has driven my politics is a hatred of discrimination against people on the grounds of their colour, their religion, or indeed their sexuality. And I thought that, if I could do one thing as Home Secretary, it would be to get some sense of justice, not only for the Lawrence family but for people who are non-white, black or Asian. And one of the most remarkable things that happens to me is people coming up to me, still today, black or Asian people, and saying, 'Thank you'. And I sort of look at them, and think, what are they thanking me for? But they're thanking me for Lawrence.

### HENNESSY

History will always linger on one particular patch of your career, which is as Foreign Secretary in the run-up to the Iraq War. And you've said publicly, you've written it too, that you could have stopped that, if you'd resigned – and I suspect even you alone, not relying on Robin Cook and Clare Short to be there buttressing it would have meant we wouldn't have taken part in that war. And I think, Jack, you're the only ex-British Foreign Secretary who can say that. It's the most extraordinary weight for anybody to carry, both at the time and subsequently; one of the things that will be with you till your last breath.

### STRAW

Yes, it is a great burden. I felt it at the time, and it's not a conceit to say that I could have stopped it – it just happens to be true. I was well aware that if, in those closing days to the decision that was to be taken on 18 March 2003, I had decided to resign then there would not have been a majority in the House of Commons; it's as straightforward as that. I tried to explain in my memoirs how I came to the alternative decision, and what drew me in to deciding, much later than Tony, that it was right to take military action against Saddam. But also to describe the dynamic that was taking place between myself and the French, and how angry I felt about the way that Chirac and de Villepin were operating, frustrated that they – if they'd made more sensible decisions – could in my judgement have joined with us, and we could have prevented a war, because we drew up these six benchmarks for Saddam that were going to be attached to the famous Second Resolution, and they were all benchmarks which were going to be achievable. The benchmarks were drafted by Hans Blix.

#### HENNESSY

The weapons inspector.

#### STRAW

The weapons inspector now running a mile from any responsibility, and pretending that his inspection reports had given Saddam a clean bill of health, which they certainly had not, quite the reverse. But the idea of the Second Resolution, as far as I was concerned, was to stop a war, not to start one. But I also became aware, in retrospect, of how you could be sucked into a decision-making process; and at each stage, the gate marked 'war' became wider and wider, and psychologically more enticing, whereas the one marked 'peace' became narrower and apparently more difficult. And it was that experience that significantly informed my judgement later that on no account were we going to get involved in military action against Iran, and that led to this rather unexpected alliance between Dominique de Villepin, the French Foreign Minister, Joschka Fischer, the German Foreign Minister, and myself, to negotiate with the Iranians, what became the E3 Formation.

### HENNESSY

So you drew your own lessons from it all. But can we go back to those days before the invasion? The Butler Inquiry into Weapons of Mass Destruction in Iraq showed that the Attorney General's opinion was crucial to all this and the full Cabinet only saw what I would call the shrivelled version of it, at the last minute, on March 17. Now, you're a Cabinet government man, Jack, and it's quite wrong to reduce peace and war to process, but process is also crucial at such moments. Do you not think that that was an absolute failure of Cabinet government, that the full Cabinet neither asked for, nor was given, the very caveat-laden full Attorney General's opinion that you had seen earlier, and that you didn't actually bring it to the table yourself either in the Cabinet Room that day?

### STRAW

I would not have run Cabinet in the way Tony did. And I share your view that process is profoundly important, because process gives you legitimacy. The difficulty about circulating the very lengthy opinion of the Attorney General was frankly that it would have been leaked, and it would have been selectively leaked. That was a problem by that stage.

### HENNESSY

You're saying one of the Cabinet colleagues would have leaked it?

### STRAW

Yes. If there had been a War Cabinet, and if people had been taken into confidence at a much earlier stage, I think the psychology of the way the Cabinet was operating would have been very different, and that's how I would have handled it. And I don't think, then, that it would have leaked. But at that moment, given the way Tony had run his Cabinets for the previous six years, and was going to carry on, that was the difficulty. It also has to be said that the very long letter was Peter Goldsmith debating about the issues, saying

'On the one hand, and on the other', this, that and the other. The letter statement that he made on 17 March, the day before the vote in the Commons, was a letter of decision. So, having gone around the houses in early March and before that, he then came to a decision, and he himself has said that there was a very big distinction in terms of the quality of these documents, and what the Cabinet needed to know was, was he saying yes or no to whether it was lawful, not how did he arrive at that conclusion. By the way, even if all 20-plus pages of Peter's earlier *exegesis* had been circulated, there was nothing that the Cabinet could have done about it; this was a decision for the Attorney, and the Attorney alone.

#### HENNESSY

The great Lord Bingham, Senior Law Lord, argued later that legal opinions like that should be shared with Parliament and the public, on peace and war. If that had been shared with the public, the longer one, the House of Commons wouldn't have voted the way that it did, would it?

#### STRAW

I don't know, is the answer to that. I mean, Tom was a great jurist, but he had his political views about Iraq. And one of the truths about Iraq is that the lawyers involved made their decision on the lawfulness of Iraq by starting with their political and moral position on it. It's a universal truth: you won't find a single lawyer who was opposed politically to the war who said that the war was, nonetheless, lawful, and the reverse is also true. And that's the nature of international law. So, much though I loved Tom Bingham and revered him as a jurist, I don't place any greater credence on his opinions on that than any other lawyer's.

#### HENNESSY

One of the legacies, in your own mind, of this experience is your proposal for a Cabinet Government Act, to spell out what the

Prime Minister is for, and the relationship with the collective, and including the Chancellor of the Exchequer, which is a fascinating idea – and I should declare that you and I have talked about that, and we're going to do some work together on it. But in a way it's a most remarkably ripe, retrospective commentary on Tony Blair's style of leadership, and indeed, Gordon Brown's, which we'll come to in a minute.

**STRAW**

Yes. I owe Tony a huge amount; he essentially made my career after it was in the doldrums under John Smith. But I never approved of the way Tony ran government, and he knew that from a very early stage. [*Laughing*] There's a whole series of missives from me in the system, in which, from early on, I'm saying you need to make the process more formal, you need to involve your colleagues more. And that included a very long set of suggestions in 2003–2004 about how he should formalise the way government operated. He, in retrospect, was never going to do that because it wasn't his style and it wasn't his personality. The irony is that had he done it, his legacy would have been a better one. He would have got the same decisions out of the system, but people would have respected the decisions more. People can accuse me of being bureaucratic. I don't think I am, but I certainly believe in process. One of the things I learned very early on as a bar student was that procedure is about the most important, not the least important, subjects in the legal system, because it's the means by which people can access power, access their rights. And we neglect it too much within the British governmental system. And that's why I think there ought to be a Cabinet Government Act, which lays down what are the responsibilities of the Prime Minister, what are the responsibilities of the Cabinet; which prescribes that there should be a National Security Council, a very welcome but non-statutory development by David Cameron, that there should be an Economic Council, which has to look at budget proposals and public-spending proposals, and that only after that's happened can they come to Parliament; that also lays down the process for both the Cabinet, as well as Parliament, to decide on war and peace. These are necessary parts of a constitutional apparatus, and they ought to be down in black-letter law.

**HENNESSY**

Gordon Brown – a very different style to Tony Blair's, but you didn't throb with admiration for Gordon's style as Prime Minister either did you? When did you realise that it wasn't going to work? Because there was that amazing first Cabinet meeting, which went on for ever, looking at this draft Great Constitutional Reform Bill that was going to come forward. Did you realise that day, even though you'd been his campaign manager, that Jack was making the wrong decision again about people that had come to the fore?

**STRAW**

Well, it was a sort of an inevitable decision to have Gordon crowned as Prime Minister, because he was the only candidate. And people say, why didn't so-and-so stand, why didn't I stand? Well he had got the numbers lined up … what would have been the point of standing when you were just going to get crushed? I was very taken with his constitutional proposals, and it fell to me, as kind of the point man, to implement them. I've got an abiding interest in the British constitution, and in the importance of change. I got a flavour for the chaotic way in which he made decisions in the drafting of what became the Governance of Britain proposals …

**HENNESSY**

So very early on you realised that this man, for all his remarkable gifts, was not going to be able to hack it. He couldn't decide …

**STRAW**

I mean, he did decide – even though bits were coming off the machine as he was deciding. But what traumatised the Cabinet, and led to this loss of confidence in him by his Cabinet colleagues, and in himself, was this paralysis of decision-making that took place at the Bournemouth Labour Party conference that took place in the early autumn of 2007, when he just allowed speculation about whether they should or should not call an election to take over the conference. He failed to quell that in his speech on the Tuesday, allowed that to go on right through to the following weekend into the Conservative Party conference, went off to Afghanistan in a flat-footed, ridiculous attempt to draw attention away from the Conservatives, misusing the power of the Prime Minister. And only at the end of that week, after the Conservatives had a field day with us, did he then say, 'Oh no, I've no intention of calling an election, and I don't know what all this speculation is about'. So it showed both that he was paralysed in terms of decision-making, but also had this remarkable propensity for double-think and disingenuity, which I'd not really understood was a characteristic of his until then.

**HENNESSY**

There's a very delicate question from your time as Foreign Secretary, when you authorised Secret Intelligence Service operations of the so-called rendition of the Libyan Islamist dissident, Abdel Hakim Belhadj. And I know there are legal processes going on, so you're probably mightily constrained about what you can say. But Foreign Secretaries do that; the SIS doesn't do special operations without the say-so of the Foreign Secretary.

**STRAW**

Well, let me say two things. One is, that in general I was assiduous in applying my legal responsibilities and duties to everything I did in supervising the Secret Intelligence Service, and indeed GCHQ.

The second thing is on this specific action – there is a legal action taking place at the moment, I'm a defendant in that, and I'm very sorry, but I can't say any more about that.

If you had made it to the Premiership, what would it have been like? There's an inner safe, Jack, I suspect, at the back of your mind, in which the draft Queen's Speech for the first Straw Premiership is, somewhere. What would you have wanted to do, and how would you have set about it?

I think I would have done OK. I think I would have surprised people. I would have formalised government, and I would have done a lot to hand back power to the House of Commons. My view is that the Whips' Office has over the years become far too powerful, that the crucial role of this place is legislation. And this place needs to have more power over it. So it would be all about that, making this place, the House of Commons, much more the cockpit of politics, than it is.

Would you have removed the timetable from all government business, played with the so-called guillotining? Because it was the Blair government that did that …

This was so-called modernisation, which is not modernisation at all in my view. Some timetabling is sensible, and a fact of life these days, with more women MPs and more male MPs with young families, is that they want to have greater certainty about when they go home. But you could have a degree of timetabling without putting the House of Commons programme in a straitjacket.

**HENNESSY**

Jack, what trace do you think you'd like to leave on history?

**STRAW**

First, as someone who held very high office, but who carried on meeting his first duty, which is to represent his constituents. Secondly, to have made this place a fairer place, which is what I saw as my aim when I was Home Secretary, both making it safer ...

**HENNESSY**

This place being the country ...

**STRAW**

Yes, this place, the country. Making it safer, but also giving people more rights through measures like the Human Rights Act. And as Foreign Secretary, my responsibility for Iraq is indelible, it will always be there. But hopefully people will also recognise the work I did in trying to bring Turkey into the European Union, and above all, in stopping there being military action against Iran. And as I used to say to the Iranians, Joschka Fischer, Dominique de Villepin and I were their human shield, and they ought not to forget it.

**HENNESSY**

Jack Straw, thank you very much.

# Norman Tebbit (Lord Tebbit)

Series 1, Episode 3, first broadcast 25 July 2013

**Born** 29 March 1931; **Educated** Edmonton County Grammar School

MP (Conservative) Epping 1970–74; Chingford 1974–92

Parliamentary Secretary, Department of Trade, 1979–81;
Minister of State, Department of Industry, 1981; Secretary of
State for Employment, 1981–83; Secretary of State for Trade
and Industry, 1983–85; Chancellor of the Duchy of Lancaster,
1985–87; Chairman of the Conservative Party, 1985–87

**Autobiography** *Upwardly Mobile*, 1988

**HENNESSY**

With me today is one of the most flavourful and recognisable politicians of recent times. As long as the governments of Margaret Thatcher are remembered, he will be remembered too. In fact, if any single figure apart from Lady Thatcher herself could be said to be the incarnation of Thatcherism, it's Norman Tebbit. Norman, welcome.

**TEBBIT**

Thank you.

**HENNESSY**

Napoleon once said, if you want to understand a man or a woman, you need to think about the world when they were 20. You were 20 in 1951 – height of the Cold War, still the shadow of the Second World War rationing. What were the forces which contributed to your formation, as a human being and as a politician later?

**TEBBIT**

I've always maintained that if you grew up as I did, in the tail-end of the depression and high unemployment, in a family on the wrong side of the tracks so to speak, and then gone through the war, been bombed and evacuated and all that sort of thing, and then come out through all that into a post-war era where for years after the war we still rationed sweets even – you have to have concluded by then that there really ought to be a better way of running things than that. And I'd come to that conclusion by the time I was about 14 or 15, that there really ought to be a better way of running these things.

**HENNESSY**

Just by the end of the war, in fact.

**TEBBIT**

Yes, indeed. And by the time I was 15, I'd joined the Young Conservatives, determined that I was going to change the world. I suppose to some extent I chipped away at a few of the edges. [*Laughs*] But I was determined to make things different.

**HENNESSY**

Now many people listening would think that a young man, aged 15, from your background, tail-end of the slump, the shared privations of the war, would be tilted to the left by that experience. That things would be better, but only because the state continued to organise things to make them better, and the state had been remarkably well organised for the purposes of beating Hitler. So you were going against the tide even then.

**TEBBIT**

Yes – I think I have an anti-collectivist gene. That was essentially the thing: I was not a collectivist at any time in my life. And I saw all salvation as being a matter of what individuals could do, and that the function of the state was to enhance the ability and remove the barriers for the individuals to do that.

**HENNESSY**

Do you think you always liked going against the swim, the conventional wisdom?

**TEBBIT**

I don't know, perhaps I did at that time, but it just came naturally. It was the tide that flowed against me, not me against the tide!

**HENNESSY**

You said later in your autobiography that when you were in the Airline Pilots' Association it reflected your obsessive competitive qualities. You were very honest about that. Do you think, looking back, that Norman Tebbit the trade unionist was there in formation, up against the big battalions.

**TEBBIT**

Yes, I think so. Competitive. And it sounds odd to be a trade unionist when you're not a collectivist, but I'd got into the trades union primarily through its activities on the technical front. And the more I saw of the way that a nationalised industry was managed, the more I began to realise that I was rather sorry for the management, that it was impossible to manage it. But I had to fight my corner within that crazy world.

**HENNESSY**

Do you think the experience of being in the Royal Air Force Auxiliary added another layer of formation? Because it's the Cold War; if the Cold War had turned nasty in the early '50s, you'd have been in the front line, Norman, with that plane of yours.

**TEBBIT**

Indeed, we would have been in the front line. But I think also it brought me into touch with a different group in society. I was commissioned in the Royal Air Force, and I began to mix with men older than myself, much more experienced, war-time guys, professionals – my flight commander became my solicitor, the intelligence officer on the squadron was my bank manager, and so on. A different group of society. And I think that made quite a lot of difference to me; it made me a good deal more confident. If I'd been under-confident in the past, if you're wearing a uniform with a bit of braid on the cuff and a pair of Air Force wings on the lapel, you do have a little more confidence about meeting anyone else in life.

**HENNESSY**

Was that turn of the '50s your golden age? A society in many ways at ease with itself, for all its problems, for all the loss of wealth in the war, and all the class obsessions which were still everywhere. You do seem to me to be a man of the '40s and '50s. Do you think that's fair?

**TEBBIT**

I think there's something in that. Roy Jenkins famously said that the permissive society is the civilised society; I've taken the view over the years that the more permissive it has been, the less civilised it has been. I ask myself why it was possible for me, as a child, to walk home through the black-out, through totally darkened streets, safely – how many mothers would now let their child walk through the streets of Edmonton if all the lights were extinguished? Not many, I fancy. I liked that stability that there was in society; I liked the fact that people who didn't pay their bills at the grocer's were looked down on, and indeed snubbed. I felt there was a firmness in society at that time, of shared values. I have to confess that it may be that to some extent it's the working class adopting some of the nastier habits of the upper classes, as much as the other way around, that has caused society to deteriorate as much as it has.

### HENNESSY

In the wider world in the '50s, 1953, Coronation year, the empire came home, the wonderful procession through the streets after the Coronation, troops from right across the globe and so on. Did it mean something to you? The extended Britain, as it were? Did you see it as an extended family, or great-powerdom – how did it work in the Tebbit mind?

### TEBBIT

I think I did see it as a special place, which I later explored a good deal. I was conscious from very early days that English was the greatest language in the world; that we contributed a lot in terms of decent and reasonably corruption-free administration to the rest of the world; that whatever criticisms are made of our record in our colonial empire, I don't think there's any other European country that could point to a better record than ours, and there are sort of touchstones of that even now. I mean cricket is a game which is only played amongst the old imperial powers, and it's played in a great spirit of equality.

### HENNESSY

You got into trouble on the cricket front later when you applied the cricket test – 'Which team do you support?' But if you take the extended family view of cricket it's all family, Norman, isn't it?

**TEBBIT**

Yes, there is a great deal of family. On a couple of occasions, I almost went to work out in the empire, I applied for a job in the Falklands – Lord knows what would have happened if I'd …

**HENNESSY**

What job was that?

**TEBBIT**

Flying the ambulance float-plane round the islands. But since my flying at that time had been confined to fast jets I think they thought that probably I wasn't the right guy.

**HENNESSY**

'The Biggles years', if you'd done it …

**TEBBIT**

I very nearly went off tea-planting in Assam. Very different careers that I might have followed! [*Laughing*]

**HENNESSY**

You're more of a romantic than people realise. [*Tebbit laughs*]

**HENNESSY**

The Conservative Party that you were active in in the late '40s, and ever since, really, was very big: it had one and half million members if not more in the early '50s; breathtaking to look back now, with Young Conservatives a great force in the land, and all that. But it wasn't the Conservative Party that was ideally constructed for a boy from Ponders End, was it?

**TEBBIT**

No, it wasn't; but then that's what making things happen is about, isn't it? You change things.

**HENNESSY**

Were you patronised by the others in the Conservative Party, as you rose through?

**TEBBIT**

I think if you ignore it, it goes away.

**HENNESSY**

You've always had reservations about the consensually minded Macmillan years, haven't you? I think you think quite a lot of rot set in, in one way or another, when Uncle Harold was in Number 10.

**TEBBIT**

I did indeed. I felt that the Conservative Party had lost its way quite badly in the early '60s, particularly under Macmillan. And I found his government was losing touch very badly in my view, and by that time of course I was married and had got a couple kids, and was busily earning my income, flying for BOAC. But I eventually got so cross about it that I put pen to paper and wrote to Iain Macleod, who was then chairman of the Conservative Party. And in it I set out what the government was doing wrong, and how it should be sorted out and what should be done; and Iain wrote back to me, and in essence said, 'Dear Norman, I understand you feel strongly about these things, and believe that you've got the answers to a lot of the problems. Why don't you come and help us?' And I read the letter several times, and then said to my wife, 'Damn it, I will.' I think that was in about 1964, somewhere like that.

**HENNESSY**

So Iain Macleod's letter was a trigger to tilt you from a Conservative party activist into actually pursuing a political career.

**TEBBIT**

That's right.

**HENNESSY**

It's a bit of a sacrifice, from being a BOAC pilot on the new and swanky Boeing 707, with a good income by the standards of those days, to the precariousness of being a candidate with a young family. Some say it's a chancer's profession, politics, because it's so unpredictable.

**TEBBIT**

It was a very chancy thing, because I stood in 1970 for the constituency of Epping, but because of the growth of Harlow New Town not least, it had double the appropriate electorate, about 120,000, so I knew it was going to be redistributed. I couldn't know what was going to happen; I wasn't even sure that I was going to win it in 1970, and it didn't quite accord with my game plan – I would have liked to have another five years building up my pension from BOAC! But I had to take a chance. You can't hesitate on these things. I took a pay cut of about 50 per cent and a very insecure future.

**HENNESSY**

Did you think you had a star to steer by, to use a favourite phrase of Margaret Thatcher's? Are you a man of destiny on the quiet, Norman?

**TEBBIT**

I didn't think that I was destined to be even a minister, entering Parliament with no background at all in politics really, at the age of about 40. I was just content that I was going to go there and do something to make things different.

**HENNESSY**

Well, you certainly had an impact. People were extremely offensive to you, weren't they, within almost weeks. 'The half-trained polecat … the Chingford skinhead' – that was later on, admittedly. You've always been on the receiving end as well as giving it out, haven't you?

**TEBBIT**

Well, that's true and I was extraordinary grateful to Michael Foot for that comment about a semi-house-trained polecat, because it told me that I'd got under his skin, and it told the public at large that I was a chap Michael Foot had to take seriously. Nobody had heard of me; they'd all heard of Michael Foot. [*Laughing*] It was a fundamental error on his part.

**HENNESSY**

Did you begin to form a friendship, even an embryonic partnership, with Margaret Thatcher in your early years, even though she was bound by collective Cabinet responsibility. Did you see a kindred spirit there?

**TEBBIT**

I scarcely had any contact with her, really. A few words now and again, you know, when we met, perhaps in the library reading newspapers or something like that, and naturally being a small 'c' conservative, I had not considered the possibility of a woman leading the Conservative Party at that time.

**HENNESSY**

What did you make of her in those early conversations?

**TEBBIT**

Very impressive woman, you know. I realised quite rapidly that she and I thought along pretty closely similar lines about politics as a whole.

**HENNESSY**

Did you ever talk to her, in those days when you got to know her through the opposition years, when Labour was in office, '74-'79, about how both of you couldn't really abide the post-war consensus, felt smothered by it? Because she was always very eloquent about how much she loathed that post-war consensus, which pretty much everybody else in your generation had taken in with their mother's milk.

**TEBBIT**

Yes, I found that very refreshing, that I found somebody else who felt the same way about that post-war consensus. But also, of course, I think we both felt the same way about some of the things which that early Labour government, the '45 government, did, which were absolutely right, and which it would be have been much more difficult for a Conservative government to do at that time.

**HENNESSY**

Tell me. Such as?

**TEBBIT**

Membership of Nato. It was not Churchill that created Nato, it was Attlee.

**HENNESSY**

Ernie Bevin ...

**TEBBIT**

Ernie Bevin in particular, one of the truly great men of British politics, in my judgement. And the British nuclear deterrent; again, how difficult would that have been if it had been a Conservative government trying to take that through against the Labour Party? And the Labour Party would have been against it.

**HENNESSY**

So you had conversations, you and Margaret Thatcher, about the Attlee government and the great things it did in that area?

**TEBBIT**

Oh, we did, as we got to know each other, it would come up – looking at those early post-war years, and what needed to be changed, and what was in fact a very good thing.

**HENNESSY**

And you would regard Clem Attlee and Ernie Bevin as 22-carat patriots, wouldn't you?

**TEBBIT**

There's no doubt whatsoever in my mind that in any really great *contretemps* that Attlee and Bevin and I would have been on the same side.

**HENNESSY**

In '79, you felt – you must have felt, given the financial position, the state of industrial relations – that there wasn't just one mountain to climb, there was a Himalayan range, really. And for all your combativeness, you must have felt daunted in May '79, when Mrs Thatcher came in with a 40-plus majority.

**TEBBIT**

It was clearly not going to be an easy time. What sticks in my mind about that era was that the TUC generals, not the shop floor workers but the TUC generals, had overthrown two governments running. Essentially they'd overthrown Ted Heath, and then they had overthrown Jim Callaghan. They were obviously spoiling for another fight, and seeking to overthrow Margaret Thatcher. That seemed to me something which could not possibly be allowed, so I knew it was going to be a struggle, that sooner or later they would attempt it, and I think Margaret did too.

**HENNESSY**

She first of all sent Jim Prior to Employment, who was a consensus man, and did make huge efforts to persuade the trade-union leaders that it couldn't go on like this. Do you think Jim failed, and if so why, and what lessons did you learn from Jim Prior as Employment Secretary when the job fell to you?

**TEBBIT**

My view was that it was inevitable that Jim was going to be Secretary of State for Employment – he'd been our spokesman. I think it would have been highly dangerous had we gone to the electorate saying, 'We're going to take on the unions; we're really going to sort 'em, to hell with what they think, we're going to do what we think', and all the rest of it; Jim's consensual approach was one which accorded with what most people probably thought. They thought there was a way through. Most people had bought into the idea that our industrial-relations problem was a load of Bolshy so-and-so's on the shop floor being restrained by these terribly responsible union leaders. I think that was the view that Jim had formed. My view was completely the opposite. I don't think many others held that view. [*Laughing*] And so everything I did was constructed around that belief, which I think has proved to be the correct one.

**HENNESSY**

The gods of politics were very kind to you, when you went to Employment, because as a young man on the *Financial Times*, you had been forced to join Natsopa, one of the print unions, if I remember, and suddenly, after all those decades had elapsed, there you were, in the driving seat, with the possibility of changing industrial-relations legislation – a belated justification for your loathing of what you'd been forced to do in the 1940s.

**TEBBIT**

Oh, I certainly bitterly opposed the closed shop in which I'd been involved by Natsopa, the union in those days. But there was another grudge, if that was a grudge, and that was that when my wife and I lived in London, we lived in the Barbican, and my wife had resumed her nursing career and was working at Barts Hospital. She became ill, but there was at the time a sort of Soviet that was seeking to run the hospital, and amongst the demands of the strikers involved at that time was that they were going to decide who could be admitted to the hospital on emergency grounds, and they decided, with all the wisdom of shop stewards, that my wife's case was not sufficiently urgent for her to be admitted to hospital. I think they realised afterwards that they must have made a mistake.

**HENNESSY**

Tell me about your first day in the Department of Employment, because Ernest Bevin, when he became minister of Labour and National Service, said to a journalist, 'Mr Gladstone, they say, was at the Treasury from 1868 to 1914. I'm going to be in the Ministry of Labour from 1940 to 1979' – metaphorically speaking. So you took over Ernie's legacy in many ways. But the officials probably didn't know what to make of you; they probably didn't know that you were a great fan of Ernest Bevin.

**TEBBIT**

No they didn't. Nor perhaps were they familiar with my theory of government, which is that all government departments exist to represent an interest in government; that's their being. The Department of Industry represents industrialists; the Department of Education represents educationalists, God forbid; the Foreign Office represents foreigners; and the Department of Employment thought they represented the TUC. I had to disabuse them of that. So the first thing I asked my permanent secretary was, 'What has happened to the bust of Ernie Bevin?', which I knew had always been on the ministerial floor just outside the lift. And he looked a bit embarrassed, and I said, well, where is it? 'Well, we moved it, we didn't think you'd want it.' I said, where is it? 'It's in the cellar.' So I said, 'Well send somebody down to bring it up and put it back where it should be, Ernie Bevin was the greatest minister of Labour that this country's ever seen.' So that was the first shock to them. [*Laughs*] And I continued with my shock treatment. I've always believed that you can get an idea through to somebody best when their defences are down; if they're laughing, they won't reject in a hostile manner. It'll go through, under their radar. So I got my officials around the table and told them that I was absolutely determined that I was going to change the whole of industrial-relations legislation in a way that it had never been changed before. I was going to repeal the 1906 Act, which is really like declaring yourself to be a republican while you're at church, or something.

**HENNESSY**

Protective picketing, and all that.

**TEBBIT**

Yes. So they began to blanch a bit, and I continued with my voice raising slightly. I said, 'Of course it will be difficult,' reminding them of the way that the Heath legislation had finished, with trade unionists who had got into jail and had to be released, to the humiliation of the government. I said, 'The Prime Minister knows what I'm going to do; if necessary we'll call the police; if necessary we'll call out the army; if necessary we'll build barbed wire barricades around every prison in the country, and we won't let any of those buggers fight their way in.' And at that stage they realised they were having their legs pulled. And they started laughing. And from there on I could not have had a better lot of guys working for me. I knew the basic philosophy and shape of the legislation I wanted, but it was they who turned it into legislation which has stood the test of time, in that it's not really been touched in the past 30-odd years.

It's interesting hear you say that, because in 2013 there's a lot of talk in the Coalition government – indeed it's been made public by the minister for the Civil Service – about how many ministers are disappointed with their civil servants: 'They block, they won't listen, and we've got to give them commands and it doesn't happen', and there's a move to politicise the senior civil service, in some quarters. It's not put quite as directly as that, but that's what it means. How do you react to that?

I think it would be a terribly great mistake. I don't want a politicised Civil Service. One should never forget that the Civil Service has to serve governments of all political persuasions. It must not be politicised in that sense. It would be a great mistake. I think too few ministers now spend enough time talking to their officials; they talk to their special advisers, who talk to their officials, and that's a fundamental error.

It's one of the mysteries, I think, that future political historians might toy with about the Thatcher years in government, your years, is that you didn't seek to turn back some of those liberal or conscience reforms of the 1960s that you really didn't like. You had these big majorities, and yet you didn't reverse the legislation that you disliked so much, those social reforms of the '60s. Now why was that?

I think one of the things I learned in government was that in a Cabinet of 20-odd people, it's unlikely that you're going to have more than half a dozen real drivers, a lot of competent people, yes, but people who really drive reform are in short supply. Parliament can only accept a certain amount of great reform at any time, and we had to concentrate on the most urgent issues: the trade-union problem was one of the great issues; the problem of the nationalised industries, which instead of creating wealth, actually consumed it; and the problem of the economy more broadly, the problems of inflation, and things of that kind. So we simply didn't have the manpower or the parliamentary time to conduct as many reforms as I would have liked. Indeed, probably the electorate would have said, no, no, that's too much. The electorate is 'small c' conservative in many ways as well; they don't want the whole world to be turned over at once.

#### HENNESSY

Would you like to have gone back on capital punishment, say, or homosexual rights for consenting adults, those kind of liberal reforms?

#### TEBBIT

I don't think that would have been sensible. I think there's a lot to be said for the concept of capital punishment, but I think that would have been, again, a step too far. I think there's a much greater tolerance of some behaviour which deviates from the norm, let me put it in that sense, and I think it will be difficult even if one wanted to, to reverse those reforms.

#### HENNESSY

One of your other regrets, looking back, I think, was that the pit closures were too rapid and too extensive. You've been very eloquent about the destruction of the pit communities, these fine working-class communities, and the problems it's brought. You feel that very deeply, don't you, and yet the orthodox view of you, Norman, is, 'Well, he's a hard man, that one – if anybody was going to take on the miners with Mrs T, it was him.' You do feel that , don't you – there is a scar there, a scar of regret.

#### TEBBIT

There is a scar of regret. But of course, it wasn't Mrs T that took on the miners, it was Arthur Scargill that took on Mrs T. And he couldn't carry all the miners with him. But I've always been conscious of the fact that the miners did form an elite within the working class, for want of a better expression, and a lot of what they were doing was *absolutely* that they were building their own little societies in which they behaved with enormous courage at times, and certainly with great integrity.

#### HENNESSY

The other event of the '80s that you'll always be remembered for is the ghastly tragedy of the Brighton bomb. It is impossible for somebody who hasn't experienced that to have any real idea of what people go through, particularly if a person you love dearly is seriously injured, and you were pretty badly injured too. I hope you don't think it's impertinent, but could you describe a bit how that changed you, that experience?

#### TEBBIT

I'm not sure that it changed me very much, and I don't like the idea that there was something unique about that experience. After all, an awful lot of people were buried alive in the ruins of bombed buildings between 1939 and 1945, and we're not expected to make an undue fuss about it, but to crawl out, or be dragged out, and get on. But it made a great deal of difference to me, of course, because I felt like I had to put my wife's interests ahead of my own, and I have never forgiven the Establishment, in its broadest sense, for the fact that although we've had enquiries into so-called Bloody Sunday, although we're now apologising for what we did to protect the Kikuyus against Mau Mau, whenever I gently suggest that it would be a good idea to have an enquiry to nail those who were really responsible for that terrorist atrocity, not the poor little creature that planted the bomb, but those who planned it, organised it, authorised it, financed it ...

**HENNESSY**

The army council of the IRA in other words ...

**TEBBIT**

Well, yes indeed, so I believe; they did after all claim credit for it, if credit be the right word. Whenever I suggest it would be a good idea to actually have an inquiry which named those people, so that we could all see them in their full glory, I'm told that that would be a very bad thing to do.

**HENNESSY**

Despite the strength of feeling that you've just expressed, Norman – do you not think it's remarkable that Northern Ireland has got to where it is now? If you'd been Prime Minister in the early '90s, and not John Major, and the message had come through the back-channel from the IRA that the war is over – would you have grabbed it?

**TEBBIT**

Let's be careful to get it right. What came from the IRA was the belief that they were on the rocks. The IRA had been infiltrated to a great extent; they were in deep trouble.

**HENNESSY**

British Intelligence had penetrated them?

**TEBBIT**

Indeed, British Intelligence had penetrated them. One of leading members of the IRA was about to be indicted, I believe, for no less than eight murders. He would probably have been found guilty. He would probably have gone to jail. I think the motivation was fear of what was happening to them. I like to think that had Airey Neave lived, that fear would have come much earlier.

**HENNESSY**

Mrs Thatcher's adviser on Northern Ireland, who the INLA[1] murdered.

**TEBBIT**

Indeed. Had Airey Neave not been murdered on the eve of the 1979 election, he would have become Secretary of State for Northern Ireland, and I think he would have approached the problem from a slightly different direction; and we would have got to at least where we are, perhaps a bit beyond, very much earlier.

**HENNESSY**

Of course, the other impact in terms of public and political life was that – because of the commitment you made to your wife, Margaret – Mrs Thatcher lost you as a ministerial colleague in '87, after the election. That must have been a very difficult decision for you, and indeed when Mrs Thatcher tried to get you back in again, you must have been really torn.

**TEBBIT**

Yes. I'd had to tell her, of course, that I would not be available to stay in the Cabinet after the '87 election. She found that difficult to accept; she even set Willie Whitelaw on me, [*laughing*] to try to persuade me, and as everyone knows Willie is a very persuasive man! But I had to stand by what I promised my wife. And then in 1990, when things were becoming very difficult for her, she asked me if I would go back into the Cabinet, and again I faced that

1 Irish National Liberation Army, a republican group

terrible conflict between divided loyalties. But my undertakings to my wife pre-dated, and they had to stand. And then in 1990, of course, when she was brought down, again, colleagues asked me if I would stand for the leadership; and it was a very, very difficult decision. Who knows, I might have been elected, I might not. I don't know. It wasn't easy.

### HENNESSY

Do you think you could have saved Margaret Thatcher in November 1990, if you'd been in the Cabinet with her? I've never seen a more dramatic moment in the House of Lords since I've been in the chamber, than during the tributes to her in the spring of 2013, when you said, 'My great regret is that I left her to the mercy of her friends', and you looked down to the senior Conservative Cabinet ministers on the Privy Council bench, where I notice you never sit, and there they were. It was drama with a capital D that was Norman. But do you think, if you had been with her, you could have seen them off, in November 1990 – or had things got to such a pitch that even you, if you'd interposed your body, couldn't have done it?

### TEBBIT

I think I could have held them back for a while. I don't think I could have seen them off. I've always taken the view that when somebody becomes Prime Minister and they walk through that door and look out of the windows of Number 10 – the windows are really quite large. The longer they stay there, the smaller the windows get. And I think it's very, very difficult for anyone to maintain that view of the world outside for more than about 10 years. There's also the more mundane problem that after 10 years, the back-benches are covered in people who you found wanting, and had to dump, and people who think they ought to be in the government, but who have been passed over.

**HENNESSY**

John Biffen called it 'The revenge of the unburied dead'.

**TEBBIT**

I think that was one of John's better remarks. I think he's absolutely right.

**HENNESSY**

If you had become Prime Minister, November 1990, what style of leadership would you have adopted? Collegiate but firm? How would you describe it?

**TEBBIT**

[*Laughing*] From the front, I suppose, is the answer. But always remembering what young men are taught at Sandhurst: that to lead is a huge privilege; that one owes a dual loyalty, first of all, of course, to Her Majesty the Queen, and secondly to those who you lead; and that the duty of a leader is always to make sure that the men and the horses are fed before he has dinner. And I think that's an essential part of leadership, that you should always be thinking about those who you are leading, because if not, they'll soon stop thinking very much about you.

**HENNESSY**

Who would you have made your Chancellor of the Exchequer and Foreign Secretary?

**TEBBIT**

I think probably Nigel Lawson would have been my Chancellor. Foreign Secretary – I don't really know. I think to a large extent I might have been my own Foreign Secretary. Whether that would have been for good or ill, I'm not sure.

**HENNESSY**

And the Foreign Office would have been stopped from represent-ing foreigners in London?

**TEBBIT**

I think that certainly would have been the message that got to them! [*Laughs*]

**HENNESSY**

If you had made it, what statute can I give you?

**TEBBIT**

I think it would have been welfare reform, because I think that welfarism has become the curse of this country. When I like to pull the leg of left-wing audiences, I speak about it. I always pop in those words of Professor Beveridge in which he says that the period of time for which a man may draw unemployment benefit should be limited lest men become habituated to idleness.

**HENNESSY**

The Beveridge report of 1942.

**TEBBIT**

And that of course raises the most terrible shouts and yells, and I say, 'Well, not my words, Beveridge's words.' And had we enacted the original reforms in Attlee's day more in line with Beveridge, they would have stood the test of time better, because we've created a dependency culture, and that has really been a curse.

**HENNESSY**

Do you worry about your country and the fragilities home and abroad? Are you really anxious about our prospects?

### TEBBIT

I am quite anxious about the future of the country for two reasons: one that, particularly in recent years, the Blairite, uncontrolled, uncounted and unlimited immigration has been more than our society could absorb, and therefore it's led to a fracturing of society in many ways. We can see that around us these days. That makes me anxious. Secondly, of course, is our relationship with our friends on the continent of Europe; that is again a great source of problems. And I think that fracturing of society, the culture of dependency and the problems of our relationship with Europe are the things which worry me most.

### HENNESSY

And I think in early days, you were in favour of us joining the Common Market, as it was then called, because you were a free-trader.

### TEBBIT

It was not so much that I was a free trader which propelled me into the European camp; but I found myself there for what I now realise were the same reasons as diplomats and members of major multinational companies. I had lost touch with the people of my own country, because I spent so much time abroad when I was flying; and I also, in that world, had found that my colleagues, other airline pilots, were a very congenial bunch, regardless of nationality; that we shared an enormous amount of views together, we were almost interchangeable really. And we also found that all the problems were ones which went across borders and could only be solved by trans-border authorities. Unconsciously, as in the case of diplomats and international business people, I had rather absorbed the idea that that went for everything. Gradually, as I spent more time in the Council of Ministers, where I made many friends and spent many, many congenial hours, as well as some deadly boring ones, I realised that the gulf of difference between us, because of our island history, and them, because of their continental history, was too great to be bridged. Curiously, I came to the view that we were more like the Germans than anybody else, and the more the EU seeks to expand, the less likely it is that it will be able to survive.

**HENNESSY**

Norman, I've always been intrigued by the contrast between the public image of Norman Tebbit and the private one, because those who know you to any degree know that you're jolly and self-ironic, but a lot of the public still see you as the *Spitting Image* puppet, the biker in the leather jacket. The toughie. Does that bother you?

**TEBBIT**

No, it never has. Partly because it's an image that has always appealed to young people, and that was very helpful to me. And secondly, when you think about it, that puppet was the one that always won. [*Hennessy laughs*] So there was an assumption that I was going to win the encounter, and indeed, I've always found, even when I've got mixed up with a bunch of drunken Millwall supporters on a Saturday night train from Merseyside, that they dealt with me with enormous courtesy and a great deal of fun.

**HENNESSY**

That's a very Norman Tebbit remark. How do you think you'd like history to remember you?

**TEBBIT**

I don't really mind; it'd be something to be remembered, wouldn't it? That's the first thing. I think, really, as a loyal lieutenant of the Prime Minister who stands out head and shoulders above any other in the late 20th century, except Churchill himself.

**HENNESSY**

How do you think you will be remembered?

**TEBBIT**

I think as a footnote, probably. [*Laughs*]

**HENNESSY**

A flavourful footnote, at the very least.

**TEBBIT**

Oh, I hope so, I hope so.

**HENNESSY**

Norman Tebbit, thank you very much indeed.

# Neil Kinnock (Lord Kinnock)

Series 1, Episode 4, first broadcast 1 August 2013

**Born** 28 March 1942; **Educated** Lewis School,
Pengam; University College, Cardiff

MP (Labour) Bedwellty 1970–83; Islwyn 1983–95

Leader of the Labour Party and Leader of the Opposition,
1983–92; Member of the European Commission
1995–2004 (Vice President 1999–2004)

**HENNESSY**

With me today is a politician who so loved his party that he burnt up his personal prospects of the Premiership in the course of making Labour electable once more, under a different leader. He was, too, a politician who couldn't help putting passion and exuberance alongside the cold calculations needed for success at the very top of politics. Neil Kinnock, welcome.

**KINNOCK**

Thank you very much.

**HENNESSY**

Neil, if there was such a thing as a cradle of the wider Labour movement, not just the party but the trade unions, the Co-op, the Miners' Institutes with their fabulous libraries – it was your patch, crammed into those narrow South Walian valleys atop the black gold of the coal seams. Are you still, deep down, a child of that formation, a child of the valleys?

**KINNOCK**

In many ways, yes, and I think particularly in terms of loyalties and cultural encounters. Because the point was, it was a very cultured upbringing, which wasn't anything particularly special in working-class areas of that time, the late '40s, the '50s, when there were thriving choirs and operatic societies and thespian companies and visiting celebrity artists – who weren't people, then, off X-Factor, but were actually the finest operatic singers and concert performers in the world, which collectively, the workers in Tredegar by their weekly contributions to the Workmen's Hall – which was the huge theatre, beautifully appointed theatre – could actually afford to bring for one night on every third Sunday of the month throughout the winter months – and given the length of the winters in South Wales that used to mean about nine months of the year. And so, maybe to compensate for the narrowness of the valleys, there was a breadth of experience, obviously encouraged hugely by my parents and subsequently by the school, and those things I still relate to, and feel very much at home with. And I can go to the valleys now – which have changed *hugely* of course, and in some ways not for the better because of the economic battering that they have had over the last 30, 40 years – and feel that I've been away for 20 minutes.

**HENNESSY**

There was another side to the culture of those valleys in those days: the greatest poet of post-war politics, Aneurin Bevan. And I think you used to go as a boy with your dad up to Waun-y-Pound where his memorial is now, still between Tredegar and Ebbw Vale, to listen to his open-air meetings. That must have been, for you, given your formation, and the sort of chap you are, that must have been like a shot of electricity.

### KINNOCK

It was wonderful. And you're right to describe Nye as a poet of politics because although he could be, when required, clinical and forensic, both in debate and in the way in which he established a National Health Service, was a brilliant housing minister, which people forget about, was a great local-government minister ...

### HENNESSY

The Ministry of Health did Housing and Local Government as well, which everybody forgets ...

### KINNOCK

Absolutely. And he turned his hand to the immensely practical and beneficial, benevolent indeed, enterprise of creating the health service. And so what was great about Bevan, wasn't simply his poetry, his oratory, which was obviously world-class, and maybe the best encountered in the century because it wasn't confined to open-air meetings at Waun-y-Pound above Tredegar, he was brilliant in committee, he was wonderful in Parliament, and he was great on the conference platform too. I only heard Nye speak twice in the open air; on other occasions it was in halls, particularly in the Workmen's Hall whenever he was in trouble, [*laughing*] which was fairly frequent, he would come to his constituency and not address a closed general committee meeting or even a trades council, where I also heard him speak when I was a young socialist delegate – but to 1,800 to 2,000 people packed into the Workmen's Hall, with a Tannoy system broadcasting to a few thousand more outside. And he would speak for an hour, he would use sophisticated language, he would make Biblical allusions, he would use snatches of Shakespeare or Wordsworth, and people would thrill to his every word. And by the time they left, they understood why he was in trouble, and they also understood why they were on his side. [*Laughs*]

**HENNESSY**

One of the great divisions between politicians, temperamental types, is between poets and plumbers, and from what you're saying about Nye Bevan, he could be a plumber when he had to be, but we all remember the poetry. Are you, Neil, more poetry than plumbing? Are you any good at the plumbing? Or does the poetry always intrude, trump everything else, because you can be no other?

**KINNOCK**

The people who worked with me thought I gave too much attention to plumbing; I would answer them by saying, unless the reorganisation of the Labour Party and the alteration of our policies is led from the top and undertaken in detail in every nook and cranny, it's not going to get done, and we can't afford to skimp. I need to assert my authority in the most minuscule details, absurdly sometimes, in order to win an argument, get a change, secure an amendment. So my preference is for poetry, I make no bones about that, and maybe my talent, such as it is, is more for poetry than for plumbing. But the plumbing had to be done, and when faced with that, the general assessment is, I think, that I made a pretty good job of it! [*Laughs*]

**HENNESSY**

We'll come back to what I think you once called your mid-life crisis, ie leading the Labour Party, in a minute. [*Laughs*]

**KINNOCK**

Yes, [*laughing*] few people can so accurately, almost to the minute, define their midlife crisis – mine began on 2 October 1983 and finished on 18 July 1992, and after that and before that I've had a wonderful life! [*They laugh*]

**HENNESSY**

When did you first think of becoming an MP? How old were you? Can you remember where and when, and what triggered it?

**KINNOCK**

I think it was, as a real prospect or possibility, a *real* ambition, after Glenys and I got married and we'd moved to what turned out to be the constituency of Bedwellty. We got the house there because it was midway between where Glenys worked and where I worked, and I discovered that the Member of Parliament, a very well-respected man called Harold Finch, was not in his late 50s, as I thought, but in his late 60s but nevertheless secure and unlikely to change. I will say, because of what people said to me, I *did* think 'This could occur in the next 10 years', not necessarily for Bedwellty, though the conditions were propitious. If anything, the prospect of becoming a Member of Parliament loomed larger in Merthyr Tydfil, where the Member of Parliament was S.O. Davies, rather than in Bedwellty simply because of the acquaintances I had, and the work I was engaged in was much more in the Merthyr valley, and in the town of Merthyr.

**HENNESSY**

Because you were a Workers Educational Association teacher, which of course you loved – that job was made for you.

**KINNOCK**

Oh, it was wonderful – in terms of the students, who were an inspiration; in terms of the people that I worked for – there was a genius called DT Guy, David Thomas Guy, an ex-coal miner, who'd got his way into university and graduated, and he was the District Secretary who appointed me, and I adored the man, he was a wonderful man. But for the accident of being elected to Parliament at 28 years of age, I would have continued happily for decades.

**HENNESSY**

But Finch decides to retire at the next election, which turns out to be June 1970, and you win Bedwellty in the valleys, classic Labour seat, huge majority, career there for life if you wanted it. And you make a mark very quickly in the House of Commons.

**KINNOCK**

Yes, I think ginger hair and a facility with jokes helped. And over the years my capacity for manufacturing jokes has landed me in some difficulty on occasion, but generally speaking it's been employed to make a serious point with a degree of wit. Maybe people heard that and caught on. The other thing is, as others have reflected since, I was certainly on the left, in the Bevanite tradition, and a huge supporter of my beloved comrade Michael Foot, but I nevertheless had no appetite at all for avid, sectarian posturing, and one or two of my colleagues on the left tended in that direction.

**HENNESSY**

That's very tactfully put; there were more than one or two in the early '70s, as you well know.

**KINNOCK**

Well, there were a few. They irritated me, and I could not forbear to tell them! [*Laughs*]

**HENNESSY**

You went into the Shadow Cabinet after Mrs Thatcher won in '79, and Labour's in opposition, and I think the public as a whole probably got a vivid sense of you – they had a sense of you already, because you're very good in the media, but I think it was the speech you made two nights before the poll in 1983 that did it: 'If Margaret Thatcher wins on Thursday, I warn you not to be ordinary; I warn you not to be young; I warn you not to fall ill; I warn you not to be old.' I think that's when you made your real imprint into the velcro of collective memory. It was as if everything that was in your formation boiled out, because you knew you were going to lose, big-time. Was it, as Nye Bevan would have called it, an 'emotional spasm', Neil, or did you calculate it?

KINNOCK

I did an unusual thing for that speech. I wrote it. Because I hardly ever, up until that point, had written speeches. I wrote it sitting in the back of a car that Glenys was driving down the M4 to finish the week campaigning in and around South Wales, and I felt these lines coming to me and scribbled them down. And the first 20 minutes of writing just flowed out. And then I stopped and read it back to myself, and read it to Glenys as she was driving, and she said, 'Hmm – you've gone in for blank verse.' So I wrote the second part of it consciously as blank verse. I decided to continue the rhythm of 'I warn you'. And it was a speech of defiance and, as you suggest, desperation. And I think you're right that that sort of made me recognisable, very rapidly, and then of course it was almost immediately followed by the leadership election campaign after Michael resigned in the wake of the electoral defeat.

HENNESSY

A future young historian of the Labour movement, say 30 years on, might say, 'Neil Kinnock had the perfect skill set to be a man of 1945' – the 1945 election, that combination of your formation of the valleys, the flesh of the flesh of the wider Labour movement, the style of rhetoric – that Neil would have been winner takes all in a 1945 context, but by '83, both the country and the world, and the nature of the media, and the nature of parliamentary politics had changed. Do you think there's anything in that?

KINNOCK

I think there's something in it. Yes, it is true that the politics had changed. We had the novelty of Margaret Thatcher, and what by 1983 she had become, and continued increasingly to be in the years after that. The media was changing, and that had a certain effect. But what I was trying to appeal to is the basic sense of community of interest in employment, the development of the economy for future requirements, the production of wealth and its fair distribution, and the expansion of opportunity for those who were willing to make the commitment and work hard. Now they're fairly fundamental, eternal objectives for any progressive, democratic politician, and I criticise myself for not delivering those arguments to the public in a way that was sufficiently appealing *and* reassuring to win eventually in '92.

In '87 I knew we didn't have a chance. My disappointment was that we didn't manage to win more seats, because that would have given us a different basis for attack in 1992. Many of the margins were very, very narrow indeed, but nevertheless, if you come second, that's no good. And '87 was in the least propitious circumstances, so I knew we were going to get very badly beaten then; but I really do criticise myself for not amending the message, or sharpening it, or making whatever change was necessary in order to ensure that it persuaded people that they were part of the community that would benefit from and contribute to this general advancement of people of all backgrounds in every class. And there's nobody else to blame for that.

#### HENNESSY

The gods of politics can be wrathful gods, and they were very wrathful on you in your first years as leader of the Labour Party, in terms of both the miners' strike and the Militant Tendency. The miners' strike, Neil, must have cut right into your core because it's about the communities that you lived and breathed in. Looking back, was there any way you could have shoved Arthur Scargill into having a national vote? The whole thing turned on that. This enormous strike, the vulnerability of those communities to pit closures and so on – you felt that as much as anybody could feel it, and yet here was this union leader, who in effect was running against you and the wider Labour movement – many people have thought – not having the national ballot before taking them all out, and splitting the miners depending on which coal field you were in. I mean that must have been unendurable for you, and it went on month after month after month.

### KINNOCK

It was appalling. Appalling. And the destitution – that's the only appropriate word – of what I saw in the pit communities, with people entirely dependent upon the collective effort and charity contributions to put food on the table for their children ... that was searing. As far as persuading, where Scargill was concerned I knew that was beyond all possibility. What I criticise myself for is not, as early as possible in the strike, saying this cannot achieve anything but misery without a national ballot. And what that would have done was give me the political space to confine the arguments to the case for and against pit closures. Instead of that, by not doing that, I was pulled into the vortex of the dispute itself, and it was easy for my opponents in politics and the press to caricature me as being an apologist for Scargillism, which God knows I never was.

The reason that I didn't make that assertion early in the dispute, either you have a ballot or you will be beaten in conditions of national disunity – is that the people I represented at senior trade-union level, and at neighbour level, at family level, were people who had already made months of sacrifice in the work-to-rule, lost lots of weekly pay, and were in favour of a ballot, but knew that nobody was going to listen to them unless and until they withdrew their labour. And these people, giving the finest example of loyalty, bravery, solidarity, would have been kicked in the face if I had lectured them at the beginning of the strike.

Even then I was caught unawares, as everybody else was, by the fact that a specially convened conference of the miners, over

Easter weekend in 1984, *appeared* to be called for two reasons: one, to change the constitution of the NUM so that a majority of 50 per cent plus one vote would be enough for a national strike, and that led everybody, including me, to believe that the immediate consequence of that would be to have the ballot. Well, they certainly passed the constitutional change, but we didn't even receive a motion to have the ballot. And those few weeks before that, when I lived in expectation – together with everybody else, *including a lot of striking miners* – that the great change was going to come, was the period in which I should have made it clear: it's a ballot or it's defeat. Because of course if a ballot had taken place, the whole circumstances in which the strike took place would have changed. It would have been much, much shorter. Sensible people in the government would have got the NCB to the negotiating table, and a rational, genuine trade unionist leading the NUM, which Scargill wasn't of course, would have come to compromise terms which is the essence of the purpose and strength of trade unionism. And it would have been done honourably, with a minimum of harm, and changed the political condition substantially. That's all 'if' and 'maybe'; the reality was vile and the reality was miserable.

### HENNESSY

Do you think Arthur Scargill had you in his sights, as much as he had Mrs Thatcher? That not only was it a political strike against a Conservative government, but against a certain type of Labour leadership?

### KINNOCK

Maybe. He would subsequently claim that. But most of the months of the strike were months in which what he wanted to do was have me to blame for not "winning", in inverted commas, the strike. He wanted to be able to claim that it was the political weakness and treachery of the leadership of the Labour Party that wouldn't call for a general strike nationally, if you've ever heard anything so absurd, that had really brought the downfall of the miners. Fortunately the miners are too sensible to believe that, so even though the claims were made by a few in the ultra-left, and Scargillites, I've never, ever encountered, on any coal field, at any time, any rank-and-file miner or lodge official who said that kind of thing to me. So Scargill utterly failed in that. But the worst failure, of course, was paid for by countless pit communities and youngsters and men who were out of work for years on end, and families that were desperately impoverished.

**HENNESSY**

The other great absorber of time and your nervous energy was the Militant Tendency.

**KINNOCK**

[*Laughing*] Yes.

**HENNESSY**

The Trotskyites within the Labour Party practising all these dreadful tactics of entryism. And it took ages for you to sort them out, not until you made that amazing speech at the Labour Party conference in '85, about the grotesque spectacle of redundancy notices being given out in Liverpool, Derek Hatton and Co were running that[1]. When you think about it, Neil, the Conservatives were dominating the political scene, and you had not only the miners' strike but what some would call the enemy within the Labour Party. I mean, what a double-headed blow for you, even though in the end it was the making of you in many ways with a wider section of the country – that speech, which was one of the greatest Party Conference speeches anybody can remember, in '85. But my heavens there was bloodshed on the way, wasn't there.

1 Derek Hatton was deputy leader of Liverpool Council and a member of Militant, a Trotskyite organisation.

### KINNOCK

Oh, there was; and it would have come a year earlier, but for the miners' strike. One of the things I was determined to do when I became elected leader, one of the reasons why I valued the very large majority that I got in that contest, was that I knew I needed all of the strength within the movement that I could get to take these people out. Because it was no good pulling the trigger unless there was going to be a kill, if I can speak figuratively. But I couldn't do it in the conference of '84 because of the miners' strike. At that time, for reasons I understood, the Labour movement, the whole Labour movement, was utterly preoccupied with the dispute and everything that went with it. And any attempt to try and focus attention on the wilful damage being done by the entrist Militant tendency would have just skimmed off the surface. And so the greatest test for me was keeping my powder dry for a further 12 months, which was far from easy, especially when I had leaders of Liverpool City Council [*laughs*] idiotically coming into my office and telling me that with a conjunction of defiance in Liverpool by the Militant-led council and the [*Liverpudlian accent*] circumstances generated by the miners' strike, [*back to his accent*] and a new consciousness that was arising in the working class, that if I called for a general strike I would bring down Margaret Thatcher. They sat on the other side of the table, with me with a few members of the Shadow Cabinet there, listening to this, and I said, 'There's more chance of me riding down Lime Street on a rhinoceros than any of this happening'. And of course that was further evidence of my deviationist treachery.

Anyway, I had to hang on and get to the conference, and it had to be at the conference because that was the only place to plant it right between their eyes. Even then, the difficult part was to come, because denouncing them is one thing; making it effective by expelling them from the Labour Party was entirely different, especially with a constitution that was built by a very tolerant party for tolerant and well-meaning people. So I had to use this constitution whilst fully observing the requirements of natural justice in order to arraign these people, against whom we had evidence before us, and expel them from the Labour Party. And it took hours and hours, and days and days, with television cameras parked outside Labour Party headquarters, and these clowns posturing and eventually being expelled on the basis of the evidence scrupulously observed. And it took us altogether with the first group of Liverpool militants about three or four months to get rid of them. And then there were more expulsions around the country, and we changed the constitution – what I was saying earlier about being a plumber – changed the constitution in detail, and went through the whole paraphernalia, so that we got a party which was a very unhealthy place for entrists or for people with purposes that were fundamentally divergent from those of the democratic, socialist, social democratic Labour Party.

#### HENNESSY

There was one other aspect of turning the Labour Party in new directions, which I think was difficult for you, because you naturally loathe the possibility of nuclear war. I know everybody does, but you took the unilateralist side when you were a young man, and the Labour Party for the bulk of the '80s, until you managed to amend it, was committed to that. And you suffered in many interviews from this always being brought up, and indeed I think in '83 you said that if you were Prime Minister you couldn't really authorise nuclear release, you just couldn't retaliate, whatever had happened. Now, that must have been particularly difficult for you, given that it was deep within you.

#### KINNOCK

Yes, because in many ways plain common sense was on its side. The whole thesis of mutually assured destruction requires very sensible and humane people to sustain the idea that there are circumstances in which they just might use it, maybe even as a first strike, very definitely in retaliation. And I've actually never met anybody, with the possible exception of Mrs Thatcher, but maybe not even her, who behind their eyes really acknowledged the reality that they would use the terminal weapon. And I thought, for long periods, that it was better to offer leadership that was based on the acknowledgment of that truth than the alternative. Experience taught me that it didn't matter how valid the arguments were, how impressive the facts and figures were, how excessive the expenditure is, how appalling the possibility was of use of these weapons – no one other than about 25 per cent, on a good day 27 per cent of the electorate, was ever going to listen to it. And so I had to say to the Labour Party when I changed the policy – and it was a rugged activity, it required not the winning of an argument but the displacement of an almost religious commitment that ran across the movement – I had to say to them, 'I've been where you've been on the picket line. I've been where you *haven't* been in the White House, in the Élysée, in the Kremlin, and I can tell you: not only can you not persuade people on the street, the counterparts don't even understand what you're saying.'

**HENNESSY**

In the Élysée, in the White House, in the Kremlin.

**KINNOCK**

And I said, on the basis of that experience, I'm telling you, no. I will not persist with the policy as it exists; I will only lead the party if we change the policy in the way that I've drafted. And we secured the agreement of the National Executive Committee, and a few months later the Labour Party Conference, and made a different manifesto stance. And that leadership was necessary because if it hadn't been done we would have doomed the Labour Party to maybe decades more out of office simply because it was an examination by the public, not of the validity or lack of validity of the argument about the nuclear deterrent and the readiness to use it, but the fundamental trustworthiness of political parties seeking to become the government. And to pass the test of trustworthiness you had to say there could be circumstances in which the weapon might have to be used and it was wise, therefore, for our country to retain the weapon. And we made substantial gains on the basis of that; unfortunately, not enough to win.

#### HENNESSY

Looking back, do you think it's inevitable that in the wider sweep of British political history you will be seen as a man of immense energy and commitment and courage, who immolated himself to create tarmac for somebody else to get into Number 10 under the Labour colours; that you paved somebody else's way, that somebody had to, and it just turned out to be you.

#### KINNOCK

I'm very reluctant to accept that description, though I know it's used, and it probably will be used, I know. It'd always be interesting, wouldn't it, to peep at your own obituaries. [*Laughs*]

#### HENNESSY

This is the nearest you're going to get, Neil.

#### KINNOCK

Yes, well I've written a few! But nevertheless: I strove to win. When I lost in 1992, by what Bob Worcester told me was twelve hundred and forty votes, which is the combined lowest 11 Conservative majorities, so it was pretty close out of 25 million votes, I was deeply downcast until it became apparent that the Labour Party had changed fundamentally in a more progressive and a more successful direction and there was therefore a possibility that what we'd achieved between '83 and '92 was going to be the foundation for substantial success. So I take some satisfaction from that. And despite all the miserable times, as my children occasionally remind me there were *some* fulfilling experiences that came as a result of occupying that position over those years. To see Nelson Mandela, just weeks after he came out of Pollsmoor jail, at the invitation of Ingvar Carlsson the then Swedish Prime Minister and a very dear friend of mine, to go to Stockholm to meet Mandela, to have hours with him, to be *recognised* by him, incredibly – because he'd been looking at pictures of myself and Glenys speaking in Trafalgar Square. They were nailed up on his cell wall. Those kinds of experiences would not have come about in that way. To go to Berlin a week after the wall came down, speak at the SPD congress in honour of Willy Brandt's – another great friend of mine – 75th birthday; I wouldn't have traded that for anything.

### HENNESSY

There was somebody else, slightly surprising, who said good things about you, in terms of the wider historical sweep. I think Mrs Thatcher once said to you, 'History will be kind to you', didn't she?

### KINNOCK

She did, actually. She wrote a kind and courteous note, that was dated the day that I stopped being leader of the Labour Party, and I was touched by that. She still addressed me as 'Mr Kinnock'. [*Laughs*] And I reciprocated. But that was a civilised element of otherwise, honestly, vituperative politics. And if we keep that mixture of civilised people being moved by convictions, asserting themselves passionately, but within a determinately democratic setting, that we seek to strengthen, I don't think we'll go far wrong.

### HENNESSY

Kenneth Morgan, the great historian of 20th century politics, particularly Welsh politics, and political leaders, once said about Nye Bevan, 'Like Lloyd George he was an artist in the use of power', terrific phrase. Do you think, Neil, that is what you wanted to be if you'd made it to Number 10? What would you have done, what's the style and the flavour of the Kinnock Premiership we never had?

**KINNOCK**

The only purpose of getting democratic power is to use it for the enlargement of people's opportunities and the further strengthening of democracy; and consequently, I would, for instance, have an explicit national-health and community-care tax, whose product went only to the NHS and community care. And it would have meant modifying the so-called standard rate of income tax, and it would have encountered the resistance of the Treasury – but we would have done it, and the NHS would have been assured permanently of buoyant finance.

**HENNESSY**

So quite a chunk of taxation would have been hypothecated, to use the technical term.

**KINNOCK**

Indeed. And I think that, in the modern world, where people need to see a direct connection between their expenditure and what is returned for that, we will move towards a much more specific relationship between what you pay and what you get. It won't be confined to health, it I think will extend to higher education, especially in the wake of the unfortunate changes that have taken place in this century with higher-education funding. But the buoyancy of that, including expenditure on research, is essential. And it can't afford to take second place to some other forms of expenditure and so I think democratic politicians are going to have to be able to demonstrate that the quality of what is being received by the community is in a direct connection with the quantity and quality of investment being put in.

**HENNESSY**

For all your word-power, Neil, and you do feel as a natural European now, you didn't when you were younger, but you do now ...

## KINNOCK

Well, I did – I just didn't like what I thought the Common Market was. I was wrong.

## HENNESSY

But you're a natural European now. Why is it that nobody has managed to sing a song of Europe, as it were, to the British people, the wider British people, particularly the younger ones? Why is it we have this persistent emotional deficit with the European community?

## KINNOCK

Some of it is to do with the very widespread political habit, not confined to this country, of describing any advance or success or plus in the European Union as 'their' accomplishment, and anything that is disagreeable as 'the fault of the bureaucrats of Brussels'. And cumulatively, of course, over decades, that takes on a life of its own. In addition, I don't think the argument has ever been assiduously made – and I mean decade-in and decade-out – that in the modern world, if countries want to effectively possess and use power, they increasingly have to do it collectively. And what we are doing in the European Union is subscribing to a pool of power, some of the powers previously retained in the nation state, in order that collectively in economic terms, environmental terms, in combating crime, in movement of people, in research and development, in a host of other areas where real authority to achieve outcomes has passed beyond the borders of states, that in return for pooling some power, we're actually accumulating a greater authority over our own destiny. That is the truth, it's been understood for many, many years, but it's never been effectively explained in a way that secured generation-to-generation understanding. Maybe now's the time to start again doing that, because with every year passes, with globalisation, greater integration, greater interdependence, not just of the European continent but the whole damn world, that reality of acting together in order to act effectively is becoming more and more sharp, and more and more evident. And we've already got the amenity of the European Union to accomplish those things. Other parts of the world are trying to build similar models. And the last thing we should do is put our future in that in any form of question whatsoever.

**HENNESSY**

What's it like having a daughter-in-law who's a successful centre-left politician in Denmark, is indeed the Prime Minister? This must be a peculiar satisfaction, even though you didn't make it in.

**KINNOCK**

Oh, it's wonderful, and she's a wonderful woman. Helle is a daughter to us, and happily both of our children and our son- and daughter-in-law are great friends to each other, and with us. We don't find ourselves talking such a great deal of politics, because my view is, and I think hers is too, that there are wider areas for enjoyable exchange: holidays and kids.

**HENNESSY**

What trace would you like to leave on history?

**KINNOCK**

I'd like to be remembered as a tall, slim man, with a deep voice [*Peter laughs*] who gave up the Premiership after 25 years. [*Both laugh*]

**HENNESSY**

What trace do you think you *will* leave on history?

**KINNOCK**

Who thinks in these terms? Do you think in those terms?

**HENNESSY**

Well, I think senior politicians do, a lot of them, Neil.

**KINNOCK**

I think it's important that anybody who stands for democratic office, certainly at national parliamentary level, is conscious of the fact that they are going to try to act in ways that have an effect on history. To fail to understand that is to fail to comprehend the nature of the duty and the task. But those politicians that I've encountered who think of themselves as history-makers, are very drab indeed. Very superficial. They perforce are obsessed with tomorrow's headlines and they will drift before the wind in order to make their place in history. There are very, very few people who are genuine history makers, who have performed acts with a deliberate intention of making history. They have done it either because it was the right thing, or because they *thought* it was the right thing, not because they were going to achieve a different theatrical review.

**HENNESSY**

Neil Kinnock, thank you very much indeed.

**KINNOCK**

Thank you.

# John Major (Sir John Major)

Series 2, Episode 1, first broadcast 13 August 2014

**Born** 29 March 1943; **Educated** Rutlish Grammar
School, Merton, South London

MP (Conservative) Huntingdonshire 1979–83; Huntingdon 1983–2001

Assistant Government Whip, 1983–84; Government Whip
1984–85; Parliamentary Secretary for Social Security, Department
of Health and Social Security, 1985–86; Minister of State,
DHSS, 1986–87; Chief Secretary to the Treasury, 1987–89;
Foreign and Commonwealth Secretary, 1989; Chancellor of
the Exchequer, 1989–90; Leader of the Conservative Party,
First Lord of the Treasury and Prime Minister, 1990–97

**Autobiography** *The Autobiography*, 1999

**HENNESSY**

With me today is one of our unexpected Prime Ministers. On the
evening he captured the Premiership, he reflected on how great the
three-mile journey had been from his boyhood in Coldharbour
Lane, Brixton to Number 10 Downing Street. His colleagues say
he opened his first Cabinet meeting with the words, 'Who would
have believed it?' Sir John Major, welcome. It was a long way from
Brixton to Number 10: it's an extraordinary story of a suburban
upbringing and tough times in Brixton to the highest office in the

land. When were the seeds of ambition first planted in you? When were you first aware that you wanted to do something big in public and political life?

### MAJOR

I think probably about the age of 13. And I think what influenced me most were what Harold Macmillan would have called, 'Events, dear boy, events'. It was what I saw and what I experienced that made me realise that I would like to take part in public life to see if I could change some things. I always had a fascination for history, and the first time I ever went in the House of Commons – at the invitation of a Labour MP actually, Marcus Lipton, the Member for Brixton – I felt that there is a special atmosphere in that building, and it reaches out and grabs you. And I thought to myself, this is where I'd like to work.

### HENNESSY

But where does the Conservative impulse come from? It's a crude way of looking at it, but so many do see it that way in our class-obsessed country – you were from the wrong side of the tracks, to use an American phrase, and yet you were in no doubt that you were a Conservative, that this was the way to get those beneficial changes.

### MAJOR

At the time, when I was 12, 13, 14, we lived in Brixton, five members of the family in two rooms and a little landing upon which we cooked, and the washroom three floors down. And the Labour Party in Lambeth were very big-hearted; their attitude generally was, 'Yes, you are in difficulties, and in due course we will help you, but be patient'. And the Conservative Party said to me, we'd like to open up avenues of opportunity for you to change your own circumstances, and those of your own family. And of the two philosophies, there was no doubt which one appealed to me. So I was by instinct Conservative. I'm not an ideologue in any way, and what attracts me is what pragmatically can be done not whether it meets some ideological test or other.

### HENNESSY

In your memoirs, you have a very vivid section about your hatred of class obsessions in our dear country. You said, 'I was in earnest about classlessness; I wanted to say that the subtle calibrations of scorn in which this country rejoices, the endless putting-downs and belittlings, so instinctive that we don't notice ourselves doing them, are awful.' Now, there's passion and there's pain in there. Were you patronised as a young man from south London in that old Conservative Party, by the grander figures?

### MAJOR

You see there's an assumption there that it was the Conservative Party that was being patronising. And if that was so, why would I join them? In fact, it wasn't so much that, it was more the way that life behaved. The fact that there were glass ceilings on opportunity for many people, depending upon their background; that there were different social values applied to people who had blue-collar jobs, and people who had white-collar jobs. There was a different social value placed on immigration. I saw immigrants at very close quarters in the 1950s; they shared my house, they were my neighbours. I played with them as boys. And I didn't see people who'd come here just to benefit from our social system, I saw people with the guts and the drive to travel half way across the world in many cases, to better themselves and their families, and I think that's a very Conservative instinct, to do that. That's what I saw. And it was things like that – and also the fear I saw amongst many people who had nothing, perhaps unsophisticated people as well. I saw a fear of officialdom among them. And it was things like that made me think: there are changes that can be made, and they can better be made from a Conservative attitude than from any other attitude.

**HENNESSY**

In those formative years you seemed very at ease with Harold Macmillan and Rab Butler and Iain Macleod, you're a classic one-nation formulation Conservative. And Napoleon used to say, if you want to understand a man or woman in authority, think of the world as it was when they were 20 or 21. And you are from that era, that post-war, relatively consensual era of concerned Conservatism. Is that the key to John Major, really?

**MAJOR**

Certainly I felt comfortable with it – I much prefer consensus to disagreement; if you can reach consensus, so much the better. And certainly of the politicians of those days I think above all it was Iain Macleod who most attracted my attention as a young teenager. Firstly because of what he said, which was uplifting, and secondly because of the way he said it, which was compelling. He had some form of paralysis of the neck which kept his head absolutely unmoving, and he had a voice like a ringing bell, and it was inspiring to listen to. And certainly as an 11, 12, 13, 14-year-old, if I could hear Iain Macleod speak, I would, and I drank in every word.

**HENNESSY**

You're a man of immense application and tenacity, but why didn't you work at school, at Rutlish Grammar School? Why did it all come later? I know people fire up at different points in their intellectual life, but it's a bit of a mystery, that, John.

**MAJOR**

Well, not to me. Circumstances at home weren't easy. My father was very sick, and was plainly at the beginning of dying; my mother was very sick; there were lots of domestic problems. I had to travel from Brixton to Wimbledon each day. There were difficulties that sat in the forefront of my mind, far more than studying. And so I suppose, rather in the way young people do, I withdrew from what

I should have been doing, which was studying, and concentrated on other matters. I knew I was doing it, and I knew I was foolish in doing it, but I couldn't not do it. And then the moment I left school, I knew I had to study, and I had to make up for that.

**HENNESSY**

And you certainly did, and you came in, in the great rush of new Conservative MPs in May 1979. A pretty rapid rise: you were in the Whips' Office first of all, and record has it you had the most furious row with Mrs Thatcher, quite early on.

**MAJOR**

That's absolutely true.

**HENNESSY**

Not entirely a career-enhancing move, one would have thought.

**MAJOR**

Well, it turned out to be so actually because she is an extraordinary set of contradictions. These days when you talk of Margaret Thatcher, you have to draw a distinction between the Margaret Thatcher of legend promoted by her opponents and by her adherents, and the real Margaret Thatcher, the flesh-and-blood Margaret Thatcher that I knew. It's certainly true that we had a colossal row. It was the fashion in those days for the Chief Whip to invite the Prime Minister for dinner once a year with the whips, and she came, and after two minutes she had exhausted the social chit-chat that she loathed so much. And so we sat down to dinner and John Wakeham said, well, the economy's central …

**HENNESSY**

He was the Chief Whip …

## MAJOR

John was the Chief Whip at the time. 'The economy's central', he said, 'I'll ask the Treasury whip, John Major, to talk about what the Party's view is.' So I told her, and the Party's view wasn't what she wished to hear, and so she decided, rather than enter into debate, that she would shoot the messenger, which she attempted to do in spectacular style, and I responded in equal style, saying that this may not be what she wished to hear, but that's what the party thought, and that was what I was going to tell her. And the argument went on for some time. And one or two of the Whips came up to me afterwards and said, well, that was a short career. And the following day I was the whip on duty sitting on the green benches in a sparse House, and Margaret came and sat next to me and said, "I've been thinking about what you said last night, we ought to have a further meeting to discuss it". And she went into the Whips' Office and convened a further meeting. And about three weeks later she had a reshuffle, and appointed me junior minister at the Department of Health and Social Security, in the job in which she herself had started, and which she thought was a good learning job. So there's a curious contradiction. She behaved pretty unreasonably in the conversation and then afterwards the other side of Margaret appeared. She didn't say 'I was wrong', but she put right what had gone wrong, and then promoted me.

### HENNESSY

Mrs Thatcher must have seen something very special in you from that extraordinary set-to. She said you were the one that she wanted to succeed the night you took over; but did she realise that you were quite so right-through One Nation? Did you think she was misreading you, and did you allow her to misread you?

### MAJOR

No I didn't. I mean, if she did misread me I'm puzzled as to how that happened, because both as Chief Secretary and as Chancellor, and briefly as Foreign Secretary, a glorious 94 days in which we went to war with no one, I saw a great deal of Margaret Thatcher one-to-one – and we didn't always agree. And we did have a relationship where I could say to her what I thought; I didn't have to temper what I thought, and I *didn't* temper what I thought. So I find it difficult to understand how she could have misunderstood what my views were, because they were expressed often enough.

#### HENNESSY

Do you think you were ready for the Premiership in 1990? Would you like to have done longer time in one of the big offices of state?

#### MAJOR

Yes, I would.

#### HENNESSY

Why was that? What did you think you were missing still?

#### MAJOR

I think I was missing the fact that the longer you have been in government, the more experience you have. I would have preferred it if I had become Prime Minister a few years later. I think that would have been easier in terms of how I felt about it, and I think it would have been easier in terms of the experience I was able to bring to the job. But if the ball comes your way, you grab it. There's nothing else you can do.

#### HENNESSY

When you become Prime Minister, the whole weight of special responsibilities fall upon you, including the most awesome one, which I've written a little bit about, which is having to do the nuclear weapons stuff, the 'last resort' letters. And I was very struck when David Cameron told me, on-the-record, that when he had to write about what he wanted from beyond the grave if we were wiped out by a nuclear bolt from the blue, he told me he called you in and asked for your advice. It's the most awesome thing that falls upon a new Prime Minister, so how did you prepare yourself for it, and later how did you help David Cameron prepare for writing down those extraordinary letters to go on the submarines?

#### MAJOR

It is a shock. The first time I realised that I was going to have to write post-Armageddon instructions to our four Trident submarines[1] was when the Cabinet Secretary told me. And it is quite an extraordinary introduction to the Premiership. And I remember I went away over the weekend, and I thought about it a lot, and it was one of the most difficult things I ever had to do, to write those instructions – the essence of them being that, if the UK is wiped out but its Trident submarines are at sea with their weaponry, what should they then do with their weaponry? And eventually I reached a conclusion, and I set it out, and I talked to David about that. I'm not going to say what I said, but we discussed the parameters of it, and I left him to make his own decision, as he did.

#### HENNESSY

Soon after you became Prime Minister – actually, straight away, given the condition of the Middle East – you were engaged in the run-up to the first Gulf War.

#### MAJOR

A few days before the war started, I went to Saudi Arabia to meet the then-exiled Kuwaiti royal family, and reassured them that Britain would be with the United States, because their closeness to the United Kingdom was – and is – remarkable. And I also went to visit the troops. And there were several things that

1 In fact, the letters were destined for the inner safes of Royal Navy Polaris submarines in 1990.

struck me about that. The first was how young they were. And I remember standing on a tank talking to thousands of them, and I knew, though they did not, that the war would begin on the 16th of January, and this was just a few days earlier. And as I spoke to them, all these boys sitting there, their faces metamorphosed into those of my son, whose 16th birthday was the date at which war began. A year or so older and he could have been part of them. And all their faces morphed into my son's when I was talking to them, and that is a memory of war I've never forgotten.

#### HENNESSY

There's a paradox in your Premiership in the early years, when, as you like to put it, you felt you were living in sin with the electorate because you hadn't got your own majority, which you did get against expected political form in '92, but then troubles came in battalions in late summer and early autumn of 1992. And so you had your majority, but the gods of politics can be very malign, and they dumped on you, John, didn't they? It must be quite painful for you, looking back, to see that paradox, because once you were no longer living in sin with the electorate your party erupted around you. Black Wednesday and the European question asserting itself again ...

#### MAJOR

Of course the party changed in 1992. A large number of the last remnants of the post-war generation were succeeded, those who had been in the war and who thought anything was better than having another European war – they had lived through one, and had memories of the first earlier in the century, and they were prepared to make accommodations to bring Europe together so there could never again be another European war. But they were succeeded by new young group of Conservatives who had grown up in a much more ideological age, with a much more ideological bent, and without the historic memory of the war and its immediate aftermath. So the parliamentary party that was so difficult after 1992 was a different, significantly different, parliamentary party from the party that had existed throughout the '70s, '80s, and the early part of the '90s. And then what significantly changed things was the collapse of sterling, falling out of the exchange rate mechanism.

**HENNESSY**

16 September 1992. A day which you'll always remember.

**MAJOR**

16 September 1992. I'm unlikely to forget it. [*Both laugh*] But of course, the background to it *was* forgotten. Why did we go in to the exchange rate mechanism? Why did Margaret Thatcher sign up to the exchange rate mechanism? And she did. *And – she – did.*

**HENNESSY**

You persuaded her and Douglas Hurd, the Foreign Secretary, did.

**MAJOR**

We talked to her, and she was persuaded. And she wasn't, as some have said, persuaded with a pistol held to her head. I will tell you *exactly* why Margaret agreed to go into the exchange rate mechanism: because as she came to the end of her Premiership, we were suffering the recession that so often follows a boom. There had been a boom in the late 1980s and we were now heading into the recession. Inflation, on the day I became Prime Minister, was very nearly 10 per cent. Unemployment was soaring. Interest rates were 14 per cent and we were undoubtedly heading for a deep recession. Now, Margaret cared about inflation. It hurt the people that she knew. She wanted to bring inflation down. And *that* is why she decided we would go into the exchange rate mechanism, because every time in her political life and mine we had had an anti-inflationary policy, the government had given way when it got difficult, and the exchange rate mechanism produced a clear external discipline to bring inflation down.

And so concerned about that was she that she actually wished to go into the exchange rate mechanism at a more punitive exchange rate than the one we chose. So the argument that Margaret was unwillingly pushed into the exchange rate mechanism is utterly, utterly false. But then of course, when we crashed out, it was taken by the Eurosceptics as a classic reason to pile in on Europe, on every conceivable front, and that of course is what happened. It was a great calamity, a political calamity that we came out. What is frustrating about that is that we had already been discussing privately within government – I had been discussing with the policy unit and others – how we could come out of the exchange rate mechanism without causing too much disruption and without the market believing we have given up our anti-inflationary credentials. And the crisis hit us, and we were toppled out of the exchange rate mechanism before we could reach a conclusion on how to come out voluntarily; and that of course seasoned everything that followed.

**HENNESSY**

It was almost the end of your Premiership, in that you seriously thought you might have to go, in a sort of honourable resignation, and thereafter you've always been very honest and said you were prone to depression as Prime Minister because of that calamity.

**MAJOR**

I was never sure whether I should have resigned or not. I asked the views of people I respected, like Douglas Hurd and I think Norman Fowler, and also people who were not politicians, about whether I should resign. And their view, maybe people always give this view, I don't know, but their view was unequivocally that I shouldn't, and that if a Prime Minister did resign a few months after winning an election that the government itself was doomed. Now, whether that was the right decision I have never been certain. I have never been absolutely certain.

**HENNESSY**

You're still not sure.

**MAJOR**

I don't think you can ever be certain, and it's not something that haunts me now – but the truth of the matter is I was never certain that it was the right or wrong decision. But it did have several effects. I was never in any doubt that winning the 1997 election would be very difficult. The day after the '92 election, Chris Patten and I sat in the White Room at Number 10 …

**HENNESSY**

He'd just lost his seat …

**MAJOR**

Chris had just lost his seat at Bath, and we agreed that in winning a fourth successive term, we had stretched the democratic elastic as far as it would go and, unless Labour collapsed, we would have little chance of winning the next election. I was reinforced in that view by the impact of Black Wednesday. I thought it overwhelmingly likely that we would lose. In once sense, that was liberating: Sarah Hogg, the head of my policy unit, for one repeatedly said to me, you can now do what you think is right, you don't have to politically trim, you can do what you think is right. And economically, we did. And if I may say so, people these days forget the dire economic circumstances on 30 November 1990 …

**HENNESSY**

When you became Prime Minister …

**MAJOR**

… and the fact that we handed on to the Labour Party in 1997, by common consent, the best economy any government has handed on to its successors, probably at any time in the 20th century. And people forget that. And they forget other things that happened after Black Wednesday: the Northern Ireland peace process, which was extraordinarily difficult to start, but extraordinarily worthwhile.

**HENNESSY**

I think history will linger on that, because you opened the back-channel to the IRA, after they'd approached MI6 saying the war's over, we need advice on how to finish it. That was an enormous risk, and it was kept very secret as it had to be but it started the road to where we are now.

**MAJOR**

I remember the afternoon that message came in. I was sitting in Number 10, it was a grizzly, grey late afternoon, and my principal private secretary came in bearing a message, saying, we're not sure what to make of this. And that was the famous message about bringing the conflict to an end. And I discussed it with the Northern Ireland secretary, Patrick Mayhew, and we realised that if this went wrong, it would be the end of our political careers, because we would have been seen as being dupes of the IRA and foolish and naive and all those things. On the other hand, if we made progress it would save people's lives. So that was the judgement: looking foolish on one hand, and perhaps making progress and saving lives on the other. So we were in no doubt about what we should do. But there was a lot of opposition to what we did, both within the Cabinet and in the Conservative Party particularly. I received a lot of support then from the Labour Party and the Liberal party, but I was never sure quite where the balance of opinion was within my own party.

**HENNESSY**

I'm very struck by Sarah Hogg saying, now you can be yourself; a sense of liberation, as you put it. I've always had the impression though, John, that if you could do it again, you would have been even more yourself. There are certain things you would have done if you'd followed your instincts despite, perhaps, difficulties. One of which would have been to put a lot more funding into the NHS, or another area which you've always been keen on, which is open government. Do you have some regrets that you weren't even more John Major, the inner John Major, than you actually turned out to be '92-'97?

**MAJOR**

Well, it wasn't just political inhibitions. It was money. I mentioned earlier the terrible economic recession that we had at the beginning of the 1990s: we spent the best part of five to six years putting that right. And it was very unpopular putting that right. And, of course, when you're doing that, you do not have the resources, or in some ways the political capital – with a tiny majority which was shrinking all the time – to actually make those sort of changes. And I couldn't, because we were preoccupied with the economy; we were overwhelmed with disputes about Europe; Northern Ireland also took a great deal of time. But in terms of the social reforms I would like to have made, I'm not sure we would have had the majority for them in the House of Commons. But above all, we didn't have the money for them.

**HENNESSY**

What would they have been, if I could retrospectively wave a magic wand for you?

**MAJOR**

Well, I think there are several different areas I would talk about. Firstly, education. Not having had much of it, I'm very much in favour of other people getting it, and widening it. I mean we did, for example, give greater status to the polytechnics – and many people criticised us for this; in some ways maybe they were right.

But I was trying to improve the quality of, the social ambience surrounding, blue-collar work. Certainly a lot of education changes. I would have liked to have upgraded the education profession. I think in this mercenary age we would have had to have looked at the rewards for the top of education. So I think it would have been expensive to do what I wished to, but I believe it would have been right to do it. And I think also I would have looked to the provision of more homes, largely small units in the inner cities. And there's a lot of space, idle space, in and around the cities where I would have wished to provide, probably, penalties for those who idly hung on for too long to land that ought to be developed, and incentives to people actually to develop. And of course, I would have wanted to make reforms to the health system. Now I believe, with the money that we had built up in the economy by '97, that we too, had we won that election, would have put a lot more money into the health service, and looked at reforms of the health service. So I shall live with regret to my dying day that I did not have the wherewithal, and was not in a political position, to go down the route of those reforms which were the sort of things I wished to do from the first moment I dreamed of going into politics.

### HENNESSY

Another problem which beset your government was the 'back to basics' idea, which was, I think, misunderstood.

### MAJOR

No, it wasn't misunderstood, Peter, it was *distorted*. And it was distorted because at that stage the government was the fox and the media were the hounds. In defence of the media, there was, though I did not know it at the time, a young briefer at central office who had spoken to people about it being a moral crusade, when it was never intended to be a moral crusade. If you go back to the source speech for 'back to basics', it was predominantly about education and good neighbourliness and community care. And secondly, for the first three months of it, it was very popular until events conspired to turn it into a negative. But it was distorted.

**HENNESSY**

Is it possible to have a private life as a modern politician? Because you've suffered very much in that department yourself.

**MAJOR**

It's increasingly difficult. I admire people who go into politics; I know this isn't fashionable to say at the moment but most of the politicians I know – and I make no party distinction here – the vast majority of the politicians I have known over the years go into politics for good motives, not bad. I don't subscribe to the lurid version of politicians only being in politics for themselves and for their own interests. That was not my experience during the years I was in politics.

**HENNESSY**

It's a tough, scarring business being Prime Minister, even in relatively benign circumstances, and you didn't have those. I was very struck, years ago now, when Quintin Hailsham was asked on Radio 4 by Anthony Clare, did he regret not becoming Prime Minister when he was so close to it in '63 – the Macmillan succession – and he said: 'I've known every Prime Minister to a greater or lesser extent since Balfour, and most of them have died unhappy; it doesn't lead to happiness'. Are you happy, John? Will you die happy?

**MAJOR**

Well I very much hope so! I'm not planning to do so immediately; I shall hope to hang on for a while. I think there's different sorts of Prime Ministers once they leave office: there are those for whom office never quite goes away; there are others to a greater extent, and I hope I'm one of them, who have been able to say, that was yesterday, and I now have other things that I must do with the rest of my life. So the advice I would give to anyone who wishes to be Prime Minister is, when it is over, there is a very remarkable world out there. Try and see it, and try and make up for the things you necessarily and rightly had to sacrifice when you were in politics.

**HENNESSY**

Finally, John, how do you think history will remember you, and how do you want history to remember you? Is there a gap between the two?

**MAJOR**

[*Laughs*] I have no idea, but the great comfort is, I won't be here to find out.

**HENNESSY**

[*Laughing*] John Major, thank you very much.

# Roy Hattersley (Lord Hattersley)

Series 2, Episode 2, first broadcast 20 August 2014

**Born** 28 December 1932; **Educated** Sheffield City
Grammar School; University of Hull

MP (Labour) Birmingham, Sparkbrook 1964–97

Joint Parliamentary Secretary, Department of Employment and
Productivity, 1967–69; Minister of Defence for Administration, Ministry
of Defence, 1969–70; Minister of State, Foreign and Commonwealth
Office, 1974–76; Secretary of State for Prices and Consumer
Protection, 1976–79, Deputy Leader of the Labour Party, 1983–92

**Autobiography** *Who Goes Home?*, 1995

**HENNESSY**

With me today is Roy Hattersley, a writer and politician, both a
historian of and a participant in events since first elected to the
House of Commons in 1964. In his very person he carries the
history of the Labour Party: from its shining high tide in 1945,
when he was a schoolboy, through the Wilson and Callaghan
governments of the 1960s and 1970s, becoming Deputy Leader as
Labour's internal civil war in the 1980s distracted and exhausted
the party. He has a taste for writing, political ideas, political biography and, I hope, for a dash of autobiographical conversation.
Roy, welcome.

**HATTERSLEY**

Thank you.

**HENNESSY**

Can we start with your formative influences? To use an old line, the words 'Labour Party' run through you like a stick of Blackpool rock.

**HATTERSLEY**

There's no doubt I am an environmental Labour Party member, so to speak. My mother was much more active in Labour than my father; she became the mayor of Sheffield. And I admit, until I was 17 or 18, I knew I was Labour, but I couldn't have told you in more than a couple of sentences why I was Labour. Then came the great, dare I use the word, intellectual influence of my life: I was in the lower-sixth, going into upper-sixth; the schoolmaster who was encouraging me gave me some summer reading. It had three books as I recall: Eileen Power's *Medieval People*, Kitto's *The Greeks*, and R. H. Tawney's *Equality*. And I read *Equality*, and it was as if I'd been struck by a thunderbolt. It seemed to me that the case for equality was overwhelming, there was no argument against it. I couldn't understand why people didn't accept it as an obvious matter of fact – and I feel just like that today. *Equality* seems to me to be the good life, the good society, the good nation. And I've felt like that ever since I was 17.

**HENNESSY**

What year was this Tawney moment?

**HATTERSLEY**

It would have been 1950, '51.

**HENNESSY**

'51. And you're at Sheffield Grammar School.

**HATTERSLEY**

Sheffield Grammar School. But another thing happened shortly afterwards, the following summer. I was working in a vac job on the milk round, naturally enough the Co-operative milk round, Brightside and Carbrook Co-operative Society – there's a title to conjure with. We were delivering milk to everyone who had a milk token. And one Friday morning we got to a house where a woman with two little children said, 'Sorry, no token'. And the real milkman – I was the assistant – said, 'Don't worry love', took out a bottle, said, 'Get a jug', carefully took off the sealed silver foil from the top and poured the milk into the jug, then put the foil back on, smashed the bottle, and said, 'We'll put this down as a smashed'. And I was rather impressed by the way he helped her – this is what society should be about. Two rows later, a woman comes out and says, 'I've no token.' He says, 'Sorry, can't do anything.' I said to him afterwards, 'What was the difference between woman one and woman two?' 'Didn't you notice?', he said, 'The second woman smokes. If she can afford cigarettes, she can afford milk.' And this began in my mind, and set in my heart, a dilemma which I still struggle with: whether benefits, welfare, should be a matter of need, or a matter of earning.

**HENNESSY**

The deserving poor and the undeserving poor. Very 19th century.

**HATTERSLEY**

Exactly. And I'm instinctively – I won't say on the side of the undeserving poor, but I see we have to somehow help the undeserving poor. When I hear Duncan Smith talking about people 'deserving benefits', or 'earning it', I have a vision of this archetypal layabout, the man in the singlet sitting in front of a television, watching racing and drinking beer out of a can, and won't go to work. Would we deny him benefits? Well, he's got a downtrodden wife and two neglected children, I mean, you've got to do something with those people despite their lack of 'desert'. And I don't know how you solve that problem, but I've thought about it every day since delivering milk for Brightside and Carbrook.

**HENNESSY**

You're a classic incarnation of '45 – you're a man of '45, Roy, aren't you?

**HATTERSLEY**

Well, Robin Day said this. He said, 'Mr Hattersley, wouldn't you have been more at home in Mr Attlee's government than in Mr Callaghan's?' And I said, 'No, Sir Robin, I'd have been more at home in Mr Gladstone's government.' And I think to a certain extent that's true, but I think that '45 was a shining hour of British politics. This is a time when by any standards we had a great government who changed the weather: nothing has been quite the same since '45. And therefore I'm very proud that I once delivered leaflets for the '45 election.

**HENNESSY**

Now, Gladstone's interesting, because Mrs Thatcher and her people would always quote Mr Gladstone as being the model: free trade, competition ...

**HATTERSLEY**

Sovereigns fructifying in the pockets of the people.

**HENNESSY**

Exactly. Now, your bit of Mr Gladstone is a different bit of Mr Gladstone to Mrs Thatcher's, I would imagine.

**HATTERSLEY**

Well, my bit of Mr Gladstone is not his politics, but his character. I have hanging in my house in Derbyshire a cartoon from *Punch* with a slogan underneath, 'Had he been a worse man, he would have been a better politician.' And what better could have been said about anybody than that? He was a man of impeccable integrity, enormous belief, certainty, courage, determination. Much of what he did, apart from Ireland, I disapprove of; but nevertheless he had this strange courage, strength and integrity, which I find immensely attractive.

#### HENNESSY

Mr Gladstone was a great man, obviously – but he lacked a raucousness gland. You are a very jolly person compared to Mr Gladstone. Mr Gladstone was very thin on jokes, Roy – you rather like jokes.

#### HATTERSLEY

[*Laughing*] Everybody's a jolly person compared to Mr Gladstone! And he hated jokes, he was very annoyed when people made jokes in his Cabinet, or made jokes to him.

#### HENNESSY

I have an image in my mind, of the young Roy, January '47, vesting day of the National Coal Board, and you got on your bike if I remember, and you cycled out to the nearest pit to see the notice board going up.

#### HATTERSLEY

'This pit is managed on behalf of the people by the National Coal Board', or 'This colliery is managed on behalf … *managed on behalf of the people*'. I mean, what a wonderful phrase.

#### HENNESSY

And you absorbed all of that.

**HATTERSLEY**

I absorbed all of it.

**HENNESSY**

And you're still a public-ownership man with qualifications, aren't you?

**HATTERSLEY**

Well, I was regarded as a right-wing so-and-so in the Labour Party, because I always argued against nationalising everything, and I've never thought that socialism was about public ownership. But sometimes public ownership is necessary. But public ownership is a means to an end – it's not what socialism is about. Socialism is about equality – and sometimes, to get a more equal society, something has to be publicly owned, but by and large most of the economy has to be run on the market principle. The market principle is essential for freedom as well as for efficiency. But there are some areas where public ownership is the right answer.

**HENNESSY**

Can we turn now to another great influence on you? The man concerned, who you actually knew – I don't think you knew Tawney – was Tony Crosland, and his *Future of Socialism* in 1956. Now, Crosland's notions of equality are very Tawney-like in many ways, but there's also a raffishness about Tony Crosland – there's that extraordinary sentence in the book, 'We need not only higher exports and old-age pensions, but more open-air cafes, brighter and gayer streets at night, later closing for public houses'. Now, you knew him very well – he's reacting against his Puritan upbringing.

**HATTERSLEY**

There's a classic completion of the paragraph, which says, 'If socialism is a matter of total abstinence and a good filing cabinet, some of us will fall by the wayside.' And that, in a sense, is what made the book catch on. People wanted socialism to be less grey, less drab, less austere. Tony was, notwithstanding that, a very, very serious politician. He also had more élan than any other politician I have ever known. I was at a Cabinet meeting, before I was in the Cabinet – they must have been discussing something about Europe – it began with Harold Wilson saying, 'There've been too many leaks from this Cabinet, and it's got to stop. It does the party damage, it does the government damage, it does the entire country damage, and I tell you now, it's got to stop.' A long pause – and Tony Crosland said, 'Harold, you only cause us embarrassment by behaving in this way, because we all know 90 per cent of the leaks come from you.' I don't know any other Cabinet minister who would have done that. The Cabinet were stunned. Harold said, 'Let's go on to foreign affairs.' [*Laughter*] And that was the essential, iconoclastic, daring, full-of-élan Tony Crosland, which I found immensely attractive. Very un-Gladstonian, I might say.

### HENNESSY

Deeply, deeply! Mr G would have deeply disapproved of T Crosland, absolutely. Tony Crosland had a great friend, Michael Young, who wrote *The Rise of the Meritocracy*, which was a book we all read. They thought about equality of opportunity, IQ + effort = merit, that classic formulation, and I remember reading it as a grammar-school boy and thinking, 'What's wrong with this? This is a charter for me.' I didn't realise for a long time it was a satire. You no doubt would have realised it was a satire, and a warning, and you've always had a sense of the ambivalence of meritocracy, even though you were a classic meritocrat.

### HATTERSLEY

I don't know what your background was, Peter, but I suspect it was like mine: ideal. If they wanted to form an individual who was the perfect candidate for passing the 11-plus, it would have been me:

my background, my family, my mother's aspirations, my father's attitudes, I was tailor-made to pass the 11-plus.

### HENNESSY

Snap.

### HATTERSLEY

But it wasn't enough – there are some other people to worry about besides you and me! And that was my basic feeling. But Tony's attempts to define what sort of equality he wanted was a great step forward. Tony clearly doesn't believe in equality of outcome, but he defines the equality he wants in a way that is totally sophisticated: namely, that people are always different, and we don't want to smother the differences. You are cleverer than somebody else, tougher than somebody else, more feeble – those are personal differences which can't be overcome, we don't want to overcome them. But we want to eliminate those differences that are imposed on us by society rather than by nature. And that's what Tony called 'democratic equality'.

### HENNESSY

And that explains, does it, for all your fondness of your own schooling, that you've been a comprehensive-school advocate right through.

### HATTERSLEY

Right through. I put myself back by at least five years when I was Education Spokesman, when against the wishes of Harold Wilson – I didn't know it was against his wishes – but I made a speech to the independent schools telling them that if I had my way I'd abolish them. Because I made the speech, I didn't become Education Spokesman after '74. I'd done two hard years shadowing Mrs Thatcher, and I assumed that when the election was over and won I would do the Education job; but not only did I not do the

Education job, I got no job at all for three weeks. I was left hanging about for three weeks to punish me for various sins!

**HENNESSY**

I've always felt very strongly that the one ministerial job you craved above all others – perhaps it would have been nice to be Prime Minister – but above all you wanted to be Education Secretary.

**HATTERSLEY**

Yes. I always did. The last time it was remotely possible was when John Smith was leader of the Labour Party, and he wanted me to stay on and be in his Cabinet. We were great friends, John Smith and me. And he had this view, 'Won't you stay on and see us in?' Which I assumed meant that I did one of these non-departmental jobs until they knew where to hang the coats and where the lavatories were in 10 Downing Street and then I was summarily ejected; I didn't want to do that. And when I went to see him, five days before he died, to tell him I was announcing my retirement the next day, he said, 'I would like you in the Cabinet.' I said, 'No. On no terms.' He said, 'Well, what if I offered you Education?' And I paused. He said, 'I'm not going to, so don't worry about it.' [*Laughs*] But right until then, Education was still in my mind, in my heart.

**HENNESSY**

If I could retrospectively wave a wand and give you the Education Department, tell me what you would have done; what would have been the sequence of actions, and what would have been the cumulative effect you would have sought?

**HATTERSLEY**

I wanted secondary education in particular to be unsegregated. We want all secondary schools to be similar in funding, if possible in esteem, and therefore in outcome. We want a unity in the secondary schools, rather than the divisions into various categories of acceptability and unacceptability. That means accepting that some parents will behave rather better than other parents. When you say parents with sharp elbows and determined characters push their children into certain schools, you're said to be denouncing the parents at the bottom end of the scale who don't bother doing that. Well, you may be, but it's a fact. Some parents push their children, some don't, and you don't want the education system to allow that to happen and to accentuate it.

**HENNESSY**

In effect, Roy, what you would have been seeking to do was to syringe out the class and status obsessions of our dear country from the education world.

**HATTERSLEY**

Well, as footballers say, that's a big ask. [*Laughs*] But I would like to nibble at the class system in this country. If I'd been able to just nibble away a tiny bit at the edges of it, I would die happy.

**HENNESSY**

Was Tony Crosland your route to Hugh Gaitskell?

**HATTERSLEY**

No, I was always a Gaitskellite before those days. I was always on what was called the moderate wing of the Labour Party. And I became devoted to Gaitskell's cause during the nuclear disarmament crisis.

**HENNESSY**

1960, '59-'60.

**HATTERSLEY**

At that time I almost gave up looking for a parliamentary seat. I was turned down for a very large number of parliamentary seats;

it was becoming rather a wearisome business, going around the country and not being selected. And I thought I probably didn't want to do it. I was a big noise on the Sheffield council, I was chairman of the Housing Committee when I was 25; I guess I would have been leader of the council if I'd stayed on. And then I went to a party conference, and there was a great argument over nuclear disarmament, and Hugh Gaitskell I suppose touched my emotions, by promising to fight, fight, and fight again to save the party we love. And I wanted to be a footsoldier in the battle. So I went home and said to the regional organiser in Yorkshire and said, 'I'm still in the race. If you can find a seat I can look for, I'll still go for it.'

#### HENNESSY

Did you think, Roy, in '64, even though Labour came back with a very small majority of three or four, depending on how you count, that '64 could be another shining hour, it could be '45 again?

#### HATTERSLEY

No I didn't. I thought that the next election might be; I thought that Harold Wilson was quite right to form a government and then go to the country for a second term quite soon. But in some ways, it *was* a shining hour you know: social policy was wonderful in '66. And when you think about what we did about social policy and libertarianism, Roy Jenkins' first period as Home Secretary, all that was immensely important. We made some bad mistakes over the economy, and we made a bad mistake on the first day by not devaluing – if we'd devalued, then we'd have had the economy moving forward in the way we needed to. But as a social government, as a reforming government in terms of individual liberty, it was a very, very important government.

#### HENNESSY

It's interesting you talk about the devaluation, because it's almost a conventional wisdom that it choked off all sorts of possibilities, that inflated exchange rate, it was far too high, it was not reduced until 1967. But the other aspect of you which I've noticed over the years was that if you couldn't have Education, you wanted to run a Ministry of Production, and you had developed ideas about what a production, a DTI, whatever you want to call it, a Board of Trade transformed would be. And yet there was the Department of Economic Affairs, and growth was the idea, indicative planning, a British version of the French planning system – and yet it didn't work, Roy, the growth rate stayed stubbornly where it had always been, with endless balance of payment crises.

#### HATTERSLEY

Well, I think it's all down to that basic first decision, and the first mistake. Jim Callaghan, to whom I was very close in the end, he put me in his Cabinet, Jim said to me perfectly openly when I discussed this with him, that the reason for doing it was political rather than economic. They didn't want the reputation that the Labour Party comes in and always devalues. It had devalued twice before, if it devalued a third time …

#### HENNESSY

'31 and '49.

#### HATTERSLEY

Yes. The reason was entirely political that they didn't. And Jim I think in the end regretted that they didn't.

#### HENNESSY

Yes. Looking back to those Wilson years, though – it was the social-democratic hour in many ways, not just those social-libertarian reforms that you've already referred to, but there was Wilson's rhetoric about technology and the scientific race, and where the future of world economic competition would be decided, and all the rest of it. Although people diminish it now, that 'White

Heat of Technology' speech he gave at the Scarborough Conference in '63, and the first attempts to do planning based on that, to take it a step on beyond the Attlee government, were all very promising, and many of us fell for it completely as young men. I certainly did.

### HATTERSLEY

Well, I fell for it, and I was still falling for it when I was in my 40s in the Cabinet. And had we won the election, I would have had that beefed-up department, with things taken off from the Treasury.

### HENNESSY

If you'd won in '79?

### HATTERSLEY

If we'd won in '79. Jim told me, at the last press conference at Transport House, on the Monday, that when we won he was going to divide the Treasury into two parts, David Owen was going to get one part of it, I was going to get another part, and mine was basically going to be the Ministry of Industry. And he said, 'Which part would you like?' and I rather annoyed him in saying, 'The part that's called Chancellor of the Exchequer'. [*Hennessy laughs*] Which he thought was being flippant about serious things. But anyway I would have wanted it, because I still believe in what you call indicative planning. I don't believe governments tell industry what to do, but you've got to ask industry what they want doing, and do it to the best of your ability. And very often governments don't do what industry wants, they do something that they believe to be right when it isn't.

### HENNESSY

Before '79 you had this tremendous crisis, the sterling crisis of '76, which I think you've always thought was overdone because the Treasury forecasts were misleading, I think that's been your case.

But you were with Tony Crosland in the Cabinet, not where Jim Callaghan and Denis Healey wanted you to be.

**HATTERSLEY**

I was the other boy on the bridge, there weren't three men on the bridge, there were only two. And we were right, but we were wrong. Our economics were right; Tony Crosland was prepared to gamble – I had no capability of working out the figures – that the public-sector borrowing requirement was not as large as the Treasury said – nor was it. In fact, we probably weren't in deficit at all. We argued as best we could that there should be a less austere view of public expenditure, and that to attack it in the way we eventually did attack it would undermine the Labour Party, and the idea of public expenditure for ever, as it did. But we were wrong in that we underestimated the importance of keeping world opinion on our side. I remember Professor Maurice Peston, now Lord Peston, who was then my special adviser, saying to me, 'The Prime Minister and Healey are totally wrong, but you have to support them. You have to support them because international opinion won't allow you to do anything else. If the Prime Minister says that international opinion requires the Cabinet to jump off Westminster Bridge, then the Cabinet must jump off Westminster Bridge. The merits don't matter, it's just getting international opinion on our side.' And I remember sitting in my room the night before the ultimate Cabinet meeting -

**HENNESSY**

This is December 1976 ...

**HATTERSLEY**

That's right. And Tony had been on some foreign jaunt, he was Foreign Secretary then, with Jim, and he came into my room and he said, 'It's all up,' and I said, 'What do you mean?' and he said, 'Well, the Prime Minister wants us to support him, and I knew that when he came to me and said, "You've got to support me, otherwise we're in trouble," I'd have to say "Yes". You must do the same'. And I said, 'Of course I will.' So the next day we had a very, very mild Cabinet, and we all agreed to everything.

### HENNESSY

Then Labour's civil war began, not that visibly straight away, but in '79, with the Winter of Discontent. It must have been very painful for you, Roy, because the Party of '45, that coalition of the wider Labour movement and so on began to fragment, and the malice, the sheer detestation of certain bits of the party, already talking about betrayal, started even before you'd lost the election of '79.

### HATTERSLEY

Much more painful than the divisions was the destruction of the idea. I mean, my social democracy, or Labour Party enthusiasm had as part of its bedrock the fact that the trade unions were a force for good, and that public expenditure was essential for a civilised society. Within the space of a year, we'd seen the trade unions behave hideously, and we'd seen public expenditure unsustainable. And to see those two pillars kicked away was very, very damaging, and I don't think the Labour Party's recovered from it even now.

### HENNESSY

And then after the election loss, the Party turned in on itself and the electoral college was changed to reduce the Parliamentary Labour Party's say; and there was a whole succession of set-backs for you and your colleagues that in effect, took away the '80s from you. It should have been your salad days, to use an old phrase, you would have had one of the highest offices in the land, if Labour had formed a government at any time in the '80s; but it was all taken away from you as the Party fragmented.

### HATTERSLEY

Well, we came out of the '79 last Cabinet meeting – we being the members of Cabinet of about 40, Bill Rodgers, Shirley Williams, John Smith – and we all said, well, we may have to wait five years, or perhaps 10 years, but we'll all still be 50. We all believed we'd be back soon despite all the ructions. We did lose those years – but they weren't fruitless years. In a strange, paradoxical way what made the years tolerable was having something else important to do and that important thing to do was getting the Labour Party right. I think I would have found it much more difficult just sitting there waiting for the next election, than I felt trying to help Neil as best I could to get the Labour Party back on its feet again. That gave us a purpose; it was a different purpose, but it was a purpose.

### HENNESSY

There was a fascinating emotional geography between you and Neil Kinnock, because you're very different in many ways, but I think you had that shared Tawney-ism, you had that equality impulse, and in many ways you weren't the odd couple people expected you to be.

### HATTERSLEY

Neil wouldn't mind me saying that in some ways we were chalk and cheese. But in fact I knew Neil Kinnock was the right man for the job, and that in fact helped, the fact that I knew Neil would be able to get the Labour Party right in a way that I wouldn't have been able to do.

### HENNESSY

You got on very well with John Smith, you were flesh of each other's flesh ideologically, weren't you, as well as good friends. He was the leader that was taken away in tragic circumstances. One of the New Labour arguments that one heard in 1997 quite a lot, although not in public, was that 'John wouldn't have got us a big majority'. Some people even thought he wouldn't have won in '97.

**HATTERSLEY**

Well, there's no question he would have won. He wouldn't have won it with as big a majority as Tony, because he wouldn't have appealed to those middle-class people who thought, 'Say what you like about Blair, he's not a socialist.' They wouldn't have said that about John. But he would have been sufficiently stable a Prime Minister to do the things he needed to do. And I think life would have been very different; we'd have had a proper Labour government, and life would have been very different indeed.

**HENNESSY**

It's interesting you use the words 'proper Labour government' – in what way were Tony Blair's successive governments improper?

**HATTERSLEY**

Well, let's put it this way: when I complain bitterly over the commercialisation of the Health Service, the Conservative Party say, 'But you began it'. When I complain bitterly that we're not building enough houses, they say, 'But you didn't build any houses.' When I say, 'You rely too much on the market, light-touch regulations,' they say, 'But you were the originators of light-touch regulations.' The things we started we enabled the new Tories to take on, and I think that is a very, very severe criticism.

**HENNESSY**

Did you feel that Tony Blair travelled light intellectually? That he wasn't rooted in the Labour Party in terms of loving it in the way you did, but also cerebrally …

### HATTERSLEY

The two things are different. He was a very clever man. He worked for me; his first job was when I was shadow chancellor, and he was the lad who did the running about late at night. And he was marvellous: he was lucid, he was loyal, he was hard-working, and he was very clever. But he came to politics very late: at university he wasn't really interested in politics, if at all. And therefore many books that you and I had read when we were in our teens he'd never heard of. For instance, he'd never heard of *The Rise of the Meritocracy*. And I think therefore that he snatched hold of some half-thought-out ideas, like the market, and hung on to them, without having thought about it quite so clearly as he should have done. I think that was one of his problems, that he didn't have the roots in the movement, and in the economic background to politics in general.

### HENNESSY

Now, you're an ace political biographer: if you were writing Gordon Brown's political biography, that still would be a mystery to you, would it? Why he turned out the way he did in the Premiership?

### HATTERSLEY

I have to say, because the requirement of honesty pervades the programme, I fear it was personality problems, it wasn't political problems, it was personality. I think he waited too long – the sort of Prince of Wales effect, the worst kings we've had have all been Princes of Wales who waited too long.

### HENNESSY

That's a bit disloyal, Roy.

### HATTERSLEY

Well, he's not King yet. [*Laughs*] I'm not anticipating he'll be as bad as George IV. [*Laughs*] I won't go any further in case you cut it out of the programme.

**HENNESSY**

Did your friendships with Shirley Williams and David Owen and Bill Rodgers recover? The others of the Gang of Four? Because you're of the same generation – you and Shirley in particular were very close operators together. Great friends.

**HATTERSLEY**

Great friends. We went on family holiday together. And my relationship with Shirley Williams survived the Gang of Four more easily than it will survive her support for the present Health Bill, which I find very difficult to swallow.

**HENNESSY**

She did a lot to modify that, to be fair.

**HATTERSLEY**

She did very little to modify it.

**HENNESSY**

Ah.

**HATTERSLEY**

She claims she did a lot to modify it, but if you look at the differences, the differences are *all* superficial.

**HENNESSY**

She would dispute that, wouldn't she?

**HATTERSLEY**

Well, I'm sure she would. The friendship with Bill was always an acquaintanceship rather, but with no animosity. And David and I, now we're friends again, we've recovered from it all.

**HENNESSY**

Friendship matters to you in politics, doesn't it, Roy? You've never been a loner.

**HATTERSLEY**

I'm not sure. I've never wanted to move in a clique, I've never wanted to join things. I mean, I've never been on a parliamentary excursion abroad anywhere, I've never done those communal things that politicians do. When I stood for the leadership, one of the things that was held against me was that I was never about in the Tea Room and the Dining Room, but I'm not that sort of politician.

**HENNESSY**

The next book ...

**HATTERSLEY**

The working title is *The Catholics*. But it's not a theological work, which I'm hardly equipped to write! It's a history of how Catholicism survived. My last book was the story of the Cavendish family, *The Devonshires*, and having written 250,000 words, it suddenly struck me that they spent very many years of their lives, over five or six centuries, suppressing Catholicism. It struck me, given that oppression that had gone on for 600 years, that it's a miracle, perhaps in my sense rather than the Catholic sense, that it had survived so long. And that's what I'm writing about.

**HENNESSY**

Has it anything to do with your dad as well, who was a Catholic priest as a young man?

**HATTERSLEY**

The dedication will be, 'To Father Roy Hattersley, born such a date, died such a date, ordained such a date, excommunicated such a date.' But that's only vaguely the reason. I didn't know my father was a priest until after he died.

**HENNESSY**

How did you feel when your mum told you about all of that?

**HATTERSLEY**

I felt desperately sorry I didn't know beforehand. Because I loved my father deeply; perhaps that's obvious to say, people do. But I loved him in a different way from the way I loved my mother. My mother was a very tough, demanding woman, a very hard woman in many ways; my father was very soft, gentle, yielding sort of man, and I could write down all sorts of virtues he possessed. But the idea that he committed this great act of bravery – that he walked away from the Church for love. I would have like to have known that he had a heroic moment while he was alive, and I think it was a heroic moment. I would have liked to have been able to say to my dad, 'I'm very proud of you for doing that.'

**HENNESSY**

You can say that in the book.

**HATTERSLEY**

I shall, believe me, I shall. [*Hennessy laughs*]

**HENNESSY**

Roy, what trace do you think you'll leave on political history?

**HATTERSLEY**

Very little.

**HENNESSY**

Why?

#### HATTERSLEY

Well, I've been a middle-ranking politician, I've never had one of the great offices of state. I think since you invite me to be self-congratulatory that I did something to save the Labour Party in the bad years. Before we had really begun the revival I set up a really rather ludicrous organisation called the Solidarity Campaign, which had only one purpose, which was to demonstrate to people in the country there were still reasonable people in the Labour Party. The Labour Party wasn't divided between the extremists who'd left to do absurd things or who demanded absurd things, and the moderates who'd left to be moderate. There was a core, a little flickering light of common sense and social democracy in the Labour Party. And we set it up to create that impression, and we did create that truthful impression. And I think that had I not imparted that, had we not had that idea of the continuity of Attlee socialism, as you like to call it, I think the Labour Party would have been in terrible trouble. So when I get to the pearly gates, and they say, 'Why should you come in?' I'll say, 'Because I helped to save the Labour Party in the 1970s.'

#### HENNESSY

What trace would you have liked to have left, if I could wave that magic wand again?

#### HATTERSLEY

I think I would like to have made great social changes, I would like to have changed the structure of British education; I would like to have made it a genuinely egalitarian operation. Of course, I would have liked to have been Prime Minister, everyone who gets into Cabinet would like to be Prime Minister – but I don't think I would have been a very dramatic or historically important Prime Minister. I wouldn't have wanted to do great things; I would have just wanted to make Britain a more equal society, a more compassionate society, a more amenable society.

**HENNESSY**

Roy, thank you very much.

**HATTERSLEY**

It's been a pleasure.

# David Steel (Lord Steel of Aikwood)

Series 2, Episode 3, first broadcast 27 August 2014

**Born** 31 March 1938; **Educated** Prince of Wales School, Nairobi;
George Watson's College, Edinburgh; Edinburgh University

MP (Liberal) Roxburgh, Selkirk and Peebles (1965–83); Tweeddale,
Ettrick and Lauderdale 1983–97 (as a Liberal Democrat 1988–97)

Leader of the Liberal Party, 1976–88; Co-founder,
Social and Liberal Democrats, 1988

**Autobiography** *Against Goliath*, 1989

#### HENNESSY

David Steel has been a real presence in our national political conversation for nearly 50 years, since he became a Liberal MP in
1965 at the age of 26. He quickly left an enduring mark by pilot-
ing the 1967 Abortion Act through the House of Commons, which
to this day leaves him reviled and praised by those who feel passionate about the practice. Now 76, he retains a youthful air, and
occasionally he is still referred to as 'the boy David'. He's been a
key and sustained player in the shift from two-party politics to a
multi-party system. David, welcome.

#### STEEL

Thank you.

**HENNESSY**

You were born in 1938 in Kirkcaldy, the son of a Presbyterian minister in the Church of Scotland. Do you think deep down, or perhaps not so deep, you're still a son of the manse?

**STEEL**

Oh yes, I think it never leaves you; ask Gordon Brown. [*Laughs*] I think it's just there. My father was very much involved in promoting better conditions for the miners on the Fife coalfields, in particular showers at the mines, so they didn't go home to sit in a tin bath in front of the fire. So that sort of influence was there.

**HENNESSY**

Did it make you perhaps a tad preachy as well, do you think?

**STEEL**

Preachy in a good sense, yes. Because I had to listen to my father's sermons twice on a Sunday, I was aware that speeches should have a structure, a beginning, a theme and an end. And I have to say, many of the speeches of political leaders today have no structure whatsoever, they're just a series of unconnected sound-bites. [*Laughs*] So, certainly my speeches at the party conferences, which were always the big annual event, had an awful lot of preparation put in them, and were very much structured along the lines of a sermon.

**HENNESSY**

When you were 11, your father was appointed to a ministry in what was still called 'Keenya', now Kenya, and suddenly you were uprooted from Scotland to Africa, and I know the Mau Mau emergency didn't erupt until a few years later, but again it must have been an extraordinary formation, utterly different from the one you'd experienced in Scotland.

### STEEL

It was in fact that four years that I spent in Kenya which were the most formative influence in my life, it's how I became a Liberal. It was international affairs that brought me into politics. My background of my having been brought up in Kenya – including the tail-end, when the Mau Mau rebellion was just starting – affected me because when I went to university at the time of the Sharpeville Massacre in South Africa, the Conservative government was still trying to inflict the Central African Federation on Rhodesia and Nyasaland ... these were the formative influences that caused me to be interested in party politics.

### HENNESSY

Being in favour of colonial freedom, as it were, across the piece in Africa, could have made you a Labour Party person just as easily. Why did it take the Liberal form rather than the Labour form?

### STEEL

You're quite right. Someone who became a great friend of mine later on was John P. Mackintosh, who you will remember was the Labour MP in the next-door constituency, but before that he was actually one of my lecturers when I was a student. And he tried to get me to join the Labour Party. He took me to a meeting which Hugh Gaitskell addressed and I was very impressed. And I won't say I was teetering on the brink of joining the Labour Party, but what stopped me was that the next day Hugh Gaitskell was howled down by his own party in Glasgow at a speech, and I thought, 'Do I really want to be involved in a party that spends all its time fighting its leader?' Actually, I knew that I wasn't a socialist, but it seemed to me, by process of elimination I joined the Liberal Club at Edinburgh University.

**HENNESSY**

It's to your credit: there's no trace of careerism in that decision because at that time, I think, the Liberal Party had six MPs, and it used to be unkindly said that the entire Liberal Parliamentary Party could have its weekly meeting in a taxi.

**STEEL**

I wasn't thinking about a political career at all. I mean, I was studying law at Edinburgh, but I had an interest in politics, and I had an interest in debating, and I took part in union debates, including debates against people from Glasgow like John Smith and Donald Dewar – it was that sort of era.

**HENNESSY**

So what turned you towards the idea of perhaps pursuing a political career?

**STEEL**

I was president of the Student Representative Council, which two years later was a sabbatical post, but at my time it wasn't, so I was spending all my time running student affairs and so on, and doing very little legal work. And when I completed my degree I'd decided by that time that I didn't want to be a lawyer anyway, and I didn't quite know what I wanted to do, and the Liberal Party offered me a job, as Assistant Secretary in the office in Scotland. It was supposed to be a year, but because Alec Douglas-Home put off the election, it turned out to be two years. And that's actually what led me into a political career.

**HENNESSY**

And you stood for Roxburgh, Selkirk and Peebles, in the October '64 election.

**STEEL**

Well, that in itself was another unexpected event. It was a seat where we had always been in second place, and we had no candidate. And I was going to fight a seat in Edinburgh where the main objective was to save my deposit. And I remember Jo Grimond coming into the office and saying, 'That seat has got to be fought' – in those days the Liberal Party didn't fight all its seats. 'But we cannot have a seat where we've been in second place and not fight it. And so, young Steel, if nobody else will do it, you'll have to go and do it.' And so I did. And then, six weeks after the election, the sitting MP, who was only 63, died totally unexpectedly. So there was a by-election, and I won it. So, you couldn't have planned that, Peter, it just happened. [*Laughs*]

**HENNESSY**

Like all the good things.

**STEEL**

I always say that, you know, that people like you write political textbooks, but the one word which is very important, which doesn't appear anywhere in any of your books, is the word 'luck'.

**HENNESSY**

It will from now on.

**STEEL**

[*Laughs*] Thank you!

**HENNESSY**

Can you remember the shock of Westminster? What was it like, in terms of what you expected it to be and what you didn't expect it to be?

**STEEL**

Well, it was quite a shock because, living in Scotland, I think I'd only ever been to the House of Commons once. It was also a shock being the youngest member. I was called 'the boy David', something which I hated at the time – I quite like it now! [*laughs*] – but in those days it was a bit off-putting. And intimidating, really.

**HENNESSY**

Can you remember who coined it first?

**STEEL**

It was John Bannerman, I think, who was the chairman of the Scottish Liberal Party, but it was taken up by the *Daily Express*, and in fact, when I won they had a special edition printed, and the front page headline was, 'It's Boy David!'

**HENNESSY**

How come you took up the very sensitive and delicate and controversial question of abortion when you came top, or very near the top, of the backbenchers' ballot for private-members' bills?

**STEEL**

Yes, I was number three in the ballot, and what had happened was that the Abortion Law Reform Association had lobbied all the candidates in the '64 election with a questionnaire and a leaflet, saying, 'If elected, will you support reform of the abortion law?' And I read this stuff, I didn't know much about the subject, and I ticked the box saying 'Yes, if elected, I will support it.' Vera Houghton, who was the wife of Douglas Houghton, then Chairman of the Labour Party, was hanging around in the corridors outside, waiting to see who'd won a place in the ballot. And she knew which MPs had ticked this box, so she made a beeline for me and said, would I consider doing this, and I decided to take that on. Again, luck played a part, because if you remember it was a very long Parliament that one, it began in March after the second Wilson election of '66, and if we hadn't had the full 18 months instead of a year, I don't think it would have got through.

**HENNESSY**

Did you have any feeling in the late '60s, as you settled down into Parliament and became quite a big figure, quite quickly, that the Liberals might just, in your lifetime, have a chance of a whiff of power, if not alone, then in combination with the Labour Party?

**STEEL**

I think I always assumed that on the way to the possible reappearance of a Liberal government there would have to be some kind of coalition, or partnership. It did occur to me that there would have to be a way through to government which would involve partnership with another party, and I have to say at that time I was thinking all the time of the Labour Party.

**HENNESSY**

In February '74 the prospect more than flickered of some kind of arrangement in coalition, or some kind of deal, when the Liberals won 20 per cent of the vote in the first of the elections, in February '74, and Ted Heath called in Jeremy Thorpe, the Liberal leader, for that long weekend to try and do a deal with him. Were you tempted to tell Jeremy Thorpe, 'We should go for this'?

**STEEL**

Not in the least. And in fact, it was very fleeting. I mean, a lot of people have written about that period as though it was a serious proposition. It never really was. I actually drove Jeremy Thorpe on the second occasion to go and see Ted Heath, and lurked in the car park outside. The election results were coming in on the Friday. By Monday the idea was dead. It was never a possibility, and in fact on the Sunday, Jo Grimond, myself and Frank Byers, who was the elder statesman of the party, leader of the party in Lords, had already met, and told Jeremy this was just not on. And it was not on for three reasons. One was that Liberals plus Tories did not form a majority; two, we'd be propping up a Prime Minister who'd gone to the country voluntarily seeking a mandate and lost; and thirdly, we couldn't really be associated with the Conservatives. So, it was never really a serious proposition, certainly not in my mind. In fact, one of the reasons I hastened down to London was to make sure it didn't happen. [*Laughs*]

### HENNESSY

Did you suspect that Jeremy Thorpe was rather tempted, that he'd been offered the Home Office? Temptation might have been too much?

### STEEL

I think he was a bit tempted by it. I mean, who wouldn't be? If you've been leader of the party and suddenly a place in Cabinet is being dangled before you – you might have some fleeting temptation. But by the time we met on the Monday, the four of us, he had realised it was not going to happen. And when the MPs met, if I remember rightly, on the Monday evening it was completely killed off. The MPs all agreed, and said that this was not on; we're not going to have a coalition. We had to continue the meeting because the press were hanging around outside and it didn't look very good if we all finished it in 20 minutes flat. And what I do remember about that meeting, very firmly, was Jo Grimond saying, 'Look, the decision we've made is the right one, but some of the things some of you have been saying are completely wrong. If we're a party that believes in proportional representation, and if we hope to advance towards government, then at some stage the thought of coalition has got to enter our minds. And it's no good saying that in principle you're opposed to a coalition. So he was taking some of his colleagues to task for having a fundamentalist view against having a coalition ever. And I always remembered that, and I remembered it when the opportunity came up of doing a deal with Jim Callaghan, which was a very different proposition because it was more than midway through a Parliament, and it was in the face of a no-confidence motion which Mrs Thatcher put down.

And Labour, for you, given your social-democratic leanings, would be the natural coalition or pact partner?

Yes. At the time they were trying to put through the devolution proposals – not very successfully – but we managed in the course of the Lib-Lab Pact to re-jig the whole of the legislation. They were keen on an incomes policy, which we were as well at that time. They were willing to have co-ordination on policy, help for small businesses, a little bit of industrial partnership and so on. So it seemed to me to have all the makings of a reasonable agreement, not a coalition, but just an agreement to sustain the government so that it would have the parliamentary majority and the confidence to deal with the financial situation.

Personalities matter terribly in these arrangements. You and Jim – he was Uncle Jim to you really, I mean he thought the world of you.

But he was that kind of character, wasn't he? I mean, he was the nation's Uncle Jim; he wasn't just my Uncle Jim. He was a very avuncular figure. I don't think we had any rows during the whole of that 18-month period. And in fact I remember when we finally ended the agreement and said, 'Look, you know, you really ought to be having an election', he said – which was very strange – he said, 'Oh, I really would like to have you in my Cabinet'. And then later, when he made the mistake of not going to the country in the autumn, I said to him years afterwards, 'Well, why didn't you?' and he said to me, 'Well, I couldn't be assured of a majority.' And I said, 'What was wrong with that? We were doing quite nicely.' So there seemed to be a contradiction between what he said to me in a private meeting at the time, and his public attitude later.

**HENNESSY**

I think he told me once that he'd thought of you in his own Cabinet; he was very keen if he'd won in '79 that you should be in the Cabinet. Did you actually talk about what job you might have done? How far did that conversation go?

**STEEL**

No, not at all. The conversation was not pursued in any way, no.

**HENNESSY**

Would you have been tempted? Do you rather regret it didn't come about?

**STEEL**

Oh, I think if he'd gone in the autumn and there'd been a hung Parliament we would certainly have formed a coalition then, yes. Yes, it could have been very different.

**HENNESSY**

And no Mrs Thatcher, no 1980s.

**STEEL**

Mrs Thatcher would have been deferred even more. She never forgave me for deferring her coming to power anyway. [*Laughs*] It's one of the reasons we never got on!

**HENNESSY**

You didn't get on? Because, you know, you've got quite a gift for getting on with people, most people, most of the time – but you didn't with Mrs T?

**STEEL**

Well ... I didn't take to her, and she obviously didn't take to me, for very good reason. But, you know, she had to invite me to things like dinners at Number 10 and so on, and we were always perfectly civil to each other. And in fact during the Falklands War, I and David Owen accepted her private briefings, which, if you remember, Michael Foot refused. So we used to go and have a glass of whisky with her in her room. So, we got on in that sense OK – but there was no meeting of minds.

**HENNESSY**

Labour in the 80s has a terrible time; it turns inward, turns in on itself, and has its civil war. And Roy Jenkins comes back from Brussels[1] and makes his famous speech about the possibility of an alliance, and so on. Looking back, do you not think it would have been better, given Roy Jenkins's leanings, which were very Asquithian, if he hadn't just joined the Liberal Party, and not gone down the route of an SDP?

**STEEL**

We discussed that very soon after the '79 election. I went over to Brussels to see him, and I had dinner with him. His argument was that if his idea of a new party didn't come off, then he would join the Liberal Party, but it would not be in a leading role, it would just be, you know, giving us a bit of help; and I said, 'Well I don't think you should do that. I think it's more important to cause a break-out from the Labour Party, it would be much more

1 Where he was President of the European Commission

dramatic than simply an elder statesman joining the Liberal Party. So I didn't encourage him to join the Liberal Party, and I got a certain amount of criticism in my own party for that reason. But I still think what I did was right.

### HENNESSY

And of course, you came quite close to breaking the mould, surging in the opinion polls and so on. And in the '83 election, just a per cent or so smaller share of the vote than the Labour Party. Looking back it was quite a close-run thing, the centre-left split, in terms of breaking the mould, probably perpetually.

### STEEL

It was a very close-run thing, and the person who stopped it was General Galtieri. If he hadn't invaded the Falkland Islands, and Margaret Thatcher emerged as a cross between Boadicea and Britannia and therefore made her whole reputation. It wiped domestic politics off the map. I mean, we'd been winning all the by-elections, and then suddenly that stopped with the Falklands War. So, that's politics. I talked about luck earlier on -- there's bad luck as well as good luck, and that was bad luck for us.

### HENNESSY

The Gang of Four – they were very interesting, Roy Jenkins, Shirley Williams, David Owen and Bill Rodgers – all very different characters. You seemed to get on naturally with Roy Jenkins. There was an affinity.

### STEEL

I did get on very well with Roy. Probably I was more close to him than the other three. You know, I wasn't a rival – whereas to the other three I suppose I was.

**HENNESSY**

You got on pretty well with Shirley Williams and Bill Rodgers, didn't you?

**STEEL**

I got on perfectly well with the other three. What the more perceptive writers of that period have noted was that the great division was between David Owen and the other three. They had all come round in various ways to the view that the SDP and the Liberal Party had to march together – in Roy's case towards union, and the other two accepted that it had to be in partnership, that there was no scope for a third and fourth party. That was never a view accepted by David Owen. So that was the division within their ranks, not with me – I had no problems with David Owen on that score; I accepted that his view and mine were different. But we got on perfectly well.

**HENNESSY**

You did have some problems with David Owen, because your temperaments are very different. You're essentially herbivorous, and he's a carnivore. [*Steel laughs*]

**STEEL**

Well, that's your way of putting it. That is how the press saw us. But the fact is that we did get on very well, you know, we stayed in each other's houses. We had problems over nuclear issues, but these were problems of policy. Although there was this divergence of view of how deeply embedded the alliance should be, we *knew* that was a difference of view that we had, and we just got on despite that.

**HENNESSY**

But you'll be for ever cursed in the political memory because of those wonderful puppets of *Spitting Image* of you and David Owen

– you being in his pocket and chirping away and so on. It's a cruel world, politics, for what people are remembered for; heaven forbid that it should be soon, but I can see the television the night when you go to your Liberal Paradise in the sky: that will be endlessly re-run, the *Spitting Image* of you and David Owen.

#### STEEL

Of course, of course. But I think we both enjoyed *Spitting Image* – he probably enjoyed it more than I did! [*Laughs*] But I used to watch it every Sunday evening, and you know, if you take these things too seriously, it's a great mistake. It was good fun. One cartoon I have on my wall in the flat is a cartoon of Trog, showing a great shark with the face of David Owen on it coming along towards this minnow, which is 'D Steel', with the face – and suddenly, the fish swallows, and it's transformed into D Steel's face, so that in fact it's been the other way around, the minnow has swallowed the shark. And in fact, that was what happened to the SDP at the end of the day. So it's quite a clever cartoon.

#### HENNESSY

Is this a metaphor for you being much tougher than you appear?

#### STEEL

Well, that was what the cartoon implied, yes –

#### HENNESSY

Do you think it was right to?

#### STEEL

It was not a question of toughness, it was a question of having – I think – the right judgment. I think David's judgment on that whole issue was always wrong.

### HENNESSY

A coalition happens, to everyone's amazement, in May 2010: the Liberals are there, in government, for the first time since the spring of 1945. It wasn't with Labour, which is where I'm sure your natural inclinations would have taken you, and always will. It's with the Conservatives. But was there not a little *frisson* of pride that your long-term aspiration for the Liberals to come in from the cold into office of a kind, albeit in a coalition, had been fulfilled?

### STEEL

There was certainly a *frisson* of pride; but at the same time, I had two criticisms. One was that the whole thing was done in an unseemly rush. Five days. We took 15 days in Scotland, with a much narrower agenda, to fix a coalition. So it was done with unseemly haste; it was also done the wrong way round by talking to David Cameron first, when in fact the incumbent Prime Minister should have been talked to first. And I think if that happened, Gordon Brown would probably have come out and done his statesmanlike thing, and said he was resigning as leader of the Labour Party much earlier, and the party would have had much more clout with the Conservative Party, because they'd have been seen to be talking to their more natural allies first. So, the mechanics of it I can criticise, but you're absolutely right that the principle was correct, and the principle of holding together in a coalition in order to overcome the financial problems of the country was wholly correct.

### HENNESSY

Would you rather have gone into coalition with Labour? A rainbow coalition, because you'd have needed a few others as well.

### STEEL

Well I think it should have been explored a little more than it was, but you could only have done that if you'd have started the other way around.

### HENNESSY

Haven't some of the coalition measures given you a bit of grief, though? People who look at the Liberal Democrat benches from across the floor of the House of Lords sometime see little bits of … well, your faces give it away occasionally. [*Steel laughs*] I'm trying to put it tactfully. Even you, seasoned old you, gives it away sometimes!

### STEEL

But the great thing about the Liberal Democrat benches at the House of Lords is that they're beyond democratic recall! [*Laughs*] They're free of responsibility. It must be very annoying for Nick Clegg, I have to say – I think he must look on them with a certain amount of justified disdain. But they do react. Their instinct is still very, very liberal. When things have gone wrong, for example the student fee debacle, which Nick Clegg has now called 'toxic' – I mean, I would have called it 'catastrophic' – then you could see the Lib Dem benches in the House of Lords, which contain a lot of experience, and a lot of dedicated people who came from the Liberal party and the SDP, tearing their hair out. But, you know, we're quite a disciplined lot, and we don't go around criticising.

### HENNESSY

There was a certain *froideur* between you and Nick Clegg over the question of Lords Reform, about a largely elected House. You weren't receiving the hosannas of a grateful leader of the Liberal Democratic Party for running your alternative, organic reforms, which indeed you got.

### STEEL

Our relations were a little strained; but I think one of the reasons for that was, I'd maintain, was that Nick, who's a man of great ability, doesn't really understand the constitution, and I was brought up in constitutional law. Mr Asquith never said he was going to have an elected House, he was always in favour of the supremacy of the House of Commons.

**HENNESSY**

Aren't you proud of your little bill, though? Because it means that peers who are convicted of serious offences bringing longer than one year of imprisonment will be gone; there's a dignified way of resigning from the chamber of the House of Lords now; and also, if you don't turn up, a persistent absentee without good reason, you're deemed to have gone, as it were. Now, it's all worth having, these organic reforms – aren't you proud of it?

**STEEL**

Well, yes. They're tiny measures, and they are worth having. One of the reasons I was slightly cross with Nick Clegg was that when he announced the withdrawal of his bill, I was actually sitting at home watching it on television, and some journalist, I couldn't see who it was, said, 'Well, what about the Steel bill?' And he said, 'I don't believe in legitimising the illegitimate.' And I thought that was really a bit over the top [*laughs*], and told him so! But, you know, these things are past us, and we've overcome these little difficulties.

**HENNESSY**

Isn't he a touch earnest for you, though?

**STEEL**

Well, I hope I'm earnest as well.

**HENNESSY**

You're pawky, as well. [*Clarifying*] P-A-W-K-Y.

**STEEL**

I think 'earnest' is not the right word. He's extremely able, and very quick, and sometimes just a bit too quick for his own good. [*Peter laughs*]

**HENNESSY**

Before we turn to an audit of your political achievements, can I raise a few of the difficulties that you've had? It's the problems on the personal side that the poor Liberal Democrats have seemed a bit prone to.

**STEEL**

Yes. [*Laughs*]

**HENNESSY**

Jeremy Thorpe – if I can put it tactfully – tragic business all that, in the mid-70s[2].

**STEEL**

It was a very, very sad story, Jeremy's fall from grace; and I put it down to the fact that he was very bad at choosing his friends and the people he relied on. I mean, the late Peter Bessell, who was the guy he relied on to try and deal with this unfortunate problem of this bloke ... he turned to the wrong person.

**HENNESSY**

The other personal business that's come to haunt you is in the huge figure of Cyril Smith. The allegations are being investigated[3]. And you were Liberal leader when he surfaced in a radical newspaper

2  Thorpe was leader of the Liberal Party. In 1979 he was charged with conspiracy and incitement to murder, charges relating to his relationship with a former male model. He was acquitted of all charges
3  Of sexual abuse of children

in Rochdale and *Private Eye* picked it up and so on. But that's still going, isn't it? And you're still in some people's eyes in the frame because of not gripping it as Liberal party leader.

**STEEL**

Just let me remind you what happened. This was reported, as you say, in a radical paper in Rochdale – circulation supposedly 10,000 in the town – and repeated in *Private Eye* in 1979; they related to incidents in the 1960s, which had been investigated by the police. The local Labour Party – because he was then in the Labour Party – elected him as mayor, they got him an MBE for services to local government, he'd been elected as the MP three times – and then suddenly this appears. Apart from asking him whether this was true – and he said that yes it was, that he had been investigated by the police – there was nothing more really for me to do. Now, that was my opinion, it remains my opinion, and while people are justified in saying, 'Oh no, you should have been doing more' – quite what, I don't know – what they're not entitled to say, and this is what I object to in some of the coverage, is that somehow there was a deliberate cover-up. That I do not believe. In fact, when I did a radio interview recently on *The World At One*, I said, 'Look, I was leading a political party, not a detective agency'; a former Tory Cabinet minister who'd heard that interview said to me, 'Do you know, a friend of mine was a QC in the early '70s, and he told me he'd been given those papers by the DPP[4].' And he had sent them back with the opinion that it was not a case that he could successfully prosecute. So I don't believe that there was a cover-up – I think there was just a decision that there was not enough concrete evidence to be able to prosecute at the time. And therefore, how was I, as leader of the party, 200 miles away from Rochdale, 20 years later – what was I supposed to do about it?

4  Director of Public Prosecutions

**HENNESSY**

Did you ever feel – if I can put it carefully – that he was a bit odd, Cyril Smith, a bit of an odd chap?

**STEEL**

Oh, he was.

**HENNESSY**

Were you at ease with him?

**STEEL**

He was not a soul-mate of mine. May I just remind you – because again, people forget this – when I was elected leader, he said he wouldn't speak in any constituency that had voted for me. When I was trying to form an alliance with the SDP, he said they should be strangled at birth. The idea that he was a mate of mine was ludicrous.

**HENNESSY**

What do you think has been your greatest political achievement?

**STEEL**

Oh, I'm in no doubt whatever about that. My greatest political achievement was winning Roxburgh, Selkirk and Peebles in March 1965. And I say that because if I hadn't done that none of the other things would have followed, and I would never been president of the anti-apartheid movement, I would never have gone to South Africa in charge of the Commonwealth Observer Mission at elections, I would never have done the Abortion Bill, I would never have led the party, there would never have been the Alliance. Everything stems from the fact that I had been elected to serve the people in the Borders.

**HENNESSY**

Being Presiding Officer of the Scottish Parliament must be up there as well.

**STEEL**

Very much so. When I was talking earlier about taking part in student debates, I can remember the speeches that I spoke most about were the restoration of the Scottish Parliament and the abolition of apartheid. And I lived to see both, and to play a part in both. So at the end of the day other politicians may have had power but I've had the great satisfaction of seeing my, if you like, my boyhood dreams come true, and to play a part in them. So I've had a very satisfying life.

**HENNESSY**

Looking back to the spring of '65 – very young Boy David, more than a little radical – and here you are now, Knight of the Thistle, Lord Steel of Aikwood. Do you think you've joined that mercurial thing called the British Establishment?

**STEEL**

Well, my wife keeps saying that I'm now an Establishment figure. And I suppose you can't be a Peer and a Privy Counsellor and a Knight of the Thistle and all the rest of it and not be thought of as part of the Establishment. It's rather sad, because I do remember in my campaigning days in the Borders, going round the council estates, getting all the posters on the windows and so on – I'm not sure that I could do that now, because my image is so totally changed. But I've got one political ambition left, because I was on the last train out of Galashiels, under the Beeching cuts, and I hope to be on the first train back into Galashiels next year.

**HENNESSY**

[*Laughing*] David Steel, thank you very much indeed.

# Margaret Beckett (Dame Margaret Beckett)

Series 2, Episode 4, first broadcast 3 September 2014

**Born** 15 January 1943; **Educated** Notre Dame High School,
Norwich; Manchester College of Science and Technology

MP (Labour) Lincoln, 1974–79; Derby South 1983–

Assistant Government Whip, 1975–76; Parliamentary Secretary,
Department of Education and Science, 1976–79; Deputy Leader of
the Labour Party 1992–94 (acting leader May–July 1994); President
of the Board of Trade and Secretary of State for Trade and Industry,
1997–98; Lord President of the Council and Leader of the House
of Commons, 1998–2001; Secretary of State for Environment,
Food and Rural Affairs, 2001–06; Foreign and Commonwealth
Secretary, 2006–07; Minister for Housing and Planning,
Department for Communities and Local Government, 2008–09

## HENNESSY

With me today is a politician who has a fistful of firsts to her credit:
first woman to be Deputy Leader of the Labour Party and for a
short spell acting leader, and the first woman to gain the glittering
prize of the Foreign Secretaryship, all over a long 40-year Westminster career where, but for a four-year gap, she sat in the House
of Commons as she does to this day, and served as a minister
under four Prime Ministers. Dame Margaret Beckett, welcome.

**BECKETT**

Thank you.

**HENNESSY**

Was yours a political home?

**BECKETT**

Politically aware, not politically active, perhaps partly because of my father's health, which was very poor from when I was quite small. But certainly very much politically aware, there was political chat but neither one of my parents was a party member.

**HENNESSY**

But there was a sort of leftish impulse …

**BECKETT**

Yes. My father was always 'agin the government', my mother would say.

**HENNESSY**

Whoever it was …

**BECKETT**

Indeed. [*Hennessy laughs*]

**HENNESSY**

Your mother was Roman Catholic, and I think you went to a Convent school?

**BECKETT**

I did.

**HENNESSY**

Did you lapse as a young woman?

**BECKETT**

Yes. I can identify the moment when I lapsed. I was watching Cardinal Heenan, who I think was being interviewed by John Freeman or someone like that. The final question was, 'What word would you use to sum up the Church?' And I sat there, complacently thinking, 'It will be charity or love, or something', and he said, 'Authority.' And I thought, 'That's it.'

**HENNESSY**

You're anti-authority in all its forms, that's very interesting.

**BECKETT**

It was a time of great controversy in terms of things like birth control, and a lot of anxiety about whether the Church was taking the right attitudes.

**HENNESSY**

Looking back to your higher education, you were very much part of the coming wave. Harold Wilson made his famous 'White Heat of Technology' speech when he became the leader of the Labour Party, an extraordinary, powerful speech, and you were an engineer, a trainee engineer, a woman in a male profession, and an AEI[1] apprentice. Looking back today – it's a bit of a parody – but that's exactly what we wish the country had done in abundance, produce Margaret Becketts by the score. [*Beckett laughs*] And there you were, in the vanguard, as a young woman.

**BECKETT**

Yes, and I loved it. It was quite accidental. I had realised eventually, towards the end of my sixth-form career, that if one did a degree in chemistry it seemed to me to be mostly organic chemistry, which bored me stiff. And the bits of chemistry I liked, actually, were in

1 Associated Electrical Industries

metallurgy. But in those days, there was nothing like the smooth system for applying to university that there is now, and I hadn't applied to study metallurgy. And if I'd known they were so desperate for students, I probably could have got into university in a metallurgy department. But I didn't know that, and so I started looking for employment, and I saw these apprenticeships advertised, and it sounded really interesting. So I applied, and I got one, and I ended up doing this course which was five years, pretty much – six months in college and six months on the shop floor, around the factory, which was a tremendous experience, and I absolutely loved it.

**HENNESSY**

I think you said once that it was a boyfriend who drew you into the Labour Party.

**BECKETT**

I first joined the Labour Club at college, and that was, yes, through a current boyfriend who I think was the secretary. My sister and I tried for *two years* to join the Labour Party – this was in the old days, when we were very much a voluntary organisation. Our letters and phone calls went unanswered, and then eventually we got a response.

**HENNESSY**

You came to national attention when you stood against Dick Taverne in the first of the two '74 elections. He'd won the famous by-election in '73, because he thought Labour's drift was leftward, and because of the anti-Europeanism he detected, and all the rest of it[2]. He was a great figure, Dick Taverne, and he had taken on, as

---

2 **Dick Taverne** was one of the few MPs elected since the Second World War who was not the candidate of a major party. In 1973, as a Labour MP, he was dissatisfied with the party's leftward direction, so he left the party and resigned his seat, forcing a by-election, which he won.

it seemed to some people, the mighty weight of the Labour move-ment, and prevailed. And young Margaret Jackson, as I think you still were then, was up against this shimmering figure. Did you feel somewhat intimidated?

**BECKETT**

No. [*Pause*]

**HENNESSY**

Do you not do intimidation, Margaret? [*They laugh*]

**BECKETT**

I'm not sure. I am the youngest of three sisters, and both my mother and my sisters, although they'd be quite put out perhaps to hear me say so, are, I think, quite formidable figures in their own right. So I used to say to my departments – 'Don't think you can bully me into something, because if sitting on me made me do things, I'd have given way years ago.'

**HENNESSY**

You've had always, I've felt, an instinctive loyalty to the Labour Party.

**BECKETT**

Yes.

**HENNESSY**

You're not a splitter or a quitter.

**BECKETT**

No.

**HENNESSY**

It's very much against your grain, that, isn't it?

**BECKETT**

Absolutely, I'm a team player. And, you know, you might say I'm scarred, I suppose: I did work at Party headquarters for some years when there were lots of rows and falling out, and blood all over the floor, and with people who had confidential documents leaking them to the media for personal advantage. Every weekend I would see people picking up the pieces from some disaster inflicted upon us by some conceited politician who had decided to do something to make themselves look good and do the Labour Party harm. I used to take pride in the fact I'd say, 'I'm a party hack.'

**HENNESSY**

You take it as a badge of honour to be called a party hack?

**BECKETT**

Absolutely, yes. [*Peter laughs*]

**HENNESSY**

You win in the October '74 election, you beat Dick Taverne, you come in to Westminster. Given your instincts on Europe, it must have been a bit of a strain on you in '75, with the referendum and the bulk of the Labour Cabinet saying, 'The renegotiation is fine, we've got to stay in,' and all the rest of it, and the referendum, two-thirds to one-third that we should stay in. Because you've always felt rather deeply about Europe; you certainly did in those days.

**BECKETT**

Oh yes, I did. I campaigned as vigorously as I could in the opposite direction. I wasn't alone, of course, there were quite a large number of people in the Party who campaigned vigorously.

**HENNESSY**

What was the root of your aversion to Britain in Europe?

**BECKETT**

I think the key thing that we felt was that these six countries[3] are not Europe, and that there would be a heavy price to be paid if Britain went into Europe, and also that the severing of our ties with the Commonwealth would be a major change. And we had other links – we had links with the EFTA[4] countries, the Scandinavians and so on. It seemed to us to be a step that we didn't need to take, and which would be a huge step in a direction in which we didn't particularly want to go, and a step that might be irrevocable.

**HENNESSY**

Do you think you were right? Do you think you're still the same Margaret as you were in 1975?

**BECKETT**

Well as it happens, the world around us has changed. If it was still the six, that would be different – but you're a bit pushed to say it's not Europe now there are 27 countries, and even at 12 or 15, particularly once the Scandinavians came in it seemed to me to be much more our sort of place.

**HENNESSY**

There's a Labour Party figure, Judith Hart, who's nearly forgotten now, but she was a very considerable figure, and a big shaper of you I think …

**BECKETT**

Absolutely.

---

3 France, West Germany, Italy, Belgium, the Netherlands, Luxembourg
4 European Free Trade Association

**HENNESSY**

You were her special adviser, and then her Parliamentary Private Secretary.

**BECKETT**

Funnily enough, Judith was one of those politicians who was highly, highly regarded outside this country and little known within it. She had been a minister for overseas development back in the '60s, I think, or certainly a Minister at the Commonwealth Office.

**HENNESSY**

Commonwealth Office, yes.

**BECKETT**

And she became very much involved with the whole field of overseas aid and overseas development, and thought deeply about it, wrote extremely well about it, and was a passionate campaigner – as I say, respected and loved across the world.

**HENNESSY**

What did you learn from her?

**BECKETT**

I learnt that people will always assume that a woman is not the minister, and so, although it's right to be friendly and approachable, don't you forget you're the minister, or else they certainly will. I learnt that there's absolutely no reason why ministers shouldn't write their own white papers, and that indeed they might be a great deal better phrased if they did. And the third thing I learnt, which was extremely useful, was that when we first came in, in '74, she wanted to negotiate a substantial increase in the overseas aid budget, and her civil servants were totally against it. The finance people in the department were completely against it: 'You shouldn't even try, Minister, it won't do anything, and what's more, it'll do damage to our relationship with the Treasury for no useful purpose.' Anyway. Judith knew Denis Healey rather better than they did, so she did indeed successfully negotiate an increase in the budget; and I thought, in my innocence and naivety of that time, that the department would be pleased. Were they hell! They were extremely put out, because it did damage their relationship with their counterparts in the Treasury, who were very cross about it, and also, of course, because they hadn't managed to keep control of their minister. That was really a useful lesson; I've always had high regard for the Civil Service, and their professionalism, but they're not always right, especially about politicians.

### HENNESSY

Your first ministerial office is Junior Minister of Education, when Joan Lestor resigned over the spending cuts in March '76, at the beginning of what was a mother and father of an economic crisis. But some of the left were very critical of you, because you were known to be of the left, and Joan was of the left, and you took her place, and there were some very unkind words spoken about you.

### BECKETT

As it happens I've never had to resign. But it always seemed to me that if you resign, it should be because either there's something happening that you can't stand, and so you simply just don't want to be a part of it, or else because you hope that by resigning you force a change of some kind, and that if you do that – and Joan was campaigning about funding for nursery education – you ought to hope that whoever replaces you will want the same thing that you were trying to achieve, because otherwise, you stand less chance of achieving it. So, with the best will in the world, I never quite understood why it was such a shocking thing to do. And also, when Number 10 sent for me, I was whipping the Aircraft and Shipbuilding Bill, on which we did not have a majority because as a government we didn't have a majority. So I couldn't go. So that gave me time, which you wouldn't normally have, and I rang the chair of my local party – to whom I'm now married – and said, 'I've been asked to go to Number 10, I think it must be about this job, and I'm really not keen on the idea at all'. But we had some good friends who were absolutely *passionate* about education, people on the education committee in the county, and things like that. I took some soundings; 'What does the local party think?' The message came back loud and clear – 'Fantastic! Tell her she must take it! We can't think of anything better than for her to take that job!' So I took it.

**HENNESSY**

It was a very tough time, the late '70s, for the Labour Party. After Jim Callaghan had lost the election in '79, the succession for the leadership comes up – you voted for Michael Foot without hesitation.

**BECKETT**

Yes.

**HENNESSY**

Why was that?

**BECKETT**

I liked Denis Healey very much, and if it had been a few years earlier I might have voted for Denis. You know, he was a brilliant man and all that. But – [*pause*] Denis didn't seem to be able to draw people round him, and I thought that, whatever his fine qualities, the Labour Party needed people to draw people together.

**HENNESSY**

Perhaps it's slightly more surprising, looking at it from the outside, that you voted for Tony Benn in the Deputy Leadership election, and didn't vote for Denis Healey then either.

**BECKETT**

Well, no, because I worked with Tony. When I was working for the Labour Party on economic and industrial policy Tony was the Shadow Cabinet minister that we worked with, and we all worked very closely on a whole string of economic stuff, and so I knew him well and closely. And I was out of Parliament at that time. I just thought Tony had got lots of ideas, a fresh approach to the party, and that he could be a good Deputy Leader.

**HENNESSY**

But given your instincts towards unity and loyalty, which are very powerful, as you've described them, the Healey-Foot combination would have been a much more balanced, unifying thing than Benn-Foot. The Benn-Foot combination, to some people's thinking, would have meant that the '83 loss in the general election would have been even greater.

**BECKETT**

I can see that; but there is another factor that was very much so then, and has become less so now, which was: if you were on the right, you voted for the candidate on the right whoever that was, and if you were on the left, you voted for the candidate of the left, whoever that was. Things are a little more thoughtful now I think.

**HENNESSY**

[*Laughing*] That's a very delicate way of putting it. In the '80s, the Miners' Strike had a tremendous, searing effect within the Labour movement. But if I remember, you were a member of the campaign group which supported Arthur Scargill. Did you have reservations about all of that?

**BECKETT**

It was an incredibly difficult period, and that probably was a low point, a very difficult time. I think it was hard for all of us, because none of us wanted the damage that was being done to continue, the damage to the mining community apart from anything else. And yet there was a very clear sort of feeling of, 'Were you on the miners' side or where you against them?' Whatever you thought about the judgments Arthur was making there was no question: I was on the miners' side.

#### HENNESSY

Can I ask you about nuclear weapons? You've always been by instinct a disarmer, as I think most people are, it's just the *kind* of disarmament that the argument's about, I think, multilateral or unilateral. You were a member of the Campaign for Nuclear Disarmament as a unilateralist; but Neil Kinnock managed to move the Labour Party away from that position. Did you move with him? Or did you stay a member of CND?

#### BECKETT

I can't quite remember. I think I stayed a member of the CND at that time. But bear in mind, I joined CND when there was no other game in town it seemed to me. And the notion that there would ever be any multilateral disarmament seemed so far beyond any realistic expectation that there was almost a feeling that people who said, 'Well, I'm in favour of multilateral disarmament, not unilateralism,' weren't serious. You know, it was an excuse not to say, 'Actually, I don't care about nuclear disarmament'. And if you were serious, the only way to show it was to be willing for Britain to stand alone if need be.

#### HENNESSY

Stand alone without nuclear weapons, yes?

#### BECKETT

Yes. Of course, things changed dramatically: we did see multilateral moves. The second thing that changed, I'm afraid, and this is the point at which I left the CND, was that it became clear that CND had become a pacifist organisation, because whatever I felt about nuclear weapons I've never been a pacifist.

**HENNESSY**

And I remember in December 2006, when you were Foreign Secretary in Tony Blair's Cabinet, the Cabinet takes the decision that there shall be a successor set of boats to Trident, to carry on into the 2050s if need be. Because you were one of the lead ministers, you and Des Browne, the Defence Secretary. Was there not a CND pang, Margaret?

**BECKETT**

Yes, there was a pang.

**HENNESSY**

Did you express it in the Cabinet Room?

**BECKETT**

No, no, it was a joint White Paper. We in our departments had worked on it together. So one went through the thinking and the concerns, and it seemed to me that this was not the time. However, it was quite interesting because in that White Paper we also committed ourselves to saying there should be a much stronger move towards multilateral nuclear disarmament on the part of all those who were the nuclear-weapon states. And I think people thought we'd put that in as a sop to the Labour Party, but we didn't, we meant it. And the very last thing which I did as Foreign Secretary, of which I am extremely proud, was to be able to make a speech on behalf of a serving British government, committing ourselves to a world free of nuclear weapons. Perhaps not next week, but committing ourselves to work *in government* for a world free of nuclear weapons – which actually did, I'm told, lead to a whole lot of the initiatives like Global Zero that are going on now.

**HENNESSY**

Spooling back to the '90s, you become Deputy Leader of the Labour Party, which suggests, Margaret, that you had within you some kind of desire to be Prime Minister if you could be one day. When did you acquire the feeling that you might want to do it, you might be quite good at it?

**BECKETT**

I didn't acquire the feeling that I might be able to do it and might be quite good at it until after I'd been leader ...

**HENNESSY**

Acting leader after John Smith's death ...

**BECKETT**

Yes. I had no intention of being the Deputy Leader, and no desire, either. But after the '92 defeat, when John began to run for the leadership – it was a Sunday afternoon, and we'd heard on the radio or something, or television, that John Smith and I were running as a team for the Leader and Deputy Leader. We weren't. And so I rang the BBC and said, 'I don't know where you've got that from.' And a little while later my telephone rang, and it was a parliamentary colleague, and he said, 'I've rung you about the Deputy Leadership.' And I said, 'It's all nonsense, I'm not running.' 'Yes,' he said, 'I've heard that – what I want to know is, why not?' And after that, the phone just kept ringing with people saying, 'You've got to stand.' And eventually, I gave way. And John came into my office and said, 'I came in this morning determined to tell you that you've got to run; but I gather you've already decided to.'

**HENNESSY**

I remember, when you opened your campaign, after John Smith's early death, for the leadership, you said something that struck me very much at the time, not least because I thought it was probably autobiographical. You said, 'We need to alter the political climate and set people free to have their heads in the clouds even while their feet stay firmly on the floor.' That's you, isn't it?

### BECKETT

[*Laughing*] I suppose it is! Not that I thought of it at the time.

### HENNESSY

But it's your general approach to politics, isn't it?

### BECKETT

Yes, I think it probably is. It may be because I didn't study politics. I'm just somebody who joined the Labour Party.

### HENNESSY

That's probably an advantage, not to study politics. [*Margaret laughs*]

### BECKETT

But it's one of the reasons, I think, why the feet are firmly on the ground. Because I came into politics almost by accident: I just joined the Labour Party and then people kept asking me to do things. And so I've always been there for what you can achieve; get the maximum out of it that you possibly can, but it's getting something. Someone said to me a while ago, about a different colleague: 'He's one of those people who thinks if he feels that he's won the intellectual argument, he doesn't mind whether he wins the decision.' And I looked aghast, and this person who'd worked with both of us chuckled, and I said, 'Yes, and I'm the other way around'. [*Laughs*] Of course I want to win the argument; but it's the decision I want.

### HENNESSY

You enjoyed being a minister, didn't you?

**BECKETT**

Yes.

**HENNESSY**

You were President of the Board of Trade, you were at Defra[5] ... you had a whole range of things before you went to the Foreign Office. You are a lady of government really, aren't you Margaret?

**BECKETT**

Yes. I've always enjoyed making decisions. I like the challenge.

**HENNESSY**

You became very concerned about climate change, global warming.

**BECKETT**

Absolutely.

**HENNESSY**

Do you think that's where you made the most difference?

**BECKETT**

I think it probably is, because I worked out once that – with agriculture and environment – I'd done something like 14 sets of international negotiations. So yes, I think that's where we made a substantial difference.

**HENNESSY**

What do you think it takes to be a negotiator? Because you must have spent hours in negotiations of various kinds.

**BECKETT**

You need to completely understand your own position, and what

5 Department of Environment, Food and Rural Affairs

it is that you've got to have and what you can't live with. You need to understand as much as you can the same context about other people's position, and then you need to listen. Because often what somebody *isn't* saying gives you the clue that, 'Ah, they're not quite so worried about that'. That's the opportunity, that's the opening.

**HENNESSY**

This negotiating experience is probably one of the reasons why Tony Blair made you Foreign Secretary – but you were immensely surprised. It's reported at the time that your reaction was terse, and rather in the expletive department.

**BECKETT**

I am afraid so, yes. I understand Jack Straw said much the same when he was appointed.

**HENNESSY**

You were really thrown by this, you didn't expect it?

**BECKETT**

I hadn't given any thought to where, if he did move me, he might move me to. So I was a bit stunned.

**HENNESSY**

It was a terribly difficult inheritance, the Foreign Secretary-ship always is; it's as if there's ten simultaneous chess games going. [*Beckett laughs*] And at least five of the boards are on fire, I always thought. And you have to start running, you can't just say, oh I'll think about it for a month or two.

**BECKETT**

I was appointed on Friday, and on Monday I was in the States meeting Condi Rice, Sergey Lavrov, the German and French

Foreign Ministers, and the Chinese Foreign Minister, all to talk about Iran.

**HENNESSY**

People think that Tony Blair pretty well wanted to be his own Foreign Secretary. It can't have been the easiest of jobs, being a Foreign Secretary under a Prime Minister that not only had his own advisers in Number 10, but also was quite a big player in the world and thought he should be.

**BECKETT**

I rather liked him being a big player in the world. He and I had worked together a lot on climate change because he was one of the few world leaders who'd got it, and was prepared to campaign and do the work, and do the networking and so on that was necessary. And so I admired that. I didn't feel in any way constrained or bothered.

**HENNESSY**

There was an occasion when Israel invaded Lebanon, and the Labour Party was very critical of the Labour government not coming out and saying anything about it. Was that a bit of a strain for you?

**BECKETT**

It was one of these occasions, which happens perhaps more these days in politics, where the media decide that you have to use a particular set of words, and they decide to show their authority. We had to call for an unconditional ceasefire, and everybody knew that meant Israel had to stop fighting but that Hezbollah didn't. And we all said, all the Foreign Ministers, 'Cessation of violence' ... 'End to conflict' ... all manner of words that meant both sides should stop. But that wasn't good enough. If we didn't say 'unconditional ceasefire' we wanted the bloodshed to continue. It was absolutely ridiculous. And in fact some of my staff told me that the final meeting of the Security Council, that did bring an end to the conflict, principally happened because I insisted. We were being advised that nothing's moving in New York, 'Nothing's happening – you'll be embarrassed if you come here'. And I said, 'I'm not going through another weekend. Terrible things can happen, I am going to New York.' And I rang Condoleezza Rice, and she said, 'Well my lot tell me not to go'. I said, 'So do mine, but I'm going.' And she said, 'Well, if you're going, I'll come.' And we rang round the others and we got that final decision made. And my staff tell me they thought it would not have happened then if I hadn't taken that stand. So we all cared terribly about it. But how do you get the maximum influence, to get people to listen, to stop the bloodshed? It mattered more to me that we had real influence in trying to bring the bloodshed to an end than that we got press praise for saying something in a way that might have done more harm than good. That's what always really matters to me.

#### HENNESSY

When the Blair years are looked at, however far ahead, it will be Iraq that will be up there in technicolor, as you well know. We haven't had the Chilcot Report, the benefit of it, as we are talking now; but looking back, Margaret, are you confident that the full Cabinet tested out intelligence on weapons of mass destruction and the legal opinion of the Attorney General?

#### BECKETT

I felt that we had been kept very fully informed of the progress of the negotiations, at the United Nations and wherever else they were. Both Jack and Tony kept the Cabinet very well informed.

#### HENNESSY

Jack Straw …

**BECKETT**

Yes. And so we were familiar with the issues. We didn't see the early discussions, but I mean, I have seen now some of Peter Goldsmith's opinion and you get this with lawyers – 'On one hand, on the other hand'…

**HENNESSY**

Goldsmith being the Attorney General …

**BECKETT**

But what matters is their *final* opinion. And it seemed clear to me he was an honourable man, and this was absolutely his final opinion. On the intelligence, we all had the briefings. And one thing that stuck in my mind – and he's said it publicly now, so I feel able to say it – is that Peter Hain was at that Cabinet, and he said that he was convinced by the intelligence on the weapons of mass destruction because of the time he'd spent in the Foreign Office, which was when Robin Cook was Foreign Secretary. Robin was the one who said he wasn't convinced by it, but he never said it in Cabinet.

**HENNESSY**

Didn't he?

**BECKETT**

I mean I wasn't astonished when Robin resigned, because he had *hated* being moved from the Foreign Office. But I thought, 'I obviously wasn't listening carefully enough when he'd said how important a second resolution was'.

**HENNESSY**

That's a specific UN resolution authorising the use of force …

### BECKETT

A specific one. Lots of people said how important a second resolution was *if you could get it*. Nobody dissented from that. But I never remembered Robin saying something that made me think, 'He's implying that if we don't get a second resolution, he'll go'. And when Andrew Turnbull, the Cabinet Secretary at the time, gave evidence to the Chilcot Inquiry, he said that Robin Cook had never said anything to Cabinet that gave that impression. But there's something else that comes out of some of the evidence to Chilcot. I had not known, until I read some of that evidence before I gave evidence myself, that the Foreign Office legal team *at the United Nations*, the people who were the *UN* legal experts, who'd dealt with all the negotiation on the resolutions, believed that the first resolution gave you authority to go to war. They did not agree with the people back in London, some of whom resigned over it, who said that it was illegal without a second resolution. The people who actually negotiated the first resolution and were up to their *ears* in the detail of that, and the way things work at the UN, didn't agree.

### HENNESSY

If Robin Cook had spoken up in the way that he might have done in the full Cabinet, would that have given you pause?

### BECKETT

[*Pause*] Probably not, because, with great respect to Robin, who was a brilliant man, he was disappointed and unhappy. I mean, it would have given me pause – but we believed that we were taking the decision on the evidence that was before us, and evidence that everybody else in the world believed.

### HENNESSY

You set quite a style as Foreign Secretary – people rather liked your caravanning holidays. [*Beckett laughs*]

**HENNESSY**

Did your Special Branch mind?

**BECKETT**

They loved it.

**HENNESSY**

Did they have to sit in a little caravan beside your big one?

**BECKETT**

It wasn't quite as straightforward as that, but basically they were around. They claim they thoroughly enjoyed it.

**HENNESSY**

Margaret, what trace would you like to leave on history, and what trace do you think you will leave on political history?

**BECKETT**

[*Laughs*] Probably none. I'm very cynical about how much impact politicians make, in the great sweep of history. What trace would I like to leave … I mean there are some things I'm very proud to have been involved with: the minimum wage is one; the progress we made on climate change; the stuff on nuclear weapons. I think I'd like to be remembered as somebody who tried to make the world a better place for people who need someone to speak up for them.

**HENNESSY**

If I could give you one last great reform, wave a magic wand for you, what would it be?

**BECKETT**

It would be nuclear disarmament.

**HENNESSY**

Margaret, thank you very much.

# David Owen (Lord Owen)

Series 3, Episode 1, first broadcast 13 July 2015

**Born** 2 July 1938; **Educated** Bradfield College; Sidney Sussex College, Cambridge; St Thomas' Hospital, London

MP (Labour) Plymouth Sutton 1966–74; Plymouth Devonport 1974–92 (SDP 1981–92)

Parliamentary Secretary for Defence (Royal Navy), Ministry of Defence, 1968–70; Parliamentary Secretary, Department of Health and Social Security, 1974; Minister of State DHSS, 1974–76; Minister of State, Foreign and Commonwealth Office 1976–77; Foreign and Commonwealth Secretary, 1977–79; Co-founder, SDP, 1981; Leader of the SDP, 1983–87, 1988–92

**Autobiography** *Time to Declare*, 1991

### HENNESSY

With me today is David Owen, Lord Owen, one of the most vivid and flavourful politicians of the post-war years, who, after becoming Foreign Secretary at the age of 38 in the Callaghan government of the 1970s, spent a good part of the 1980s attempting to reshape the centre-left in Britain, as one of the co-founders of the Social Democratic Party. He now sits in the House of Lords as an independent social democrat. David, welcome.

### OWEN

It's nice to be here.

### HENNESSY

Tell me about your family formation. You were born near Plymouth to a Welsh mother and with family in Wales, which I think probably had a very considerable influence on you. Were you in effect brought up in the Welsh radical tradition, even though you lived in the South West?

### OWEN

Well, in the Welsh radical tradition in the sense that politics is important and is discussed a huge amount. My father was a general practitioner and he was an independent on the parish council; my mother was an independent on Devon County Council and an alderman, and a real independent. In those days, she wasn't a closet Tory, she had her own views, and was very powerfully involved with the mentally handicapped and with health issues for the county council. So politics was discussed, but very rarely in a party-political sense. But my father summed it up pretty well by saying, 'Nobody in our family has ever voted Conservative without a stiff drink before and afterwards.' I think that was basically our attitude.

### HENNESSY

But you spent holidays with the Welsh family?

### OWEN

Yes, in the early days we used to always try and spend Christmas together, and in the summer we'd often go to Tenby, or particularly to Aberporth. And I lived with my grandmother and my grandfather, who was a clergyman, blind, in the Welsh church but basically a Methodist, needed the Welsh church, therefore was very keen on disestablishment. And I went to the local school every day with him, as he tapped his way on the road down to the village church. And I learnt Welsh, but I've forgotten every word of it! So I do identify with the Welsh; I feel Welsh, I have no English blood in me at all.

#### HENNESSY

There is, I think, an ancestor of yours, your great-grandfather, who had early things to say about remaking the centre-left in Britain.

#### OWEN

Well, he was chairman of Glamorgan County Council, as a prominent Liberal. I mean he really did know Lloyd George.

#### HENNESSY

Early part of the 20th century?

#### OWEN

Yes, he died in 1923. He was the Chairman of Ogmore Vale Liberal Party; but also, interestingly, he was Chairman of Ogmore Vale Divisional Liberal and *Labour* party, and before that mid-Glamorgan. Those were the days when a strong Liberal Party, the government, was still ready to do seat deals with the small Labour Party, if it would increase their representation.

#### HENNESSY

The NHS has, I think, been your life-long cause, and I think you picked it up around the table at home, didn't you? Were your mother and father shot through with the altruism of the NHS in its original conception?

#### OWEN

Yes, my father came back from the war, voted Labour because he wanted a national health service; he genuinely wanted to give up having to charge patients whom he knew couldn't afford for him to come and have a consultation with them in their home.

And all his life he supported it, though he was critical of it from time to time. So it is, if you like, in my DNA, and I couldn't have imagined what's happened to the health service since about 2002: it started under Tony Blair, and it continued under Cameron, and who knows, but I personally think we have destroyed the National Health Service.

**HENNESSY**

Through market-isation, a terrible word.

**OWEN**

Yes, but it's accurate. 'Privatisation' isn't quite correct. There was very little privatisation. They've kept the assets, they've kept the name, 'the National Health Service'. But what they've brought in is the American market structures, and it's a recipe, actually, for spending far more of a percentage of GDP on health, but inefficiently and unfairly. Any health service is going to be rationed; the key thing is, do you ration it through the market or do you ration it through a combination of democracy, good health priorities and a little flexibility. I am quite keen on the idea of looking now at devolving big chunks of the Health Service to some of the big city conurbations in England, and I'd do it to the Mayor of London as well. So in that sense, I suppose, I'm a radical; I've been arguing this for quite some years.

**HENNESSY**

Was your radicalism enhanced, as a young man, by the Suez Crisis? It affected your generation pretty strongly.

**OWEN**

It hugely affected me. I remember it very well. My parents believed that you should work your way through university, and so I was working at Costain, the builders, on the sewage plant in Plymouth – which, when we go past it, my children all think I built

single-handedly [*laughs*], they pull my leg. However, it still exists.
But the Suez Crisis broke ...

**HENNESSY**

You were 18 ...

**OWEN**

I was 18. Nasser nationalised the Suez Canal and he was ready
to pay compensation to all shareholders at the same price as the
day before nationalisation; it seemed to me, therefore, that it was
something not to get this worked up about, and the idea of going
to war over it seemed ridiculous. So I went with my workers, fellow
workers, having sandwiches for lunch, and I was staggered to find
that they were totally on the side of the Tory government and Sir
Anthony Eden, and against the 'gyppos' as they called them, and
all in favour of sending troops in to the Suez Canal. And I first discovered what you could call 'working-class Toryism' – in which the
dockyard cities, Plymouth of course being famously one of them,
are very strong. And therefore you have to get to grips with the fact
that you couldn't assume liberal views, liberal with a small 'l', were
always going to be held by members of the Labour Party, far from it.
I remember first canvassing in my constituency in Plymouth in the
'66 election, and the door being slammed in my face, saying, 'We're
for Queen and Country here'. That meant they were Tories. I soon
learned to put my foot in the door and say, 'Well, I'm for Queen and
Country too!' [*laughs*] and then to try and get an argument going.

**HENNESSY**

What made you want to be a medical student? Was it the family
tradition again?

**OWEN**

I changed late, really. I was nearly 17 before I decided to do
medicine. I was going to do law but I took a rather prissy view;

I discovered that you have to defend people even if you thought they were guilty – probably a rather simplistic view. I think initially I didn't want to just do medicine – there were a huge number of doctors and clergymen in our family, typically Welsh, and I thought law was going to be more interesting. My grandfather was also very keen on the law at one time. But I switched and I've never regretted it. My wife jokes that when an election was called – and Plymouth was a pretty marginal seat for a while – I would look up the vacancies for neurologists in the back of a *British Medical Journal*, just in case. I never could take it for granted that I was going to win my seat. The majority was down to 400–700 … pretty tight at times.

### HENNESSY

It must have been an advantage, though, knowing that you had a proper profession to fall back on if the caprice of the electoral system or your electorate threw you out.

### OWEN

Yes, you could earn more money, and you would go back to something you loved. Yes it was a tremendous – and I suspect it's been one of the reasons why I have felt freer. I've not felt that the party Whip was an absolute in my political life.

### HENNESSY

You made rapid progress, having come in in the '66 election; Minister of the Navy about two years later, Harold Wilson appointing you. And you worked with the extraordinary Denis Healey in the Ministry of Defence.

### OWEN

Well, 'extraordinary', I don't know if that's the right word for him. I think he's a fantastic character, I love him to bits, really. He was a wonderful boss, I learned a huge amount from him.

**HENNESSY**

What did you learn from him?

**OWEN**

I think an integrity of ideas. The trouble with Denis is that there are two Denises: in opposition, you can do anything you like, it doesn't matter; in government, you've got to be very serious. [*Laughing*] But I don't think you can be quite so dismissive of what you do in opposition. But he is both an intellectual and a man of the people. Long may we have people like him in politics. And I respect and admire him. Of course we've slagged each other off in public, we've had some quite serious rows. But underneath it, my wife and his wife, and Denis and I, have always got on.

**HENNESSY**

He could be fairly rude about you: he once called you Mrs Thatcher in trousers, which for him was not a compliment.

**OWEN**

No. And I didn't accept it as a compliment. But it was at a time when I was fighting the Labour Party, and Denis had decided to stay. I respected those people who had broadly the same views ...

**HENNESSY**

This is the mid-80s now ...

**OWEN**

I mean, if Denis had fought Michael Foot in '80 for the leadership of the party, which he'd have lost, but if he'd fought him on the issues instead of trying to stand as a compromising candidate, I think he would have very soon – certainly before the election – replaced Michael Foot and become the leader of the Labour Party, and we would have been standing with somebody who had been fighting for the things we wanted, and I certainly don't think I would have left to join the SDP. The appalling problem that we were faced with was the 1983 manifesto. People find it very difficult to remember. I could never have fought the election, on the '83 manifesto in Plymouth – they'd have voted me out. And they should have voted me out! I'd been asked to support giving up on nuclear deterrence, which went right to the heart of the nuclear-submarine build ratè; to come out of the European Community, as it was then called, without even a referendum, which Labour itself had only given seven years earlier in '75; and I'd been hugely involved in these issues as Foreign Secretary. To suddenly turn 180 degrees on two major, massive, issues of importance to Britain, to fight on that manifesto in '83, I couldn't have done. So, for me, the issue was 'Do I stay in politics? Or do I stand and fight with a new party?' And that was the issue.

**HENNESSY**

You made great cause early on in your parliamentary life with another very great figure of the centre-left, Roy Jenkins. And I think you resigned with Roy over the idea of a referendum on Britain's membership of the European Union when you were in opposition in the early 70s. You were very close to Roy Jenkins.

**OWEN**

Yes, I was very close to him, and we did resign. Actually, we disagreed: I argued on paper, in detail, for accepting that referendum, Roy argued against, very powerfully. And at one stage I could see he wasn't taking my argument seriously, because I think he thought I was trying to hedge my bets and not have to resign. And I said to him, 'Look Roy, I am resigning anyhow. If you resign, I'm going too. That's out of loyalty. Let's argue this issue out on its merits.' In these sort of areas he was very good, and he saw the issue straight, and I resigned with him. I resigned a number of times, actually, probably a little too often. [*Hennessy laughs*] But I always think you resign for a purpose, and that was certainly a resignation for a purpose; in fact, they've all been for a purpose, my resignations.

#### HENNESSY

It's interesting because your critics, David, say that it's a great characteristic that you do feel things very strongly, hence all those resignations, but that in argument, in which you're very powerful, you don't just want to win but you want to flatten the opposition. Do you think that's true of you? They've always said that about you, because you have a force field around you.

#### OWEN

You frequent these circles of people who say this about me. [*Laughs*] I don't think that's true. I mean, sometimes, in government I quite often took on an issue which I didn't totally agree with myself, but in order to provoke an argument. I enjoy argument, personally; I also find it clears my mind. I like the confrontational side of politics. I like the House of Commons as it used to be. Nothing is more thrilling really than winding up a debate, in the old days, at 9.30pm, speaking for 29 minutes and having to sit down, to shouting and cat-calling and a great many people who are not just at the bar, but they've been at other bars before they're at the bar – and the thing is a cockpit, and that's a part of politics I still think needs to be retained in part. I'm not wanting the flattening out of all differences. I don't – I'm a militant moderate.

#### HENNESSY

[*Laughs*] Who loves a scrap.

#### OWEN

I don't mind a fight.

**HENNESSY**

You again rose rapidly in the Wilson and Callaghan governments as Minister of Health, and then when Tony Crosland dies in '77 you become Foreign Secretary, at a very young age, 38, I think the youngest since Anthony Eden. Do you think, looking back, that it came to you too soon?

**OWEN**

Well, in part it did, obviously, because you haven't got the same maturity and length of history. On the other hand, you've got courage, vigour, and capacity for hard work. It's a stretching job, and in those days there were a lot of very nasty world confrontations that needed a great deal of travel, yet you also have young children and a family. Personally it was a great decision to be given that responsibility – but I think on balance it was a good thing to have it young.

**HENNESSY**

Do you think you were a bit rough on the officials?

**OWEN**

No, I don't think so at all.

**HENNESSY**

Some of them thought you were.

**OWEN**

They did, yes, but then some of them find a difficulty in accepting the policy of the government – not my policy, the policy of the government – and particularly so on Europe. Actually, I had no problem with the diplomats on Africa, and they were solid to a man. I was the first Foreign Secretary to be utterly clear: one person, one vote, no A-rolls, B-rolls ...

**HENNESSY**

In Rhodesia …

**OWEN**

In Rhodesia, and also in Namibia, which was another big issue, and South Africa itself … you know, the whole of southern Africa was in flame, it was a very tricky issue. But we were also dealing with real issues with the Soviet Union and the Cold War. But on Europe, these people who'd spent many years negotiating and having to renegotiate – a rather strange and not a very significant negotiation happened in 1975 – found it difficult that the Labour Party was still not a federalist party. That was a Cabinet decision, and I'm very pleased to have been asked to present the papers for that Cabinet decision in the summer of 1977. I think it's the only time where there has been a very coherent strategy of how we saw our membership of the European Union. I was in favour of Europe, and remain in favour of Europe; but there is no way that I'm going to be integrated to such an extent that you end up in a federalist Europe, and you've lost the sinews of nationhood, if you like, of being an independent state.

**HENNESSY**

If Jim Callaghan had won the '79 election, I think he would have asked you to be Chancellor of the Exchequer. He was going to split the Treasury into a Ministry of Finance and then a Bureau of the Budget, and put Roy Hattersley into one and you in the other. Did he tell you that you were going to be Chancellor if he won?

**OWEN**

No, but I think there are some signs that that was what he was going to do. But who knows? These are the 'ifs' of history.

**HENNESSY**

Yes, we have to be careful with the 'ifs' of history – but if Jim had won, and you had become Chancellor of the Exchequer, you'd have been on a pretty good glide path, albeit with others wanting to be on the glide path too, to replace him, and become Prime Minister one day.

**OWEN**

Look, I gave up the possibility of being Prime Minister the day I agreed to join the SDP.

**HENNESSY**

Yes, but that came a bit later.

**OWEN**

That came later, yes, two years later. I think it's easier, actually, to give up these possibilities, and they are only possibilities, if you've had one of the great offices of state, and I remember when ambition changed a little for me. One night, Field Marshal Carver, who was then the designate Governor for Rhodesia, and Sir Antony Duff who later came to head up MI5 – these two very senior and very admired-by-me men came to see me, and they said, 'You always said you wouldn't call a conference at Lancaster House until you were sure it would succeed,'[1] and at that stage, in October, November of 1978 everybody was wanting it. Callaghan wanted it, Jimmy Carter wanted it. But there was only one answer to that question: it won't succeed. So I said, 'Well, I'll think about it.' And I decided that it couldn't go ahead, and I had to persuade Jim against having that conference. And from that moment on, I passed a certain threshold. It was strongly in my interests to be the chairman of that conference, but it was premature, and these people were right. And I think that, when you've taken office like

---

1 The conference was tasked with settling the Rhodesia crisis and bringing internationally recognised independence, following Ian Smith's unilateral declaration of independence in 1965. It would finally take place – under a Conservative government – in 1980

that there are moments when you do stop being a purely partisan, party politician – you have to look at the wider interests. Not being pompous about it at all, you do grow a little in stature and in worth, and I think that was a moment. And from then on I always felt, 'Look – I've had this fantastic experience, I've had this fantastic opportunity, it's not the end of the world if you don't become Prime Minister'. Of course I'd like to have been! But it didn't eat me up.

**HENNESSY**

Labour in '79 is in bad shape after the elections, going into a civil war, and you leave, for reasons we've already talked about. Was it a wrench, leaving the Labour Party, David? Didn't you really rather love the Labour Party?

**OWEN**

Huge, huge wrench. About the middle 1990s, '95, '96, Jim Callaghan used to say to me, when we'd meet, 'David, I think it's time you came back to the Labour Party, come back to us.' He never criticised me for joining the SDP. And I suddenly had a leaflet in an envelope, not a single sign of who it came from, and it was the leaflet of the young Dr David Owen, fighting Torrington in the 1964 general election, pristine new leaflet, just folded.

**HENNESSY**

You never knew who sent it?

**OWEN**

I never knew who sent it. It had a North Devon postmark on it. It came from someone in the Labour Party. I have a few ideas of who it could have been. And … and I wept, actually, when I looked at that. Even to talk about it is quite difficult, quite emotional. These were wonderful people in the Labour Party. Largely non-conformist, very Welsh in a way, holding their faith. The only issue for me then was whether I could save my deposit. There wasn't the slightest chance of winning in '64 in that particular seat. And it was very medieval England, you went into a square with a loudspeaker, it was a one-man-and-a-boy organisation really. You'd start speaking about the Labour Party and the Labour slogans, and you'd see the curtains just move. They wouldn't come out to see you, but they would come and listen. If you held your faith in those sort of constituencies, all through those years, it was a deep faith, and it was a good faith. It was about trying to achieve a fairer world, a fairer country, a fairer town, city; these were people who were often practising their religious views through their political party. They were really good people. And they still exist, let's be clear about that – they still exist in the Labour Party, and the Labour Party has to ignite their commitment and their passion again.

**HENNESSY**

I can see it's affecting you; as we Catholics say, there's a twitch on the thread. Would you go back? Can you go back?

**OWEN**

To the Labour Party?

**HENNESSY**

Yes ...

**OWEN**

I consider that I'm more or less back with the Labour Party. To join the Labour Party officially would mean, because I'm in the House of Lords, taking the Whip. I don't really like the House of Lords, I think it's there for a purpose, which in my view is a few debates on foreign policy a year and some other ethical and moral issues. I don't really want to go back to voting on a Whip, and that's what it would mean. But I have given the Labour Party money in the last couple of years. I was deeply upset that they couldn't campaign with the passion and unity which I wanted it to on the National Health Service. I was very sad. I think it would have given them the edge, but they were still hung up with one section of the party wanting markets in healthcare, and another section not wanting to, and I hope they resolve that issue in at least the next few months. No, I want to see them back. I'm in mourning, really. I still wish that Ed Miliband would have been in Number 10, and it wouldn't have worried me at all if you'd have had to work with the SNP, and Greens and the Liberal Party and Uncle Tom Cobley and all.

**HENNESSY**

Looking back to the SDP experience, the Alliance came very close to getting the second-largest share of the vote in the '83 election. It was a close run thing – the mould nearly did fracture. And yet you fell out amongst yourselves, particularly you and Roy Jenkins, which will mystify people looking back because the difference between you on policy – style is a different question – was minute. And here was this great figure, who'd been a bit of a beacon for you – it must be very tough, David, looking back at that.

**OWEN**

[*Pause*] Yes, it's tough. The issue was a very simple one. We who were young and had a lot to lose were giving up the Labour Party, giving up the chances of being in senior office, because we thought we could recreate an opposition as a Social Democratic Party that would be identified with Socialist International. That was the party that Roy Jenkins joined with me. And within weeks we discovered it was actually that they wanted to have a party which could have joint membership with the Liberals. If that had been on offer, a lot of us wouldn't have dreamt of joining it. Now, I'm not regretting the SDP, the SDP was in many ways a marvellous vehicle for bringing people into politics who'd never been in it before, particularly women; and giving women a strong stance in party policy.

But Roy was a Liberal, and wanted a joint party with the Liberals. That's absolutely fine, but don't fly under those colours. That was not what we signed up for, the Gang of Four. The Gang of Four was for a social democratic party.

## HENNESSY

It was painful reading, reading his memoirs, and yours. There was the question of nuclear weapons and so on – he was rather direct about you, claiming you were building a philosophy around a weapons system. He was very cutting to you, and you were really quite cutting back. Do you think there was any way you could have avoided that falling-out?

## OWEN

I think sometimes in politics these deeper divisions that exist in the group are highlighted by the personalities of the leaders – in a way you see that with Lloyd George and Asquith – and maybe … maybe it could have been different, I don't know. Of course I believed it would have been different: I didn't want to be the leader of the SDP, I wanted Shirley Williams to be the leader, I begged her to stand, I begged her to stand, she and Roy. However, she wouldn't stand, and it was for me a huge tragedy. If she'd stood then, she'd have been the leader of the party, we'd have been a clearly social democratic party, we'd have had much more appeal to the Labour Party in the North East, to women in the Labour Party, we'd have done even better in the election of '83, and I think she would have stayed. I would have supported her right the way through to the next election in '87. But, you know, these are the 'ifs' of history, and there were a lot of personal reasons, which I am now much more aware of, why Shirley didn't want to take the leadership, and I respect those; but it was a tragedy. Then she quite understandably moved more towards the Liberals and towards Roy Jenkins's few, because she was out of Parliament, she was looking for a seat. And it was perfectly understandable. But what do I do? I'm in a seat which I have taken away from the Labour Party. I could win Plymouth, Devonport as a Social Democrat; I couldn't win it as a Liberal. The Liberals are strong in Devon, Cornwall and Somerset, but they're nothing in Plymouth. Callaghan used to say that in politics everything depends on where you sit, by which he meant which constituency you're in. If you're very ambitious in the West Country, in my day when the Liberals were getting the seats, and you are on the progressive side, become a Liberal. But I didn't become a Liberal, for a lot of reasons: I respect the collective decision-making, the collective nature, of the Labour Party. I'm not at all ashamed of the links between the Labour Party and the trade unions. I find myself now being looked on as wildly left [*laughing*] by quite a lot of my friends. I don't think I've really shifted my position. But you're right; Roy and I did break our relationship, from being very close. It was not easy, probably, for him to become President of the Commission and find that this young political figure, to whom he was really a mentor, was suddenly the Foreign Secretary, chairing the Council of Foreign Ministers. So that tension started from '77 … it was there a few years before that.

#### HENNESSY

That's when Roy Jenkins went to the European Commission …

#### OWEN

He went there, and I thought rightly, and I think he was a good President of the Commission. I think it would have been better, in retrospect, if he had joined the Liberal Party a little earlier, while still in Brussels, and come to an agreement with David Steel; and if we had broken off, we would have been much clearer that we were people doing a deal on seats, a pact. This merger – I don't understand where it comes from. We were told you couldn't have more than three parties; now you've got five or six.

#### HENNESSY

Ralf Dahrendorf, a great observer of British politics and, I suspect a friend of yours, once said that the SDP promised people a better yesterday.

#### OWEN

It was a wounding phrase, and it was, unfortunately, too true. And there again, the problem really was Roy. Not totally him, by any means, but he came of an age where he was very committed to certain things, and the party wanted to move towards more of a market in the private sector. He wanted a prices-and-incomes policy. That was ridiculous; we'd been through prices-and-incomes policies. They had patently failed by then. The last thing we wanted was a new party to saddle itself with that commitment, and there were a lot of commitments which we made for the '83 election which had a sort of passé feel about them already. It was a shame, really. We revived from '83 to '87 the idea of the SDP being the party of ideas. We still did quite well in that election you know; only 2 per cent less. If we'd held our nerve, in 1992 a deal would have been done if the Alliance had kept its position. A great, missed opportunity occurred in 1992, because you had a Labour leader who would have given you proportional representation, and that's where we'd have ended up, we'd have done a deal with Neil Kinnock, even though we could've realistically looked as if we could have talked to John Major. And that's when you get the best deal, is when the two leaders of the bigger parties need the third force. And we would have been a third force. David Steel would have stayed leader of the Liberals, and I'd have been leader of the SDP. Of course the Liberals would have been the stronger party, because we would have not been able to get enough seats, enough members of Parliament; but we'd have still been a broad enough coalition to have been holding the balance in 1992. But these, again, are the 'ifs' of history.

**HENNESSY**

There's one party leader we haven't talked about, the great figure of the 1980s, Mrs Thatcher. She took rather a shine to you, didn't she? Did she have a shine for you before the Falklands War, when you did rather think alike?

**OWEN**

I think it was probably the Falklands. We didn't think rather alike; we were totally alike. Both of us knew that if the mistakes that we made in the early stages of that war were not changed, then Britain would be the lesser. That was a war we had to win, actually. There was no nonsense about it. We had to be able to get the Argentinians back off that island. It was a great tribute to our armed services that they did so. And it was a good thing for the SDP that we supported them; but it probably did a great deal of harm, because electorally she was unbeatable after the '82 Falklands War. The '83 election was always going to be won by them.

**HENNESSY**

Did she call you in for private chats during the war?

**OWEN**

Yes, she did.

**HENNESSY**

What did she ask you?

**OWEN**

Well, it was just on privy counsellor terms, to discuss the situation, sometimes with David Steel. Sometimes we'd just bump into each other and she said, 'Come and have a word?' I remember once, when one of our ships had been very seriously damaged, we lost a lot of people on it, that there was not the slightest hint of hubris or jingoism about her. She was facing a hugely vulnerable situation. I remember once she said, 'We could never bomb the Argentinian airfields on the mainland,' and I went in and I said, 'Be careful, Margaret. If you've got a Super Étendard that has hit the back of one of our aircraft carriers, with *Ark Royal* limping out of the area, and you know they're coming in after you, you'd have to bomb those airfields, you'd have to render them not viable.' She didn't bite back. She took it, you know, she didn't say, 'Nonsense, nonsense!' It troubled her I was saying that. She put up some arguments against it, but I think it was helpful she had a contrary argument put to her on that particular moment.

### HENNESSY

That's why the Vulcan did the bombing of the Falklands airfield; it showed that it could reach Argentina. She probably listened to you.

### OWEN

Exactly. I think it was a mistake she said that – she was under great pressure to say it, and she probably oughtn't to have said it. But overall, she handled it very well, and the military found her rational, careful, cautious, and she proved to be a good leader in the Falklands.

### HENNESSY

What are the ingredients of your admiration for her?

### OWEN

Well, I think it was necessary, unfortunately, given where we were over groups like the miners and others, to make changes to the union regulations. They had got too powerful, and they had to be checked. That isn't to deprive them of their rights, their basic rights, their important rights. And I think that was a necessary change, the trade-union reform package which she put together, and the SDP supported it. And there were some elements of markets where we had forgotten that the prosperity of the Victorian period was in our capacity to sell into world markets. I'm a social market man; I believe some things are social, and you don't have markets in them, like the health service and social provision, and in some things you are a world competitor and you have to have market disciplines, like engineering and building aircraft, and cars and things like that. So I believe in the tough and the tender. There are a certain areas where a market operates, where Britain is ruthlessly out there building markets and building its prosperity; and there are other areas where there are no markets, where you're looking after your own, your disabled, your sick, your mentally ill. And the two are not the same, and pretending they're the same and introducing the market everywhere is wrong, and it is *wrong* that the Labour Party went down that route, and Blair has a lot to answer for. It's not just the Iraq War which went wrong. A lot of these changes in the social-care provisions and the attitudes were basically, fundamentally wrong. The Labour Party should not have gone down that track, and I hope the new leader of the Labour Party gradually puts things back so we can have a passion about some of these things.

#### HENNESSY

Let's turn to Tony Blair. He tried to get you back into the Labour Party, didn't he? Shortly after becoming leader.

#### OWEN

Yes, in 1996. I wished him well, we had a very nice conversation, friendly, went on for probably too long for his purposes, because we'd got on to the Euro. And I suddenly realised that this man was totally in favour of us joining the Euro. And the more I talked to him, the less he seemed to know about it. And by this time I'd become absolutely convinced that we shouldn't touch it, that it was flawed intellectually, and in its financial model was flawed, and we shouldn't go near it.

## HENNESSY

You became very critical of Tony Blair later, in your book on leaders' psychology and so on.[2] You called him a victim of the hubris syndrome. Do you see him essentially as a tragic figure – all that promise?

## OWEN

Well, to be fair, there were things which he did as Prime Minister which were good, and there isn't all together a bad record. It's a tragedy that his conduct since he left office has, I think, made it very difficult for people to be generous enough to him for the good things he did as Prime Minister. It's a terrible ending. But I think he did make a mistake over Iraq, but I made that too. I supported the Iraq war. The actual military invasion went technically quite well; what was terrible was – and I think we'll see when the Chilcot Inquiry comes out – that the conduct of the aftermath was appalling, and both Bush and he were so hubristic they thought the war was over. All the experience of the Balkans was that the war isn't over after the peace is signed, the war continues. It's the troops you have on the ground, how you remake peace on the ground when the fighting has stopped, that is absolutely crucial.

## HENNESSY

If you'd become Prime Minister, David, how would you have made sure you didn't succumb to the hubris syndrome? Because it quite often goes with the job, particularly if you're there for a long time.

## OWEN

Well, I've got a very wonderful wife, who is perfectly prepared to criticise me very seriously, and particularly one-on-one. There is barely a moment when she is not pulling me down, not in the

2 David Owen, *The Hubris Syndrome: Bush, Blair and the Intoxication of Power*, (Methuen Publishing, 2012)

nasty sense, but in the sense of quietly saying to me afterwards, 'David, you never gave him enough time to take his viewpoint', or 'You can't speak to people like that'. There have been other people in my life too who've been what I call in the book 'toe-holders'. The wiser you are, you encourage around you people who are strong enough to hold you back, who will challenge your views. I've been extremely lucky in all my jobs in government that I've had civil servants in my private office who are very, very high calibre, who are perfectly prepared to argue with me, and I encouraged it. That's one of the ways that you can stop hubris, is to have people around you who love you but who are strong with you, tough with you, and who are not prepared to let you have your own way. But of course it's better if you've got that control in yourself; but unfortunately, a lot of us get … I'm certainly vulnerable to hubris syndrome, I don't deny it, that's why I write about it. I think it's so important.

**HENNESSY**

What would an Owen Premiership have looked like? What would you have done on day one? What would have been your style of government?

**OWEN**

I … don't really want to go down there.

**HENNESSY**

You must have thought about it, David, come on.

**OWEN**

Of course you've thought about it, but I don't want to go there, that's … presumptuous. You didn't make it, and don't start believing or thinking that you did. You didn't. Probably the reason you didn't make it was part bad luck – luck plays a huge role in politics – but sometimes, part of it was probably your own deficiencies.

And so you can't ... That's life. I have no regrets. I thoroughly enjoyed my period in politics.

### HENNESSY

What trace would you like to leave on history?

### OWEN

Who knows what trace one has left, or will leave? I'm not sure. I think one thing is this. That when the politics gets tough and rough, it's perfectly legitimate, proper and right that you should put policies and principles above your party, and that worship of the party is absurd. A party is a vehicle. Be loyal to it, and like it, love it – but don't get into a situation where to leave a political party is treason. You're not a traitor if you take a different political view from your party. Politics is about give and take. I think overall we have a good political system. It's not performing very well at the moment. It's had a bad period, I would say probably since 2003.

### HENNESSY

Since the Iraq War.

### OWEN

Since the Iraq War, and Afghanistan. These are two defeats. Afghanistan was appallingly handled. We have to learn these lessons. Libya: mistake. I wanted a no-fly zone, it didn't work. I thought the best decision Parliament made in the last five years was to not go into Syria and to allow America to have time to think, and then decide themselves they wouldn't go into Syria. So if Ed Miliband is given not much credit, I hope he'll be given credit for that one at least. That was not going to be a proper military intervention; it was going to be a gesture politics. And now we have this Islamic Republic sitting there in a third to two-thirds of Syria. It was always there. If we had gone in, a military intervention, everybody in the Middle East would be blaming the British, the French and the Americans for going in, and they would say we brought on Isil or Isis. We didn't, it was there already, we weren't going to stop it. Now they have got to have an overall regional solution to this issue, and again we can help them, but we should avoid 1919 Peace Conferences; it was that map which landed Syria in the mess that we're in today.

**HENNESSY**

If I could grant you one last reform, what would it be?

**OWEN**

To bring back the National Health Service. The National Health Service came out of the flaws of the private-market system all through the 1920s and 30s, the degradation and the deprivation of not having an overall National Health Service. Bring it back, take out this marketisation. But I am pretty sure the NHS is going to go on deteriorating over the next few years, sadly.

**HENNESSY**

David Owen, thank you very much indeed.

# Nigel Lawson (Lord Lawson of Blaby)

Series 3, Episode 2, first broadcast 20 July 2015

**Born** 11 March 1932; **Educated** Westminster
School; Christ Church, Oxford

MP (Conservative) Blaby 1974–1992

Financial Secretary to the Treasury, 1979–81; Secretary of State
for Energy, 1981–83; Chancellor of the Exchequer, 1983–89

**Autobiography** *The View from No 11*, 1992; rev.
edition as *Memoirs of a Tory Radical*, 2010

### HENNESSY

With me today is Nigel Lawson, Lord Lawson of Blaby, a self-proclaimed Tory radical, and one of only a handful of post-war Chancellors of the Exchequer who, during the Premiership of Margaret Thatcher, truly changed the nature of Britain's political economy with his tax reforms. Nigel, welcome.

### LAWSON

Thank you very much, Peter.

### HENNESSY

Tell me about your home background: was it a political family in north London, in Hampstead?

**LAWSON**

No, not at all political. Indeed, I didn't intend to go into politics myself. It was a very conventional, comfortably-off, middle-class home.

**HENNESSY**

Was it a religious family?

**LAWSON**

Not at all.

**HENNESSY**

Slightly impertinent question, but are you a religious person?

**LAWSON**

No, I'm not. I used to think about these things and didn't come to any conclusion. When I became an undergraduate at Oxford, reading mainly philosophy – but it wasn't mainly because of that – I thought about it very hard, and I used to discuss these things very deeply with a number of my Catholic friends in particular. And I came to the conclusion that I couldn't believe in God; and I used to call myself an agnostic, but then later on I thought, 'Well that's pretty gutless; if you're an atheist, you should call yourself an atheist'. So I've been an atheist ever since, and that's a long time ago, that was since I went up to Oxford in 1951; and I've seen no reason whatsoever to change my view. But I'm not an aggressive atheist because I've had so many religious friends who are good people, and the last thing I want to do is offend them.

**HENNESSY**

Was Oxford a fairly exotic experience? You'd been at Westminster School in London, and I think you got a scholarship in Mathematics and changed to PPE, but concentrated on the linguistic analysis – pretty austere stuff – but did you have a kind of lotus-eating existence on the side, if I can put it like that?

**LAWSON**

Oh yes, I spent most of my time going to parties. Indeed, I was warned by one of my tutors, a particularly silly man, that if I didn't stop going to parties I would only get a Third for my degree. And I didn't take any notice of him. No, the party life was great.

**HENNESSY**

Napoleon had this dictum that if you want to understand a man or woman in authority, as you were to be later, think of the world as it was when they were 20. And if it works in your case, it may not, it was the gradual ending of austerity, the Attlee government was just over, Churchill setting the people free and all that. Did you absorb political instincts and views at that time? Was that part of your formation at Oxford, having been apolitical at home?

**LAWSON**

Yes, I was very critical. The first government that I was aware of, really, was the post-war Labour government, the Attlee government of 1945. And I could see that socialism didn't work.

**HENNESSY**

Which bits in particular?

**LAWSON**

The economy was a disaster. But also it was clear to me that they had no understanding of human nature, and that they were trying to change human beings in a way that suited their ideas, that were no doubt very high-minded – but you can't change human beings, at least, very rarely. Some people think about progress, and there is a lot of progress, largely in technology; but I don't think there has been any progress whatever in human nature.

**HENNESSY**

That's rather a bleak analysis, Nigel.

### HENNESSY

No it isn't, human nature has its good and its bad aspects, but there is absolutely no progress in human nature. People today are not any better than people in the past, but the technology is better, so we live more comfortable lives.

### HENNESSY

Did you absorb what used to be called the post-war consensus? The Churchill government, Rab Butler being particularly influential, accepted the welfare-state aspect of the post-1945 settlement, and many of the nationalisations. So there was a very powerful relative consensus, I think one would call it, in the early '50s, between the two front benches. Were you Keynesian, were you welfare-state-ish? Even though your view of human nature was not perhaps that of Stafford Cripps, who was a saintly figure?

### LAWSON

I was never welfare-stateish. I was brought up, as everyone was at that time, with Keynesian economics, maybe particularly so in my case because my economics tutor, Roy Harrod, was a great disciple of Keynes, and indeed wrote the first biography of Keynes. And he thought Keynes was a very great man, and I liked Roy a lot; but I have a naturally sceptical mind, and therefore I never did take when I was young whatever my tutors told me, I thought, I'll reserve judgement. That was the only economics I knew at the time. And then time passed, and it was clear that the Keynesian policies being pursued by that time by the governments of both parties were not outstandingly successful. And this was a very sad thing for this country. We'd won the war, and we thought we could be successful in the peace after the war, and we were markedly unsuccessful in the economic sphere, and it was a great concern.

**HENNESSY**

We had growth and we had full employment in the '50s, however
...

**LAWSON**

It began well but it rapidly went south at the start of the '60s, which
were a very bad time.

**HENNESSY**

So it's the '60s when you began to realise that there may be some
flaws in all this?

**LAWSON**

That's right.

**HENNESSY**

In a very interesting lecture in 1988 at the Centre for Policy Studies,
'The Tide of Ideas From Attlee to Thatcher', you talk about the two
great weather systems in post-war British politics: the Attleean
settlement – the mixed economy, welfare state – and Mrs Thatcher's rolling back the state, and to some degree the welfare state,
though never really touching the health service. Do you think
those are still the great weather-maker premierships of our post-
war politics?

**LAWSON**

Yes I do. It is quite clear that the Attleeite settlement long outlived the Attlee government, and the broad lines of that were
largely followed by the subsequent Conservative government, by
Winston Churchill, who was not particularly happy with it, but
he was only a shadow of his former self when he was the post-
war Prime Minister. But the rest of the Conservative government
accepted this as a change because there had been this theory, this
belief, that somehow the Depression of the 1930s had destroyed

the old idea of the capitalist free-enterprise economy, and indeed the descent into depression in the 1930s was a terrible experience. But I think the analysis of *why* it happened was wrong; still, that was the conventional analysis, and it was on that basis that the Attleeite settlement wasn't really rejected at all by the Conservative Party and consecutive Conservative governments. And it was not until Margaret Thatcher came into office in 1979 that a radical change was introduced, and it *was* a radical change. And the subsequent Labour government in effect endorsed that; Tony Blair basically endorsed it. And so it has survived in the way that for a long time the Attleeite settlement survived. These are the two great weather-changers, to use your expression, Peter, in post-war British politics.

#### HENNESSY

It intrigues me, what you just said, because one of your strong characteristics, Nigel, if I may put it this way, is that you cannot see a consensus without wanting to biff it; you don't like going with the tide of ideas if you think that people are getting carried away with an orthodoxy. And yet your time as Mrs Thatcher's Chancellor, particularly those tax changes which have been only partially reversed, means that you're one of the architects of the current consensus.

#### LAWSON

But that's what I sought to be. I was not anti-consensus, Margaret was. Margaret hated the idea of consensus *in itself*. I just hated the idea of the consensus we'd had before, which clearly was mistaken. No, I did hope that there would be a consensus around what you might call Thatcherite policies. I very much hoped that. Because after all, when you're in government you are working very, very hard, and you're trying to achieve something, but you're not trying to achieve something just for your term of office, you're trying to achieve something which will endure after you're out of office because everyone comes out of office sooner or later, and sometimes sooner rather than later. And so I was very anxious that our approach to economic policy in particular would endure, but also it was within a wider framework of understanding what a government is about and what a free country is about. And indeed, one of the things I was always keen to do, like in the privatisation programme, was to entrench the privatisations by having the widest possible spread of shareholdings, so that it made it much harder for a subsequent government to reverse it.

**HENNESSY**

So I must see you now as Nigel the consensualist.

**LAWSON**

Absolutely.

**HENNESSY**

There's another element in your Conservatism, which I trace a long way back, certainly reading your memoirs, which is patriotism, good old-fashioned patriotism.

**LAWSON**

Yes.

**HENNESSY**

And I remember you expressed it very vividly once, when we were talking about the pride, the legitimate pride, you hold in being one of the few national servicemen in the Royal Navy to command your own vessel.

**LAWSON**

Yes, I was lucky.

**HENNESSY**

The motor-torpedo boat named …?

**LAWSON**

*Gay Charger.*

**HENNESSY**

How terrific.

**LAWSON**

But 'gay' in those days meant something different from what it means today.

**HENNESSY**

Certainly in the Royal Navy. [*They laugh*]

**HENNESSY**

You left Oxford and went into journalism – why was that?

**LAWSON**

Because I was always interested, like you, in public affairs. And I felt that I would enjoy that more than anything else. I also, I suppose – I don't want to sound pompous or priggish – but I always felt that I would like to do something for the public good, and since I can't do anything creative or artistic for the public good, the one thing I could do was maybe contribute to public affairs.

**HENNESSY**

And was the worm of political ambition at work already as well?

**LAWSON**

No, I didn't particularly want to enter politics. I thought my contribution to public affairs could be the best done by writing, critical writing; and indeed, I also, I think, had the prejudice which is frequent among the young in general, and among young journalists in particular, that politicians are a disreputable lot of people. And indeed I think the only thing which really, completely, got rid of that feeling for me – although as I'd been a journalist and got to meet them and I realised there were all sorts, and there are some extremely decent people – was working for Alec Home, who was a man of such complete integrity and he had also done well in politics. The integrity had not prevented him getting to the top – and so then I took a different view of politics and politicians.

**HENNESSY**

Were you for Mrs Thatcher from the beginning?

**LAWSON**

I was, really, yes; and this was not just because of her political views, but her personal qualities. I didn't know her, really, very well. I came across her slightly and she had impressed me, when I was asked to write the 1974 manifesto – I had at that time decided that I would like to go into politics, and therefore I was working for the Conservative Party, and they asked me. There was a draft manifesto already in existence, because they prepare for these things, but it had been written a long time ago, and the world had changed, and politics had changed so much, that it had to be completely redone afresh. And so one of the first things I did was to write to every member of the Cabinet, and I said, 'I would like you to let me have a draft of what you would like to see in your area of policy in the manifesto.' And they all sent me things which had clearly been written by their officials, they were absolutely useless. The one person who had written her own, clearly, was the chapter I was sent on education policy; Margaret was at that time Secretary of State for Education, and it was clearly written by her. Indeed, there were crossings out, and changes in her own hand. And it was quite different from what all the others had sent me. I had never met her then; that made an impression on me.

**HENNESSY**

And she becomes Prime Minister in '79 and you go to the Treasury as Financial Secretary. How would you sum up her style as Prime Minister? As manager of Cabinet, for example.

**LAWSON**

She certainly didn't see herself as just a sort of non-executive Chairman. She had this engaging habit of summing up at the beginning, and then seeing if anybody had the guts to challenge her summing up. That was how she approached it. She also, sometimes, didn't know what she wanted. She didn't always know what she wanted. And when she didn't know what she wanted, the meetings could go on and on and on, going round and round and round. And that was particularly true in Cabinet committees. And so I had to suggest to her that I would have, in-between meetings with the committee, a committee of my own to try and make progress, because otherwise we were going to go round and round for ever. But she was very strong, she had very strong views. She liked an argument, and the people who got bullied by her, like Geoffrey Howe, they never argued with her, that was the problem. I mean, he would stubbornly persist with his own views, but he would never actually argue. She loved an argument; obviously, she wanted to win every argument. But she didn't just want, as it was popularly known, a Cabinet of 'Yes Men'. It was helpful to me because, although she and I had very different personalities and characters, we were at one on a number of ideas. I came into Parliament late in life, I was over 40 before I became a Member of Parliament, and I'd been writing all the time; so my ideas on the need to break away completely from the old failed consensus – it was not just negative, I had a clear idea of what we needed to do – chimed very well with what she'd come to think and believe.

**HENNESSY**

As an old journalist, you were quite a connoisseur of watching her press operation, weren't you. Her press secretary, Bernard Ingham, would do the cuttings, leading with *The Sun*.

**LAWSON**

Yes.

**HENNESSY**

Can you describe how you rumbled that particular operation? Because it needed a journalist's eye to see what was going on.

**LAWSON**

She didn't read the newspapers, except on the weekend. She relied entirely on Bernard Ingham's press summary, and Bernard Ingham's press summary was delivered not only to Number 10 but to Number 11 as well; so I didn't have to be very clever to know what he was feeding her with. And he would always lead with *The Sun*, and there was a curious circularity about his press summaries, because he would have been the person who'd told *The Sun* what to write in the first place. So [*laughs*] all that was happening was that he would then say, 'Prime Minister, very important, this is what *The Sun* has to say, and they are most closely in touch with the people of this country, as you know.'

**HENNESSY**

So she thought she had a unique access to the minds of the British people because of this particular operation?

**LAWSON**

Absolutely, yes.

**HENNESSY**

Very clever. Not many people rumbled that at the time.

**LAWSON**

I don't think so.

**HENNESSY**

No. Going back to the Keynesian orthodoxy that you were instrumental in puncturing, if I can put it that way – how tough was it to turn around that orthodoxy?

**LAWSON**

It would have been very tough but for one thing, and that was that the experiences of the Labour government in the 1970s, before we came into office in 1979, had been so bad that the Treasury officials – for whom I have a very high regard, and I couldn't have done what I did without them – but those officials were, fortunately, completely demoralised. They were shell-shocked. They were shattered, particularly after the experience when the British government had to go cap-in-hand to the IMF.

**HENNESSY**

In 1976.

**LAWSON**

In 1976, the first industrialised country that had ever done that. And that was a humiliation. So they didn't believe at all in what we said we were going to do – maybe one or two did, but the majority of the mandarinate in the Treasury didn't – but they had nothing else to offer, and they were as I say completely demoralised and shell shocked, so we were able to have our way with much less difficulty than what would otherwise have been the case.

**HENNESSY**

Did you expect with the set of policies that the first Thatcher government brought in – loosely labelled Monetarism which is an inadequate label, but there it is, that's what it was called – would produce quite such high unemployment?

**LAWSON**

No, we never expected that to happen. But what it demonstrated, of course, was the huge inefficiency in so much of British industry, worst of all in the nationalised sector, but also in other large companies. There was huge over-manning in the nationalised industries, and in most large corporations. When there was a clear financial discipline applied, and the government was no longer going to be a soft touch, there was a shake-out of the over-manning, so unemployment rose to a very high level, which was very distressing, we didn't want it. But it was a necessary part of the correction. We weren't going to be deterred from pursuing these policies because of the high level of unemployment, which governments in the past, when they tentatively tried, on the few occasions they had tried what we were doing, were so terrified by that they always thought that they could not go ahead; and of course it all worked out very well, and unemployment eventually came down. But it took a long time, and it required a lot of nerve, which is a great credit to Margaret Thatcher, again.

**HENNESSY**

Can we turn now to your refashioning of the political economy? I think economic historians will see it probably in two parts: liberalising the City, the 'Big Bang'[1], and then later the tax changes, the standard rate and the highest rate and so on. Did you have an idea in your head of a new political economy, in the way that Mr Gladstone would have had in the 19th century?

**LAWSON**

Oh yes, there was certainly a need for deregulation. Not solely the

1 The deregulation of financial markets in 1986

City. The deregulation went across the board. The fact was that we had two problems with the economy, stemming from the semi-socialist way in which it was organised. What it meant was that not only did we have a union movement which was harmful, but that management on the whole was lousy. Because if you were a businessman you were so hamstrung by regulations of one kind or another that you decided that the best use of your time was to lobby the government for more favours – regulation which might put your competitors out of business rather than you, or permission to do this or permission to do that. And that is the death of good management. So we were suffering not merely from a bad union movement, but rotten management. So a real change had to be introduced, and I was determined to do it. On banking and the Big Bang, incidentally, I was very concerned that the quality of the necessary regulation for the banks, that is to say prudential regulation, was inadequate; and I introduced what became the Banking Act of 1987, which greatly increased the quality of banking supervision and banking regulation. Unfortunately, when Gordon Brown took over in 1997, he first of all neutered it and then abolished it, and put in its place a totally ineffective and dysfunctional form of bank supervision and bank regulation. And it is possible, who knows, that if the system that I put in place had persisted, we would not have had quite such a bad experience in 2008.

**HENNESSY**

So there's the privatisation of the nationalised industries, which we've talked about, there's the Big Bang, and then there's the tax changes in 1988, which probably will be seen as your greatest legacy.

**LAWSON**

Well, I'm very happy to have any legacy at all. But politics moves on. Privatisation was a very radical policy. It had never been done.

There had been progressive episodes of nationalisation, but when the Conservatives got in, they never unwound them. So nationalisation grew and grew. The idea that you could somehow go back from state ownership to private ownership – that had never been tried at all, and had never been tried anywhere in the world. And we were the pioneers in this country, and it was subsequently followed all over the world, first of all in the Western world, and then subsequently in the countries which had escaped from the Soviet Union, the Soviet Empire, rather. And they went in for privatisation. And indeed it was this country which not only gave the policy to the rest of the world, but it gave the word 'privatisation', which is now used in every language under the sun.

**HENNESSY**

Perhaps your one big failure, when historians look back, will be the Poll Tax, because I think you could have killed the Poll Tax. I think in your memoir, you almost say that if you'd turned up to a meeting at Chequers, and made the Treasury's case against it, you might have stopped it.

**LAWSON**

I don't think so. She was determined to do it, and I was the only opponent. It was a big mistake, you're quite right, not to be at that meeting, which was the first collective discussion of it. But I don't think it would have made any difference. I fought it very hard. The problem was that it was local taxation. And the Chancellor of the Exchequer's writ runs as far as national taxation is concerned, and Margaret couldn't have done anything in the field of national taxation which I disagreed with. She could not have done that. But local government taxation is a different matter. I argued with her, first of all in private, very strongly that this would be a disaster; when the Cabinet committee was discussing it I wrote the most hostile memorandum because the Treasury has the right to put forward a Cabinet paper on any legislation, uniquely the Treasury, on anybody else's legislation. And I put it in the paper, which was the most hostile paper that I ever put into Cabinet. And so she knew fully my view and so did all my colleagues, but none of them were prepared to stand up and be counted. And I also signalled my opposition, but it was perhaps too subtle, by the fact that when the Bill came forward I was asked as Chancellor to put my name on it because there'd never been a tax bill of any kind that didn't have the Chancellor's name on it. And I refused to do so. But nobody picked it up – the press are very dozy and very lazy.

**HENNESSY**

You should have leaked it.

**LAWSON**

I was never a leaker.

**HENNESSY**

No, you weren't.

**LAWSON**

I was never a leaker. I was opposed to leaking. I didn't want to leaked against, and therefore I felt it would be wrong for me to leak. But my opposition was well known. Margaret knew – and indeed, she used to see journalists and say, 'I've seen off Nigel.' You know there was no secret of it. So I don't think it is right, Peter, to say I didn't fight it.

**HENNESSY**

Relationships were souring, I suspect, by this time with Mrs Thatcher generally. One of the most striking things in your memoir is when you say how you went to see the Queen to brief her on the '89 budget and said, 'I can only say this to you privately because you won't leak, you don't leak. This will be my last budget, it's all becoming impossible.'

**LAWSON**

At the end it did. I mean I had a number of very good years with her, and I admire her enormously. She was a great Prime Minister, there's no two ways about it. I don't think she was as great in her latter years as she was earlier on, but we were very, very close, fighting shoulder-to-shoulder, both in opposition and then in government for many years. And it only went sour at the end.

**HENNESSY**

What was the reason for it? There must have been multiple reasons, I suppose ...

**LAWSON**

I suppose so. I think ... that the fact that I was frequently critical – I always had expressed myself, I hope, in an acceptable way but often in a critical way, when we were discussing things. If I thought that she was mistaken I think that she had earlier on quite welcomed it, she liked argument, and she did see herself during the earlier years as the captain of a team. At some point – and these things are gradual, they don't happen suddenly – she saw herself less and less as a team player, and more and more as the great leader, and the team were really surplus to requirements. And so that changed her relationship, not just with me but her relationship with her Cabinet colleagues altogether, I think, changed. And I think that the Poll Tax – which is a huge political misjudgement, and I think most people, if they weren't architects of the Poll Tax, recognise that now – was a misjudgement she would not have made in the early years. She would have been far too cautious. She became – to use the word said to me by a Permanent Secretary – she became careless. And in the early years she was *anything* but careless, she was extremely careful. She was radical, but she was not careless.

**HENNESSY**

And the last straw was the Alan Walters business, her personal economic adviser at Number 10, who you thought, I think, was having too much say.

**LAWSON**

No, it was not that he was having too much say. I'm always happy to debate anything. But he was not saying it just in private, he was saying it publicly. And that is unacceptable for an adviser to be doing that, and it is particularly unacceptable in this area, because when the financial markets don't understand what the policy is, because they have two different policies coming at them, one ostensibly the Prime Minister's policy because it's from the Prime Minister's special adviser, and the other from the Chancellor, then they don't know what to believe. And so this complete failure to have the financial markets on our side, which we had had in the past, makes the conduct of economic policy very, very much harder. And so I said to her, 'Look, you know, this is an impossible situation. Either Alan has to go or I will go, and I will quite understand it if you want me to go, because you're the Prime Minister and he is your adviser.' And she said, 'Oh no, I don't want you to go, you mustn't go, you mustn't go.' And she thought I was bluffing. She thought that it was a bluff. But you know, I didn't make that statement in private without having thought it through, and you don't do that unless you are prepared to go if the thing goes against you. The irony is that the hullaballoo in the markets in the wake of my resignation was so great that he had to go as well.

**HENNESSY**

And just over a year later, she was gone too.

**LAWSON**

And she was gone too. I don't think it was because of that, but I don't think that helped.

**HENNESSY**

Economic historians looking back might say that one of the paradoxes of your time in the Treasury was that in the end it created what in the shorthand was known as the Lawson Boom. That here were you, who kept your nerve and so on in the early '80s despite the high unemployment and all the rest of it, but you let it rip, a bit, towards the end.

**LAWSON**

No, I didn't let it rip; it ripped. I actually secured a budget surplus, which the present Chancellor, whom I have a high regard for, would give his eyeteeth for. I eliminated the deficit and got a surplus. I didn't let things rip. I think that in so far as I did make a mistake, I perhaps contributed to a mood of overconfidence by making confident speeches, because the conduct of economic policy is not science. There is a kind of scientific dimension to it, but there also, perhaps even more important, a psychological dimension to it; and if I got anything wrong, which I probably did, it was not the economics, it was the psychology. Actually Keynes explained the economic cycle entirely in terms of psychological mood swings.

**HENNESSY**

Animal spirits and all that.

**LAWSON**

Well, more than that. In those days there was no such thing as consumer credit except for the wealthy, the borrowing was all done really by business, borrowing to invest; if you're not investing, you don't need to borrow. So it was this cycle between business being extremely optimistic about the future and so borrowing an awful lot in order to invest for the future, in plant and machinery and so on, and then suddenly getting worried they've done too much, and so they get unconfident, they don't borrow any more, indeed they may repay any borrowing if they can. And that is what, in Keynes's analysis, determines the economic cycle: it's mood swings, basically psychology. And to the extent that I got something wrong, I think that I should have been making rather bearish speeches towards the end instead of saying, 'Look how well the economy's doing.' But it's natural when the economy *is* doing well for ministers to say, look how well it's doing. I'm not the first minister to have done that. [*Laughs*]

**HENNESSY**

Nigel, you've remained a man of causes, right through the years, since you left high office, left the Treasury. One of them is global warming. It's very interesting, reading the book you wrote on it, I think, in 2008 …

**LAWSON**

Right.

**HENNESSY**

… *An Appeal to Reason.* Your natural scepticism is there, which we've talked about. But you've always talked about the need for realism in politics, and indeed human nature doesn't change and all the rest of it, you're very eloquent about that. But an overwhelming proportion of the scientific community do think something very serious is happening that we can't ignore, and that adaptation – which human kind always goes in for anyway – won't be enough, that you need mitigation. But you have you come out very strongly against that, and some people would say – is your view evidence-based policy or is it policy-based evidence?

**LAWSON**

No, the conventional wisdom is policy-based evidence. I am on the evidence-based policy side. You talk about the overwhelming majority of scientists. That is not true; there may be a majority, but some of the best scientists in the world – including, for example,

Freeman Dyson, of Princeton, who is widely regarded as the greatest living physicist – is on the academic advisory council of my think-tank, and I have other great scientists.

**HENNESSY**

Having said that, Nigel, there's a great many very senior scientists who have been very concerned about this increasingly for a very long time, and you're implying that they're suffering from a Grand Delusion, with a capital G and a capital D.

**LAWSON**

Well, they're not economists. And there are three dimensions, four dimensions really, to the global-warming issue, which is one of the reasons why I was attracted to it: there's the scientific, there's the economic – what policies make economic sense, which are cost-effective and so on; and there's the political dimension – can you get a global agreement, and if you can't get a global agreement, what sense is there in the United Kingdom going ahead when we're responsible for less than 2 per cent of global carbon emissions; and then there's the ethical dimension, which I think I've come to feel most strongly about. The only reason we use fossil fuels is that they are by far and away the cheapest and most reliable source of energy. That may not always be the case. But it is the case now, and it will be for the foreseeable future. That's why we use them. And this has a huge bearing on the alleviation of poverty, which is particularly important in the developing world, although obviously there are pockets of poverty in the developed world as well. And therefore you want to get people out of poverty, and you need to use the cheapest and most reliable form of energy. And to say that you don't give a damn about the people who are alive today, yourself, your children, and in my case, my grandchildren, but that for people hundreds of years hence, people who will in any case because of economic growth be considerably richer than those alive today, in order *possibly* to be helpful to them, you've got to do harm to the people and the poor people alive today – that strikes me as profoundly unethical.

**HENNESSY**

You've got another great cause as well, which is Europe, the European Union. Is it true, by the way, that when you were asked why you live such a high proportion of the year in France, you replied, 'Because I like to live outside the European Union'?

**LAWSON**

I did say that, but that was something of a joke; but the point was – it's not entirely a joke – the point was that the European Union legislation, which is terribly bureaucratic and so on, is taken much more seriously in this country than it is in France. But no, France is my home, I love France, and far from being anti-European, I love France, and I live there out of choice. But one must never make the mistake of confusing Europe with the European Union.

**HENNESSY**

Nigel, what do you think history will remember you for? What trace will you leave on history, your public and political life?

**LAWSON**

I don't know. You said earlier on that maybe it's the tax reforms which will endure; and I think they were tremendously important, and I think that to a considerable extent, not totally, they have outlived my time in office. And the approach to taxation, which sounds small, but it affects everybody, and has a considerable bearing on the success of the economy, and it has influences overseas. But I'd like to think there was more than that, but what it is, I wouldn't know. You know I think that's for historians like you; it's not for humble people like me to define what posterity will say.

**HENNESSY**

I should say you're smiling at this point. [*Nigel laughs*]

**LAWSON**

But I do think that you refer to me, because I refer to myself, as a Tory radical, and I do think that's a pretty good combination, Toryism and radicalism.

**HENNESSY**

Do you have one great regret in your public and political life?

**LAWSON**

Well, my regret … my regret is clear. My regret is that circumstances arose in which I felt I had no alternative but to resign.

**HENNESSY**

In 1989 …

**LAWSON**

In 1989. I regret that those circumstances arose. But if they had not arisen, I would not have resigned; and equally, if they had arisen at a later date, I would have resigned. It was not that I think that my reaction to the state of affairs in which I found myself was a mistaken one. It wasn't an easy one, I thought long and hard about it, and the arguments were balanced on each side – but what I really regret is that that state of affairs arose in the first place.

**HENNESSY**

If I could give you one last reform, what would it be? What would you want?

**LAWSON**

Well I think two reforms I would like relate to the two main causes which I have been fighting now, even in my great old age, which you've mentioned, although there is a third.

**HENNESSY**

So that's Climate Change and Europe, but a third one?

**LAWSON**

The third one is banking. I think the lessons of the banking melt-down, and the appallingly bad behaviour of the bankers, which led to the meltdown in 2008 – they've not been sufficiently learned. OK, there were certainly mistaken policies, and the Labour government's abandonment of the stronger supervision that I put in place was a huge error. But there's no getting away – the bankers behaved very badly, and this has to do with the culture of banking. And I firmly believe that we need to have a complete separation between what used to be known as High Street Banking, which has to be terribly prudent, must be prudent, and investment banking, which used to be known as merchant banking, which is exciting and creative and all that, and that's all very well and good, but it's anything but prudent. If you have the two things together, if the culture of imprudence and risk-taking – particularly because banks know at the back of their minds that if the risk goes sour the taxpayer will bail them out – if that infects the main body of banking, the joint-stock banking, and destroys the prudence there, we're in deep trouble. We're in even deeper trouble, because, of course, it is the joint-stock banks, which have the deposits from the public, and so those are at risk, and ultimately the taxpayer stands behind them. So I believe you need a complete separation. The government, who set up the Vickers Commission, which was asked to look into this, the government has accepted the logic but not the conclusion. They've accepted that there must be a ring-fence between high-street banking and investment banking; that's never been done anywhere in the world, for a very good reason: I don't think it's workable. You have to have a separation. So that's one reform that I would like to see. The other two are the repeal of the Climate Change Act and Britain's exit from the European Union.

**HENNESSY**

You're as radical as ever. Nigel Lawson, thank you very much.

**LAWSON**

Thank you, Peter.

# Clare Short

Series 3, Episode 3, first broadcast 27 July 2015

**Born** 15 February 1946; **Educated** St Paul's Grammar School, Birmingham; Keele University; Leeds University.

MP (Labour) Birmingham, Ladywood
1983–2010 (Independent, 2006–10)

Secretary of State for International Development, 1997–2003

**Autobiography** *An Honourable Deception?*, 2004

### HENNESSY

With me today is Clare Short, a politician of often outspoken passion and individuality. Not always at ease with the disciplines of party politics or collective Cabinet responsibility, she first stayed then resigned from the Blair Cabinet over the invasion of Iraq. Clare, welcome.

### SHORT

Thank you.

### HENNESSY

Tell me about your early life. I think your political values are very much embedded in your family. And you were born the second of seven children in a Catholic family; your father was originally a teacher in Crossmaglen …

### SHORT

He came from Crossmaglen, but he came to London to study as a teacher. I think he was meant to be a priest if he'd stayed in Northern Ireland. And then he taught in Britain.

### HENNESSY

So it's a classic Catholic, religious family with a lot of Irish influence in it? In the early '50s ...

### SHORT

That's right. My Catholic childhood is a deep part of who I am; the belief that you have to try and be truthful and care for people and be fair, and the poor should be looked after. And of course later I gave up the Church, because of ridiculous teachings on contraception and all the rest; but that core of me comes from that childhood, and that best side of Catholicism, I would say.

### HENNESSY

So it's still there, deep within you ...

### SHORT

In fact I love Pope Francis; [*laughing*] if only he'd been around a lot earlier.

### HENNESSY

Your father had a strong sense of injustice about the treatment of Ireland by British governments over the years; that's another part of your formation.

### SHORT

Indeed; and that led to a belief that the British Empire wasn't a good thing, and a sort of sense of solidarity with Africa and Asia in so on. We weren't hectored at; these were just deep values that trickled through the family, and if you met my sisters and brothers, we're all different, but we've all got this core in us of similar values.

I think these core values erupted, if that's the right word, at the time of the Suez Crisis, when you were only 10. I think you took a different view in the playground about the invasion of Egypt from some of the other school kids.

**SHORT**

That's right. This is St Francis Catholic Primary School in Birmingham Handsworth, and the children are singing, 'We'll throw Nasser in the Suez Canal!', which must have been going around. And I got them all together and said, 'Listen, that's wrong. This canal is in Egypt, and if they want to take control of it they're entitled to their canal. You shouldn't sing that song.'

**HENNESSY**

That was very precocious, and somewhat brave, wasn't it?

**SHORT**

Well, I don't think it was brave really, they just listened to me. I don't know if they carried on singing it when I wasn't there! I suppose it was precocious but I still think it.

**HENNESSY**

You went to grammar school in Birmingham; did you flourish there? Were you one of those classic products of the 1944 Education Act who went up the ladders of opportunity that simply weren't there for previous generations? Did you feel that at the time?

**SHORT**

My mother went there and had to leave early because my granny had a difficult pregnancy with her youngest child. So I knew that, and I'd had aunts who went there; it's the girls' Catholic grammar school in Birmingham. I flourished, I liked it, but I got lots of order marks. I was often the elected prefect but I had to write down the order marks, and sometimes mine were more than anyone else's.

**HENNESSY**

Order marks being tickings-off ...

**SHORT**

Yes: three and you have to stay in half an hour and write out lines or something. They put us into an A Form and then two alphabetical B Forms, and I was in the A Form, and I'd do reasonably well and work reasonably hard and have a lot of fun and play a lot of netball. And then, when I came to 16, I said to my dad, 'I don't want to stay at school any more.' And he arranged for me to do my A levels in a local FE college. So I thrived, but I wasn't a sort of goody-goody. But I enjoyed it.

**HENNESSY**

It seems to me you're a natural-born member of the awkward squad ...

**SHORT**

Yes, but I don't hate anyone, I never have. I used to get into trouble for talking too much, we used to bag seats at the back of the classroom, and they'd always bring me to the front in the end. I was just a bit exuberant, and a bit un-deferential, but not completely uncooperative. Which I think I'm probably still.

**HENNESSY**

You did Politics at Leeds – were you active in the Student Union, with Jack Straw? I think he was president of the Student Union at the time.

**SHORT**

No, I wasn't active in the Student Union. That was the time of Enoch Powell and those sort of racist politicians, and there were demonstrations against them. They'd come and speak and I'd go to those meetings. I sometimes thought the way the protests went was a bit silly. There was a sit-in at Leeds, and I can remember Jack standing on a table reading out telegrams in support of the sit-in, and it was a silly sit-in. There was cause for it in other parts of the country, with files being kept on students; it was purely imitative in Leeds. So Jack Straw, the sensible man, was a bit on the silly side then, [*laughing*] from my 19-year-old point of view.

**HENNESSY**

Do you think because of having a political formation at home, you weren't going to succumb to what Nye Bevan would have called in a different context 'emotional spasms' of the late-adolescent kind?

**SHORT**

I think I was a bit too grown up for some of the silly side of student politics. I joined the local Labour Party in Chapeltown, the 1970 election. We really thought that, Keith Joseph[1], we were going to defeat him. And of course we didn't. [*Laughs*]

**HENNESSY**

Why on earth did you join the Civil Service, with these characteristics that you describe so vividly? You're not a natural fit; you weren't a sort of Permanent Secretary in the making, were you?

**SHORT**

No ... But there is a serious side to me. You know, I did my work at university, I read the books, I still refer back to some of what

1 Conservative MP for Leeds North East and later Margaret Thatcher's Industry Secretary and Education Secretary

I learned. There's another side of me, I'm not just a sort of troublesome person, I think. And why I took the exams for the Civil Service, which was the old 'privileged entry' system, was that I really wanted to have a look at the British Establishment at work.

#### HENNESSY

Did you find it? Did you find that elusive thing called the British Establishment?

#### SHORT

I did. And I found that some sides of it were very honourable and decent – public servants helping to run good constitutional arrangements. I mean, they were a bit conservative for my view, but I came to respect them.

#### HENNESSY

That's very interesting. Were you tempted to join the British Establishment? Not that there's a form you can fill in.

#### SHORT

I could have stayed; I got promoted to the next rank, and so on. But I loved the policy stuff and, you know, when I was Private Secretary to a Minister I was in the Home Office, which did Northern Ireland then, and prisons and police and so on. But when I went with my ministers to the House of Commons, and gave them the pieces of paper telling them what to say, I thought, if I were there I could *do* the policy, and be myself, and speak my mind. So it was when I saw politicians at work and experienced the tantalising interest of getting better policy that I decided I wanted to get into politics in order to do policy with my own perspective and views.

#### HENNESSY

I think you fell in love with one of your Ministers.

**SHORT**

Well, I married Alex, yes indeed, that's right. My previous one was Mark Carlisle. We got on fine but I didn't fall in love with him. [*Laughs*]

**HENNESSY**

Alex Lyon is remembered very warmly by people who knew him. What influence did he have on you, apart from the fact that you fell in love? Did he teach you anything about politics? What were his special insights?

**SHORT**

He was a very committed Methodist, and he was very principled and decent. We had this massive backlog of immigration cases with divided families, and he worked incredibly hard trying to reunite divided families. This was before DNA-testing came along and showed that, sure enough, they were real families. The system had become quite cruel in separating families. And I admired his work and his principled-ness. And that might have influenced me – I think, *did* – to think you can, with honour, serve in politics and become a minister, and do good and be a decent person.

**HENNESSY**

Not the view that the public has of the political class these days; but you saw the very best of the public-service political tradition, as you've just described it.

**SHORT**

Indeed, though I was there in the two elections in 1974 in the private office and so on; so I saw deep contention in politics. I do think, with the public, that things have deteriorated. It's a complex thing to explain, but I think it has to do with leading figures having to be media people, and the media being the dominant discourse. As less and less people read the press, it becomes more and more powerful, it's a very odd thing. So long-term thinking, principled positions, all go out of the window for tomorrow's headline, and nothing is thought through. So there's been a grave deterioration, it seems to me, and we need to think more about why it's happened, and how we could correct it.

### HENNESSY

You come into Parliament in 1983, representing the area of Birmingham in which you grew up; that must have been rather an exquisite pleasure, and also, presumably, it creates an extra-special bond.

### SHORT

I think that's right. It is a great pleasure, you know, 'That's where my granny lived, that's where I went to school, that's the church where I was baptised, made my first Communion', da dee da. I still do love the place and feel a lot of respect for the people. And although we were of Irish origin but born in Birmingham – my mother was Potato Famine Irish – the new migrants that became in the end the predominant population I saw as on the same journey as we had been. Same people from different continents, maybe different religions, but same story. So I felt very close, and identified with my constituents. And I had hours-long advice bureaus, and I felt honoured the way people trusted me, and I learned a lot from what was hurting them about what was wrong. It was good, I enjoyed it.

### HENNESSY

You came in when Mrs Thatcher was at her zenith as Prime Minister. Even though your politics were and remain, I'm sure, very, very different, was there a little bit of you that was terribly pleased there was a woman Prime Minister?

**SHORT**

No, not a little, little bit. I mean, unemployment in my constituency went shooting up, we had terrible riots, and there was the miners' strike. I always saw Scargill and her as kind of similar characters, but I think a decent government would have tried to bring it to an end more quickly. And no, I didn't respect her, I'm afraid, at all.

**HENNESSY**

Do you think she respected you? She liked women of strong opinions, didn't she?

**SHORT**

I was a blip, probably, on her consciousness. She used to say hello in the corridor, kind of thing, but I was a young, new backbench MP on the other side. I don't suppose she thought much about me.

**HENNESSY**

You'd seen the Commons in operation as a civil servant in the in the officials' box in the Chamber, and I'm sure you had a very considerable feel for the place; but it's the never quite the same as being in there in your own right. What was it you learnt about Parliament, once you'd got in, that you hadn't entirely sensed before?

**SHORT**

I think the drama and the power of standing up and making your speeches. I think it's been limited by so many debates being guillotined, and so many short speeches, but I started to see what you say in a committee or a meeting, and then what you say in the Commons, and finally what you write, is of more and more import. What you write, lastly, because it's there for ever. But making speeches that are recorded in *Hansard* in a kind of dramatic forum: there's a power in it even when you don't get your way. I mean, just saying the truth as you see it is important. It's part of the unwinding of how our society comes to terms with where it's going, I think. So I took it all fairly seriously and spoke fairly often. And in those days, of course, some of the big figures, Denis Healey, Michael Foot, Enoch Powell, would stay in the Commons when they were out of power and come in to the latter end of a debate and make big speeches, and everyone would scuttle back in to listen – that's all gone. Some of that discourse, and debate, and listening, has gone.

### HENNESSY

The nature of the tabloid press being what it is, I think you first came to wider public attention because you clashed with the extraordinary Alan Clark about his behaviour in the House of Commons; and also the Page 3 girls in *The Sun*. The nature of the press is that whatever you say about high policy and politics and the condition of people's lives, it's that sort of thing that the media latch on to.

### SHORT

Indeed.

### HENNESSY

Now it must have been galling for you that this was so. The Alan Clark one, I think you were suggesting that he might have been a little bit squiffy on the night ...

### SHORT

And he was. I mean, everyone said how outrageous I was to say it. I said, 'I know you're not allowed to accuse people of being drunk, but I do think the Minister has, you know, been imbibing', or something to that effect. In his memoirs much later he said he'd been to a wine-tasting. He was a new Minister, he was a Parliamentary Under-Secretary in Employment, he was reading an order about equal opportunities which, of course, wasn't him at all, and was reading in a sneering way, making jokes of it that were very disrespectful. So yes, I got attacked for it, but I don't regret it, and as I say, later he kind of admitted that he had been drinking.

**HENNESSY**

Tell me about the Page 3 Campaign, the *Sun* Campaign.

**SHORT**

Well, I stumbled into that again, which is my way. I was in a debate on a Friday about private-members' business and there was Winston Churchill's grandson putting up a Bill that would have outlawed any sexual imagery, any pictures of violence and so on in the media, that really would have outlawed war reporting, sex education – crazy. So I got up and said, 'This is very silly and very dangerous, but if you really want to do something about the dignity of women, I think we should take this Page 3 out of the press, and we can do that without endangering any freedom'. And I hadn't really been aware of the thing, but when you come to the Commons there are these racks of newspapers, and you flip through them when they're having a go at you, and it's really quite stunning how many of those pictures there are. And it does degrade our press I still think; although there's much less of it now, indeed, including *The Sun* giving it up. So, as I spoke, I said, 'I think I'll introduce my own Bill.' And then I got, what seemed like a lot of letters, a few hundred from women, and I'm not aware that it was widely reported, saying 'Please do, please do.' So I did, and then it was thousands, and then it was *The Sun* on my back, wouldn't leave me alone. I still agree with it, and others took it up – but it became a burden, yes.

**HENNESSY**

You come into the Commons at a time when the Labour Party – well, I think the politest way to describe it is 'engaged in a civil war'. You were a politician of the left, and yet the left, in the eyes of many in the middle ground, was making Labour unelectable. It was a terrible time for the Labour Party, the 1980s.

**SHORT**

Well, I'm of the left, Attlee left. I'm a Social Democrat of a radical perspective. I'm not a Trotskyist, I never have been. Later, I think it was '87, I was elected to the National Executive and we started to do the reforms of policy, and it became clearer and clearer – I think most of us hadn't understood how all the different Trotskyist groups had come into the Labour Party. And I still really disdain them for their belief in transitional demands, you know, they don't say openly they believe in Revolution, they try to get people to sign up to policies that are unachievable in order to make you into a revolutionary without realising you are doing it. And I really disrespect the dishonesty of that. So I became clearer and clearer about what the problem was; I think lots of us hadn't understood what the problem was. By the time the militants had two MPs in Parliament, they'd started running candidates against us in by-elections. So we had to get those people out, they had to choose the Labour Party or their factions. And I was part of that. It's not nice, but it was necessary to get back to sanity, and an honest Labour Party.

**HENNESSY**

Neil Kinnock put you on his front bench. What did he ask you to do?

**SHORT**

Well, it was a shock to me: you get into the Commons and in no time at all they put you on the front bench! But of course, there's hundreds – people don't realise – well, a hundred or so people in positions on the front bench, Whips or whatever, in any government or opposition. So I'd been doing youth unemployment and unemployment before, so I think John Prescott asked me to be a junior spokesman and I did Wage Councils, then I tippled off, I resigned over something, and then I got invited back on to do environmental protection I think, and so on. I took my front-bench responsibilities seriously, but if I disagreed with the party line, I would speak up and tipple off the front bench, and come back again. [*Laughs*]

**HENNESSY**

A nice verb. I think you tippled off first over the renewal of the Prevention of Terrorism Act in 1988. Now, why was that?

**SHORT**

Well, I'd been in the Home Office and in the box on the night the Bill was passed, and it had been cobbled together -

**HENNESSY**

That was on the back of the Birmingham Bombs.

**SHORT**

Yes, indeed. And my city – my family thought one of my brothers, he used to use that pub and might have been in it, so it was quite close to me, I knew how dreadful it was. But then they'd put together this Bill in that searing reaction to a dreadful event, and there were people in the box with me saying, this is not well thought out. This isn't good legislation. And you remember it was temporary, and it had to be renewed. And then they wanted to make it permanent, you get the escalation. And also there was an element of Neil proving he was a tough guy, and it wasn't considered policy, it was gesture politics and you had to toe the line. Well, these two things offend me. Gesture politics and just having to toe the line to toe the line, rather than be persuaded. So I wasn't persuaded and I didn't.

### HENNESSY

Now, your critics might say that you have a penchant for resignation. That in some ways you devalue it – though it's always a great personal step, I'm not in any way diminishing that – by doing it as often as you did. Or were you like Martin Luther, 'I can do no other.'

### SHORT

I'm a bit 'I can do no other'; it's not calculated in my case. I don't say, 'Is this going to help my political career or not help my political career?' And I think I was willing and happy to be a back-bencher speaking my truth. I wasn't trying to climb the greasy pole. It's just they kept inviting me up it. So yes, I understand what you mean. I think I'm probably not calculating to a fault. I think maybe one should think about how can you best deploy your influence. I tended to go in, do my work, take it very seriously, but if I was deeply offended by something that was wrong, then I'd walk off, and think that was what I should do.

### HENNESSY

It says a lot, that they kept wanting you to come back, doesn't it?

### SHORT

I suppose so. But then, as I keep saying, there are loads of people on the front bench. People don't realise how many.

### HENNESSY

After Labour's second defeat under Neil Kinnock in 1992, John Smith becomes leader of the Labour Party. I think you had a lot of time for John Smith, rated him very highly. And of course he died tragically, just two years later.

### SHORT

Absolutely. I didn't support John for the leadership. I supported Bryan Gould, being of the same but more leftist position. Then

John took over the leadership, and he was a man of such comfortable intellectual self-confidence that he didn't have to crush people. He liked having people round the table who put forward ideas, had discussions, and that's of course the politics I like. And I came to really admire and respect him. And I think it's a tragedy for Britain that he didn't survive to become the Prime Minister. I think the '97 Labour government would have been a much more significant, transforming government if John had been the Prime Minister.

### HENNESSY

John Smith made you Shadow Minister for Women. He wanted Labour to be a women-friendly party. Do you think something shifted as a result of that? That it did become so?

### SHORT

John Smith – I think because of his daughters, and his respect for his wife – he had an instinct that we had to change, and of course Labour hadn't won the women's vote, and the evidence from other countries is that when there's more and more women's participation in the labour market, the voting pattern shifts. So there was what's right and big politics at stake. The only way we could get more women elected was the all-women shortlists which we always twinned with a mixed shortlist in another seat; so we weren't squeezing out men, we were just delivering some women. And we improved our policies in all sorts of ways – domestic violence, childcare etc. And in '97 we won the majority of the women's vote. And yes, he liked me and I liked him. He loved vigorous discussion of policy and so do I. And there's no doubt we would have won under him in '97. Less big majority, but we would have won.

### HENNESSY

Some people in the Labour Party said after '97, that under John we wouldn't have won ...

### SHORT

But that's not true. I mean, this is the 'Pol Pot' New Labour thing; everything started with them. All the basic reforms of the Labour Party had been done under Neil and John to get us back to sanity and electability with some integrity. And the polling was absolutely clear that we were *en route* to win: we had the 'More trusted on the economy', that crucial one. If anyone looks at the evidence, it's not true that we wouldn't have won under John. It is true that Blair, with the purple posters if you remember, and the young attractive family, added more to the majority. Maybe not good, actually. But we would have won under John, there's no question, the evidence is there.

### HENNESSY

Am I right in suspecting that there were always one or two things about New Labour that set your teeth on edge, right from the beginning?

### SHORT

Yes. Tony and Gordon came on to the National Executive late on. I remember Gordon saying, you have to choose which way you want to make a mark. And there was some argument about reform of the trade-union voting, that perennial chestnut, and Tony adopted some positions, and some positions in the media, that I disrespected profoundly. So I got to know what he was made of, and was not a fan from the beginning.

### HENNESSY

Were you worried about the propensity to spin, which you became very critical of later? You talked about people who live in the dark, spinners and so on. Do you think that was a factor from early on in your unease with certain aspects of New Labour?

**SHORT**

I remember John Smith saying, 'I don't ask my advisers on presentation to tell me what to sell, I want them to help me to sell what I'm in favour of'. And he said, 'I don't suppose people who sell baked beans say, "Should I sell baked beans, or should I sell something else?"' And he was making the point that first you should get some integrity into your policies, and then you should present them as well as you possibly can. I think the spin under New Labour went across that line, and became 'Tell me what you like and I'll advocate it'. And then at some point there becomes little point in being in government ... if you don't have any depth and integrity in the message that you're trying to convey, in the policies you're trying to take forward.

**HENNESSY**

Yet Tony Blair offers you what in many ways, I suppose, might have been your dream job: Secretary of State for International Development in '97, and you did it for six years.

**SHORT**

Indeed. Well, I was elected to the Shadow Cabinet; he wouldn't have offered it to me otherwise. And obviously he dropped Michael Meacher who was elected to the Shadow Cabinet. But I think it was a judgement that it would cause more trouble to drop me than not. Yes, it was my dream job, and I got really stuck into it and I did it in an old-fashioned way, that is, I respected my civil servants, they respected my leadership, we wrote papers, read them, I got a bigger table in my office, we discussed everything and thrashed out policy, we transformed all the positions of the department, and I was very lucky that at that stage, Number 10 wasn't interested in International Development, unlike, say, Education or Health, where they were telling the Secretary of State what to do. And we developed deeply thought-through, radical policies. We were the leading edge on getting the Millennium Development Goals, to get the whole world to work together to systematically and measurably reduce poverty. We took those from UN conferences. But it was a wonderful experience, a fabulous job, a brilliant department, superb civil servants, and I'm very lucky that my political career included those six years.

**HENNESSY**

I think also you struck up really rather a good relationship with the Secret Intelligence Service that used to brief you, which might surprise some people.

**SHORT**

Well, yes. Sierra Leone peace – I was very involved in that. You know it was difficult to understand what that civil war was really about. At first, actually, the successive Cs used to come and see me –

**HENNESSY**

That's the Chief of the Secret Intelligence Service.

**SHORT**

Yes, and in the early days their budgets were being cut, this was the end-of-the-Cold War optimism. And I said, well, what do you want me to do? Do you want me to have you spy on governments that I'm working in partnership with? Really, thank you, no! And then along came – maybe I shouldn't name him – and he said you do realise all those presidents ask to see us all the time?

**HENNESSY**

This is one of the Cs, one of the chiefs?

**SHORT**

Well, it was one under him.

**HENNESSY**

Yes, I don't think we want to use his name.

**SHORT**

No.

**HENNESSY**

Very charming.

**SHORT**

Indeed.

**HENNESSY**

Particularly charming officer, I think.

**SHORT**

And very well read, and knowledgeable. When I realised that, and he gave me some books to read about Sierra Leone, I thought yes, I want this relationship with these people. After the end of the Cold War, lots of civil wars and conflicts broke out in Africa as the two sides pulled back from every tension on that continent, and that was hurting people and holding back development. And we wanted to do better at ending those conflicts. The Foreign Office didn't care about those conflicts, but they hated me [*laughs*] being concerned about them. But I had a good working relationship with the intelligence agencies, right up to Iraq. But I saw them malfunction around Iraq – getting excited by going with the Prime Minister to the White House, and so on, and lose their way. So I've seen the best and the worst of them too.

**HENNESSY**

When the question of Iraq begins to make a good deal of the political weather, and the weather inside the Cabinet, the Prime Minister sets up a Ministerial Group on Iraq, which wasn't a proper

Cabinet Committee, if I remember. But you were never on that group. Did you feel that you were deliberately excluded from that inner group of ministers on the run-up to the war in Iraq?

**SHORT**

You have to know that under Blair the Cabinet did not function as a Cabinet. It became a dignified part of the constitution – I suspect that's still going on, actually, that the Cabinet as it used to be is no longer of significance in the governance in this country. But Blair did everything informally; if he ever thought you were going to say something at the Cabinet that might be contentious, he'd ask to see you first and square it. He was the opposite of John Smith, who liked the discussion and to hear everybody's views. I'm not much bothered with status and so on, and people hovering around Number 10: I'd enjoyed being semi-detached, being able to run my department. But I spoke up in the Cabinet from the beginning, and I thought from the beginning that if we hold on to Blair's ankles he can probably hold on to Bush, and we can probably get a more intelligent policy here. And of course, as you know, you'd have one set of assurances in discussions in the Cabinet and then another set of screaming headlines in the media. I still thought we might be able to avoid rushing to war without thinking through what we were doing, and I tried for that. And there was a lot of duplicity, I'm afraid.

**HENNESSY**

Did you get a special briefing on the Iraq Dossier, as it became known, in September 2002? The collation, which wasn't done classically by the Joint Intelligence Committee, as these things normally are ...

**SHORT**

Alastair Campbell never liked me, because of my independence and non-adoration, I suppose, and not always asking his permission to say anything to the media. So when he was in charge of the dossiers I stayed out of them. You can only fight on so many fronts, and I thought, they're just presentational.

**HENNESSY**

Coming right up to the rim of the war now ... The Cabinet of 17 March, when the Attorney General's opinion is brought to the Cabinet ... It's very short, it's very terse by the standards of these things. Did you not feel that, and did you not raise it, at that very last minute?

**SHORT**

Yes. It was a special Cabinet that I'd asked for. There'd already been rumours in Whitehall that the Attorney General had said there's no clear legal opinion, the military had said they wouldn't go without it. Then he suddenly comes ... Robin Cook's gone by then, he sits in Robin's seat ... He's got this one-and-a-half page typed document, and he starts just reading it. They'd put it round the table, so we all said, 'We can read'. And then I said, 'But why so late? Have you changed your mind?' And things were so tense by then that people were saying, 'Clare, be quiet! Leave it!' So we didn't have any discussion. And it was all very fraught, very last-minute. And now we know it was concocted. And it was drafted as an answer to a parliamentary question I think tabled first in the Lords, then in the Commons. It wasn't the full legal opinion, or anything like. And he didn't talk about any process of consideration, and where his doubts ... there was none of that.

**HENNESSY**

Did you ask for the longer document that you assumed must be there, that had been made earlier? And indeed, now we know there was one ...

### SHORT

No, I didn't know there was a longer document, I was just astonished, and I asked, 'What's happened? Did you change your mind?
How come it's so late?' and they all said, 'Clare, be quiet, leave it,
leave it, leave it.' There was no discussion.

### HENNESSY

Do you think you should have resigned at that point? Robin Cook
had gone a day or so earlier, I think.

### SHORT

He hadn't gone yet. You know, you booked to give your resignation
speech, and I'd done that, and then I did this radio interview to say,
I'm still thinking that at the last minute, hold on, maybe we can
stop this. And then Blair had me in for repeated negotiations, and I
was thinking, 'We can't stop the war, but we could reconstruct the
country better, and differently'. And there had been careful prepa-
rations in the UN led by Louise Fréchette who was Deputy Secre-
tary-General, all under the radar, and if we could internationalise
the reconstruction I thought we could probably avoid a disaster.
And actually, he promised me that, and of course, it was just to keep
me quiet. But I thought – and this was a big pain for me – I thought
it was utterly wrong to go to war without the UN resolution.

### HENNESSY

A specific resolution authorising it ...

### SHORT

As promised, as had been promised. And I hadn't then read the
'Project for the New American Century'[2] and that should have

2 The founding principles of a neoconservative think tank of the same name.
Its stated goal was 'to promote American global leadership'. Many signatories
went on to serve under President George W. Bush

been circulated in Whitehall, I think it's shocking that it never was. But of course, the Foreign Office wasn't really much in charge either, it was all being run out of Number 10, directly on the phone to the White House and so on. I thought, I'll stay because we can still retrieve what otherwise is a disaster. And it's another of those moments of not calculating my position. But I don't feel bad about it. I mean, it didn't work – but I did it for the best of reasons, and if he had done what he'd promised, I think Iraq would be in a different place today.

**HENNESSY**

But you'd booked your resignation slot speech in the House of Commons, you got that close?

**SHORT**

Yes, yes, same day as Robin, I would have come on after him, which would have been quite something, wouldn't it?

**HENNESSY**

And you don't regret that? Because it would have had a very powerful impact if two of you had gone on the same day.

**SHORT**

I still think it wouldn't have stopped it. It would have made the vote close – even the vote from the Labour Party was a massive majority. People talk as if that was close. I mean, there was lots of arm-twisting and lots of Labour MPs voted against where their instincts lay. It would have been much better for me. It would have been much happier for me, it would have been better for my political career, but I don't regret it. Of course, I regret it in that the promises he made to me weren't fulfilled, so it didn't have any effect – but I know that I did it for the right reasons, and if he had kept his word – a reconstructed Iraq with big international support and probably the replacement of American and British troops by forces from Muslim countries and so on – it would have been a different Middle East today. So I regret that what I did didn't have any effect, but I'm glad I tried.

**HENNESSY**

How much later did you go, and what was the reason? What triggered the actual resignation when it came?

**SHORT**

Well, then it's this promising a UN resolution for reconstruction, which you have to do to comply with international law or otherwise you're not allowed to change the institutions of an occupied territory. There are the breaches of international law in Gaza and the West Bank that goes on to this day with no action. So then I was focused on that, as part of it being absolutely necessary to internationalise reconstruction. And remember Bush came to Northern Ireland, and he said 'UN' about six times and Tony told me, 'Look! Bush is saying UN!' and stuff like that. And then the actual resolution we got was very weak, and the arrangements being made were not to re-internationalise the reconstruction. So I'd completely failed, it was a disaster, and I went.

**HENNESSY**

There was a lot of attack on you from various quarters, over Iraq and so on. How do you handle attacks, Clare? Are you sensitive?

**SHORT**

Yes, it hurts, it hurts like … it hurts a lot. But you know, if you can't stand the heat, keep out of the kitchen. It seems to me these things have to hurt you, to have any sensitivity and concern about what's going on. But yes, it's horrible, I hate it. But this is my Catholic childhood, isn't it? If it's right, you have to do it, whatever the pain.

**HENNESSY**

You resign from the Labour Party in 2006 and become an independent on the back benches. Why did you do that? Because that's severing flesh of your flesh?

**SHORT**

Yes.

**HENNESSY**

The Labour Party had been part of you for a long time …

**SHORT**

Yes. You know, the Catholic Church had been my formation, and then when I decided it was at fault, I gave my heart and soul to the Labour Party, as an instrument of moral advance for Britain and the world. But through Iraq, and then the failure of the party to come clean on it and sort it out and hold to account the lies etc, I thought 'It's lost its way'. And I remember saying to some of my close friends, 'I don't want to lapse again.' That is, you know, what you call Catholics who stop being Catholics. But I did. And actually, I resigned the Whip, but I didn't mean to resign from the Party; but you pay your money to the Parliamentary Labour Party, so if you stop that, it stops your membership. And then I was shocked to find that, even though I'd resigned from the party, I didn't mind.

**HENNESSY**

Really?

**SHORT**

Yes, that was the shock.

**HENNESSY**

You felt so estranged?

**SHORT**

Yes. You see, I went to a couple of conferences afterwards, and the whole thing's transformed. I mean, you know, there's not much voting, no democratic debate, not much of a fringe. I know the old Labour Party with all the Trotskyist groups in it became screaming and nasty, but the democratic structure of the conference, which is shaped around the model of the Methodist Conference actually, was crucial to a democratic party that brings everyone together with their consent and through debate. That had all gone. And there was no holding to account what had happened on Iraq, and then I thought, 'I don't belong here any more'.

**HENNESSY**

They must have been lonely, those last four years in the Commons?

**SHORT**

Yes, indeed. And, you know, I spent nearly 30 years there, and 10 years on the National Executive of the Labour Party. I sort of divorced a lot my friends, really. But I don't regret it.

**HENNESSY**

Have you not come back to membership?

**SHORT**

No.

**HENNESSY**

Not tempted?

**SHORT**

No. I quite admired and respected Ed Miliband, but no. I think the left is reshaping. The social democrats are in trouble all over Europe. I think we desperately need a change in our electoral system, and then we'd get Greens, SNP, Welsh Nats etc and Labour.

I think we need a pluralised left rather than a party dominated by Blair and Alastair Campbell and everyone having to toe the line and please Mr Murdoch and his papers. I don't like those politics, and I don't think they're good for the country.

**HENNESSY**

Can I ask you about a story that the public was deeply moved by and loved, which was when you rediscovered your son in the 1990s, who you'd given up for adoption when he was very small?

**SHORT**

Well, I regretted him being adopted from weeks, months after it happened, after it was done. And I think it's another side of the bad and good of me – I was too rational. It was a rational thing to do, but it was painful emotionally. I was young. And in those days you weren't even on the telephone, I didn't talk to my mother, all that stuff. And I wrote and tried to sort of see if I could retrieve him or see him … There's a system where you can register now, and I did, and lo and behold, he turned up. And I love him to bits, and we're still very close. So, I'm very lucky he came back.

**HENNESSY**

Wonderful. Looking back over the sweep of your career, what's the greatest satisfaction?

**SHORT**

My service to my constituency, and all the people that live there, and my respect for them, and my efforts to care for them and represent them. And my six years in International Development – it was the germ of what Britain's foreign policy could be. The way we can make the world safe is to make it more evenly developed, more just, particularly in the Middle East, which is a disaster that's going to go on for years. And the third thing is, using the Commons to speak the truth as I understood it. I'm proud of that, too.

**HENNESSY**

What's your greatest regret?

**SHORT**

I really regret that Blair did what he did on Iraq. I think that was a disaster for Labour, and for the world, and for the Middle East. I've got lots and lots – you know, 'Regrets. I have a few'. I mean any serious human being has a lot of regrets, but that's the big one.

**HENNESSY**

What trace do you think you'll leave on history?

**SHORT**

I don't know. That's what I think immortality is, everybody leaves scratches behind them, for good and ill, both on the personal level and in the work they do. My international development goes on, and I think that will leave some scratches. I don't know what else. The kind of style of politics that's gone, that might come back? A more honest style of politics? Maybe?

**HENNESSY**

Finally, if I could grant you one last reform, just like that, wave a wand – what would it be?

**SHORT**

I'd go for electoral reform to get this pluralisation of British politics that, I think, would lead to a more thoughtful, considered, more progressive, better Britain. Britain playing a better role in the world. I'd go for that.

**HENNESSY**

Clare Short, thank you very much.

**SHORT**

Thank you.

# Michael Heseltine (Lord Heseltine)

Series 4, Episode 1, first broadcast 2 August 2016

**Born** 21 March 1933; **Educated** Shrewsbury
School; Pembroke College, Oxford

MP (Conservative) Tavistock 1966–74; Henley 1974–2001

Parliamentary Under-Secretary, Ministry of Transport,
1970; Parliamentary Under-Secretary, Department of
Environment, 1970–72; Minister for Aerospace & Shipping,
Department of Trade and Industry, 1972–74; Secretary
of State for the Environment, 1979–83; Secretary of State
for Defence, 1983–86; Secretary of State for Environment,
1990–92; President of the Board of Trade, 1992–95; First
Secretary of State and Deputy Prime Minister, 1995–97

**Autobiography** *Life in the Jungle*, 2000

## HENNESSY

With me today is Michael Heseltine, Lord Heseltine, one of the
most flavourful politicians of recent times. He was that rare thing,
a minister known instantly by his nickname. Sometimes Hezza,
sometimes Tarzan, with his forceful speaking style topped off by
what an admiring Cabinet colleague describes as 'Michael's mane
waving.' He has causes, lifelong causes. Above all, the regeneration
of British industry and what he calls the forgotten people. He is

one of the most fascinating of the nearly-Prime Ministers of the post-war era. Michael, welcome.

**HESELTINE**

How nice to see you again.

**HENNESSY**

You were born in Swansea. Welsh by birth, family history Welsh, and I think you're very proud of your Welsh ancestry, aren't you?

**HESELTINE**

I'm very proud, but I have to be upfront. My paternal grandmother was 100 per cent French. My maternal grandfather I think had at most half Welsh blood. So I'm frankly that very common phenomenon of the United Kingdom, a mongrel.

**HENNESSY**

But a proud Welsh mongrel.

**HESELTINE**

But a proud Welsh mongrel, that's true.

**HENNESSY**

I think you still have a feel for Swansea and indeed I think you bought yourself out of the army, national service, to stand for a South Walean constituency in 1959.

**HESELTINE**

It was the Gower Peninsula. Now a Tory seat, but of course they've lost the Swansea valley where all the mines were and where the huge Labour majority was.

**HENNESSY**

I think Nye Bevan picked you out, didn't he, in the '59 election if I half remember a story?

**HESELTINE**

It was certainly a wonderful moment for me to be so publicly humiliated by so great a figure. I did the thing that all aspiring politicians do, you know. No one came to my meetings. There were no Conservatives in any numbers in the Gower Peninsula, so I tried to get into a joint meeting with Ifor Davies, the Labour candidate, and I went to any lengths, I challenged him to meet me, you know, I accused him of being a coward and all that sort of thing. Anyway, he very rightly had nothing to do with me. But then I saw this advertisement in the *South Wales Evening Post*: 'The Labour Party of South Wales. The Rt Hon Aneurin Bevan will address the party in the Elysium Cinema on the 10th of October, 1959.' So I thought, well, this is too good to be true. And I, in the rain, in the dark, thousands of us descended on the Elysium Cinema and I took my seat on the back of the third tier and on they all came, and Nye Bevan came and introduced them one by one and he –

**HENNESSY**

All the Labour MPs?

**HESELTINE**

All the Labour MPs, one by one, and then he said, 'And we have Ifor Davies, the candidate for Gower here tonight,' whereupon a voice was heard at the back of the third balcony of the Elysium Cinema, 'You have both the candidates for Gower here tonight.' Nye crouched over the microphone: he said, 'Ah, I hear the voice of an Englishman.' I didn't actually win the seat, you know.

**HENNESSY**

Good start though, good start. What sort of upbringing was yours, Michael, what did your parents do?

**HESELTINE**

I think you'd call it a middle class background – comfortable, not rich. My father was a structural engineer by profession. He was in the Royal Engineers as a result of his Territorial experience and then of course the Second World War. We were hugely fortunate in that we had the Gower Peninsula as our playground.

**HENNESSY**

Your earliest memories I suspect are of the transition to war and your father going off to war.

**HESELTINE**

Certainly very clear memories of the Chamberlain broadcast, standing at Number 1, Uplands Crescent, in the kitchen that morning.

**HENNESSY**

Sunday, 3 September 1939.

**HESELTINE**

Indeed, listening to the broadcast. I can remember the bombers because Swansea was one of the most heavily bombed towns in the country. They came at nine o'clock and our little dog knew exactly when they were coming, he was always at the top of the cellar stairs waiting to go down. I can remember standing in the garden with my grandfather watching the searchlights trying to pick out the bombers.

**HENNESSY**

What was your family's politics?

**HESELTINE**

Politics didn't seem to play much part. I don't remember any political debates, but I do know very clearly that in 1951 my father was Chairman of the local Conservative campaign in Swansea West. Oh, and I do remember he did say to me once that in 1945 he was the only officer in his mess to vote Conservative.

**HENNESSY**

Yes, very interesting.

**HESELTINE**

Yes.

**HENNESSY**

But you have a great political hero out of the Welsh political pantheon, who's not a Conservative. Am I right, Lloyd George?

**HESELTINE**

Of course. A great war leader. You know, he was a hugely impressive character with many great weaknesses, but nevertheless a leader amongst men and of course exactly the sort of person that you would expect to find in a war circumstance. But he had a great record of social reform and I would identify of course with the Welshness, with the passion. What I'd have thought was the conviction and with the humanity of understanding, although I never personally experienced it, but I was close enough to see the social conditions against which he revolted.

**HENNESSY**

I remember I came to see you as a young journalist, just after you got to the Ministry of Defence from Environment and I noticed you'd brought that huge portrait of LG with you, Lloyd George, and I remember you saying to me, Michael, I think I can say this now after all these years, 'It would be very nice if you didn't mention that too much because you understand why, Peter, but I'm not entirely sure the Conservative Party will understand why he's up there.'

**HESELTINE**

Well I think that's right. I've always had that problem that there are those who doubt my credentials as a member of the Conservative Party. They're quite wrong, of course, because I would argue that without people like me the Conservative Party shrivels to the right and becomes unelectable. But the One Nation Conservative, which I represent, Macmillan, the obvious starting point of my earliest life, that is very much the Conservative Party that I belong to.

**HENNESSY**

You went to a very English public school. Your parents sent you to Shrewsbury. Did you fit in?

**HESELTINE**

I don't think so, really.

**HENNESSY**

Why not?

**HESELTINE**

You can't make these judgements about yourself. I wasn't interested particularly in lessons. I never got enthusiastic about what I was doing. I wasn't ever in a school team and I just don't think I was a sort of clubbable person. And actually that's quite an interesting observation because that's what people have said often about the rest of my life. Anyway, I had good friends, but limited in number and it was not until my last year when I got hooked on history that things began to change academically.

### HENNESSY

You did well enough to get into Oxford, after all.

### HESELTINE

That was a different world. I can't overstate the gratitude I feel to that university for just enabling me to become me. I did have quite a lot of confidence actually when I think back on it. You know the first day I joined the Oxford Union, I joined the University Conservative Association and I joined the City Conservative Association, so it was quite obvious by then that I knew where I was going.

### HENNESSY

You said a moment ago, you were not clubbable, and yet you were a very social President of the Union. You opened up a nightclub in the basement and you had great friendships, life-long friendships. Tony Howard, the journalist – marvellous man – and Jeremy Isaacs, very distinguished journalist and many other things too. You had a gift for friendship, so I'm interested that you still think you were not a naturally clubbable person. Or was it that you said other people think you're not?

### HESELTINE

I was not the sort of person you'd find drinking in the bar. It was just not an ambience that attracted me, and you can translate that into the tea-rooms of the House of Commons. I had things I wanted to do. I had a sort of work-stream, whether it was in the voluntary side of the Conservative Party or in my garden or in the business I created. There was always something to do. And that's what I did. My motivations, if they were associated with ambition, were to do the job I'd been entrusted with, or selected to do myself, to the best of my ability, believing that if I made a success of it, it would lead somewhere.

### HENNESSY

Now after Oxford, though you had the political career in your sights, I think you were determined to have a good business career so you could be financially independent to pursue your public service.

### HESELTINE

That is true and it took an interesting form. I'm not one of those who thinks that life is planned. I think that there's a heck of a lot of luck for all of us, but it's spotting the luck. My father wanted me to be an accountant. I think I wanted to be an accountant too, and he was going to get me articled. He'd agreed this with Deloitte's in Swansea, which is a five-year articled clerkship. And something or other made me say, look, I'd like to go to university. He hadn't been to university and it wasn't something that was absolutely built into my family's assumptions. So that meant three years articles, three years at university. But at the end of my time at Oxford I went to London and I was earning £7 a week, which was half what my peer group of graduates would earn – they got about £12, £13 a week. But my grandparents had left me a thousand pounds. So I found another friend who had a thousand pounds and between us we bought a boarding house. And we had I think 13 rooms. We lived in two and let out the other 11. And we lived rather well.

### HENNESSY

In west London?

### HESELTINE

In Notting Hill Gate – not just Prime Ministers live in Notting Hill Gate.

### HENNESSY

Not just Etonians. [*Heseltine laughs*]

**HESELTINE**

And the year later we sold the boarding house, we'd doubled our money and we bought a 44-bedroom hotel. And I was in property. So I worked as an articled clerk all working hours and then I painted this building, sort of renovated it all the weekends and evenings.

**HENNESSY**

And you did quite well out of that?

**HESELTINE**

Well, it was the beginning.

**HENNESSY**

You took the traditional route for a Conservative aspirant, in those days anyway, you fought a seat you couldn't win. But you made it in 1966 in the West Country in Tavistock.

**HESELTINE**

Well, within no time at all I was adopted in very early January '65 for the wonderful constituency of Tavistock. It was a huge nostalgic privilege to be the last Honourable Member for Tavistock where Drake was once Member of Parliament.

**HENNESSY**

You are a romantic, Michael, aren't you?

**HESELTINE**

Well, wouldn't you be romantic about that?

**HENNESSY**

Were you already self aware, I'm sure you were, about your gifts for moving an audience, because for all the doubts that some kinds of Conservatives have about you, you know how to move an audience and work a crowd. But was it apparent when you were talking to the good Conservative people of Tavistock, trying to persuade them to choose you as their prospective parliamentary candidate?

#### HESELTINE

Oh yes, yes, yes. The speech I made at the Tavistock town hall – that was quite an evening. Because well, you know, I don't need to describe what the Conservative Party in those circumstances would have been like. It would have been heavily military orientated I think we can say and I had a magazine called *Man About Town*.

#### HENNESSY

You were a publisher by this stage?

#### HESELTINE

We were publishers by this stage, and we had a magazine called *Man About Town* and this was when Hugh Hefner and Guccione were launching the revelatory nude magazines and the word got out that ours was in this genre, which it never was, I have to say.

#### HENNESSY

That you were a mild pornographer?

#### HESELTINE

That's what the rumour said, but it was never true. But anyway it electrified the Tavistock constituency and so this huge audience, 600 of them packed the town hall at Tavistock and when I – you know what it's like, you're left outside to be called in, and all these macs hanging in the hall, they all had copies of *Town* magazine, and I was told I was going to be cross-examined and all that. Anyway, it caused me no problem whatsoever. I got a rapturous response and they were very good to me all the way through.

### HENNESSY

Now, Ted Heath is having a tough time as Leader of the Opposition after the '66 election. Harold Wilson is making the political weather. It's a difficult time for the Conservative Party, but did you get close to Ted in those years, when he was rather an embattled figure who was wrong-footed all the time by slick and clever Harold?

### HESELTINE

My memories of Ted Heath are very clear and they're very focused in time because I got married in 1962, met Anne I think in 1960, and one of the very first things I said, which perhaps should have warned her, is 'You really must come and have dinner with the Coningsby Club because Ted is speaking and this is tomorrow's Tory Party.'

### HENNESSY

You were a natural Heathite in the sense that you've always had – if I can put it this way Michael – a public-private impulse. You're not a mixed economy man in terms of nationalisations and all that, but you are in terms [of] public-private and industrial intervention when necessary.

### HESELTINE

These slogans are so dangerous. I've worked with Conservative Party ministers from all persuasions and, faced with the real world, practical decisions, most of these slick generalisations disappear. And because of my political experiences and my commercial experiences, I know that every government intervenes. They may not know they're doing it, they may not think of it as intervention but do it they do. So was Ted Heath right to save Rolls Royce? Look, Pratt and Whitney, General Electric, they'd have bought it in the morning.

**HENNESSY**

1971, when he nationalised it, yes.

**HESELTINE**

Indeed, indeed. But looking back was he wrong to do that? Well of course he wasn't wrong.

**HENNESSY**

Ted made this – well, it's used against him, although I think it's simplistic – U-turn in terms of prices and incomes policy when unemployment is rising and inflation is rising. Did you have any doubts about that, his swivel as it were in 1972, '73?

**HESELTINE**

I think that there was a sea-change in politics shortly after I went into the House of Commons. When I first went in 'My Right Honourable and Gallant Friend' was a very common form of address for the field officers who had served in the Second World War, and my generation, of course, didn't undergo that experience. But those who did, brought up in the '30s, remembering the '30s, the poverty, the unemployment, the near annihilation of the reputation of the Tory Party which even Churchill's incredible achievements were not able to eclipse in 1945 – the men who came through that experience had developed a comradeship across the classes in the most horrendous of circumstances. And that's what you have to know about Ted. Facing the rising unemployment – we'd had boom years, post-war reconstruction and suddenly it began to look very different and the memories of yesteryear became sharp. So Ted, essentially a rational person, said, 'I must use every known device I can to find a way of reasoning my way through this appalling crisis.' He delayed the decision to have a 'Who governs?' election, I think, for the same reason, because his colleagues, Willie Whitelaw, Peter Carrington, both in the Brigade of Guards in the Second World War, they had the same experience.

And they hesitated before indulging in what they could have felt and others would have said was a sort of political civil war. So that government ended, it was bound to end after the oil hike of 1973; there was no way back for popular support after that, and the next incident was of course the destruction of Callaghan's government by the same forces. And then Ted's government was re-elected, that's the interesting thing, under a different leader, but in 1979 we were battle-hardened troops. We'd been through it all. We knew what had to be done. And there was no demur from Willie or Peter who'd served in all these different circumstances. We knew the law had to be supreme and Margaret led the party through that experience.

**HENNESSY**

So in that sense she's the daughter of Ted?

**HESELTINE**

The continuum is fascinating. You see the speeches of 1978, read 'Selsdon Man' of 1968–9.

**HENNESSY**

Which was the think-piece before the Conservative Manifesto of 1970.

**HESELTINE**

Yes, yes.

**HENNESSY**

Yes, a re-balancing of the economy and the power of trade unions. Yes.

**HESELTINE**

Yes.

**HENNESSY**

Of course, in the spectrum of popular political memory, Michael, there's an episode in those mid-'70s which you're forever part of, which is the Mace waving. What was it that overcame you that evening when you literally picked up the Mace in the House of Commons and swung it around?

**HESELTINE**

I can deal with people in debate, discussion, I can win, I can lose. What I cannot stand are people who cheat, and that was the issue of the Mace. There is the strictest, clearest parliamentary convention that you don't break pairs and I –

**HENNESSY**

This is the arrangement whereby you don't turn up, if a Labour opposite number doesn't turn up?

**HESELTINE**

You've done a deal. You say we can't, for whatever reason, I can't be voting tonight, will you keep out of the lobbies 'cause you can't as well, and that is a binding agreement. I was responsible for leading the opposition to one of Labour's flagship bills, the nationalisation of aircraft and shipbuilding, and we were going to win. And the Chief Whip for the Labour Party found a guy who had paired with one of my people and he pushed him through the lobbies. And the Labour Party then came back into the Chamber to hear the result and stood on the green benches singing the Red Flag. And I didn't wave the Mace. I picked up the Mace and I said, 'You have usurped the authority of this House, you'd better share the symbol.' And then I put it down again. And the cartoonists are very interesting. There is the cartoon with the wild Dervish waving the Mace, but there's the cartoon that was on the front page of *The Sunday Times*, which is this heroic figure standing against the mobs. You take your pick.

Going back to Ted. How did you handle the vote for the succession? He actually stood, didn't he, in February '75 against Margaret Thatcher. How did you vote, Michael?

I abstained.

Did you? Why did you abstain?

Because he invited me to be a member of his Shadow Cabinet in 1974 and I sat alongside Keith Joseph. Keith is one of the nicest men in politics and he tried to get Ted to have a discussion in the Shadow Cabinet about what had gone wrong, what needed to be done, how the party should reposition itself, the basic answers to very sensible questions. And Ted's treatment of him was brutal. And I remember sitting there saying, this party has to come together, we have to reunite. This guy cannot do it. And so I abstained in the first vote and then voted for Willie Whitelaw in the second. Margaret then became Leader, and she had a hit list. She was going to sack Peter Walker, Paul Channon and myself. This appeared in the press. And the day, the great sacking day came, and Peter and Paul went. And she was about to do me when someone said, 'Well, there's a small problem, Leader, he's actually speaking at a meeting with you in front of a couple of thousand small businessmen in Westminster Hall at two o'clock and then he's opening for the opposition against one of the government's principal pieces of legislation. Of course, you can sack him, but maybe a little delay?' And so I survived that day. Then I made one of those speeches. It was quite difficult to sack me after that.

**HENNESSY**

One of your special speeches.

**HESELTINE**

Yes, the first of them.

**HENNESSY**

She made you Environment Secretary in '79.

**HESELTINE**

I then had this massive department. And I got the numbers down, and I got the right-to-buy through. I created the London Docklands Development Corporation – interventionism on a massive scale, with her explicit support, overruling Keith and Geoffrey.

**HENNESSY**

That's Geoffrey Howe the Chancellor.

**HESELTINE**

Chancellor and the guru –

**HENNESSY**

Keith Joseph.

**HESELTINE**

The guy in charge of the conscience of the party.

**HENNESSY**

I think you had a ruse in persuading her about the Urban Development Corporation, London Docklands, because of Reg Prentice, who'd been a Labour Cabinet Minister and had come over to the Conservatives. And if I remember, Michael, I may be wrong, he said, 'The way to persuade her is to tell her all the Labour local authority people there are Communists.' Is that what you did?

**HESELTINE**

I did.

**HENNESSY**

It wasn't entirely true, though, was it? Or was it?

**HESELTINE**

Well, I mean, you know, in the way politicians talk about things it was true. [*Laughing*] And this is what Reg had told me. He'd been a Labour MP in the East End.

**HENNESSY**

In Newham, yes.

**HESELTINE**

Yes, and he then crossed the floor. And I had this problem. I mean, I knew there were six thousand acres of derelict land, and I knew that they were Labour authorities, and there was no way they were going to regenerate that area. And so I had a very clear idea of the Development Corporation that I'd worked on in earlier years. But I couldn't see how to win. Geoffrey was against it. Keith was against it. The four of us ended up in Downing Street, and Geoffrey said, 'Margaret, you've got to stop this, this is – there's no money.' Keith said, 'This is exactly what you said you won't do.' And she turned to me, and I said, 'Look, I can't tell you, Margaret, how I've been agonising over this. I've promised Geoffrey that not a penny more than the budget I've agreed with him will be spent. I'll find all the money that's necessary.' So that was all right. 'Keith argued – no one is keener on the great vision that Keith has brought to bear in this party – but the problem is, Margaret, I've been talking to Reg Prentice and he's told me that they're all Communists down there.' It's like lighting the blue touch paper on a rocket. And there it was, we got the Development Corporation.

### HENNESSY

When you went to Defence, I think there were two big things: the rise of the Campaign for Nuclear Disarmament and the move from Polaris to the Trident system was under way. I think Mrs Thatcher wanted you to do both, see through both. I remember actually getting the story in *The Times*, that you'd set up a new Defence Secretariat to counter CND. Some people thought that was a bit iffy. It's propagandist really rather than being Secretary of State-like. Other people thought it was exactly what was needed. But it was a sort of private initiative within the MOD, and I think you're very proud of that aren't you?

### HESELTINE

We did have the meeting you discussed. Well, of course you would. I mean, we were besieged by this particular movement, wherever we went, every journalist would ask and this sort of thing. So of course one had to take it extremely seriously. It was my job as Secretary of State for Defence; I had to facilitate the arrival of the cruise missiles. And so we did meet, once a week I think, to discuss all the problems, all the agenda items, the meetings, how to handle it. And out of that meeting came another vital change. We stopped talking about unilateral disarmament and we began to talk about one-sided disarmament. And if you did the polling, if you asked the population at large what they thought about nuclear disarmament, 70 per cent were in favour of it and 30 per cent were against it – disaster for me. If you asked them about one-sided disarmament, 70 per cent were against and 30 per cent for. So we never talked about nuclear disarmament again, always talked about one-sided disarmament. And the game was ours.

### HENNESSY

The other thing you're remembered for on defence is the Westland crisis, which is quite hard to encapsulate now. It's about the fate of a helicopter company in the west of England.

**HESELTINE**

No, not really.

**HENNESSY**

Well, that's the occasion rather than the cause.

**HESELTINE**

Of course.

**HENNESSY**

Was it really about the antipathy that had built up between you and Mrs Thatcher, I remember –

**HESELTINE**

No.

**HENNESSY**

Wasn't it? What was it about?

**HESELTINE**

It was very simple. What rights have you got as a Cabinet Minister? Now, my view is very clear: that I have the right to be heard in a Cabinet. And what happened over the decision about Westland is that Mrs Thatcher, perfectly legitimately, favoured an American solution. I had been invited by Leon Brittan, the Trade and Industry Secretary, to see if we could put together a European alternative. I produced an alternative, led by GEC and British Aerospace and European players that I had negotiated the Eurofighter deal with. And quite properly, Margaret Thatcher had a meeting with a small group of us. And she tried to argue for the American solution, I argued for the British-led European solution. And she lost. So she then called a meeting of the Economic Committee of the Cabinet. She brought Cuckney, who was the Chairman of Westland to that committee – very unusual.

**HENNESSY**

Sir John Cuckney. Yes.

**HESELTINE**

Very, very unusual. And she lost. And she was furious. And she summed up that meeting by saying, 'Very well, we will meet again after the Stock Exchange closes on Friday to hear what Heseltine has got to say,' because my scheme was unfolding. That was not recorded in the minutes. But I have a letter from an official who took the notes confirming that that's what was said. I know it was said but I've now got the letter.

**HENNESSY**

That's the Cabinet Secretary, Robert Armstrong, I would imagine.

**HESELTINE**

No, it's not the Cabinet Secretary.

**HENNESSY**

Oh.

**HESELTINE**

And I had promised I will not publish that in my life. But it's there.

**HENNESSY**

It's a smoking letter.

**HESELTINE**

It's a smoking letter. And the meeting that we were promised on the Friday was set up by the Cabinet Secretariat on, I think, the Monday. It was cancelled on the Wednesday. And so it never took place. As a result of which I had no choice but to try and raise the matter in Cabinet. And Margaret wouldn't allow the matter to be discussed.

**HENNESSY**

This is 9 January 1986.

**HESELTINE**

I think there was another meeting as well in the meantime. But this is the issue: have I the right to be heard or can the Prime Minister, having lost the argument on two occasions with colleagues, simply say, 'I'm going to go ahead in this way.' And my view is very clear, that if I had agreed to that, I would have had to say to the European Defence Secretaries that I'd worked with, 'I'm sorry, the Prime Minister wouldn't let me talk about it.' I would have been finished. Number 10 would have briefed every journalist in sight saying 'A man of straw'. You know, just one puff of smoke and he's gone. That's what they'd have done. That was the issue. And if you actually want to see the inside of it, there were two further stages. The first was the behaviour of Charles Powell and Bernard Ingham, as described in Charles Moore's book, and even –

**HENNESSY**

This is the Press Secretary, and the Foreign Affairs Private Secretary at Number 10.

**HESELTINE**

Correct, and you can see that even Charles Moore, her official biographer, is ashamed of what he found out. And anyway, I then resigned. And the only reason the Americans got Westland is because friends of the Prime Minister organised a concert party to buy the Westland shares.

**HENNESSY**

That's a big accusation, Michael.

**HESELTINE**

It was made by the press at the time. And it was – there are the records, that's when you saw Hanson, Goldsmith –

**HENNESSY**

Businessmen.

**HESELTINE**

Yes – suddenly came together to buy Westland shares. The Americans won. They failed in their mission, which was to make the Ministry of Defence buy the Black Hawk helicopter, and so they sold it again and went away. I had the most profound regrets that I had to resign, but I have never had a shred of doubt.

**HENNESSY**

It's very interesting. You didn't turn up at that Cabinet meeting that morning expecting to resign, did you?

**HESELTINE**

No, I didn't. No I didn't. But I knew that something was up. I'd been in Cabinets a long time, I know how they work. The secretariat produces a brief for any chairman of a Cabinet Committee saying, 'These are the issues, this is where the debate will go, there are two or three outcomes. Here are the alternative summaries where you may be able to sum up.' It was when Margaret reached down into her handbag and produced a scrappy piece of paper from which she read the conclusion of the Cabinet that I knew that something was up.

**HENNESSY**

You had been set up, do you think, Michael?

**HESELTINE**

Oh yes, of course, and the set-up was very simple. This is what the conclusion was: the Cabinet now agree that in any future questions about the affair of Westland, no Cabinet Minister will answer questions without reference to the Cabinet Secretary. To which I intervened to say, 'Do you mean, Prime Minister, that if I'm asked the identical question I was asked three days ago, I have to say, the answer, 'I've got to refer to the Cabinet Secretary?' 'Yes.' You know, just think what Bernard Ingham would have done with that.

#### HENNESSY

The Press Secretary.

#### HESELTINE

The Press Secretary. So there was no compatibility with honour to remain in that Cabinet.

#### HENNESSY

So you felt like Martin Luther, you could do no other?

#### HESELTINE

I never put [it] in such a dramatic, religious context, but I certainly believed then and certainly nothing has changed my mind that I had to go. It was this, frankly, the cheat. You cannot allow that to happen to you in public life.

#### HENNESSY

Not getting your discussion that Friday.

#### HESELTINE

That is the issue.

#### HENNESSY

Yes. I remember at the time thinking, I related it, perhaps wrongly – others did too – to your efforts as Environment Secretary to regenerate Liverpool. And you wrote, after those riots, the most remarkable Cabinet paper of the era I think – not that I've seen all of them of course – called 'It Took a Riot', which you brought to Cabinet in 1981. And I remember I got a copy at the time, and it was the most extraordinary thing because it's not just analytical in the way that these Cabinet papers are, but it's full of passion, it's you, it's everything you've been describing to me – and it had a great impact. But you didn't prevail. And some people think a fuse was lit in your relationship with Mrs Thatcher that summer and autumn of 1981 when you didn't get your way on the regeneration of Liverpool and other inner cities, which was your great cause at the time.

**HESELTINE**

No, that's not true. It was 1981 as you rightly say. And I did write a paper that was designed to shock as well as inform. Because that's what everybody said, everywhere I went, 'You've only come because of the riot.'

**HENNESSY**

In Liverpool.

**HESELTINE**

Yes. And that's why I did come. That's why I said to Margaret in 1981, 'Look, we can just treat this like yobs on the street, we can say public law and order demands backing the police, and we all understand and feel the importance of that. But I think there's something worse here, I think there's something more profound and I want your permission to walk the streets of Liverpool and come back and tell you what I think it is.' She gave me permission to do that. I spent three weeks doing it. And began the process, which has had, I hope, some success. The next 18 months I went to Liverpool every week. She knew that. And it wasn't extra money I was looking for. I think I got a little extra money, but I had so many levers within the Department. But what I did in Liverpool in those 18 months, from the middle of '81 to '83, I proved that little things could be done that worked. And that was the heart of the problem in Liverpool, that confidence was bombed out. Everybody knew what was wrong, and it was you, never them. So showing them that if you took a project and worked on it you could get the phoenix out of the ashes was a psychological process that I had to do. I felt, frankly, there's no one else who's going to do it, so I'd better do it.

**HENNESSY**

You lost the argument over that document, but you did it anyway?

**HESELTINE**

No, but I don't think I did lose the argument, you see. I think that they didn't stop me, and I've forgotten the debate now, because I know that nothing stopped me doing Liverpool. And I got promoted at the end of it, you see. So it's quite wrong to suggest that something had gone wrong in my relationship – we were never friends, but we were colleagues.

**HENNESSY**

Did you think your political career was finished when you left the Cabinet in January '86? It's very hard to be a comeback kid in the British system.

**HESELTINE**

I believed all the way through I'd be back.

**HENNESSY**

Did you?

**HESELTINE**

Yes.

**HENNESSY**

Why were you so confident?

**HESELTINE**

I think it's very difficult to know the answer to that question, but within no time at all, the volume of support had its own eloquence. The letters flowed in, the invitations came. I got one or two speeches that were cancelled. But I was making 12 speeches a week. And so it gathered its own momentum.

**HENNESSY**

Then Mrs Thatcher falls into trouble over her management of Cabinet and the European question, the curse of so many British Prime Ministers, I suppose, in the autumn of 1990 and Geoffrey Howe resigns, for whom you had a great deal of time and affection, I think.

**HESELTINE**

Oh yes, a great friend.

**HENNESSY**

And then you were there, ready to challenge her. Did you have any hesitations about that, because I've heard it argued by, I think, very wise Conservatives that if you'd just waited it would have fallen into your lap, the premiership, or at least the leadership of the opposition, once Mrs T had lost an election, and then you would have been Prime Minister that way. So it must have been a very difficult calculation for you.

**HESELTINE**

Well, it was summed up within minutes of Geoffrey's speech. And I walked out of the chamber past another friend, Michael Jopling, and I said, 'Michael, what the hell do I do now?'

**HENNESSY**

Former Chief Whip.

**HESELTINE**

Yes. And he said, 'You do nothing. You'll be Leader of the Opposition in 18 months.' And I said, 'I don't want to be Leader of the Opposition.' And the –

**HENNESSY**

Why did you say that?

**HESELTINE**

Well, I didn't want to be Leader of the Opposition. I wanted to be Prime Minister.

**HENNESSY**

Did you think you'd win the leadership contest?

**HESELTINE**

No, I don't think I did think I would win. But I was much impressed by the argument of – I had many followers who said, 'Look, if you're going to be a leader, in the end you have to lead. And if you run from this, that will have its consequences in people's judgement about your fitness to be a leader.' And I did hear that argument and it did make sense to me. There were two absolutely fundamental disagreements: the European issue, which was Margaret was completely out of sympathy with what most of the parliamentary party thought; and the poll tax was just bleeding support. And so there were two huge issues of difference. And here was the opportunity that Geoffrey had created, not in any way my doing. Frankly – I may be quite wrong – but I think she knew that there was a high chance that I would be her successor, and that she was determined to avoid at all costs. Quite wrongly, for the reasons that she believed, because she had completely misunderstood what my industrial regeneration views actually were. And I actually privatised more of the state, I think, than any other minister.

**HENNESSY**

What would you have done if you'd become Prime Minister, Michael? What was the first thing you would have done?

**HESELTINE**

I would have got rid of the poll tax, and I would have had an election.

**HENNESSY**

Wouldn't you have gone on, I think once we talked, a speaking tour?

**HESELTINE**

Ah, that would have been the election campaign. It would have been called 'The Forgotten People.' And I'm very interested to see how those words have suddenly started emerging. But you and I know, because we talked about this many, many years ago, my election campaign would have begun in the more remote parts of the United Kingdom – not in Central Office, not in the middle of London.

**HENNESSY**

The western isles or the northern isles?

**HESELTINE**

It could have been even as dramatic as that. But I would have been out there in the most remote parts of the United Kingdom, and my campaign would have criss-crossed the country from one area of deprivation to another, to one community that felt forgotten, gradually closing in on London, with the ultimate eve-of-poll meeting in the capital, which I was going to change.

**HENNESSY**

You'd worked it all out. This was like your Liverpool walkabouts but on a national scale.

**HESELTINE**

Yes. That's not a bad example.

**HENNESSY**

And what would have been the gist of the speech you would have given to 'The Forgotten People'?

**HESELTINE**

Oh, what I've had the privilege of doing for David Cameron and George Osborne, which is restoring power to the people from which it has been eroded over the last 100 years.

**HENNESSY**

They would have said, 'Well, show me, Michael, how do we do that?'

**HESELTINE**

I'd have shown them London Docklands and Liverpool.

**HENNESSY**

So your great cause of regeneration has run on, but your other great cause in your life, Europe, Britain's place in Europe, there's this great *caesura*, this referendum result, which does change everything. How do you think it's going to play out?

**HESELTINE**

Well, we'll see. The jury's out.

**HENNESSY**

Explain.

**HESELTINE**

The referendum has said Brexit, but no one knows what Brexit is. And so I think Theresa May has been absolutely right in putting three of the principal Brexiteers into the key jobs. They argued the case, let us see what they mean. But in the end Parliament is sovereign, and that's where the ultimate decisions will be taken.

**HENNESSY**

Didn't the British people think that they were the sovereign body when they took that decision?

**HESELTINE**

Yes, but we all know that they're not. Parliament is supreme.

**HENNESSY**

I'm not sure they know that.

**HESELTINE**

Well, wait and see. Wait and see what people think when they know what the alternative they voted for is.

**HENNESSY**

You've been very rude in a way – certainly by your standards, because you're a very courteous man – about the new Foreign Secretary, Boris Johnson.

**HESELTINE**

I – I was deeply shaken by his references to Hitler.

**HENNESSY**

Yes. Do you think he's fit to be Foreign Secretary?

**HESELTINE**

He is Foreign Secretary.

**HENNESSY**

That's not what I asked. [*Laughter*] Michael, if I could wave a magic wand for you – you're in your eighties now – and grant you one last great reform, what would it be?

**HESELTINE**

I think that it would be a process whereby I could remove the head teachers of failing schools.

**HENNESSY**

That would be the reform?

**HESELTINE**

I think so.

**HENNESSY**

That's critical for you, is it?

**HESELTINE**

I think it is the beginning and the end of everything. If you don't educate the kids, what chance have they got? And that is true today, it will be doubly true tomorrow, and triply true next week.

**HENNESSY**

What trace do you think you'll leave on history, Michael?

**HESELTINE**

My trees.

**HENNESSY**

Your arboretum – in Thenford.

**HESELTINE**

Yes.

**HENNESSY**

That's your immortality?

**HESELTINE**

It's the only thing that people will remember.

**HENNESSY**

Are you sure?

**HESELTINE**

Yes.

**HENNESSY**

That must be in some ways a great consolation to you.

**HESELTINE**

Yes.

**HENNESSY**

Because you love that arboretum, don't you?

**HESELTINE**

Yes.

**HENNESSY**

You and Anne have built this extraordinary thing.

**HESELTINE**

Yes, the book is coming out in late September, and Anne and I worked on it – well, effectively we've worked on it for forty years. And we treasure it and it is a life's work.

**HENNESSY**

Putting that great legacy on one side, what political memory would you like to leave?

**HESELTINE**

Oh, the 1981 October speech at the Tory Party conference. 'They're black, they're British, they were born here, they vote here.'

**HENNESSY**

That was a brave thing to do in those circumstances, was it not?

**HESELTINE**

It was. I felt it was a make or break speech.

**HENNESSY**

How did it go down?

**HESELTINE**

They cheered to the echo.

**HENNESSY**

Yes.

**HESELTINE**

A standing ovation. And David Dimbleby said, 'Michael Heseltine picked up the Tory Party, shook it, and put it back down where he wanted it to be.' That's not a bad thing to have said.

**HENNESSY**

Michael Heseltine, thank you very much indeed.

# Vince Cable (Sir Vince Cable)

Series 4, Episode 2, first broadcast 9 August 2016

**Born** 9 May 1943; **Educated** Nunthorpe Grammar
School; Fitzwilliam College, Cambridge

MP (Liberal Democrat) Twickenham 1997–2015; 2017–19

Acting Leader of the Liberal Democrats, 2007; Secretary
of State for Business, Innovation and Skills, 2010–15;
Leader of the Liberal Democrats, 2017–19

**Autobiography** *Free Radical*, 2009

### HENNESSY

Sir Vince Cable is a late-flowering politician. He didn't reach the
House of Commons until he was 54, at the fifth attempt under
three different party labels. As the Liberal Democrats' economic
spokesman, warning 'there may be trouble ahead' of the great crash
of 2008, he aroused public attention and respect. His prowess on
the dance floor won him public affection. His five years as Secretary of State for Business, Innovation and Skills in the Cameron-
Clegg Coalition brought him sustained public attention. Vince,
welcome.

### CABLE

Thank you.

**HENNESSY**

You were born towards the end of the Second World War in York. What kind of a household was it?

**CABLE**

Well, it was sort of upwardly-mobile. My parents came from a working-class background, they left school at 15, worked in factories – my mother on the production line at Terry's in York, and my father at Rowntree's. But they – my father in particular – were very ambitious, anxious to get on in life, to progress into the middle class, which he did through hard work and self-education, became a lecturer at a tech college and we gradually moved up through the classes from a terraced house with an outdoor loo and a tin bath to the respectable semi-detached house. And having a successful eldest son at school and passing the 11-plus and going to Cambridge was very much part of that kind of ethos.

**HENNESSY**

But reading your memoir, *Free Radical*, it wasn't a particularly happy home was it?

**CABLE**

No, I mean, it wasn't catastrophic. I mean, but there was a lot of tension. I think my parents were of a generation where you didn't divorce, even though relations got very strained and difficult, and certainly my teenage years were memories of tension. And my mother had quite a bad nervous breakdown after my younger brother was born when I was ten and went off to a mental hospital for, I think about a year, something like that. And that was partly a reflection of the environment in which she lived, where she was a, you know, housewife, you stayed at home, you did the washing, you did the cleaning, and were respectable and didn't socialise very much. And I think the loneliness of it sort of got to her and that was the consequence. But later in life, I mean, I think, you know, where these things come out in the wash eventually, she turned herself round, mainly through adult education actually, learned to paint and study history, poetry, things she'd never encountered before, and became more self-confident. And the relationship with my father, which was quite strained when I was young, in their sixties and seventies became more kind of close and affectionate and it went round in a circle.

### HENNESSY

There's one very sad and searing line in your autobiography when you talk about, 'something happened in childhood that cauterised my emotions' – that you didn't feel particularly emotional at all when your mum and dad died. It's a very sad line that, Vince.

### CABLE

Yes, I think when you hear a lot of rowing and argument, how do you deal with it? You can explode yourself, or you just turn inward and just shut out the noise, which is what I did. So I rather switched off. And that was when I was a teenager, and of course the problems became more serious later. I married somebody who I'd actually met in York but who was an East African Asian by origin. And this was at a time when, you know, interracial marriages were not acceptable in that kind of society. We split from my parents for several years, and indeed from her parents too, because it was equally unacceptable in her Indian culture. And that in a way created a big divide for me, particularly with my father. I mean, subsequently he became friendly and, you know, started to value my wife and our children. But a wound was there and never, never went away.

### HENNESSY

You sought a bit of faith didn't you? You were one of those seekers after faith. Again, I think it's one of your most interesting phrases, you talked about faith as you found it 'a particularly elusive bar of soap,' which in theological history is a very unusual metaphor.

**CABLE**

Yes.

**HENNESSY**

Are you still searching? Is there something within you?

**CABLE**

Yes, I think I'm still what would be regarded as a searcher. I do go to church from time to time and there's something about the Church which I value. I mean, I don't have spiritual experiences and I wouldn't subscribe to doctrine in any sense, but I do feel whenever I go to a church I tend to sort of light a candle and experience some of the atmosphere. But when I was young, I mean, I did the lot actually. I started with the Baptists with my parents, and then the Methodists, and then went off to the Quakers, pursuing an attractive teenage girl at the time, but got quite captivated by the Quakers. Then married a Catholic, and in between I sort of dabbled in some of the others – went to see what the Mormons had to offer and various others. So I thought there was something there that I was missing out on and that I needed, but I never quite found it and that's the slippery bar of soap.

**HENNESSY**

A kind of spiritual market testing?

**CABLE**

Yes it was, exactly what it was. And I think that, if you remember the late Bishop of Woolwich, who was a very influential theologian.

**HENNESSY**

John Robinson.

**CABLE**

Yes, John Robinson. He had a phrase about a God-shaped hole. And I had that hole and I was trying to fit God into it and never quite succeeded. But I still, you know, attend church from time to time. I value the insights of people with a kind of spiritual background, and so I wouldn't describe myself as an atheist.

**HENNESSY**

You have, I think – I think you've talked about this in the past – a restlessness which your father had. And also I think you said he drank deep in the bottle of workaholism.

**CABLE**

Yes, he –

**HENNESSY**

You do as well don't you?

**CABLE**

Yes, indeed. He was very austere. I mean, hardly drank, worked very, very, very hard, was very polished in everything he did. And I suppose he passed on that rather kind of puritanical streak to me, because I do work extremely hard and, I mean, otherwise I would have not been able to cope with the job of Secretary of State, which is the most difficult job I ever had to do, but it was very intense. But it was the habits of youth. And that's why I have somewhat ambiguous views about my father. I mean, we did fight each other, about politics and other things, but I am indebted to him in many ways for the traits that I've inherited.

**HENNESSY**

Did it make you a shy boy? I think it probably did. You had a schoolmaster who brought you out by making you Macbeth in the school play.

### CABLE

That's correct. Yes, I was paralytically shy, I think, as a lot of teenagers are. I don't think it was unique. But when I was 16, the teacher who did the annual school play auditioned us. I was hoping to be a spear carrier or a tree at the back of the chorus or something. But he had heard something that other people hadn't heard – I did have a good way of speaking poetry – and he gave me the lead role, and it was a while before I could conquer the terror, but I did eventually learn how to speak to an audience and look at the back of the hall and declaim, and I grew in confidence. And without that I would never ever have been able to speak in public.

### HENNESSY

It's very interesting. So you wouldn't be sitting here with me but for him.

### CABLE

No, I wouldn't. It was one of those transformational experiences.

### HENNESSY

I think the grammar school, the post-Butler Act, Rab Butler Act, was made for you wasn't it?

### CABLE

Yes, it was. I mean, I was one of the ones who passed the 11-plus. I still have vivid memories of the 11-plus day when we announced our results and the class was split in two. And you know, some of us, the sheep, went off to grammar school and the goats went off to secondary modern. It was a very searing occasion, and I remember the people sitting next to me who'd failed and I never saw them again, actually. It was a terribly divisive thing. But it was personally fantastic for me, and I didn't go to one of these very high-pressure public schools or direct grant schools, and you had the benefit of being a big fish in a small pool, and getting – certainly in the sixth form – far more attention than I'd have ever got and support, and which is why ultimately, I went up to Cambridge. I was one of a small number of Oxbridge products of the school.

**HENNESSY**

Did you feel that you were, when you got to Cambridge, I think in the early sixties, the rising force, the gritty northern meritocrat? Did you read Michael Young's *The Rise of the Meritocracy*?'

**CABLE**

Yes, I did, and I suppose we were part of that. And I suppose people like me, we had a bit of a chip on our shoulder, you know, we'd come from fairly ordinary northern schools. In my case I was a scientist and my first year was spent miles away in digs, and I used to look at these posh boys at the posh colleges and, you know, this was the enemy. So there was a little bit of the class sense that I brought down with me from the north of England.

**HENNESSY**

Do posh boys still actually give you a little ripple now and again?

**CABLE**

Yes.

**HENNESSY**

A little atavistic ripple?

**CABLE**

Yes. I suppose I've never quite – I mean, obviously you grow out of these things, but I still recognise the differences, and certainly I was working with the Bullingdon Club in the Cabinet, and yes, it did – I did occasionally notice the difference.

**HENNESSY**

And how did you manifest yourself in the Cabinet room? Are there certain forms of language or secret codes that you detected on their part that would get Vince to say things in a rather blunt northern way around the Cabinet table?

**CABLE**

Yes, I think probably I wouldn't make too much of that. I mean, there were people like McLoughlin, the Transport Secretary, who was a miner actually, much more working class than me, and Pickles who had his Bradford accent. So we were quite a mixed group. So I would. But I did belong to the proletarian tendency. [*Both laugh*]

**HENNESSY**

You got to know quite a lot of Conservatives through the Union, I think. Ken Clarke and Norman Lamont and so on. Did you strike up reasonable relationships with them?

**CABLE**

Yes, I got to know Norman Lamont well because he was in the same college and a year ahead of me. And I admired him actually. I mean, he was a brilliant performer. Ken Clarke was a bit of a late developer, I think. He subsequently did brilliantly in public life, but he wasn't a great orator, whereas Norman Lamont could command an audience and was always interesting and took a slightly different take on things. No, it was a very, very good experience, because I went there as a scientist, I worked in the labs, and then to go off in the evening to be exposed to big ideas and debate was a great mind-opening experience.

**HENNESSY**

When you switched to economics after two years doing natural sciences, I think, did you have already in your mind father figures, as it were, were you Keynesian or were you influenced by Lloyd George?

**CABLE**

Yes, I think Cambridge in the sixties – and the legacy's still there, but it was particularly then, it was dominated by the heirs of Keynes. You know, there were people who had worked with him. Richard Kahn, Joan Robinson and her husband. They were the kind of intellectual leaders in Cambridge. There were people with other views, but they were dominant. So I did inherit that, I think. The economist who most impressed me was one of the Nobel Prize winners called James Meade, and he was interesting because he was, apart from being a brilliant man, he was trying to reconcile the ideas of having a market economy that was open and competitive, but also a state that redistributed income and wealth and provided good public services. That kind of practical social democratic model was something that attracted me from quite an early age and stayed with me.

**HENNESSY**

That's interesting because it sounds like you, actually. But before I come back to that, you watched those Cambridge dons going down in the Wilson government to advise, and you thought they went into a cul-de-sac with the National Plan of '65 and the incomes policy, which is unusual really, because your generation was rather swept away by Harold Wilson.

**CABLE**

Yes, yes –

**HENNESSY**

Another gritty northern meritocrat, with that fabulous speech at the '63 party conference about the white heat of technology and harnessing technology and economic prowess to great advance. And yet you were a kind of in-house sceptic.

### CABLE

Yes, I dabbled with the Liberals when I was a student, partly because of the fact that Jo Grimond had led the way on Europe and they were internationalist and had a lot of very attractive values. But when Harold Wilson came along it was very clear that this was *the* serious political force of the future. And you know, science, technology, upward mobility – the kind of things that embodied what I was about essentially. So I was quite attracted to the Wilson revolution, but then you know, we all felt let down subsequently because in office [he] didn't accomplish anything like what had been hoped. And the country drifted into economic crisis.

### HENNESSY

Cambridge left quite a mark on you really in all sorts of ways. You obviously gained more in confidence and it's a great preparation for political life, even a slightly artificial replica House of Commons of the Union, and so on. But you were not a fully-formed chap really – well, bloke – by the time you finished. And I think, I suspect it was when you get into Africa, it's Kenya…

### CABLE

Yes. I think one of the things I was very, very anxious to do was to see the world. I travelled round India on my own, and I became utterly absorbed and fascinated by that and wanted to do more. So I then landed a wonderful job in Africa, in the Kenya government, working for the Kenyatta administration in the Treasury.

### HENNESSY

It's a great responsibility at a young age, in some ways more responsibility than you perhaps had till you were Secretary of State for Business.

### CABLE

Yes, indeed. I mean some years later, it must have been over a decade later, I went into the British Foreign Office for a couple of years; I was a sort of middle-level British civil servant and you're doing fairly menial things, you know, organising *placements* for diplomatic dinners, whereas when in Kenya in my early twenties I was being sent out to negotiate with big investors and aid donors on, with what were then, enormous sums of money.

### HENNESSY

You ceased to be a neutral civil servant for a while and became a special adviser to John Smith, who was Secretary of State for Trade and Industry, at the end of the Callaghan government. Now, you'd been a Liberal at Cambridge, were you a Labour man by this stage?

### CABLE

Yes, I was and I'd been reinforced in that by the fact that I'd lived in Glasgow for six years, I'd stood for Parliament for the first time in Scotland. And I'd been a Labour councillor in Glasgow, and it was a real 'university of life' experience and I had quite serious responsibility on the council and in many ways became very much part of the Labour culture. I mean, I was on the kind of social democratic wing, I suppose, of the party, but I fitted in comfortably enough. And then when I went to work for John Smith, similarly, he, you know, he gave me a responsible job as a special adviser. I was a great fan of his, I thought he was a really great, great man – a pity he never became Prime Minister. And he had that kind of balance of pragmatism, that conviction which I, you know, greatly admired and tried to emulate.

But what I did discover about the Labour Party at that time was that – with his help and support – I was trying to get a nomination for a parliamentary seat, and contested several in north London and ran up against Jeremy Corbyn, Ken Livingstone. It was the point where the hard left was starting to take over the Labour Party, and until I'd run into them and competed with them, I hadn't realised how far the rot had gone. And I suppose that sowed the seeds in my mind that there was a battle coming up and when it reached its peak a couple of years later with the SDP breakaway I decided to join it.

**HENNESSY**

A historian, I think it was Paul Addison, once described Winston Churchill as a 'politician of no fixed abode'. Do you think that's true of you?

**CABLE**

No, I wouldn't actually. I was a Liberal student, moved to the Labour Party and then moved back into what's now the Liberal Democrats, through the SDP. I think what happened was that my views are remarkably, indeed boringly, similar to what they were half a century ago. My view of the world hasn't changed very much. But the political landscape has changed, and the party boundaries have changed, and I've been on that fault line. And there has been a big fault line running through British politics and what you could call the centre-left. And it's been dependent on what's happening with the Lib Dems or the Labour Party, and I've crossed that boundary. But my broad approach to life and, you know, how you do economic policy is not vastly different from what it was when I was first introduced to these ideas half a century ago. I read Crosland's *The Future of Socialism*, which is the kind of social democratic bible. And I think probably my views are pretty much there.

**HENNESSY**

I think you were very much influenced in the wider world since by your first wife, Olympia, weren't you? It opened up thoughts and so on. She sounds a remarkable lady.

**CABLE**

Yes, she was. Partly because my personal upbringing wasn't

terribly happy, when I sort of fell in love with her and we had a very deep and happy relationship, and young children, it became a dominant feature in my life. And probably one of the reasons I took so long to get into Parliament was that I wasn't able to be single-minded about the politics, and I did feel, you know, because of my closeness to her, because I valued family life, I often didn't turn up to meetings, I wasn't that sort of 100 per cent committed career politician. But she encouraged me nonetheless and even – she got cancer I think about 14–15 years before she eventually died in 2001 – and even when she was very ill, she told me to keep going, never give up. And her moral support was fantastically important, and a lot of people would have given up in my situation, but she, you know, she helped to keep me going.

**HENNESSY**

There's a side of you, Vince, that everybody's intrigued by, almost to the level of absurdity I would have thought, which is your ballroom dancing. Now, was it Olympia who suggested you should do it?

**CABLE**

Yes, it was, yes, when our kids were growing up as teenagers and we wanted to do things together, this – I think it was her idea actually, because when we'd first met we'd danced in nightclubs in Nairobi and we said, 'Well, we'll go and learn to do it properly.' And I think, partly because of our temperament we didn't just do it as a hobby, we had to do exams and progress through the hierarchy of exams; it's a bit like learning the piano, you get to grade eight. So we did lots of dancing exams. Unfortunately she then became very ill and couldn't do it, and I had to drop it. But when she died, after she died I was a bit lost emotionally, I was looking for things to do to occupy me, and I started dancing with my teacher, and that led – one thing led to another. I got onto *Strictly Come Dancing* for the winter show. And since then, when I was a Cabinet Minister, I always used to try and protect my Friday afternoon lesson; it was one of the things that kept me sane. And now I've moved out of that world I do it competitively actually. I've been to Blackpool for the national championships. I'm not brilliant by any means, but it's a brilliant hobby. You know, you're using your brain in a totally different way, it's a way of keeping fit. I love music, I love rhythm. And it's something I strongly advocate and encourage other people to do.

#### HENNESSY

It does fascinate people. I'm sure you're being modest, because to use a phrase that Bertie Wooster used of Jeeves, you swing a dashed efficient shoe on the dance floor, don't you?

#### CABLE

Well, I did get a 10 from Len, that goes down on my CV as roughly equivalent to being Secretary of State. [*Hennessy laughs*]

#### HENNESSY

But it does intrigue people. When you read Roy Hattersley, who's rather a connoisseur of Yorkshire males – being one himself – and he's intrigued by this. He had a rather unkind line in the review of your book about you having the demeanour of a Yorkshire undertaker on a day out at Bridlington, which I thought was a bit uncalled for. [*Cable laughs*] But then he contrasts it with the dancing and says he still can't work out – Roy – whether it's an aberration or integral to you. What's the answer?

#### CABLE

Yes, well, they're both parts of me. I am in some ways quite staid and orthodox and reflect my, you know, nonconformist upbringing, but I do love dancing and I do love music. And yeah, my current regime, I'm now in my seventies, you know, keeping fit is terribly important and I do the gym, you know, I do all that stuff and also cycling, but dancing isn't boring like those things. It's stimulating.

**HENNESSY**

You've almost converted me, Vince, you've almost converted me. Was it an advantage to come into Parliament so late? You'd been around the block at bit, in a good sense of that phrase. It must have been quite difficult for you to adjust to these rather pushy young men with their obsession with tactics and spinning and so on – I'm being slightly unkind to them.

**CABLE**

Well, the Lib Dems are quite a good party in that sense, because there were quite a few of my contemporaries who had come into the Lib Dems because they'd, you know, their politics in local government, and they came in, like me, in middle age. I think it's a mixed story. I mean, there are advantages in having done other things. And the fact that I'd had senior jobs in government and business and travelled the world and, you know, all this helped me to deal with problems in a perhaps more mature way than many others. But the problem about coming in late is that people very quickly pigeonhole you as past it. You know, pensioner.

**HENNESSY**

Which happened to Ming Campbell after all –

**CABLE**

Yes it did.

**HENNESSY**

For all his remarkable array of gifts, it happened to him.

**CABLE**

It was indeed, and that's partly why I wasn't able to pursue the leadership after him, because people had collectively made up their mind we can't have old people doing this, got to have the young bloods. And I think that kind of stereotype was very powerful. I think probably less so now because of course the younger generation have rather screwed up –

**HENNESSY**

So let's hear it for gerontocracy –

**CABLE**

And one of Theresa May's attractions is she's a serious grown-up and I think that age may be less important in future.

**HENNESSY**

Was it difficult for you, given your experience, to see the kind of playground politics at its worst, which the House of Commons can produce at its worst? At its best it's remarkable, but at its worst it's not edifying. That must have been quite galling for you, plus also the fact that I suspect, Vince, that you thought you could do certain people's jobs better than they could.

**CABLE**

Yes, there's probably an element of that. I think the playground politics is very, very, very tiresome – you know, this idea that humanity is irreconcilably divided into these tribes and we've got to fight each other morning, afternoon – I find that just very, very tedious and unproductive. And probably my impatience with it showed in Parliament, because my instincts were always to agree with people on the other side if they said sensible things. And that's why, in a way, I relished the Coalition. And I had a very simple philosophy in my department, although I had strong disagreements with a lot of the Tories, that you leave your guns at the door and we just get on with the job of work and we work together, and achieved a great deal actually. And I mean, I look back on the five years I had, you know, the whole industrial strategy, the creating new banks for business, and the sort of social legislation that we did, reform of corporate governance. An enormous amount was achieved, and it was done through people being grown up and getting rid of the tribal nonsense and just getting on with the job.

### HENNESSY

We'll come back to the Coalition in a minute, but what really made your name with the public was the warning about the inflated bubble in housing and so on, in an era when certain politicians, I think the Chancellor, Gordon Brown, was claiming that boom and bust were over.

### CABLE

Yes.

### HENNESSY

But your instincts told you otherwise. Now, what was it with your inner gyroscope, Vince, that put up this feeling that it was *not* so?

### CABLE

Well, I think a sort of bit of basic economics. [*Laughs*] But you just looked at some of the indicators, you know, the growth of personal debt in relation to people's income, the relationship between the price of housing and the trends in people's income. There was something not right about it. And I think even three years before the crisis I was going around banks saying, you know, 'Do you not realise there's a problem?' I remember going along to meet the head of HBOS at one point, and he said, 'Yeah of course there is, this is all very dangerous. But if I don't do it, I lose my job. The shareholders want high returns.' So there were people even in the City, I think, who realised they were sitting on a bubble and it was dangerous. But there was a lot of abdication of responsibility. I remember going to the Bank of England and saying, 'Look, for goodness sake why don't you blow a whistle?' And the response was, 'Well, it's none of our business. It's not part of our mandate, we're not allowed to.' And of course the government were in denial, for political reasons, because Gordon – for all his positive side and there are a lot of very good things about Gordon Brown – he'd bought in, I think, to this myth that, you know, they'd abolished boom and bust forever and found it difficult to admit that there was a problem.

**HENNESSY**

Didn't you feel the flame of the scholarship boy flickering though, 'I could do this job better than Gordon? I'm hearing and feeling things that he's not.'

**CABLE**

Well, I've often felt that about – about people in all parties. [*Hennessy laughs*] But no, I think, I just want to leave the thought that he was a serious guy actually. He's a man with convictions. He's still passionate about world poverty.

**HENNESSY**

Any profile or any biography of Gordon Brown will have your killer line in the House of Commons, 'Am I alone in noticing the Chancellor's gone from being Stalin to Mr Bean in a matter of weeks?' I think I'm paraphrasing it a bit. But that was a killer line. Did you prefabricate that one, Vince?

**CABLE**

Well, I did make it up myself. I know people think that everything said in Parliament is scripted by researchers and so on. I did do my own lines. I have mixed feelings about being remembered for that because, as I've already said, I have very mixed feelings about Gordon Brown, he had his weaknesses but he had his strengths too, and I – I wouldn't like to be thought of [as] the person that just assassinated him.

### HENNESSY

No, but it's the nature of political memory, isn't it? If you've got a killer one line, that's right at the top of the memory bank.

Historians will probably look back on your career – they'll be very interested in it – but one of the aspects they'll look at is could Vince have been Liberal Leader? I think twice probably you could have been: when Charles Kennedy was unwell and standing down, and I think you were partly instrumental in persuading him to go. And then later in the Coalition when your friend Lord Oakeshott was organising a coup, to put it no higher than that, against Nick Clegg, what was the real Vince doing? It's not entirely clear how close you were to doing the Brutus bit.

### CABLE

Well, the Charles Kennedy episode was, I think, very, very painful and difficult for all of us involved, because we had a great affection for him and he was a lovely man and extremely talented. But when it became clear that he couldn't do his job properly, you know, we had this awful problem of communicating it to him. And he didn't want to hear. I mean, it's one of the problems of people who've got alcohol problems that they won't accept it. And I had to go along and lead the group, and say that sorry, you've lost our confidence. And that's not an easy thing to do. So I think for those of us who were involved in it that was much more the issue than, you know, who comes next. And actually Ming Campbell was in a way the natural successor.

I think during the Coalition, I mean, there wasn't really a coup, I mean, that's overstating it. There was a lot of dissatisfaction with – in the party – with Nick, which is in many ways unfair. I mean the guy had made the big decision to go into the Coalition that was right. There were people who were promoting me as an alternative, but when it came to it, I thought it was very, very important that we stood together as a team, actually. We'd taken collective responsibility for going into this Coalition, it had exacted a heavy toll, but I think if we were going to maintain the respect of the public, the last thing we should do is start fighting each other. And you know, Nick had started this project, taken us into the Coalition and was clearly determined to see it through. And I didn't think it was helpful to the party or me to have broken ranks at that point.

**HENNESSY**

Conventional wisdom amongst the political journalists is that – this is probably very unfortunate for you – is that I think Nick Clegg's communications director said to you in so many words that if you don't actually stop this we'll out you and Lord Oakeshott as plotters, or words to that effect.

**CABLE**

Well, I don't – that's a very strange account of what happened.

**HENNESSY**

It wasn't like that?

**CABLE**

No, it wasn't like that.

**HENNESSY**

Wasn't like that. You've obviously got a tinge of regret about that, though, the whole episode, because it wasn't very seemly was it?

**CABLE**

Well, there were some, you know, very difficult episodes throughout the whole Coalition government. I was involved in the thick of a lot of them. But there was a very real problem that, you know, a year before the election we'd suffered terrible losses in the European elections at that time, there was a lot of frustration in the party. People wanted a change, and I think it wasn't just Matthew

Oakeshott, but various other people were punting around alternatives. And it was inevitable I was going to get drawn into it. But I think, you know, I did the right thing.

While we're on the regrettable side, perhaps as you might see it, of the Coalition – everybody will remember the tuition fees: the pledge of the Lib Dems, unequivocal, you all signed up to it, literally signed up to it, to abolish tuition fees, and then they went up to £9,000 and you were the Secretary of State in the lead on this. That must have been very difficult for you.

Well, as I said a few minutes ago, we had a whole lot of very traumatic episodes during that government. The pledge was a terrible mistake. I mean, we'd discussed this a lot in opposition, our party activists were passionate about the tuition fee issue, I think quite wrongly, but anyway they were passionate about it, and we were committed to this policy which was, you know, not – really not possible to deliver in an environment where there's severe cuts in public spending. When it came to it, I mean, I was in the hot seat in the sense that my department were responsible for universities as well as further education, science, industry among other things. And the practical choice I was faced with was, do you take money out of universities and replace that with a sensible system of basically a graduate tax – which is what we've got – or do you take money out of further education for people who don't go to university, do you take it from scientists and so on? And I thought that the system we devised and which I worked on with David Willetts was fair. It was progressive in the sense that people who graduate pay more. We protected funding for other aspects of government that were less fashionable but very important for the country. But the problem is we were stuck with this public pledge which Nick had felt he had to endorse and that was enormously damaging. So the hurt was not the policy. The policy was actually perfectly sensible and most people who analysed it, as indeed the students did, could see that they weren't paying fees, it meant they pay a tax later in life dependent on their income. But it was the loss of faith because a public pledge had been made. And I think actually we've been very unfairly dealt with because the Labour Party made, twice made pledges on tuition fees and broke them. The Tories did as well. Mr Cameron broke pledges on immigration quotas and lots of other things and they got away with it, whereas we were hammered mercilessly because a pledge that we had made – foolishly – was held against us for the rest of our period in government.

### HENNESSY

Though in some ways the Lib Dems are bound to suffer aren't they, Vince, in those terms because you tend to be the ones who talk about a cleaner, more decent and different approach to politics, 'we're not like the others'. So having preached heavier than your weight perhaps, the vengeance of the electorate was going to be that much harder, wasn't it?

### CABLE

Yes. I think when people have analysed the way in which our standing with the public deteriorated, tuition fees has often been cited, but the evidence doesn't really support this actually. We lost a large part of our support when we joined the Coalition. You know, half our voters were people who were anti-Conservative and suddenly they see us in the Coalition government. And so we lost them at that point. So they'd already gone by the time the tuition fee problem arose, and I think what we didn't do was we didn't really explain to the country why the Coalition was necessary.

### HENNESSY

'Cable-watchers' I think, at the time, thought that you instinctively, because of your patrolling that fault line that you've talked about of the centre-left, would have much preferred to go into coalition, other things being equal, with a left party, Labour Party. And that in human terms it was quite difficult probably for you to make the adjustment to working closely with a party that had never warmed you, had never fired you up.

### CABLE

No, absolutely and I would have been more comfortable, but you know politics isn't decided on the basis of people feeling comfortable. It's decided by brutal arithmetic. In the 2010 election it simply wasn't possible to construct a stable coalition of non-Conservatives. I certainly talked to Gordon Brown about it, other people did. We explored it, but it wasn't a viable option and we could have walked away altogether and said, you know, 'Nothing to do with us, Guv, let the Tories sort out the mess.' I think that would have been deeply irresponsible, and I think what people had not appreciated and where the Lib Dems have probably not been given the credit we should have done, is that what motivated us was not a wish to get into ministerial cars or anything like that. I mean I think it was a feeling that the country had an emergency, we had to deal with it and it involved working with people who had traditionally been our enemies. And it was a big thing to do; it wasn't a petty thing to do.

### HENNESSY

What about the Chancellor and the Prime Minister because it was not cabal government, or cliquey – one can exaggerate that – but there was very much a sense of insiders and outsiders, inner rim and outer rim, and you weren't on the inner rim, were you? You weren't on 'the quad' that tried to resolve the disputes and so on.

### CABLE

No, I wasn't. My relation to the Prime Minister was perfectly cordial. He's an extremely courteous man and I can never remember him sort of losing his temper, certainly not with me. He was always very polite, but you know, we were somewhat distant. I had closer relations with George Osborne because we were, I suppose, two of the major economic ministers, approaching this from different departments and in a somewhat different way, so certainly in the earlier stages of the government we worked very closely together. The government was a bit beleaguered at that point, you know, we were still stuck in recession. We knew we would hang together or hang separately, and I found he was very businesslike and if you had a good proposition he would listen and you could make things happen. Subsequently I think our different views about how the economy should be managed became more apparent and we sort of rather drifted apart. But he was extremely bright and I think our relationship was pretty cordial and businesslike for most of the Coalition.

**HENNESSY**

But not excessively warm from the way you've put it.

**CABLE**

No, I mean it wasn't friendship, but that wasn't the point. I think one of the strengths of the Coalition government was that it was businesslike and we knew how to make decisions and they happened.

**HENNESSY**

We're talking, Vince, in the aftermath of one of the great disruptions of post-war British politics, perhaps the greatest, which is the Brexit vote. How anxious are you about what might become of us?

**CABLE**

Well, I'm very anxious, because I think a lot of the warnings that were given were genuine. I mean it was said with some truth that the tone of Armageddon was overdone, but many of the warnings, the warnings given by the Governor of the Central Bank, by the head of the IMF and other people, they were kind of professional judgements that, you know, this is going to cause very serious disruption, it's going to cause major uncertainty and it will do a lot of harm. And I think we may well find ourselves in a Brexit recession before very long and we may well find, as we warned and as I was told by the people in business I dealt with, that some of the big investors in this country who've committed themselves to the aerospace industry, the car industry, pharmaceuticals and the rest of it will start leaking away. I think that's plausible. I don't think it was scaremongering, that's just real. But you know, we've made the decision. It's gone against Remain and I take a fairly pragmatic view of it. We've now got to think about how to protect the good things about the European Union, that's going to be the big battle over the next few years.

**HENNESSY**

Do you think it's triggered an opportunity to remake the centre-left, where you've spent all your life trying to reconcile the various elements of the centre-left into a centre-left grouping, and how would you do it? And there must be one or two subjects that the centre-left has always had a difficulty in handling, like immigration which was a big factor in that vote, that the centre-left will have to think about in a slightly different way probably?

**CABLE**

Yes, I think that given the way that the vote happened, the public have spoken and one of the key concerns was freedom of movement. I think it's very difficult to believe that the principle of free movement within Europe can now be protected. I think one just has to accept the reality of the matter that that was not politically doable. The system was not very defensible in any event. What we'd been doing is we'd been saying to people from Bulgaria and Lithuania 'You're free to come here,' but people from Canada or

India, who have much more in common are treated quite harshly. And certainly under Theresa May's stewardship it was extraordinarily difficult for – even for skilled people and students – to come here from those countries. So the present system I think is going to have to change and we've just got to face the fact that migration from the European Union is going to be managed in some way. I don't have any theological problem with that.

**HENNESSY**

Now amidst all these anxieties are you finding solace in writing your novel?

**CABLE**

I'm told by the publisher they like it and they're going to try and publish it next year, but I'm dissatisfied. I constantly want to update it and rewrite it and I hope I finish it.

**HENNESSY**

Is it a thriller?

**CABLE**

Sort of, yes. I don't want to take – say too [much] more, but that's, yes, it is that.

**HENNESSY**

And you find that faintly cathartic do you?

**CABLE**

Yes, I like writing, and I don't think I'm bad at it, but one of the things I have realised [is] that writing fiction is a very, very, very different skill. And I read people like Le Carré and I think my God, how wonderful it would be to write like that.

**HENNESSY**

Is the hero a Vince Cable type figure from the north?

**CABLE**

No, no.

**HENNESSY**

No, it's not semi-autobiographical?

**CABLE**

I think I'm not so narcissistic I think. It is much more detached.

**HENNESSY**

If, Vince, I could grant you one last reform, if I could give you all the parliamentary time you needed, I know you're not there yet, you're not in the House of Lords actually which is a pity so many would think.

**CABLE**

Well no, I chose not to go in.

**HENNESSY**

Let me ask you about that, because you've actually been quite nice about the Lords in some ways. You've said it's a very good brake on deficient legislation, but you don't want to come in.

**CABLE**

Yes, I think it's terribly in need of reform. I don't think you can have an upper House which is based overwhelmingly on patronage. I think that's fundamentally a wrong system and it needs changing. And on a personal level, I've discovered the merits of Tony Benn's adage, that politics starts outside Parliament actually and I'm doing quite a lot of political things outside. But to go back to your question – this may sound a very politically correct answer, but it is true – I think what we desperately need now is to reform the voting system. We're producing bizarre and damaging outcomes. I mean one of the reasons we've got this Brexit disaster is because you had a government elected with the support of 36 per cent of the public, 25 per cent of the adult population, without any checks and balances of the kind we had in the Coalition, when we would have stopped Cameron doing some of the things that he's been able to do, and getting much more responsible, balanced government than we've got at the moment.

### HENNESSY

What trace would you like to leave on history?

### CABLE

Well I'm pleased with my legacy in my years in Coalition government. I think we achieved a great deal – a mixture of laws and institutions, and I helped to make the Coalition government work; I was one of the key players within it. I could have been much more destructive than I was, but I took the view we've got to make it work, and of course Nick Clegg led it on our side, but I think I made a significant contribution to that and I'm proud of having done it.

### HENNESSY

What trace do you think you will leave as opposed to the one you want to leave?

### CABLE

That I don't know and I'm not the best placed to judge. And I haven't given up yet. I mean I'm still active in public life, I'm still writing, I'm still doing all kinds of things, so who knows? I mean you know, 73 is the old 50.

**HENNESSY**

Vince Cable, thank you very much indeed. Thank you.

# Margaret Hodge
# (Dame Margaret Hodge)

Series 4, Episode 3, first broadcast 16 August 2016

**Born** 8 September 1944; **Educated** Bromley High School;
Oxford High School; London School of Economics

MP (Labour) Barking 1994–

Leader of Islington Council, 1982–92; Parliamentary Under-
Secretary, Employment and Equal Opportunities, Department for
Education and Employment, 1998–2001; Minister of State, Lifelong
Learning, Further and Higher Education, Department of Education
and Skills, 2001–03; Minister of State for Children, Department
of Education and Skills, 2003–05; Minister of State for Work,
Department for Work and Pensions, 2005–06; Minister of State,
Department of Industry and the Regions, 2006–07; Minister of State,
Department of Culture, Media and Sport, 2007–08, 2009–10; Chair
of the House of Commons Public Accounts Committee, 2010–15

**HENNESSY**

With me today is Dame Margaret Hodge. She made her name in
the battles waged by some Labour local authorities against the local
government reforms of the Thatcher years, when she appeared to
be on the harder rim of the soft left. Yet she was a supporter of Neil
Kinnock's leadership in his drive to make Labour electable once
more. And such is the rollercoaster journey of her party, she was in

the forefront of the challenge to Jeremy Corbyn's leadership inside the Parliamentary Labour Party. In between, she held a wide range of mainly social policy jobs in the Blair and Brown governments before becoming chair of the powerful House of Commons Public Accounts Committee, when even the most seasoned permanent secretaries anticipated their evidence sessions before her with a high degree of anxiety. Margaret, Welcome.

### HODGE

Thank you.

### HENNESSY

You were born in Alexandria in the late 1940s. Is your earliest memory there? Can you actually see it, feel it, even now?

### HODGE

I can't feel it. I've got memories of it. My really strong earliest memory was actually becoming an immigrant and coming into the UK. So I remember the journey from Egypt to the UK. In those days the planes had to stop to refuel in Rome. We arrived here, we went into bed and breakfast, and I remember the horror of the food. I'd never had porridge before. I was used to exotic, succulent fruits. The vegetables were all sort of shrivelled up and I was used to something very different. I remember all that. That early memory of being an immigrant has stayed with me and I think has influenced me hugely in my politics.

### HENNESSY

And you would have picked up very quickly, I'm sure, the fact that your father had left Germany because of the persecution of the Jews and gone to Egypt for safety, and after the state of Israel is created anti-Semitism breaks out there. So you were double refugees in a sense.

**HODGE**

Yes, actually my father had left Germany during the depression because he couldn't get a job. My mother had left Austria, really just before the war, and gone down to Egypt. And I lost a lot of relatives. I had a grandmother – my mother's mother – who was shot at the doors of a concentration camp because she was considered too old. And an uncle of mine, my father's sister's husband, had this horrific experience actually. He hid in France and he was sent to Auschwitz at the very end of the war, and when I went to visit Auschwitz and you go through these horrific – the rooms – there is this one room where you've got the children's clothes on one side, the hair and the suitcases, and as I came across these suitcases there was a suitcase with my uncle's initials on it. I'll never know whether it was his or not. So all that background really, really influenced me. My father and my mother coming to the UK were really desperate to integrate. I think because they had been rejected by two countries. My father had lived in Egypt for, you know, 20 years, so had been there for a long, long time, but being rejected by two countries their real sort of imperative was to integrate. So we didn't move to north London, where most of the Jews had congregated, we moved to south London. And I never had religion, it was never part of my life. Although I discovered later, when my parents died, that German had been my mother tongue, we never spoke German at home, we always spoke English.

**HENNESSY**

That's very interesting. And you went to Bromley High School for Girls, I think.

**HODGE**

I did.

**HENNESSY**

Did you feel at home? Because I suspect you were a clever girl, and you probably were much more grown up than your own age group because of what you'd experienced.

### HODGE

I didn't like school very much. It was a quite traumatic time for me because my mother died when I was ten. And in those days I think parents weren't very good at dealing with death, so, you know, I never went to the funeral, I was never told she had died. I'm a September-born baby and top of my class, so my father got me to skip a class just six months after she died. So I lost my mother, lost my friends, went into another class. I then became a completely unruly teenager and I was sent off to boarding school for a couple of years, which I completely rejected. I think that had a huge impact on my politics as well. Because I arrived there and in those days the school was a direct grant school, so it took a lot of children who came in through the 11-plus. And there was a mix of sort of kids from – whose parents worked at Cowley in the car factory – and with the daughters of academics at the university. And it was quite extraordinary how the two groups of young women just couldn't mix, they couldn't mingle. And I felt in the middle of that. I didn't feel I belonged to either; I felt the outsider to both those groups. And I just realised then how sort of entrenched the class system was in British society, and I hated that – it was part of my immigrant background – and it sort of strengthened my determination to fight for equality, which has been the driving sort of value that has influenced my life and influenced my politics.

### HENNESSY

So you were quite a formed political character by the time you got to the London School of Economics.

### HODGE

I was. I'd been on CND marches, I'd sold the CND newspaper outside Foyles Saturday upon Saturday in the pouring rain. I'd gone on anti-apartheid demos and things like that. But I was never in any of the extreme left groups. I was also into theatre quite a bit. I always say politicians tend to be failed actors and actresses. And so I did quite a lot of drama in my early days at LSE. I was a terrible student – and I still have nightmares about those days – in that I never worked, I did one essay in my three years at LSE.

**HENNESSY**

One essay? In three years?

**HODGE**

One essay, outrageous. I had a wonderful time. I mean, I developed as a person, you know, read a lot of poetry, went to a lot of cultural events in London, had a lot of deep, meaningful conversations with all my friends.

**HENNESSY**

But no essays. Or just one.

**HODGE**

And I only went to the lectures that interested me.

**HENNESSY**

How did you get a degree?

**HODGE**

I have no idea. To this day I have nightmares about it. I should have failed. I walked out of one of my finals. It is very odd that it is my recurring nightmare, doing badly in those exams. I feel really bad about that.

**HENNESSY**

Why was it you couldn't buckle down?

**HODGE**

I think that the death of my mother really damaged my academic progress. I think I was just so thrown by that at the age of ten, and then being taken out of my school at 11, and then again at 13. I think it just damaged my confidence and my focus. Although I'd like to think now I've got all that back again.

**HENNESSY**

I think you've got it now. [*Both laugh*]

**HODGE**

But in those – when I think back that's probably what caused it.

**HENNESSY**

Yes. How did you get involved in politics first?

**HODGE**

I mucked around after university, because I'd done so badly, really. I tried an MA in philosophy, but that didn't really grip me because I think I'm too practical. So whilst sort of thinking about theoretical constructs was intellectually challenging, I just wanted to always impact on the world and make the world a better place. So I went into an international market research company just as they were being founded and I speak three languages because of my background, so we were doing multi-country studies. When I started having children, in 1971, travel was very difficult, those were different days, really. You were expected to stay at home really until the babies were about four or five years old. I am an absolutely committed mum. Being a mother is a really important bit of my life, but I was a frustrated stay-at-home mother as well. I did various things, I did bits of teaching, I tried to sort of do market research work at home, but I like to get out and mix with people. And I was in the Labour Party. And one of my friends in the Labour Party – a vacancy came up on the local council because she was moving – and she said to me, 'Go on Margaret, go on the council. It'll keep you sane whilst you're changing nappies.' And I thought, okay, I'll give it a go. And from starting off perhaps not from the best of motives, it became a passionate drug and has given me an incredibly interesting and fulfilling life.

**HENNESSY**

You came to public attention, I think, as Deputy Leader of Islington Council, didn't you? And in shorthand memory people remember it as the time when the red flag flew over the town hall in Upper Street.

**HODGE**

Yes. Actually, do you know, one of my lasting achievements – everything I've done has always been in a team – but one of the things I'm most proud of, which has stood the test of time was before I became Leader of Islington Council, I actually chaired the housing committee. This was in the mid-'70s. We'd bought all this stuff and it was sitting there because we couldn't devise a programme to rehabilitate it and bring it into use. And in a year we went from creating 12 homes to creating 1,600 homes out of this renovation programme. And we also were constructing them, so probably in Islington in the mid-'70s we were creating something like 3,000 decent homes every year at a price people could afford. And that has stood the test of time. And we tackled the old inter-war estates and created decent housing out of that. And I think that investment was brilliant.

I became Leader in 1982, after a bit of a difficult period. This is a sort of pattern in my life, because when we arrived in Islington politics – I got there about 1971, '72, '73, Islington Labour Party was full. You couldn't become a member of the party, and that was because it was run by a very small Tammany Hall cabal who were very old-style, old, old-style Labour. So we spent those early '70s opening up Islington Labour to a new group of probably trendy young people like myself moving into that part of London. And we took over. We were much more radical.

**HENNESSY**

So by the time you become Leader, the Conservative government – Mrs Thatcher's government – is imposing a whole set of reforms on local government. And you were very much in the vanguard against them. I think I can remember, just about, as a young journalist reporting a meeting when I think you had a go at Michael Heseltine, the Environment Secretary.

**HODGE**

I did. Do you remember that?

**HENNESSY**

I think you did. I know you did, because I was there.

**HODGE**

I walked out on him, do you remember? [*Laughs*]

**HENNESSY**

I remember that. I can see you now, blazing you were.

**HODGE**

In 1982 we were in this position where there was a coalition really between the soft left and the absolute mixture of ultra left groups. We came into office and we took on the Thatcher cuts. It was a time, remember also it was the miners' strike, it happened in '85, rate capping happened around then. And I think we did some very radical things. Which were considered completely off the wall at the time and have become accepted orthodoxy today. So let me give some examples. For instance, we did the very early childcare provision; we set up a council nursery. At that time it was seen as an obscene waste of ratepayers' money. But actually today it's considered commonplace. We started monitoring to make sure that there wasn't discrimination against people in the allocation of housing or in jobs. And that was seen as political correctness gone mad. I sometimes laughingly say we invented Private Finance Initiatives, something that I today think is a terrible mistake. But in those days, I'd got this big housing capital programme, I was determined to keep it going; providing decent homes at a price people could afford was absolutely central to my ambitions. And there was no money. So there we were, the City down the road from Islington, and there were a lot of financiers came to see us and they found a way of borrowing money which would be paid back by future generations, to maintain the housing capital programme today. I still think it was the right thing to do because we invested all the money in capital. And then we did some mad things, you know, we were successful in staving off the worst excesses of the cuts. We did some radical stuff that is now accepted. And then we did some mad things.

### HENNESSY

Do you think, Margaret, there are two sides to you? One is the Margaret who does veer – the harder edge of the soft left, as I think I was describing you a moment ago, and you rather regret that now, and you were dealing with some groups that you really find deeply uncongenial now, Trotskyite groups and so on. And yet then there's the sensible Margaret Hodge, the administrator, the one who actually will make coalitions with, say, City financiers. Do you think there's always that tension within you?

### HODGE

I always felt uncomfortable in that coalition with the hard left. The day I became Leader and we were sitting in this meeting and somebody said, 'Let's put the red flag on top of the town hall,' my heart sank, and I thought this was a silly bit of gesture politics which wouldn't get anywhere. But the reality – you know, you have to deal with the reality of the political situation in which you find yourself – and the reality there was that if I was going to get anything done I had to work with the people who were a pretty strong presence and had a good power base in the party. And I just remember it so well, that London at the time Ken Livingstone was controlling it, John McDonnell was always the brain behind what was happening there. There were people like Ted Knight around.

**HENNESSY**

Red Ted.

**HODGE**

Red Ted, you remember him. And the clever thing they did, particularly in '83, was they always, after a general election, set the agenda. And they set the agenda immediately after we'd completely been smashed, the Labour Party had been smashed in the '83 general election. Before it came to '87 it was absolutely clear that it was going to be a disaster for Labour. But I was absolutely determined that this time round we were going to set the agenda. So I wrote a paper before the election which talked about [how] it was pointless passing resolutions in the town halls, that didn't change the life chances of poor people in any way. If we were going to re-build trust in Labour, we had to start answering the phones and emptying the dustbins. And I got that out before the hard left had any chance to get at that. And interestingly enough, that strategy worked, because it set the agenda so they were always having to respond to it. And then we spent those years building support for Neil Kinnock, who was very brave.

**HENNESSY**

Neil Kinnock made his famous speech at the party conference in '85 denouncing Militant. I mean, it's one of the great post-war speeches. And that would have resonated for you, wouldn't it? So you had gone through a transition, you realised that you couldn't actually accommodate these left groups.

**HODGE**

Yes, I think –

**HENNESSY**

So in the mid-'80s the Margaret Hodge that sits before me now was created out of that.

**HODGE**

Yes.

**HENNESSY**

There's one dark side to your years which is dark in so many ways across our land really, is the child abuse question.

**HODGE**

Yes.

**HENNESSY**

And I think you regretted publicly that you hadn't picked up on this.

**HODGE**

Yes –

**HENNESSY**

– when you were running Islington.

**HODGE**

Yes. I've learnt, you know, there are lessons you learn in your political life, and that's the one I regret the most. But it's an interesting story because it's – what do you learn from it? So I'd been Leader of Islington for 10 years, we'd lost the '92 election, that was the fourth general election I'd lost. I was giving up on politics. And the *Evening Standard* did an investigation in which there were allegations that there was paedophile activity in our children's homes. And I did what every responsible person would do at that time. So I called two or three meetings, I had the police in front of me, and I had all the leading people in the social services world. I had the Chief Executive. We went through each of the allegations and the officials told me that there was no basis to them. I mean, I held two or three meetings, I did take it seriously. My mistake was I only talked to the officials, I never talked to the children. That's the lesson you learn from that. And I think people today would think that was unconscionable, you wouldn't imagine doing it that way. But in those days that's how we operated. And I was fed up with the press because we'd had years and years of attack, sometimes for things we'd done, often for things that were invented in pubs in Fleet Street by journalists. And I was fed up. One of the social workers said to me that the children had been bribed to give the stories. And that flipped with me. And so I just challenged the story. And I was wrong. I was wrong. And I think the lesson I've learnt, it's made me – maybe it's helped me become a more effective chair of the Public Accounts Committee because it made me much more sceptical –

**HENNESSY**

Very interesting –

**HODGE**

– when I was given advice and evidence by people who were responsible for – for jobs. But my real regret was not talking to the kids at that time.

**HENNESSY**

Is that your greatest single regret in your political life do you think?

**HODGE**

Yes, yes, yes . It was a huge error, yes.

**HENNESSY**

You make the leap to national politics when you replace Jo Richardson as MP for Barking, at the by-election after her death. It must have been a great moment for you really. They were big shoes to step into but you probably had the self-confidence and the zip to do it by then didn't you?

**HODGE**

Actually, do you know, the interesting thing is I'd never gone into Parliament before, because I wasn't terribly attracted by Westminster.

**HENNESSY**

What was wrong with Westminster in your view? A bit blokeish?

**HODGE**

I'm a doer. I like doing things. And the pomposity of debate in the chamber was never greatly attractive – it wasn't an attraction. It isn't debate that changes the world; it's political action that changes the world. And that's, you know, where I get my satisfaction. But politics is a drug, and I'd done local government for 20 years, and then I thought, if I don't do it I'll regret missing the opportunity, and I think that judgement was right. I was the first person to do it on 'one member, one vote,' which had been a recent reform that had been introduced by John Smith.

**HENNESSY**

You admired John Smith, I would imagine.

**HODGE**

I did.

**HENNESSY**

Do you see him as the lost Leader?

**HODGE**

I felt the Labour Party did have to reform beyond where he was prepared to take it, to really connect with people and, you know, secure government over a long period. Which we did.

**HENNESSY**

Who did you vote for in the succession to John Smith?

**HODGE**

Oh, Tony Blair.

**HENNESSY**

Without hesitation?

**HODGE**

Well, I'd known Tony Blair forever.

**HENNESSY**

You were near neighbours weren't you?

**HODGE**

We were neighbours and he was a lawyer, my husband was a lawyer. They're all part of the sort of left law establishment. So we'd known each other, we'd been friends. I admired him. I thought he was a real radical thinker. Blairism has been so tarnished, mainly by Iraq and also by the way Tony Blair has chosen to lead his life after leaving office, I think those two things have tarnished it.

**HENNESSY**

The money-making side.

### HODGE

The money-making side. But at that time this sort of concept of saying that economic prosperity and social justice weren't competing with each other, but were inextricably linked to each other was a pretty radical idea. It was articulated in different ways by different people, but it was a radical concept and I bought into that in a big way. And I think that really was the sort of underpinning value.

### HENNESSY

You had a whole range of social policy posts, posts designed for a doer like you, a self-described doer – Minister for Children and so on, and indeed for the universities. And the old Margaret still was attracting a bit of attention by the press on one or two occasions weren't you? For example, you got a lot of flak from your own side in particular about tuition fees for university students. And your argument, if I remember, was that this could help poorer students, that it was not an inequitable reform.

### HODGE

My argument was more if we were looking where we were placing our education expenditure, we were putting a heck of a lot of money into the Higher Education part of the whole budget. And even to this day money put into Higher Education, public money put into Higher Education, is a subsidy to the middle classes. Again, back to my driving value, I believe in equality, and the way that you can best – through public intervention – achieve that is high-quality investment in the early years. And the money we put in that is abysmal. You know, we pay people appalling sums of money. It's childcare on the cheap. So what my argument was always, if you're a real socialist and you want to strive for equality, shove all the public money into the early years and find a way in which the middle classes can contribute in those later years. I mean, we would all have loved to have gone for a graduate tax – that would have been the most equitable way of going forward. And the only reason we couldn't was the high upfront cost was never affordable in the public expenditure envelope that was available to us.

### HENNESSY

Do you have any regrets from your ministerial days in the Blair and Brown years, those posts you held, something that you really think you should have tilted at and had a real good go at which you didn't for whatever reason?

### HODGE

I'll tell you my greatest regret. I was never left in a job long enough to see things through. Because when you get into a new job, it takes you six months or so to get to understand the portfolio. Then you start thinking through and talking to your stakeholders as to what you could do with it. I mean I loved all my jobs, you know, and I like to think that in every one, working with others, I was able to change the world a little bit. But if I take the children's job, getting that early years offer of a sufficient quality to really transform people's lives, that never happened. And I was there two or three years but it wasn't long enough really to embed it. And in those days I used to go round making speeches saying this is the new frontier of the welfare state, thinking no future government could ever tear this down. And of course they have; they've dismantled and destroyed Sure Start and a lot of the stuff we were doing. So that's my regret there. And I suppose in the culture job, one of the responsibilities I had was to appoint people to the boards. When I arrived, 25 per cent of the people on all these boards – be it the museums or the big theatres and concert halls – 25 per cent were women. And this is shocking. And we set about trying to improve that. There's plenty of really talented women who have the background and the capability to contribute as board trustees. And within a year, I was very proud, we'd got it up to about 46 per cent. And then my husband fell ill, and I took a year off of compassionate leave, came back after he'd died. And a year out and it was back to 26 per cent again.

**HENNESSY**

Yes.

**HODGE**

And it showed me how –

**HENNESSY**

How sloggy reform is –

**HODGE**

Sloggy reform, how, absolutely – you know, the impact of ministers can be very, very ephemeral.

**HENNESSY**

You must regret not getting up to the Cabinet level, after all this experience.

**HODGE**

Well, you know, I mean, I don't think – you said I attracted the press every now and then. I say it as it is, it's one of my hallmarks. I'm not very good at keeping my mouth shut. And I think every job I had was interesting. Every job I held was – I learnt something. And if you're below the radar that little bit, you can probably get on with doing things in a way that you can't if you're up at the Cabinet level. So in an odd way, although you sort of think, 'Oh well, I didn't get to the top of the greasy pole,' actually probably that was a good thing.

**HENNESSY**

Where were you on the Iraq War?

**HODGE**

Well, remember my background was the CND.

**HENNESSY**

Yes.

**HODGE**

And I hated Tony's foreign policy. I absolutely hated the interventionist policy. It seemed to me that there was a missionary zeal to impose our form of democracy on other countries which was –

**HENNESSY**

The Chicago speech and so on, about intervention.

**HODGE**

Yes, I – I couldn't – I couldn't buy into any of that. But in the end the thing that decided me was that I thought, we've put this guy in as our Leader, we have got to trust him, that he has got information that we haven't got access to that drives him to this view. So I put trust in my Leader before my sort of instinct, which was to be sceptical, and I voted for it. And it was a terrible decision.

**HENNESSY**

Do you regret not resigning? One or two did.

**HODGE**

Yes, I do. I think if at that time we'd been bolder, ministers had been bolder, the course of history might have been different.

**HENNESSY**

What do you make of your two Prime Ministers? Very different styles, Blair and Brown, the way they conduct business. How would you sum up their styles, given the flavour of the Blair-Brown Number 10?

**HODGE**

Oh goodness, that's a clever question. I think Blair was a brilliant communicator. I liked him. He was a good friend, you know, he was easy to get on with, easy to talk to. I think he wasn't a really good listener. I think he sort of – as time moved on – he got sort of more locked into that sofa in his little room, and I think failed to listen to outside, more determined to pursue – not just in foreign policy but actually I think in public service reform – he became sort of obsessed that structural reform was a way of achieving better quality, which I would challenge; and that privatisation was also a way of improving quality, which again I would challenge. So I think he got locked into a route that was, you know, that meant the legacy was less good than it could otherwise have been. Gordon was just sort of paranoid. I was a friend of Tony's so I was never trusted by Gordon, full stop. But on a personal level... I'll tell you a story about Gordon on a personal level. I had just become an MP and my 16-year-old daughter at that time had lost the sight of an eye. She had a detached retina and she lost the sight of an eye, and you can imagine, it was a huge trauma in the family. And I happened to get into the lift with Gordon – our offices were in the same building at the time – and that thing was on the top of my mind and I said, 'What do I say to her? How do I help her work through this?' And he sort of chatted to me, you know, in this ten seconds going up in the lift, and then he said to me, 'What's her name?' And I told him. And within two hours a four-page letter came to her about how to cope with being blind in an eye.

**HENNESSY**

Which, of course, he'd suffered himself.

**HODGE**

Which, of course, he'd suffered himself. That was why I asked him. And that was incredibly... And when my Henry was ill, and I went to see him and asked for compassionate leave – which had never happened before, no minister had ever had compassionate leave, so it's a good first – he gave it to me. He gave it to me. I mean, it was Harriet Harman's idea, but he gave it to me, and that was sort of a sensitive side of Gordon. But there's also a really paranoid side of Gordon, and I just think he was locked, so locked into his sort of internal turmoil that he never could relax. And I think the really sad thing about him was, you know, that he was so driven into becoming Prime Minister, he'd been this sort of – that's what he'd wanted all his political life, and he got there and the impression he left was he didn't know what to do with it.

**HENNESSY**

So both your Prime Ministers are tragic figures, but for different reasons.

**HODGE**

Yes, but – but, but, but, I'm not one of these people that will write off – I think those 13 years of a Labour government achieved fantastic change, which since we lost power in 2010 has been just written off in the most appalling way by too many of my colleagues. I think, you know, there's a lot of which we can be proud. I mean, I can give you lists if you want, but I am proud of a huge number of social reforms that we did in that time. I think the way that we tackled inequality, began tackling inequality at that time, whether it was through tax credits or whether it was through investment in education. So don't – don't write off that 13 years, they were important.

**HENNESSY**

Your friends thought, when you came into the chairmanship of the Public Accounts Committee in 2010, that this was a great late flowering for you. They were very pleased, and also you seemed to relish it from the very first moment. Did you actually take yourself by surprise?

**HODGE**

Yes.

**HENNESSY**

I thought you had.

**HODGE**

I went into that job in my sixties, and life is a marathon, it's not a short sprint, and I think for too many people they think if you haven't done it by the time you're 35 you're never going to do it. And I hope that I'll keep going for many years doing new things, but it is a marathon and I think it's important to see people who, you know, start doing well in jobs in their late sixties, which is why I did so –

**HENNESSY**

It's very interesting that, because you've had some sharp things to say about the cult of youth and special advisers and rising up and all the rest of it. It's a very interesting perspective. It's not an argument for gerontocracy quite, is it Margaret?

**HODGE**

No.

**HENNESSY**

But you need more seasoned people at the top is what you're saying.

**HODGE**

And for women it's quite important because women do go through their lives, through these phases of their lives where they, you know, will have care and responsibilities, whether it's for elder relatives or whether it's for children. And they feel that therefore, you know their ability to succeed in work is curtailed, and it just isn't. You've just got to think you're going to be there for a long time, and if you don't do it – I mean my contemporaries in early politics were Jack Straw, David Blunkett, people like that and I've succeeded perhaps a little later than they have, but you know, I got there in the end. [*Laughs*]

**HENNESSY**

And those special five years on the Public Accounts Committee, your critics thought that you had only one style which was very effective, but it was attack and that you were not accommodating of perhaps the good practices that Whitehall throws up, that you were there as the tribune of the people. I think the head of the Civil Service, Gus O'Donnell actually wrote you a letter saying that. Looking back, do you perhaps think you overdid it a bit?

**HODGE**

No.

**HENNESSY**

You don't?

**HODGE**

No. No. I mean at first, we did – I think it was the way in which people chose to engage with us. I think, you know, it's really important on behalf of the taxpayers to hold people to account for the way in which they spend money and there is a reluctance on the part of senior civil servants to engage openly in that debate. You've got the whole issue of ministerial accountability – they hide behind that really to talk openly about how particular projects went. Now by its nature the Public Accounts Committee will tend to look at things that have gone wrong.

**HENNESSY**

Yes.

**HODGE**

By its nature. However we did look at success stories. We did have very open sessions, even where there had been mistakes, where those giving evidence were willing to engage in an honest and open and direct way with us and we did produce reports which praised competence. Of course they never get coverage in radio and television. You know, renewing of the Prison Estate, you may not have – actually that was done by a guy who had been there for a long time so he didn't shift jobs every couple of years. He had a lot of experience, he did it quietly and it was done within budget and within time. Delivering the Olympics. We looked at 16 to 19-year-old education – there were a lot of good things to say about that. You could never get them on the *Today* programme. And the other thing is we did introduce a PAC award scheme in the Civil Service Awards and that was an attempt to get recognition. But, you know, when I look back at those five years – and I have just written a book which is going to be published at the beginning of September about those five years – I think there is unconscionable waste of public money. And as somebody who believes in the importance of public money to invest to transform people's life chances, I can't tolerate it. And I think there is an inability to learn from past mistakes in a way, for all sorts of complicated reasons. And I think there is a sort of silo mentality within government. I think there are all sorts of things that are wrong in the way that we run these programmes.

**HENNESSY**

Let's go back to something we touched on briefly. The hard right in your constituency – you and John Cruddas in the East End of London, others too, had to deal with widespread concerns about immigration amongst your own working-class vote. It was very difficult for a long time for people on the centre-left, wasn't it, to talk about this candidly and openly. I think most people regret that now. But you had the real-time problem of dealing with quite a strong BNP presence as you've described. Now how did a left liberal with your formation, particularly your sensitivity to migrants and so on, your family story, cope with that, Margaret? What strategies did you develop?

**HODGE**

It completely changed my politics. It completely changed the way I do my politics. Barking and Dagenham has been transformed by migration so when I arrived in 1994, and I have this memory of coming out of the tube station from Islington where I lived, and it was completely white and I'd never met so many great-grand-mothers who lived within 10 minutes of their great-grandchil-dren. So it was a very close knit, East End community. That was transformed, right-to-buy brought in new people and Ford's dis-appeared, and you had a Labour Party in Barking Dagenham that were used to weighing the votes in rather than counting them, and locked into internal politics rather than communicating with the electorate. And all that allowed the emergence of the extreme right. And in 2006, when 12 BNP councillors were elected to the council, I just thought, we've got to change how we do things. So I just changed my politics. I stopped cutting ribbons at Town Hall events, I don't focus on internal Labour Party meetings, and everything I do in the constituency is about reconnecting with people. How can I reconnect with them? So I have a whole series of strategies and I'm always looking at new things to do. A typical one is, I will invite a thousand people to come and have a cup of coffee with me. Seventy or so show up and they get a decent cup of coffee and a chocolate biscuit and I go table to table. So I don't bring the latest Westminster bubble issue to them, whatever it is. I just say, 'What's bugging you, what's the top of your agenda?' And then I bring them together after an hour of that. I always start with a local issue, so whether it's the traffic scheme, or whatever it is. And quite quickly it will move into a really difficult conversa-tion about immigration, and there have been some really, really, really powerful exchanges in these forums. But I have never ever said I'll turn the clock back to the 1950s and '60s when this was an all-white closed community. But what I have said is two things: a) I want to make it to work for you and the other thing is I listen to them so I can deliver on some things. I can deliver on the local issues, and the mere fact of listening, delivering where you can and communicating with people means that you start rebuilding trust. And that's really been the way I've done it. But that has changed and that – I took all that experience into the Public Accounts Committee. So I was very much asking the sort of questions that I knew Barking and Dagenham people would want me to ask, and rebuilding trust meant that we could then tackle the extreme right. And I never once gave into the racism. I mean at the time I did say controversial things, but I think, you know, if you can't deliver on numbers, which I think you can't, you've got to think what makes it work for people? And the thing that really struck me is there's a deep sense of 'It's unfair. It's unfair if a new person comes into the borough and jumps the housing queue because their need is greater and I've been waiting patiently for years and years and I'm born and bred in the borough and I don't get access to housing.' It's not very good for communities because we want to keep these strong communities together. So I think there is nothing wrong with saying you put a bit of time in before you can access limited resources that are always going to have to be rationed. Now, when I originally said that it was horribly controversial and people accused me of all sorts of racist attitudes. Actually it has again become accepted orthodoxy today.

**HENNESSY**

The other thing you've been in the forefront of recently is the Corbyn question, which has riven your party, and you and Ann Coffey were the ones who pushed the no-confidence motion in the Parliamentary Labour Party. Now what drove you to that, Margaret, because you love your old party, don't you? You're a natural loyalist in many ways.

**HODGE**

Oh, I'm tribal. [*Laughs*]

**HENNESSY**

Yes, I wasn't going to quite put it like that. I'm glad you've put it like that rather than me. So it must have been quite something for you to do that.

**HODGE**

Well, that was my experience of the '80s. I know John McDonnell, I know Ken Livingstone, actually I've known Jeremy Corbyn for 35 years, I was there when he first became the MP for Islington North and I was Leader of the Council in local government. I know what they're about.

**HENNESSY**

What are they about?

**HODGE**

They want the party to be a movement. They're interested in not reforming capitalism, as Ed Miliband was trying to do, but in overthrowing capitalism. And they put in a series of transitional demands until you get to an impossible position. So, you know –

**HENNESSY**

It's regarded as an old Trotskyite ploy.

**HODGE**

Absolutely.

**HENNESSY**

Would you agree with that?

### HODGE

Yep, completely. And I wasn't going to have my party, I'm not going to allow my party that I, you know, believe is so important in being *the* political institution that will always promote equality, and I wasn't going to allow it to be taken over as a plaything for a whole load of Trots. So – and I'm clear that's what they want to do. Actually it's very interesting, because you know I welcome the young people who've joined, it's not just young people who've joined the party, some of my very old friends voted for Jeremy Corbyn because we'd reached a very bad point in the development of the Labour Party. Blair and Brown never really tolerated dissent and they never allowed debate. And that meant refreshing our ideas was limited. The room to refresh our ideas was limited. So when we came to 2010 and we had a leadership contest we had a lot of people who had held managerial jobs in Labour government or had been political advisers to people who'd held managerial jobs in Labour government, but who had never really developed a sort of value system, particularly in the context of, you know, post the 2008 crash. And that was what let Corbyn through, and I can understand. It's a bit like us in '79 when we thought we'd been let down by Anthony Crosland and the party was over and the IMF and all of that. So I could get that, but to allow that debate to be dominated by a bunch of people who have no interest in really striving for a Labour government is unconscionable to me. I couldn't let it stand.

### HENNESSY

Margaret, if I could give you one last reform, wave a magic wand for you, what would it be?

### HODGE

I think for me the most important – if my driving value is equality – I think investment in high-quality early years experiences for *every* young child, that new frontier of the welfare state, would be the lasting reform that I would really love.

**HENNESSY**

What trace do you think you'll leave on political history and what trace would you like to leave on political history?

**HODGE**

Oh, my God, I don't think any of us leave – we're all ephemeral, we're all ephemeral. And can I just say, it's not the 'I,' it's the 'we'. So you know nothing in my life has always been me on my own, it's always been with others. So there's so much I'm proud of. I mean I think our battle against Nick Griffin was very important, fighting off the extreme right and the new way in which I did politics out of that. I hope that there is a new era of resurgence of parliamentary democracy through the select committees. I hope we've opened up the debate about taxation in a much more public way than we've ever done before. But, I hope actually, for women, this idea that it's a marathon not a short sprint is something that will impact on how politics is seen. I hope the Labour Party as a really important force coming back into government to fight for equality will be a legacy for the future.

**HENNESSY**

Margaret Hodge, thank you very much indeed.

**HODGE**

Thank you.

# Kenneth Baker
# (Lord Baker of Dorking)

Series 4, Episode 4, first broadcast 23 August 2016

**Born** 3 November 1934; **Educated** King George V
Grammar School, Southport; Hampton Grammar
School; St Paul's School; Magdalen College, Oxford

MP (Conservative) St Marylebone 1970–83; Mole Valley 1983–97

Parliamentary Secretary, Civil Service Department, 1972–74;
Minister of State, Department of Industry, 1981–83; Minister
of State, Industry & Information Technology, 1983–84;
Minister of State for Local Government, Department of the
Environment, 1984–85; Secretary of State for the Environment,
1985–86; Secretary of State for Education and Science, 1986–89;
Chairman of the Conservative Party, 1989–90; Chancellor of
the Duchy of Lancaster, 1989–90; Home Secretary, 1990–92

**Autobiography** *The Turbulent Years*, 1993

### HENNESSY

With me today is Kenneth Baker, Lord Baker of Dorking. Ken
Baker is a politician with a sense of history. During this extraordinary summer of high political drama, and abundant political
haemorrhage, he told the House of Lords it possessed more than a
whiff of the Middle Ages. 'When a dynasty changed,' he declared,

'a new guard came in and the old guard went out and some poor wretch was executed in Pontefract Castle. The only difference today is that political assassination takes place in prime time in television studios.' Ken Baker knows a great deal about political dynasties, having worked closely with three very different Prime Ministers: Ted Heath, Margaret Thatcher and John Major. Perhaps his greatest personal mark was scored across the historical page by his core curriculum as Education Secretary in the late 1980s and the fires of educational reform still burn fiercely within him. Ken, welcome.

### BAKER

Thank you very much.

### HENNESSY

Let's begin with your personal history. You were born in Newport.

### BAKER

Yes.

### HENNESSY

The Welsh borders. Was the influence of Wales powerful upon you?

### BAKER

Not really. We moved from it when I was only five or six years old to London. And so I have very few recollections of Wales, but I had a Welsh grandfather who was a docker.

### HENNESSY

Your grandfather, I think, worked in the docks at Newport and knew the great trade union leader Ben Tillett.

### BAKER

Yes.

**HENNESSY**

Do you think that somewhere within your make-up your passion for technical education comes from that self-help, Workers' Educational Association tradition?

**BAKER**

It might do. Yes. The Bakers rose through education. They thought education was really the most important thing in life and my father felt that because my grandfather was a docker. He was made the secretary of the dockers' union because he was the one who had beautiful handwriting and kept the records. And he was actually offered a seat to stand in Parliament by Keir Hardie. But he couldn't afford that, he'd got two young boys – three young boys, one died – two young boys and he didn't do it. But he was a very active member. Though, at the end of his life, he ended up managing part of Newport docks during the Second World War.

**HENNESSY**

Do you think it's given you some empathy for Labour? Why were you not an aristocrat of Labour yourself with a background like that?

**BAKER**

Yes I suppose there was a bit, really. And my father was sort of Conservative only on some days, other days he was certainly Labour. I remember him, after the War, explaining to me Stafford Cripps' budgets and how necessary they were and that sort of thing.

**HENNESSY**

It's quite interesting, it should be a balance because he was a career civil servant –

**BAKER**

Yes he was.

**HENNESSY**

– so part of him should be one and part of him the other.

**BAKER**

Yes he was.

**HENNESSY**

Ministry of Supply?

**BAKER**

Yes he was.

**HENNESSY**

What did he do in the Ministry of Supply?

**BAKER**

He was involved in supply, basically of foodstuffs, I think. And they went – the whole department was moved up to Liverpool during the war, so we were evacuated. And I was brought up in Southport where my father got a flat for us. And I had a very good education. I went to an ordinary primary, Church of England primary school. There was no field, there was a brickyard with brick walls around it, glass on top of it, which we used to climb and we'd try and chip the glass off. And we were taught in the very traditional, old-fashioned way, and it was the basis of my education.

**HENNESSY**

And then grammar school?

**BAKER**

I went to a grammar school in the north for a year, King George V, and I went to a grammar school in Middlesex, Hampton Grammar School, which is now a private school, for two years. They were excellent schools.

**HENNESSY**

Why on earth did you transfer to St Paul's when you had such an excellent grammar school?

**BAKER**

Well you might well ask. Because one day my father said, 'Do you want to go to St Paul's?' I said 'Well it's a church, isn't it?' I had never heard of the school. But he'd heard of it, and my father was a great sort of mover-on and he knew that going to that school might be better for me than going to a grammar school, that's what he thought, so I didn't take Common Entrance, I'd probably have failed that. I had to go along and write an essay for a teacher in St Paul's on Shelley and do some sums, and they said, 'You're all right, you're literate and numerate, you can join.' And so I joined. And I was there for four years.

**HENNESSY**

Not rigorous testing by your subsequent standards was it?

**BAKER**

No. No not at all, no. But they knew talent when they saw it. [*Both laugh*]

**HENNESSY**

Do you think you'd have gone to Oxford if you'd stayed at Hampton Grammar School? You almost certainly would have done.

**BAKER**

I might have done or might not. I think the teacher I had in history, P D Whiting, was a very gifted man indeed. And he placed people in Oxford in those days. And he got me into Magdalen, I think. Because he knew I liked history and I think he thought I would do well at it.

**HENNESSY**

And of course Magdalen was just made for you because you had stunning teachers. You had the medievalist Bruce McFarlane, whose legend lives on, and the very famous A J P Taylor, the first telly don.

**BAKER**

Well I was very lucky. McFarlane was the creator of bastard feudalism, a great medievalist. A J P Taylor was another kettle of fish; a wonderful historian and he would sit with his cat in his lap and you'd go for an hour, as it were, and he was very good on general politics. And he also had a wonderful series of lectures on the First World War. And he gave them at nine o'clock on a Wednesday morning, in the examination halls. It was packed. And I went to him afterwards, I said, 'Why didn't you do it at 11 o'clock?' He said there was no hall in Oxford big enough to take the audience who would come.

**HENNESSY**

Were you a fledgling Tory by this time?

**BAKER**

Sort of. What I did like, I liked debating. When I was at St Paul's, John Adair and I created the public school debating society that led to the Observer Prize and all that sort of thing. I always liked debating and arguing and standing up and expressing my views. So I suppose that sort of attitude is generally quite good if you're going to be a politician.

**HENNESSY**

But what made you a centre-right person rather than a centre-left?

**BAKER**

That is quite interesting actually.

**HENNESSY**

And when? What was the formation of that?

**BAKER**

I suppose it entered probably at Hampton Grammar School, and a bit later at St Paul's. I felt that socialism at the beginning was far too controlled and restrictive; I gathered that from what I read about it in the papers. I didn't want that. And I think reading J S Mill's *On Liberty* was one of the most important things that I read, actually. And that might have turned me into a Liberal, quite frankly, but it made me more of a Conservative. The elevation of the status of an individual in society is the thing that has, I think, dominated my political thinking.

**HENNESSY**

How old were you when you read Mill for the first time?

**BAKER**

I should think I was about 15 or 16, that sort of age.

**HENNESSY**

Now Alan Taylor was a man of the Left, did you have little clashes with him? Did he sense a Tory in the making in you?

**BAKER**

No, no he rather, he rather liked it. One of his great heroes is Charles James Fox.

**HENNESSY**

Yes.

**BAKER**

And I handed in an essay on Charles James Fox and he said, 'Ah, what you haven't realised, he was the first Leader of Her Majesty's

Opposition, though unrecognised.' And he absolutely was, of course, because Fox turned up night after night in the House of Commons arguing against [the] very popular Pitt. And that required a great deal of attitude and energy from a wonderful man who was a wastrel as well and a libertine, but a great orator. I think one of the things that has attracted me always in politics was great oratory.

**HENNESSY**

Yes.

**BAKER**

And there were some great orators in the House of Commons in my time.

**HENNESSY**

When you first arrived in the '60s...

**BAKER**

Yes, when I first arrived there was Michael Foot, who was brilliant. There was Iain Macleod. But there were people who used words in a way... they used the sort of things that have dropped out completely – satire, and sarcasm – brilliantly. And that is hardly done in the House of Commons today. Dryden said it very clearly when he said, talking of satire, that there is a vast difference between the slovenly butchering of a man and the fineness of a stroke that separates the head from the body and leaves it standing in its place. But the butchery, it is butchery, it would take a club today; this is the Trump approach, it's totally club-like. And quite a lot of the question time is club-like.

**HENNESSY**

Let's go back to somebody who wasn't an orator, but you met when I think you were still an undergraduate, Clement Attlee. I think you sat next to the Attlees at dinner. That must have been a fairly terse occasion, Ken, wasn't it?

**BAKER**

It was at the Oxford Union. He turned up in a little, tiny Austin 7 car, driven by his wife, and their main preoccupation before dinner was where they could park so they wouldn't be fined anything. This is the former Prime Minister of Britain. And he was a very, very nice, courtly man, I liked him very much indeed, very humble. You could see in the speech that he made at the Union that night was a very traditional, go along with the traditions of life speech, if you like. It was, observe things sensibly. I remember him saying something about referendums – he said, 'Referendums? I think Hitler did four, didn't he?'

And you don't really want them back and that sort of thing. And he was, I thought, very effective. I liked him as a person. I could see how he had managed to survive as a Prime Minister, because he was very clear-minded.

**HENNESSY**

What mark did National Service leave on you? You were in the desert, in Libya, teaching the Libyans artillery, weren't you?

**BAKER**

Yes, I was an artillery instructor, yes. I was trained in mortar gunnery. I actually enjoyed my National Service. Two years after school, you grow up. You grow up enormously. You meet people from other walks of life that you would not have met at St Paul's or even at Hampton Grammar School. You learned about comradeship, which is very, a very important thing to learn about in life. And working with others, and taking responsibility. I was responsible for 30 men and had to deal with them. We were only partially on active service. The guerrilla activities in the Canal Zone – because Nasser had just come to power –

**HENNESSY**

Suez, that's Egypt –

**BAKER**

Yes, Egypt, in the Suez Canal Zone – had just come to power. And then Eden negotiated withdrawal from the Canal Zone – went to Cyprus. And I was then sent off to Libya because Libya had been given some mortars by Turkey, American mortars, and I was asked to train the army. But it was really a sort of parade army, nothing more than that.

**HENNESSY**

So you felt quite grown up when you turned up in Oxford?

**BAKER**

Yes. You'd lived a bit, which is important, you know, you'd drunk perhaps a bit too much on some nights and you knew about girls and things like that, yes. Yes you'd lived a bit, which was very good. And that's a good way of enjoying Oxford.

**HENNESSY**

Who were the most exotic people you knew in Oxford in your time? Brian Walden, is a fairly interesting man wasn't he?

**BAKER**

Brian Walden is probably the most exotic. He was the greatest orator. He was one of the best, he was the President of the Union and he was brilliant. Two weeks running I heard him, one week defending censorship and the following week saying it was absolutely unacceptable. And both were such convincing speeches – quite striking. He was the chairman of the Labour Club when I was the chairman of the Conservatives. And during the Suez Crisis, all work stopped for a fortnight in Oxford. And we were only concerned about the Suez Crisis, and also at the same time Hungary was being invaded by the Russians. It was an incredible –

**HENNESSY**

November 1956.

**BAKER**

And there were huge meetings and all the time it was the only subject talked. That was quite an exciting time in politics.

**HENNESSY**

You got involved very early on, I think, and were one of the founders of the so-called Bow Group of progressive Conservatives.

**BAKER**

Yes indeed.

**HENNESSY**

They're almost forgotten now, but it seemed to me looking back, that what you were interested in was the West German model of the social market that Adenauer and Ludwig Erhard, above all, had introduced, and applying it to British circumstances. And you were young, you were graduates and I think you were called the Bow Group because you met in Bow in east London.

**BAKER**

We met in Bow in the Bow Road. 153 Bow Road. And it was an old, Victorian house, right next door to Poplar Town Hall. And Geoffrey Howe was there, and Leon Brittan and John MacGregor, people like that. Quite a clutch of people who wanted to, as it were, change the attitude of the Tory Party. And it was very invigorating to go down there because this was a working class area, old fashioned, working class area, I canvassed in it enormously because I stood in the Conservative cause in the 1964 election in Poplar. Poplar and Bow.

**HENNESSY**

You must have been an exotic bird of paradise, given your dress sense down there, weren't you?

**BAKER**

We were rare birds, but we were respected rare birds. People would answer the door in their shirtsleeves with shaving foam all over their face, 'What do you want mate, what do you want mate, eh?' And then you'd explain, 'Ah, not one of ours, but thanks for calling.' And that old working class area's disappeared totally in the redevelopment, I would say.

**HENNESSY**

Clearly you enjoyed all that.

**BAKER**

And so I enjoyed all that enormously. But in those days, you see, to aspire in politics – well, first I was a ward member going canvassing and collecting subscriptions, then a councillor, then you fight a safe Labour seat, which I did. I fought Ian Mikado. He was a sort of hate figure on the Tory side. And then you fight a marginal. I fought a marginal in the 1966 election for Acton which we'd just lost. Could I win it back? No, I didn't. And then I was still the sitting candidate when the member committed suicide, Bernard Floud. And I had to decide then should I go into politics or not, by going on and winning the seat because I was bound to win the seat. And at that time I was the chief executive of a publicly quoted company. A company that had three factories supplying Marks & Spencer's – I pulled it round from bankruptcy. And I had to choose that night, do I go into business or politics? And so that was the choice. Given that choice today, I don't think anybody, hardly anybody would make the choice I made to go into politics.

**HENNESSY**

Would you, if you faced it again?

**BAKER**

I think I'd have to think quite hard again about it.

**HENNESSY**

Why's that?

**BAKER**

Because the political life has certain great advantages, there's no question about that, particularly if you're reasonably successful it has great advantages. And it's interesting because you're dealing with big issues and you meet interesting people. But on the other hand the way that politicians are exposed today by living permanently in a goldfish bowl, everything is known about them, their lives, their children, their wives. The press are out to get them if they possibly can. And the rewards are not very significant compared to a successful businessman, quite frankly. And so I think a lot of people will be deterred from going into politics today, given that choice.

**HENNESSY**

When you came into the Commons in '68 there were, on your side, great orators at the peak of their powers. One thinks of Enoch Powell and one thinks of Iain Macleod who I suspect was a bit of a hero of yours.

**BAKER**

Yes he was.

**HENNESSY**

What was special about him?

**BAKER**

He was a most attractive figure in every possible way. First he was a great orator, he had some lovely things to say, you know. When Wilson was in the devaluation crisis, he sort of said that he was a very honest man and Iain Macleod said, 'When the Prime Minister talks of honesty, we have to count the spoons' – wonderful way of putting it. I remember another time on Wedgwood Benn, 'There was Wedgwood Benn flying a kite and there were we watching it thud to the ground.'

**HENNESSY**

Do you think he would have made a better Leader of the Conservative Party than Ted Heath?

**BAKER**

Yes, without any shadow of doubt.

**HENNESSY**

And it was a great blow to Ted Heath when he died in a few weeks of the '70 government being formed.

**BAKER**

Yes he died in 11 Downing Street one night. And that was a blow to the whole Heath administration, actually. I think that if he'd lived, it would not have got into the mess that it did get into.

**HENNESSY**

How would he have prevented that? Because he could have told Ted anything directly in a way that other people were put off –

**BAKER**

Well he was, the Chancellor of the Exchequer, the second most powerful man in the government, and it was basically on economic policy that we went badly astray. We tried to introduce prices and incomes policy because Nixon had done something rather similar. The Counter-Inflation Bill, it was called. And by that time I'd joined the government as the most junior minister, the Junior Minister for the Civil Service. But I was Ted Heath's own minister because he was the Minister for the Civil Service. So I was sucked into a lot of what was happening in the centre. I also saw what went wrong, because on the Counter-Inflation Bill, which had set up The Wages Board and The Prices Commission, we had the best orators in the house against us. We had Nicholas Ridley, Enoch Powell, Brian Walden, really brilliant people, and they criticised the whole concept. And I think Enoch Powell's greatest contribution, actually, to British politics was his destruction of the concept of a prices and incomes policy as being totally unworkable. His best speeches were on that.

**HENNESSY**

You were very loyal to Ted.

**BAKER**

I was very loyal to Ted, yes. I felt loyalty to him because I was his minister and he'd appointed me. And after he lost in 1974, February '74, Tim Kitson, his PPS, approached me and said 'Would you help Ted and be another PPS?' I said 'Come off, Ted is going to lose. He's had it; he's not re-electable. And if I join him it's a classic case of a rat joining a sinking ship. Do you really want me to do it?' And he said 'Yes, yes.' And I said 'Well I will do it.' But I was always very clear that Ted was not going to win another election.

**HENNESSY**

You were next to him, I think, when the word came in that he'd not made it in...

**BAKER**

We were waiting – when he saw that Margaret had got more votes than he did, I was sitting in his room with him. And Ted accepted immediately, actually, and wrote out in his own hand his resignation statement.

**HENNESSY**

And by a kind of symmetry you were with Mrs Thatcher when she went under.

**BAKER**

Yes. Exactly so, yes.

**HENNESSY**

You're a dangerous man to have next to you in bad times, aren't you? I mean there's a kind of Ancient Mariner touch.

**BAKER**

I'm in at the death. [*Both laugh*]

**HENNESSY**

The undertaker. Ken Baker, the undertaker –

**BAKER**

Absolutely, yes.

**HENNESSY**

– of political lives.

**BAKER**

Absolutely.

**HENNESSY**

But Ted Heath will always have that great place in history, despite the referendum result to leave the European Union, because he got us in.

**BAKER**

Yes.

**HENNESSY**

And it's thought at the time, certainly the French have always said this, that Ted Heath was the only British political leader at that time who could have engineered the British accession to the Treaty of Rome.

**BAKER**

That comment is right because Macmillan failed. And there's a wonderful cartoon, drawn I think by Illingworth, of the 'No', of the barrier coming down, de Gaulle's great nose being the barrier and stopping Macmillan going through.

**HENNESSY**

The customs barrier.

**BAKER**

Yes, the customs barrier. But Ted did do that and this all comes from the fact that he was in the war and he felt a real consciousness that Europe must not fight again, we must all be together. And I respected him for that. And I think that was the great gain in the first stage of European association, quite frankly. That was the great, great political gain. And no one can take that from him at all.

**HENNESSY**

And he did try to modernise the machinery of government and local government, he was a great technician of state, wasn't he?

**BAKER**

He did. But he also established an extraordinary relationship with his chief civil servant.

**HENNESSY**

William Armstrong.

**BAKER**

William Armstrong. And in those days when the prices and incomes policy was falling apart, Ted would have meetings at one of the great houses in London, public meetings, and William Armstrong would be on the platform with him.

**HENNESSY**

Lancaster House.

**BAKER**

That had never happened before. And William was spending all his time in Number 10 trying to shore up the prices and incomes policy. And the trouble with all of that was that the most effective minister, after Ted, would have been Willie Whitelaw. But Willie Whitelaw was diverted to go and run [Northern] Ireland for two years. And it took him off the eye of British politics in London and in Westminster. And he was only able to come in just before Christmas in 1973. And it was all too late because the calibre in the Cabinet was not strong enough to do what they were doing. He was let down by a lot of his colleagues at the critical time when he needed help.

**HENNESSY**

You weren't a natural Thatcherite, as these crude labels of politics are applied.

**BAKER**

No.

**HENNESSY**

But you're very good at surviving, you're a great survivor, Ken, aren't you, because you shimmered like Jeeves, eventually, from being a Heathite to being very close to Mrs T. Now what is it in your character that enables you to do these shimmering routines? [*Laughter*]

### BAKER

After Ted had lost I was out in the doghouse because I'd been trying to get him re-elected. I'd worked loyally for him and tried to get him – I knew it was a hopeless task but I did all I possibly could to get him elected and he failed. And I was looked upon as a Heathite. But, strangely enough, I was a member of an extraordinary body called The Economic Dining Club. And this was a group of people including Margaret and Enoch and John Nott and John Biffen. And we met at each other's houses once every two months, where the host would give a dinner, a supper, and we would talk about economic matters. And I found myself to be very sympathetic to what they were saying, because the old method of prices and incomes didn't work – you needed something else. And that group went on for quite a long time. And when Margaret was host, we went to her house in Chelsea and she'd always do shepherd's pie, which she said she cooked herself, and we talked about the free market and privatisation and de-nationalisation. And things like that. And I was very switched on by that. I would go –

### HENNESSY

Was this the first time you'd encountered free market ideas in the flood?

### BAKER

No, I was in fact, when I first got in, back in 1968/69, there was a Bill before the house to make the Post Office a nationalised industry, and I was on the committee for that. And I then moved amendments in that committee to actually privatise the telecoms side, not the post side.

I approached it as a businessman. Telecoms was a business and should be run by business people, not by ministers and civil servants. So I was an early privatiser, if you like, and this group that met was in favour of that. I rather liked all of that. But even so, despite being a member of that club, when Margaret was elected in 1979, she didn't offer me a job. I was a backbencher.

**HENNESSY**

I think you came in as the IT man.

**BAKER**

Yes.

**HENNESSY**

Before IT was generally perceived as the transformer it was going to be. I think you came in to Keith Joseph's Department of Industry.

**BAKER**

Correct. I did that because, being on the back benches, and a businessman, I took an interest in computing. And in the '70s I went to Japan a lot to look at the VLSI, that's the chip development that they did, and I got to know what was happening in computing and I became a shareholder when Logica was a private company, the great software company. And I got to know a lot about all of that world and I decided that you needed a minister to actually promote the changes that were just about to happen. And so I wrote out a manifesto, if you like, ten points for a Minister of Information Technology. One of which was to get one, single computer into every school; one to give financial support to early robotic development; one to support the English invention of fibre optic and also the paperless office in Whitehall. And I worked up schemes and ideas and put these to Margaret, and she appointed me. And I then put that into practice. And I was given quite a lot of leeway in getting money for that. Margaret came to me – I joined in January '81, and in the summer of '81, when she was [a] very unpopular, one-term Prime Minister, a 'witch' and all the rest of it, the recession of '81 was much worse than 2008–2009. As a minister in the Department of Industry, when you arrived in Manchester or Leeds or Birmingham, you were met by your senior local official who'd give you the factories closing that day. It was a dreadful, deep recession. And right in that deep recession Geoffrey Howe introduced a budget that in fact decreased public expenditure, increased taxation, but Margaret wanted something nice to say, so I gave her a little package of technology measures, one of which was computers in schools, another one was supporting robotics.

### HENNESSY

Didn't you develop a technique for handling Mrs Thatcher? I think you had a kind of Baker style.

### BAKER

Yes.

### HENNESSY

What was it?

### BAKER

I think, a) you must be fully boned-up on your subject, whatever it is, that's being debated of the day. I'd seen ministers and civil servants absolutely destroyed by Margaret because they weren't in charge of their briefs one way or another, or careless. And so I was always very prepared for all the issues that [she] could raise in case I ever discussed [them] with her in committee or in Cabinet. And therefore when I wasn't winning – sometimes that happened quite a lot – I would not sulk and get angry, I would try and humour her slightly. And I remember on one occasion she said, 'Kenneth, why are you still smiling when you haven't won any of the points you've raised this morning?' And the point is you have to – when you're dealing with a very forceful personality like that – know how to cope with it. And therefore I would come back a week later or a fortnight later, and perhaps slightly modify it and come back and try and persuade her again. But I wasn't, as it were, daggers drawn with her. And so I was able to humour her more.

### HENNESSY

Was it a particular problem when you became Education Secretary, because that's the job she'd held in the Heath Cabinet and quite often Prime Ministers think they have a kind of proprietorial right over their old territory? Was that a problem?

### BAKER

When I went to see her when she appointed me, I expected to be given a list of things to do. Not at all; she said to me, 'The problem in education at the moment is the teachers' strike. It's been going on for 18 months – this is something that must be resolved, settled. And on all the other issues I want you to think about them and come back to me in six weeks' time and tell me what you think you want to do.' I was a bit flabbergasted, quite frankly, because I knew what I wanted to do. I wanted to get more technical schools, I wanted to get computers into schools in a much bigger way. I wanted to make some schools independent of local authorities, and I wanted a national curriculum. And I took them back to her and she said she liked what she saw and she was going to support them. And I had to do papers on each of them, of course. And that formed the basis of our policy for the election, and we had nine pages on education. And we had things like National Curriculum, we had tests, we had league tables, we had City Technology Colleges independent of local authorities, we had grant-maintained schools, parents electing to come out, as it were, from state control. We also had delegation of budgets to schools, that was a great change. That wasn't my invention, there were experiments going on in Cambridge, and I saw how good they were, I spread it to many more schools quickly.

**HENNESSY**

And you achieved political immortality as well in a very rare way, with the Baker days, the in-service training days. Only Leslie Hore-Belisha with his Belisha beacon –

**BAKER**

Yes, that's right –

**HENNESSY**

– had ever given his name to an artefact.

**BAKER**

Yes I suppose I might be remembered. It was a sort of a decision that was made late on a Friday afternoon, as it were. But there we are. I'm better known for that.

**HENNESSY**

One of the great spinal cords in your career, Ken, is the passion for technical education. Now why is it that we didn't get it right? It's there in the 1944 Education Act which was Rab Butler's great monument. Sir David Eccles, Minister of Education in '55 really wanted it, as did his Prime Minister, Anthony Eden. And yet it didn't happen. Now what is it about our country that is resistant to this concept of technical education, which many people would say is absolutely critical and always was to our industrial and economic future?

**BAKER**

Snobbery is the answer.

**HENNESSY**

Simple as that?

**BAKER**

There were 300 technical schools in existence in 1945. And they were closed over the next five or six years because everybody wanted to go to the school on the hill, like the grammar school – the trees and the flags flying and all the rest of it – and they didn't want to go down to the school in the town with shabby premises, dirty jobs, greasy rags. And very extraordinarily the Labour Party never supported technical education. So it came to Tories like Rab Butler and David Eccles and now me, as it were, supporting technical education. And it's still desperately needed.

**HENNESSY**

And you're still in the process of actually building technical schools aren't you –

**BAKER**

Yes, absolutely –

**HENNESSY**

– in your early eighties.

**BAKER**

Yes.

**HENNESSY**

Michael Gove was very resistant as Education Secretary to your technical colleges.

**BAKER**

Yes he was.

Why was that?

He didn't really understand technical education and he succumbed to the teachings of an American philosopher, educational philosopher, called Hirsch who said that the way you can really improve the lot of the working classes of the poor people is just to concentrate on academic subjects, that's all you have to do. Well, there's no evidence that this works. Because that's all right if you've got a grammar school approach and you've got a certain level of education, as it were. But maybe somewhere between 40 and 50 per cent of the young people in our country don't want to just do academic subjects. And it's gone back to that at the moment, and it's completely wrong. The actual curriculum that is now being imposed upon the education system consists of nine to eight subjects. And they're word for word the subjects that were announced in 1904 by Dr Morant, the Secretary of the Board of Education.

The great Robert Morant.

And it didn't work. And so I've always believed there should be a mixture of technical and academic. And I think it's even more important today because we're now on the edge of a digital revolution which is going to change absolutely everything in my view. It's going to change employment; it's going to change education. And you've got to give kids today, when they leave school at 16, a series of skills. For example, as part of the academic subjects they should have worked in teams, which we don't in schools at all; they should deal with problem solving, which they don't really do in schools at all; they should be making projects so that they can then present them to others and talk; they should talk to lots of adults other than their parents and their teachers, like business people who come in to school to teach them. These are the sort of skills youngsters should leave school with today, at 16 or 18, because in the future there's going to be much more – as a result of digital revolution – self-employment and part time work. Uber's part time work. There'll be lots of these sort of things in the future. And therefore you've go to give people a lot of talented skills, which they can then link themselves to a personal income stream. That I think is the test of education in the course of the next ten years. And I'm fighting for that. We've got 43, 45 technical colleges [which] will now be open in September of this year, dealing with 15,000 students. And my target for these youngsters – they go from 14 to 19, not 11, we're the only country left in the world with a transfer age of 11. It's ridiculous, it's entirely history. It was the fact that historically the grammar schools started at 11 that we got 11. We're about the only country left with the 11 transfer, most countries moved to 13, 14.

### HENNESSY

You've been thrown at several of the perpetual problems of British politics and government, haven't you? One of the others was local government finance.

### BAKER

Yes.

### HENNESSY

It's probably scored on your heart.

### BAKER

Yes. Yes, to some extent.

### HENNESSY

The poll tax, it will always collapse into 'I name the guilty men and women on the poll tax'. Are you a guilty man?

**BAKER**

I could see the advantages of it and was one of the ministers involved in actually devising it. William Waldegrave was, I think, the person who now is prepared to take the full blame for it, but that's not entirely – it was a joint effort. It was an attempt to replace rates with a more sensible system of taxation. And of course personal charging has become much more sensible now. The Congestion Charge is a poll tax. Parking charges are [a] poll tax.

**HENNESSY**

So what went wrong?

**BAKER**

Well what went wrong was that when the scheme that we introduced first was to be phased in over ten years, it would start at £50, no more than £50, and it was going to be linked with property and personal taxation for ten years. And I also recommended that anybody under 21 should not be included, no students should be included. That was dropped out by people after me, as it were. Nick Ridley thought it was such a good idea, the poll tax, so wonderful in itself, it ought to be brought in at once.

**HENNESSY**

He was Environment Secretary.

**BAKER**

And he was the Environment Secretary. I protested to Margaret and to the Chancellor that it would be absolutely disastrous, because it would throw up huge increases for little old ladies in Lancashire and Yorkshire and all the rest of it. And it was implemented incredibly badly.

**HENNESSY**

So you're a qualified guilty man?

### BAKER

Yes sort of – well, no I don't try to shed my guilt as I could see the advantages of having personal taxation for charging, because I think that's going to be how much of it's going to happen in the future.

### HENNESSY

Then there's the Home Office. Do you think you left a mark in your Home Office days?

### BAKER

I set about prison reform. Because I had to deal with the consequences of Strangeways and I dealt with the Woolf Report. The Woolf Report was the best report we've had on prison reform –

### HENNESSY

Strangeways was a prison riot.

### BAKER

A prison riot that David Waddington had to take when he was Home Secretary and they were on the top of that jail for nearly a fortnight – really unacceptable. And following that, Lord Woolf, later the Lord Chief Justice, produced a report, which I accepted in its totality and introduced it. And that changed all sorts of practices, like allowing telephones in prisons and things of that sort, trying to improve education, that sort of thing. And making it – the real punishment for a prisoner is the deprivation of liberty, you don't have to make them live in squalor, as it were. And I felt that really strongly. And I set in train quite a lot of prison reforms. But the prison population is twice what it was in my time. Far too many people are put in prison today in Britain. 86,000 when I was dealing with 41, 42,000.

**HENNESSY**

How did you get on with John Major? Your third Prime Minister.

**BAKER**

*Quite* well. When John Major had his first Cabinet after the election, he looked around the table and he said 'Who'd have thought it?' And I think it's fair to say quite a lot of them would not have thought it was him, quite frankly.

**HENNESSY**

Why is that?

**BAKER**

Well it was quite a quick ascent, as it were, in the pattern, and he was never really a Thatcherite. I think Margaret Thatcher thought he was a Thatcherite, but he really wasn't a Thatcherite. He, for example, had been a great believer in going into the ERM.

**HENNESSY**

The Exchange Rate Mechanism.

**BAKER**

And I remember that episode very clearly, because it was never debated by the Cabinet. There was no paper on it. But I learned overnight that it was going to be done the following day and I was Party Chairman. And the Party Chairman does have right of access to the Leader straight away, so I went to see Margaret and I argued against it very strongly, on the grounds that it would restrict her capacity when it came to the election with interest rates and it was quite the wrong rate to go in, all the rest of it. And she said 'Oh no, no.' She listened for a bit. She had Charles Powell and Bernard Ingham in as her advisers, who were supporting, nodding every time when she sort of countered my arguments. And I could see I was going to get absolutely nowhere. But it was a huge mistake. And she said 'Well you know Kenneth, they're going to reduce interest rates by 1 per cent tomorrow, that's a great gain, you know. And I've been told it's all very flexible, we can go up and down as we like.' Well you just couldn't do that. And that was a huge mistake that she made right at the end of her premiership, actually.

### HENNESSY

There wasn't much speaking truth unto power to Mrs T at that stage was there? It was a fairly supine Cabinet.

### BAKER

Yes.

### HENNESSY

In her last, rather crudely called, 'bunker' phase.

### BAKER

I think it was.

### HENNESSY

She was on transmit rather than receive, to use the jargon.

### BAKER

Yes I think so. Because quite a few of my colleagues were thinking what was going to happen afterwards, I think, quite frankly. And I could detect quite clearly that some of the strongest Thatcherites were falling out of love with her. And, strangely enough, I was quite cool at the beginning with Margaret, but I came to respect her more the longer she was there. And as I was going along my road to Damascus, all the others were moving back on their road to Damascus the other way. [*Laughs*]

**HENNESSY**

Why did you stick by her through thick and thin at the end?

**BAKER**

I'll tell you why, because the great thing about Margaret, that really did mark her out from all the other Prime Ministers I've known, I've known them since Macmillan – well Eden really – was her willpower. She had enormous willpower. It didn't come from great intellectual distinction, it came from a whole lot of instincts, really. To understand Margaret you have to understand Grantham, I think, and all of that. And her instincts were there, and the willpower –

**HENNESSY**

The influence of her father and so on.

**BAKER**

Yes her father.

**HENNESSY**

And the nonconformist upbringing.

**BAKER**

And all of that, and living within your means and being careful. There was a great deal of carefulness about Margaret in the way she approached things. And I came to respect her in coping with all of this, and coping so well on the world stage as well. What she did in all of those negotiations as the East was crumbling was quite remarkable, actually. And she was very proud of her role in all of that, she was seen as almost a patron saint in Ukraine and in that part of the world. And that's why she went, in her last election, when she was challenged in that election which she lost for the leadership –

**HENNESSY**

By Michael Heseltine.

**BAKER**

By Michael Heseltine. I tried to persuade her not to go to a great meeting in Europe, which she wanted to go to on the Monday night.

**HENNESSY**

It was the ending of the Cold War meeting, wasn't it?

**BAKER**

And it was the ending of the Cold War. And she felt she had to be there. And I begged her not to, but just stay in London and canvass some rather awkward Tory backbenchers. But no, she felt she had to go. And she said, 'Surely, can't they show me gratitude? I won them three elections.'

**HENNESSY**

There's no gratitude in politics, as somebody once said, Asquith I think.

**BAKER**

No gratitude, that marble-hearted monster.

**HENNESSY**

But all three of the Prime Ministers you've watched carefully and worked with and for have come to a tragic end in one way or another.

**BAKER**

Yes. They all have done that. Margaret was – you know, that was matricide. And when a party commits matricide you only have to have a slight knowledge of Greek tragedy to know what happens. And then John Major, really, led the party to a massive defeat.

**HENNESSY**

He seems to be more cheerful than perhaps the other two were in their last years, not that he's in his last years, he's some way to go, I hope.

**BAKER**

I think yes. I think that he slightly reinvented himself as an international businessman, and his views are respected. He was campaigning quite a lot in the referendum, I noticed, and trying to persuade people to vote Remain.

**HENNESSY**

Were you a Remain man, Ken? Because it's very difficult to decode you sometimes.

**BAKER**

No, I was a Brexiter.

**HENNESSY**

How interesting. Because nobody was entirely sure, were they?

**BAKER**

No. Well I didn't talk about it.

**HENNESSY**

How did you camouflage yourself?

**BAKER**

I didn't talk about it very much. But I really fell out of love when I was a minister by going to meetings in Europe, and I could see what was happening. The ministers would only meet maybe once every two or three months. So you get to know the other ministers. The next meeting, some had been promoted, some had been defeated, some had been arrested. They weren't the same people that you were talking to in the past. And you're up against a very solid and very competent Commission secretariat. And I saw papers produced where ministers at one meeting would say, 'No we don't quite agree with this,' then the papers would come back with barely changes in punctuation, but subtle changes for the next meeting. And the ministers had all changed. This wasn't a way to run things in my way at all. So I really began to fall out of love with it.

And the balance has all got wrong. I didn't mind it when it was a much smaller group of six to nine. But I think the expansion has brought in economies of such huge difference from ours, quite frankly. And I think the great achievements of Europe, the European Union, has been the democratic ones and bringing people back into democracy like Spain and Portugal, and things like that.

#### HENNESSY

And the former Eastern Bloc Soviet satellites.

#### BAKER

And the former Eastern Blocs coming in. That is their great thing. They just tried to be far too ambitious. I think the actual Euro is a complete disaster. And will be seen to be a disaster.

#### HENNESSY

What would you have done if you'd been Prime Minister? Is there a Baker plan still in the back of your hippocampus, the historian's bit of the brain?

#### BAKER

No, no, no. I'd have done some of the things that Cameron's done. I think Cameron is now, because of the defeat, is looked upon as an underrated Prime Minister. I think in fact he was quite a successful Prime Minister in very difficult circumstances. There was a bit of lack of follow up and all the rest of it, but he had some very good ideas. I rather like the 'Big Society'. Because, in fact, you've got to find a way of bringing the poor and dispossessed, as it were, much more into the benefit of our society than they have at the moment. And this is going to become a major problem in my view. One of the reasons why I think the north voted so clearly to leave just wasn't Europe, it was a whole host of things. I go to the north a lot and, you know, you go through towns that look poor and are poor. And the disparity now between the very rich and the rest is actually socially not acceptable, and will cause a great deal of trouble.

**HENNESSY**

If I could give you one last great reform, Ken, magic wand waving and so on, what would it be? Will it be in this area? Which is the one that you think would most matter to the problems you've just outlined?

**BAKER**

I think it would be education, because I think the challenges of the digital revolution are so great that a lot of jobs will disappear on a very quick scale. And this isn't a sort of a lunatic personal view of mine. There was a great report at Davos this year which talked of the hollowing out of middle management. And there were two reports from McKinsey – they talk of millions of jobs being lost. The economic adviser to the Bank of England says automation will cost British society 15 million jobs. And that is going to be a huge problem for the next ten years, really a huge problem for us. What are these people going to do? Young and old. And the jobs that are missing out are sorts of students who did humanities subjects and moved into middle management of large companies. Nice house, nice mortgage and all the rest of it. Those sort of jobs are largely going to disappear, on quite a big scale. Automation will do for them, artificial intelligence, big data, will remove them as it were. And this is going to raise huge social problems in my view, because you're going to need a larger number of highly skilled people up there, really digitally aware people up there, really clever people. And quite a large number of semi-skilled people here. For example, if you take a driverless lorry which is being experimented with in America. There are three million truck drivers in America and eight million people running sandwich bars and stopovers. Well most of those will go with great automated trucks going across America. This is going to happen in our society in a very considerable way. And, therefore, unless you leave the education system with a range of skills, you could be earning very little for the rest of your life. And people who earn very little usually have poor lives. When there's a lot of money in society everybody seems to float up. When there's less money in society, there will be quite a lot of people floating down. And I think we're going to have quite difficult social problems in the course of the next ten or 20 years.

**HENNESSY**

What kind of trace will you, Ken Baker, leave on history?

**BAKER**

Well, I think education is what I might be remembered for. I like writing. I've produced 15 books; I did five poetry anthologies for Faber. I do very much believe that a politician's got to live in a world a bit outside politics.

**HENNESSY**

So you'd like your trace to be a bit of Secretary of State for Education, and the books?

**BAKER**

Yes. Books do survive. You know perfectly well because you're a scholar, we turn up a book written by somebody whose name has totally disappeared, but it's really rather a good book.

**HENNESSY**

We all live in hope, Ken, don't we?

**BAKER**

Yes.

**HENNESSY**

In addition to your scholarly appetites, you've had this love of political cartoons, haven't you?

**BAKER**

Yes.

**HENNESSY**

Why?

**BAKER**

Well almost by accident. I bought my first political cartoon, must be 50 years ago now, I went into a shop and I saw this little picture of the state coach, as it were, with someone sitting in it who I thought might be the King, wasn't sure who he was, with people driving it – recognisable politicians – people throwing stones at it. And I bought it for a fiver, and that would go now for about £600. And I found out what it's all about. It was Pitt supporting the monarchy, driving the King to the opening of Parliament when the King was shot at and Fox's followers throwing things at it. So it is a good story, I think.

**HENNESSY**

And who was the cartoonist?

**BAKER**

Gillray.

**HENNESSY**

The Great. Greatest of them all.

**BAKER**

And this is where I picked up cartooning and I found it, and I found it absolutely wonderful. It's given me enormous pleasure. I've written four books on cartooning – *The Life of George IV and George III in Cartoons*, and *The History of the Premiership in Cartoons*, *History of the Monarchy in Cartoons*. And I find them very vivid. It's a very good way of learning history.

**HENNESSY**

Have the cartoonists been kind to you as a subject?

**BAKER**

Oh no, you don't expect cartoonists to be kind to you. That's not their purpose in life. And so I've been depicted in various stages as a lion – not very frequently but occasionally – as a lion; various sinuous cats and things; snakes; once as an eagle, that wasn't for very long.

**HENNESSY**

There was a terrible one of you as a slug in *Spitting Image*. Of all things.

**BAKER**

I was a slug, I was a slug, but I didn't mind that, you see, having written about satire I'm not worried about satire. I'm not worried about the attacks. Because I know how wrong they are in many cases and they were wrong about me. I didn't mind about that. So I didn't care. You have to have a thick skin in politics.

**HENNESSY**

Ken, thank you very much indeed.

# Tony Blair

Series 5, Episode 1, first broadcast 10 August 2017

**Born** 6 May 1953; **Educated** Fettes College;
St John's College, Oxford; Lincoln's Inn

MP (Labour) Sedgefield 1983–2007

Leader of the Labour Party, 1994–2007; Leader of the Opposition,
1994–97; First Lord of the Treasury and Prime Minister, 1997–2007

**Autobiography** *A Journey*, 2010

### HENNESSY

With me today is Tony Blair, a bedazzling politician who as Prime Minister for ten years with his energetic policies at home and abroad gave his name to an era. Like other Prime Ministers whose personality creates an aura and whose name acquires an 'ism', few people are neutral about him and his legacy, especially the Iraq War and its aftermath. Historians will linger long over the Blair years in Number 10 between 1997 and 2007, his policies, his style of government and his attempts to remake the centre-left of British politics almost from the moment he succeeded John Smith as leader of the Opposition in 1994. We're meeting in the Tony Blair Institute for Global Change in central London.

Tony, you were born in 1953 in Edinburgh. Tell me about your family.

**BLAIR**

My family was unusual in the sense my father was a foster child, who was brought up in a very poor part of Glasgow. In the 1930s he became Secretary of the Young Communists. He was virtually the only person I've ever come across who went off to serve in the war as a confirmed socialist and came out the other end as a Conservative in 1945. [*Laughs*]

**HENNESSY**

Unheard of.

**BLAIR**

Right, so. And my mother was from Irish stock, from Protestant southern Irish stock. So it was – they were both, although not originally from Scotland, brought up in Glasgow. That's where they met, that's where they married. And you know, my father was a fascinating man, a very brilliant man who would have been, I think, a very successful Conservative politician. He was due to stand for Parliament in the 1964 election, for what was a relatively safe Conservative seat and then tragically had a stroke at the age of 40 which finished his political career.

**HENNESSY**

It greatly affected you as well, didn't it?

**BLAIR**

It affected me in a number of ways, but most particularly obviously our family income then declined significantly. I learnt the vagaries of life at a pretty early stage. And you know, I was always very conscious of a certain desire to fulfil what my father had been unable to.

**HENNESSY**

You had a spell in Australia as a family, in the late '50s…

**BLAIR**

Yes, we went – Dad was a lecturer at university.

**HENNESSY**

Law lecturer?

**BLAIR**

Yes, a law lecturer, and actually knew Bob Hawke, the then future Labour Prime Minister in Australia, and he very nearly stayed actually, very nearly stayed, but in the end decided to come back to the UK. We had a spell again in Scotland as a family, and then we settled in Durham.

**HENNESSY**

How did your schooling shape you? There was the Durham chorister school first and then Fettes with the very influential, extraordinary Eric Anderson as your teacher. But do you think your schooling shaped you? Did it bring out both your gifts, your performance, your great style that you have as well, and also your rebellious streak, which I think you're quite proud of aren't you?

**BLAIR**

Well, I certainly did have a rebellious streak, particularly when I was at Fettes. But I think the most important impact is that it gave me a really good education. And one of the reasons why I've remained so passionate about the importance of education is that I don't think I was particularly naturally clever, but a decent education just opened up horizons for me and even today you think of how many millions of young children never really get the chance to think about what they could do, because they never have these horizons put before them. And the great thing about education – and you know, it was a private education, it was a very good quality education, I had remarkable teachers like Eric Anderson, someone who inspired me a lot – is you realise what you can do.

And many people go through their lives never understanding what they can achieve.

**HENNESSY**

Were you a popular boy at school?

**BLAIR**

Reasonably popular, yes, I think, on the whole.

**HENNESSY**

When did you discover the great gift you have for explanation and performance? Conversation, chat, call it what you will.

**BLAIR**

I was very keen always on acting, and I did a lot of acting at Fettes, and actually for various reasons I never continued it at Oxford. I would have liked to have done that. So I guess there was always a certain – and, you know, I was in a rock band and all that sort of stuff – so there was always a certain performer element of my character that was obvious from an early age. I think, in terms of explanation and communication, the other really influential figure on me was Alexander Irvine, who was my pupil-master.

**HENNESSY**

Better known as Derry.

**BLAIR**

Better known as Derry Irvine, who then became Lord Chancellor in my government. But he was the first person, I think, who really – I would say he was the person who taught me how to analyse and how to think in a completely different way from even anyone who had taught me in the years before. So that was a hugely important formative time, my time spent with him, because he had such an extraordinary and masterful intellect. And so I think added to the sort of, the characteristic of being prepared to go out and perform, was added that sort of lawyer's ability to analyse and get to the heart of problems and consume a lot of information and turn it into something quite quickly, which was of enormous benefit to me in later life.

### HENNESSY

That's quite an implied criticism of Oxford University, because you were three years there studying law and you had to wait till you went to Derry's chambers to learn how to analyse.

### BLAIR

Yeah, but it's entirely my fault. Because, you know, it would be... [*Laughing*] I was not always completely diligent, let us put it in that way, particularly in my second year when I was much more interested in rock music than frankly, going to lectures.

### HENNESSY

I think you told Roy Jenkins, a man you greatly admired, that you wished you'd read history at Oxford, not law. Is that right?

### BLAIR

Yes. I actually wanted to read English originally, because I was so keen on acting. But I then got in to do law and my father was a lawyer and my brother was a lawyer and, you know, law was in the family, as it were. But no, I always – I think law as an academic subject never really interested me, never excited me. I mean, law practising, by the way, did. I really enjoyed my seven years as a lawyer. But I think I would have enjoyed much more and been much better at the – if I'd studied history.

### HENNESSY

Better in what way?

### BLAIR

I think it would have – well, first of all, I would have been really passionate about the study of history in a way that frankly I wasn't about the study of law. And secondly I think a sense of history is very important to be a successful political leader.

### HENNESSY

Churchill once said to a schoolboy, 'In history lies all the secrets of statecraft.' Do you think so? Not all perhaps, but many...

### BLAIR

Yes, I think all the – I mean, some of those, well, not all, because some of those secrets are only learnt by experience. But it does help if you have an historical perspective. And, you know, despite what people often think, I did – despite reading law – I in the end and in later times studied the history of the Labour Party and the history of the country very, very deeply. But I think I would have, I'd just have enjoyed history more.

### HENNESSY

Yes. Oxford – you did have somebody who influenced you greatly, Anglican priest Peter Thomson. Tell me about him, because I think he had an acute sense of the social gospel didn't he?

### BLAIR

Yes, Peter was an extraordinary man. I mean, one of the most extraordinary people I have ever met. He was the antithesis of what you might expect a Church of England vicar to be. I mean, he was extraordinarily iconoclastic. He was a deep socialist. He was part of that, at the time, that whole movement, which was given expression in the book *Honest to God* by John Robinson, which was really about how you redefine the whole theology of Christianity and make it much more attractive to young people, because it had the idea of the divine as very much set in the human condition.

And that led a group of people, not merely to be quite distinctive in their assault on traditional Christian doctrine, but then become radical in the social activism that came from that perspective on the world. So Peter was, you know, he was a genuine revolutionary, an extraordinary character, a brilliant sportsman, an immensely charming personality. And you know, I kind of fell under his spell really, and I think my ambition in politics and my attachment to the left of politics, not the right, came really from his influence and the influence of another Australian actually, Jeff Gallop, who then went on to become premier of Western Australia.

**HENNESSY**

When did you discover – was it at Oxford? – that you had quite a deep instinct for faith? And there was a religious element in your make-up that was really quite powerful?

**BLAIR**

Yes, I came to religion and politics at the same time, and in a way through the same gateway, which was really Peter Thomson. And so the two were always connected with me, so my politics was of the more communitarian sort, and it was based on a sort of philosophical position in relation to the world rather than – even though I'd sort of toyed with Marxism, as everyone did at the time, the attraction for me was never really profound.

**HENNESSY**

What was the attraction at all, some might say?

**BLAIR**

Well the attraction – the first political book I ever read, by the way, was Isaac Deutcher's trilogy of Trotsky.

**HENNESSY**

Yes. Not many jokes in Trotsky.

**BLAIR**

No, but it was remarkable – I remember because literally I had no interest in politics at all – and I actually remember, we were playing some gig that night, me and my rock band. And I'd actually had the first volume of the Deutscher trilogy of Trotsky, lying in my room unread, that I think Jeff Gallop actually had given me. And for some bizarre reason, when I got back I picked it up and started to read it, and I literally didn't stop reading it all night. And I suddenly – it just gave me a completely, it opened a different world to me. I suddenly thought, the world's full of these extraordinary causes and injustices, and here's this guy Trotsky who was so inspired by all of this that he went out to create the Russian Revolution and change the world. And I think it was a very, very odd thing, just literally it was like a light going on. And even though, you know, over time I obviously left that side of politics behind, the notion of having a cause and a purpose and one bigger than yourself or your own ambition, and I think probably allied at the same time to coming to religious faith, that changed my life in that period.

**HENNESSY**

Would it be fair to say that you were very briefly a Trot?

**BLAIR**

Yes, in that sense I was actually. And I – [*Laughs*]

**HENNESSY**

Not many people know that, Tony.

**BLAIR**

No, no, that's, that's right. And it was reasonably brief, let's say. But I kind of really understand that politics, by the way. I mean, because I was in and around it for long enough – I mean it wasn't longer than a year probably – but in and around it long enough to understand it and then come finally to the conclusion that it wasn't right. And there was another very important moment when again – and the odd thing about my time at Oxford is that the most influential people to me were all non-British – so there was also an Indian graduate student there, Anwal Velani, I remember, who was a very, very bright guy and who had a long conversation with me, in which he said to me – and it's stuck with me all the way through my political career – he was disputing my kind of Marxist analysis and he said, 'Look, you've got to understand that the state too can become a vested interest. You know, yes, it's true that capitalism gives rise to all sorts of interests, but the state can adopt its own set of interests, and the state can run the state for those interests rather than for the people, and unless your politics takes account of that and the dangers of it, then your politics is incomplete.' And it was a very profound insight for me.

**HENNESSY**

You joined the Labour Party, I think, only when you left Oxford though, didn't you?

**BLAIR**

Well, when I was in the early '70s and when I was at university the Labour Party was regarded as a kind of anathema. These were the betrayers of socialism, these were the people who, you know, didn't really believe in the way that you should believe, and so when I left and I joined the Labour Party, I joined it very much as someone who was very critical of the Labour leadership at the time, and that it wasn't producing socialism and so on.

**HENNESSY**

Harold and Jim?

**BLAIR**

Yes, Harold Wilson and Jim Callaghan. So I mean, people forget that at that time – as of course people have been with Attlee, by the way – those on the more far-left were deeply critical and many people thought joining the Labour Party was an act of betrayal in itself.

**HENNESSY**

Of course you met Cherie in the chambers didn't you? It wasn't just Derry Irvine who shaped your life in chambers, you met Cherie. Was she influential in steering you towards more mainstream Labour politics?

**BLAIR**

Yes. The great thing about Cherie is that she's literally never changed her politics from the first time I met her. She'd complete contempt for the far left then, which was an unusual position for young people, because she'd been brought up in a working-class part of Liverpool and realised you actually needed people to govern and govern sensibly to improve people's lives. And yet, she was absolutely, you know, she would rather have given up the ghost than vote Tory. So she was a sort of mainstream Labour person then, and remained that literally all the way through. And that was influential because obviously when we started going out together she was extremely critical of what she regarded as my sort of Oxford student socialism. [*Laughing*] So she made that very clear.

**HENNESSY**

You had a stab at Parliament in the Beaconsfield by-election of '82, when Michael Foot was Leader, and the '83 election, which was disastrous for Labour – 'longest suicide note in history' manifesto, as Gerald Kaufman called it and all that – and you were elected for a Durham seat. Now, how would you depict the Tony Blair that came into the House of Commons? Where were you on your journey from, some might say, the wild left frontier to the Labour mainstream?

**BLAIR**

By the time I entered Parliament I was definitely in the Labour mainstream. I had been the Labour Party's lawyer, Michael Foot's lawyer, with Derry Irvine in the case to expel Militant.

**HENNESSY**

Yes.

**BLAIR**

So you know, I tried for about ten seats before I got Sedgefield. I mean, if I can go back a moment, standing for Beaconsfield was the thing that really set me on my way. Because even though it was a strong Conservative seat and I was fighting in the middle of the Falklands, you know, the Conservatives won a vast majority, all of which was completely expected, I made the connection with Michael Foot. Michael Foot, because frankly he'd been meeting Labour candidates of varying hues of sort of unacceptability around the country, and then suddenly he had a conversation with me and I remember talking to him all about P G Wodehouse and Lamb and the books that he'd written about literature –

**HENNESSY**

Hazlitt and so on.

**BLAIR**

Yes, and Hazlitt and so on and I think he was so bowled over by the fact he'd met someone that he could have a reasonable conversation with that he was extremely complimentary about me, and that then set me up for Sedgefield. But I had been trying for seats and failing all the time because I would do extremely well up until you then got asked the question at the time – are you in favour of expelling Militant? Because of course the Tony Benn position was, 'No, you can't expel them, you've got to defeat them politically but not organisationally,' and literally the moment you gave the wrong answer on that you could just feel a significant part of the room just moved away from you. So I was trying and failing all the time. And then I actually found a constituency in Sedgefield which had been sort of untouched by the Bennite revolution and who just – because I was the last candidate in the country to be selected, the whole selection process took three weeks just before that May '83 election and I think they just regarded me as a smart young guy that could help them.

**HENNESSY**

You rose very fast once you were in. You were in the Shadow Treasury team pretty quickly with Roy Hattersley. Roy's become critical of you in his old age, but you got on pretty famously at the time I think.

**BLAIR**

Yes, he was fabulous to work for and, I mean, for me it was just a great learning experience; learning, because I was learning about the economy through doing the Treasury brief and learning because I got to see him first-hand and, you know, could see a top politician at work.

**HENNESSY**

What did Neil Kinnock teach you – Michael Foot's successor as Leader of the Opposition?

**BLAIR**

Well, Neil taught me political courage, because you know people forget this too easily now, but he was extraordinarily courageous in the way that he took on the far left. And you know, the fact is the Labour Party needed to undergo this long process of change. And I often think the problem is that Neil just was there at the moment when the Labour Party was ready to change but not ready to change enough. And so again I learnt a lot from him and I saw what he also had to go through and the viciousness of the attacks upon him and the power of the media – which probably I became too affected by, to be blunt – but, you know, I watched what he went through and could see how incredibly destructive it was. Because at that point the media was immensely powerful in its ability to shift opinion and it was so negative on him that it really didn't matter whether what he said was sensible or not sensible by the time they'd finished with it. He literally had to stand out against, I would say, I don't know, it must have been 70 per cent of the media, 80 per cent of the time.

**HENNESSY**

We'll come back to the media in a minute. But you were a great John Smith man weren't you? Got on very well with him…

**BLAIR**

Yes, sure, because John – John of course was a close friend of Derry Irvine's, so I knew him in that connection. I'd known him before I came into Parliament. And John was just this extraordinary person, I mean a brilliant debater, I mean razor-sharp mind, absolute no-nonsense type of person, and very tough to work for because he was so demanding, but absolutely brilliant.

**HENNESSY**

Yes. The tragedy of his death in '94, and suddenly there you were, within touching distance of becoming Leader of the Opposition. Now, historians get fetishist about certain things, and you know what I'm going to ask you about, don't you, this Granita restaurant conversation with Gordon Brown. Now, have you ever read an accurate account of what went on in that restaurant? And if you haven't, tell me, give me the accurate account.

**BLAIR**

Well, the truth is it wasn't in Granita restaurant. We did have a dinner in Granita, but by then we'd already decided what we were going to do. The actual conversation I think took place in a couple of different places in Edinburgh.

**HENNESSY**

Ahead of Granita?

**BLAIR**

Yes, ahead of Granita. So –

**HENNESSY**

I think we ought to – historians need to know the location. Where were the crucial conversations?

**BLAIR**

Well, one was definitely at a friend of mine's, an old school friend of mine's house. And in fact I think both of them were at two different old school friends of mine's houses. That's if I recall it right. So we had a conversation going – I mean, it was going on all the time – about how we would resolve the question of which one went forward.

**HENNESSY**

And what was the crucial bit?

**BLAIR**

Well, the crucial bit was really –

**HENNESSY**

How did it resolve itself?

**BLAIR**

The crucial bit was who had the best chance of winning, I think, for the country.

Did you simply say, 'I have the best chance, Gordon, I have to be honest.'

**BLAIR**

More or less I did. And to be fair to him, he accepted that in the end and it was extremely difficult for him. And it's very hard to understand this properly now. I mean, we were so close, we were – we would speak to each other several times a day. So this was a very close political relationship, personal relationship. I found him, you know, he taught me an immense amount, Gordon. I mean he taught me how to make a speech, for a start. You know, I remember the very first time I had to get up and address the Labour Party conference. I was Employment spokesman, I was finally given a spot at the Labour Party conference, it was a big deal. You were going to get one of the prime spots. And I showed him my speech, which was, you know, written by a lawyer. I mean, it was a very – if I may say so – very intelligent analysis of what was wrong with Conservative employment law and how we were going to change it. [*Laughing*] But in terms of a conference speech it plainly didn't work. And he said to me, 'Oh my God, you can't say this, it's ridiculous,' and then literally sat down and wrote out the first opening lines. And I remember thinking well, he knows more about it than me so I'm just going to go and give it, and then being absolutely astonished at the extraordinary reaction I got from the conference. And after that I thought, yes, well that's obviously the way to do it.

**HENNESSY**

Let's come back to the media, because you're Leader of the Opposition at a time when John Major is having the full weight of the media thrown at him. And I always thought at that time, observing you a bit from the outside, that you and Alastair Campbell were determined that you'd never have the press doing to you what they were currently doing to John Major and had done to Neil Kinnock. And you had rebuttal schemes, you changed the nature of political communications between you, and it made you a very effective Leader of the Opposition, the most effective since Harold Wilson, I think. But wasn't there a price, Tony, in the long term? You've often talked about public trust and trust in politicians, but wasn't that the era in which the natural reaction of the public on the receiving end of political communications was, 'What really is going on, what's behind this?' The corrosion of spin and how that word took on a life of its own. And it began in many ways when you and Alastair and Peter Mandelson were making sure that your opposition leadership was not destroyed in the way that others had been, or partially destroyed. Is that fair?

**BLAIR**

I think part of it's fair and part of it's not. I think what's not fair is I think in today's world if you don't have a strong communications strategy and capability, I mean, you're finished. And that was happening as we were coming into these positions of authority, because it was clear that the way the media could drive the agenda meant that if you weren't able to protect yourself against that and turn the fire on your opponents, you were going to be savaged. And, you know, in 1992 the Conservatives did that job on Neil Kinnock. So it's not that we invented the concept of – we invented it from the Labour perspective, that's true. But the Conservative campaigns under Margaret Thatcher and indeed the 1992 [campaign] were pretty full-on brutal. And their capability was very strong. I mean, Saatchi and Saatchi, and all of that. So that bit of it, I think, is not fair. It's just that people were unused to the Labour Party having that capability. I think what is true, and I've thought a lot about this over the years, is that what we should have been doing is trying to get to a situation where the media were not so empowered, and instead what we did was empower them significantly, because we played into that – that theme or that climate that they operated in. And, you know, this is something that I think now with social media, I think it's become an even bigger problem. I mean, I think it's the central difficulty in modern politics, is how you actually communicate with people today in a situation where the media is fragmented, polarised and where social media, so far from being a discipline on conventional media, has actually just put booster rockets on all the worst aspects of the conventional media. And this is, I think, a big problem today, I think it's a far bigger problem than me or what happened to us or what happens in Britain, it's a western political phenomenon that I think is really, really serious and dangerous actually. But we back then were just determined on one thing: we weren't going to be kicked around in the way that, frankly, Neil and his team had been.

**HENNESSY**

It was very interesting the way you operated as Leader of the Opposition. A small group of you transformed the Labour Party from within. And as many saw it, when you went into government it was rather like Lenin's sealed train; it was still a small group of you who were going to transform British government from within as you already had the Labour Party. And it's interesting now when people look back – for example, recently was declassified a very personal note [by] Richard Wilson, the Cabinet Secretary, sent to you about your use of power, in which he said you choose not to use the levers of government, you don't use the machine, and he advised against all of that. So historians again will linger long on that style of government, the command style. I think it was Jonathan Powell, wasn't it, who said that it's got to be a Napoleonic system of government and therefore he was called Napoleon ever after in Whitehall, if I remember, rightly or wrongly. [*Blair laughs*] But the point is, Tony, that some people think that the model that was so successful and transforming within the Labour Party when you were Leader of the Opposition, it didn't fit the naturally collective nature of government, the sheer weight of government once you're Prime Minister.

## BLAIR

Well, this is something, Peter, you're an expert on, so I will choose my words carefully. And it's a debate I have with myself even about this. I do think that there was a sense when we came into government that we carried on in the same mode that we had been in opposition. But I think the problem with that was more that we carried on campaigning and it was only after a time I realised – I remember when somebody said to me, 'Look, you've got to go out and make another speech on the Health Service,' and I said, 'I don't want to make another speech on the Health Service, or indeed on anything, I actually want to get something *done* in the Health Service.' So I think that was more of our – you know, we came in as this group of people that had changed the Labour Party and up-ended British politics and so for the first period I think, yes, we governed more in that mode. As time went on though, I think we came to a more measured position. I mean, I do think there was a genuine problem with the way the bureaucracy in government operated. What I learned about bureaucracy is that it's great at managing things but not great at changing things. If you had a crisis, there was nothing better than that British system. It kicked in, it operated to a high degree of quality, and on numerous occasions I had cause to be really thankful to it. But when it came to how do you do health service reform or education reform, or I remember in the early battles I had on reforming asylum and immigration policy, I found it frankly just unresponsive. I remember one of my very early presentations that I got in Downing Street was when they came in to give me a presentation on crime, and the system basically said, 'Look, when unemployment goes up crime goes up.' Which is the usual thing. So I said, 'Well, unemployment's falling.' And they said, 'Yes, but when unemployment falls then people are more wealthy, they've got more consumer goods and there's more to steal.' So, I said, ' So basically crime just carries on going up.' And they said, 'Well, more or less.' But I always say this about *Yes, Prime Minister*, it is part documentary. I mean, the system can be like that. So I don't accept that we were wrong to bring in special advisers and to make the system work differently, and this was a constant debate between myself and people like Richard Wilson. What I do accept is that you can get – but I think we did, by the way, in our last… certainly in my last six, seven years, we were operating in this way – you can get to a much more balanced perspective, where you're liberating those people within the bureaucracy who actually do want to make change and who are enthusiastic behind an agenda of change. But I just say this, because I say this to governments around the world, you should always treat the bureaucracy with respect, you should recognise what it can do, but if you become a prisoner of it, believe me, you'll achieve nothing, you'll just go round in circles. So it's a longer debate to have and it's a very important debate to have, because I think re-inventing government has fallen off the political agenda in recent times, and it really shouldn't because today, especially with changes in technology, this whole concept of how government itself works is in my view fundamentally important. But, as I say, I love the integrity of the Civil Service and in a crisis it was brilliant. But when it came to trying to make change – I'm being very honest here – I found it inadequate.

**HENNESSY**

Where it did work very well, I think, is the constitutional revolution. I think that is the right word, which the formidable Derry Irvine drove through for you very quickly: devolution to Scotland and Wales – we'll come to Northern Ireland in a minute, because it's very special; Freedom of Information, about which you had some retrospective doubts –

**BLAIR**

Yes –

**HENNESSY**

– Human Rights Act incorporation. By any criteria, that was an extraordinary change in UK politics, and the architectonics of the state, and it was done very quickly. So the machine seemed to work for you there, very well indeed.

**BLAIR**

Yes, it did, but it did only because, one, we had someone of the intellectual quality and drive of Derry Irvine making it happen. But secondly because, frankly, we were doing things politically that were not particularly welcomed by the bureaucracy. So, for example, we made sure that on devolution we had referendums in place in Scotland and Wales that overcame the opposition in the House of Lords and elsewhere to devolution. Northern Ireland, I have to say though, the Whitehall machine was superb all the way throughout. And that's what I mean, if you've got a specific problem, I think Whitehall is – I mean the British system by the way, I've seen systems all round the world now, the British system is up there with the top of the top globally, there's no doubt about that at all. I just think there's a general point about bureaucracy.

**HENNESSY**

I said in my intro that you were a controversial politician, but the one area where I think there is a consensus is that your handling of Northern Ireland was crucial, that only a Prime Minister could have done that. And the way you picked up the hand that John Major passed onto you – because they'd done a lot of the preparatory work, back-channel stuff and all that – really did justify what your critics criticised you for in other areas. That prime ministerial government could only have done it, to use the shorthand.

**BLAIR**

Yes, I think it could only be driven from the very top in the government, from the Prime Minister. Also I sometimes think that it was only in that first flush of assuming power, with all the kind of ambition and hope that comes with that, that I would have tried anything as seemingly impossible as make peace in Northern Ireland. Because when we came to power the peace process was in embryo form – had broken down. And actually shortly after – I think my first days in office – there was the murder of policemen in Northern Ireland and the ceasefire had finished and so on. I think if I'd tried – if someone had suggested doing that in year seven or eight of the government, I would have said, 'Well, that's just too impossibly ambitious, I've got more experience now and I know that that sort of thing can't be done.' Whereas then we just, literally – it was a confluence of events and circumstance and leadership, by the way, from people in Northern Ireland that gave us the ability to do it.

#### HENNESSY

Was there a particular moment when you thought – to use a phrase Roy Jenkins liked – that there might be a favourable curve through all this, that you just might be able to cut through to get the deal that you did get?

#### BLAIR

Yes, we thought it was possible to do when we turned up in Northern Ireland in April 1998. We thought that favourable curve was there. But then I have to say, in the first day of negotiation it seemed to have disappeared. And we just slogged it out over the course of three or four days. And, I remember, we got about a couple of hours' sleep every night and we were just negotiating and negotiating. One of the strange things about it that just shows you how weird politics can be sometimes is that what became the power-sharing arrangement between the DUP and Sinn Fein – you often forget this, the DUP were protesting the Good Friday Agreement and Sinn Fein never actually signed it. But it set in train the process. But then it took frankly another nine years to deliver it properly.

**HENNESSY**

And of course however long your premiership is studied, which will be a very long time indeed, the other great area of concentration will be Iraq and the world after 2001. Tony, when things go wrong for people I sometimes think that we do a kind of audit in our own head first, there's an inquest in our own head long before – if you're in public life – there's an inquiry. Did you 'Chilcot' yourself in your own mind before Sir John and his colleagues were commissioned to do the big inquiry?

**BLAIR**

Yes, of course. All the time. And it would be very odd if you didn't do that. And you know, I always say to people about this that the mistakes that we made I have owned up to on many occasions and own the responsibility for those. Some of the intelligence turned out to be faulty. And in the aftermath there was, I think, an absence of the knowledge that we needed to have about what would happen once you removed the dictatorship. And this is the lesson that we've learnt now from the Arab Spring again, and we've learned in Libya and in Syria and so on. So yes, of course, that critique has been there all the time. I mean, at the same time obviously, the thing that is I think difficult for people to accept is that I haven't changed my view that it was better that we removed him than not.

**HENNESSY**

Saddam, yes.

**BLAIR**

Yes.

**HENNESSY**

When you 'Chilcotted' yourself, as it were, which areas of the whole story were you hardest upon yourself about, toughest on yourself?

**BLAIR**

Not understanding the depth of the problem within the world of Islam and the Middle East. In other words not understanding that even though rationally, as indeed we had done in a sense in the Kosovo conflict, if you remove the dictator you give people a proper democratic process, you give them unlimited funds to rebuild the country, rationally that should take care of the problem and the country can build itself. But it was not understanding the deep forces at play in the region and in the broader world of Islam that meant that that was not going to happen, that there would be groups of people – in this case Iran on the one side, Al-Qaeda and others on the other – who were going to subvert that entire process. And that's why it's commonly said nowadays in the West, well look, it's better to leave the dictatorships in place. Now what I would say to that is that the Arab Spring shows you that's not going to happen in any event. But that is the – it's realising that once that oppressive hand was removed, all those forces that had been suppressed by it were going to come out and disrupt. And that was the gap of understanding.

**HENNESSY**

I remember talking to somebody very close in with you on all this, when it was quite plain it was going wrong, the aftermath. And I said, 'If I'm still breathing in 2050 and have PhD students what will they need to know about this that isn't obvious to them?' And he said, 'If we were going to make an example of one third-world WMD proliferator it had to be Saddam, because he had so little left.' Do you recognise that analysis?

**BLAIR**

Well, I recognise the analysis that since he was the only person who'd actually used them we thought that he was the person to make an example of. And, you know, look, what happens – obviously I can talk about this for a very long time and have on many occasions. Now people tend to think, 'Well was the whole thing just sort of made up about Saddam and WMD?' But we forget that he used those not merely against his own people but in the Iran–Iraq War in the '80s when, after all, there were somewhere in the region of a million casualties in that – significant numbers of whom came through the use by Iraq of chemical weapons – and actually it was out of that that Iran's nuclear programme was born. So I think that's – the reason was the history. I don't think it was because he had so little of it, it's because he actually used it and, you know, look, I always say to people if you want to know whether there was a deception or not, the intelligence reports that I received you can go and read them online, so you can see what I was receiving.

**HENNESSY**

Do you think, as some still do, that he had a little bit of it left and he'd spirited it over the border into Syria so that it wouldn't be found by the weapons inspectors?

**BLAIR**

I don't know because it's a mystery, because the one thing is we know he had them because he used them and we know we haven't found them, so that's – you can't dispute that – and certainly some of the intelligence obviously turned out to be wrong. And again, there's been a whole lot of information on that. But I think the central thing for me if you take in the broad perspective of history – because we have to work out and see what happens and whether Iraq can stabilise and give its people the future that I think undoubtedly the people actually want there. But the thing – because I spend so much time in the Middle East now, I mean I'm there twice a month and have been now for almost ten years – this is the origins of the problems of terrorism and extremism. There is a problem with the politicisation of Islam by a group of people who have turned it into a totalitarian ideology of which its most extreme product is ISIS and these groups, but whose support for that ideology goes out I'm afraid deeper and wider than that. I mean that is now how I see the region, and actually, bizarrely given everything that's happening there, I think there are real signs that in the region there is a coming together of the modernising forces within Islam who in the end will be the people – with us in alliance with them – who will sort this out.

**HENNESSY**

There's a big hope for the future. Looking back through the Chilcot Report I was very struck by the Crawford meeting you had with President Bush in April 2002 on his ranch – what I would call the Crawford Criteria. And you worked out between you how you would handle it: the UN inspectors needed to be given every chance of success; the United States should take the multilateral route, which would be done within the framework of international law; there should be a blueprint ready for post-attack Iraq; that action should enhance rather than diminish regional stability. Now those tests you set for yourselves, those are the ones that history has been very hard on you so far – contemporary history – because in many ways you can argue all sorts of things about the legal opinion, whether you needed specific authorisation from the Security Council or not, but many people thought you did, certainly in Whitehall and elsewhere. And when you applied the Crawford Criteria that you and President Bush set for yourselves, albeit in private, because we only knew what they were when Chilcot reported, it's a tough call Tony to justify that. You didn't meet your own requirements, did you?

**BLAIR**

Well I would say we met our requirements in terms of going down the multilateral route, because we went to the UN and we got a further resolution. What I can't argue obviously is that you ended up with regional stability. On the other hand I think – and you know this is a much longer conversation, which I always say to people I'm very, very happy to have because I have thought about this and I study it a lot, and you know, you can come to this discussion with whatever preconceptions you want, but I really have thought about this a lot – in my view, the question in the end is, because I can argue about each one of these criteria, the question in the end is, you know, was it a mistake to remove him or not? That is the ultimate question. And my answer to that, and I would reference the state of Syria today, is that it's actually better to have these dictators out of power than in power. But that's a debate that's obviously going to be strongly contested. I think what is not contestable though is either that we underestimated the problems that we were going to encounter – and that is the thing that I reproach myself for – and these problems, being so deep, are going to take a long time to work through. But I would argue it's strongly in our interests as the West to be in alliance with those modernising forces within Islam and resolving them, because otherwise the problems will come back on our own doorstep. And what you can see from the terrorism today – here and around the world – is that this is attacking countries some of whom supported Iraq, some of whom didn't, some of whom have never been near any western military intervention. You know, you see what's going on in the Philippines today, which is a dispute going back 30 years. And I think my understanding of what is driving all this is much greater, and I think in the end when history finally comes to judge all of this, they'll look at the whole issues to do with Iraq in that context.

**HENNESSY**

There's one very powerful piece of paper in the Chilcot Report which is you to George W Bush on 28 July 2002: 'I will be with you whatever.' That's the bit that's clung to the memory of people who've read Chilcot, the summary and so on, and the newspaper accounts. And I think, Tony, it relates to that bit of Crawford, the multilateral route, the UN route, because it implies that even if you didn't get a specific UN resolution authorising force – which is what you were seeking, and which Lord Goldsmith said, in one of his earlier opinions, that you really needed to have (I'm paraphrasing here) the feeling was that whatever the circumstance, even if there were no other allies, you would be with George Bush, that the post 9/11 world meant that you would be beside him. And that conditions, I think, the way your conduct of the war, and the run up to the war, and the aftermath of the war is seen. Do you think that's fair?

**BLAIR**

Yes – no, I think people do see it in that way. I mean obviously if we hadn't gone down the UN route, we couldn't really have been with the US in those terms. It would just not have been possible. But, you know, I completely aver that I was – I took a decision after 9/11 that we should be shoulder-to-shoulder with America in dealing with this. I thought it absolutely essential. I still think this alliance with America is fundamentally important to our security. I don't think we would ever have got the Americans to do the things that they did post-9/11, which includes far more than simply Iraq, unless we had been alongside them in that way. But that's a decision many people would disagree with. But no, I was absolutely clear that the attack of 9/11 changed our whole security perspective. It was an attack not just on America but on our world and our values and that we had to be with them. And, you know we forget this now, but we formed an alliance which had over a half the European Union in it with us, as well as Japan and Australia and other key allies. But I don't think it would have been as easy to have assembled that alliance if Britain hadn't been very strong with America. And, you know, that relationship with America was such that there was no big decision that America took in those years that didn't have British input. And when it came for example to the G7 summit in Gleneagles in 2005 I don't think we would ever have got the US to what was a revolutionary package in respect of Africa and debt and so on and aid if we hadn't been their strong ally. So, you know, this is really – this is where politics comes to a set of decisions that in the end I think it's the responsibility of the Leader to take. Now I'm not saying those decisions are right, but I think you've got to take them. And I was very clear in my own mind after 9/11 it was essential that we bonded with America in a deep way and historians will argue whether that was right or wrong, but it's not something I look back on and think, 'We shouldn't have done that.'

### HENNESSY

Can I ask you about another element of the special relationship with the United States – the nuclear? In your memoir, it's very interesting when you're talking about another set of boats to carry the Trident Missiles into the 2050s, a decision you took to Cabinet in 2006, and you said, 'I did think seriously and talked to Gordon Brown about it whether this might be the moment to stop, but we decided it wasn't.' Am I right in thinking you've toughened up your view a bit? That you wouldn't quite be – there's a slight element of ambiguity when you were Prime Minister and took that decision and steered the Cabinet through it. Have you hardened your view on that since, given the world has changed?

### BLAIR

Possibly a little, but I still think there's a case for saying: 'Don't have an independent nuclear deterrent, you just come under the American umbrella.' But that's the alternative by the way. You know, you wouldn't get rid of Trident and then have no form of protection. It just means you won't have an independent form of protection. No, I think you can still make a case for that but I think on balance I still believe it's right to renew Trident.

### HENNESSY

How did you feel early in your premiership when you had to sign those last resort letters and put your instructions for retaliation or not from beyond the grave if you were wiped out? It must be the most extraordinary thing to have to do. It's fallen to very few people.

**BLAIR**

It is, but it's slightly surreal at the same time. I mean, I guess – and at that particular time I thought it was a very, very remote contingency. And also, how on earth do you know, really?

**HENNESSY**

How on earth do you know what?

**BLAIR**

Well, how on earth do you know what the right thing to do is in those circumstances? It's extremely difficult, so you tend to follow advice and precedent, which is what I did.

**HENNESSY**

Did you talk to Jim Callaghan about it, as a former Prime Minister who'd had to do it?

**BLAIR**

You know, I have a vague recollection that I did, but I certainly took a lot of advice from the senior Civil Service and the people who, frankly, at that point knew a lot more about this than me.

**HENNESSY**

Yes. The European question runs right through your premiership as it runs through everybody's; it's a great destabiliser of British politics, as we've seen. Do you regret now that you didn't take on your Chancellor on the question of the Euro? Could you have taken him on, because there was a kind of division of labour in your government which is very interesting, which you've touched on briefly but not deeply?

**BLAIR**

No. I mean, at the very beginning, by the way, if anything I was somewhat more reluctant on the Euro, but people always thought that the economic tests that we devised were really just a sort of cover for essentially a political decision. And I was always – I remember writing this in a note to my team – politically, I've always been in favour of Britain integrating with the mainstream of Europe. And politically I always thought it was important if we could that we became part of the single currency, because this also then would completely consolidate our ability to influence Europe and to take it in the directions that we wanted. But the economic tests were real, for him and for me. So there was a disagreement between us sometimes about what we emphasised. So I would say, 'No it's important that we prepare to have the possibility of joining,' and Gordon would perfectly understandably say, 'Well, that's going to give people a sense you really are going to do this thing.' But actually we were in agreement on the economic conditions. And the truth of the matter is, as I used to say to people, it may be a project driven by politics but it's expressed in the economics, so if the economics aren't right then this is going to be dangerous. And the reality was and is that the convergence that is necessary was not there. And the reason why the Euro and the single currency has got so many problems is precisely because these countries came together in the Euro – inspired by politics – when their economies weren't really ready to be pulled together in this way. And the whole of the Eurozone crisis is really, in my view, a kind of balance of payments crisis that comes about because countries like Italy got a vast reduction in interest rates without really doing anything other than joining the single currency, and countries like Germany got the advantage of a much more competitive exchange rate in the Euro than in the Deutschmark. So this is for me – this was always for me a decision that had to be economic as well as political and in that sense we were agreed.

## HENNESSY

Can we come back to the other great disturber of our times which is the fissile nature of British politics, I suppose. Are you really serious about helping remake the centre-left in the UK? You've said some interesting things. What are you going to do about it?

## BLAIR

I am really serious about remaking the centre-left in British politics. I think there's an urgent need for progressive politics to recapture its traction – modern progressive politics. What I can do about it is, what we will do within the Institute is to try to shape a policy agenda for the future. Because the truth is if the centre wants to regain its position, it's got to be the place of change. Post-financial crisis, post-9/11, people want change. And the stresses of globalisation – culture and economic – are severe. But the change has got to be change that's sensible and modern, and the truth is this populism of left and right, where the right essentially blame the immigrants and the left go anti-business, I mean this will not produce solutions. This is riding the anger, not providing the answers. So I am unapologetic, even though it looks like the centre has been marginalised in British politics today, that it is the right solution and I still think even after this election there are millions of disenfranchised people.

## HENNESSY

Tony, how would you like to be remembered?

## BLAIR

Don't know – always never know how to answer that question. [*Laughs*]

## HENNESSY

How do you think you'll be remembered?

**BLAIR**

Well, and I don't know how to answer that one either [*Hennessy laughs*] because I think – I'm a very not retrospective person. I mean, I do think a lot about things in government, but I only think about them in terms of where the future lies. So I really don't know, and if you press me hard on it you'll just get a kind of politician's answer.

**HENNESSY**

I won't press you hard then.

**BLAIR**

Yes, right. There's no point. [*Laughing*]

**HENNESSY**

But I will press you hard on this one. If I could give you one last reform, if I could wave a magic wand for you, what would it be?

**BLAIR**

That I'm very clear about. I think there is in all western societies there is a problem with a group of people right down at the bottom of the heap that get excluded from society's mainstream, that really go generation-to-generation without hope or opportunity, and I think you require a radically different set of measures around intervention and support that deal with those people. And in our last couple of years before I left office we started to work on this, but after that the impetus behind it seemed to drain away politically, but I still think this a major, major problem. It's not maybe a huge number of people. They're people who probably don't even vote, so they've got no real political voice, but their existence and this propagation generation-to-generation, I think is a severe problem for them and for the country.

**HENNESSY**

Tony Blair, thank you very much indeed.

**BLAIR**

Thank you.

# William Hague
# (Lord Hague of Richmond)

Series 5, Episode 2, first broadcast 17 August 2017

**Born** 26 March 1961; **Educated** Wath Comprehensive School; Magdalen College, Oxford; Institut Européen d'Administration des Affaires

MP (Conservative) Richmond 1989–2015

Parliamentary Under-Secretary, Department of Social Security, 1993–94; Minister of State, Department of Social Security, 1994–95; Secretary of State for Wales, 1995–97; Leader of the Conservative Party and Leader of the Opposition, 1997–2001; Foreign Secretary and First Secretary of State, 2010–14; First Secretary of State and Leader of the House of Commons, 2014–15

### HENNESSY

With me today is William Hague, Lord Hague of Richmond, former Leader of the Conservative Party and Foreign Secretary for most of the 2010–2015 Coalition government. He first came to fame aged 16, with a boy-wonder performance at the 1977 Conservative Party conference, calling for the old political establishments to make way for the freedom-loving rising generation, all delivered in a voice and with a maturity older than his years, and with that perfect timing which is one of his oratorical hallmarks. He was a Cabinet Minister at 34, party Leader at 36, and has now, at 56, morphed into an elder statesman of his party and an accomplished political biographer. He was probably the best House of Commons orator of his generation, and it's now the House of Lords that relishes the Hague performances, which have kept their old wit and bite. William, welcome.

**HAGUE**

Thank you.

**HENNESSY**

You were born in Rotherham in March 1961. What kind of family was yours?

**HAGUE**

Well, a very conservative family in terms of values. Not political in the sense of taking part in elections or political parties, but certainly one with conservative attitudes, in a very industrial, Labour-dominated area. It was a striking thing to me that I grew up in the constituency which then had the biggest Labour majority in the country.

**HENNESSY**

32,000 I think.

**HAGUE**

32,000. And I was quite proud, it was a badge of honour, you know, for a Young Conservative that it was *that* difficult where I lived. It was overwhelmingly the other way.

**HENNESSY**

Now, the old Conservative Party over 100 years ago relied on what used to be called the 'Beerage', the great brewers. But you come from the pop, the soft drinks tradition.

**HAGUE**

Yes, and not even the great ones, really. This was a small business. My great-great-great-grandfather, if I've got that right, was a miner who started making lemonade in 1870. And the family business carried right on through to 1990, when my father retired and I'd clearly gone into the House of Commons by then. And it was a manufacturer of soft drinks, a wholesaler of beers and wines and spirits. So I was brought up really around the pubs and clubs of Rotherham and Barnsley, that was the clientele of our business.

**HENNESSY**

Some say that you've got a touch of the northern clubs in a way, because you're very funny and you've got this great sense of timing which I was mentioning a moment ago. Do you think you picked up some of that from doing the clubs' deliveries?

**HAGUE**

Well, maybe. I mean, there are a lot of highly amusing people among all these, you know. These were really the miners and steelworkers' clubs. And I used to go around – that was my vacation job from when I was 15 years old, I used to work on the delivery lorries. That's the first time I got fit, actually, by delivering big kegs of beer to these places, and then I used to sit and talk to them. So I – I don't know if – I think these sorts of things are partly one's natural aptitude and then partly education. I was very fortunate to go to a school – Wath Comprehensive School – where debating, acting, speaking was highly encouraged. I think I must have given some speech or performance every week from when I was 13 years old. So it possibly came from that sort of experience in education as well.

**HENNESSY**

I noticed in your dedication in your Pitt biography that it's to your mum and dad for teaching you a reverence for books. So they were obviously quite a formative influence on the scholarship as well.

### HAGUE

Yes, and I'm one of those people who was the first in my family ever to go to university, though that's not unusual for somebody of my age. But although that was true, my mother read books at a terrific rate, my late mother. And she would take me every week to the library in our village to get two or three more books for me to read that week. And my father, who was a great devotee of American history, would always be there reading about one American President or another. So I did grow up surrounded by books and learning, not in an academic way, but that was the atmosphere in our house.

### HENNESSY

Having three elder sisters myself, I always think it's sort of winning the lottery in life if you have three older sisters, did you think that? Were they jolly?

### HAGUE

Well, I didn't think so at the time. But I do now. I'm deeply fond of my sisters. I suppose I was then, but there was a bit of rivalry. And they're significantly older than me. I was seven years younger than my youngest sister, you see. So I was a bit separate from them.

### HENNESSY

I think one of them – was it Veronica? – used to write to you as 'Dear Tory pig.'

### HAGUE

Yes. They all left home at 16–17 years old and went into their careers, so there was a lively correspondence then between me, the ten year old, and all my sisters scattered around the country or the world, and yeah they made relentless fun of me starting to be interested in politics. [*Laughing*] 'Dear Tory pig' was a regular introduction to sisterly love through the letters.

**HENNESSY**

Were they proud of you when you made that stellar opening in your political life at the party conference in '77 at the age of 16? I mean, it was an amazing thing. I can remember it to this day.

**HAGUE**

They were I think, they were proud of me. They all took [it] in their stride. You know, my sisters saw it as their job to bring me straight back down to earth; we're that sort of family. I didn't really know what a big thing I was doing, I just – I went to the conference, I decided I ought to say something and I put in a slip of paper saying I wanted to and suddenly there I was in front of thousands of delegates and a live television audience. It just came about in a very straightforward way. But after that, you know, *News at Ten* followed me for my first day back at school, a crowd of hundreds of pupils at school following me around. And I was offered newspaper columns and so on. It was my mother who said, 'Right, now you've had a few days of this, you're going back to your A Levels and back to normality. And okay, you might become a politician one day, but not now.'

**HENNESSY**

That's a good mum. I remember when you got the Longman History Today book prize for your biographies of Wilberforce and Pitt, you recalled that moment, and you amazed your listeners – of whom I was one – by saying you didn't recall it with particular pleasure. Can you remind me why?

**HAGUE**

Well, I think this was when I was explaining that having made the infamous – the, speech I was taken – the boy wonder, the wonder kid, the ways the media were describing me – straight to see Margaret Thatcher. And the first thing she said to the media was, 'We may be standing here with another young Mr Pitt.' Now, I had no idea I was the future biographer of Pitt, and indeed I had only the haziest idea who Mr Pitt might be. So my first reaction was 'What is she talking about?' And the second thing she said, which was much more irritating, was, 'You must go and telephone your mother.' Now, of course, I would want to telephone my mother, but being instructed by the Leader of the Opposition in front of the world's media to telephone your mother when you're a teenager is not really, you know, that's not a very comfortable situation. So it wasn't a great first encounter with Margaret Thatcher.

**HENNESSY**

There's a danger, William, I think, that when your biographer gets to work on you, as it were, he or she will be so carried away with the politics side of your adolescence and your formation they'll forget the other bit of the adolescence. Now, you're a Meat Loaf man aren't you?

**HAGUE**

Yes, I am. Yes, absolutely. I've just been to see the *Bat Out of Hell* musical that is on in London at the moment.

**HENNESSY**

So what was it about Meat Loaf? With whom I'm not exactly familiar, I have to admit.

**HAGUE**

I can tell. [*Laughing*] Well, I didn't have a very developed musical taste myself at that time. That really followed from the age of 40, when I learnt to play the piano. The thing I started on the day I resigned as Leader of the Opposition in 2001 was learning to play the piano. I did have some taste for very lively, striking music before that, perhaps because I wasn't familiar with much other music. And I'm colour blind, and Ffion, my wife, always remarks on how I like lurid, very brightly coloured paintings. So I think it was the same sort of thing. I was a bit tone deaf. But once I became 40 and learnt to play the piano, which I was mathematically attracted to, then my musical taste really changed and I became a great fan of Bach and Chopin and Beethoven and played some of those.

**HENNESSY**

[*overlap*] And jazz too.

**HAGUE**

And jazz, which is harder to play.

**HENNESSY**

Yes.

**HAGUE**

From then on I could be found occasionally, once I was released from party leadership, late at night in the jazz bars of central London, sitting behind the piano whenever I could so I could really see a pianist's fingers at work and witness their extraordinary talent.

**HENNESSY**

Now, Oxford must have been fascinating for you. Well, it's fascinating for anybody really when they go to university. But to be the first from the family and to do the classic PPE and all the rest of it, and to be active in the Union... it was, in many ways, it was an adventure playground just ready for you wasn't it, Oxford?

**HAGUE**

Oh, it was, it was wonderful. And I could really not only do the academic side of studying politics, which I did in a very practical way. I didn't want to study philosophy – I soon dropped that part of it. I wanted to know about elections and the machinery of government, and economics insofar as it would be useful to a politician. You know, I was there with a purpose. But I not only did that, I also took part in as many elections as possible. I ran for office in the Union and the university Conservative Association, eventually became president of both of them, and I feel I learnt an enormous amount from that, that no-holds-barred student politics. You know, student politics is rougher than Westminster politics. There's far more skulduggery than in Westminster.

#### HENNESSY

What gifts did you discover in yourself when it came to the roughhouse of politics at Oxford?

#### HAGUE

Well –

#### HENNESSY

Are you not as nice as you look, William?

#### HAGUE

[Laughs] Actually one of the lessons was that 98 per cent of the time you don't need to be a plotter, most of what you need to do in politics is having good relations with – in a perfectly normal, civilised way – with as many people as possible. But then you do need 2 per cent of ruthlessness at crucial moments. You know, you do need to know when you need to remove someone from your team, from your Shadow Cabinet or Cabinet eventually, for the collective good. Or when you've got somebody who is about to do something to you and you need to act first.

#### HENNESSY

Why did you become a management consultant straight away?

#### HAGUE

Well, I – went at the very beginning after leaving Oxford, to Shell.

I realised then that actually what I ought to be doing was joining a company where I would really learn as much as possible about business and the economy. So I went to McKinsey, and found that was a tremendous crash course in business. And I went to do an MBA, a second degree at the European Business School in Fontainebleau. And I enjoyed the great variety and the very hard work. This was the sort of job where you work late at night, sometimes all night, to complete a key report. And I worked in brewing and banking and retailing and a great variety of industries and I enjoyed that. And for me it just meant that whenever I've stepped out of the political front line, as I have done twice, I then have work I can do in the private sector. And that's why I say to young people, make sure you have your MBA or you're a lawyer or you're whatever you may be. Many different things. You have to have that alternative. Politics is a really unpredictable profession.

**HAGUE**

And you fought a very tough seat, I think the seat of your birth place really, Wentworth, didn't you, twice?

**HAGUE**

Yes, which is part of Rotherham, one of the Rotherham constituencies. The Wentworth seat, a very safe Labour seat. And of course my game plan then was, after another Parliament, to try to get a seat where a Conservative could win, unlike part of Rotherham. But in fact a year and a half after that a by-election came up in North Yorkshire, not too far away, and I found that irresistible. So I left McKinsey earlier than I had really planned, and at the age of 27 found myself in Parliament.

**HENNESSY**

It was 1989 wasn't it?

**HAGUE**

It was 1989. And I won the last by-election that the Conservative Party won at all for eight years.

**HENNESSY**

Yes.

**HAGUE**

In fact, the next time we won a by-election I was the Leader, it was such a long gap. So I feel I scrambled over the drawbridge just before it slammed shut on the Conservative government then, which was entering a period of great unpopularity. And so what I witnessed in my first year in Parliament was the last year of Margaret Thatcher. The crises of –

**HENNESSY**

The *Götterdämmerung.*

**HAGUE**

Yes. The resignations of Nigel Lawson and Geoffrey Howe, a long-standing government falling apart.

**HENNESSY**

And the poll tax and all that.

**HAGUE**

And all of that. Yes. Which brought her down.

**HENNESSY**

Now, why did you go for John Major in 1990? Because Michael Heseltine and Douglas Hurd, in their different ways, were formidable contenders.

### HAGUE

I'd got to know John Major because I'd become PPS to Norman Lamont, who was Chief Secretary to the Treasury. John Major was Chancellor. So it was the Treasury team, really, gathered around John Major. So there was already a personal connection with him but I also thought he was the best candidate to hold the Conservative Party together at a difficult time. Divisions on Europe were widening. So I had no hesitation supporting John Major, and no regrets about doing that, he did very well to go on to win the '92 election and he introduced me to government and speedily promoted me through the ranks in the 1990s.

### HENNESSY

And you were the youngest Cabinet minister since Harold Wilson, I think – thirty-four when you took over the Welsh Office in '95?

### HAGUE

Yes. And I was very surprised to be Secretary of State for Wales. I didn't know Wales very well. But he [John Major] gave me a very clear instruction, he said, 'I want you to take Wales to your heart.' And I did. Within –

### HENNESSY

Literally.

### HAGUE

– 18 months I was engaged to my Welsh private secretary and I did take it to my heart and today my main home is in Wales, you know, so it had a very big lifelong effect on me, appointing me Secretary of State for Wales. Hopefully it did a bit of good for Wales as well.

### HENNESSY

Is it true that your wife, Ffion, one of her early tasks, because she's a

Welsh speaker, was to make sure you could sing the Welsh national anthem properly the way your predecessor, John Redwood, had been a bit challenged in the national anthem stakes hadn't he?

### HAGUE

Yes, he, poor man, has been labelled with that as much as I have with the teenage speech. And of course it meant that whoever replaced him, that the Welsh media then immediately had to find out and publicise if the new Secretary of State could sing the national anthem. And it's quite difficult when you don't know what any of the words mean, to begin with. But it's true, although it sounds an incredibly soppily romantic thing. Ffion and I sat on a churchyard wall on a hill in North Wales through one summer's evening and she taught me how to sing the Welsh national anthem. And the next day I was bathed in TV lights at a major event while I sang lustily the Welsh national anthem, proving that, you know, this Secretary of State was different. That was the test I had to pass. It's amazing what you have to do in politics.

### HENNESSY

A marriage made in song, it's quite wonderful.

### HAGUE

A marriage made in song, as is appropriate to Wales.

### HENNESSY

It was a mystery to me at the time, if I can be honest, and to many others, why you went for the leadership in '97, because I think you were supporting Michael Howard originally. So why did you cease to support Michael Howard and go for it yourself? Because the Blair ascendancy was – you didn't have to be that subtle a political analyst to know that the weather was going his way, at least for a good while. And I know you had lots of years on your side, but it was going to be an absolute torment, wasn't it, to be Leader of the

Opposition at that point? But you did it. First of all, why did you not carry on with Michael Howard, as it were?

**HAGUE**

Well, there's a very clear reason for that. My inclinations were not to stand myself, and I thought, if we can get a, you know, a ticket together with Michael Howard... And we discussed that and then I went back to my team, the people, the MPs who were encouraging me to stand, and I said, 'I've decided to support Michael Howard. So we'll all join together with his team.' And they said, 'Well, that's very disappointing; we want you to be the Leader. You can support Michael Howard, we're all going off to support different people.' It became clear to me within a couple of hours that the Howard-Hague ticket wouldn't necessarily win, whereas actually I could win myself. Funnily enough we never shook hands on it. And it's one of those funny little things; had we shaken hands on it, I wouldn't have changed my mind. It's a little lesson in life: when you've agreed something with someone, shake hands on it, it might mean something significant to them.

**HENNESSY**

Fascinating. Yes.

**HAGUE**

And I think it was still right for me to become the Leader then, even though it was this then very difficult experience and as it turned out impossible to defeat Tony Blair in the election four years later. And I think all of the other candidates would have had a much harder job keeping the Conservative Party intact through that period than I had. I feel I did the night shift in leading the Conservative Party. But somebody had to do it. And it got it out of the system for me, you know. The experience of being Leader of the party at a young age, for four years, fighting an election, absolutely got that out of the system for me. I had no remaining ambition to be Prime Minister. And so I stepped back in 2001 from the frontline of politics to enjoy and develop other skills and passions. And I thought, well, I'll only go back if I feel that I can do it on a different basis. I'll go back into the frontline without any ambition to be Prime Minister, and that will actually allow me to be quite strong in politics. And to leave again whenever I want to. And that was the basis on which I went back when David Cameron asked me to become the Shadow Foreign Secretary in 2005.

**HENNESSY**

The bit as Leader of the Opposition that you seemed to enjoy most was Prime Minister's Questions, because you had a capacity to deflate. Again, it's what I would call your northern music hall turn side. And the one I remember very early on, right at Tony Blair's ascendancy, he was walking on whatever political water was around – was when you said, if I remember, you said that no hospital is safe from a sudden midnight visit from St Tony, the Angel of Islington.

**HAGUE**

I think I made *him* laugh the most when I said if he was having such difficulties with the job of Mayor of London he could split the job and Frank Dobson could be his day mayor and Ken Livingstone could be his nightmare. And – and Blair himself really had to laugh a lot at that one. No, this was partly my own natural tendency, that I like to put some life and energy and humour into parliamentary proceedings. But it was partly that I had nothing else going for me at the time.

**HENNESSY**

Yes.

## HAGUE

You know, there was the Conservative Party that had had a total drubbing, lost half its seats, we were way behind in polls. Well, at least on a Wednesday afternoon I had to show there was some fight in us, that I could raise the morale of my side. I had very few other ways of doing so. So I think it was part of my natural tendency to be like that in Parliament, but partly it's the guerrilla psychology. You know, if you can't win overall you start looking for ways you can win little victories. And I always enjoyed speaking in the House of Commons. In a way I feel a bit like Pitt, who I wrote about, that I gave full vent to whatever is my personality when speaking in the House of Commons more than on almost any other occasion.

## HENNESSY

Now, there was an argument at the time, William, when you were Leader of the Opposition, that you wanted to modernise the party – pretty well every party Leader wants to modernise the party, I suppose – but that you were drawn into buttressing the core vote through taking a hard line on certain policy questions, not least the question of the pound and Europe and all the rest of it. But the other way of looking at it is you actually believed all that. You believed in the values that the core voters believed in.

## HAGUE

Well, I believe in both these things. Actually the party needed to modernise and change: needed to have many more women at senior levels; needed to be more ethnically diverse; attract young people. But I also believed that some of these issues, that tax was too high, that we were signing up to too many European treaties, went beyond our core vote. Now it turned out they didn't go much beyond that, at the time. But I didn't see these things as contradictory, as some observers saw them. I do wish I'd pressed even further on the modernisation agenda, when I look back on it. That is a regret. My successors completed that and by the time of David Cameron the Conservative Party has looked very, very different. And felt and sounded very different from the time when I was the Leader. I think we could have pushed that even further, faster and if I had my time to do again I would do that.

**HENNESSY**

Tell me about the pleasures of authorship, particularly biography. When the attraction of the library trumps the attraction of the green benches of the House of Commons.

**HAGUE**

Well, this is something you know well, I think. And this was to me one of the most satisfying things that I've ever done, to go into writing first a biography of Pitt and then of Wilberforce. To me the great fun and satisfaction is writing history as if it's a novel, you know. Not in terms of – you're not making it up of course, hopefully, but you're really pulling the reader on. The chapter ends in a way that makes you want to – I must read the next chapter, this is so exciting! Because history and real life is like that and we should try to convey that in the way that we write.

**HENNESSY**

Were you in two minds about coming back to frontline politics?

**HAGUE**

Yes, I was in two minds about it and had David Cameron not been elected I probably would not have come back. I had no fixed plan to come back. But when David Cameron was elected I thought, well, we really could make a go of this. Now here is a leader who can take the Conservatives back to power. So he said to me, 'Will you come back?' And I said, 'Well there's only one thing. There's only one job I'm going to come back for and I don't want any other job. You're not going to be able to move me around 'cause I'll just leave if you put me in another job. There's only one.' And he said, 'I know what that one is. You'll be the Shadow Foreign Secretary, and, you know, eventually the Foreign Secretary if we win.' And he was as good as his word. In my mind I was going to give him a decade and I did give him a decade. I spent ten years back in the frontline of politics and he always said to me, 'You can do this for as long as you like, you know, you can be Foreign Secretary for as long as you want.' But I felt that a decade back in the frontline was enough for me and certainly between four and five years as Foreign Secretary in the modern world of a major country I think is just about as much as you should do. You start to lose your edge after that.

### HENNESSY

I think you were pretty crucial to the negotiations with the Lib Dems that produced the Coalition, weren't you?

### HAGUE

Well I chaired the negotiating team, although it was a team and George Osborne was a big part of it and we reported back every few hours to David Cameron. But yes, that was a momentous few days, five days, creating the Coalition. A big shock to us, actually, that the Liberals wanted a coalition. You know we thought it was more likely, given the arithmetic, that they would want a confidence and supply arrangement – the sort of thing that's just been agreed with the Democratic Unionists. But they were very clear in the first few minutes that if we're going to do anything we want a coalition. We want to be in government with you. And that was fine with us. Thinking back on history with my historian's hat on I almost felt like saying them, 'Do you know what's always happened to the Liberal Party whenever it's entered a coalition with the Conservatives over history?' But I decided not to mention that point to them.

**HENNESSY**

How tactful.

**HAGUE**

That it was up to them to know their history and we set about creating a coalition. And I think they knew the risks they were taking. Perhaps they underestimated them, but they knew it was a risky exercise.

**HENNESSY**

If I remember there was one thing that really hurt you in a way, or horrified you perhaps when you came in as Foreign Secretary, you found that the fabulous Foreign Office library had been sold off, or given away?

**HAGUE**

I was distraught actually. I believe very strongly in the importance of institutions in government and I think this is an under-debated topic. Ministers pass through often for two or three years, doing their best, but not really giving attention to the long term capabilities of their departments. Government benefits enormously from departments like the Treasury and the Foreign Office being strong institutions that people have pride in, that they learn in and they want to belong to for most of their careers. So I was upset at the state of the Foreign Office and its lack of confidence institutionally. On my first day, I can't remember now what it was that happened, but something happened and the officials said, 'We'll get the line to take on this from the Cabinet Office.' And I said, 'No, from now on the line to take comes from the Foreign Office. This is *our* job. Of course we will consult the Cabinet Office and so on, but we have to do the thinking ourselves. We're a big thinking department with a small budget. Not small thinking with a small budget.' And so I really did my best in four-and-a-bit years to build up that confidence in the Foreign Office again; I hope all my successors will continue that.

**HENNESSY**

Are there particular scars, William, you'll carry from your time as Foreign Secretary? For example, Libya. There was much thought – it was collective discussion in the Cabinet, there was a legal opinion that was published and there was – it was different from Iraq, of course it was, but it seems that the Brits have lost the gifts perhaps they once had for dealing with countries where sand meets oil meets politics. And Libya and Benghazi – all that – probably is the scar on you from those years, isn't it?

**HAGUE**

Actually I think there's a bigger scar, which is our failure to resolve the conflict in Syria. Which is still going on now. That is the thing over which I have the most regrets. I'm not sure there's much more I could have done over that, but it is the great frustration. You know we came quite close in 2012 to agreeing with the Russians a settlement of the Syrian War and that's, I think, the biggest scar. But on Libya, yes that became very controversial. But I still think that was the right thing to do, to intervene in Libya. We did so with UN authority. And I don't subscribe to the view that it's what we did in Libya that has produced chaos in Libya. I think it's chaos in Libya that produced the need to intervene. And it's all very well for people to say afterwards you know well you weren't sufficiently prepared for that, or you didn't know everything you were going to do afterwards. In reality though, in government, when these situations arise and there are thousands of lives at stake just outside you on the doorstep of Europe and you've got Colonel Gaddafi's tanks heading down the highway towards the city where they *say* they are going to carry out great reprisals on the population, you know then you do have one of the classic ethical and diplomatic dilemmas, as we've had through the ages. You know I went to stand as Foreign Secretary in Rwanda at memorial events where you stand on the grave – the mass grave of hundreds of thousands of people who were killed because the West did not intervene. And then we stand there and say, 'Never again.' And when a situation arises in Libya people say, 'Oh you shouldn't have intervened.' So it's as if you can never get it right. But these are the awful decisions that you face and I'm afraid there is no perfect answer.

### HENNESSY

You used an interesting phrase a couple of years ago to the Westminster Abbey Institute about the need for a 'restless conscience', I think was your phrase, in foreign policy. You've got that. What form does it exactly take? Obviously it plays into the way you look at these circumstances when they're unfolding, when you look at the intelligence and the risks and so on. Tell me more about the 'restless conscience.'

### HAGUE

Well here I'm – *I'm* influenced enormously by studying Wilberforce, you know, who saw it as a crucial mission of Britain on grounds of religious principle, but actually that coincided with national interest, to end the slave trade. And Britain had the power to do so once it had resolved to do so. Now we don't have that same global power as we had then to enforce our will, but I think it's still right in principle to save lives, to prevent conflict and it's usually in our national interest to do so as well. Otherwise greater disorder in the world comes to get us in the end. You know it doesn't mean you can do that everywhere because people then say, 'Well, why can't you create human rights in China or Saudi Arabia?' Well this has to be what is practical. This has to be what it is within your power or the power of your allies to do. But within the limits of that power I think it's very important to have that – that foreign policy with a conscience. And I tried to extend that further. I launched a preventing sexual violence and conflict initiative as Foreign Secretary and I strongly supported our spending of 0.7 per cent of our national income on development aid. This is part of being human and I don't think that governments can live separately from that, without the principles and motivations and ethics of human beings.

**HENNESSY**

Is another regret the Syrian attack-that-was-not, that never happened, which was when the HMS Tireless was just minutes away waiting for the instruction from the Cabinet to launch its cruise missiles on Syria after the chemical weapons attack and the House of Commons stopped it. But do you regret that? Because you've always thought Parliament should have the final say. You were quite keen for a while on a War Powers Act weren't you? Not just the convention that the Commons is consulted –

**HAGUE**

[*overlap*] Yes.

**HENNESSY**

– before military action's taken. So it must have been a very strange experience that for you, 'cause you wanted parliamentary sovereignty to be the key factor and yet at the same time you really did want those cruise missiles to fly from the Royal Navy submarine, didn't you?

**HAGUE**

Yes, I did, and it was very frustrating. And I think I hadn't anticipated that when chemical weapons had been used – and we were confident that they had been used – that in those circumstances the House of Commons might still not vote even for limited military action. Perhaps that shows how separated I had become from public opinion. Dealing with these foreign policy questions all the time, steeped in the history of these things and the chemical weapons conventions and treaties of the last few decades, I had come to think that if they used chemical weapons, really people will rally around saying... doing something to show they can't do that again. But it turned out no, the public were *so* fed up after the Iraq War and many MPs in all parties so rattled by the public concern that they wouldn't vote even in those circumstances for a limited military action. And that's very disappointing to me. Now subsequently of course there has been such action. President Trump actually has launched action in response to the use of chemical weapons and of course the UK is now involved in that region in military action, in Iraq and Syria against ISIS. So I think we've moved on from that disastrous vote. But it was disastrous. It showed the rest of the world that the West would let anything happen. And that emboldened Russia to come to the rescue of Assad. In my view it has prolonged the war. It showed allies of the West in the Middle East that we could not be relied upon. It certainly strengthened the position of Assad. So I think it was quite a calamitous error that the House of Commons made on that occasion.

#### HENNESSY

And now we're, in geopolitical terms, in a very strange position, aren't we? We're about to engineer the greatest shift in our position in the world since we gave up on the territorial empire, with Brexit. Now you've been around the block a bit now, William. Can you see a way through that can be consensual, that can carry the parties and the public into the kind of relationship with Europe after what will be 46 years of aberrational membership of an integrating community? Is the Hague wisdom just lurking in your frontal lobes?

#### HAGUE

Well it's easier out of government to say what to do than it is to do it in government. There is a narrow way through, I think. There's a very narrow path here, particularly for a government without a majority or without a majority for its party. And I speak as someone who – I was not – I did not agree with leaving the EU. I favoured remaining in the EU, despite all my Euro scepticism. But I agree that we have to do it now. I think the process of trying to go back on this decision would be so divisive in this country and probably not even successful, that that's not an option. It has to be delivered now, Brexit. There is a way through, actually, because there is *just* sufficient space or common ground among the positions of the various political parties, the factions within parties, the business world and that can be negotiated with the EU. And to me that means taking powers back, the sovereign powers back to the UK, leaving the EU, leaving the single market, but then using those in a very constructive way. Which means continuing to have quite a liberal approach on migration, which is essential to our economy, in the short term anyway. So we take back control but we use that to enter a strong free trade agreement. You know you can take back control of a gun but it doesn't mean you use it to shoot your foot off. So let's take back control but enter willingly as a sovereign nation into a very robust free trade agreement, and with the right attitude on migration I think it's possible to reach the right solution on trade. And I think that's something that the Conservative Party could support across the board and that many business organisations and people in other parties could then support. So there is a way through, but I'm not pretending this is easy to arrive at, to negotiate exactly in that form. The government faces the most complex task of any government since the Second World War. It is a very difficult one.

#### HENNESSY

Do you think that one of the side effects of Brexit is that Brexit is absorbing so much time and nervous energy and concentration that we're losing sight of other things in foreign and defence policy that we should be worried about?

#### HAGUE

Yes, I do. That is my main concern. That's the main reason

actually why I was against Brexit. You know I'm no fan of the European Union in many ways, but we are seeing now the strategic division and divergence of the western world, the fragmentation of the western world. And we're adding to that. This is not just about Britain leaving the EU. You can see greater differences between the United States and Europe on many issues. As the United States becomes energy independent and as Europe faces a huge future migration crisis from Africa and the Middle East that America doesn't face, you can really see the strategic priorities being pulled apart. And so for Britain that is the crucial hinge between America and Europe, to leave the EU and then spend the next few years heavily devoted to the mechanics of that, is contributing to that division. But it has to happen and so we have to make sure that we are maintaining our strong cooperation in every other way. In NATO, that we work with European nations in *their* common foreign policy and I think it's a major mission of this government, although it has this incredible test of delivering Brexit, the biggest test of all actually is making sure that this country's in a strong position whatever happens on Brexit. And that means it has to devote a lot of attention to these wider international issues.

**HENNESSY**

Do you have, William, in your own mind your own formulation comparable to Douglas Hurd's well-known appetite that we have for punching heavier than our weight in the world? What's the Hague formulation about that?

**HAGUE**

It's actually to be at the centre of the networked world, I think is the best way that I can put it. And that's why I spent my time as Foreign Secretary opening new embassies around the world, actually expanding our diplomatic footprint, visiting countries that had never been visited before by a British Foreign Secretary, some of them hadn't existed before of course. It's very important in a world that is less based on blocs and alliances, but is a mass of shifting overlapping networks to be at the heart of all those networks. And there are many ways in which we can do that – strengthening our links with Latin America and Asia, even as we go through this process with Europe. I think that's how we have to think about it and re-orientate ourselves.

**HENNESSY**

What trace do you think you'll leave on history?

**HAGUE**

Well you see there is exactly the sort of thing that I haven't bothered myself to analyse, and it doesn't bother me greatly whether I've left a trace or not. And I really don't think about it in those – I'm not a politician, a former politician who's obsessed with legacy and so on; I did my best at the time. But I hope, I suppose I hope that I helped to make sure the Conservative Party is a strong, modern force for the future. It's often said to be the world's oldest and most successful political party, but it came closest to disaster or annihilation at the time that I was senior in politics. And now it is most of the time again the governing party and it's increased its vote in five elections in a row, in its proportion of votes, which hasn't happened before. So I hope my 20 years or so in and out of the senior ranks of the Conservative Party has helped it to do that. Otherwise when I look at specific – going back to your question about trace on history, there are specific things I've done, such as designed and passed the Disability Discrimination Act in 1995, which are among my proudest achievements. Things I didn't expect to do when I went into politics. So there are some things like that that I look back on. They may be a small trace on history but one I've been happy to leave.

**HENNESSY**

If I could give you one last reform, wave a magic wand for you what would it be?

**HAGUE**

A reform now? Well that would be a global – I've now gone global in my mind since I was Foreign Secretary – and that is for the architecture of global diplomacy and security to swing behind what I've campaigned on, preventing sexual violence in conflict. Because the right combination of judicial and political and diplomatic and military commitment can actually end one of the greatest injustices and horrors of the world: mass rape in many conflicts. So I know that sounds a bit ambitious for a reform but we've started the work and it's one of the things I continue to work on even though I've left politics. And there's every reason to be ambitious about it.

**HENNESSY**

William Hague, thank you very much indeed.

**HAGUE**

Thank you.

# Harriet Harman

Series 5, Episode 3, first broadcast 24 August 2017

**Born** 30 July 1950; **Educated** St Paul's Girls'
School, Hammersmith; York University

MP (Labour) Peckham 1982–1997; Camberwell and Peckham 1997–

Secretary of State for Social Security and Minister for
Women, 1997–98; Solicitor General, 2001–05; Minister
for Constitutional Affairs, 2005–07; Justice Minister,
2007; Leader of the House of Commons and Lord Privy
Seal, 2007–10; Women and Equalities Minister, 2007–10;
Deputy Leader and Chair of the Labour Party, 2007–15

**Autobiography** *A Woman's Work*, 2017

**HENNESSY**

With me today is Harriet Harman, former Deputy Leader of the
Labour Party and twice its acting Leader. She's left a distinct mark
on her political generation, for there has been no more doughty,
determined and persistent an advocate of the place and quantity
of women in public and political life. She's also lived through all
the highs and lows of the Labour Party and the Labour movement, both the infighting and the governing achievements, over
the past 40 years. She's one of those politicians who arouses
strong feelings, inspiring both admiration and criticism. Earlier

this year she published her memoirs, *A Woman's Work*. Harriet, welcome.

**HARMAN**

Thank you.

**HENNESSY**

Tell me about your family and your formation. What kind of family were you?

**HARMAN**

Well, we were a middle-class family, and like middle-class families in those days, my father, who was a doctor, had as his housewife my mother, who although she very unusually had been to university and qualified as a barrister, had given up work, like married women, if their husband could afford to, for them to stay at home and look after us four girls. And when I look back on it, I find it quite poignant that she'd qualified as a barrister, but her wig and gown was in our dressing-up box. Because of course, much more important than being a barrister was that she should cook my father's breakfast, run the house and have his supper ready on the table when he came home from work. And really it was at a time when the whole vocation and aspiration for a girl was to get a good husband. And, once you'd achieved that wonderful ambition of getting a good husband, to be a good wife to that husband and everything else was secondary to that. And one of the things that was absolutely transformative was that the women's movement said, 'No, no, actually that's not the way we see it. We see your own ambition and your own achievements in life to be about you, not just triangulated through whether you please men.' And that was a very stunning change from my mother's generation to mine. So I was brought up at a time of very mixed messages. You know, be attractive to men, be careful not to be too educated, because if you were you might be regarded as too clever by half, and no husband would want a wife that would overshadow him, so therefore you wouldn't get the best man around. And that attitude started to change and that is what I grew up in and it was a very exciting and transformative time.

**HENNESSY**

Your mother did have a career as a lawyer, though, didn't she?

**HARMAN**

She practised just for a few years before she started having us children. And then it was a combination of my father not wanting her to be travelling to different courts round the country, and also solicitors, most of whom were men, didn't want to advance to their clients the notion that there might be a woman barrister in case they thought they were getting second best and they would want the real thing, which was a man. So external discrimination and internal discouragement put paid to my mother's legal career. But, looking through the women's movement's eyes to my mother's life, I looked at her and I thought, I am not going to do that. You know, she's been a great mother and I've got no criticism of her, but my life is going to be different.

**HENNESSY**

Your mother did stand as a Liberal candidate in Hertfordshire, in the '64 election, and that showed, by the standards of the day, considerable spirit, didn't it?

**HARMAN**

Yes, she was very, very political. Not that we four daughters took much notice of what she was doing. She was a strong supporter of Jo Grimond. I can remember one time when she was standing as a candidate, that we were folding up her election address into envelopes ready to be delivered – she was standing for the Liberals of course – she was standing in a seat which they had absolutely no hope of winning, otherwise of course it would have been a man standing. But because it was a – regarded as a hopeless seat it was all right for her to stand in that seat. But I think she did love politics and loved being a candidate, but again not compatible with being a wife. You know, you can't be out at public meetings inciting people to vote Liberal when your husband's waiting for his dinner on the table. And my father discouraged her from doing it again. So you know, she was a woman who in my generation she would have been a high court judge, or she would have been an MP and she would have been in the Cabinet.

**HENNESSY**

There's a lot [of] family politics in your deeper background isn't there? There's lots of political dynasties. There's the Chamberlains, there's the Pakenhams. How conscious were you when you were forming your own political views of this great inheritance, some might say, from these big political families?

**HARMAN**

Well, not at all. Partly because I was not into listening to my parents' generation, because why would we listen to them? We weren't going to do anything like they'd done, we were going to do everything completely different. And it's hard to describe how much of a transformative change it was, but it was basically about the role of women. If the role of women hitherto had been above all to be a housewife and to be a mother and for us that was not going to be the determining factor in our lives, then why would you listen to anything else? We were like a fresh start. We had nothing to learn from anybody, we were going to remake the world. So the idea that I could look at some ancient, dusty old Chamberlain and lead my life in some way related to that, or the Pakenhams, I mean, it was a completely different era. I sometimes look back at the people that I came across and think, if only I would have listened to what they'd said and tried to draw on their experience

I might have done much better and done much more. But it's part of forming yourself, is to reject what is different and what's gone before. We were going to do things differently. And that locked us out of any received wisdom, any inherited wisdom.

**HENNESSY**

Do you think – it's very interesting what you said a moment ago – that perhaps if you had listened to some of the ancestral voices you might have done even better?

**HARMAN**

Well, I think I would have done a lot more. And I probably would have not felt so alone with my struggles. I mean, reading Barbara Castle's book, which I only did after I'd left the front bench, I mean, how stupid was that? I should have read it straight away when she gave me a copy. But we were so busy remaking things we didn't have time to look back, or the inclination. But seeing her describing going to bed at night with her husband Ted, saying, 'I'm a complete failure I've messed everything up.' And if I'd have known that there was other women who I regarded as highly successful who'd had those same doubts and doubted themselves I might have felt a bit better about my own struggles.

**HENNESSY**

Very interesting. You had a prominent suffragette in the family too, I think, didn't you? Was that an inspiration?

**HARMAN**

Louisa Martindale?

**HENNESSY**

Yes. Even if the others weren't, was she?

## HARMAN

She was an inspiration to my mother, and my mother said Louisa Martindale gave her the sense – and this was a highly subversive thought – that women could do things outside of the home. The only problem was that you had to have no children to do that. And therefore, because my mother had children, then she couldn't do these things. I'd never heard of Louisa Martindale. I was – had no interest in the suffragettes. It was all about the peer group, it was all about the sisterhood. We were going to do things in our own way and differently. And I remember how widespread this was. I remember once seeing a TV programme that Germaine Greer was on, and she'd written her book, *The Female Eunuch*, and she was speaking to all these kind of, you know, frightfully entitled young white male students, and she was, you know, giving her pitch and they were sitting there looking highly sceptical, and one of them in the question session said, 'Well, I don't know what it is you want.' And she said, 'Neither do I, but sure as hell I know it ain't you.' And it was like – I was so shocked, it was so electrifying and exciting because the whole thing about women is we were programmed to please men, and here she was saying she didn't know what she wanted but she knew it wasn't him. It was like, 'shove off.' And it was subversive beyond belief and very exciting and very shared. So we were all working together on it.

### HENNESSY

Did you have these burning convictions *fortissimo* in the way you've just described them to me by the time you arrived at St Paul's School for Girls in Hammersmith?

### HARMAN

I always had this sense of railing against hierarchy. So I was in revolt mode, really from the time when I got to secondary school. Unless you were in a submissive mode to hierarchy they couldn't be dealing with you. So me and my friends we just didn't fit in and so therefore, you know, I was very pleased to leave. But then I didn't fit in in university either –

**HENNESSY**

I was about to ask you.

**HARMAN**

– so it's probably something to do with me rather than the institution.

**HENNESSY**

I would have thought that York University and studying politics might have been a liberation?

**HARMAN**

Well, it wasn't really. I think actually I was, quite young and quite homesick for my family. But also I mean, I was doing a politics course and I just found myself completely uninterested in learning the structures of different legislative assemblies round the world. But the politics, the student politics, was divided into the Tory Party on the one hand, and I wouldn't be seen dead anywhere near them, I thought that they were really weird, and I wouldn't want to have anything to do with them. And then on the left it was various Trotskyite factions, all knocking six bells out of each other. And then there were some who were, through the Students' Union, fighting for students' rights. But the reality was that students in those days, we were incredibly privileged, we were a tiny minority from a very narrow class background. We were not the people who had problems. We were the kind of gilded generation, and the idea that we should turn ourselves into suffering victims when we had the whole world at our feet and all you had to do is get a degree and walk into a decent paid job, I couldn't see us as the reason to have the struggle.

### HENNESSY

In your memoirs you reveal a shocking incident where one of the politics teachers said you'd get a 2.1 if you slept with him and you'd get a 2.2 if you didn't. I mean it's amazing. Why didn't you shop him at the time?

### HARMAN

Well, there're two things that are shocking about that. One, that it happened basically – it was towards the end of my third year, heading towards my degree, this professor called me in and said, 'You're borderline. But you know, if you have sex with me it'll be a – definitely a 2.1 and if you don't it'll be definitely a 2.2.' So the idea that I would have sex with him, I thought absolutely repulsive. But it was endemic. The idea that this was somehow something unusual or one-off – I think it was absolutely endemic, and the idea that I should complain about it – I mean, to who would I complain? To all the other men in the department, who were all his mates? Again it's the hierarchy that was so prevalent at that time. The lecturers were up here and we were down there. And the idea of accusing them of doing something which was obviously wrong and known to be wrong, I just would have totally assumed that he would deny it, they'd take his side and I'd be labelled as even more of a troublemaker. It just did not even for one second occur to me that there was any point in making a formal complaint, and that was the experience of all girls at that age.

### HENNESSY

So liberation, as it were, or feeling more at ease with yourself and perhaps the world, you have to wait until you're working in the Brent Law Centre, in the late '70s.

### HARMAN

I wouldn't describe it as feeling 'at ease' because we weren't at ease,

we were arming ourselves for the revolution. It was a very energetic and exciting time.

But you were the kindred spirits, I suppose, that's what I mean.

Yes, I found my spiritual home. I found a team of people who,
like me, wanted to change society, who disagreed with everything about it. I mean, for example, I got together with – who then
became my husband – Jack Dromey. He was from a working-class
Irish Catholic background, and I was from a middle-class professional Protestant background. I mean that was, like, shocking.
We met when he came to do the annual general meeting of the
Fulham Legal Advice Centre where I was a volunteer. But we then
were together on the Trico picket line, which was one of the first
equal pay disputes after the 1975 implementation of the 1970 Equal
Pay Act. Then we were on the picket line of the Grunwick dispute,
which was largely Asian women who were regarded as the least
militant, and yet they refused to be bullied and they walked out
on strike. And it became a *cause célèbre* because they were only
asking for trade union recognition.

What was the attraction of working at the National Council of
Civil Liberties, which was your next job?

Well, because my sort of ideology was all about people's rights.
And one of the ways to get your rights was to use the law. And
I wanted to use the law to empower people. And that started off
with Brent Law Centre in a local area, but then in the National
Council of Civil Liberties, which then became Liberty, to use the
law on a national basis to empower people. So I took the first cases

under the Sex Discrimination Act asserting the rights of women as part-time workers not to be treated as second-class citizens, for example. We campaigned as well as enforcing people's legal rights, for things like the Freedom of Information Act, a Human Rights Act, for longer maternity pay and leave. All the injustices we saw, we were taking legal cases to try and take forward, but we were also campaigning for them.

### HENNESSY

Had you always had it in mind to go into frontline mainstream politics, mainstream in the sense of Parliament? Was that part of the plan, as it were? Or are you not the sort of person that has plans, you have causes but perhaps not plans?

### HARMAN

Yes, I've been very lacking in plans, but very full of causes. And having qualified as a lawyer, I could use my legal qualification to commit to those causes. Which I did in Brent Law Centre and then Liberty. And then, being involved in the women's movement, we were, like, outraged by the fact that there were so few women MPs. It was 97 per cent men in Parliament, only 3 per cent women. The same as it had been since 1950.

### HENNESSY

This is the early 1980s now.

### HARMAN

Yes, in the 1980s. And late 1970s. Only 3 per cent, a tiny, tiny minority. So we've all got to get into Parliament, shake the whole thing up and make sure women's voices are heard. So it was part of that argument for change and we were all like, women have got to put themselves forward. And it's like, oh, who's going to do it? Oh, well we'd better. So it was a bit like that. You know, you can't argue for change and expect other people to do the fight, you've got to do the fight yourself. And I got in in 1982 expecting that I would be joined in 1983 by a monstrous regiment of women who would all be there with me to shake things up. But because Labour did so badly in the 1983 general election I kind of turned round and discovered I was the only one. So then it was a very tough battle inside the House of Commons, but strong, strong support, motivation and sisterhood outside the House of Commons. So I became like, the political wing of the women's movement.

**HENNESSY**

December '81 I think you were adopted for Peckham as prospective candidate, then Harry Lamborn, the incumbent MP, dies unexpectedly, I think, in October '82. Some would say it was very brave of you, Harriet, to as it were, run for a by-election although you were already [the] candidate, because you were expecting your first child weren't you? It must have been a tremendous effort of organisation and determination to do that.

**HARMAN**

Well, the thing is that we didn't make any calculations about whether anything was doable. Because if we'd have done that we'd have never done anything. So to be a younger person, to be a younger woman, and to be pregnant, I was nothing like what people expected an MP to be. But that was like, well if that was their expectations we were going to change that and show a woman, a young woman could be an MP, and if she was pregnant she could have a baby and do it all as well. And once we all set our faces in this direction we couldn't back down. So that basically, although it became unbearably overwhelming, especially once I had three children and the House of Commons would be sitting through the night, and I felt it was unbearable, wanted more than anything to throw in the towel and just say, 'No, sorry it's just not doable. It's just not doable. I can't reconcile my vocation as a mother with my vocation in politics, I'm going to have to give up being in politics.'

Once you've raised the flag you can't just say, 'Sorry, I can't hack it,' because you'd know that everybody would turn round and say, 'See, I told you, you can't have a woman who's pregnant or a woman having children.' And it would set back the cause. And I just felt I couldn't set back the cause. Once I'd like, waded in I had to stick it out. And I'm actually glad I did, although I think if there'd have been more women like me at the time we could have leant on each other and supported each other and it was the kind of isolation that made it so hard to really cope with.

### HENNESSY

You came into a House of Commons in which there was a woman Prime Minister, Mrs Thatcher. Did she talk to you? Did you talk to her? Was there a flicker of sisterhood between you, ever?

### HARMAN

Absolutely not. And I was very tribal Labour and the pinnacle of everything I objected to was a Conservative Prime Minister, and the fact that it was a woman, well, she was no sister, and we had banners, 'The first lady puts women last,' we marched against her. So I didn't have any difficulty feeling that she was the enemy and I was fighting against everything she stood for. She was reinforcing the notion of the housewife. Although she was Prime Minister for heaven's sake and had two children. She was still reinforcing all the traditional notions. That's what we felt. So we were very opposed to her. And in fact I remember one time when we were voting very late at night and unusually I had my baby with me, which usually I didn't have, but I had my baby with me on that occasion. I saw her down the end of the long corridor and she was walking in my direction towards me as I was walking from the other end of the corridor and she had her sort of two aides with her and was walking down the corridor. And I could see she'd spotted I had the baby with me and was bearing down on me. Now normally the most instinctive thing for a mother is to show your baby. You're so proud of your baby. It's the most beautiful and wonderful thing in the world. You want nothing more than everybody to look at it and admire its perfection. But I had this feeling that I didn't want her eyes to fall on my perfect baby. That – that it would be horrific. And I saw a little room off the side and I dived into it in order that she shouldn't actually see my baby. And I think perhaps if I hadn't have been able to find that room I would have literally drawn the cover over the baby's face for her eyes not to fall on it. Now when I look back on that I think that's quite weird really, but it – it tells me not only how obsessed I was with my baby at the time and how completely smitten and my brain turned upside down, but my visceral hostility to the Prime Minister.

### HENNESSY

You were eloquent a moment ago about the hostility all this aroused. How did you cope with it? Because it was very fierce and it was very personal and sometimes it still is. Some of the reviews of your memoir show that it's still there. How do you cope with it, Harriet?

### HARMAN

Well, it was very personal, it was very virulent and it was also very public. Because one of the things that was the case at the time, is we not only had an overwhelmingly male Parliament – 97 per cent men, 3 per cent women – but we had an overwhelmingly male press gallery. And the journalists whose job was to report on Parliament were 95 per cent men, 5 per cent women. So they were not interested in my agenda, understanding the importance of it, thinking about what it was based on, thinking about the support there might be outside, they were strangers in my ideological world. So I got it in the neck in the press very publicly, but what that did is it aroused amongst the women of my generation who were in the women's movement all wanting to have more aspirations and to change their lives from that that their mothers had led, they were active in my support. So if I'd be going on a train somewhere to visit a group of women councillors in Manchester or something, women would come up to me on the train or at the station or clipping my ticket and they would say, 'Keep it up. Keep what you're doing up. Good on you'. So it was a bit like the irresistible force of the women's movement meets the immovable object of Parliament and me being squashed in between, but actually it was the absolute solidarity of women all around the country, from all walks of life, you know, from people who were cleaners to people who were professionals saying 'You're fighting for us'.

**HENNESSY**

I think when you were first offered a place on the front bench by Neil Kinnock in '84 you had some thoughts about not accepting. What was that about?

**HARMAN**

Well, it was 1984. I'd only got in the House of Commons in 1982. I'd had my first baby in February 1983. I was trying to be a new mother. I was trying to be a new Member of Parliament and doing both at the same time and finding it all pretty overwhelming. And I was called down by Patricia Hewitt who was then the Press Secretary to Neil Kinnock to have an appointment with Neil Kinnock and I thought, oh dear, I must have done something terrible, I must be in for some major telling off, 'cause I'd never been called to see him before. And I was feeling very ill at the time and he said, 'We'd like you to be on the front bench.' I was completely shocked and said, 'Oh well, can I think about it?' And I said to Patricia as I went out, who'd been General Secretary when I was at NCCL and was a very close friend of mine, 'I can't do it. I'm, you know, I'm just, new baby, new work in Parliament, it's just – go on the front bench, take on national responsibility? I couldn't possibly do that and I feel really, really ill anyway.' And Patricia said, 'Oh it's probably just flu. Take it, you know. There's hardly any women on the front bench. Women outside need to see you on the front bench, you know, it's your responsibility really to step forward,' and I was like, 'Oh God, all right I'll do it then.' And she said, 'Look, just go home to bed and I'll tell Neil you'll do it.' So I went home to bed and told Neil I'd do it and then the next day it was in the papers and then a few weeks later I discovered that I was not actually going to feel better for another about eight months because I was pregnant and was having, you know, a very full-of-sickness pregnancy as well as a new baby. And actually I felt I had to do even more than what the men on the front bench did. I had to go all around the country, be highly visible, be encouraging in supporting Labour members all around the country. Every council by-election, every parliamentary by-election, elections in Scotland and Wales. I had to be there to show that if you had a young woman with children as an MP on the front bench you weren't getting second best. You were getting the real thing.

**HENNESSY**

Was John Smith, Neil Kinnock's successor as Leader, a sympathetic ear for you and your causes? How did you get on with him?

**HARMAN**

Well, I didn't really know John Smith very well. He was part of the Scottish Labour establishment which was a formidable and, you know, very coherent, strong force in Parliament at that time. But he was very supportive of me. I mean extraordinarily supportive. Even to the extent that I did, you know, a series of disastrous interviews and really messed things up and fell off the Shadow Cabinet, not least because I'd had so many arguments with so many of the men and they voted me off the Shadow Cabinet, partly because I'd done some displays of incompetence which would have been fine if I'd have been a man, but as a woman it gave them the opportunity to kind of exact their revenge and knock me off the Shadow Cabinet. And the Shadow Cabinet in those days was voted for by the Parliamentary Labour Party. And he extraordinarily said, 'Well, I don't care what the PLP think, I as Leader am going to put her back in the Shadow Cabinet.' And I think that, you know, he had three daughters and I kind of think that he probably was the sort of man who if a young woman was going to be slighted was going to be there for them and back them up. So I absolutely upped my game and did a whole load of things which then worked out really successfully. So he really stuck his neck out for me, but I felt such a responsibility. And I said to him, you know, 'I will make sure that the risk you've taken on me that I will deliver for you.' I was very explicit. I knew what a risk he'd taken, so I had to deliver. I was constantly finding there were reasons that I had to step up all the time. But that's what I did.

### HENNESSY

After the great Labour victory of '97 Tony Blair makes you Secretary of State for Social Security and Minister for Women. I think you've talked, Harriet, I think it's in the memoirs, at how unprepared you were for this huge workforce you inherited, this 80,000 people and so on and the nature of the job, it must have been daunting. Yet another challenge to you as it were, 'cause when we've been talking your life comes out as a series of challenges that you've had to overcome and your determination burns through to actually make it. Now that must have been a very big one?

### HARMAN

Well it was, and remember we'd been out of government since 1979. And here we were in 1997. And I made a major miscalculation and misunderstood that actually what happens when you're in opposition is you all work as a team. You're the team that is working to get the government out and to get yourself into government. But once you get into government things are different. You are not a team, you are holders of big public offices. The Prime Minister, he has his role. The Chancellor, he has his, well normally his role, and the Secretaries of State all have their role, and I sort of thought it was me and Tony and Gordon like it had always been. And it hadn't been. And so as things got worse and the problems in my department multiplied, one of my special advisers said to me, 'I think you're in real danger of being sacked.' I mean you didn't need that much insight, it was on the front pages of the papers – 'Harman to face axe.' So he said you know, 'I think you're in real danger of being sacked in the first reshuffle.' And I said, 'No, no, Tony would never sack me, you know, he's my friend.' And my special adviser said, 'He's not your friend, he's the Prime Minister. And the Prime Minister has no friends.' And that was so true, and nor should it be the case that the Prime Minister runs things by friendship, but I kind of felt that that team which had been so coherent to get Labour into government was somehow still there. And I hadn't clocked that actually it was each man or woman for themselves fighting their own corner and if trouble was coming from my department there was a way to solve it! And the way to solve it was to sack me and start again with a new Secretary of State and that's the solution they found.

### HENNESSY

You were in office for about a year as Secretary of State for Social Security I think. In essence, very briefly, what was it that went wrong? You had the extraordinary Frank Field as your Minister of State who had a great welfare reform brief and there was tensions there, but all sorts of other things went wrong. In essence what was the problem, Harriet that led you to be sacked in 1998?

### HARMAN

Well, I think there were – there are a number of things that went wrong. I think that appointing me and Frank together with me as the Secretary of State and he as the Minister of State was wrong from the outset, because Tony Blair had wanted to appoint – I didn't know at the time – but he'd wanted to appoint Frank Field as Secretary of State for Social Security and send a huge message that there was going to be a transformation of social security. But Gordon had not wanted Frank Field to be Secretary of State. Not least because Frank Field believed in universality rather than –

### HENNESSY

Selective, selective welfare, yes...

### HARMAN

– means testing and therefore that would have spent too much money because we'd got a commitment for the first two years to stay within the Tory spending limits. So to move to a universal system you have to spend loads more money and obviously Gordon didn't want to have a Secretary of State for Social Security who was going to come in with a massive bill and demands for more money at a time when the budgets were going to be very tight for the first two years. But Frank was – so he'd originally been offered Secretary of State and then Tony said, 'Sorry, I'm afraid I can't give it to you, it's got to be Harriet who's the Secretary of State.' I had been doing the job in opposition, but [he told Frank], 'Don't worry, you know you'll be Secretary of State shortly, so just take the Minister of State for a bit and then you can be Secretary of State.' So Frank took the job expecting it would only be temporary and then I would be off somewhere and he would then take my place and [he] told the department this. So the department were very confused. So I went along to Tony, although I was very reluctant to bring problems to him 'cause we were – you know he's about to be changing the whole country and I said, 'There's this problem.' And he was, 'Oh dear, well, just do your best to try and keep it under wraps, it will be absolutely terrible if Frank resigns.' So it was really wrong at the outset, both for me and for Frank, caused great instability, everybody said we were feuding. But it wasn't really that we were feuding, it was just that we were very badly matched in the department and also then of course there was the lone parent benefit cuts. So we came in with a commitment to the public in our manifesto, which had been a very big part of us getting elected, we will not spend more than the Tories. Now in other departments that meant they could just defer projects. They could just not fill vacancies. They could defer capital projects. But *my* department was about weekly, fortnightly, benefit entitlements to real people and it was actually in legislation. So to change that, real people had to have less money and it had to be done in Parliament. We couldn't take money away from pensioners. Pensioner poverty was a massive problem – they were the biggest group of the poorest. We couldn't take money away from pensioners and they had no ability to work. We couldn't take money away from disabled people, but the thought was, well, new lone parents who are coming onto the books they can have £6 a week less than existing lone parents and we'll help them with childcare so they can then go out to work. And actually that was wrong because childcare wasn't properly established. Some of them would have had very, very tiny children, and anyway lone parents had so little money as it was. I mean £6 was a big amount less for people who already couldn't live on that amount. So even though it was new claimants it was not right to do it, it was mean and not right for the Labour government to do it. And I raised it with Gordon and said, 'This is terrible, it's the wrong thing to be doing, everybody will be up in arms,' and he basically said, 'This is a really huge manifesto commitment and if we break this manifesto commitment that we're going to keep to the Tories' spending limits, the money markets will panic, the pound will collapse, economic confidence will drain away that we've spent so long building up and the government will fall.' And having struggled to get into government, the idea that I should be somehow the reason why the whole Labour government fell, I just didn't feel I could have second-guessed Gordon's economic sense of what would happen. What I should have done is said 'Well this is a big problem, why don't you use all your Treasury brains to find a way to solve it?'

**HENNESSY**

And this was the showdown that led to your sacking?

**HARMAN**

Well that and the turbulence with Frank Field, which meant that I lasted 15 months. So having 15 years of slaving all around the country to get Labour into government so that we could start changing things which were so problematic for my constituents, we were in government but after 15 months I was not part of it. However, I was still part of the team, weirdly, so I was writing papers on maternity pay and leave for – for Gordon. I was in and out of the Treasury – I was like, every time there was a budget there'd be childcare tax credits and the things that I'd pressed for were all rolling forward. I wasn't carrying the red box, but I was carrying forward the ideology with the New Labour team and things were really improving in my constituency. So the idea that I would rebel would be absolutely unthinkable.

**HENNESSY**

Can we now leap forward to you becoming Deputy Leader of the Labour Party when John Prescott stands down in 2006? It showed that you had great following in the party. But also it must have been quite difficult really being Deputy Leader to Gordon Brown, given his mercurial character?

**HARMAN**

Well, I'd worked with Gordon Brown, he got in in '83, him and Tony and we were kind of part of the same project and I'd actually been his deputy when he was Shadow Chancellor and I was Deputy Shadow Chief Secretary – I was Shadow Chief Secretary to the Treasury at the time, so I was used to working with Gordon and was full of admiration for his intellectual prowess, his absolute political energy and commitment. He was absolutely a force of nature about getting us tackling the problems that were shackling us into opposition and getting us into government and I admired that enormously. And he transformed the way people saw the Labour Party in terms of our economic policy. And he wasn't the easiest boss to work for by any stretch of the imagination, but you know I supported what he supported and we shared the cause.

**HENNESSY**

So you had a good relationship?

**HARMAN**

Well, I think – yes and no. Over the years he supported me a great deal in ways that are not generally known or visible. Like he supported me to go on the National Executive Committee and said 'You've got to stand for the National Executive Committee' and I'm like, 'I've got too much on my plate. Got three children, I'm a Shadow Minister, I can't be on the National' – 'Oh,' he said, 'you must go on, stand for election, I'm sure you'll get elected' and you know, so he was always pushing me forward as part of his team and supporting me and I'm sure he was key to John Smith rescuing me after I'd been sacked off the Shadow Cabinet by my colleagues in the PLP. So he supported me a lot over the years. There were many things that he did which were not supportive and which he should have done I think, like for example making me Deputy Prime Minister. But over the course of decades of working together yeah, I think we did some really good things. He did some really good things, I did some good things.

**HENNESSY**

When he stands down after losing the 2010 election you become Acting Leader of the Labour Party and in fact you were to do it twice. When people write your biography, as I'm sure they will, they'll say, given that Harriet was a great crusader of women in the top of political life and public life, why didn't you go for the leadership? What held you back?

### HARMAN

Well, I think you know all the expectation was that you know, one of the young Turks would be Leader, you know. Would it be David Miliband, you know, would it be Ed Balls? There was no sense anywhere, as there often isn't with women, that I was leadership material. That it's very easy to see men as leadership material. Somehow it's more difficult to see women as leadership material, and therefore you're being counterintuitive as putting your forward – yourself forward. But when I became Leader of the Opposition on an acting basis, and really worked my socks off to do the best for the party who were like raw and miserable with the 2010 defeat and being chucked out of government, and I was like, I've got to step up and really nail it in Prime Minister's Questions, in the Budget response, in the Queen's Speech response, going all around the country, speaking at regional conferences, and actually to my internal surprise, in a way, I found I was really nailing it. And going around the country party members were saying, 'You're nailing it, we're so proud of you, why aren't you standing for leader?' And I was so relieved not to be cocking the whole thing up that I took it as a great compliment, but I didn't go that next step and think 'They're asking me why I'm not going for leader. Why aren't I?' I just never got to that point. I think if I'd have stood, I definitely would have got it. Whether I'd have made a success about it well, we never know, but I think I would have got it.

### HENNESSY

I'll ask you about the Prime Minister that might have been in a minute, but looking to where we are now, women in politics, the scene as you've described it when you came in it's been absolutely transformed between now and then but you're not one for resting on your laurels, are you? I think the fires still burn. They're not banked, are they, Harriet?

### HARMAN

No, they're not. I think that it is right to recognise how far we've come, but actually we – we can't just rest on our laurels and think that it's all been achieved, 'cause it so evidently hasn't. You know if you think of the kind of daily toll of broken ribs and black eyes and punctured lungs of domestic violence, if you think of the weekly toll of women killed by their husbands and former partners, if you think of women tearing their hair out trying to find decent childcare. If you look at the decision making which is so male-dominated, if you look at Labour's last manifesto, the one in 2015, it had more about football supporters and animal rights than it had about women. And so we clearly on all fronts have still got a long way to go, but my goodness me, the women in Parliament now are utterly proliferating – still outnumbered two to one – but very strongly assertive and determined to find their place and to fight for other women in the country, so I think that there are attempts always to push things back and the kind of cloud of misogyny that comes across the Atlantic from Trump is a threat that the clock can always be turned back. But I think that we've got the basis for going forward but we still do have to go forward because we're still nowhere near on equal terms.

### HENNESSY

If retrospectively I could make you Prime Minister, what would you do on day one?

### HARMAN

I think what I'd do on day one is think, blimey. I am Prime Minister. I'd better live each day as if it's my last because you never know when you're Prime Minister it might be, and crack on with it and actually not be too reasonable. But I've always thought that today's unreasonable demands are tomorrow's conventional wisdom. So get out all the unreasonable demands that everybody has said are absolutely bonkers, get them out on the table and do them.

**HENNESSY**

If I could grant you one last reform, another wave of the magic wand, what would it be?

**HARMAN**

I think to implement Clause One of the Equality Act. What we did in 2010 is we brought in the Equality Act, the Tories have implemented quite a number of things in it, but one of the things they haven't implemented is Clause One and what that does is say that the government, every government department, every quango, every public organisation, every health authority, every school has got to, when they are making decisions, take into account narrowing the gap between rich and poor. That would transform the way public policy and public organisations make us a more fair and equal and meritocratic society.

**HENNESSY**

Harriet Harman, thank you very much.

**HARMAN**

Thank you.

# Michael Howard
# (Lord Howard of Lympne)

Series 5, Episode 4, first broadcast 31 August 2017

**Born** 7 July 1941; **Educated** Llanelli Grammar
School; Peterhouse, Cambridge

MP (Conservative) Folkestone and Hythe 1983–2010

Parliamentary Under-Secretary, Department of Trade and Industry,
1985–87; Minister of State for Local Government, 1987–88; Minister of
State for the Environment, 1988–1989; Minister of State for Housing,
1989–90; Secretary of State for Employment, 1990–92; Secretary of
State for the Environment, 1992–93; Home Secretary, 1993–97; Leader
of the Conservative Party and Leader of the Opposition, 2003–05

**HENNESSY**

With me today is Michael Howard, Lord Howard of Lympne,
former Leader of the Conservative Party, and before that a flavourful and combative Home Secretary. He rose up by the clas-
sical meritocratic route through grammar school to Cambridge
and on to a career as a lawyer. He arrived quite late for his generation in the House of Commons in his early forties, in 1983, a well-
established QC whose forensic gifts swiftly marked him out as a
coming man almost from the moment he took his seat as MP for
Folkestone and Hythe. Michael, welcome.

**HOWARD**

Thank you very much, Peter. Very good to be with you.

**HENNESSY**

You were born in the war, early part of the war, in Swansea in Wales.

**HOWARD**

Born – born actually in a village called Gorseinon, very near, between Swansea and Llanelli, where I grew up and went to school.

**HENNESSY**

Tell me about your mum and dad and your family.

**HOWARD**

Well, they – they were shopkeepers, basically. My father came to this country in his very late teens, from Transylvania, which was then in Romania – it's been tossed about a bit between Romania and Hungary. And my mother came to this country when she was a six-month-old baby, a babe in arms. My mother lived in Llanelli. She was brought up by her mother, who was a single parent, having lost my grandfather. I think he was 32 or something when – when he died, and she remained a widow for the rest of her life, my maternal grandmother. And my mother grew up in Llanelli and – and when she met my father he came to live in Llanelli too.

**HENNESSY**

Were – were they drapers' shops?

**HOWARD**

Yes.

**HENNESSY**

Was it a political household?

#### HOWARD

It was political in the sense that we often talked about politics at mealtime, but it wasn't in any sense party political and I don't think my parents actually ever voted Conservative until I got involved with the Conservative Party. I think they voted Liberal in those days.

#### HENNESSY

Were you a precocious boy in the sense you read the newspapers and the political columns early on?

#### HOWARD

Probably. [*Laughs*] I can't quite remember, but it wouldn't astonish me if that turned out to be the case, yeah.

#### HENNESSY

Now, I know one must never categorise generations or localities, but to be a Conservative in your generation, in the war and after the war with the great social solidarity of the war, which of course was cross-party, but even so to be a Conservative at a young age in a grammar school in South Wales, it meant there's a streak of steel in you really.

#### HOWARD

Well, I had a – I had a lot of Labour friends at Cambridge, and they attributed this to the fact that I was a natural rebel. I tried to start a soccer team at Llanelli Grammar School –

#### HENNESSY

Now –

#### HOWARD

– which was as close to heresy as you can conceivably get, and I was almost expelled for my pains.

**HENNESSY**

That was brave, because there's sacred properties to rugby union in Llanelli.

**HOWARD**

Absolutely, absolutely. And the Scarlets have recently won the Pro12 title, and I watched them with great glee as they did it. But I always preferred soccer and wanted to play it and so that perhaps supports the view that I – I – I wanted to go against the grain.

**HENNESSY**

You're a classic meritocrat, I mean, you're the classic product of the 1944 Education Act. I mean, but for that we wouldn't – we wouldn't be talking in this way would we?

**HOWARD**

Absolutely not. I mean, I owe a huge amount to Llanelli Grammar School. In fact, just a couple of weeks ago I hosted a reception in the House of Lords for the old boys of Llanelli Grammar School, and we had a very good time.

**HENNESSY**

Tell me about the roots of your patriotism, because you've got a very strong Welsh patriotism, you've got a very strong British patriotism, and the combinations are always very interesting within the UK, at least I think they are. Tell me about yours.

**HOWARD**

Well, look, I mean, I owe this country everything. And in a way I owe Winston Churchill everything. I've made quite a study of the first three weeks of Churchill's prime ministership, and as you know, but not all that many people know, we came quite close during that period to doing the same kind of deal with Hitler that France did. And I'm totally convinced that if Churchill hadn't been there that's what would have happened. Now, had that happened, I probably wouldn't be alive to tell the tale today. And so I owe everything to this country, and my father always impressed upon me how much we as a family owed to the country, and that has certainly stayed with me for the whole of my life.

**HENNESSY**

Now, tell me about the Cambridge you came into, in the late 1950s I think it was.

**HOWARD**

It was a great mix. In all sorts of ways. My college had a rule –

**HENNESSY**

That's Peterhouse.

**HOWARD**

That's Peterhouse. That you had to do National Service before you came up. Now, I was, I think, the first year which got to the relevant age after National Service was abolished. So when I went up to Peterhouse the college was a terrific mix of people who'd done their national service and those like me who hadn't. It was also a social mix, because there were quite a few people like me who'd come from grammar schools, but there were also a lot of public school boys, and probably a predominance of public school boys. So it was a great mix in all sorts of ways. It wasn't, unfortunately, much of a gender mix in those days.

**HENNESSY**

Women's colleges were separate –

**HOWARD**

Much to my regret. But in other respects it was.

**HENNESSY**

There's one episode in your Cambridge life which intrigues me, and it's when the Conservative Association – your great friend Ken Clarke, I think, invited Oswald Mosley to come and speak, and you were enraged by this and I think you resigned from the Association, because Mosley had been standing on a kind of – not National Front, I forget what he called it – British Movement, ticket, hadn't he, in the '59 election and was still quite a figure. And you felt this very deeply didn't you?

**HOWARD**

Well, it – well it was a little bit more complicated than is normally described, because he'd been invited the previous year to the first meeting of the academic year, of the Cambridge University Conservative Association, and I didn't really object to that. But Ken, as chairman, then invited him to the first meeting of the second academic year, and I thought, if this is going to be a regular thing, a regular fixture, this is too much. I can't be part of this.

**HENNESSY**

Did it affect your friendship with Ken Clarke, as you – I think you've been buddies really from the beginning haven't you?

**HOWARD**

Yes, we have. And I think there probably was a sort of little bit of friction immediately after that. In fact we stood against each other for the secretaryship of the Union not long after that. But, as with the other members of the Cambridge mafia, our friendship has survived our differences of view on lots of things. We have an annual reunion dinner, which John Gummer organises, and so we – we have retained those bonds of friendship over the decades.

**HENNESSY**

It's quite a mafia isn't it, because I think it includes Norman Fowler and Norman Lamont...

**HOWARD**

Yes.

**HENNESSY**

As well as the ones you've mentioned.

**HOWARD**

Leon Brittan...

**HENNESSY**

Leon Brittan.

**HOWARD**

Now sadly – sadly departed.

**HENNESSY**

You were very active in the Union. Was this because you liked debating? Was it because you saw it as a help to a future political career or a legal career? Or you just couldn't resist it?

**HOWARD**

I didn't go to the Union at all in my first year. There was – rather bizarrely there was a course on existentialist philosophy which absolutely clashed with the main debates in the Union, and I chose to go to that. But please don't ask me any questions about the course that I followed.

**HENNESSY**

Now that was – that was – that's quite remarkable, Michael.

**HOWARD**

Well, I mean...

**HENNESSY**

What on earth was the appeal of existentialist philosophy?

**HOWARD**

Looking back on it I'm astonished and I don't think I could tell you the first thing about existentialist philosophy. But anyway I went to that course of lectures and I didn't go to the Union. At the beginning of my second year I decided I would have a go. And then I found that I could do it, more or less, and then I decided that I wanted to go to the bar.

**HENNESSY**

What attracted you to the law?

**HOWARD**

By that time I had become very interested in politics, but I was never sure that I was ever going to get into the House of Commons. And I thought that the bar was the next best thing. It would give me, I thought, a pretty satisfying career if I was never able to get into Parliament.

**HENNESSY**

About that stage in one's formation one is very much open to influence. Who – who shaped your thinking, your Conservative thinking? Was it Macmillan and Butler, the big figures of the time, or Iain Macleod in particular?

**HOWARD**

It was Iain Macleod – we were all, I think practically all of us, we were all acolytes of Iain Macleod, he was our great hero. He seemed to have everything. He was a wonderful orator, he was entirely pragmatic, he achieved great things as Secretary of State for the Colonies, when he put in train the process of independence. And to this day I believe that had he lived, not only was he the best Prime Minister we never had, but had he lived as – when he was Chancellor of the Exchequer in 1970, I believe the whole history of the 1970s and thereafter would have been very different.

**HENNESSY**

It was a very liberal-Conservative hour, wasn't it, those [of] you who were Macleod acolytes, including Europe. At that stage.

**HOWARD**

Yes.

**HENNESSY**

You all saw Europe as part of this modernising theme...

**HOWARD**

Yeah.

**HENNESSY**

The Empire was going and Macleod had made that stunning speech at the party conference, taking on those who were reluctant to shed empire. So you were realists about the fading British Empire and you were very much Europeans. This was going to be the new basis of British influence in the world.

**HOWARD**

Yes, I campaigned in the 1975 referendum for remaining in the European Economic Community, which it then was. And yes, I was even a member of the committee of what was called the Conservative Group for Europe.

**HENNESSY**

We're jumping ahead a bit, Michael, but as we're talking about Europe, what was it that changed your mind about Britain's place in Europe and the nature of the Community? And when was it? Was it a gradual process?

**HOWARD**

Well, my position always was that I wanted the United Kingdom to remain a member of a reformed European Union, because I believe that the European Union in its current form is a flawed and failing project which desperately needs reform. Reform which would not only be good for the United Kingdom but would be good for the European Union itself. I had very high hopes that when David Cameron said in his Bloomberg speech in 2013 that he was going to argue for fundamental and far-reaching reform – that was his phrase – that at last we were going to get somewhere. And I was intensely disappointed by the failure of his negotiations. I mean, he came back with a deal, but it wasn't a substantial deal. And so, really rather reluctantly, faced with the prospect of remaining a member of an unreformed European Union or leaving, I thought the best course for our country would be to leave.

**HENNESSY**

Hence the change from the early '60s optimism to – well, now.

**HOWARD**

Yes.

**HENNESSY**

You had a good '60s didn't you? You liked the '60s. You loved pop music.

**HOWARD**

I love –

**HENNESSY**

I gather you're a bit of expert on pop music in that era...

**HOWARD**

I wouldn't claim expertise but I love the '60s. I saw the Beatles perform several times. I even – the first time I saw them they weren't even top of the bill. I have a – an album at home somewhere, their first album, and the sleeve says at the back, 'the Beatles are the biggest thing to hit British show business since the Shadows.'

**HENNESSY**

Do you sing along when you play your CDs?

**HOWARD**

Occasionally.

**HENNESSY**

Do you practise the air guitar?

**HOWARD**

I don't, no. I used to play the guitar, I used to play in a skiffle group.

**HENNESSY**

Did you? A skiffle group past. I don't think that was known about you.

**HOWARD**

That was when I was at school.

**HENNESSY**

You also stood for a Liverpool seat, your first attempt to get into Parliament. I think it was Edge Hill in the '66 general election. And you rather fell in love with Liverpool, didn't you?

### HOWARD

I'll tell you a story about my selection meeting, because I had always been, since I was a small boy, a passionate fan of Liverpool Football Club. So when I went to the selection committee they said, 'Do you have any connection with Liverpool?' And I said, 'Well, not really, but I have this great support, which is [a] life-long passion of mine, for Liverpool Football Club.' And there was a deathly hush in the room, because every member of the selection committee was an Everton supporter.

### HENNESSY

A Blue.

### HOWARD

And I always thought that the fact they selected me despite that was probably the greatest single achievement of my entire political career.

### HENNESSY

It is quite something isn't it? And you used to go to the home matches didn't you?

### HOWARD

I did. Yes. I used to stand on the Kop. I used to go – I fought two elections, I was a candidate for quite a long time, and rather unusually as a candidate I used to hold surgeries. Monthly surgeries. And I'd go up, I'd hold my surgery in the morning and I'd go and stand on the Kop in the afternoon.

### HENNESSY

On Saturdays, yeah. Did you learn anything from the great Bill Shankly about how to manage a political party, or to manage a government department do you think?

**HOWARD**

Oh, I think Bill Shankly was in an entirely different league from mere mortals like me. No, I couldn't – I couldn't begin to compare myself to the great Bill Shankly.

**HENNESSY**

The other great memory of the '60s is the easing-up of certain social constraints. The conscience bills, as they were called in Parliament in those days. The reform – homosexuality law reform, abortion and so on. And there were a number of them. Capital punishment. Were you by and large a straight-down-the-line social liberal Conservative on those questions?

**HOWARD**

No. Certainly not on capital punishment, although I changed my mind later. I'm not sure that I had very strong views either way on the – on the – on the other things.

**HENNESSY**

What changed your mind on capital punishment and when?

**HOWARD**

What changed my mind on capital punishment was what happened to the Birmingham Six and the Guildford Four.

**HENNESSY**

Yeah...

**HOWARD**

The great argument against capital punishment was the possibility of mistakes. And I had previously thought that if you had a kind of second-tier appeal against a guilty verdict on murder, not just on points of law or misdirection of the jury, but the appeal court really looking again at the evidence in some detail to examine the possibility of a mistake, that you could effectively rule out mistakes. But that was more or less what happened in the cases of the Birmingham Six and the Guildford Four, and it wasn't enough to preclude a mistake. And I therefore concluded that there was no way in a system that is in the end administered by fallible human beings to rule out the possibility of mistake. And I changed my mind.

**HENNESSY**

Now, you were very successful in the House of Commons straight away because you have a great natural debating style and you're very forensic, you're naturally forensic, I suspect, as well has having been trained to be. But...

**HOWARD**

So my wife tells me.

**HENNESSY**

Well, she would know, wouldn't she? She would know. I've often wondered though, Michael, because you're one of those politicians – I hope you won't mind me saying this – whose public persona is very often out of – really out of kilter with the private persona. That all your friends say the Michael Howard the public got an impression of, being very tough and relentless, is in many ways quite the reverse of the way he really is. A) Do you think that's true, B) do you think it comes from your legal training, plus a bit of your temperament, and C) has it been a burden for you?

**HOWARD**

It probably is true. It probably comes more from my temperament than my legal training. And yes, it's been a burden. I think the reason is that, I mean, throughout my time in government – although I wouldn't presume to say I was alone in this – but throughout my time in government I had pretty difficult jobs, and to do what I thought was the right thing for the country more often than not meant overcoming quite a lot of vested interests. And they were really tough battles, especially at the Home Office, and I think I'm probably more widely known for my time at the Home Office than for my time in other departments and other jobs. And in the Home Office I was really trying to change things quite radically, and there were a lot of really well-entrenched vested interests. Not just in the Home Office, but in the wider criminal justice world.

**HENNESSY**

Prisons and police.

**HOWARD**

Yeah. Who were horrified I was trying to change what had been a sort of high level of political consensus for a long time. I'm not sure that it ever had much public support, but it had a high level of political level of agreement, and I was trying to change it.

**HENNESSY**

To toughen it up in other words?

**HOWARD**

Well, in some respects. I just wanted to make it more effective. It wasn't, it – to the extent that it involved toughening up, that was a means to an end. The end was to turn around what was presented to me as the inevitable continuing rise in crime. When I arrived in the Home Office I was shown a graph by the civil servants which showed crime going up at an average rate of 5 per cent a year, and they said to me, 'This is what's happened to crime over the last 50 years and there's nothing you can do about it. Your job, Home Secretary, is to manage public expectations in the face of what will continue to be this inevitable rise in crime.' Now, I didn't take that advice and I set about, across the board, I had rather a comprehensive plan to try and reverse that, and some of it involved toughening up. But that was a means to an end, the end was to bring crime down, to reduce the number of victims of crime. And it's the poor in our society who are disproportionately the victims of crime.

### HENNESSY

You did become known for your very direct style, you admitted a moment ago it's a bit of burden, this. Why is it Michael you couldn't do as some people would have done more perhaps, a bit of light and shade?

### HOWARD

I don't know.

### HENNESSY

What is it in your temperament? You said it could be – it was really your temperament, you said a moment ago...

### HOWARD

Well, I wanted to get to the crux of the – I wanted to get to the crux of the argument. There was an argument. You know, the – the people on the other side had reasonable points. I had reasonable points. I wanted to get to the argument. And I thought I was right and I wanted to – I wanted to try and persuade, if not them, at least other people who were listening, watching this debate, I wanted to persuade them that I was right and so I wanted to get to the crux of the argument. Now, I'm sure it would have been more effective if I had been able to introduce light and shade as you suggest, but that's the way I looked at it.

### HENNESSY

Because the – the collective memory, political memory is very cruel. Your Home Office years will be remembered probably for the Derek Lewis affair, the directorship of the prisons...

**HOWARD**

I hope not. I hope they'll remember me for the fact that for the first time for around 50 years we did turn round the rise in crime.

**HENNESSY**

And you got it down quite a bit.

**HOWARD**

Yes, it had been going up and up and up. It came down by 18 per cent in my time, so there were nearly a million fewer crimes being committed a year when I left the Home Office in 1997 than when I got there in 1993, and however you look at the measurements, whether you take the recorded crime figures or the crime survey they show that during that period the trend in crime turned. It stopped going up and it started to come down. And it's come down pretty well the whole time since. And the changes that I made and the reforms that I put in place are still there; they haven't been reversed by my successors of whatever party.

**HENNESSY**

What was the key to your reforms?

**HOWARD**

I tried to take a comprehensive approach. I wanted to try and stop crimes being committed in the first place, so I encouraged the use of closed-circuit television cameras, which had an impact. I wanted to try and make sure that if crimes were committed those responsible were apprehended and brought to justice so we established the first DNA database in the world, which made a big difference. I wanted to try and make sure that if they were apprehended and they were guilty they were convicted, and I wanted to do that in a way which didn't obviously imperil the innocent, and so we changed the right to silence, which remained but could be commented upon in court because previously if you were silent and you then came up with a cock and bull alibi you couldn't be questioned on the fact as to why you hadn't said this at the time. So we changed that. And then finally, probably the thing for which I will most be remembered, is that I thought that if – if professional repeat criminals were convicted and were a clear danger to the public, not necessarily in a physical sense, but a danger in the sense they'd commit more and more burglaries and so on, that danger was removed by their being sentenced to imprisonment and that's what I meant by prison works.

#### HENNESSY

Prison works, your great phrase.

#### HOWARD

Yes, in the sense that while these repeat professional criminals were in prison they simply weren't at liberty to commit more crimes against the public.

#### HENNESSY

And it was prison escapes that's caused the bit that became the *cause célèbre*, didn't it? It's quite a complicated story I think because the prison service had been hived off to a so-called 'executive agency,' and the idea was –

#### HOWARD

Yes...

#### HENNESSY

– that operational control would be the director and that you as the minister would have a supervisory role and all the rest.

#### HOWARD

And would set the policy.

**HENNESSY**

Would set the policy, exactly. And after some escapes, I think two batches of escapes, there was an inquiry and the famous show-down – this is the bit – this is where I'm alluding to that you'll be remembered for because it's bound to be shown on the night, heaven forbid that you perish, when they have the clips, the film clips it's bound to be Jeremy Paxman asking you 14 times is it not – you have to live with this – 'Did you threaten to overrule the Director General of the Prison Service and get that Governor of Parkhurst sacked?' And that's the awful nature of political memory is it's bound to focus on that interview, isn't it, Michael?

**HOWARD**

Well you know the reason why he asked the question 14 times.

**HENNESSY**

Because he had to fill in a bit of time, didn't he, because the other interview had fallen down.

**HOWARD**

Hadn't turned up, yes, that's the reason, it's not unusual –

**HENNESSY**

But history doesn't remember the caveats does it?

**HOWARD**

Of course not. Look, I was being asked these questions by Jeremy years after the event. This interview took place during the 1997 Conservative leadership campaign.

**HENNESSY**

That's right, yes.

### HOWARD

These events had happened two years earlier. I'd been campaigning all day, I hadn't remotely been thinking about Derek Lewis or prisons, I'd been thinking about the Tory leadership. And I knew that every word I'd said had been crawled over and I, you know at the end – this is not an excuse but perhaps an explanation – the end of the day, long day when you're tired, you know what these days are like, I wasn't able to go back over the history and so I answered in my own way, as the phrase goes. But I mean the questioning was – in a way it was – it was slightly absurd because what I was not supposed to do was to overrule Derek Lewis and I didn't overrule Derek Lewis and no one has ever suggested that I did overrule Derek Lewis. So I didn't break any of the rules or the conventions and there's no question that I did. Now my recollection, going back over things, is that I didn't threaten to overrule him either, but whether I threatened is really a bit beside the point because I didn't do it.

### HENNESSY

And also it was allied to that remarkable lady, Ann Widdecombe, who'd been your Prisons Minister I think saying, famously saying there was 'something of the night' about you. One of the most devastating lines of post war British politics in a way, Michael. You must carry a scar from that.

### HOWARD

Well – you know Ann and I disagreed about Derek Lewis. We had an inquiry. After the first batch of escapes I said, 'This, you know, can't carry on,' and he gave me all sorts of assurances and said, 'It won't carry on, and we're going to tighten up in the following ways.' And then the second batch of escapes occurred, they were very high-level escapes, very dangerous people escaped and it turned out that the system hadn't been tightened up and I commissioned an independent inquiry and it came to the conclusion that changes had to be made from top to bottom of the Prison Service, which obviously meant including the man at the top going. And that was the conclusion I came to and I thought it was my duty to implement that and to ask for Derek Lewis' resignation and Ann profoundly disagreed with that. She didn't of course resign at the time over it, but she disagreed with it and that was the source of our disagreement.

**HENNESSY**

Have you got on all right since? Do you talk?

**HOWARD**

Well, we don't – I don't see her much now, because she's – she's not around at Westminster. We served in the same Shadow Cabinet for a while after that under William Hague and obviously I had some dealings with her when I was later Leader of the Party in a perfectly sensible way.

**HENNESSY**

I think she was, Ann Widdecombe, was very touched, Michael, by the letter you wrote to her on the death of her mother.

**HOWARD**

Well we'd worked pretty closely together until we had this disagreement. We'd worked together for a number of years and I knew what it was like to lose a parent.

**HENNESSY**

The other thing you probably will be remembered for is your part in the poll tax, 'cause you were an Environment Minister and that's another great disrupter. There was a scene of multiple disruptions really, the political ecology of that era, but looking back now on the poll tax question, how do you feel about that? If you could rerun the Movietone what would it be like?

**HOWARD**

Well the poll tax, as has often been said, had many fathers. My – my job was to take the bill through Parliament, through the House of Commons, I was made Minister of Local Government after the 1987 election and so I had the task of steering the bill through the House of Commons. And that I did.

**HENNESSY**

Loyally?

**HOWARD**

Yes.

**HENNESSY**

With anxiety?

**HOWARD**

I could see its merits. Intellectually it was a sensible solution to a particular problem. But I could also see that it had political difficulties, but those political difficulties were to be considered by people above my pay grade.

**HENNESSY**

Michael, you'll remember, as everybody will who was in her Cabinet, the fall of Mrs Thatcher in November 1990. It's one of those vivid memories that's obviously scored itself in people's minds and I think you went to see her, as did all the Cabinet Ministers, to give her advice. What did you say to her and how did you feel and how did she take it?

**HOWARD**

I said to her that if she decided to stand in the second contest I would – I think the phrase I used was I would 'die with her in the last ditch.' But that I was very worried that she would lose rather badly in that second contest. And that was my honest opinion. I thought there were a number of people who had voted for her in the first round –

**HENNESSY**

When she ran against Michael Heseltine, or Michael Heseltine ran against her to be a bit more accurate.

**HOWARD**

Yes, yes, but in the first round I think there were a number of people who felt bound to vote for her on grounds of loyalty – ministers and some other people – who would feel free of those bonds of loyalty if there were a second round. I was and remain an enormous admirer of Margaret Thatcher who I think was a kind of peacetime Churchill in her achievements, and the last thing I wanted was for her to be humiliated. That's what I told her.

**HENNESSY**

Were you very moved?

**HOWARD**

Of course.

**HENNESSY**

You're moved in the recalling it, I can see.

**HOWARD**

Of course.

**HENNESSY**

Talking about being Secretary of State for the Environment I think later as you were, I think there's one aspect of it that you're particularly proud of, that political history hasn't recorded that well.

## HOWARD

Well it led to the single most fascinating day in my entire time in government. Immediately after the 1992 election I was made Environment Secretary and the Rio Summit, the first big United Nations gathering on climate change was a few weeks away. And it was very uncertain whether the President of the United States, George Bush Senior, would go to Rio and sign at least one of the conventions that were being negotiated. And so I was told go to Washington and persuade the United States that he's got to go to Rio and sign the Convention. Quite a tall order. So I got to Washington and in the most extraordinary way for the government of another country, I saw the political heads of various departments, they were entirely open with me. One of them would say, 'I think it would be a disaster if we signed this Convention, the Climate Change Convention, but whether we do or not depends entirely on your meeting with the State Department at the end of today.' And then the next person I saw would say, 'I think it's *essential* that we sign this Convention, but whether we do or not depends entirely on your meeting at the State Department at the end of today.' I had lunch at our Ambassador's residence, there were two aides from the White House there with diametrically opposite views, the only thing they could agree on was that it all depended on my meeting at the State Department at the end of the day. So eventually I got to the State Department and I sat down with Bob Zoellick, who later became President of the World Bank, and we went through the Climate Change Convention line by line and he – and we sort of changed a comma here and put a parenthesis in there and changed the order of various things, changed the wording a little bit, and at the end of the exercise he said, 'I think we've cracked it.' And I went off to the White House and I saw Brent Scowcroft –

## HENNESSY

The National Security Advisor?

**HOWARD**

Yes, and he said, 'Well I think you know, if Bob says it's okay I expect the President will think it's okay too.' I went to Dulles Airport and I flew back. I went into the office next morning. First thing Bob Zoellick was on the phone and he said, 'The President wants a change.' And I said, 'What's the change?' And he told me what the change was and I said, 'No way, that's completely unacceptable.' And he said, 'I knew you'd say that, it'll be all right.' And it was. And the United States signed the Climate Change Convention and George Bush Senior went to Rio.

**HENNESSY**

One of your proudest moments?

**HOWARD**

It is in a way, yes, because I am not a climate change denier. I think it is largely man-made and I think we have to take action to deal with it and yes, I am quite proud of the part I played in that.

**HENNESSY**

Do you regret now the pretty unequivocal support you gave as an individual, but also as your party did, to the invasion of Iraq in 2003?

**HOWARD**

Well obviously it's worked out disastrously. I believe, and this is controversial, that the main cause of the disaster was what happened afterwards. And this is not entirely with the benefit of hindsight because Michael Ancram was Shadow Foreign Secretary at the time and was constantly saying, and it's on record in the House of Commons, 'Where's the plan for what happens afterwards?' And there was a plan. This is the tragedy of it. Colin Powell, who was Secretary of State, had a plan, and Cheney was Vice President, and Rumsfeld the Defense Secretary –

## HENNESSY

Yes.

## HOWARD

– said, 'We don't need a plan, we'll be greeted as conquering heroes, liberating heroes, we don't need a plan.' And my main criticism of Tony Blair – because he had a lot of leverage with George Bush at that time – is that he didn't say we must listen to Colin Powell and we must implement his plan. And I really do think that if that plan had been implemented everything would have been different. Now that didn't happen and given what happened it would have been better for the invasion not to have happened. So to that extent, yes I regret my support for the invasion. But Saddam Hussein was a really bad man and it was not a happy situation for him to remain in control of Iraq, so if the carefully prepared plan of Colin Powell had been implemented, I think things would have turned out differently.

## HENNESSY

In retrospect are you worried though about the intelligence that was provided for the House of Commons? If you'd known then what you know now about the reliability of the intelligence, or indeed if you'd seen Lord Goldsmith the Attorney General's rather fuller first opinion, earlier opinions on the legality of it, without a specific UN Security Council authorisation for the use of force, would you not have had doubts about that?

## HOWARD

Well look, I said at the time, or not at the time but when I was Leader of the Opposition, I got into a lot of trouble over it which shows that you can never predict the way your – what you say is going to be interpreted, but I said, 'If you look at the motion which the House of Commons passed in 2003, it refers to the intelligence in a way that is completely unsustainable by what we now know of the intelligence.' And so I said when I was Leader that if we had known at that time the scanty nature of the intelligence, which was thoroughly misrepresented to the House of Commons by Tony Blair, if we had known at that time how scanty the intelligence was no one could have voted for that motion in 2003. Maybe they'd have voted for a different motion which would still have led to going to war, but no one could have voted for that motion.

**HENNESSY**

Did you want to always to lead your party one day and perhaps become Prime Minister?

**HOWARD**

No, I never thought it was – it was remotely possible. When I eventually got to the House of Commons and as you say it took me quite a long time to get there, my ambition was to become Attorney General. An ambition I never actually realised.

**HENNESSY**

No, you didn't, did you?

**HOWARD**

No.

**HENNESSY**

No. Why didn't you want to become Leader and Prime Minister? Most people do to some degree.

**HOWARD**

Well it wasn't that I didn't want to, it was that I never really – I never thought of it as a remotely practical prospect.

**HENNESSY**

Why not? Not just because you came in late, surely?

### HOWARD

Well partly because I came in late. Partly I suppose I thought people had had enough of lawyers at that stage. They probably would want somebody different. I wasn't sure I had the ability to do it. You only discover both your abilities and your limitations when you've been tested in office. I hadn't been.

### HENNESSY

Were you reluctant to take over from Iain Duncan Smith as Leader of the Conservative Party in 2003? It was a bit of a surprise, wasn't it? It's not something you could have anticipated.

### HOWARD

Not at all.

### HENNESSY

And you were *nem. con.*, you were a shoo-in as it turned out.

### HOWARD

To be honest, I didn't have the same enthusiasm for it in 2003 that I had in 1997, so I wasn't full of enthusiasm for it, but we were in [a] terrible mess as a party. I was the third Leader in two years.

### HENNESSY

Yes.

### HOWARD

And the fourth in seven, if you take it back to 1997. And people had said, 'You've got to do it,' and so yes, I did it. And I obviously didn't win the 2005 election, but I think we made some progress and I like to think that I established a platform from which David Cameron could go on to become Prime Minister in 2010.

**HENNESSY**

You got 33 seats back, didn't you, if I remember?

**HOWARD**

Yes, more than Jeremy Corbyn got at the recent general election.

**HENNESSY**

How interesting. You did have your moments though didn't you as Leader of the Opposition. I think it was when you were Leader of the Opposition you had a tremendous put down of Tony Blair about not taking lectures, this grammar school boy isn't going to take lectures from a public school boy like the Prime Minister. You must have enjoyed that one.

**HOWARD**

Well I did and, you know, it was in the context of educational opportunity. And no one cares more about educational opportunity than I do, not surprisingly given my background. I'm absolutely passionate about giving everybody, from whatever background they come, the greatest possible opportunity to realise the most of their talents. Everybody's good at something and it's the job of a good school to find out what that person is good at, what that child is good at and encourage them and to make the most of what they're good at. And so I am passionate about that and I didn't take kindly to being lectured about educational opportunity by someone who'd had the gilded background of Mr Blair.

**HENNESSY**

You're still relishing it even now, aren't you?

**HOWARD**

I suppose so.

### HENNESSY

I was reading the other day your prospectus, your speech when you became Leader of the Opposition. I was wondering if it would be an indication of what you would have done had you become Prime Minister, because I think you said in a nutshell that you hoped to do for public service in the quality of them, the improvement of them, what Mrs Thatcher and her governments did for improving the basics on which business operated. Would that have been the keynote, the hallmark of a Howard government if you'd formed one?

### HOWARD

I would like to think so. It is something that we badly needed then and which I think we still need because there's been considerable progress in some areas, but there's much, much more to be done. And it's a challenge that all countries face and we do better than some, but not quite as good as others and there's much to be done still.

### HENNESSY

Did you ever think in your head, Michael – it's a rotten thing to ask really – what you would have said on the threshold of Number 10 if you'd gone to kiss hands with the Queen and she'd asked you to form an administration? What would you have said on the step which is, would have set the tone and the pitch for what was to come?

### HOWARD

I don't think I ever got quite as far as working that out. I'd like to think I'd have said something similar to what I said in that speech to which you've just referred but I never got quite as far as working it out.

## HENNESSY

In your retirement from frontline politics you've done a lot in the hospice movement, haven't you and I think you've made that very much a focus.

## HOWARD

Well it's a huge privilege. I chair Hospice UK which is the umbrella organisation for all the hospices in our country.[1] They are just fantastic organisations. They're all independent of course and because of what they do we are world leaders in palliative care. And no one should underestimate the importance of palliative care, of looking after people at the end of their lives in a way that really minimises their pain and mitigates the bad things which are inevitable, but also if you go into a hospice there's such a wonderfully cheerful atmosphere. It's the most wonderful movement of which we should all be hugely proud and I regard it as a fantastic privilege to be associated with them.

## HENNESSY

If I could be a magic wand waver for you, a fairy godmother, and grant you one last reform I would guarantee that could be implemented, what would it be?

## HOWARD

I'm currently in discussions with – I probably shouldn't make this public but anyway I'm going to since you've asked.

## HENNESSY

I can be terribly discreet.

---

1 Lord Howard retired as chair of Hospice UK in November 2018, after two terms in the role.

### HOWARD

I'm currently in contact with Simon Stephens[2] about changes that can be made in relation to the NHS. One directly involves the hospice movement. We have put an offer to the NHS that of the 250,000 people who die in hospital every year, most of whom don't need to die in hospital and shouldn't die in hospital, don't want to die in hospital, we in the hospice movement can take out and look after 50,000 before they die and I hope we're going to be able to get that up and running next year. Quite ambitious. And then there's another plan for digitalised care plans which could actually not only transform care but save the NHS literally hundreds of millions of pounds. And I think there is huge scope in the NHS for operating more effectively and more economically. And digitalisation is one way forward, making full use of what the hospice movement can achieve is another way, and these are really practical things which can be done and I hope will be done in the very near future.

### HENNESSY

How would you like to be remembered by history?

### HOWARD

Well, when you, as you know, Peter, from your own experience, when you go to the House of Lords you are asked whether you want to have a coat of arms and with the coat of arms goes a motto. And I took as my motto the Latin for a phrase that originally was used by President Teddy Roosevelt. He said, 'It's better to take part in the action than to be a spectator.' *Melior conatus quam spectatio* I think is the Latin. That's been my guiding light.

### HENNESSY

How do you think you will be remembered?

2 Chief Executive of NHS England since 2014

**HOWARD**

That's for others to decide.

**HENNESSY**

Michael Howard, thank you very much indeed.

# Paddy Ashdown (Lord Ashdown of Norton-sub-Hamdon)

Series 6, Episode 1, first broadcast 31 July 2018

**Born** 27 February 1941; **Died** 22 December
2018; **Educated** Bedford School

MP (Liberal Democrat) Yeovil 1983–2001

Leader of the Liberal Democrats, 1988–99; International
Community High Representative and EU Special
Representative for Bosnia Herzegovina, 2002–06

**Autobiography** *A Fortunate Life*, 2009

**HENNESSY**

With me today is Paddy Ashdown, Lord Ashdown of Norton-sub-
Hamdon, who led the Liberal Democrats for 11 years between 1988
and 1999. His was a highly unusual formation for a politician of
his generation. He caught this in his memoir, *A Fortunate Life*, in
a neatly-crafted paragraph of autobiography, 'I was a soldier at the
end of the golden age of imperial soldiering, a spy at the end of the
golden age of spying, a politician while politics was still a calling,
and an international peace builder backed by western power
before Iraq and Afghanistan drained the West of both influence
and morality.' Paddy, welcome.

**ASHDOWN**

Nice to be with you, Peter.

**HENNESSY**

You were born in India in 1941. Who were your parents and why were they in India?

**ASHDOWN**

I'm sort of a child of the Raj, I suppose... My family went out as merchant adventurers, Irish merchant adventurers – says a great deal – in 1805, and basically stayed in England and India one way or another through until we left in 1946 when the British left. So I am born to the son of an Indian Army colonel, whose name is John Ashdown. He always used to say to me that he had been involved in all the great retreats of the war and had a son after each of them. I'm the eldest and I am Dunkirk, I suspect, probably conceived on the very day my father got back with his Indian regiment – by the way, without losing anybody. And the consequence is that nine months later, when I arrived in Delhi – I was born in New Delhi – there's a little riot outside my father's house from the Indian Army troops that he brought to Dunkirk, who turned up and said – because my real name's Jeremy, as you know – and they turned up in front of the house and said to him, 'Oh sahib, this is very bad news. We are fighting Germany and you are calling your first son Germany.' [*Both laugh*] So I was brought up until the age of five – for the last, I suppose two years, my dad was behind Japanese lines in Burma, and my mum went down to the plains to wait for him – he came out very sick actually. So I was brought up by the family servants and it meant that I was brought up to rhythms of Islam. And you know, it's always been sort of part of my background. When I came back to Britain, to Northern Ireland, I could actually speak Hindi rather better than I could speak English.

**HENNESSY**

Your mother was bitten by a rabid dog when she was carrying you wasn't she?

**ASHDOWN**

She was – the day before I was born.

**HENNESSY**

That's extraordinary.

**ASHDOWN**

You may draw what conclusion you wish. [*Hennessy laughs*] My father was typically shooting snipe in a jeel, an Indian marsh, and my mum was out with him and she was bitten by a rabid dog. And I was born the next day. There may be some connection there.

**HENNESSY**

When the family come back to Britain they go to Northern Ireland, and I think your father was a pig farmer in quite a big way – a thousand pigs? That's a lot of pigs isn't it?

**ASHDOWN**

It is a lot of pigs and they were part of my early upbringing. And he was a wonderful man and I admired him all my life and he's still a sort of model for me. Even after he died I can remember asking myself, 'What would Dad have done or expected me to do in these circumstances?' But he wasn't a good businessman, and the business went bust. I was 18, the eldest of seven, but by that time one had died, six. And the rest of my family sailed down Belfast Lough on their way to Australia as 'ten-pound poms', leaving me behind. But the 'Paddy', Peter, as you know of course, is a nickname, because I went to my father's school and my grandfather's school in Bedford, a sort of public school for the sons of the Raj. So I went with a broad Northern Irish accent, and it was drummed out of me, and I'm rather sad.

**HENNESSY**

Before we leave Northern Ireland and get to Bedford School, your dad engaged in a bit of smuggling across the border with the Republic didn't he? What did he smuggle?

**ASHDOWN**

Margarine and beer.

**HENNESSY**

Margarine and beer. And he taught you how to throw nails in the road to stop the pursuing police.

**ASHDOWN**

He did. He did. My dad, though a colonel in the Indian Army, was a very unconventional man. He particularly believed that God made fish and it was unreasonable for any man to claim them, and he taught me poaching at an early age and various other faintly illegal pursuits. But he was a wonderful man indeed, and he was – although he would never have admitted it – a classic liberal. He taught me the habit, which I've never forgotten, of never being afraid to be alone in holding an opinion, and he taught me the art of – he would always take sort of ridiculous positions just for the process of arguing them out. He taught me the passion of argument and debate. And he really strongly influenced me, as indeed did my mum. My dad gave me, as indeed I try to give my grandchildren, adventures. My mum – it's funny how you sometimes repeat your own parents in the woman you marry – my mum dished out love in unconditional great dollops like cream to everybody around, including us. So we'd come in battered and bruised and a bit sort of low because we had had an argument with Dad and she would see this and held the family together.

**HENNESSY**

Did you enjoy Bedford School?

### ASHDOWN

Not much if truth be known. I can remember learning the art of scrapping, fighting, in the little prep school that I went to first, at the age of 11, missed my mum and dad a lot, suffered badly from homesickness. Then I managed to settle into it okay, and in truth I was not very good at school. I was not interested at all, I was much more interested in the athletics track and the rugby pitch and the girls at the local high school. Until one day – and how many times have you heard this? That quite literally changed my life. I had a friend come to see me, he said, 'Paddy, come to the poetry society.' And I said, 'The poetry society? Poetry society?!' Anyway, I went because I liked him very much, and I met a remarkable man called John Eyre, who was my teacher, and that evening he gave me a lifetime's love of literature and poetry.

### HENNESSY

Can you remember the poem that most excited you that evening?

### ASHDOWN

Oh, I think probably – the ones that I absolutely fell in love with, it probably was that evening, was John Donne. I mean, I memorise poems, I must have a hundred in my head and my favourite ones are John Donne. I think it probably was 'I wonder, by my troth, what thou and I / Did, till we loved? Were we not weaned till then? / But sucked on country pleasures childishly?' But of course I was 16–17, the hormones were coursing through my blood, so the Donne love poems were ones which struck me… He remains my favourite poet, from that evening. There's a wonderful one of his which has been – actually much later, because of course he wrote sacred poems as well as love poems, and there's a line of his which goes, 'On a huge hill / Cragged and steep, Truth stands, and he that will / Reach her, about must and about must go.' It's wonderful. About the eternal search for truth.

**HENNESSY**

Talking about your teenage hormones, they had a bit of a surge when you had a fling with your maths coach lady, didn't you?

**ASHDOWN**

Yes, I've covered this story – it wasn't necessarily – I was trying to protect the person that, um –

**HENNESSY**

In your memoirs.

**ASHDOWN**

Yes. It wasn't exactly the maths coach, but yes, it was an interesting early experience of my life.

**HENNESSY**

You left Bedford without taking your A Levels because you got a place in the Royal Marine Corps.

**ASHDOWN**

It's a bit more complex than that actually. My dad was running out of money and he really wanted to send my brother, his second son, Timothy, to Bedford, and so I took a naval scholarship at the age of 16 which paid for my school fees, which enabled my brother to go to the same school as me at least for a bit. So I was then locked into a career in the Royal Navy. It would have been a Royal Naval scholarship, but in the end my maths wasn't good enough so I went into the Royal Marines. You know, almost all the things that have happened in my life have happened by luck, by happenstance. I could have gone to university at that stage, probably, I think – that's what my teacher said – but my dad didn't have the money. I could have gone to the Royal Navy, but I'd have been very unhappy because I discovered later, for all sorts of reasons, the Navy at that stage was very snobbish, very class-ridden. And so because of exigency really I went into the Royal Marines and it was by far the best thing for me.

It suited you really down to the ground, didn't it?

Oh yes, absolutely. I mean I left my school with two things. One, with an overbearing sense of my own importance, which was very soon knocked out of me in the Royal Marines, and the second was a desire to go on learning all my life. And I've undoubtedly learnt more since I left school than I ever learnt at school, and the Royal Marines really knocked the edges off me and taught me all sorts of things which, you know, have sustained me in many ways ever since. It annoys me today, to be honest, Peter, that people always remember Paddy Ashdown, ex-Royal Marines. It's an important, but probably the least important, part of my life. I'm actually Paddy Ashdown, ex-unemployed youth worker when I came to Parliament.

Yes, we'll come to that.

But the friends I made, by the way, in the Special Boat Service, which I eventually went into and commanded a Special Boats unit in the Far East, I learnt my politics [from] as well, because I was in charge of men, who by any standards at the profession we were involved in – the profession of soldiering, sometimes in quite difficult circumstances – were better than I was. And I thought what kind of country could we have if it was a genuine meritocracy? And what that made me was a Liberal. I mean we were working in very small teams, sometimes three or four in quite difficult circumstances and I relied for them on my life and they relied for theirs on me, I suppose in a way, and it gave me a tremendous sense of the equality of human beings.

It must have been a bit difficult in the officers' mess sometimes –

It was –

– because you were a Labour supporter in the Wilson years and then a Liberal, and I don't want to be unkind to the corps of Royal Marines but they don't normally exhibit the views and prejudices of Hampstead, do they?

No, no they don't, although the odd thing is that if the nation passes through real war, it nearly always turns left afterwards for precisely those reasons.

Yes, yes, exactly.

But by 1959, 1960, it was not a very popular thing to be a Labour supporter. We're all entitled to the errors of our youth, but on the other hand it was the Labour Party of Shirley Williams and of Roy Jenkins, who of course I got to know very well later on. And so no, it wasn't a popular thing at all, but I've always [had] that old habit my father taught. Blondie Hasler, the great leader of the Cockleshell Heroes raid once said, 'When all of the world is going in one direction it's time to follow the reciprocal.' He was a classic liberal.

**HENNESSY**

You like all that, don't you? You take great pleasure in being perverse in that way.

**ASHDOWN**

No, no, I don't. I mean I take great pleasure in defending opinions even though they may not be popular ones. I do take pleasure in that, and sometimes, you know, when people see my style of politics they find it quite passionate in the present climate. I remember saying to a friend not long ago, 'You need to remember I was trained as a Commando officer, I know of no other way of dealing with a problem, but to fix bayonets and charge at it.' In that sense, I suppose I'm slightly diminished as a politician because I don't do subtlety terribly well. On the other hand, probably it hasn't stood me in much harm that I tend to see a problem quite clearly and then tend to worry away at it. The one thing that I cannot resist as a temptation – throughout the whole of my life – is when somebody says to me, 'Paddy, this is impossible, it can't be done.' That becomes irresistible.

**HENNESSY**

You're a natural special operator. Do you think learning how to throw nails underneath police cars was your first taste for special operations –

**ASHDOWN**

No, I think –

**HENNESSY**

– and it's stayed with you ever since?

**ASHDOWN**

I found adventures irresistible, of one sort of another.

**HENNESSY**

I think that's what I meant by the question actually.

**ASHDOWN**

I thought you probably did. And by the way politics gives you a huge amount. I think – I remember saying to a friend once that of all the things I've done, there's nothing which matches so closely active service, because the bullets are always flying. The good thing is in politics you can get up, dust yourself down and try and do better next time. But, you know, it is an adventure, it's a great game. It is the great game. Spying isn't the great game; politics is the great game.

**HENNESSY**

Very interesting. We'll come to spying now, because you went to Hong Kong to learn Chinese. It's interesting how you were hopeless at languages at Bedford School, but then you subsequently learnt eight others.

**ASHDOWN**

Well actually when people ask me how many languages – I've forgotten six is my answer. Eight's a bit of an exaggeration. I think the reason why I can do languages, at least moderately, is because I learnt Hindi first and it had opened up channels – by the way, I can speak no Hindi now – but it opened up channels in my brain that enabled me to pick up languages.

**HENNESSY**

Very interesting. And then the Secret Intelligence Service and the way they have of keeping an eye on you as a potential recruit and you had frontline experience, tough circumstances and then you had the language. So I suppose it was almost inevitable that the pass was made at you. Tell me how the pass was made.

**ASHDOWN**

Be very careful, Peter. If you cause me to say too much I have to eat you at this stage. I'm only allowed to say –

**HENNESSY**

I'm aware of that, I'm being very brave.

**ASHDOWN**

I know you are. Well, somebody toddled along and said, 'I say, come out to lunch.' And I went out to lunch, and they said 'Well you have an interesting background and you can speak Chinese, you're learning Chinese, would you like to go into the Foreign Office?' Quite a conventional approach really, nothing special.

**HENNESSY**

And you knew what he meant though?

**ASHDOWN**

It didn't involve beards or false moustaches really.

**HENNESSY**

But you knew what he meant by something in the Foreign Office, didn't you?

**ASHDOWN**

I sort of knew what he meant, yes, because if you work in the SBS you're living quite close to that milieu and you quite often have contact with it. So I had a broad idea of what they were about, yes.

**HENNESSY**

And you had no hesitation in saying yes?

**ASHDOWN**

No, I didn't really because I knew because I knew my next stage of soldiering was going to be in staff offices and behind desks, and I knew I'd probably had the best time in soldiering that I could have and I had – does this sound a bit sort of pompous? –I had a sense that I could work on a wider horizon instead of the one I was working in. So I went out to Geneva with my wife and family – halcyon days – we had a wonderful villa on the shores of Lake Geneva. And we had a wonderful two years. I was a British diplomat, working in the United Nations with several of the –

**HENNESSY**

That was the day job, wasn't it?

**ASHDOWN**

That was the day job. It was –

**HENNESSY**

You can't tell me much about the night job, but just give me a flavour.

**ASHDOWN**

Well it was the Cold War. It was the height of the Cold War and you'll know, as I think most of the world does, that around the international organisations, the UN in Geneva, the UN in New York, spies circle. And it's an interesting milieu to establish, I suppose, what's going on in the world. In the end, however, we had a wonderful two and a bit years there – you know, the children are young, we're walking in the Alps in the summer, skiing in the winter, we've got a boat, this fabulous interesting job. But it's 1974 – three-day week, two elections – and I felt it exceedingly painfully that the country which I was representing in the day job, Britain, was the object of derision and disrespect and jokes; it was 'the sick man of Europe.' And both my wife and I decided that however fine, nice, pleasant life was at the time – I mean, this does sound quite self-righteous, but it genuinely was – we wanted to do something to make sure that we played a part in trying to ensure Britain got out of the mess it was in. So I went into politics. And not, I should say, just any old politics; Liberal politics – at that stage we were 3 or 4 per cent in the opinion polls, my party Leader was being arraigned for conspiracy to murder at the Old Bailey.

**HENNESSY**

Jeremy Thorpe, yes.

**ASHDOWN**

In my constituency, Yeovil, it had been Tory since 1910; they didn't count their majorities, they weighed them. We were third when I went to the constituency, ready to turn up and be duly elected to Parliament, I discovered there were about ten members of the Liberals – most of whom, I used to joke, the average age was deceased. And I suddenly realised what a huge and very potentially dangerous decision I'd taken, irresponsible decision I have to say – though undoubtedly the best of my life – with a wife and two children. I couldn't get a job, I was unemployed for six months. The Tories did everything they could to stop anybody giving me a job locally and I wouldn't move elsewhere. I wouldn't go elsewhere, that was where I lived, I was going to represent where I lived; that was what I'd chosen as my home. So I lost. I improved the Lib Dem position to second, but I lost.

**HENNESSY**

In '79.

**ASHDOWN**

In '79, lost to the great John Peyton, who I liked very much. And then I was unemployed for a second time, for a year. I applied for a hundred and something jobs in 1981–82, in the first recession of the Thatcher government. And then I finally got a job on what was then called the Community Programme, which was an unemployment assistance programme as the youth worker in Dorset. And until the end I really didn't think we could do it. And yet – is this strange? – looking back I suspect building the team, winning Yeovil against the odds at the time I think it probably was, was the most enjoyable part of politics. It just seemed much simpler then. And if I look back, if someone says to me you can have one line on your tombstone – why would you want more? – I think Member of Parliament for Yeovil because it is a unique and extraordinary privilege to be able to represent the community you live in and love and one so wonderful as the one that I live in in the Parliament of your country. What greater accolade can there be? Is that the right word?

**HENNESSY**

It is. You're a romantic in politics really, aren't you?

**ASHDOWN**

I am, I am.

**HENNESSY**

You are.

**ASHDOWN**

No, I'm incurably romantic, you're quite right.

**HENNESSY**

Would you, Paddy, have had second thoughts about going into politics if you'd known how intrusive into people's private lives the newspapers were going to become?

**ASHDOWN**

No. No, I mean did I know that when I went in? No, but I recognise from the bruising experience to which you are referring that that's part of the territory. I think probably my skills such as they are, gifts such as they are, were gifts best satisfied, best exercised in politics. I said a moment ago, in battle if you stand up and do the wrong thing at the wrong time you're liable to get a bullet from somewhere. The same is true of politics. If you act stupidly you're going to put yourself in the position where that comes to light. So it was undoubtedly, I suspect, for me and my family the most painful period of my life but I don't blame anybody else for it.

You've always been very interesting about Westminster because you've always described yourself as not clubbable, and you've been quite honest about not adapting to the conversational style of British politics in either of the Chambers. I think you've written somewhere that you can sound shrill and a touch self righteous. It's very candid of you, but what surprises me a bit Paddy is that you didn't learn to adapt to the ways of Westminster for the sake of being more effective in your oral contributions.

To be honest, I never much liked Westminster, Peter, and it never much liked me. For me politics was outside Westminster, not just in it. I had to work there. We often have to work in places we don't find terribly congenial. I never liked the atmosphere of Westminster and I never thought it necessary to really adapt to that. Probably it would have been, I might have been more successful if I had, but in the end I learnt how to do it better. But, you know, I'll let you into a secret – I'm sure no one else is listening – if you're standing up in the House of Commons it can be quite frightening and so there are times when your voice goes up because you are pushing against six hundred voices. And very frequently, particularly over Sarajevo, particularly over this thing that I went back to time and time again about the need to intervene in the Bosnian War, I would be shouted at by six hundred people and it can be quite an intimidating experience. The main thing is not to give in to that and just to make sure you continue to make your point as best you can.

**HENNESSY**

This is also the era when the mould of British politics looks as if it just might be breaking. You were a great admirer of Roy Jenkins and Shirley Williams and Bill Rodgers weren't you?

**ASHDOWN**

I was.

**HENNESSY**

David Owen perhaps less so?

**ASHDOWN**

David Owen less so.

**HENNESSY**

There's always been a bit of something between you two, hasn't there?

**ASHDOWN**

Yeah.

**HENNESSY**

What is it?

**ASHDOWN**

Well, I mean when we launched the Liberal Democrats and he launched the continuing SDP, you know only one of us would survive. I knew that. It was, you know, the O.K. Corral. If he had won with the continuing SDP we would have ceased to exist, and it was a pretty head-to-head confrontation. Yes, I suppose there has been a bit of needle.

**HENNESSY**

Have you both mellowed a bit since?

**ASHDOWN**

Probably.

**HENNESSY**

Good.

**ASHDOWN**

You do get older.

**HENNESSY**

It's not for me to say good, sitting here as a kind of care worker.

**ASHDOWN**

No, he's a formidable man. He's a really formidable man. You know whenever he spoke he spoke with great authority. The thing he couldn't do, David Owen, respect him though I do for many of his positions – Roy Jenkins got it right – he was not a team builder. He used to call him 'the upas tree' – do you remember? – under which nothing would ever grow. You know I've no doubt whatsoever if David Owen had been in American politics, he'd have been the President, without a shadow of a doubt. But because he couldn't build a team, couldn't work a team and couldn't create a team, he couldn't get as far as he should have done in British politics.

**HENNESSY**

Can we talk now about one of the really deep passions in your life which is the consequences of the former Yugoslavia breaking up. Your detractors used to shout at you, 'You're the MP for Sarajevo, the member for Sarajevo.' But where did that start and how?

## ASHDOWN

By mistake. It's another one of those times you know when it's a pure happenstance. I'm walking down the corridor – I could even take you to the place – after the 1992 election, and you know, Peter, you've made a very deep study of these things, after an election there's no role for the Opposition. You've got to stand to one side, you've got to let the government have its honeymoon. There's no point in popping up and starting to… So I'm walking down there – I can't stand being bored – so I say to my good friend and close *consigliere*, Alan Leaman, 'What do I do now?' He said, 'Well you know about wars, why don't you fly out there?' So I did. I flew out – hitched a lift on the Special Forces Hercules flying into besieged Sarajevo and saw what was going on. And I'll tell you what I thought, and I still think it's true, that this was in some ways a Spanish Civil War of our time. It was the predictor of what was coming in terms of conflict, internal conflict, inter-ethnic conflict, conflict across borders, within borders and across borders; and the second was that it was a profound moral challenge to our time. And the third reason why is I'd often go round Bosnia in the middle of these battles, and in the middle of these battles I'll see a little sort of pottering van that came from somewhere like you know Ledbury which was full of stuff that had been gathered in a Ledbury garden fete to be sending out to Bosnia. The people of Britain I think understood the consequences of this and what it really meant in Bosnia far better than the politicians. And that's very similar to the Spanish Civil War.

### HENNESSY

Can we return now to breaking the mould, remaking the centre-left. You started trying again, didn't you when John Smith was Leader of the Labour Party? You got somewhere but not that far if I remember.

### ASHDOWN

Not with John Smith, no, not at all. Look, my first job with the Lib Dems was to ensure they survived. We were once represented when I took the party over by an asterisk denoting that no detectable support could be found for us anywhere in the land. So up until 1992 the job was to make sure the party survived and it did. And then I remember saying to my colleagues, 'Now we've survived, we're on the field of play, we're now going to play.' And by play I mean we're going to start working with other parties and doing what we can to change the context in which we were, because only if we changed that context could we begin to create a space in which we'd continue to prosper. But secondly because the Tories had been in power for so long it occurred to me that Britain needed an opposition and the parties of opposition working together was a sensible thing. So I went to see John Smith and he said, 'Yeah Paddy, I can see your point. I'm Labour through and through and I'm going to be Labour through and through and if you can make your own way by yourself, fine, help yourself, but I'm not going to do this in the way' – and it was, I mean I loved John Smith, a lovely man, wonderful parliamentarian and he was just being straightforward with me. When he tragically died, Tony Blair took over. Here was a person of a completely different view who, you know, he used to say 'I could never see any difference – you know, when the SDP was formed – I could never see any difference between the policies of Roy Jenkins and the policy of me and I used to ask myself why aren't we in the same party?' So over a series of dinners we got to know each other quite well and we agreed that we would work together and to give Britain an alternative to the Conservatives. Remember in those days we genuinely wondered whether we would ever have anything but a Conservative Party, whether they could ever be defeated. And so we put a process of cooperation together which got closer and closer right up to the '97 election. And I think doubled my seats – we went from what was it, 20 to 50 something or other, and helped to deliver a massive majority for him, which was the problem.

**HENNESSY**

Exactly. Did you really think in the run up to the election that there would be Liberal Cabinet ministers and a *de facto* coalition of the centre-left?

**ASHDOWN**

I was much less interested in Liberal Cabinet ministers than I was in two parties working together around an agenda that we agreed on. I mean obviously Liberal Cabinet ministers was the product of that, it was the only way you could deliver that, but the thing that I saw and I think he saw too was that if two parties worked in coalition when they weren't forced to by the electorate, you did it from the position of moral high ground, and provided that you had the same broad agenda – what was necessary for Britain – that was a perfectly sensible thing to do.

**HENNESSY**

Came quite close, didn't it? I think it was only John Prescott, wasn't it and Gordon Brown who – because he was taking the proposition to them if I remember.

**ASHDOWN**

Well they were the ones in the end who blocked it, yes. But I think that one of the most baleful constitutional instruments in Britain is the Downing Street removal van. Because here you are, you've finished an election and if it passes from one Prime Minister to another the removal van turns up next day. And you are asked then to take decisions with your bloodstream swilling with, you know, testosterone and exhaustion and adrenalin. You're not in a position to take long-term decisions. And I think that having a certain interim to settle a government in is probably a much better thing. But this is a very clear example of it. So the following day, I spoke to Tony Blair from a school in Somerset about midday on polling day and I said, 'You're going to win it, Tony.' The first time he ever actually thought he was going to, oddly enough, or at least said so. And so we agreed to speak the following morning in the expectation that what we had planned we'd put into operation. And the following morning I met Roy Jenkins in the Leader's Office in the House of Commons and I said to Roy, 'You know, this is going to be an indecent majority' – what did he have, 170?

**HENNESSY**

179 or something.

**ASHDOWN**

179. We had 50 on top of that. And do you know, very seriously, both of us reached the conclusion that to have a coalition adding my votes to his would leave too weak an opposition and it was an undemocratic thing to do. He seems to have come – I never quite know what happened that night because certainly Cherie said to me later on that it all changed that night. Something happened during the night. But by the time I rang him the next morning I could tell absolutely, he didn't say the words, but I knew him well enough to be able to read them clearly enough to say 'Not yet, perhaps later', and the best opportunity was lost.

**HENNESSY**

Yes.

**ASHDOWN**

By the way I think that if he had done that, he had the authority to carry it through, I do think it would have provided a new basis which would have been acceptable for coalitions in British politics, and I do think it would have been – am I being a bit, a bit sort of self aggrandising to say so? – but I think if the two parties had worked together some of the mistakes, particularly the early triumphalism of Labour and the classic decision to go ahead with the Dome, if you remember, which I thought was the first –

**HENNESSY**

The very first Cabinet meeting.

**ASHDOWN**

The very first and I thought it showed – I think Blair revealed the weaknesses of his administration within [the] first five or six months. I think that would have been different.

**HENNESSY**

And perhaps no British participation in the Iraq War? It's not for us to speculate too much.

**ASHDOWN**

No it's not for us and you need to remember that I wasn't in Britain, I was away.

**HENNESSY**

You were in Bosnia.

**ASHDOWN**

I was in Bosnia, yeah. And by the way I got that judgement wrong. I think it's the one judgement looking back in foreign affairs that I think I got wrong. I was trying to hold together an international coalition in Bosnia with the Americans and the French and therefore divided by the Iraq War. Viewing it from a distance, I watched the great debate, When I heard him [Blair] say that he's [Saddam Hussein] got weapons of mass destruction I accepted that as indeed did many others, though my party did not, and they were right and I was wrong.

**HENNESSY**

What did come out of the 1997 election was the Joint Cabinet Committee on Constitutional Matters which built on the Bob McClennan–Robin Cook talks before the election, which produced a remarkable range in the late 1990s – which is all too easy to forget – of constitutional reform: devolution all round, Freedom of Information Act, the incorporation of the European Convention on Human Rights into UK law, and that was very much the fruit of the collaboration. But it didn't endure. I think when Charles Kennedy succeeded you it rather faded away. You must have rather regretted that?

**ASHDOWN**

No, I didn't actually. I thought it had gone already. Let me explain. I mean you're absolutely right, Peter, most people say oh we got nothing. Yes we did. By the way Blair wasn't really interested in constitutional reform, he really wasn't, I'd see his eyes glaze over when it came to talking about – he was a man who wanted to control things and quite right and proper, I'm not critical about that. So he did the constitutional reform you referred to, Wales, Scotland – by the way proportional representation at the European election. I think he did believe in the European Human Rights Commission, I'm sure he did. Freedom of information, I'm not sure. He was quite – he was quite equivocal about that.

**HENNESSY**

He's been very shirty about it since as well.

**ASHDOWN**

Exactly so. So I think those were the fruits of that cooperation. The one thing that I – I knew that cooperation could not last, could not lead to the kind of things we wanted to see in government unless you had proportional representation. And Roy Jenkins then produced the Roy Jenkins Report, it came out with a conclusion, not perfect but good enough, pragmatically I think necessary and a good first step to take [before] proportional representation. At this point Tony, who again wasn't tremendously keen, took it to his Cabinet. I had a call from Robin Cook – actually I've never said this before – that night before it went to the Cabinet and he said, 'Tony's not going to back it.' And against the opposition of John Prescott and others who did not want to have proportional representation, and Jack Straw, he then basically ditched the Jenkins Report. And at that stage I knew that the direction of travel that I'd been following had fulfilled as much as it could, there wasn't any more to do. I felt that it was time for me to stand down as Leader of the party and hand over to Charles. And I think actually to give Charles his credit, I suspect I would have removed myself from the Cabinet Committee even a little before Charles did, who did it in a sort of more gentle and I think probably wiser way. So no, I don't think that it was Charles. I think it was Blair rejecting the consequence of proportional representation and therefore, whether he recognised it or not, leading Labour back into the psychology of we are the masters now, and you can't build a partnership on that basis.

**HENNESSY**

And then the Balkans calls again. The UN's High Representative. I suppose we can call you a Peaceroy, not a Viceroy.

**ASHDOWN**

Well I hope so.

**HENNESSY**

But it was an extraordinary job to do and the fires in you really burn when you write and talk about it, Paddy, almost more than anything else.

**ASHDOWN**

No, not more than anything else. I'm more passionate about trying to do what I can to more sensibly play my part in rearranging British politics. But yes, I mean I was very privileged. Blair, by the way, when asked – he proposed me as the High Representative

– the European Union said 'Look, who's Paddy Ashdown? Is he up to this job?' And Blair said, 'Look, this guy's actually run the Lib Dems for 11 years, the Balkans are going to be a doddle after that.' [*Hennessy laughs*] And then I went out there. And do you know what I did? I actually, I actually pretty well enacted the Lib Dem manifesto of 1997 and it worked. I mean we managed to pull the country –

#### HENNESSY

You mean rebuilding civil society.

#### ASHDOWN

Rebuilding civil society. I found myself – heavens above, how many times in politics do you have to do this? – completely reversing my position which I opposed Mrs Thatcher on – I found myself stripping down the barriers to business, lowering taxation, making sure the economy gets working again, encouraging entrepreneurs. And so I was extremely privileged to be able to spend four years in a country I learnt to love very much, and to help it towards peace – a stabilised peace, I should say. The sadness is that because the European Union has now lost interest it's all going backwards very badly.

#### HENNESSY

Why did you decline Gordon Brown's offer to be Secretary of State for Northern Ireland in his government?

#### ASHDOWN

[*Laughs*] Because I didn't agree with what his government was doing. Gordon – I mean, I said to him, 'Gordon, look, you know, you can't expect me to be a sort of Liberal Democrat bungalow in the garden of Number 10 Downing Street. You know, there's a thing called Cabinet solidarity and I don't agree with what you're doing.' And Gordon, bless him, said to me, 'Well couldn't you just keep quiet about it?' And I said, 'No Gordon I couldn't.' So the answer – it was very – I like Gordon very much and it was very decent of him to offer and it showed a rather surprising non-trib-alism, because Gordon's a classic, very deep and highly effective Labour politician. So that was very good I thought, but you know clearly I could not have taken a Cabinet position unless I agreed with the policies of the Cabinet.

### HENNESSY

I think you said after the European referendum that you didn't recognise your own country.

### ASHDOWN

Yes, I didn't, and there was a moment of despair. I was driving back home, I hadn't had any sleep the night before, obviously, I was driving back with Jane over Salisbury Plain, down towards Amesbury and there before us was laid the wonderful rolling hills of Salisbury Plain, covered in the blazing yellow of mustard seed or rape as I remember. And I turned to her and the tears were rolling down my face. I said, 'I don't recognise my country anymore.' Well, that's how you feel. You will know how politicians feel the morning after a political defeat on something that you really –

### HENNESSY

What was it you didn't recognise? Because many people think looking back it was a lightning flash that illuminated an extended family, if you want George Orwell's metaphor of the country, that no longer knew itself.

### ASHDOWN

Yes it did, it did illuminate an extended family, and one that had largely I think hidden below the surface before and now it's had permission to come out into the open. Look, let me start off by saying many millions, probably the clear and maybe even vast majority, of those who voted Brexit did so for perfectly good, genuinely patriotic means. They believed that was the right future for our country. But there were some less fragrant people in there too, and I see the rise in hate crimes, I look at the retreat from this great British position that has made us great in the world which is our internationalism, our sense of engagement, into a sort of proto-isolationism. And that's not my country. It really isn't. And obviously I love it and I'll go on serving it as best I can, but the country that I know and believe in is internationalist, we've become less so; is famous and properly so for its habit of compromise, for its relative politeness in the public discourse and for its respect and tolerance of others. Insofar as those remain attributes, and of course they do in Britain, they seem to be attributes much diminished by the new mood that has taken hold post-Brexit. Maybe it will go away, maybe we'll come back to our senses. I hope we will. But I'm dedicated to providing a force in Britain that can genuinely offer effectively, which we're not doing at present, an alternative to that.

### HENNESSY

If I retrospectively could wave a magic wand and make you Prime Minister, what's the first thing you would do in entering Downing Street, after your well-rehearsed spontaneity on the doorstep? [*Ashdown laughs*]

### ASHDOWN

I'll tell you what. I think – the thing that I've been – I remember when Blair was elected and we were thinking about a Millennium project and he chose the Dome. I said to him, 'Why not recreate the British Museum technologically? Why not use the massive force of the internet to put all the information in the known world and make it accessible to every British citizen and we could become information brokers in the world as well?' The one thing that drives me in politics, Peter, is that I believe profoundly in the empowered citizen, not the powerful state. And so what would it be today? Probably that moment has passed, but it would be something that would confer power on ordinary citizens in Britain. We live in an internet age which has hugely empowered ordinary individual activity and yet our politics remains stuck into a position of the 1870s – furtively hierarchical, tending to exclude people rather than include them. So have I given you an answer? I know what the aim would be.

**HENNESSY**

The aspiration, yes.

**ASHDOWN**

The aspiration would be: I would want to lead a government I suppose that was dedicated to empowering ordinary citizens to make their own decisions. Devolution of power is very important in that, giving them a space in the economy, fighting monopolies, building up consumer power, all those things that are classically Liberal.

**HENNESSY**

What trace do you think you'll leave on history?

**ASHDOWN**

I haven't a clue.

**HENNESSY**

What trace would you like to leave on history?

**ASHDOWN**

Well I honestly don't know what trace I'd like to leave.

**HENNESSY**

Have a go, have a go.

**ASHDOWN**

Hmmmmm. I suppose when in due course all this agenda, what I've referred to as the sort of liberal agenda comes back into play, when the age of populism has passed and we reassert those old liberal, small 'l', liberal internationalist values then I would be very satisfied if somebody reading the footnotes of history, tiny down the bottom, recognised me as one of those who had fought to preserve that and give the opportunity to return it.

**HENNESSY**

Your dad would approve of that, wouldn't he?

**ASHDOWN**

My dad would certainly approve of that. Perhaps one of the sadnesses of my life is my dad was dead before I was elected. But he's driven me, he's driven me ever since.

**HENNESSY**

When the time comes for your biography – your biographer will have quite a time with you, as biographers always do – but there's one thing that's run right through: you've been passionate about pretty well everything you've done. And that's a great bonus in life, isn't it? You're not an indifferent sort of chap are you?

**ASHDOWN**

Do you know, that's such an interesting question, Peter, because it's actually true. I think we are exceedingly fortunate, and by the way I am exceedingly fortunate – if the dreadful thing happened and I suddenly curled up my toes tomorrow afternoon, I'd obviously be pretty upset and it would probably spoil the day a bit, but I wouldn't have reason to complain. I've managed to fit a huge amount into my life. And so I sort of see it in this rather, you know, the Almighty, whatever Almighty you happen to believe in –

**HENNESSY**

You do believe in the Almighty *en passant* don't you?

**ASHDOWN**

I do, yes, I do. But I don't allow anybody to ask me what – you know, what kind of Almighty. I mean it's my Almighty and I suppose I'd have to say I'm a Christian because I find that a suitable moral code in which to live my life in these times, although I could have been probably a member of any of the Abrahamic religions. Yes, I do believe in the Almighty, but it's Paddy Ashdown's Almighty and if someone says, 'Is it Protestant?' I'm not going to tell. I don't know. So you have been given this extraordinary gift of life parcelled out in 24 hour chunks, and I have been lucky enough to have the opportunity to sort of devour it day by day and get as much in as I possibly can. And it seems to me a waste, almost an insult, not to be passionate. Why would you want to be lethargic? Why would you want to be apathetic in these circumstances? So yeah, I suppose I can get a little too passionate, sometimes get in the way of good judgement, but frankly I wouldn't have lived my life any other way.

**HENNESSY**

Paddy Ashdown, thank you very much.

**ASHDOWN**

Thanks.

# Sayeeda Warsi (Baroness Warsi)

Series 6, Episode 2, first broadcast 7 August 2018

**Born** 28 March 1971; **Educated** Birkdale High School;
Dewsbury College; Leeds University; College of Law

Vice Chairman of the Conservative Party, 2005–07; Minister without
Portfolio and Co-Chairman of the Conservative Party, 2010–12;
Senior Minister of State, Faith and Communities, Department
for Communities and Local Government, 2012–14; Senior
Minister of State, Foreign and Commonweath Office, 2012–14

**HENNESSY**

With me today is Baroness Warsi, Sayeeda Warsi, a lawyer, politician, and the first Muslim to sit in the Cabinet. In her own words, she's the girl from Dewsbury who ended up at the top table in the land, and a northern mum with five kids. In 2010 she became Co-Chairman of the Conservative Party and Minister without Portfolio. Two years later she was appointed Senior Minister of State at the Foreign and Commonwealth Office and Minister of State for Faith and Communities. In 2014 she resigned over the government's policy on the Israel-Gaza conflict. She's the author of *The Enemy Within: a Tale of Muslim Britain*, and sits in the House of Lords as a Conservative peer. Sayeeda, welcome.

**WARSI**

Thank you.

**HENNESSY**

What kind of family was yours?

**WARSI**

Big, loud, female, argumentative. I'm one of five girls and debate and discussion was a huge part of growing up. Dad's a great story-teller, and we were always encouraged really, from quite a young age, to have an opinion. And so yes, there was always a lot of noise.

**HENNESSY**

Was it unusual, do you think, amongst your friends and people from your own faith community in those days to be a family that did have this kind of continual running conversation about matters of public affairs and so on, and being argumentative, and being *encouraged* to be argumentative I would imagine?

**WARSI**

I think what was different about us was that first of all we're an all-female family, and I think had there been boys *and* girls maybe the rules or the culture at home would have been different. So there was no hierarchy really in the way that maybe sometimes in conservative families you do have, where the men would be considered to have an opinion and the women may not be allowed to. And the other thing is we came from quite a plural religious upbringing, so we had very strong Sunni roots, very strong Shia roots, grew up in a local community which was again different, Tablighi Jamaat.

**HENNESSY**

That was Savile Town in Dewsbury.

**WARSI**

That was in Savile Town, Dewsbury. We came from a Pakistani background, whereas the local community was predominantly from an Indian background. So there was lots of difference and in many ways [we] always felt like slight outsiders, which I think meant that the rules about what we could and couldn't do were far more relaxed, because the sense of immediate community censorship wasn't there for my parents. And I think once they'd had five girls they'd kind of felt like they'd failed anyway, so, you know, shrug shoulders, let's just get on with it. [*Laughing*] It can't get any worse than this.

### HENNESSY

I think, from having read your book, your mother's a very powerful person and was very ambitious for her girls. And I think you might have said once she 'thought middle class' in terms of wanting you all to be professional ladies, is that right?

### WARSI

Oh yes, Mum absolutely thinks we're middle class, and whereas, Dad, I think still thinks working class. And I think it was this sense of – she had to better herself, so she very early on, in the early '70s, was driving, she passed her driving test, she bought herself a car. She wanted us to go to college and university. She wanted us to be dressed right. So one of the things she'd do is she'd go along to – I think it was a C&A at the time – and she'd buy a dress that had just come out and then she'd go down to the market and buy fabric and stitch the rest of us the same dress, so it looked like we all had C&A dresses on but we didn't. So she was always wanting us to look as if we were far more successful than we were, behave like we had far more than we had. Always keep your best clothes for going out in, so it looks like we were doing well. Always buying the next house. So they traded properties every three or four years and each time bought a slightly bigger house, put an extension on it, sold it and made some money, bought the next house. So she was very, very pushy and vocal as the middle class, and in many ways was the driving force alongside my Dad's hard work that really changed our lives.

**HENNESSY**

What about the income flow, because your dad, when he first came over, I think, worked in the mills, the way so many immigrants did in West Yorkshire, and was a bus driver, and then got into business in his own line and I think – and did extremely well, does extremely well I think, 'cause he's still with us isn't he?

**WARSI**

Still works.

**HENNESSY**

So was it the rising level of income as well as a rising level of ambition in your household?

**WARSI**

Dad comes from real poverty. I mean the kind of poverty which means they couldn't guarantee three meals, two meals a day. They couldn't guarantee clothes for all the kids, shoes for all the kids at all times. Whereas Mum actually came from a much more comfortable family. So I think Dad's work ethic is quite raw. There's always the feeling that, you know, things could go back to the way they were, and so just feels the need to work every hour that he had, worked double shifts in the mills, worked – even when he started his business continued to minicab for three nights a week – as well as running the business for many years. And still now goes to work, gets in before everybody else. You know, I roll my eyes because, you know, he's on the phone, 'Where are you, why are you not in the office?' first thing. You know.

**HENNESSY**

And he's 82 isn't he?

**WARSI**

He is.

**HENNESSY**

Tell me about school.

**WARSI**

School was the local comprehensive. I don't think I was properly stimulated in school. I was quite naughty. And I think part of that was because I just felt that I wasn't getting pushed as much as I probably should have been. Got great O Levels, in the end. But I think, you know, talked far too much and caused far too much trouble whilst I was at school. But in the end I think the fear of what could happen at home if I didn't get the grades meant that I actually got the grades. And then went on to college and then the University of Leeds.

**HENNESSY**

I think your mother decided that you would do law.

**WARSI**

She did.

**HENNESSY**

And so you did law, you did what Mum said. Do you regret that? Do you not think you might have wanted to say to Mum, 'I want to be something else'? In fact, I think you had a taste for the theatre.

**WARSI**

I did. I wanted to take the old English classics and really give them a modern twist and put them on stage. So I probably would have been the person that should have made *Bride and Prejudice* or something. And she made it very clear that there were a handful of professions that we were going to go into. It was medicine, or dentistry, or accountancy, or law, or pharmacy, or teaching. I mean, these were the – and in retrospect it was absolutely the right thing for us, because I ended up doing what I really enjoy doing and have had such an amazingly varied career already, because I had a very stable, well-paid job in my twenties and thirties.

**HENNESSY**

Tell me about your own Conservative philosophy, your political Conservative philosophy, because in your age group, with your faith background it's quite unusual isn't it, to be a Conservative? At what point did you realise you were one, and at what point did you realise what kind of one you were?

**WARSI**

Dad was a member of the trade union when he worked in the mills. He voted Labour most of his life, although has voted for other parties. And Mum voted Margaret Thatcher. And I over time started to wonder what it was that my ideological kind of home lay in. And for me, I suppose the overwhelming factor was this sense of if you got the opportunities and you were prepared to go out and work hard then there was almost anything that you could achieve. And in many ways, even though it was Mum that voted Conservative, that was an ethos that we got from my Dad. Because he, you know, one of the overwhelming messages we got from him when we were young was, 'If I ever see you in the Social Security queue I will never forgive you. Don't ever do that to me. And I don't care if you sweep the streets. You sweep the streets but you get yourself a job.' And I think that work ethic and that sense that there's dignity in work and work is the only way of changing your life and it can absolutely change the course of your life as it changed his. For me I saw that very much as a Conservative principle. And I fundamentally believe in a low-tax economy. I was brought up in a faith where tax is set at 2.5 per cent, and then there are dozens of other ways in which you can give. I mean, the number of words in Islam for giving and charity are just numerous. And invariably I found my parents, who didn't have a lot, would always give their 2.5 per cent, but they would always give more to lots of other causes. And I realised early on that actually if you keep tax rates low and incentivise people to give, and this, obviously with Islam it was incentivised by your faith, then there are many ways in which you can give. So I think it was – it was a really interesting early way of looking at how society works and what is most effective and what is the role of the safety net. And having personal responsibility, but also freedom, I sensed very much was part of Conservative principles, family values, Conservative values, which again were very much part of the way I grew up. So I don't think there was a moment when I thought, 'ping', I'm actually a Conservative. I became involved with the local party initially.

**HENNESSY**

How old were you when that happened?

**WARSI**

In my late twenties.

**HENNESSY**

Yes.

**WARSI**

And I found some really interesting individuals who allowed me to see the world in a different way. And I think over time then I realised that actually if I was more comfortable it was going to be in the Conservative Party. It's the only party I ever joined as a member.

**HENNESSY**

Were you a bit bedazzled by Mrs Thatcher when you were young?

**WARSI**

My mum certainly was. And she instilled in us a sense of – I'm not even sure she understood her policies – but she instilled in us a sense that strong women need to look like this. And she – I remember her talking about the way she – Mrs Thatcher – was turned out and how her hair was always immaculate and how she looked. She liked the way she spoke, she liked the way she felt she was in control. And so I think she was very much held up to us as a role model.

**HENNESSY**

You married very young, didn't you, your first marriage?

**WARSI**

I did. 19.

**HENNESSY**

Was it an arranged marriage?

**WARSI**

It was. It was, it was –

**HENNESSY**

So you went back to Pakistan and the family arranged it for you, as it were?

**WARSI**

Yes. I went to Pakistan when I was 16. A number of options were presented to me. Of the options he seemed the most obvious. And now, you know, my children will often ask me, 'How did you do that? Why would you even do that at that age?' It was just what happened. And it wasn't forced and it wasn't – I didn't feel traumatised by it. It was just something you did. You know, you went along and you kind of felt your parents directed you towards somebody and you said, 'Oh, okay, that's fine.' And – and I was probably a fairly docile teenager in the sense that I wasn't really into make-up and boys and partying. You'd invariably find me stuck in a book somewhere. And so this was just something that you kind of just did. And at a time when lots of girls from the community that I grew up in were being taken out of school, were not being allowed to go to college, you know, had no sense of direction and ambition for the future, were not being allowed to have an opinion, I felt that we were in a really liberated space. So I didn't see my parents going out and directing us in this way as being anything but them doing their duty.

**HENNESSY**

Do you regret that it didn't work out?

**WARSI**

I regret the fact that the marriage broke down. I think divorce is probably one of the most traumatic things that will happen in anyone's life, even if the relationship is completely over and it's right for that relationship to end. I think the – just the wrench of divorce is something which –

**HENNESSY**

And you had a child too.

**WARSI**

And we have a daughter. But do I regret that that marriage happened? No, because I wouldn't be the person that I am today if I hadn't had that experience. And yes, a lot of it was bad, but I think it's an experience which formed who I became. And I don't think I would have been either as successful or as considerate or as knowledgeable on really important issues if I hadn't been through that experience.

**HENNESSY**

Tell me about your progress through the law. After Leeds, what did you do?

### WARSI

So I went on to do my finals as a solicitor, my professional exams, and then went on to do my training with the Crown Prosecution Service, the Home Office Immigration Department. Then went into private practice. Ended up working for the last Conservative Member of Parliament for Dewsbury, before I stood. And was there for a very short time when one of the senior partners there had left to set up his own, quite niche legal practice. And I was a newly qualified solicitor. He asked me whether I would come and work for him when he went off to set up this new firm, and I was very cheeky and I said to him, 'Well, why would I come and work *for* you? This is a new practice. I could come and work *with* you? I think we should go in as a 50–50 equity partners and we should set up this firm together.' I think he was quite taken aback. But I got that in the end. And so in my kind of mid-to-late twenties I had my own practice.

### HENNESSY

One of the great dramatic events in the world that also very powerfully affected you was 9/11 – the attacks on the twin towers and the Pentagon. It seems to me, Sayeeda – extrapolating a bit – that your whole life has been an attempt to ease the relationship between your country and your faith. And it must have become harder to do that in that very instant of that day in 2001, September.

### WARSI

I think it definitely changed the course of my life forever. When they say a single event can change where you go and what you become. I think up to that point I felt that if there was a point of difference it was race. And certainly by the time that September 11th came around I felt very comfortable being British and Asian. I'd been a positive story, a positive social mobility story. I'd done well, I had a great job, we were having foreign holidays. I was even thinking about buying a classic car. Life was good! And then things changed and I was no longer British and Asian. And those battles that we were still fighting on race now took on a completely different face with religion, and I became British Muslim. And all those questions about loyalty, belonging, identity, started all over again. My marriage by that time had practically broken down. I suppose I had an early midlife crisis, and I just wasn't sure I wanted to fight those battles all over again. I felt – I wasn't sure whether I belonged in Britain at that time. I wasn't even sure where I belonged, I think, there was so much going on in terms of my own personal life. And so I packed my bags and I picked up little one and I went to Pakistan. I left, I checked out and I checked out for about nine months. And I suppose I went to find myself in some ways, and I realised, having been away for nearly nine months, that I'd taken the easy option. I'd run away rather than face up to both my personal life and the challenges that Britain presented at that time. And I could either be a bystander or I could be an upstander and I could play my part. And that's when I came back and really threw myself into politics.

**HENNESSY**

Before then you hadn't really considered a political career, even though you had pretty strong Conservative convictions?

**WARSI**

No. I hadn't. I mean, I'd been vice-president of the Students' Union at college, so I'd always been involved in some sort of politics, and I'd been on lots of demos and had spent six years with the Joseph Rowntree Trust and looked at interesting ways in which we'd fund it. Actually people went on to become great activists and –

**HENNESSY**

What kind of demos did you go on?

**WARSI**

Oh God, I just dread one day these photos are going to appear. I went on the poll tax demo. [*Laughs*]

**HENNESSY**

That was taking a walk on the wild side –

**WARSI**

It was! [*Laughing*]

**HENNESSY**

– for a loyal Conservative.

**WARSI**

But I wasn't a loyal Conservative at that time was I, I was at university. I mean, it was quite – if you didn't go on a poll tax demo, it didn't matter who you were, there was something wrong with you wasn't there? [*Laughing*] It was the obligatory demo. I suppose grown-up politics, as I call it, serious politics, for me started post-Pakistan. Which sounds really odd, right, because it sounds like I went away, had my jihadi gap year, became completely radicalised and then joined the Tory Party. [*Laughing*] I'm sure that Conservative colleagues of mine will wonder what I was doing for nine months wandering around rural parts of Pakistan!

**HENNESSY**

It was quite a brave thing to do because you would have had a comfortable and successful career. You already were having one in the Crown Prosecution Service and then in your private practice. So it really was quite a step to take.

**WARSI**

It was, but I was also very lucky in the sense that my legal career and owning the practice and then selling the practice put me in a place where financially I was probably much more stable than most people in their early thirties. And also I realised, I think, having spent nine months in Pakistan, that you really didn't need that much to live on. You know, all the plethora of clothes and lotions and potions and technology that you thought you needed, suddenly spending time in rural Pakistan made me realise that you could probably live out of a rucksack. And I think it did make me think again about what was important in life.

**HENNESSY**

You stood for Dewsbury in the 2005 election and you got into a bit of trouble I think, that you now regret. Something you said that was deemed to be homophobic.

**WARSI**

I think there's a lot about that campaign that I regret. Particularly the comments that were in my leaflet around Section 28 and –

**HENNESSY**

Age of consent and Section 28, yes.

**WARSI**

And at that time I think that kind of comment was what was kind of mainstream in the Conservative Party, or it was acceptable to say it. Ultimately I take responsibility for that campaign and I should have directed it rather than allowing it to be directed by my then campaign manager. Whether it was political naivety, lack of experience, whatever it was, I think there were sections of the way in which that campaign was run which if I was to do it now would have been done completely differently. And I also, in retrospect, having spent time understanding, genuinely understanding the equalities framework rather than the equalities framework as it uniquely and acutely applies to me, made me realise that those positions were deeply hypocritical and it was right to say they were wrong and it was right to apologise.

**HENNESSY**

Yes, you did apologise directly for them, didn't you?

**WARSI**

I did.

**HENNESSY**

Michael Howard, the then Conservative Leader, you came to his attention. How did that happen?

**WARSI**

I think it was either the back end of 2004 or early 2005, before the election. Where we had a fundraiser in Yorkshire and Michael was coming as Leader. And I was asked to do an introduction and again I had no idea what I should have been saying, so I went up there, told a few jokes and –

**HENNESSY**

At his expense?

**WARSI**

Not at his expense actually. They were quite self-deprecating jokes. He thought it was hilarious. I think he thought I was slightly mad. He just said he thought I had huge amounts to offer the party, and he rang me a few days later on my mobile. He said, 'Hi, it's Michael.' I said, 'Oh, Michael who?' 'Michael Howard.' And you could almost hear my head going, 'Michael Howard, who?' Until it occurred to me it was *the* Michael Howard, and you know I was a little minion in the party in a seat which we probably weren't going to win, whatever I was telling people. Then after the election I came to see Michael and he said, 'Look, I'd like you to become

Vice-Chairman of the party.' And he just kind of – I suppose brought me in and kept me in. He always said you should have fought another seat and you should have been in the Commons and when, I remember, the opportunity to join the Lords came up he said to me, 'You're writing off your opportunity to take up one of the big offices of state and you could go all the way to the top. Why would you do this?'

**HENNESSY**

So you regret it?

**WARSI**

No, *he* told me I would regret it.

**HENNESSY**

And do you?

**WARSI**

No, not at all, no, I don't, because I think the Lords for me at this age – I mean I think six months after joining the Lords in my mid-thirties I woke up every day thinking have I made a huge mistake? Is this really the place for me? I took the Equalities Bill through actually on the frontbench immediately I think after joining and I just remember a couple of times my colleagues saying, 'You know, calm down, at the despatch box, you know. You don't need to go in for the kill, this is not court.' You know and it was a completely different way of politics. I was much more suited to the Commons I think at that age. Whereas I think once we came into government, for me the part of the job that I really enjoyed was the despatch box, especially at the Foreign Office.

**HENNESSY**

You like the performance aspect too, don't you?

## WARSI

And I like the advocacy. It felt natural to be back at court effectively and to be able to make the argument. I think often at the despatch box as ministers we don't make the argument and say look, we disagree but this is why and this is the thinking behind why we're doing what we're doing. And to me I really enjoy doing that at the despatch box, making the argument for the points that I was making, rather than just surviving the questions which I think sometimes ministers do.

## HENNESSY

Tell me about your first meeting with David Cameron.

## WARSI

So I met David briefly before the 2005 election and then I met him immediately after because Michael said, 'There's a young man who I think you really should get to know.' And that young man turned out to be David Cameron. And then before David did his big speech at Blackpool declaring his interest as Leader and asking conference to – to support him, he came to Dewsbury. So I took him to see one of the social action projects that I was running, I took him into the home of a Pakistani, British Pakistani family where I was running a reading project where women would go in and – women from the English community would go in and work with the kids from a really young age so that when they went into school they were reading English and understood the language much more than what was available for them in the home. And Samantha came as well and then we went onto the [stage at] Blackpool and then I introduced him at conference. And I always say to him, 'I was your good luck charm because you stood up and said, "You know, when Michael Howard first mentioned Sayeeda to me,"' – so he tells this story about what Michael had said to him, saying, 'If you don't get your skates on, David, she'll get into Parliament and she'll wipe the floor with you.' And so we had this joke that, you know, subsequently he had to send me to the House of Lords 'cause clearly I was much more of a threat if I'd gone to the Commons.

### HENNESSY

A defensive measure. You became well known in many ways to the wider British public, I think, through your television appearances, particularly one: *Question Time* when Nick Griffin of the BNP was on.

### WARSI

They had a huge audience for that, I think eight million people tuned in. And it was a moment when I think the far right in this country was trying to go mainstream. I remember being asked to do it and David was really keen for me to do it.

### HENNESSY

That's Cameron, not Dimbleby.

### WARSI

No, David Cameron was really keen for me to do that. I remember speaking to George Osborne at the time and going through the briefing and I just thought, I'm just going to go on there and be myself rather than try and be a politician. And I remember initially being sat next to him, that's the way they'd formatted the panel and I said I didn't want to sit next to him, I wanted to sit on the opposite side of him and they said, 'Oh is it because you're – you know you're worried?' I said, 'No, because I use my hands a lot' and I thought, I'm going to get quite animated during this programme and I'm going to look like I'm about to slap him. And that is not – that is not the image I wanted to project, you know, I wanted it to sound like rational debate. So I wanted to sit on the opposite side so I could kind of reach over and speak to him. I absolutely felt we needed to go and take his arguments on. And I genuinely believe it was the beginning of the end of the BNP.

**HENNESSY**

What was the main point you made to him?

**WARSI**

A point which I continue to make, which is I'm not going to take lessons on loyalty from the far right. For somebody whose grandfathers, both maternal and paternal, served in the British Indian Army and fought fascism, who actually protected the values that we now talk about as dear in this country. For somebody whose family have been giving blood, sweat, life, loyalty to this country for over a hundred years I'm certainly not going to have somebody who are the descendants of the very fascism we were fighting telling me that I've got to pledge my loyalty, or even questioning my loyalty. And that's the message I gave to him to say, you're no representative of British patriotism.

**HENNESSY**

It was a special day when you were the first Muslim to sit around the British Cabinet table. How did you feel? How did you prepare for it? And of course the photographers loved it too because you did look very distinctive.

**WARSI**

After the election there was that whole period of forming a coalition, so it wasn't immediate. So I wasn't really sure what he was going to ask me to do, if anything, or whether it was even going to be at Cabinet level. And so I hadn't prepared and I remember when the call came I looked in my wardrobe and I thought, I haven't even got anything to wear. And the only outfit that was new was that pink outfit. And I thought, well at least the weather looks all right, so I'm going to kind of just wear this and for me I wear a lot of you know kind of quite ethnic looking clothes in the summer, they're just so much more comfortable to wear. And I don't even think I thought about the fact that walking down Downing Street looking like that was such a big moment until afterwards when I saw the pictures all over the papers the following day. But when I went in and you know David asked me to do the job, I suppose two things – I had no idea what he'd ask me to do, he said, Minister without Portfolio. I had no idea what that meant. And secondly, the over-whelming emotion was I thought I was going to cry, because it was being overwhelmed by the moment, but also I suppose a sense of fear. You don't ever lose that fear that somebody's going to walk in and tap you on the shoulder and say, 'What are you doing here? Wake up. This really isn't happening'. I remember speaking to the press outside saying I just feel really humbled and privileged to be able to serve my country.

**HENNESSY**

Did David Cameron tell you what *he* meant by you being Minister without Portfolio?

**WARSI**

No, he didn't. I remember him saying something like, 'Yeah you're going [to] just do the kind of stuff you're doing and keep doing it.' Which I –

**HENNESSY**

That's pretty imprecise!

**WARSI**

Yes, but it was brilliant, because it was so broad that effectively the way I interpreted that role was that I could be chief interferer.

**HENNESSY**

And were you?

**WARSI**

I was, of course I was. I loved it because there was no sense of – no boundary of where I could go, which brief I could get involved in as long as you know the PM was happy with what I was doing. I could just go anywhere really, so I ended up doing domestic stuff, foreign policy stuff, issues around you know Cabinet Office, constitutional stuff. I started travelling. There were certain parts of the world which he asked me to take responsibility for – the 'stans'. So I was the one who very early on developed the relationship with places like Kazakhstan, parts of the world which were really difficult to get to and people didn't realise they were countries, I think. So I spent time there. Uzbekistan, Tajikistan. I went out to Pakistan actually within months of taking on the role, because William went out.

**HENNESSY**

William Hague.

**WARSI**

He was Foreign Sec[retary] and he came back and he said, 'You really need to go out, Sayeeda. They absolutely believe you're a part of them, and what you could do out there, and the boundaries we could push on our diplomatic work is worth doing.' So I went out there very early on. Became involved in integration stuff, faith stuff, the counter-terrorism stuff, so it was such a broad brief and, of course, all the Chairman's work as well.

**HENNESSY**

Chairman of the party, yes.

**WARSI**

The Co-Chairman's work with Andrew Feldman. So it was brilliant yet brutal because I think from the day I took the job certain parts of the party decided they didn't want me to be Chairman. I think from day one it was like, 'No, don't want her,' you know, 'She doesn't represent what we want the party to be.'

**HENNESSY**

Oh really? Straight away you felt that?

**WARSI**

Oh, it started very early on. So, long before I was even in Cabinet the articles had started about why I was an unacceptable Conservative.

**HENNESSY**

That must have been quite hard to take.

**WARSI**

Yes, but I suppose it's no different to what I've seen all my life, you know where you turn up somewhere where people like you don't normally turn up and then somebody tells you you don't belong and you just say, 'Okay,' shrug shoulders, keep moving on. 'You'll get used to it – your problem, not mine.'

**HENNESSY**

I think you got increasingly worried about the attitude of some people in our country towards the Muslim community. You made a remark in 2011 that the Islamophobic mindset had passed the dinner-table test. What did you mean?

**WARSI**

That phrase, 'Islamophobia has passed the dinner-table test,' has almost become a line in the sand. Even now academics, and we're taking evidence in Parliament on this very issue, will say that was a moment when actually publicly there was an acknowledgement that it was now being found in the most respectable of settings. So the kind of racism that I'd been used to growing up, which was much more brutal, the 'P' word on the street, you know, people chasing you down the street, we'd kind of come to terms with and realised that some people were just not very nice people. But this form of Islamophobia, this pernicious form that you found in the media or in think tanks or in politics, the language, the discourse, the way in which people were being demonised and – and clumped together as this block and then given these tropes around that community [which] were being peddled – for me was deeply worrying. And I said it, you know, Islamophobia was the way in which the respectable rationalise racism.

**HENNESSY**

Do you still feel that?

**WARSI**

I think it's far worse. I actually think that Islamophobia is Britain's bigotry blind spot. We actually even fail to see it now. We open the papers every day, deeply appalling Islamophobic stories, comments, incorrect many of them which have to subsequently be corrected and we just say, 'Okay, this is what happens'. You know we now hear Islamophobic discourse in Parliament, in the House of Lords. The most awful comments are sometimes made in debates from some of my colleagues, not necessarily Conservative but UKIP and some Conservative colleagues where I'm astounded that this is not the kind of discourse that we would ever tolerate in relation to any other minority race or religious community. So I actually say it's our bigotry blind spot.

**HENNESSY**

I think recently – we're leaping ahead a bit – you've suggested that the Conservative Party needs to take a long look at itself on that question.

**WARSI**

It does, it does and I think very publicly it manifested itself in the mayoral election with Zac Goldsmith.

**HENNESSY**

In London.

**WARSI**

Yes. I think anybody on any measure would look back at that campaign and should be thoroughly ashamed, as I was of my 2005 campaign. It shouldn't be wrong for us to say we got it wrong and I'm sorry. I've done it, I think other people should have the confidence to be able to do that.

**HENNESSY**

In 2012 there's a reshuffle and you're part of the reshuffle. Why do you think David Cameron moved you to the Foreign Office to be the Senior Minister of State? What was behind all that? Did you want to be part of a department, as opposed to being a –

**WARSI**

No. I mean I was happy to stay on as Chairman but I think that the calls from Parliament at that time to have a Chairman from the Commons were too strong. And I certainly hadn't endeared myself to the right of my party. So initially he offered me another job, which I refused.

**HENNESSY**

Which was that?

**WARSI**

It was a Commonwealth role and an Equalities role and I just felt that, you know – I said to him, 'Do you not understand what's tokenistic about a female offspring of Commonwealth immigrants doing Commonwealth and Equalities? Do you not get how that would just kind of stick in my throat, to say really? Why am I even doing this job? You know, where does my kind of expertise lie?' So I said to him, 'Look, you know, no hard feelings,' it was just not the kind of job I wanted to do and I really didn't want to be away from my family and doing 85 hours a week in a job that I really wasn't even happy doing. So for me just having a job in Cabinet wasn't the be all and end all. It had to be a job I really loved. So I left and I said to him it wasn't a role that I wanted. I haven't even talked about this before actually because – and I told him that you know my husband was coming down, I was going to talk to him – 'cause he said to me go away and think about it. And I said, 'Iftikhar's coming down, I'm going to talk to him about it, but I really think it's going to be a no.' So we talked about it and I called back and I said, 'Look, it's definitely a no.' And I said, 'Iftikhar's going back north because he had some work and I'm going to jump in the car with him and head back 'cause I just want to get away from London if I'm going to be leaving, I don't want to be the story tomorrow.' And I got a call in the early hours of the morning saying – and I checked out, I said, you know, 'Checking out as Tory Chairman and it's been a great time,' and somebody at Number 10 picked that up and said, you know – I got a call in the early hours saying, 'Where are you and what's this about you leaving?' And I said, 'Well, I told you last night that I was leaving and I'm just kind of north of Leicester on the motorway where I told you I was going home.' And [they said], 'No! David needs to speak to you. Turn round and come back.' You know it was just a bizarre kind of moment.

**HENNESSY**

Who was it who actually made the call?

**WARSI**

Ed Llewellyn.

**HENNESSY**

Ed Llewellyn, his Chief of Staff in Number 10.

**WARSI**

And he kept saying, 'Why are you going home?' And I kept saying, 'Because I told you I was going home, what did you think I'd said?' I kind of thought, am I not communicating here? So then I just went home, and they said, 'Well, you've got to come back,' and I said, 'Well, I'm not coming back today.' I said, 'I'll come back tomorrow now. I'm halfway home, I need to have a day off.' [*Laughing*] So I then went home to Yorkshire and then came back the following day.

**HENNESSY**

How did you craft, or did David Cameron craft – Ed Llewellyn helping no doubt – the job you actually went into, which was a very interesting one combining Foreign Office and Communities and Local Government? It looked at the time as if it was bespoke for you.

**WARSI**

It was. So he said, 'Well what do you want to do then?', 'cause, you know, David said, 'Look, I don't want you to go and I don't want you to leave, why would you even do this?' So he said, 'You know what you'd like to do?' And I said, 'Oh I'd really like to do this, this and this and I'd really like to do this' and it just – they just gave me what I wanted really.

**HENNESSY**

And there it was.

**WARSI**

And there it was, yes. It was very bizarre. I mean I now talk to people sometimes, you know young politicians, to say how this all works. And I say, 'You know, some of it is just farcical really, the way in which politics works.'

How did you get on with the Civil Service? I think you were a bit critical of them actually after you'd been in that job for a while.

Look, the Foreign Office is so slick and you know, ministers in the Foreign Office are just a simple inconvenience you know, we're there to just keep the seat warm until the next minister arrives. Whereas the sense I got from William was absolutely this was going to be the way he was going to shape this. We weren't just –

William Hague.

Yes, William Hague. We weren't just going to stand by the sidelines and let the Civil Service run the Foreign Office, and he wanted to take back, which he did, he took foreign policy back to the Foreign Office rather than let it sit in Number 10. And he was always clear, look let's get some scratches on the Rolls Royce that is the Foreign Office.

Was that his phrase?

That was his phrase. And I used to say, yeah you know the Foreign Sec wants us to get some scratches on it – let's put some dents in it. You know let's really go the extra mile. So he was an amazing guy to work with, so bright, so kind of visionary and I always say that, you know, had he still been Foreign Sec in 2014 I'm not sure

I would have been able to walk past him and leave. I think just the level of respect that I had for him, even when we disagreed, and the faith that I had in him I think would have probably been far greater than my kind of deep-rooted instinct to walk away.

#### HENNESSY

What do you think you achieved with the faith job in the Communities and Local Government Department and the special Minister of State job in the Foreign Office? What will you look back on when it's all over and tell your grandchildren, even your great-grandchildren this is what Great-Granny did?

#### WARSI

I met two popes. I took the largest delegation ever to the Vatican with six Cabinet ministers and as a Muslim I led that, and I spoke at the Ecclesiastical Academy and asked the cardinals assembled to be sure of their Christian heritage. And I presented a copy of the Koran to the Holy Father. I think that was definitely one of the high points. And also taking away [the] often kind of sniffy approach towards religion in government. The last Archbishop of Canterbury put it really well, he said, 'Faith is seen as the preserve of minorities, foreigners and oddities,' and I suppose because in some ways I was all three, I didn't really care, and I mainstreamed a lot of the thinking around faith being an informer of the debate. You know we're not talking about theocracy, we're talking about being an informer of the debate and an important voice around the table on so many issues, as it has done for hundreds of years. And probably one of the strongest statements that I was moved by when I left government was, I think a couple of days after my resignation, an article which said, 'Today the Church has lost its strongest friend in government.'

#### HENNESSY

You're quite a fan of the Church of England being established, aren't you? Do explain why.

**WARSI**

Absolutely. I think its role as the established church and its responsibility to all of its parishioners whoever they may happen to be allows something for all of us in a multi-faith, multi-religious society to coalesce around. I think it's an important convenor for issues like interfaith action and interfaith dialogue. And so I just think it's a real – like the monarchy – a stabilising force in what sometimes certainly in the political space can be quite fraught.

**HENNESSY**

What went wrong in the end? Why did you leave the Foreign Office?

**WARSI**

Because, as somebody who had practised human rights, as somebody for whom international justice and accountability, international institutions, human rights, were an integral part of who I was. I loved the human rights brief. I know lots of colleagues before me have just hoped that they survived the human rights brief but I really embraced and loved it and it was a big part of who I was. I found that at that moment during that Gaza conflict everything that we had preached for years, and I genuinely believed, we neither believed nor practised. And whether it was the way in which we wouldn't allow the Palestinians to take the UN as a space to resolve these issues or we didn't want them to go to the ICC or we went to the –

**HENNESSY**

International Criminal Court.

**WARSI**

The International Criminal Court, or we went to the Human Rights Council and abstained on a resolution on accountability on both sides for any human rights abuses that may have been committed.

Absolutely no political commitment or vision for accountability, post this crisis. No private conversations happening about how we were appalled about what was happening in Israel and Palestine. It was almost as if we'd wiped the slate and thought, no, none of the normal rules of the game now apply.

**HENNESSY**

You said this directly to the Foreign Secretary, Philip Hammond, did you?

**WARSI**

I mean, I said this directly to the Prime Minister and I said it in the National Security Council and I said it informally and I tried to persuade my colleagues and I tried to speak to my colleagues who were friends of Israel to say, 'This is a moment where you've got to give the Prime Minister the confidence to be able to say he has to do the right thing.' And I realised that being in position meant I had absolutely no power on some of the biggest things that mattered to me, and so therefore the position really didn't matter anymore and I felt that I needed to hand over power and retain my principles.

**HENNESSY**

So no regrets?

**WARSI**

Absolutely no regrets. I mean every single day I look back at that moment and I'm grateful that I made the right judgement, because it would have been so easy, as, you know, the working class girl from nowhere who ended up in this amazing place to have been tempted at that moment just to stay a little while longer because it was just a great place to be. But no, I look in the mirror and I can live with myself and that matters so much more than holding onto power.

**HENNESSY**

Would you like to resume your Cabinet career?

**WARSI**

I always say that [at the] age of 47 I probably should never say never, but certainly not now.

**HENNESSY**

Why?

**WARSI**

Because I'm having a ball of a time outside of frontline politics. We're in an interesting stage in our life, our children have all grown up, we had our kids very young, we're empty nesters. I'm back in business, so I'm working with Dad and my sister and my brother-in-law, who I get to see every week now because of the work that we do. I'm travelling and speaking on issues that really matter to me. I'm deeply involved in charitable work, I've set up a foundation. We're doing some fantastic work with young kids from working-class backgrounds and difficult backgrounds and trying to change the course of their life. I loved writing. I think there's so much going on, I feel like I'm living life and I'm not sure that government allows you to do that. So yeah, maybe when I'm older and wiser and feel that there's a different way of doing politics, but I don't feel that's a space for me right now.

**HENNESSY**

Now I know you're only 47 so this is a premature and cheeky question. What trace would you like to leave on history?

**WARSI**

That she survived politics with her principles intact. That's probably the nicest way of putting it.

**HENNESSY**

Very succinct. What trace do you think you will leave?

**WARSI**

She's the awkward Yorkshire woman who we could never get to do what we wanted her to do probably. [*Laughs*]

**HENNESSY**

What if the awkward Yorkshire woman had actually made it to Number 10 and you'd become Prime Minister? What would you have done on the first day?

**WARSI**

Oh God. Leave. [*Laughs*] I think it's just such a difficult – I mean a privilege but it's not a job that I would ever either do or want to do.

**HENNESSY**

If I could grant you one great reform what would it be if I could wave the magic wand for you?

**WARSI**

That we should change the laws so that we don't sell arms to regimes with dubious human rights records.

**HENNESSY**

Thank you very much, Sayeeda Warsi.

**WARSI**

Thank you.

# David Blunkett (Lord Blunkett)

Series 6, Episode 3, first broadcast 14 August 2018

**Born** 6 June 1947; **Educated** Royal National College for the Blind; Sheffield University; Huddersfield Holly Bank College of Education

MP (Labour) Sheffield Brightside 1987–2010; Sheffield Brightside and Hillsborough 2010–2015

Leader of Sheffield City Council, 1980–87; Secretary of State for Education and Employment, 1997–2001; Home Secretary, 2001–04; Secretary of State for Work and Pensions, 2005

**Autobiography** *On A Clear Day*, 1995 (updated 2002)

**HENNESSY**

With me today is David Blunkett, Lord Blunkett, who served as Education and Employment Secretary, Home Secretary and Work and Pensions Secretary in the Blair Cabinets. Admired across the political spectrum for the way he tackled a series of immensely demanding jobs, he regards his blindness as an inconvenience rather than a disability, believes we should all be judged by what we do and how effective we are. David Blunkett brought a passion for reform and social justice to every task, becoming a Sheffield City councillor aged 22, while still a student at Sheffield University. David, welcome.

**BLUNKETT**

Thank you, Peter.

**HENNESSY**

Now, you were born in Sheffield in 1947. Tell me about your family and where you lived.

**BLUNKETT**

We lived on a council estate, as they used to be called, in the north of Sheffield, in the area which I was proud to represent both on the city council and then eventually in Parliament. And my dad worked in the gas industry. My mum had worked in the wartime industries in machine tools and then in producing tracer bullets, but she wasn't working because she'd been quite seriously ill. In fact, when I was nine she had breast cancer. In those days it was almost always fatal, but she lived another 27 years.

**HENNESSY**

But you also had your granddad with you, who I think was quite an influence, because he'd read you things from the *Daily Herald*, David.

**BLUNKETT**

He was a character. He'd lived through the pre-war recession in the 1930s, travelled the country for work, read me the paper, got very disgruntled, was often quite cantankerous, but an influence in the sense that he taught me the importance of understanding history, not to live in it, but to learn from it.

**HENNESSY**

Do you think because of being blind you acquired a pretty fabulous memory right from early on? Because one of the people who worked with you said many years later, 'David never takes notes, he remembers everything.' Do you think it comes from sitting there with Granddad?

### BLUNKETT

Oh, I probably pretended not to take notes. I took notes in order to be able to remember. My memory was absolutely crucial to me, but it was focused. I couldn't remember a Shakespeare sonnet any better than anyone else, but facts and detail, I had to, because that was the only way I was going to survive, and I never wanted anyone to say that I wasn't on top of the job or on top of the facts because I couldn't see. And so I probably went beyond the extra mile, you know, the extra hours in the evenings and weekends, determined that, for instance, when I sat in Cabinet, whilst people were flipping through their papers I'd already read them.

### HENNESSY

You mentioned going to school across the other side of Sheffield, a boarding school when you were only four. It's a most extraordinary, wrenching read in your *On A Clear Day* book, in your memoir. It must have been frightful, David.

### BLUNKETT

Looking back on it, I can tell it was, because I can still remember the emotion at four, five, six, passing the Sheffield Cathedral on a Sunday evening. I always remember the dappled sun touching my face, getting on the second bus, normally with my mum, because my dad worked shifts and had very few weekends off. He, as you know, Peter, was killed in a works accident when I was 12, but while I was at the school in the south of Sheffield it was my mum who took me. And we'd arrive and I had to just say, 'bye,' and find the dormitory and learn to make my bed and clean my shoes. It sounds dreadful, and in some circumstances it was, because the food was very much Dotheboys Hall. But actually when you're that age you adapt. You learn to play cricket, with bell in the ball, kick a ball about with ball-bearings in it, to learn to ride a bike. You just mucked in. And for you that was life. You weren't thinking 'Oh, goodness me, I wish I was at home.' You were thinking, 'How am I going to survive with this little kid crying in the night?'

## HENNESSY

Yes. You referred to your dad's terrible accident in 1959 when you were 12. It's another horrendous part of your upbringing, a terrible tragedy, and he died shortly after falling into a vat of boiling water, I think, in the gas-works.

## BLUNKETT

Yes, he lived a month. He was working over retirement age – my mum and dad had me post-war when they were both – well, my dad was in his fifties, my mum in her forties, which was highly unusual in those days. And my dad had wanted to continue working, as I do, and unfortunately got caught up in what was a process called water gas plant, and he fell into a vat, and lived a month, and I went to see him on a number of occasions in hospital, which rests with me. And the main thing that I remember was that I had to look after my mum. I mean, I was only 12 and I had to go to boarding school in Shropshire because it was just at that moment that the changeover was due to take place and I was going to the secondary school, and I remember my mum ringing me – we had no phone at home, ringing me from a phone box – trying to get through to the phone box in the school, and I used to think, 'How on earth are we going to survive this?' But somehow we did.

## HENNESSY

It left a mark on you, though, didn't it? It made you a very determined person when it comes to health and safety, for example.

## BLUNKETT

Yes, I had a brief spell in charge of the Health and Safety Executive and I've long been committed to good occupational health and safety, not messing about with silliness, but the really serious issues.

I think in two ways it affected me, my dad's death. One, it did make me determined that the world was going to be a better place and I was going to make a difference. And that was true of my grandfather as well, who died in a geriatric hospital, which we don't, thank the Lord, have any more. And secondly, I think for a time it made me extremely edgy. I think there were a lot of rough corners on David Blunkett until quite late into my midlife. And I'm a – I hope I'm a slightly more tolerant, gentler person. I certainly had some of those rough edges rubbed off. But in another sense it was crucial, because it made me determined, slightly pig-headed, sometimes arrogant, which saw me through. I don't know how I would have achieved what I've done, good or bad, without that tenacity.

### HENNESSY

You mentioned going to school in Shropshire. Why, David – because you were a bright boy – why didn't you go to the grammar school for the blind in Worcester? I know there was only one grammar school for the blind in the whole country, if I remember, then. Why didn't they send you there?

### BLUNKETT

They didn't put me in for the final exam. They thought I was disruptive and that I would not settle there. I don't know whether they were right or wrong, but it was an extraordinary decision and it was in keeping, remember, with a very distant time. People do forget how people made judgements about children at a very early age and presumed that there was going to be a different trajectory in life for them, and that's what they thought about me. I mean, another part of my tenacity was to prove them wrong. So, you know, at 16 the school I went to, the guy had a PhD who headed it, but didn't think that blind children could be put in for external exams. So at 16 I didn't have any O Levels, as they were in those days, I had to start going to evening class down at the local tech. And there were a group of us, it wasn't just me.

**HENNESSY**

So you went into Shrewsbury?

**BLUNKETT**

Yes. Into the town, into the technical college, a small group of us determined to do something with our lives. I don't think if I hadn't passed the first two O Levels I'd taken, just one evening a week for a year, if we hadn't passed – and a number of us did – I don't think I would have been able to carry on. You wouldn't have had the confidence to do that. So it was a miracle that we got through the first two. And we got some help. There was a guy called Wilf King who was a teacher at the college. I remember writing an obituary a few years ago for him in the *Guardian* because he was an example, like *How Green Was My Valley*, of someone who went the extra mile and made a massive difference to my life, and I hope to others. He came down to the college with me to do O Level physics, would you believe? I don't think that the college were too keen on me doing chemistry in case I blew something up. But he came down, voluntarily, without being paid, on wet nights and fine, and he helped me get that O Level in physics. Now, that is a fantastic example of someone who believed in education but believed in others.

**HENNESSY**

Yes. There's another very interesting description in your memoir about how the BBC Home Service, the precursor to Radio 4, on which we're now speaking – with a nice piece of symmetry – was your kind of university of the air even before you went to university.

**BLUNKETT**

Very much. I leant about oratory, about language. I had a love of learning, which is something that I believe in very strongly. The ability to inspire youngsters to have an inquiring mind, to light that candle, is something that overrides anything else that I think we should do in our education system, and I had it in spades. I think that's probably what saw me through in the end. I just hoovered up knowledge, information, how people spoke, the history they talked about. That is radio at its absolute best.

### HENNESSY

But also it was your great source of entertainment, wasn't it? Because there were extraordinary series, *Hancock's Half Hour*, *The Navy Lark*, *Round the Horne*.

### BLUNKETT

I used to love those Sunday afternoons. There was a group of us at school made a point of actually saying that we weren't going to do anything else until we'd listened to that hour of comedy, which certainly cheered us up. What it did for our knowledge of outside life Lord only knows.

### HENNESSY

It's interesting, the sequence. So it's Dad and Granddad getting you interested in current affairs and you had a great sense of injustice and the difference between those with wealth and power and those with none because of your upbringing and schooling and so on. But what turned it into a political interest? What crafted your party political side?

### BLUNKETT

Reading history. We had another teacher – I think now he'd have been described as a communist. He was called Rodwell, and he taught me to read history, to understand and try and learn from what had happened in the past, and the way in which change had been brought about.

**HENNESSY**

Your socialism owed more to Methodism than to Marx, to use the old line of Morgan Phillips, the General Secretary of the Labour Party – do you remember?

**BLUNKETT**

I do.

**HENNESSY**

Because you were a good Methodist family weren't you?

**BLUNKETT**

Yes, my mum took me to church every Sunday when I was at home, and I went down from the school when I was in term time. And for a very short time I became a Methodist local preacher, as we call them, lay preachers, as the Church of England would have it. And I was taken aside one day and said, 'Really enjoyed the service and the sermon, but don't you think you'd be better in politics than you would be in the pulpit?'

**HENNESSY**

Who said that to you?

**BLUNKETT**

One of the church elders. [*Hennessy laughs*] And I said, 'Well, I'll think about – '. He was right. I was preaching politics from the pulpit is the honest truth. But it did give me a foundation, and so did my mum's belief, a work ethic. I think my mum really instilled into me, and my dad's example, obviously, the work ethic. And it's still with me today.

**HENNESSY**

Did you acquire a faith, do you believe now?

### BLUNKETT

I believe in a spiritualism. I believe in a force of good and evil, a force of nature. When things have been really bad for me I've loved walking in the Derbyshire countryside, just outside Sheffield – we have the Peak District both inside the city and immediately surrounding it – and that love of nature, that listening to birdsong, that wonderful hearing the breeze in the trees and feeling the sun on your face, that's as close as you can get to understanding the spiritual and how you can be renewed and refreshed.

### HENNESSY

Coming back to your early political formation, you were very taken with Harold Wilson as Leader of the Opposition weren't you? He was a real dazzler between '63 and '64, as our generation remembers. But you were very much caught up with his new style of socialism –the white heat of the technological revolution – weren't you?

### BLUNKETT

I thought he was breaking with simply being stuck in the past. I thought he was talking about a new era, a different era. Bear in mind this was a time of, again, very rapid change. In terms of our social wellbeing everything was beginning to change. We had really all sorts of challenges in terms of the world of tomorrow, and he was trying to get to grips with that. Not terribly successfully in practical terms, which has always been something that's rested with me, including when I got in government, there's no point in having aspiration if you can't deliver it. And his belief that we had to look to tomorrow rested with me when I did have the opportunity to do something.

### HENNESSY

And you acquire the set of qualifications you need, through night school and so on, to get to university and you go to Sheffield, your great city university and you come across Bernard Crick, who became a lifelong influence on you and a great friend I think, the Professor of Political Theory and Institutions, which was the degree you took. Now, tell me about Bernard Crick. He was a most extraordinary man wasn't he? What was special about him?

#### BLUNKETT

Bernard taught me that it was really important to be able to understand how to translate values into practice. He'd written a book called *In Defence of Politics* in the early '60s. I think it's still a seminal read. And that was all about how politics was inevitably a messy business. If you were going to reach agreements with people, and it's appropriate, post-Brexit to reflect on this, you're going to have to get your hands dirty, you're going to have to do things that actually make it possible to achieve the goals you've set out. But you can only do that if you have an understanding of where power lies and the international pressures and how you countervail them or at least influence them. And more critically than anything else – and this really influenced my politics – you can only do it if democracy is participative, if people are engaged, if they actually believe that politics, democratic politics is something to do with them and that they can have a say in it, not just in voting but in their lives. And that's a difficult one because people just want to get on with the day-to-day life that they're living, and very often just surviving, as certainly was true in my early days of the upbringing in Sheffield, and still is for many people in my old constituency.

#### HENNESSY

You were very brave as a student in taking on the Sheffield councillor's job at the age of only 22, I mean you were reading for a demanding degree in a very high-quality politics department yet you took on this extra work. Now, what was that? Because you describe in your memoir that you always had this sense of obligation.

### BLUNKETT

Yes. It came from that work ethic, that desire to make that change as fast as I could. I've always been in too much of a hurry, certainly my Cabinet colleagues in the eight years I was in Cabinet thought so. I wanted to get on with it. And tutors said to me, 'It's not very wise,' and of course it wasn't, you're quite right, it was not a wise thing to do. But I valued it because I was learning about the practice and having some of the spots knocked off and learning about the reality of not getting your own way all the time, at the same time as studying political theory and institutions, which was giving me a much clearer picture of how the world worked, what the processes were, how I was going to proceed if I wanted to make that difference in the future.

### HENNESSY

How did the older councillors react to you, because you were a young firebrand? They must have been quite irritated.

### BLUNKETT

Yes, I did have a propensity, as I did later, to get up people's noses. And the one person who really saved me was the Leader of the Council, a guy called Ron Ironmonger, who got a knighthood. Fantastic local politician, who understood that he had to teach me that I was no better and no cleverer than anyone else, and that certainly not being able to see wasn't going to get in his way of putting me in my place, but then to come round afterwards, put his arm round me and say, 'Come for a chat, let's talk about what you did, why you did it, why it didn't work, why you didn't win the vote,' and that stood me in enormous good stead later in life. I didn't always remember it, as you probably know, Peter. But it helped.

### HENNESSY

Another great influence on you, I think, was Enid Hattersley, Roy's mother, who was a long-standing Labour councillor and became [Lord] Mayor of the city, I think, in the early '80s.

#### BLUNKETT

Yes, she was [Lord] Mayor of the city when I was leading. She was a character with a mission, and her mission was art and culture, which wasn't easy in Sheffield. I see Roy every home game and some away games with Sheffield Wednesday, because we're avid supporters. In fact, we get on better now than we ever have.

#### HENNESSY

You're friends these days, because you had a great falling out over education policy.

#### BLUNKETT

We had a falling out over education. Roy's great love was education. And I was struggling to get some kind of agreement before the 1997 general election about where we were going to go, not that we were just simply going to go backwards, to reversing the policies that had been brought in by Ken Baker, but that we were going to pick them up and reshape them and do something with them. And we had this clash at Labour Party conference where I actually made a slip and I missed out a crucial word in terms of describing what we were going to do about grammar schools, and Roy was very angry with me and so were my special advisers, because whilst it didn't matter in the greater good of things sometimes missing a word out, like 'there will be no *more* grammar schools,' rather than 'there will be no grammar schools,' is a really important change.

#### HENNESSY

Interesting. In terms of your own position within the wide spectrum of the Labour Party, I think, David, you always strike me as very interesting because you have great respect for what Jim

Callaghan used to call original Labour. Remember Jim used to say 'I'm neither old nor new, I'm original.' But at the same time you thought that the old generations who tended to dominate local politics, when you obviously were a young man just coming in, were very staid and in many ways paternalistic. For example, Sheffield would insist that all the council houses had the same colour paint on their doors.

#### BLUNKETT

Believe it or not we had 94,000 houses under the municipality at the time, and I always used to reflect how on earth did anybody ever vote for their landlord? Because that's what we were. People were not allowed to do their own homes up. They didn't get a choice in those days, when the houses were being renovated, in terms of what went into the kitchen or the kind of doors they wanted. It was well-meaning paternalism that was completely out of its era. And the tragedy for me was that Margaret Thatcher was able to pick up on that. Sadly that had a resonance with the population as a whole who were moving on, who wanted choice. They wanted to be able to make decisions for themselves. And in many ways old Labour stood in the way of that. It was trying to prevent change rather than roll with it and shape it with our values for the future. And that rested very strongly with me and that's why we did clash from the time I got on to the council in 1970 through to when I became leader ten years later.

#### HENNESSY

When you're Leader of Labour in Sheffield it's the height of the recession of the early '80s. I think Sheffield lost 50,000 manufacturing jobs inside three years – it must have been very difficult to cope with. And of course the film *The Full Monty* has caught that forever.

### BLUNKETT

Yes, people thought it was funny. I mean, there are funny Sheffield bits of humour in it, but actually it was to me a tragedy, because it did reflect the enormity of what had hit the city, and part of the task that, as Leader with a team of people around me – because you never do things in life on your own, I've always believed strongly in the values of mutuality, reciprocity with a team. We were trying to hold the banner high, we were trying to give people hope. We were trying to say there is a third way, before Anthony Giddens invented the term, which is not market-driven, Thatcherism, free-for-all, and isn't old paternalistic Labour, it's about engaging with people and our values shining through, allowing them, as part of our democracy, to be able to influence what's happening in their own lives. And we were trying to do that against the odds. It did involve raising the local rate, the council tax as it is now – we had the business rate as well – by eye-watering proportions. I mean, how we got away with it and increasingly won seats in the city I still don't fully understand. We evangelised, we had street meetings, workplace meetings, and we put the council tax up by 40 per cent in one year and people stood it. But it was a difficult time.

### HENNESSY

The moment you really came to public attention, I suppose – really quite intensely – was the famous Labour Party conference in '85 where Neil Kinnock made one of the speeches of his life about Militant Tendency in Liverpool and Derek Hatton and all that, 'the grotesque spectacle of redundancy notices being taken round by taxi.' But then you came up with a compromise, asking Derek Hatton publicly and out of the blue if he'd let other Labour councillors audit the books in Liverpool, and he accepted. Now, was this a cunning plan of Baldrickian proportions on your part or was it spontaneous?

## BLUNKETT

It was spontaneous, about half an hour before the debate started. And I fortuitously met a guy called Tony Mulhearn, who was Chairman of the Liverpool Labour Party in the gents. And I said, 'You're going to have this motion defeated, because we have the trade unions with us, but I'm going to put to Derek from the rostrum that if he withdraws the motion you'll have won a partial moral victory, but the *quid pro quo* is that we actually are able to engage with you and have an investigation.' 'Well, I don't know about that,' he said. Anyway, I just chose to do it. I'd never do it again, it's a once-off. It was an incredible risk. Not only a risk in terms of whether this wasn't going to come off and I was just going to look a bit of a twit, but also because not being able to see, I couldn't tell whether he was actually agreeing to this when I was putting it to him from the rostrum. And he was walking up and the tension was absolutely incredible, and much to my relief, and much to his chagrin later on, he agreed, and as a consequence we opened the books, we saw that they weren't actually telling the truth, that it was impossible for them to survive, and the inquiry then led inexorably to the investigation of the Militant Tendency and the expulsions.

Neil Kinnock said to me on the day, immediately after the debate, which was electric, 'You skate on bloody thin ice.' And I said, 'I know, Neil, and one day I might go through it.' [*Hennessy laughs*]

## HENNESSY

You must have irritated him that day.

## BLUNKETT

Yes, he was very angry. The only redeeming feature was that the National Executive was so finely balanced that my vote counted, so he invited me round to stay at his house, because I didn't live in London, of course, I lived in Sheffield. And my dog eating his cat food sort of healed the breach a bit. [*Hennessy laughs*]

**HENNESSY**

It's a wonderful image. One of the problems, if you've had a great career in local government and become a national figure is when you come into the House of Commons for the first time, as you did for Brightside, Sheffield Brightside in 1987, is there's a kind of stored up resentment waiting for you.

**BLUNKETT**

Yes.

**HENNESSY**

Did you suffer from that?

**BLUNKETT**

Yes, I did. But here's a twist in life. Two things happened to me – two illnesses. One, I had a gall bladder operation, and I had viral pneumonia, all in the first nine months. And the paradox there was that it got me out of the place sufficiently and calmed me down sufficiently not to do what Ken Livingstone did, which was to *really* irritate people. And so by the time Neil had decided that having me in the tent rather than out was a good idea people were prepared to tolerate it, so very quickly put me on the front bench in the team that were dealing with local government. And of course people didn't really want to touch the poll tax within the echelons of the Labour Party, because whilst we knew we had to tell people to pay it, the campaign outside was 'no pay.' So there I was with the opportunity of doing something that could have been suicidal politically but with a great opportunity, and I just grabbed it with both hands and said, 'Yeah, I'll take on the issue of the poll tax, let's see if we can manage to work our way through it.'

**HENNESSY**

The '92 election: there's this great rally in Sheffield, in your own city, very close to the poll. Did you have doubts that night?

### BLUNKETT

Oh terrible. I welcomed people as the Leader at the beginning of the rally – no idea about this flying in in a helicopter and it all coming up on the screen.

### HENNESSY

This is Neil and Roy.

### BLUNKETT

And then Neil comes on and he does this terrible, 'Are we all right?' and I just felt this is not us, it's not Labour, it's certainly not Sheffield. But the ten thousand people in the arena were carried away. The polls had already started to move – I mean, the rally wasn't responsible for us losing the election, we were already sliding, and the soap box that John Major stood on in the pedestrian precinct in Sheffield was more in tune with people out there than the rally in the arena.

### HENNESSY

Very interesting. After the election Neil Kinnock stands down. You became quite close to John Smith, I think, didn't you? What do you think he – he would have made quite a considerable Prime Minister?

### BLUNKETT

Yes, I do. He wouldn't have been as reformist as Tony, and we may not have won a majority of 179 and then 165 in the following election, but John had a deep, deep-seated set of values rooted in his Scottish Labour heritage.

### HENNESSY

Who did you vote for in the succession?

**BLUNKETT**

I voted for Tony. Tony Blair. I'd just got to know him reasonably well. I'd met him on a train actually for the first time, going to a conference, and we'd had a proper conversation about education – which is why, I think, when he had the opportunity he asked me to take on the shadow job, because he had understood that I had the same reformist zeal about what was happening to children in schools, where they were being, in old Labour terms, patronised. It was almost, 'Well, these youngsters from this background aren't going to be able to make it are they, so let's look after them.' In my own constituency, in Brightside, at that time only four out of about a dozen primary schools actually got anywhere near the standard that we would expect. In fact, a handful of them were as low as 20 per cent of children getting to level four by the time they were 11. It was a scandalous neglect, and if I had my time again as Leader of Sheffield – and we were counted as being in the top three education authorities in Britain, Lord help us – I would have really gone to town on the education system back in the 1980s.

**HENNESSY**

It's very interesting, coming out of the first of the Blair governments, because somebody who worked very closely with you said to me, 'It's interesting to see how David and Tony, though from very different backgrounds, coalesce on education policy.' Because he wanted choice and you wanted those basic values, those basic capacities given to children to give them a start in life.

**BLUNKETT**

Yes.

**HENNESSY**

And so your origins meant that you came at it from different angles but you ended up in the same place, and really quite an extraordinary team.

### BLUNKETT

And it worked, because Tony had decided that it was education, education, education and it was absolutely seminal to the wellbeing of individuals, but also to our economy and our place in the world. And I was obsessed with standards. I used to say standards not structures. The real thing is what happens in the classroom: excellent teaching, great leadership in schools. We were able to bring in Professor Sir Michael Barber immediately, day one after the general election to head the Standards Unit. And with Michael Bichard, who's now in the Lords with us, as the Permanent Secretary, we were really able to drive that forward. And when you've got the backing of the Prime Minister and you've got the zeal to do it, and you've got expertise around you, it is possible to bring about real change.

### HENNESSY

Was that your happiest job?

### BLUNKETT

Oh by far. Education's still my great policy love. It was a joy. Every time I went into a school or college, every time I met young people in a job centre, because we were transforming *their* lives as well, you came away re-energised.

### HENNESSY

Sure Start's the other great thing from your time as Education Secretary.

### BLUNKETT

Yes, I was able to work with my friend the late Tessa Jowell. Tessa and I talked before the general election about what we might be able to do, because we both heard about what had been experimented with in Seattle in the United States. And she became the Public Health Minister, Junior Minister in Health, but a very, very useful post. And I was the Secretary of Education and I was the one who was able to get the money, and so Tessa and I worked together across departments and we were able, just by force of will, to get everyone to agree that we would do this as a cross-cutting, cross-departmental energising effort linked up to local communities and the voluntary sector.

**HENNESSY**

It was all about pre-school wasn't it?

**BLUNKETT**

It was immediately a child is born what happens to them. That's at the moment when the great divide, the inequality is reinforced. Could we do something to reverse that long-term? And I still believe that that was a really seminal piece of policy change and I hope that in future we'll be able to return to the original programme, because it really did make a difference. Not just to the children – the nurturing, the development of the child – but it was also a transformation to the parents, mostly women, not always but mostly, who suddenly started to believe in themselves and to learn alongside their children and believe that they might go to university as well as their child.

**HENNESSY**

How did you get on with the career Civil Service, because there was a famous occasion at Cabinet – which came to my attention by one means or another – where you had a bit of an eruption, to everybody's surprise, because you were normally – you quite relished working with officials. I think it did take people's breath away. Now, what was behind all of that?

**BLUNKETT**

I didn't have a conspiracy theory like Tony Benn, that they were against us. My frustration was with the inertia. And in the early days there was no inertia, we were actually really moving, as I've described. And then, as things do, governments start to slow and things become more difficult to change. One day I found myself in Cabinet – I do from time to time lose it – breaking a pencil that was in front of me and throwing it across the table. Tony asking me very gently if I would calm down, and talking to me afterwards about how you can't take on Russian fronts, you can't take on everybody at the same time. And the reason I was annoyed was because I was deeply committed to the kind of reforms that came in later, when Gus O'Donnell, who became head of the Civil Service, was beginning to bring about change in project management, in the delivery – not the individuals, very bright, policy savvy individuals, but actually to be able to implement. And there are two different things there. The delivery is not the same thing as the development of the policy papers and the minutiae of the mandarins within Whitehall. And you obviously, in the real world, need both.

## HENNESSY

You described becoming Home Secretary, and almost immediately the world changes, quite literally, with 9/11, 2001, and you have to go into the emergency mode with COBRA. It must have been extraordinary, that first day, because nobody knew if we were going to have attacks on our own territory. Can you relive that moment for me?

## BLUNKETT

I was on a train coming from a police superintendents' conference and I received a phone call, firstly from one of my sons who had seen the television through a shop window. And the next thing I get a phone call from Downing Street saying 'You've got to come back.' I said, 'I'm on my way back.' And the carriage started to erupt because people were receiving messages. And we met at the Cabinet Office and what impressed me was not just the calm, thoughtful way in which both Tony Blair and Gordon Brown handled the situation, but the Cabinet as a whole. Nobody panicked. People were discussing the reality of the potential for attack on the City of London, because that was the presumption. The steps we'd have to take, the speed that we needed to move to reassure people, but the calmness we needed to evoke, so that we used to talk about people being alert but not alarmed. And to ensure that people were going to go to work the following morning and that they continue going to restaurants and cinemas and that life went on. And that was important not just for the obvious economic disaster that would have befallen us, but it was important in terms of the symbol and the signal that it sent to the rest of the world.

#### HENNESSY

You had very quickly to put together what I think was described as a new protective or new protecting state to face this terrorist threat in all sorts of ways, including new counter-terrorism legislation; which led you to have quite profound disagreements, I think, with certain people or certain colleagues in the Labour Party and beyond. And you denounced them a bit as airy-fairy civil libertarianism didn't you?

#### BLUNKETT

Yeah.

#### HENNESSY

I mean, you felt very strongly about this.

#### BLUNKETT

I did. I was making a point. It took me four weeks to produce a statement to the House of Commons on the 15th October in that year, and then another three weeks to actually get under way with legislating. And they were difficult decisions and I understood as well as anyone else the balance, the proportionality between retaining freedoms and civil liberty and the security of the nation. But my job was to try and argue that through Parliament. And actually I believe that our democracy worked extremely well. I was irritated at times, but I've reflected since in the House of Lords in speeches that actually the House of Lords played a really seminal role because there were people in there with genuine expertise who helped to shape the way in which the laws that we were passing would not infringe our basic liberty but would enable us to do what we were setting out as the objective. And I think that that was a great example of democracy at its best.

How did you feel when you had to step down as Home Secretary? It was to do with a work visa wasn't it? Work permit?

Well, it was a deeply personal matter, which is something I think people understood later. People in my city understood almost immediately, it was fantastic; press and media came up and got a flea in their ear, of which I'm very proud. It was a terrible moment because I should have stood down three months earlier, in the September of 2004. It was at that moment that I knew that there was going to be the most terrible trauma in my life and I was going to have to go through –

In your private life.

In my private life. And I had to take decisions that other politicians historically and even today find it difficult to take: ie. to take responsibility for their own personal actions and not to walk away from them. And I was offered the opportunity to walk away and

I wouldn't. And I should have known then that this was going to come back to bite very hard, and Tony, who I talked to, suggested it probably would. And three months later it did.

### HENNESSY

You come back as Work and Pensions Secretary. What was your main thrust, what did you want to do with that job in 2005?

### BLUNKETT

I wanted to reinforce and accelerate welfare reform, because I knew it was going to happen eventually and we needed to do it with the grain of helping people to help themselves and not take away the props and the support. And secondly, to sort out the pensions system. I'd got agreement with Tony and just about with Gordon that people would automatically enrol in pensions, that we would have to extend the retirement age, difficult as that was, and that we would have a major campaign with young people to get them to understand the enormity of what was going to hit them down the line. And that was then carried forward by John Hutton and others, and that's another part of my philosophy, that you don't do things on your own, you do things as a team. I wasn't good as a team player in Cabinet. I think I was a lot better at building a team, in terms of that ministerial –

### HENNESSY

Inside the department. That's very interesting.

### BLUNKETT

Inside the department. And I also had another great asset, which was the most wonderful family and circle of friends. You can only survive what I went through if you have that family and friends around you, people who believe in you through thick and thin. And I think that one of the great disadvantages of politics is that you're so often immersed that you lose touch. You know, one of my closest friends said to me, 'Welcome back,' when I came out of Cabinet. And I didn't understand immediately but I did later.

**HENNESSY**

Later on. And you had to stand down from Work and Pensions because of some alleged business interests.

**BLUNKETT**

Which was utter rubbish.

**HENNESSY**

You were cleared eventually weren't you?

**BLUNKETT**

Yes, I was. But it was too late by then. And in a sense that was again the aftermath of the previous year's events. So they all went together. And once you're on a rollercoaster then it's very difficult to get off it. And all sorts of things I could think of now that I would have done differently, but actually you live your life, don't you? We're not automatons. And if I hadn't been the human being that I am I wouldn't have got where I got and I wouldn't have had the traumas that I've experienced.

**HENNESSY**

Yes.

**BLUNKETT**

Thick and thin.

**HENNESSY**

Would you like to have been Prime Minister?

## BLUNKETT

I didn't think so at the time. I didn't think that a blind person could ever be Prime Minister – I didn't think people were ready for it. I'm not sure they are. Now, when I look at the mess that's occurred since, I think well, although I thought at the time that maybe I'd extended as far as I could go and with the ability to read the material and to be at the cutting edge and to work 16 hours, could I have done it? And I thought at the time probably not. Now, in retrospect, I think well, if this bunch can manage to do it I probably could have done. [*Laughs*]

## HENNESSY

What would you have done on day one, if I could make you Prime Minister retrospectively what's the first thing you'd do?

## BLUNKETT

I probably would have said we needed to change the nature of government. Firstly, we needed to engage much more with the idea of this being outward-facing participative government – devolve, decentralise, very quickly. And secondly, we needed to equip the Civil Service for delivery and not just for deliberation.

## HENNESSY

What trace would you like to leave on history, David?

## BLUNKETT

I'd like people to have judged what I managed to achieve in Cabinet, in local government and today and beyond as me, not as a blind man in politics, not as a politician who was blind. And I probably – and this is the paradox – will have left something that had to do with me being blind and achieving at the level of Cabinet, and that is that families with a disabled youngster, youngsters growing up with a disability, people in broader society – particularly employers – might just think that someone that is struggling to make their way in life can actually do it if they get the helping hand, that mutuality and reciprocity that I so care about. And that probably will be the lasting legacy.

**HENNESSY**

If I could wave my magic wand one more time for you, and give you one last great reform guaranteed, what would you want it to be?

**BLUNKETT**

I probably want it to be in the Health Service. I'm married to a GP. I think health is so central to everything that we value, and I would want it to be that we actually have transformed our health service into a preventive public health service. And my small part in banning smoking in public places was really a gesture to the past where clean water, decent housing, the ability to live in an environment that you could breathe, actually made the difference to changing the life chances of the people I grew up with.

**HENNESSY**

David Blunkett, thank you very much indeed.

**BLUNKETT**

Thank you.

# Iain Duncan Smith
# (Sir Iain Duncan Smith)

Series 6, Episode 4, first broadcast 21 August 2018

**Born** 9 April 1954; **Educated** Bishop Glancey Secondary Modern, Solihull; HMS Conway, Anglesey; Royal Military Academy, Sandhurst

MP (Conservative) Chingford 1992–97;
Chingford and Woodford Green 1997–

Leader of the Conservative Party and Leader of the Opposition, 2001–03; Secretary of State for Work and Pensions, 2010–16

**HENNESSY**

With me today is Iain Duncan Smith, who led the Conservative Party for two years between 2001 and 2003, when he famously described himself as 'The Quiet Man.' He entered Parliament as MP for Chingford in 1992 and swiftly made his name as a critic of the Major government's European policy. His political life has been devoted to getting the United Kingdom out of the European Union. Yet perhaps his 'quiet man' side meant that his country has never fully seen the real Iain Duncan Smith and his passion for social policy reform, which he had a chance to pursue as Secretary of State for Work and Pensions in the Cameron government. Iain, welcome.

**DUNCAN SMITH**

Peter.

**HENNESSY**

What sort of family was yours? What's the family background?

**DUNCAN SMITH**

Well really, I think, on my father's side, very service-orientated. Military service and public service. My grandfather had been both in the Indian Army and also in the Indian Civil Service and retired eventually in India and is buried to this day [in] Ooty; he never came back. My father was born over there. A whole line of coffee planters, tea planters and family basically have been born and served in India, but in public service. On my mother's side, similar but my great grandfather was a bit of a Raffles figure, who travelled the South Seas, etc – ended up captaining the King of Siam's yacht, at the time of *The King and I*, by the way.

**HENNESSY**

I was going to say there's a great musical in that.

**DUNCAN SMITH**

Exactly at the same time. And his first wife died and he travelled up to China where he set up a small trading company and then became Deputy Consul, I think, in the area that he was. And he married then a Japanese woman who was from Samurai background, and of course the Samurai at that stage, after the Meiji restoration in 1860, had lost all of their privileges and their weapons, and so many of them took up painting and various other things. And this brother and sister came over to China and he was a painter and he got on very well with my great grandfather and he then married his sister. So it's, I guess, a story of British imperial past.

**HENNESSY**

Yours is a late imperial childhood.

**DUNCAN SMITH**

Yes, I think so.

**HENNESSY**

And a Second World War one because your father was a much-decorated pilot wasn't he?

**DUNCAN SMITH**

Indeed, yes. He wrote actually a rather good book which one of the journalists described to me as a mini-classic, and I think it is, because it's written quite late after the war, called *Spitfire Into Battle*, and it's just gone on being reprinted and sold all over the world. He allows himself to dwell on things like the loss of friends and what fear is like and how you cope with it and, you know, how you manage in those incredible situations and to that extent, therefore, I think it's better than many of the kind of books that came out that were all gung-ho. I found it a very moving book actually.

**HENNESSY**

How much of his approach to life – shaped by the war – rubbed off on you as a young boy do you think?

**DUNCAN SMITH**

It's difficult to say. I do know this much: my father generally had a very low opinion of politicians. He was from that generation that felt they had been betrayed. And he –

**HENNESSY**

By appeasement?

**DUNCAN SMITH**

Yes, by the nature of politicians' failure to take the right decisions. He was, as so many were at that stage, passionate about Churchill, but generally didn't put him down as a politician. He thought he was a – kind of had risen above politics. And I do remember him saying to me time and time again, you know, 'Politicians lost the lives of many of my friends by not taking early enough action.'

#### HENNESSY

Your mother was a Catholic and you were brought up as a Catholic, was that a tussle between your parents about the faith you should be nurtured in?

#### DUNCAN SMITH

I'll be quite frank with you, my parents married without the permission of the Catholic Church.

#### HENNESSY

Shock horror in those days.

#### DUNCAN SMITH

Very much so. My mother was essentially excommunicated from the Catholic Church because she chose to marry a man that had been married before. And my mother, as she always did – she was an incredibly strong-willed woman – said, 'Well, if you will force me to make a choice between the Church and the man I love I will take the man I love.' And so for, I think, for 40 years she didn't take communion in the Catholic Church – still remained a strong Catholic, but wouldn't take communion. And I had huge regard for her strength. And when the time came for me, the rest of my brothers were Church of England, because my father said he would take them to church, and my two sisters were brought up as Catholics. And then I ended up at a kind of Catholic school, when I was much younger, I think about ten or 11, and my mother said, 'Do you want to come over?' Because I was going to church with her all the time, and my father had ceased going to the church quite a while ago. And so yes, I became Catholic and it was kind of more, I'd been doing it already so it wasn't a – didn't seem like

– a Damascene conversion; it was – life had already become like that so it seemed reasonable for me to do it. And then later on one of the great moments in my family was when – and my father later, much later on, converted to Catholicism. I think principally because he felt at that stage he could bring my mother back to the Catholic Church, which is where she wanted to be.

**HENNESSY**

Did Catholicism shape you powerfully as a young man? Did you pick up Catholic social teaching, for example?

**DUNCAN SMITH**

I think you can't avoid picking it up as a Catholic, it's there and you know, the discipline of the Church is also there about, you know, reaching conclusions, reaching decisions while still being compassionate. I think that flows through Catholicism.

**HENNESSY**

You've never lapsed?

**DUNCAN SMITH**

No, I still go to church. I have my differences with the Catholic Church on a number of issues and I think they have their differences with me. But I principally remain a Catholic.

**HENNESSY**

Your schooling was at a Catholic school, Bishop Glancey Secondary Modern in Solihull. Then you went to HMS Conway in Anglesey, which is a naval, merchant naval training establishment. What led to that?

**DUNCAN SMITH**

I sat the Common Entrance to go there and then went into the school. When you're that age you're kind of very much guided by your father's view on it, and he was quite keen on the idea. There was a lot of – obviously a lot of naval stuff in there, but the core of it was still essentially a school and education was done like any other school really, in a sense. You know, you did your exams and everything else. It was quite straightforward really.

**HENNESSY**

Now why did you go for the Scots Guards? Because your dad was an airman, you went to a naval establishment, was it an outburst of IDS independence of spirit?

**DUNCAN SMITH**

Well, it was, because my father considered himself as, and was, Scots, he was passionate about Scotland. And I remember talking to him, because I said that I thought I wanted to go and do something which was, you know, action, and not just spend my time sitting down studying. And we talked about it and he said, 'Well, you want to go to –' you know, what he considered to be the best in the army, and he'd had friends in the Scots Guards and he had family who'd been in the Black Watch and stuff like that. And intriguingly he just said, 'The Scots Guards will be a really good regiment to go in.' And so I looked at it and thought about it and I thought, yes, I was happy to [go] into a Scots regiment. And that's how it all developed really.

**HENNESSY**

Did you enjoy Sandhurst?

**DUNCAN SMITH**

Well, it's changed a bit now. It was very intensive at the time. I had to do – if you go into the Guards in those days you had to do brigade squad. Brigade squad was you did about nine weeks, I think, of being trained as a recruit. So you had to experience recruit training, you know, the bellowing, the shouting, the getting up early in the morning.

**HENNESSY**

Good practice for politics.

**DUNCAN SMITH**

Well, in a funny sort of way it was really fascinating. I – now they've stopped it because people don't like doing it. But you know, you did at least experience what the people you then had to lead had to go through to get to the point where they got through into the Army. And I think that helped you a lot really [to] understand where they came from and everything else. And I think to that degree it was hard, toughens you up a lot actually, when some-one's walking in at four o'clock in the morning picking all your boots up, throwing them out the window and telling you you're not worth anything, go and pick them up and start again, when you'd been up all night with about 20 minutes' sleep. And you get men weeping in the corner because they've been taken to the brink of despair and then rebuilt. And you suddenly see just what your limits are. And I thought it was – it taught me a lot actually.

**HENNESSY**

Then you go to Northern Ireland as a very young officer, don't you? The troubles are still very severe at that point.

**DUNCAN SMITH**

Yes, we were positioned in the Bogside, which was considered dangerous enough that no police went to the Bogside unless they had military escorts at that stage. We had the first Sunday on which the anniversary of Bloody Sunday fell since Bloody Sunday. I remember the march that took place, well over 100,000 people there and I remember being in a complete state of permanent panic because I had these patrols of men around it, knowing full well there was absolutely nothing we could have done had they decided to get violent and angry. But worrying all the time, where is so and so, what are they doing? I can't see them. You know, you're constantly worried about the men that you're leading. And we had, you know, moments where we found stashes of ammunition, stuff like that. So, you know, it's a time when you're on edge. I lived in a small caravan with a hole in the side of the wall. So it was in the winter and so it was damp and wet and none of my clothing really dried throughout the whole period that I was there. But in a funny sort of way, again, you know, doing that helps you understand a lot about yourself, but it also helps you understand a lot about the way that people behave. I mean, intriguingly, as a Catholic it was a big eye-opener to see that even people who are the same religion can be incredibly divided from each other in aspects like that. It makes you grow up quite a lot really.

### HENNESSY

What did you learn about your fellow countrymen, because the army's a great bringer-together of all sorts and conditions of people, and in peacetime, post 1945, and particularly when National Service had ended we'd rather lost that shared formative experience. So what did you learn as a young man that you didn't know before?

### DUNCAN SMITH

The truth about the army is people talk about King or Queen and Country, but the reality is that when you're in difficulty it's the person next to you. That is why you fight, or why you do what you do, because everything breaks down into that. And that's what the army more than anything else teaches you, is that *in extremis* you look after each other. And every other principle goes out the window, but you look after each other. You will find that relationships struck in the army remain often so strong because you've often operated *in extremis* and you – you know that you can trust that individual to a certain degree and how far you can take each other. I think if that teaches you anything at all it's that, it's the simple ability to just believe in somebody enough to know that they won't let you down. And letting somebody down is the biggest cardinal sin. My father taught me that. You know, he talked about in combat, if somebody turns and goes and you leave and let somebody down, that's the biggest sin of all in anything you do, whatever else happens. And I think that is the truth. I mean you let somebody down, it's – it's very difficult to forgive somebody when they let you down.

### HENNESSY

You had another little flourish of late imperial experience, when you went to Rhodesia, about to become Zimbabwe, with General Acland, and you had [to] disarm the guerrilla armies, if I remember.

### DUNCAN SMITH

We did, yes.

### HENNESSY

That must have been quite precarious as well.

### DUNCAN SMITH

There were some really key moments. And again you learn a lot. I was very close to the politics for the first time. It's that that tipped me over the edge to go into politics.

### HENNESSY

Is it? Do explain.

### DUNCAN SMITH

I went to the Lancaster House Conference, I went to all those areas with him, and I was watching what happened. And while I was out there I reached the conclusion that actually I had much more interest in making the solutions than I had in implementing the solution itself, and I realised at that stage that if you want to do that there is only one place to be, if you want to make change rather than be told how to make that change then you have to go into politics, because politics is where that whole set of ideas comes from and is driven. And it was, actually, literally a moment when I was out with him in some quite far-blown place in what was then Rhodesia and seeing these little kids who were being fed and supported and for the first time – they'd had real problems. And I thought to myself if that's the end result of good policy then I want to be the person that decides how that policy works rather than the person that implements it.

**HENNESSY**

So that's why you didn't carry on in the Army.

**DUNCAN SMITH**

I don't think I ever would have done. I was not really cut out for the Army, I was not very easy to discipline and I used to – I suppose I don't suffer fools gladly.

**HENNESSY**

You're painting a picture of yourself as sort of awkward squad really, aren't you?

**DUNCAN SMITH**

Well I – yes, a little bit I suppose I am to be fair. I suspect my friends would probably say the same too. But I think I wouldn't have been a great peacetime soldier, but what I did learn from it was invaluable.

**HENNESSY**

You went into industry after leaving the army. GEC I think.

**DUNCAN SMITH**

Yes.

What did you do for them?

**DUNCAN SMITH**

It was with the Marconi set-up. It was all the electronics. It was fascinating work. I went into industry because I still wanted to go into politics but I did feel that I needed to develop a hinterland much more and understand industry having come out from the armed forces, you know, really important to try and get my feet down to earn a living to discover what it was like. I learnt quite a lot of lessons actually before I came into politics. I was made redundant. I made people redundant. It was worse making people redundant than it was being made redundant – horrible time when somebody I made redundant, a few months later they died of a heart attack, and I went to his funeral, and, you know, you can't help feeling that you know you had to do it because you had to tighten up on the administration, the company was tightening up, but – and also being made redundant you know it stays with you because you drive home, all your aspirations have just fallen through a hole in the floor. You arrive home and you have to tell your wife, or whatever, you know, the bottom just fell out of my dreams. I don't know what I'm going to do. I've got to find another job, you know. And you realise now –

**HENNESSY**

And you were only recently married then I think.

**DUNCAN SMITH**

Yes, yes, very much so. And you know you then start the process of trying to get yourself sorted and back into work. But I think, as a result of that, I do know just how difficult it is, and I often think politicians who haven't been through that – that experience – it's difficult for them to understand just how human this experience really is, and they're just not numbers on a board, that being unemployed is a devastating sense to somebody and it can damage everything to do with their lives. And so, you know, working to that end and understanding it is vitally important. I do remember somebody once in a meeting saying when I first arrived in politics – I think it was, well we came in in '92, so it was the tail end of another downturn –

**HENNESSY**

Recession, yes.

**DUNCAN SMITH**

Recession. And somebody said at a meeting, 'Well, people, you know, just have to get used to this, we have to make these decisions, this is part of re-building and difficult as it is, it just has to happen.' And I remember rounding on them and saying, 'Don't you ever say that to somebody who's been made redundant, because you have no idea how devastating it is to be made redundant. They are not just numbers on a board. They are human lives that are being put there and it is our responsibility to make the economy right so that we don't do this to them, and when we do, you have sympathy. Don't lecture them.'

**HENNESSY**

At this stage you're quite influenced by Mrs Thatcher who was getting into her stride.

**DUNCAN SMITH**

Yes.

**HENNESSY**

And Mrs Thatcher's critics always argue, do they not, about that early '80s recession, that the government's policies made it worse. There was a great row in the Cabinet about public spending cuts and so on, and monetarism. So what was it about Mrs Thatcher's conservatism that appealed to you, given your eloquence now about redundancy? I'm not arguing in any way that Conservative economic policies produce recessions, of course not, but it's slightly surprising that you took the Thatcher philosophy almost in full – at least, that's what people describe you as doing.

### DUNCAN SMITH

Well, she inspired me very much to get involved in politics once I'd been in Rhodesia, and looking at how it was done, and it was her, of course, at the Lancaster House set-up with Carrington. So I think more than anything else, you know, we're both old enough to remember what life felt like in the 1970s and particularly towards the end of the 1970s. I mean it was a pretty dull and depressing grey period, and I can remember even while I was in the Army just thinking to yourselves well, nothing seems to go right here. This country seems to be sliding, sliding, sliding. If you're patriotic about your country, if you care about it, you worry that we just don't seem to have the answers and everybody else seems to be going past us, and why can't the UK, you know, just get its act together? And along comes this woman who seems just to say 'I don't agree with any of that, what is required is a clarity and leadership.' And you respond to leadership in a funny sort of way. If somebody says, 'I do know how to do this and I know that we're going to get through this, but we have to rebuild so that the future is better,' then your tendency is to say, 'Well, they know where they're going and I'm going to give them the leeway to make those changes.' And so it was her sense of leadership and a sense of determination and vision.

### HENNESSY

You're chosen to replace Norman Tebbit, a very primary-colours politician, almost totemic in those years of a particular kind of conservatism. You're not quite so primary colours if you don't mind me putting it like that. You're a very different sort of person from Norman Tebbit, but did you by and large feel that you were 'son of Norman' in a way – that his instincts were your instincts – when you took over Chingford?

**DUNCAN SMITH**

I was a huge admirer of Norman's – it's difficult not to be an admirer of Norman's – and also subsequently since the Brighton bomb, I mean every day goes by I know that Norman is in pain himself, which is hardly ever reflected on, and looking after Margaret and that had huge issues. So I admire Norman enormously. You don't have to agree with him on everything, but I think on essentials we pretty much line up close to where we might be normally – may not approach, may not come at it in quite the same way at times.

**HENNESSY**

Your language is somewhat different.

**DUNCAN SMITH**

Yes, Norman is someone that likes to stir the argument up and then pronounce. Sometimes I think you need to just step away slightly and reshape it in different ways, but you know, more often than not as I say Norman – I'm a huge admirer of Norman's. I mean he became a bit of a political mentor to me. I hadn't known him before, but you know he was very helpful, not in party politics sense, but just helpful in shaping my understanding of what it is to be a constituency MP, how you operate in Parliament. I do remember he gave me one bit of advice, which is, I said, 'Norman, it's very difficult to know sometimes' – this is after I'd been elected – 'you know, when you're a little unsure whether you're saying the right thing.' And he said in that wonderful whisper of his, he said, 'Well, Iain, it's as simple as this.' He said, 'If you're speaking and the other side are smiling and cheering at you, sit down.' He said, 'If you're speaking and the other side are shouting at you, keep going, you're doing the right thing.' [*Both laugh*] I often find myself evaluating myself by that very judgement, suddenly saying 'Stop, this is too simplistic'.

## HENNESSY

Vintage Norman Tebbit. You broke parliamentary convention in a way with your maiden speech, because you're meant to be pretty bland in your maiden speech, but you weren't, you really biffed them. And it was the time of 1992 when John Major had come back to everybody's surprise with a majority – not a very big one. And yet you went straight for the jugular. And there you were, and you tore into the Hurd-Major line on Europe, didn't you? All about the danger of a super-state, if I remember.

## DUNCAN SMITH

Yes, I did. I remember writing the speech. I just felt that I had made it clear before the election that I didn't think – I thought the direction that Europe was going in was a wrong direction and I thought that it was wrong for us. And I'd looked at the Maastricht Treaty and I thought that generally this just made it worse and I just reached the conclusion that really it was time for the UK to re-evaluate why it was in the European Union. I'd voted to join, by the way. I'd not been opposed to it all the time. It was as I got towards politics I started looking at it more and I realised there'd been the beginnings I think – the Single European Act was the big change.

## HENNESSY

1986.

## DUNCAN SMITH

Which Mrs Thatcher herself was persuaded to put through, but the more I looked at it, the more you realise that people like Altiero Spinelli, who was one of the great architects of this – much not known about here in the UK, but I think arguably more influential than Monnet and Schuman were in the direction of which you went. And his design for it, the more you read about him you realise his design was literally to take more and more power from the nation states to central control. That was the only way that you could overcome the fallibilities of politicians who would never take the big decisions at national level. I can understand that, but I disagreed with it and I felt that was the direction we were going in with the qualified majority voting. So when I arrived to make my speech I felt it important just to state that this was my position clearly because it became apparent to me that if I didn't do it then, once you start just giving in on that issue then you never stop really. And I've always come up with one simple conclusion. There's lots of things when you're in government you have to put up with, you don't agree with – I accept that's, you know – we always say, that's collective responsibility. But as a non-governmental person, as a backbencher, you should always hold onto the simple fact that you enter Parliament with your character, and what you leave with is how you behave with your character. And if you spend your time selling your character for just little bits and pieces here and there and privileges from government, then when you leave the only thing that sustains you at the end of the day is that you still hold your character, and you can look yourself in the mirror and say, do you know what, at the end of the day I think on balance I was about right.

**HENNESSY**

Being such a consistent Maastricht dissenter in terms of casting votes and all that –

**DUNCAN SMITH**

I wasn't quite as big as Bill and the others –

**HENNESSY**

Bill Cash and some of the others, no, but you were pretty well up there Iain, I think. Do you not think – not that you probably, well perhaps you were anticipating being Leader one day – but the trouble is if you behave as that kind of awkward squad, it stores up a lot of resentment amongst the middle ground in parties and certainly the whips. And so when you need the loyalty, the unquestioning loyalty, as a leader yourself it can quite often flow back on you, can't it? Do you think you suffered later as a result of your Maastricht pattern of voting?

### DUNCAN SMITH

Almost certainly, yes. That's the honest and unequivocal answer. But then again I hadn't planned to be Leader at the time, so I was trying to do what I felt to be right. And you only have to look back in history; you can see how Churchill was not at all accepted by the Conservative Party after Chamberlain went, there was still anger over his behaviour. I'm not comparing myself to Churchill for God's sake, no, but I'm simply saying that it is of course inevitable that people who all through have said they've done what the loyal thing is feel bitter about somebody who then ends up as Leader who hasn't. And I can understand that.

### HENNESSY

You became Shadow Social Security Secretary when William Hague became Leader. Did you ask for that job?

### DUNCAN SMITH

No. It actually came out of the blue. I hadn't expected any job. Bear in mind I hadn't done any government jobs at all at that stage and to go into the Shadow Cabinet was a bit of a jolt really. When I did take up the post it had a massive influence on me because I spent a lot of time travelling around visiting communities that, you know, were often blighted in difficulty, etc, talking to people about where it had gone wrong. And I started to think carefully at that stage where this wealthy economy was, and how sometimes we needed to look at ways in which that spread, etc, of wealth and aspiration could be moved around and communities that lived next to each other that were – one was you know poor and the other one was rather wealthy – and we were dividing ourselves. All that started when I was in that post.

### HENNESSY

Was there an epiphany moment, because many in your own generation of Conservatives or some have certainly said to me that they noticed a change in you, that you suddenly became much more sensitised to the wider 'condition of Britain' question, to use a Disraelian phrase.

### DUNCAN SMITH

A lot of my direct interest in the social justice end of things started with my Shadow Cabinet position as Secretary of State for Social Security. I'd already made comments about it before but I was able then to start developing it. I'm not very good at these ideas that there's a moment of epiphany, does it gradually grow on you that there is a big challenge here that needs to be met? A lot of my early period had been really dominated by the Europe argument, and I moved away from that at that point and chose actually to park that. I said, 'I'm not going to stay involved in that at all, I want to get on with this,' and I realised that there was an agenda. My biggest issue was the Conservatives had become quite narrow and we had, as a party, failed to recognise that there were big issues around poverty that we needed to look at and to see whether or not, as Conservatives, we should have vacated the field in the way that we had and left it solely to the Left to discuss, to debate, to argue and at the same time to provide solutions. And it more and more grew upon me that the idea was that if any – in any political debate – if one side leaves the agenda what happens is the whole thing tilts and can often go badly wrong. And my feeling was that a lot of what was going wrong was because, you know, Conservatives had not entered that debate and felt there was nothing important to them. I was then trying to get across the idea that this was different. I met Bob Holman, I admired him enormously, he was a remarkable man. He lived his life as he believed in his own philosophy, but he lived it. And to his day, he believed that there should be a simple limit to income, that everything should be shared, and you have to admire somebody that lives their politics. But he was very good in explaining that life change was really what they were after, not politicians just placating them with money and bits and pieces, they wanted a real change in the way that their lives could be lived, and those that they were serving. And he had this project in Easterhouse that he'd set up, and I went to visit it [and] met some really interesting people, like the Baptist Minister Sandy Weddell and others. And it did strike me that there was a lot in here which really doesn't necessarily have to be pigeonholed as a particular party's view of life. It's actually universal, it's about the condition of man rather than the idea that, you know, we believe in free markets or we believe in state control and all the other kind of normal political debates. Something in here was about people. And that's what really drew me to it. So Bob had a huge influence on the way I looked at this. I met some others too in Glasgow that were really good, again in the same area, often not talked about, in Gallowgate. But all of that was part of what I was trying to do when I was Leader, trying to discover what it was that we could, you know, take forward. And I didn't want to get bogged down in Europe when I became Leader. In fact, everyone expected me immediately to start talking about Europe, and I said, 'I'm not going to talk about Europe, we're going to get everybody out there and we're going to look at things like why does the Health Service have problems, why do people's lives look so blighted so near others that have great expectations and aspirations, a walking distance away?' All of that, I wanted to do that. That angered, I know, a lot of my colleagues who wanted to talk about Europe.

**HENNESSY**

Some were surprised, some were surprised indeed that you were doing it.

**DUNCAN SMITH**

Some got angry actually, yes.

**HENNESSY**

Now, why did you decide that you were the one to go for the leadership when William Hague declared his intention to stand down?

**DUNCAN SMITH**

Well, I tried to get William not to stand down. It wasn't over simply because he lost an election, which was lost pretty much from the day we lost the last election. Nothing changed in the public's view, they thought Blair needed more time, didn't matter whether he'd made mistakes.

**HENNESSY**

This is 2001.

**DUNCAN SMITH**

I hadn't actually any plans to be Leader, but I just had a number of people calling me up and saying, 'You've got to stand,' which was rather peculiar, because there were lots of people more senior than me that could easily have picked up the baton. But in the end I thought, well, at least I need to try and make the case for certain key elements of the things that I believe in now and I want to make the party change. And so I thought it would be useful to do that. I didn't have any expectations that I would be Leader. After all, there were two enormous beasts in the field and I –

**HENNESSY**

Clarke and Portillo.

**DUNCAN SMITH**

Yes. And I was still, not relatively unknown, just unknown.

**HENNESSY**

You were fairly cutting towards Michael Portillo, many would argue, at the time. I think you talked about – or maybe you weren't thinking of him – about the danger of emoting in politics and 'pashmina politics', and so on.

**DUNCAN SMITH**

Yes, actually that was –

**HENNESSY**

Because he's quite a social liberal, isn't he, Michael Portillo? Or maybe that was a wrong interpretation. Do you think you were a bit harsh on him?

**DUNCAN SMITH**

We may well have been. I mean, leadership elections are not – any election like that is not a pleasant process because, of course, particularly in parties, because it's always personal, you can't help it. Actually I didn't come up with that phrase. I'm not going to tell you who did, but –

**HENNESSY**

Come on, you can say now. Time has elapsed…

**DUNCAN SMITH**

It was Bernard actually that came up with it.

**HENNESSY**

Bernard Jenkin.

### DUNCAN SMITH

Yes, yes.

### HENNESSY

Your campaign manager.

### DUNCAN SMITH

It was. I think Maurice Saatchi said that it was one the best advertising catchphrases he'd ever heard. Well, I think if you're trying to describe something you need to come up with some kind of sense of what it is you're describing. It wasn't really describing social liberalism, it was that you need also at the same time to give some leadership and sense of direction, rather than just, you know, empathising and saying, 'I feel your pain.' That was the main point to make. It's all very well to keep going round saying, 'I've discovered what life is like, to have, you know, to have been a porter,' or whatever it is. The key element is to understand more fundamentally what the roots of the problem were. So there was a difference between us. I have a huge respect for Michael and, you know, thought he was an excellent politician and I was sorry he chose to leave politics. I always felt he had more to give. So I don't think it was personal, but it was about picking on what kind of agenda were we going to be going towards, between the two. After all, I was the outsider and I was having to show that the two others were, in effect, dyed in the wool in an area that would have made it very difficult to run the party. That's what you have to do. And then you have [to] say, 'Well, you know, you have an alternative.' But in those days I didn't think for one moment that I would have been elected at the time.

### HENNESSY

Were you ever at ease as party Leader?

### DUNCAN SMITH

It was very difficult, I have to tell you. And I think whoever had been elected would have had real trouble. My sense was the party really didn't want to get back into power. I mean, they said they did, but they didn't want it enough to be able to say we're going to have to come back together again and make compromises. So everybody was set in their own positions and it was quite difficult to get them to do it. And when I said, 'I want us to go out and look again and think about the conditions that – where the big problems are, in these estates etc, and to look at the Health Service,' there was quite a lot of resistance to that at the time. 'You know, well, we've got to make the point about taxation, we've got to make the point about Europe, we should be on Europe and it's all going wrong.' And the answer was, 'Look, that's how people see us, but we've got to broaden out now and show that actually we really do care about these things.' But when a party decides arguments are no longer the key but power is, that's the moment that you can lead them back to power, as Blair found and as David Cameron found. You know, there's a moment when suddenly the party says, 'Do you know what? We really do need to get back to power.' And that collective moment, it kind of just happens, and it wasn't there when I was there.

### HENNESSY

Do you regret the 'Quiet Man' self-appellation?

### DUNCAN SMITH

It was meant to be a juxtaposition with the razzle-dazzle constant comment –

### HENNESSY

Of New Labour.

**DUNCAN SMITH**

Of New Labour.

**HENNESSY**

Yes.

**DUNCAN SMITH**

The total politics, which was new. There was a sense that out there, there was the beginnings of an idea that maybe there was too much politics and that you needed a more calm sense to it, and a more considered sense, and somebody who really said, 'You know what, I just want to find the solutions and I want to take us somewhere,' rather than somebody who constantly had a comment or a view. As a statement it stayed.

**HENNESSY**

It stuck.

**DUNCAN SMITH**

I'm not sure how successful it was.

**HENNESSY**

What went wrong at the end, Iain?

**DUNCAN SMITH**

I just think – it's very difficult to say. I clearly didn't manage to get the party across the line on the things that I wanted to do. They obviously felt that I clearly wasn't going to be able to take them to success at the next election. And, you know, it's difficult to put your finger on it. It was quite early for me, because you know, to be Leader of a party sometimes you need quite a lot of political experience, and I'd had quite little, not a lot. And so when you look back you know that there are things you know now that you would have done differently. But that's the nature of the game.

You can't finesse this, you do what you do when the moment arrives.

### HENNESSY

Do you still carry the scar?

### DUNCAN SMITH

It's difficult. Not really now, I move on. I never try and sit in judgement on it. There are people who I thought behaved badly, but I don't think there's any point in vendettas, vendettas destroy you more than they destroy anybody else, and you simply have to accept the fact that it didn't work but you need to move on. There were attacks on my character which I felt were unfair, and I set myself the task of regaining my character really, which is important.

### HENNESSY

It gave you a chance to set up the Centre for Social Justice, but also you had the chance, when David Cameron forms the Coalition government, to actually put some of this into practice when you were appointed Work and Pensions Secretary. I've often [thought], Iain, how strange it is that no government since the Coalition government in the war has done a Beveridge, has looked at every aspect of deprivation. The argument being you've got to hit all those five giants simultaneously: ignorance; idleness; squalor; disease; want, to break the crust of deprivation. Do you not regret, looking back, that you didn't have a kind of new-Beveridge look at all this before you set about those reforms as Work and Pensions Secretary?

### DUNCAN SMITH

Well, I believe that we did, because while I was at the Centre for Social Justice we undertook a monumental task of looking at what had happened to society and where the damage was and where the problems were. We published a two-volume report called

'Breakdown and Breakthrough Britain,' and there we looked at what I call the five modern pathways, which were family breakdown, debt, failed education, worklessness and addictions. Having talked a lot to the voluntary sector groups, these are the ones that kept coming up again and again. So we redefined that as those were the modern-day pathways. And from that we then set up five task forces to look at it. And they're very big volumes and they came up with a lot of evidence – sent them out to the country to talk to all these groups. So that work I believe had been done, and we came up with a number of ideas to try and reinforce and improve that.

### HENNESSY

Universal credit was the key was it not? This was your way of modernising the entire welfare system. You had real problems with that –

### DUNCAN SMITH

Yes. I mean, there were lots of other things, you know. Free schools were one of the policies. There were lots of areas across the board – better involvement with kids who had been in care, replicating family structure much more, getting them involved longer. All these sort of things were things that percolated through all of the government policy at the time, and I think were very helpful and successful. We did a number of things when I was at the Department of Work and Pensions. One of the big problems, of course, is that when we came in we had this economic crisis and that meant everybody was tightening up financially. And it's always difficult to implement stuff if you're spending your whole time also taking money out of systems. Now, I don't make any comment other than of course the government had to do that at the time, that's why there was a coalition. But we did things like the work programme. Also we looked [at] things like the benefit cap and bits and pieces, which were all aimed at trying to say, 'Look, the balance between work and being out of work, when the choice arrives, is one that you need to take the choice to work. And so we need to incentivise people to work.' Universal credit was looking at the problem as we had done in 'Breakthrough Britain' and saying that there is a real problem of complexity in the benefit system which makes it very difficult for people to navigate. Those six benefits, you try and merge those together so that when people make a claim everything they want to do was done at that same point and that all the way through they can then understand how much money they are due, which is immediately told to them, and if they take a certain amount of hours' work they can figure it out for themselves because the tapers are straight and flat and there are no cliff edges and no disincentives. So those two things. And there was the third and fourth elements, which one is that you will then stay with the same adviser all the way through. This brings it all together, so you always have somebody to go and see if you have a problem. The human interface to me was very important, it's very little talked about. And the last element was we designed around it a thing called universal support, which is about once you identified some family has a problem, councils and the department should work to get them into things like rehabilitation or debt counselling and/or drugs [rehabilitation]. You know, whatever it happens to be: stabilise the exceptional families but set a system up that allows those who are not in that to be able to flow in and out of work very quickly.

#### HENNESSY

Were the criticisms of the National Audit Office, which were quite severe about all this, justified?

#### DUNCAN SMITH

Well, the early implementation I stopped, because I set up my own panel to look at it and they told me that the way the civil servants at the time were designing the system wasn't going to work. So we stopped it and redesigned it at the time. What we did was we said we'd roll it out stage by stage, which was very unusual. So that every time you roll it out to a group, you can check to see whether there's a problem as it hits the human interface, and make the changes. And that's what's happening at the moment. Big changes were made in December, which are already now having an impact, and I argued for a lot of those. The truth is, and I stand by this, that as has often happened to be the case, the Work Programme was highly criticised when it first started, and then two years later the same office had come out and said it's the best, most effective back-to-work programme that's been instigated by a government. I believe the same will be said eventually of Universal Credit. I resigned because I thought taking money out of a system like that as you launch it is quite the wrong thing to do.

#### HENNESSY

You said it's balancing the books on the back of the poor. You'd had a huge run-in with George Osborne, the Chancellor, hadn't you? There's an element that seems to be quite unpleasant, there seemed to be an animus. It must have been quite difficult for you.

#### DUNCAN SMITH

Yes, I had a vision about how I wanted this to be, and I still do, I still think it's wholly achievable. My problem was that I'd never been in favour of the next tranche of cuts, reductions. I thought we'd gone far enough and that we now had to safeguard the rollout of programmes and we needed to look again at the sickness and work process, which is the big reform that had to be done, and therefore coming back into government in 2015 was a difficult moment because we were set on a £12 billion reduction, and I didn't think that that was doable.

#### HENNESSY

Yes.

### DUNCAN SMITH

And I didn't think it was the right thing to do and I think we should have looked again. But, you know, you have these differences in government, and we did, and as the year went on I realised more and more that I was no longer able to use allies that I had in Cabinet prior to that, when we were in coalition. And therefore I was not able to win these arguments any longer.

### HENNESSY

So you left. Just a few weeks later, after your resignation in March 2016, we had the European referendum. We vote to leave. You and I bumped into each other in Westminster the day after and I remember you said something very interesting about people coming out to vote who'd never voted before.

### DUNCAN SMITH

On the day I spent my time knocking on doors. But my agent had gone off to talk and look at other areas because I thought, well, we're losing. I need to get a perspective on this because I've got to do this ten o'clock interview. So as I was literally just going in to do the interview at about a quarter to ten or something, and he rang me and I said, 'What's happening?' He said, 'Well, I've been in politics a reasonable amount of time,' he said, 'I've never seen this before.' I said, 'What?' He said, 'They're queuing at the polling stations in the housing estates, which never happens. And some people who never voted before are being taught how to vote.' And he said, 'These are people that were never registered before.' And he said the turnout on two of the estates, he said, was already over 80 per cent. Now, I put the telephone down and I knew that that is also not my experience of politics, and I went in and I spoke to a couple of people about it. Tom Watson was one of them actually. And I said to Tom – I've known him for ages, he's an old friend – I said, 'Tom, what do you make of this?' He said, 'Well it's exactly what I found up in the north-east.' And I said, 'What do you make of all of it? I don't know.' And he said, 'I think there's going to be a big surprise tonight.' So I went on to the Dimbleby programme and the first question they asked me was, Nigel Farage actually said we'd lost. And I said, 'I make a special effort not to listen to what Nigel Farage says when he forecasts stuff.' But I then relayed this story, and to be fair, David Dimbleby said, 'Oh, that sounds very interesting,' and he said, 'So we don't know where we are.' I said, 'I don't,' I said, 'but I have to say if that is the case then it could change everything.'

### HENNESSY

Do you think there's a danger that your life's cause might be caveated away? That the settlement we'll finally have, the post-Brexit settlement, will not be what you wanted all your life?'

### DUNCAN SMITH

Well, we voted to leave. I still think this will be best for the UK. My instinct is that the European Union won't want us to leave without arrangements, and politics being what it is, we'll come up with something at the end. I was with a group of European ambassadors, funnily enough, about ten of them, and I said to them, 'I wonder if you're in a position to take a pace back and just ask yourself the simple question: isn't this a case of UK exceptionalism?' And they said, 'What do you mean?' And I said, 'Well, the UK was never a very easy partner with the European project. You all sign up to this, you all think that, you know, this stops the war and everything else. The UK is an island nation and has a different view of the world to a degree. Wouldn't it be better now to accept the fact that we're not going to lead loads of countries out of Europe but that you'd like to remain on good close terms with us and we with you? It's just that we're like the neighbour next door now. We don't live in each other's lives, but we certainly recognise the way we affect each other. Wouldn't it be better for the Commission to stop messing around worrying about whether we're going to damage the European Union and accept the fact that actually a really good, strong friend next door may be worth more than one that's been captured inside the European Union, unable to influence things sometimes for your benefit?' And there was complete silence amongst them all, and one of them said, 'Only a British citizen could say something like that.' And they all roared with laughter. But I did think that that was a case we haven't made to the European Union. Which is: if we're friends why can't we do this properly?

**HENNESSY**

If you had made it to Prime Minister, what would you have done on day one?

**DUNCAN SMITH**

The first thing I would have done was restored the money back to Universal Credit that was taken out of it just before I left.

**HENNESSY**

Your big cause.

**DUNCAN SMITH**

Yes.

**HENNESSY**

Iain what kind of trace would you like to leave on history? How would you like to be remembered?

**DUNCAN SMITH**

That I came into politics to make a difference, and I hope that it's seen that we did make a positive difference to the way that people live their lives. If you want to ask me, of the things that I've done that I want to see work more than anything else, it's the changes that I made to social structure and the Centre for Social Justice.

I do genuinely really, really, really care about the fact that some people's lives are blighted from the day they're born and they don't reach the kind of level of aspiration that my children will have done. And it drives me more than Europe does, I have to tell you. If there's anything at all that I want to leave behind, it's that.

**HENNESSY**

Iain Duncan Smith, thank you very much indeed.

# Chris Patten (Lord Patten of Barnes)

Series 7, Episode 1, first broadcast 29 July 2019

**Born** 12 May 1944; **Educated** St Benedict's
School; Balliol College, Oxford

MP (Conservative) Bath 1979–92

Director of the Conservative Research Department, 1974–79;
Parliamentary Under-Secretary of State, Northern Ireland Office,
1983–85; Minister of State, Department of Education and Science, 1985–
86; Minister for Overseas Development, Foreign & Commonwealth
Office, 1986–89; Secretary of State for the Environment, 1989–90;
Chairman of the Conservative Party and Chancellor of the Duchy
of Lancaster, 1990–92; Governor of Hong Kong, 1992–97; Chairman,
Independent Commission on Policing for Northern Ireland,
1998–99; European Commissioner, External Relations, 1999–2004;
Chancellor, University of Newcastle, 1999–2009; Chancellor,
University of Oxford, 2003–; Chairman, BBC Trust, 2011–14

**Autobiography** *First Confession: A Sort of Memoir*, 2017

**HENNESSY**

With me today is Chris Patten, Lord Patten of Barnes, whose political career can only be described as broad gauge, embracing as it
has a seat in both Margaret Thatcher's and John Major's Cabinets,

the governorship of Hong Kong, the shaping of the Police Service of Northern Ireland, the chairmanship of the BBC Trust and the chancellorships of the universities of Newcastle and Oxford. He has also been a European Commissioner and has worked for the Pope. Some years ago, Chris Patten was the first person I heard describe the relationship between Britain and the European Union as a 'psycho-drama.' Chris, welcome.

### PATTEN

Thank you very much indeed. The drama continues.

### HENNESSY

Never-ending. Tell me about your early drama, the kind of family you came into the world with and your early formation.

### PATTEN

I'm often described in the tabloids, which pretty well covers all newspapers in this country now, as a 'Tory grandee', which is slightly wide of the mark. I'm the only 'Tory grandee' to have been born in Blackpool, I think, and brought up in the suburbs of west London. I'm middle class, but it wasn't middle class as in Surrey and large gardens and tennis courts; it was middle class as in the pre- and post-war estates, which were built along the arterial roads out of London for the workers at Glaxo, at Rockware and Heathrow, now with a large formerly immigrant community. My dad was a music publisher. He'd been, before the war, a drummer in a band; went into the RAF. While he was a drummer in a band he met my mum in Exeter, playing at a gig. And her parents found, to their horror, that their beautiful actress daughter, in all the best amateur productions in Exeter, was marrying not just a drummer in a band but a Catholic Irish drummer in a band. [*Hennessey laughs*] My grandparents were head teachers at Catholic primary schools in Manchester, and my great-grandfather was born in Boyle in county Roscommon in 1829. I noted recently that the population of Boyle is lower today than it was in 1829, and he was one of many who escaped the famine in the 1840s by fleeing, emigrating to Britain. He worked first of all as somebody who repaired cane chairs and then got into a better job as a weaver in the textile industry. So I came from a sort of Irish [background], on that side, like millions of others in this country. My mum's father was a – started off as a clerical officer, working for Heavitree Breweries in Exeter. Her mum was a milliner. And my grandfather on my mother's side finished up as the company secretary of Heavitree Ales. No, I come from a fairly standard, first-generation-at-university, family. I was brought up at Catholic schools: primary school, scholarship to a direct grant independent school. And I've often said that I wish that I could sue for deprivation of literary royalties, because I had an extremely happy childhood and time as a schoolboy.

### HENNESSY

Your dad's profession, drummer then music publisher, is fairly raffish actually, in a nice sort of way, wasn't it? And I remember, when I was reading your memoir, *First Confession*, how I was very struck by, he managed to persuade Guy Mitchell – a great singer in the '50s, in our childhood – both to buy and sing *She Wears Red Feathers and a Hula-hula Skirt*.

### PATTEN

Absolutely.

### HENNESSY

I think that's quite something to be proud of actually, isn't it?

### PATTEN

Absolutely. He also published the music – popular music – of one or two other people, including – I think he was called Johnnie Ray, who used to weep while singing.

**HENNESSY**

Used to cry on stage, yes.

**PATTEN**

Yes, exactly.

**HENNESSY**

The crooner who cried.

**PATTEN**

It's not too unpopular these days to cry if you're British, but it used to be in those days. Anyway, he wasn't British, he was American, so you can allow that, I suppose. Yes, it was a bit sort of raffish. There were some good sides about it. First of all, my dad had a lot of Jewish friends, so any idea of anti-Semitism in my lower-middle-class, middle-class family would have been thought to be astonishing. Secondly, he and my mum gave me a love of music. Most of the music he loved was big band American, but also singers like Ella Fitzgerald, Frank Sinatra and so on. So I grew up very happily with them. And my dad was very keen on sport and used to bowl endlessly at me in the gardens as I scored centuries for England against Australia. So very happy and pretty normal, and my primary school, ditto – a very traditional Catholic, rather rigorous education. But it meant – as I've told people from time to time, and they look slightly surprised – it meant that when I go into a gallery now or a church on holiday, I sort of know the story behind the paintings. And I remember going – when I was doing a job in Rome for Pope Francis and the Vatican and when I had plenty of time on my hands one afternoon – I was going around churches looking at Caravaggio paintings. I went into the great French church, and there's a series of paintings of the life of Saint Matthew, including one which is called *The Calling* or *The Vocation*, and it's Jesus coming into the sort of VAT office in Palestine and pointing at Saint Matthew and, you know, saying in effect, 'You're coming with me.'

It's Pope Francis's favourite painting, apparently. I can remember the day that I was told that story, sitting on Mrs Williams's knee aged about seven. And it came back to me straight away. I knew *exactly* what had happened, and I knew when I was looking at the painting how Mrs Williams had explained to us that that was what it was like. You were told you were a follower of Christ and you, it might be painful, but you had to do it. And of course, in Saint Matthew's case, he finished up on a cross.

#### HENNESSY

You had what one would call a deep-immersion Catholic upbringing, which I had too, in pre-Vatican II north London, just around the North Circular, in my case, in Finchley. And there's a wonderfully evocative photograph in your memoir of you leading the May procession of Our Lady of the Visitation with heroic quantities of Brylcreem in your hair. [*Patten laughs*] It brings it all back.

#### PATTEN

My hair flattened, flattened. It was only – and it was clearly regarded in Greenford as a rather exotic event, the May procession. We would wander out into the street with a couple of police officers – in those days you occasionally saw police officers – holding back crowds who watched this strange sort of freemasonry going past with its mumbo-jumbo language and the odd autocratic figure in Rome whom nuns would kneel [to] in order to telephone. So it was – one was regarded a little, as a little strange in those days. I think it's all changed hugely thanks, not least, to Pope John XXIII and the Vatican Council. And I've never in public life really felt any antipathy to me or curiosity about me being a Catholic.

#### HENNESSY

Do you not think it's given you a bit of an edge in a good sense, as a kind of insider-outsider in British society? Because we *were* regarded as somewhat odd.

**PATTEN**

Yes, I think that two things helped, well three things helped. First of all, the Vatican Council; secondly, I think some of the appointments – I think Basil Hume and Cormac Murphy-O'Connor were so obviously part of the mainstream of British public life.

**HENNESSY**

Vatican Cardinal and Archbishop, yes.

**PATTEN**

Yes. And [thirdly], I think our society has just become more open and more tolerant. I think that – while there are some things that worry me about life today – I do think that, when you look at the treatment of minorities, it's on the whole been transformed.

**HENNESSY**

You've talked in the past about your faith being your personal lifeboat. I thought that was a very interesting concept, because it's stayed with you throughout, hasn't it?

**PATTEN**

Yes, it has. And I'm not one of those people who thinks that your politics is in one box and your faith in another. I feel able to talk openly about both. Not in a way which suggests that, because I'm a Christian, because I'm a Catholic, there is something superior about my views on political issues, but I couldn't separate the two. And I sometimes think as well it's not only a lesson for politicians, it's a lesson for some churchmen that the laity have every right to speak out on issues, which aren't matters that are written on tablets of stone as though there ever were such things. And I've got every much a right to express my views on homosexuals or on divorce or on gay marriage or on contraception as any Cardinal.

**HENNESSY**

St Benedict's, Ealing – your direct grant school, down the road from Greenford where you grew up – obviously again left a big mark on you. They lit fires in your mind, didn't they, your history teachers, Mr Wilding and Father Brown, who used to reduce everything, I think, to cricketing metaphors?

**PATTEN**

Yes, I think –

**HENNESSY**

Thomas à Becket bowling the king a googly and that sort of thing.

**PATTEN**

That's right. I think there is something else which it taught me apart from moderation, which has always been – though they've had some difficulties recently – a Benedictine desideratum. I think that they were very happy that I should have my own views, provided I was serious, provided I'd thought about them. A great friend of mine, and probably one of my two closest Irish friends, was saying this to me the other day, that it's so important to be serious – I don't mean not to be larky, not to have a sense of humour. But one of the things that worries me about Britain today is we're *not* serious any more in the way that some other countries still are, which enables us to watch the degradation of political debate in the way it has happened in the last few years. But I think to be taught to be serious, to think things through... If you've got lots of opinions – and it goes for people who have different opinions from me as well – if you've actually *thought* about them and you've got a good case, then that's fine.

**HENNESSY**

Were your teachers at St Benedict's surprised when you got your exhibition to Balliol? I think they thought you were going to do English at university –

**PATTEN**

Yes, they were –

**HENNESSY**

– and you suddenly did history.

**PATTEN**

I had a wonderful, wonderful English master who brought sarcasm to a high art. He was a wonderful man, and [he] got me and got us reading all sorts of people that we wouldn't have read otherwise. I mean, I don't just mean poets like John Donne; I don't just mean George Eliot – who I think is the greatest English novelist – and others, but Christopher Isherwood I remember he was very enthusiastic about. And the idea was that I was going to try to get a scholarship at Peterhouse at Cambridge, but my history masters thought that, since in those days the Oxford scholarship exams were just before Christmas and the Cambridge ones afterwards, they should put me in for history first at Oxford. And, to everybody's surprise, I got an exhibition. I went up without having revised any – much – history, but having loads and loads of English quotations in my head. So I got a scholarship when I was sixteen and a bit, and then wasted the next year and a half playing cricket and doodling.

**HENNESSY**

You weren't particularly political at Oxford, I don't think. I think you wrote reviews and things – theatrical rather than political.

**PATTEN**

Yes, to say I wasn't particularly political is an understatement. I went to the Union once and thought it was pretty boring, and took

Chris Patten (Lord Patten of Barnes)

against some of the people who made the Union their career. But I wrote a lot of reviews. I edited a satirical magazine called *Mesopotamia*, which had been started by some of the people who went on to start *Private Eye*, one of the great institutions of our lives. I played a lot of cricket, quite a bit of rugby, I acted. I used to go on a touring review every year, in which we'd take a Greek play and rewrite it as a jolly review to music. And then we'd go round public schools and private parties and the law, the Inns of Court and so on, performing. It was great fun.

**HENNESSY**

Tell me about your politics, as you were finishing in Oxford; you were attracted by Tony Crosland's book *The Future of Socialism*. I think you once said you would have voted Labour in '64 if you'd had the vote.

**PATTEN**

I think I would. But I was swiftly put off by, I have to say, Harold Wilson. And I also became extremely sceptical of the idea that you could systematise politics. I became extremely sceptical about the notion that there was a way of ordering society which would answer all our problems. And that turned me, inevitably, into a sort of Oakeshottian Conservative. I wouldn't have been able to put it like that when I was 21, 22. The real reason why I got into politics rather than the BBC – because, in 1966, I got an offer of a graduate traineeship at the BBC, largely I suppose because of my acting and writing – but what really turned me onto politics was I had a scholarship to go to America, a travelling scholarship, and while I was there got involved in an American political campaign, working for the successful Republican – though very moderate Republican – candidate in New York, John Lindsay.

**HENNESSY**

Before I ask you about that political awakening, Chris, I was very interested in what you said a moment ago about your sceptical side. You've written about – in your memoir – 'most of us hide parts of ourselves in dark burrows like John le Carré characters, manipulating others by what we think they want or expect to see.' There's something of the Kantian line there, which Isaiah Berlin used to call it, do you remember, 'out of the crooked timber of humanity nothing straight is ever made.'

### PATTEN

Yes.

### HENNESSY

It gives you a kind of detachment, doesn't it?

### PATTEN

Well, we're probably going to talk about him – the politician to whom I was always most attracted was Rab Butler. Rab Butler: people used to celebrate the fact that he was so wickedly ambiguous. Actually, the most important thing was he was ambivalent. And he would say things which had a profound truth, because they recognised the complexity of life and that you couldn't always be on the one side or the other. I remember a friend of mine telling me that he'd been in Rab's garden in Essex – beautiful garden – and he'd been working on a speech with Rab, and before he went Rab said, 'I'll cut you some flowers, take them to your wife.' And as he was doing so, my friend said to him, 'Rab, what was the most important lesson that you learnt in politics?' And Rab said, 'Oh, that's easy,' he said. 'It's more important to be generous than efficient.' And he didn't literally mean that efficiency didn't matter, what he was really saying in his Rab-ish way, is that politics is about values and not just price, and if it's just about price it's a pretty worthless pursuit, and economics is a pretty worthless pursuit as well. But he had that terrific quality – as well as being a master of efficiency himself, because I don't think anybody in the post-war years was as good at translating policy ideas into legislation. He did it brilliantly. So, I think I've sort of found, as I've spent more time working in the Conservative Party and the Conservative Research Department, that it met my requirements that political parties shouldn't be too dogmatic, that there should be a sort of a common-sense pragmatism about them. Not to say there shouldn't be principles to which you stick, and I can recite mine, I've done it often enough. But that ultimately there is a sort of majestic pragmatism about the most successful politics, I think.

**HENNESSY**

I think you carried a picture of Rab around with you from one job to the next, didn't you?

**PATTEN**

I did. I even had a picture of him in Hong Kong. He was a real hero for me.

**HENNESSY**

The Conservative Research Department was a fascinating place. I think you said it was slightly batty. You give an impression of a kind of inspired eccentricity. Give me an example of the battiness of Old Queen Street.

**PATTEN**

It was a rather sort of doggy smell in my early years, because the establishment officer – who'd, like her successor, I think, been a Lieutenant-Colonel or Brigadier in the women's army – used to turn up to work with a large, slightly mangy hound and one of those dogs whose smell rises through a building. The building itself was a wonderful 18th-century, or two 18th-century houses, with a wheezing and grunting and grinding lift which made its way slowly from floor to floor. It couldn't have been said that people kept the most demanding, Protestant-work ethic hours.

There were some who got in at normal times, there were some who would arrive rather later in the day, and it always reminded me of those stories about the Alexandrian poet C P Cavafy, who used to hire somebody to put a jacket over the back of the chair in the early morning so that nobody would know that he wasn't getting in until 11 o'clock or whatever. And I mean, a lot of people from there went on into politics, as you know. The one thing most people had in common was they were pretty smart. But you also had this tendency of people to [say] 'on the one hand or the other', and a very nice atmosphere, I would never have dreamt of asking too many questions about people's personal lives – but they were, some of them I know, were moderately rackety, a bit louche. It could have been the stage for a very funny novel. And I'm still surprised nobody's ever written it.

**HENNESSY**

You came in, I think, to the Conservative Research Department in '66, which is Ted Heath's first general election, the one he lost rather heavily to Harold Wilson.

**PATTEN**

Yes.

**HENNESSY**

And your view of Ted Heath changed over the years, I think. You rather got put off by his curmudgeonly phase, his Easter Island-statue phase, as I think Douglas Hurd once called it. But when you think about it, Chris, your politics and Ted Heath's were pretty coterminous weren't they, when you first came in?

**PATTEN**

Yes, they were. And I think he was right about some important big things. I think he was right about Europe. I think he was right about race and racial issues. The trouble was, I think, that his ambition meant that there was a period in his life when he was prepared to embrace almost anything in order to stay in office or run the country, and I think it rather confused the Conservative Party. By the end, during the long sulk, he became horribly servile to China. So when I was Governor of Hong Kong, even though when we were negotiating the [handing] back of Hong Kong to China he'd made speeches in the House of Commons saying how important it was that Hong Kong should be given democracy, when we actually tried to introduce a few smidgeons of democracy in Hong Kong, he was a loud detractor. And he could be extraordinarily ungallant and uncivil.

### HENNESSY

How did you make the adaptation, the transition to Mrs Thatcher, for whom you wrote speeches? You had a very good observation post to see that sea-change in the Conservative Party, which she and Keith Joseph engineered.

### PATTEN

I think it was made easier for me by the fact that she was always very civil and that, unlike Ted, she would smother you with gratitude and offers of hospitality. You couldn't possibly spend much time in her company without being offered sandwiches, which she would go and cut herself, or tea or coffee or whatever. She was only really rude to people who were [laughs] supposed to be her peers and her colleagues in government. I didn't agree with her on a lot of things, and she knew that. But she also recognised, and you can see it in the careers of people like Ken Clarke as well as me, that she actually realised that the Conservative Party was a broad church not a narrow sect. She knew that one of my arguments with her was her enthusiasm for trying to find an 'ism' for Conservatives. You know, the Labour Party had 'socialism' so we needed something the same. And I was always very sceptical of that. And I was also sceptical of some of the extremes of monetarism. I didn't doubt that we had to make the private sector more vibrant in Britain and that we had to deal with some of the abuses of trade union power, but I think there was an early flirtation with the more extreme forms of monetarism, which helped to destroy part of British industry.

### HENNESSY

You go through a succession of junior posts, getting ever more eminent, really – Northern Ireland, Education. And she brings you into her Cabinet towards the end of her time as Prime Minister in '89 as Environment Secretary, with the most poisoned of poisoned chalices to be dealt with: the poll tax. It was a tremendously difficult inheritance for you, Chris. Did you think of saying 'no' to that job offer because of the poll tax?

### PATTEN

I didn't really, perhaps I –

### HENNESSY

Should you have done?

### PATTEN

I don't think so. What happened was that I'd been Britain's Development Minister for three years. I'd been in Northern Ireland, then Education and then I did that job. I was known to be rather keen on environmental issues and I'd made one or two speeches. And in the European Parliament elections in 1986, the Green Party did fantastically well and the Conservatives badly. So I was really put in the Environment Department – which was then the biggest domestic department in government, so it was quite a promotion – in order to produce an environmental White Paper. But it also involved, as soon as I got there, my discovering – which I hadn't really spent much time thinking about, because I'd been Development Minister and I'd been going around the world for years – to discover that actually the biggest issue in the department was this wretched poll tax, which had been designed by very clever people with the best intentions in the world but was probably the most unpopular single policy in British politics since the war. I mean, it was like being responsible for the Black Death.

**HENNESSY**

It was one of the contributory factors to her fall in November 1990. What did you say to her that evening when she saw Cabinet Ministers individually?

**PATTEN**

I think it was more attributed to her fall than Europe.

**HENNESSY**

Yes.

**PATTEN**

I think it was much more important and significant, because it had a really big impact on particularly floating voters in marginal constituencies, as I pointed out the first time I had a discussion with her about the poll tax. What I said to her that evening – I mean I'd voted for her in the first round – is that I didn't think she was going to win. And I thought it would be demeaning for her either to lose or only win marginally, that it would turn her into exactly the sort of thing she wouldn't want to be, which was a lame duck. So I said that I thought the dignified and sensible thing for her to do was to step down. Now, to some extent, as things have turned out, I've sometimes wondered whether that was actually the right advice, because there was a myth created that she'd been defenestrated because of Europe, that she'd been ganged up on by a lot of pro-Europeans. If you actually looked at the people who were – [who] used to vote against the government and so on – they were, as is so often the case, a lot of them were right-wingers.

But I think that it would probably have been better for the Conservative Party if the electorate had dealt with her rather than the Conservative Party. But, at the time, it didn't feel like that. At the time, it felt as though we were all of us heading for a really big and humiliating defeat, and in particular that would affect her.

### HENNESSY

You voted in the next round for Douglas Hurd rather than Michael Heseltine or John Major. Why was that?

### PATTEN

Margaret Thatcher drove the bus at a hell of a pace, round bends, up and down hills. Nobody had done anything like that, quite, before. And it seemed to me that what we needed was a rather sort of calmer period with somebody who would take things – going back to something I was talking about earlier – a bit more seriously, a bit more calmly; who would know when the time – to mix my metaphors – when the time had come to sit under the tree rather than to rush around. Douglas was one of the two best people I've ever worked for. Peter Carrington and Douglas Hurd were wonderful. And I thought he would be the right person to do it. I thought that Michael Heseltine would make a huge impact, but that slightly worried me because, after all, she'd made a great impact and I thought it was time for a bit of calm. But he might have been able to carry it off. And as we know, John Major was able to carry it off and he was a very good Prime Minister.

### HENNESSY

One of the intriguing partnerships of post-war British politics is yourself and John Major. You became very close and you've always been very loyal to him. And the bad times began pretty quickly after the unexpected victory of the '92 election, the bad times crowded in with Black Wednesday, and then all the fights over Europe. And he came to depend on you to quite a high degree, I think. I think it's quite well known that he did. What was the key to the relationship?

I think John knew that I was always going to be completely loyal to him, that I wasn't ever going to connive at undermining him or trying to follow him. I think he recognised that I thought he was the cleverest member of my generation. I'm absolutely convinced that he's the most decent person I've worked with in politics. Of course he had a downside – we all do. He was incredibly thin-skinned, and I used to try to persuade him not to worry about what the young fogies, not-so-smart young fogies, on the *Daily Telegraph* were writing about him. I used to try to persuade him not to look at the first editions of the newspapers every night before he went to sleep because it would stop him sleeping. But I suspect that he needed a bit more of the carapace which managed to ensure that Margaret Thatcher endured and succeeded in what is primarily a man's world. I think he needed a bit of a harder and tougher skin in order to enjoy being Prime Minister, because I don't think he ever enjoyed it very much. He was right about all the big issues, as I think time is showing now, and very, very nice to be with. I used to feel sometimes a bit guilty that I'd lost my seat and gone off to Hong Kong. He'd wanted, as had others, he'd wanted me to fight a by-election, but I remembered what had happened in 1964, '65, when somebody slated for the Foreign Office had –

**HENNESSY**

Patrick Gordon Walker –

**PATTEN**

Patrick Gordon Walker, indeed. Others wanted me to stay on in the House of Lords and be a senior minister there. I thought all that was pretty unseemly, and I thought that I should just quit. But he would have liked me to have been around, and I still wanted to –

**HENNESSY**

He wanted you to be his Chancellor, didn't he?

**PATTEN**

Yes, he did. And that might have been a success, but I might have been swept away by the ERM debacle.

**HENNESSY**

Black Wednesday. Now, Hong Kong's fascinating. You were obviously going to be the last Governor. And you executed quite a big change in policy over it. I remember the great Foreign Office sinologist, Sir Percy Cradock, a very imposing man who negotiated the final deal, and set about you in public in a way which is most unusual. Now, what was it that annoyed Percy Cradock?

**PATTEN**

Well, I think it was both a matter of policy and, to be frank, a matter of vanity. The truth is that all I was attempting to do was to put some flesh on what had been in the joint declaration – the treaty between Britain and China – which was supposed to guarantee Hong Kong's way of life for 50 years after 1997. The fact that I was attacked so vigorously by some Chinese propagandists made me out to be much more of a democratic hero than I deserved.

**HENNESSY**

You were trying to extend the franchise a bit.

**PATTEN**

Only a little bit – I mean, I wasn't trying to increase the number of directly elected legislators. Perhaps I should have done. I was trying to make sure that those who were elected by what are called 'functional constituencies', rather as in the 18th century in England, that their numbers should be as substantial as possible and that, wherever there was an opportunity of tweaking things in a democratic direction, we should take it. But I was also very keen that we should protect Hong Kong's way of life, human rights there, by getting rid of any colonial-era legislation which was left which the Chinese could abuse, by ensuring that there were at least two foreign judges on the court of final appeal in Hong Kong. And each of those efforts, and others, was as part of an attempt also to make the last colonial Governor seem to be more prepared to reflect personal views in Hong Kong about social problems as well as political problems.

**HENNESSY**

The day you left Hong Kong, with the Prince of Wales, on the royal yacht *Britannia*, you wept quite copiously, Chris. What were you crying for? Obviously you'd had an extraordinary time there. Were you weeping – was it a kind of elegy for the lost empire, the best bits of the British Empire?

**PATTEN**

It was partly because 'Nimrod' always makes me cry.

**HENNESSY**

Elgar.

**PATTEN**

Yes, exactly. No, it was partly that it was a hugely emotional moment because I realised it wasn't just sad for me, sad for my family. I wasn't just worried about leaving behind so many friends, but I was really concerned about whether we'd done all that we could for Hong Kong to keep alive the balance between economic and political freedom in one of Britain's greatest colonies. Two things: first of all, it was always going to be difficult for China and Britain, for China and Britain politically and morally. For China, it was a reminder – Hong Kong – of one of the dark periods in Chinese history, the unequal treaties and imperialism; but also difficult for them because they knew that more than half the population of Hong Kong were refugees from Communism in China. Difficult for Britain because of both the history, the way in which we'd acquired Hong Kong. And because we were never going to be able to do what we'd done in every other colony, which was prepare it for independence, because that was never the deal. And any time we'd tried in the past to make faster progress democratically, the Chinese had said to us, 'Don't do that, because people will start to think that they're going to be like Singapore or Malaysia and they're going to become independent, and they're not' – which was true. So the most difficult question I had to answer ever, and it made quite an impact on me, was phrased perhaps most directly by a guy in a mental hospital when I was visiting quite late in my governorship, maybe only two or three months before I left, who said to me – very politely in English, a Chinese guy in a three-piece suit, I remember – and he said to me: 'Tell me, Governor, you'd agree, would you, that Britain is the oldest democracy, parliamentary democracy in the world?' And I said, 'Well, yes, I mean we'd certainly make that claim.' And he said, 'You'd agree with me that China is the last great Communist tyranny in the world?' And I said, 'Well, some people would say that.' So he said, 'Well, can you explain to me how it is that parliamentary democracy in Britain is handing Hong Kong back to China, without ever asking people in Hong Kong what they want?' It was a savage question which went right to the heart of things. It was the sort of question which Emily Lau, whom I always much admired, used to ask as well to visiting British Foreign Secretaries. So there was that moral issue all the time. But I think we did a pretty good job in managing it, and I don't think it was inevitable that when we left people would cheer. Indeed, I remember a lunch with Max Hastings before I went when he said he thought it was 50:50 whether I'd leave on the *Britannia* or leave in a helicopter from the roof of Government House. So, we left in good shape and the Chinese subsequently treated me with considerable respect, even warmth.

### HENNESSY

You moved from one great geopolitical post to another: you become European Commissioner for External Affairs in 1999. I think you had all sorts of difficulties in that job because you're not quite a Foreign Secretary for the EU but you're expected to be – the Iraq War, you had all sorts of difficult things on your watch. Looking back on that time, what is at the root of the problem of Britain and Europe?

### PATTEN

It's always been there. I mean, Jean Monnet thought the problem was we'd won the war.

### HENNESSY

He said we didn't have to exorcise our history, didn't he?

### PATTEN

Yes. I think that we've always had a problem in adjusting to being a very successful middle-sized power with a terrific history, but without an empire and without always having inevitably a seat at the top table. And one shouldn't forget that, when we joined the European Union, people were describing us as 'the sick man of Europe.' And the crazy thing is, we're leaving it when we're actually in a rather better position – or have been until we leave, I think. So we always had that feeling of great superiority. We didn't think it would work. We were surprised when it *did* work. And we were amazed when our greatest success, which was the single market, resulted in a lot of decisions being taken at the European level (thanks to Margaret Thatcher) which we would have liked to have taken presumably in the House of Commons – like, I don't know, motor bike noise or the colour of lawnmowers or any of these other issues which are – which apparently are part of 'taking back control'. So there was a slightly romantic view of what parliamentary democracy really meant. There was a sort of mindless criticism of Brussels and anything foreign. And I think that quite a lot of our history played into that, and it was made worse by the fact that most of the newspapers which had previously supported our membership of the European Union went over to the other side, and by the fact that British politicians never, ever stood up for the European Union. Tony Blair, to his credit, made one or two speeches, very good speeches, about the importance of the European Union. He tended to make them in other countries rather than in Britain. And when the craziest things were being said about Brussels, not least by a notable former *Daily Telegraph* correspondent in Brussels, Boris Johnson, when those things were being said, people didn't immediately bang them on the head and point out what was really happening in Europe. So I think it was part of the creeping lack of seriousness in British politics which contributed quite a bit. But [it's] certainly true that it became rather a toxic issue and was blamed for everything that went wrong.

## HENNESSY

We've talked about the high points in your career, Chris. Can I touch briefly on one of the low points, which was, as Chairman of the BBC, when the Jimmy Savile business unfolded? The sheer accumulation of dreadful events, which should have been discovered by a whole range of people, was on your watch. Is that one of the great low points of your public life?

## PATTEN

Yes it is. I think it's fair to say that the job was impossible and I should have turned it down, as several friends suggested to me. Because you fetched up having responsibility for things that you couldn't control. I mean, I wasn't Chairman of the BBC, I was Chairman of the BBC *regulator*. And the BBC largely ran itself with the Director-General taking most of the big decisions, and we were left carrying the can. And partly, I think, because I was well known and because I was a passionate believer in public service broadcasting, and still am, I found myself in the firing line quite a lot. Now, I don't mean to be rude about anybody. [*Laughs*] Why not? But I haven't – it's a long time since I heard any member of the BBC board, or even the Chairman being interviewed on the radio or television, whether it's about pensioners and free TV licences, or whatever. The can tends to be carried by Tony Hall, who I think is very good.

**HENNESSY**

The Director-General.

**PATTEN**

But it's – it wasn't like that, I have to say, when the Jimmy Savile case broke. And the Savile case – what took place on my watch was a *Newsnight* programme on Savile which was thought to have been dropped. It wasn't Savile's actual *behaviour* during my time, it was what the BBC was prepared to *say* about his behaviour. And the Director-General at the time denied knowing anything about this. He left the BBC not very long afterwards and has done very well as the *New York Times* Chief Executive. The guy who took over from him, whom I thought was an extremely nice and decent man and a good broadcaster, was overwhelmed by it. And we went back to appointing Tony Hall, who should have probably got the job much earlier, when Mark Thompson got it. So it wasn't a very happy period and my health took a hit. And I fetched up being able to resign as BBC Trust Chairman from the cardiology department in the Royal Brompton Hospital.

**HENNESSY**

Looking back on the great long sweep of your career, Chris, do you think that political historians will regard you as one of the 'nearly' men, one of the 'nearly Prime Ministers', along with Rab Butler, Michael Heseltine, Denis Healey, Roy Jenkins? It's a very distinguished group of people, the 'nearly' men.

### PATTEN

I'm not sure I'm that distinguished! But I suspect so, I suspect so. And I think very often people say nice things about you like that, 'you'd have been a wonderful Prime Minister' or whatever, because you never got the opportunity. So they never actually saw what a terrible job you'd have made, or you were making, of it. I think it is true that I'll be remembered for, to some extent, for what I didn't do as for what I did. But I'm very proud of some of the things I did in Hong Kong, not just on the issue of Hong Kong's freedoms but other matters as well. In some respects, the thing I'm most proud of is the reorganisation of the police service in Northern Ireland, which was the most difficult job I've ever had and I'm delighted it's worked as well as it has. It stopped policemen being killed.

### HENNESSY

Would you have liked to have been Prime Minister?

### PATTEN

Yes, but I never thought, interestingly, that I would be – partly because I've always been on the left of the Conservative Party and I think it's difficult. Even though I don't actually think there's much difference between my views and John Major's, he wasn't perceived as much as I have been as being on the left of the party. So I've always thought it would be difficult in the long run of things. What I'm – if I'm honest with you, and why not? – I think I'll always regret the fact that I didn't have one of the great offices of state – that I wasn't Chancellor or Foreign Secretary or Home Secretary. And I had some big jobs in government, but I'd loved to have been the Foreign Secretary, but that was not to be. I remember, shortly before he died, having lunch with Peter Carrington, who was the best part of my education, both in politics and as a man, and he kept on saying, asking me – I mean, he had all his marbles – but he kept on saying to me, 'Are you happy?' And I'm not sure I ever gave him the right answer. Part of what he was saying was, would I have liked to have been Prime Minister? And the only answer I eventually gave him was I'd liked to have had the job he did. But he did it brilliantly, and he was then brought down by circumstances rather unfairly.

### HENNESSY

The Falklands War.

### PATTEN

The Falklands War, for which he certainly wasn't responsible. But a man of huge honour and decency, and I think I learned more from him than anybody else.

### HENNESSY

If I could wave a magic wand for you and make you Prime Minister retrospectively, what's the great reform you would want to have introduced as Prime Minister?

### PATTEN

I think that I would want to do all I could to restore Cabinet government. I think I would want to have Cabinet ministers who understood that they were responsible for what happened in their departments and they weren't going to be constantly chased by Number 10. I think I would greatly reduce the number of staff in Number 10 and beef up the sense that the Cabinet is responsible for the governance of this country. The biggest reform I would make straight away is to introduce the Andrew Dilnot proposals on care of the elderly, which I think has been a shocking failure of nerve on the part of politicians. And I'd also – which may surprise you – I've sort of got an obsession with education and research, perfectly understandably given my relationship with Oxford for the last 16 years. But my great reform wouldn't affect higher education. What I would really do is something about further education. When I was briefly a Schools Minister, I used to think that

FE colleges were one of the jewels in the crown, which was being underfunded spectacularly year after year. And the one bit of the Augar Report I agree with, I guess it's –

**HENNESSY**

That's on student fees, yes.

**PATTEN**

It's on student fees. I guess it's the bit which was written by Alison Wolf, who's a very good education economist, [and it's] the suggestion that we should spend much more on FE. If you're interested in productivity in British industry and the British economy, one very good way to start is by doing something about FE and vocationalism, which we've always been rubbish about in the British education system.

**HENNESSY**

Chris Patten, thank you very much indeed.

**PATTEN**

Thank you.

# Alan Johnson

Series 7, Episode 2, first broadcast 5 August 2019

**Born** 17 May 1950; **Educated** Sloane Grammar School

MP (Labour) Hull West and Hessle 1997–2017

Parliamentary Under-Secretary, Department of Trade and
Industry, 1999–2001; Minister of State, Employment Relations,
Industry and the Regions, 2001–03; Minister of State, Education
and Skills, 2003–04; Secretary of State for Work and Pensions,
2004–05; Secretary of State for Trade and Industry, 2005–06;
Secretary of State for Education and Skills, 2006–07; Secretary
of State for Health, 2007–09; Home Secretary, 2009–10

**Autobiographies** *This Boy: A Memoir of a Childhood*, 2013;
*Please, Mister Postman: A Memoir*, 2014; *The Long and Winding
Road: A Memoir*, 2016; *In My Life: A Music Memoir*, 2018

#### HENNESSY

With me today is Alan Johnson, whose extraordinary life, lived
within the Labour movement, took him from the Post Office to
the Home Office, from delivering mail in southwest London to
the Home Secretary's desk in SW1. Perhaps the last of a line of
trade union General Secretaries to be recruited – in his case by
Tony Blair – to the life of high politics. But for all the width of

his political experience, which embraced the Department of Work and Pensions, the Department of Health and the Department of Education as well as the Home Office, he's perhaps best known for his acclaimed autobiography, especially the first volume dealing with his childhood and the story of how his gem of a sister saved him from an orphanage after the early death of their mother. Alan, welcome.

**JOHNSON**

Thank you, Peter.

**HENNESSY**

Tell me about the family into which you were born. Where was it and what kind of family was it?

**JOHNSON**

So, it was North Kensington. And when the childhood memoir you just mentioned was first published in 2013, I had to go to some lengths to rescue North Kensington from this generic term 'Notting Hill', which has covered this whole swathe of west London, and I had to explain, look, North Kensington was very different and very poor and always has [been] – was then and is now. Sadly, Grenfell Tower came along and now everybody knows where North Kensington is because that's where Grenfell Tower is. So always a very poor area of London, the area where Rachman eventually came and, you know, gangster landlords –

**HENNESSY**

The property speculator –

**JOHNSON**

Absolutely –

**HENNESSY**

The racketeering landlord –

**JOHNSON**

Yes. The so-called Notting Hill race riots were really the North Kensington race riots. And the house that we lived in, in Southam Street, I was born into, two houses there were, immortalised by the great photojournalist Roger Mayne, who came and took photographs there in 1955 when he left Cambridge. And these photographs of Southam Street, I found out years later, were very famous – V&A exhibitions and big coffee table books. And he captured the squalor of these awful conditions, condemned as unfit for human habitation in the 1930s. We were living in them in the 1950s, and Dickens would have recognised all of that. And my father was a pub pianist around North Kensington. There were plenty of pubs; one on every corner. A piano stool in the corner of every pub, on which my father's posterior usually rested, with the piano. But he was a womaniser, he was a gambler, he was a drinker, he used to come home drunk and beat my mother up. And so when he went off with the barmaid from the Lads of the Village pub in 1958, it was a cloud lifted from our lives. But for my poor mother, who'd had this terrible life – she was one of eleven children in Liverpool who – because her mother had died, had eleven children by the age of 38 then died at 42, and because *her* mother, my mother's grandmother, had died at 42 – my mother was always convinced there was some curse on the female line, that *she* would die at 42. And she had a heart disease called mitral stenosis, so shouldn't have been living in those terrible slums. The damp was awful. She shouldn't have been doing six or seven jobs charring and cleaning down the kind of posh end of South Kensington, that was bad enough for her health. But having this feckless husband as well who, when he went, left her with a whole new set of problems, because women in the mid-50s – it was post-emancipation but it was pre-'equal opportunities.' So she had a very hard life – and she and my sister protected *me* from having a hard life. You know, when people say, 'you had a hard life,' no I didn't. I was protected by these two incredible women.

**HENNESSY**

You said of your dad that 'Steve was a dark shadow in our lives.' Reading your memoirs, Alan, is that shadow still with you? The way you talk about him now. It's bound to affect you right through your life, really – or is that a bit of an exaggeration?

**JOHNSON**

I think it's an exaggeration. I don't think it has. I met him once more, and I suppose then – which was a big mistake. That was –

**HENNESSY**

That was at a family wedding.

**JOHNSON**

That was at a family wedding. Here was a man who was supposed to be my father, who I didn't know, I don't remember ever having a father. And that was fine by me, you know. My mother and my sister bringing me up was wonderful. And so it was the embarrassment of being forced to meet this man who I didn't know, who I was supposed to call 'father.' The words couldn't pass my lips.

**HENNESSY**

You mentioned already the Notting Hill riots, as they were called, in '58. The first so-called race riots in the United Kingdom, right in your area. How much did you witness of all that? What was it like?

**JOHNSON**

I remember seeing some of the debris as we walked to school, but not much about that. It was a year later, when Kelso Cochrane, a young West Indian carpenter, was murdered on the corner of our street, on the corner of Southam Street. And suddenly there were television crews – such as they were in those days – BBC and ITV. Southam Street was in the news, and of course it reverberated all around the community, and my mother had witnessed the start of the altercation as she came home from serving at table for one of the women she cleaned for. And so my mother came back at midnight, saw the lads, these teddy boys surrounding this black guy, shouted, 'Leave him alone!' One of them looked up. She recognised him, thought he recognised her, dashed back to the house, and then found out next morning Kelso Cochrane had been murdered. My mum never went to the police with that information. Nobody had a phone. And you, kind of, wouldn't do that, and she was very frightened as to what would happen. We were on our own then, the three of us. And that murder is still unsolved. And indeed it brought Oswald Mosley out of retirement in France – the fascist leader. He came and stood in North Kensington, in the general election of '59, and said he wasn't exploiting Kelso Cochrane's death – but what else was he doing? He stood on the spot where Kelso Cochrane was murdered to have his street meetings. The '50s wasn't a period of peaceful innocence for me. I don't know where these people get this idea that it was, you know, a wonderful, beautiful cohesive society and where everybody – where crime was non-existent. I don't know where they were in the '50s, but I know where I was. And it wasn't anything like that.

### HENNESSY

You went to the local primary school. Did you have teachers who inspired you? Because you – on Sundays you'd go to the museums. You'd walk down to the Victoria and Albert, or the Science Museum, or the Natural History –

### JOHNSON

Well, my mother cleaned around Church Street in South Kensington. So, during the summer holidays, we used to go to Kensington

Gardens and, if it was raining, we would go to Exhibition Road and into the museums. So that was fun. But at school, a great head teacher at Bevington called Mr Gemmill, so, you know, 'i before e, except after c', the line of the planets. He was very interested in the planets, and all of that [was] drummed into us from a very early age. And he was unforgettable. And then, at my grammar school, just before I left, in the fourth year – I left when I was 15 – but [in the last year] came a great English teacher called Peter Carlen, and he had the whole class reading *Animal Farm* by George Orwell, passing the book between us to read a couple of pages each. And he took us to the theatre, and he saw that I was a voracious reader and got me reading Geoffrey Household and C S Forester, and Arnold Bennett and Dickens.

**HENNESSY**

I think your three great passions in life were, they were music – rock music in particular – reading and football. Queen's Park Rangers.

**JOHNSON**

Yes, spot on.

**HENNESSY**

And there's one very special moment, 1967, March, when QPR win the League Cup and you in your band play in Shepherd's Bush to a jolly but inebriated audience. And the way you've described that in the past makes it almost seem as [if] it's the high moment in your life, despite everything else you've done since.

**JOHNSON**

Well, it was! What else has happened? – Rangers were at Wembley. I was interested in football *per se*, but of course QPR, my local team, who I supported and went to watch. I mean, it was a very memorable moment. And the fact that I was playing in a pop band at the time – The Area, which was, you know, a good mod band around west London, and was playing at a do in Shepherd's Bush, I think it was a wedding, and everybody was just euphoric about Rangers' victory.

#### HENNESSY

The listeners can't see it, but you're glowing in front of me as you recall it. [*Johnson laughs*] But I'm jumping ahead too much, because I must ask you about the tragedy of your mum dying very young in 1964, and Linda, who I think is a couple of years older than you –

#### JOHNSON

Yes –

#### HENNESSY

– your sister, who was at grammar school persuading a local welfare officer that you shouldn't both of you go into an orphanage, that she could look after you if the council could find you a flat. And Mr Pepper, I think, was your saviour. He did it.

#### JOHNSON

Mr Pepper, yes, but –

#### HENNESSY

Linda caught everybody's imagination when that book came out.

#### JOHNSON

Oh, she was the heroine. I mean, Lynn Barber when she reviewed it for the *Sunday Times* said, 'Never mind all this nonsense about "Alan Johnson should have been Prime Minister" – *Linda* Johnson should have been Prime Minister, I think.' I agree, I agree with her 100 per cent. And by the time my mother died – aged 42, as she always thought she would, with this, you know, groundbreaking heart operation. And Linda had actually left school at 15 to train to be a nursery nurse and Mr Pepper had – it wasn't an orphanage, he was going to put me into foster care – he'd found the foster parents in Chelsea; and Linda, he said, you can go to Dr Barnardo's at Barkingside – so she was going to an orphanage – and you can continue your training at Dr Barnardo's big headquarters there. And Linda just tore into him and said you're not going to split us up. You know, I can see her now, hand on hip, finger wagging in poor Mr Pepper's face. So he went away with this giant Linda-shaped flea in his ear. He came back and said I've got a deal, I've got you this flat. So not only did Linda get Mr Pepper to negotiate to get us a council house, when she went to look at it, it was in such a state. Linda said, 'You go and look at it, if you think you can live there with your family, come and look me in the eye and tell me, and I'll think about it again.' And we never heard of that place again. We got a lovely, two-bedroom maisonette in Number 11 Pitt House on the Wilberforce Estate in Battersea, which meant we had to go south of the Thames, which was traumatic for us, but we got over that. And we always say that *one* decision by someone in authority, who *listened* to us, really was the most important decision on what direction our lives would go in.

#### HENNESSY

Why didn't you flourish at grammar school? Because you'd got bags of intellectual curiosity, you're bookish, you like museums, you've got heaps of energy. I would have thought a grammar school was tailor-made for you.

#### JOHNSON

Well I wasn't there a lot of the time. I used to make excuses. There were bits of it I liked, Mr Carlen I liked. I liked economics, funnily enough, and a teacher called Mr Pallai, a Hungarian guy, who'd escaped the Hungarian revolution. I learned a lot about politics from Mr Pallai and Mr Carlen, and a lot about totalitarianism because Mr Pallai was a socialist – he'd escaped Hungary as the tanks came in.

**HENNESSY**

In '56? –

**JOHNSON**

– Budapest in '56. And he had a story to tell which was very influential for someone like me who was starting to think about politics. Because of Mr Carlen, I was reading Orwell. I was mad about Orwell. I read everything, you know, from *Keep the Aspidistra Flying* to *Road to Wigan Pier* and so he was an important influence on me.

**HENNESSY**

Tell me about your early experience of work, because you got radicalised by Tesco's I think.

**JOHNSON**

Yes that's true.

**HENNESSY**

Which not many people can say, really.

**JOHNSON**

That's true. Well apart from helping on the milk float and the 'paraffin' round two nights a week which I'd started when I was about 12, when I left school at 15 I worked for Remington electric shavers for a little while, all the time wanted to be a rock star, was in bands all the time. But I had to have a day job. A friend of mine worked at Tesco's, said come and work with me there. The money was better. And, in the end, there was an altercation with the big regional manager [who] came round at Christmas and the warehouse was in a mess, and the manager shouted at me to cancel my lunch and come and sweep the warehouse. And I told him where to go and he said, 'Well if you go to lunch don't come back.' And I gave him a two-fingered salute. But those were the days. You fell out of one job and into another.

**HENNESSY**

And then the Post Office comes in, which was the making of you.

**JOHNSON**

Well that was when – this crime wave followed my bands around. So, one band was broken up because we had our gear nicked. But then this In-Betweens, who asked me to join them – proper band, manager, little fan club, bit of money behind them. And the bass guitarist, West Indian guy called Sham, worked for Royal Mail as a postman, higher grade. And when we got all our gear nicked, Sham wanted me to start another band, and I was just about to get married at 18, and I said, 'I need to go and earn some money.' And he said, 'Why don't you join the Post Office, become a postman? They can't recruit for love nor money, which means there's loads of overtime.' So I joined the Post Office, thinking it would be a temporary sojourn from my music career.

**HENNESSY**

And it made you. It made you.

**JOHNSON**

Yes, I loved it as well. I mean I didn't join the Post – I joined the *General* Post Office, I'd joined the GPO.

**HENNESSY**

Big civil service department –

**JOHNSON**

Uniformed civil servants –

**HENNESSY**

Yes.

**JOHNSON**

And I signed the Official Secrets Act. You know, and it felt like you were a proper public servant. And then when I went – started at Barnes in London, southwest 13, with 30 blokes, all blokes, 28 of them had fought in the war. There I was working amongst these guys that were in their early 40s, who'd served at Monte Cassino, who'd been at Dunkirk, and the union rep was a guy called Billy Fairs. And Billy Fairs was so decent and so respected – unlike the manager, by the way, who when something went wrong in the sorting office, the manager would go and shut himself in his office. And Billy Fairs, from the union, would sort it out. And I had such respect for Billy Fairs that, in a sense, that got me interested in representing, you know, your work mates. And six years later, after I'd transferred out to Slough, where me and my first wife got a council house on this big council estate, I became a union rep for the first time.

**HENNESSY**

There's one memory I think you have of those really rather warm days in Barnes which you plainly enjoyed, and that was Ted Philpott, I think, who didn't come out on strike in a one-day solidarity strike with another part of the union and was sent to Coventry. Nobody spoke to him, nobody played billiards with him, and I think the dark side of trade unionism – that's always stayed with you hasn't it, that incident?

**JOHNSON**

Always stayed with me, I've never forgotten that. Because if you're in an office, just 30 of you, and in those days you used to go out and do your first delivery and then come back, go up into the canteen where there was a little snooker table, half-sized snooker table, you were all, you know, there was [an] air of camaraderie which, once again, was very attractive to the ex-servicemen. And Ted Philpott, another ex-serviceman, who smoked a kind of Sherlock Holmes-type pipe, was the best snooker player in the office, and he would be at the snooker table all the time taking on different people. And we had a one-day strike – in support of overseas telegraphists, by the way, that were a very small part of our union. But that's what the union was about: you all supported the minorities. They had a pay dispute; we came out for one day. My first experience of any trade union action, and Ted Philpott was the only person not to come out. And the way everyone ignored him – actually it would have been less cruel if people had shouted at him and argued with him and remonstrated with him. They just didn't talk to him at all. He'd stand up with his snooker cue and everyone else would just put their snooker cues down. They wouldn't play him. They wouldn't sit with him. And I left – that was in February of '69. But I made contact with Billy Fairs when the memoir that this was in, *Please Mr Postman*, was published. But I asked Billy, 'How long did that go on for with Ted Philpott?' He said, 'At least another four years.' Four years of being 'sent to Coventry', as they called it, was not a glorious part of trade union history. But I don't think anyone was coordinating it, certainly not Billy Fairs. So, you know, I say it was an awful part of trade unionism, but I guess there'll be, even without an organised trade union that kind of thing would happen. It was a terrible, terrible lesson that I never forgot.

#### HENNESSY

Yes. There was a clandestine element to your existence, then wasn't there? You read *The Times*, but not when the blokes were watching.

#### JOHNSON

[*Laughing*] No.

**HENNESSY**

What was all that about?

**JOHNSON**

There was one other guy called Vic Osborne who read the *Guardian*. And he was – he flourished the *Guardian* – but Vic was about 54, 55. I felt so uncomfortable, as a youngster, reading that newspaper when everybody else read, most of the other people read what we'd now call tabloids, they read the *Mirror*, the *Sun* –

**HENNESSY**

*Sketch* –

**JOHNSON**

– was around by then. There's this thing in working class culture, and maybe in other classes as well, I wouldn't know, where if you're seen to be too big for your boots and if you're seen to be getting above yourself, I mean I don't know whether it's a good thing or a bad thing. It's obviously a good thing in the sense [of] the modesty, the kind of inbuilt modesty. The bad bit is, of course, sometimes it holds you back. You don't realise what you can achieve. It was only because Tom Jackson – you know, with the handlebar moustache, that great trade union leader we had in the Union of Post Office Workers as it was – came to my delegation. He claimed he was talent spotting. I'd actually made a disastrous contribution from the rostrum, but he came over to where my delegation sat, and he said, 'Alan, don't worry about that, you know, you'll be fine, everyone has a few setbacks if you're speaking in front of 2,000 people. You know, doesn't always go right.' And he said, *sotto voce*, with my union secretary listening, 'Why don't you go forward for the Executive Council?' And once he said it, it became Joe Paine's idea and the branch's idea. But I could never have done that myself.

**HENNESSY**

Very interesting.

**JOHNSON**

I'd have felt inhibited, yeah.

**HENNESSY**

Very interesting. Before we come to Tom Jackson and the great strike of 1971, postal strike, you liked living in Slough, didn't you? The police – when you were asking [for] directions for the Britwell Estate when you and your wife, Judith, got off the train – sort of warned you about what a terrible place it was. But you loved it, the Britwell, didn't you?

**JOHNSON**

I loved it. No, I said, 'Excuse me, do you know the way to the Britwell Estate?' And this copper said, leaning up against his blue and white striped Ford Anglia police car, 'Should do, we have to go there often enough.' That was the first, actually, sign of council estates getting some reputation. I grew up *longing* for a council house. My mother *longed* for the council house that never arrived, to get her out of the slums. That was the only route out. So it was my first indication that actually council estate people were being looked down upon. Now I think in Slough, it was because that guy was a local, and whole swathes of west London had moved out to the big council estates, the Britwell Estate and the Trelawney Estate. But, you know, there we were with two kids in a beautiful house, front garden, back garden, well made. And, you know, there I was, with a job for life – provided you could get up at four in the morning – with the Post Office. I had a house, council house, and I had a strong union to represent my interests. Now all three of those things have eroded to some extent or other. And it's a cause of great unhappiness, I think, amongst people.

**HENNESSY**

I think your Britwell years were your Marxist years as well. Where did all that come from?

**JOHNSON**

Well no, I wasn't a Marxist – it was reading Orwell that stopped me going the full tilt to that, dictatorship of the proletariat, but I was interested in Marx. Unlike Harold Wilson, I'd got past the first page of *Das Kapital*, I read *Das Kapital*. I loved the kind of –

**HENNESSY**

What all of it, all of it?

**JOHNSON**

I read the first volume.

**HENNESSY**

Ah.

**JOHNSON**

– Surplus Value, so –

**HENNESSY**

The one with the jokes?

**JOHNSON**

[*Laughing*] Yes, yes. His analysis, and the idea of a workers' state attracted me. What always pulled me back from it was Orwell and democratic socialism. I mean, as Shostakovich said when he was told that Pablo Picasso [was] a Communist: it's easy to be a Communist when you don't live under Communism. And so I was, I was with Orwell, and in fact Orwell's great gift to so many generations of people on the left, including me, was to make the argument that you can be on the left without going down that route towards totalitarianism. So I never became a Marxist. I had a lad who sold *News Line*, which was the paper of the Workers' Revolutionary Party; he was a teacher from Kingston-upon-Thames who travelled round the Britwell Estate on a Saturday bringing our copies of *News Line*, and he would chat on the doorstep to – I mean it was actually saying, you know, we should bring arms to the working classes. And I would say to him, 'Have you seen that sign down the road there, that big white sign, "Keep Britwell white"? You know, there are people on this estate who, if you gave them guns, I know who'd they be going out and shooting, and it wouldn't be the upper classes.' So actually, the more I dealt with Richard, selling me *News Line*, the more I became a supporter of the Labour Party.

### HENNESSY

You've got a wonderful line about the 1971 strike, when public school Marxists came to your aid in the trade unions, and you said, 'They dress scruffy and talk posh, we dress posh and talk scruffy.' And I thought that was a wonderful juxtaposition. [*Johnson laughs*]

### JOHNSON

Well, we were going down from Slough on a coach to London to support our union – we had rallies. This was a seven-week, all-out strike. No strike pay. And swarming around us were International Marxists and the International Socialists and, you know, the Red Mole group and Tariq Ali's mob all coming up to us with scruffy clothes. I mean, we dressed smart because we were on union business, you know. We were mods, most of my mates. And we couldn't understand why these guys who had all this money were wearing such shabby stuff with badges stuck all over it. And of course, they wanted us to be cannon fodder in the class war. That was another great lesson for me, that seven-week strike, when I was 20 years of age. It was part of my education.

**HENNESSY**

Now how come Tommy Jackson picked you out? Tom Jackson was a great figure, national figure, much loved really –

**JOHNSON**

Yeah, much loved by me. I mean he led that strike, the first strike we'd had in the Post Office in the union's existence – and most working days lost since the general strike in 1926. You know, quarter of a million people worked for the Post Office then. But you know what, when it became obvious that we weren't going to win it, he led us back. On a kind of trumped-up committee of inquiry thing, that everyone realised wasn't going to do much for us, but he had the guts to stand up and say, 'We've got to go back.' Now, if you compare that to what happened with the miners – where, in the end, they were starved back after a year – to me, that was leadership. As soon as I say to people when I'm doing these book festivals, you know, 'with the handlebar moustache', they remember Tom. He was better known than most Cabinet ministers. How did he pick on me? I don't know. I'd made a couple of speeches at conference, because I liked this – a bit of, I suppose, you know, the roar of greasepaint and the smell of the crowd – whichever way round it is – having, you know, failed to be a rock star. Making speeches in front of 2,000 people, who were telephonists and postal workers and clerks just like me, excited me. The trade union movement excited me; the fact that you could do any course under the sun on any subject free of charge through the TUC – not for anything other than a little certificate of merit – but having left school at 15, that was a vehicle to have another chance at education. It opened up a complete new world for me. And trade unionism is the untold story of social mobility, and Tom was very big on that – about education within the union. So I'd made these couple of speeches, he came over and said what he said, 'why don't you nominate Alan for the Executive' sort of thing. And when he said that – and he told me, 'Look, you won't get on for the first two years, but three years' time there's a number of retirements, you stand a very good chance.' Sure enough, I got on, while he was still General Secretary.

**HENNESSY**

Now if I were your biographer, Alan, I'd place a lot of emphasis on your charm. And there's a wonderful bit, a bit later on in your story, when you're working with Charles Clarke at Education, the Secretary of State for Education, and it's top-up fees for students – which had a great bite on the back benches of the Labour Party, it was hardly getting through the House of Commons – and you had a charm offensive and you said, 'I did the charm and Charles did the offensive.' Which I suspect annoyed him greatly. [*Johnson laughs*] Now –

**JOHNSON**

Charles was 'offensive', yes –

**HENNESSY**

But you are naturally charming. What are the ingredients of your charm? Have you ever analysed yourself?

**JOHNSON**

God no, not at all.

**HENNESSY**

Have a go.

**JOHNSON**

No, I mean, the only thing I would say, I don't take myself too seriously, you know? And in politics sometimes, I suppose people do, a bit 'up themselves', as we used to say. No, I can't possibly self-analyse – I've been on *Desert Island Discs*, that was bad enough, with Kirsty, I'm not going to do it with you, Peter. [*Both laugh*]

**HENNESSY**

You know how to work a crowd though, don't you?

**JOHNSON**

Well, you learn that in the trade union movement, you know, you learn all these skills – it's a great apprenticeship for coming into politics. You have to learn public speaking, you have to learn to write, because you're writing to managers all the time. You have to learn to negotiate, and negotiating is one of the great, almost ephemeral, skills that no one can teach you, you just pick it up by doing it. And charm is an important part of that, I suppose. Although, I'd like to think I'm never knowingly charming. I mean, you know, it's the kind of thing you can't put on. So no, I don't know, all I know is I've had this charmed life, if you like, if you want to use the word 'charm': Tom Jackson coming and helping me and suddenly I was there; Tony Blair asking me to come into Parliament. I didn't have to go and move my family into a constituency hoping that the incumbent was going to kick the bucket, which is what some people do. You know, to get a parliamentary nomination, you have to go knocking on doors. All I had to do was wait for the phone to ring.

**HENNESSY**

Why did Tony come looking for you?

**JOHNSON**

Well, I think there was a certain *savoir faire* about our union because we'd beaten Heseltine and Major when they tried to privatise the Post Office. We ran a – even though I say it myself – an excellent campaign. Michael Cockerell made this wonderful documentary about lobbying and made our campaign, half an hour, a central feature of an hour-long television documentary – prime time telly. And I was on the NEC of the Labour Party. And Tony was keen to have – because we were coming up to '97, so this was early '97 – he was keen to have people in Parliament that hadn't spent all their lives trying to get into Parliament. But for me, you know, I couldn't go for a seat and not get selected, because I had to get re-elected every five years in the union. If my members had seen me trying to become an MP it wouldn't have, you know – I said to Tony, 'Look, I can't, you know, I can't be left dangling in the wind.' So it was halfway through the '97 election, when my predecessor retired to spend more time with his peerage, and the local party then couldn't – we were in the general election, the posters were up –

**HENNESSY**

This is Hull – this is Hull West and Hessle.

**JOHNSON**

Hull West and Hessle.

**HENNESSY**

Yes.

**JOHNSON**

So I sort of arrived three weeks in, into Hull. It's the best move I ever made. I mean, when Tony asked me about it – he said, 'I hear, someone told me, you wanted to be an MP.' I said, 'I don't know who told you that. I don't want to be an MP.' I mean, I was General Secretary of the sixth biggest affiliated union. And so, initially I was hostile to it, but the more I thought about it and this idea that we would be back in power, the *chance* to be part of that! And I've always been interested in the constitutional issues like reform of the Lords, like proportional representation, like a Scottish Parliament. You know, Keir Hardie's original vision for the Labour Party was a national minimum wage, devolution to a Scottish Parliament and control of working hours. All of that became possible and, almost, you could reach out and touch Labour in government, the *things* we were going to do. So, in the end, I was very grateful for Tony, and to get that constituency, Hull West and Hessle, a marvellous, marvellous place. I mean I had to eulogise it when I was the MP, I don't have to now, but it's – that's where I *live*. And because they had this big issue about trawlermen. It was the biggest distant water port in the world until the settlement of the cod wars, which the British government agreed with Iceland to a 200-mile fishing limit round the coast of Iceland. 8,000 fishermen lost their – that was Hull's fishing grounds, that's where they fished, the only place they ever fished – and the men were promised – a government minister stood up in Parliament in the early '70s and said, 'You'll get redeployment, retraining and compensation.' They got *nothing* and were still fighting 20 years later. And everything they asked for, I'm very proud to say, a Blair government conceded. But it was an issue I could get my teeth into, that I wasn't unfamiliar with the issues, because it was about an industrial injustice.

**HENNESSY**

Your ministerial rise is quite rapid; it takes a bit to kick off but, once it started, it's quite swift. Were you chuffed when you became Minister for Higher Education, not having been to a university?

**JOHNSON**

I *was* chuffed, 'cause I'd spend all my time at DTI, Department for Trade and Industry. I'd spent four years there as a junior minister. And I fancied a change and actually, from the moment the Dearing Report came out – and I knew Dearing, because he was –

**HENNESSY**

– on student finance.

**JOHNSON**

– on student finance, Ron Dearing was the Chairman of the Post

Office, I'd negotiated with him as Chairman of the Post Office. And
Dearing's report – supported by both parties of course, it started
under Major and then Blair took it on – what he recommended
was initially not what we did. We introduced a thousand-pound
fee up front, because we couldn't afford the whole system. What he
recommended, from the moment I read it, I was convinced: free
higher education with generous grants wasn't progressive, it was
regressive. In 40 years since the Robbins Report, the social class
gap in higher education hadn't closed, it had widened. So all this
rubbish about working-class kids won't go if they have to make a
contribution, so Dearing said everyone should make a contribution. If we want to really expand higher education and, you know,
something like 50 per cent of 18-to-31-year-olds getting a higher
education, we have to make it affordable. And so students make
no contribution; graduates, once they've graduated, once they're
earning, should put some money back. I was *seized* by that. But,
you know, I felt that very strongly, particularly as we were going to
use half of these fees for grants for poorer kids. And we'd already
introduced the Education Maintenance Allowance, so now you
could see poor kid – bright kid from poor family – doesn't have
to leave school to go and work in Tesco's because he can say to
Mum and Dad, actually, I get this EMA, you know, about 30 quid
a week, that brings it into the family, and then when I'm 18 – and
you don't make the decision to go to university at 18, you make it
when you're, you know, much younger – I don't need your help,
there's no up-front fee, Mum and Dad, you don't have to pay anything to this. *I* take on the cost myself, after I've graduated, and
I get a very good maintenance grant to get me through without
the bank of Mum and Dad. Because that's the biggest problem for
poor kids, getting through three years of higher education. I think
it was a no brainer, to me. Of course it's been distorted since, by
some of the things George Osborne did. But the basic principle is
still the same and, of course, what do we see? Since those fees were
introduced, the number of kids on free school meals in higher

education has gone from 10 per cent, prior to fees, to 27 per cent now. So, I didn't need to be persuaded of the argument, I needed to go out on that charm offensive with Charles to persuade enough of our colleagues to get it through, and it only went through in the end – we had a 175 majority, I think it was – and it went through by four votes.

**HENNESSY**

Yes, very close. You weren't in the Cabinet until September 2004, so you weren't there when the Iraq War discussions took place at the Cabinet table.

**JOHNSON**

No.

**HENNESSY**

How did you feel about the Iraq War, Alan?

**JOHNSON**

I supported the Prime Minister, I supported what we were doing. I was Minister of State, so I wasn't in the Cabinet, but I was in Parliament, and this was the first time that Britain had ever gone to war on anything other than a royal prerogative, so it was –

**HENNESSY**

– with a proper vote, yes –

**JOHNSON**

– with a proper vote in Parliament.

**HENNESSY**

Yes.

### JOHNSON

And it was incumbent on us to know what we were talking about in that vote. And my great mentor and friend, Robin Cook, who was – had a big effect on my political life – we came together because he was Heseltine's shadow when we'd led the campaign to stop the Post Office being privatised. So I got to know him as well as anyone could know Robin, and we were both proponents of PR, proportional representation. And Robin took a different view. But he didn't take that view and say, 'Oh, and Blair's a liar,' and all this other rubbish we got. He just took a different view on what we should do at that time. To me, it wasn't even about weapons of mass destruction. We knew he had them because he'd used them against his own people. Everyone knew he had them. Countries that weren't going to war, Germany and France, knew he'd *had* weapons of mass destruction. Did he have them now? That was the question. Was he allowing full and unfettered access by the weapons inspectors? He'd been running rings round the UN for ten, twelve years. And to me, that was the big issue, as we discussed it in March 2003, the deadline having run out for Resolution 1441 at the end of 2002, and he still hadn't complied with it. How long do we let this guy and his psychopathic sons run rings around the United Nations? That was the big issue. So, you know, there's lots of people who were in that debate who voted the way they did who are now running away from it and suggesting they were misled or misinformed. No, they weren't. They weren't misled or misinformed. What we did then was make a very serious decision. Given the same circumstances and the same information, at that time, I'd have done the same thing again.

### HENNESSY

You have an extraordinary array of Cabinet posts. I think you have five Cabinet posts inside six years, once you make the Cabinet level under both Tony Blair and Gordon Brown –

**JOHNSON**

Yes.

**JOHNSON**

It's an extraordinary way we do our government, isn't it? Just when you master something – or about to master something – you're moved on. Now, does that suggest you're a safe pair of hands?

**JOHNSON**

[*Laughing*] I hope so –

**HENNESSY**

– or you're a good front man, or what is it?

**JOHNSON**

– goodness knows –

**HENNESSY**

– you're a kind of a fireman they rush into the breach –

**JOHNSON**

– or they always wanted to get rid of me! Well, it always seemed to be an upward trajectory, so that wasn't bad but, you know, I'd have liked to have spent more time at Work and Pensions, where I started. I mean, we introduced the idea of auto-enrolment. I know it doesn't set the blood racing through the veins, but auto-enrolment's very important for people to have a pension plan, an occupational pension plan. *Everyone* should have one, it came from the big review –

**HENNESSY**

– the Adair Turner Review.

**JOHNSON**

The Adair Turner Review.

**HENNESSY**

– yes –

**JOHNSON**

And I sort of pressed the button on that and I'd have liked to have seen that go further. And to have been Home Secretary for a year was a great privilege. Once you hit a position like that, I doubt if you'd be talking to me now if Gordon hadn't made me Home Secretary, because there is something about those offices of state –

**HENNESSY**

Big offices of state, yes –

**JOHNSON**

– yes, Chancellor, Foreign Secretary, Home Secretary, that do kind of round off a career nicely.

**HENNESSY**

You have a certain skill at getting on with people, which you've already talked about. You're one of the few, aren't you, right at the top of the Labour Party in that generation, your generation, who got on with Tony *and* Gordon.

**JOHNSON**

I did, because I wasn't in the TB or the GB camp.

**HENNESSY**

How did you avoid that?

**JOHNSON**

I don't know. I mean, it helped that I stood up to Gordon on one particular issue – pensions. So, Gordon didn't like the fact that the Turner Review was almost contracting out our responsibility on pensions, we should have done it ourselves. So he had a thing about that and I opposed him on that. And, with Tony, he wanted to time-limit benefits at the time, at the same time, and Gordon was against that and I was against it, so I argued with Number 10 on that. So I think, you know, as long as you do it, you're not throwing your toys out of the pram or being a prima donna, you just – when you meet the Prime Minister you argue why you believe that this is right or this is wrong. And I didn't go along with a Brownite line or a Blairite line. And I respected the two men immensely, and I still think it's a great sorrow that the two of them came to such an impasse in the end. And I observed that kind of first-hand. And, to me, you know, it was the Lennon and McCartney of Labour politics splitting apart where they could have done so much if they'd stayed together.

**HENNESSY**

When Labour lost in 2010, one got the impression from the outside that you didn't much care for opposition; you're a man of government doing things, practical things, and you retired from being Shadow Chancellor. Why was that, Alan? Because people also saw you as a future leader, after all.

**JOHNSON**

Yes, I know, but they didn't see me as a Deputy Leader, the one time I did stand. I had no ambition to lead the party.

**HENNESSY**

Why not?

**JOHNSON**

– I didn't want to be the leader.

**HENNESSY**

Why not?

**JOHNSON**

I don't know. I wanted to be the leader of my union and I achieved that, and I didn't want to be the leader of the Labour Party. I think because I realised all that it would do to me and my family for ever more. I mean Home Secretary was enough for me, and Prime Minister's a different level completely. And also, whenever people were talking about me being the leader, it was always to knife the current leader in the back. They wanted me to step over Gordon Brown's prostrate body or step over Ed Miliband's. And, you know, I just, I'm not into that kind of thing and, anyway, both men were doing a good job. Gordon grappling with leading the G20 on dealing with the financial services meltdown. So I would never have been able to do that as well as them. So, as I didn't want to do the job, I felt I wouldn't have done it well – no point taking on a job that you don't want to do. It'll show.

**HENNESSY**

If you had been Prime Minister, what's the big thing you would have done?

**JOHNSON**

I don't know about a big thing – I would have tried to ensure there was a collegiate Cabinet rather than –

**HENNESSY**

– proper Cabinet government.

**JOHNSON**

Proper Cabinet government. But if I was to focus on one thing, it would have been health inequalities. We've got the world's greatest expert in Sir Michael Marmot. Michael Marmot talks about the social determinants of health: the fact that a boy born in North Kensington, as I was, will die – today, not in 1950 when I was born, *today* – will die on average 16 years before a boy born in South Kensington, the same London borough, is an obscene statistic. And we set out in government to close that social class gap in health inequalities. And do you know, we failed, but as Michael Marmot says, the health of the poorest, by the time our 13 years finished, was at the level that the health of the most prosperous was 13 years before. What happened is that the health of the most prosperous improved as well, which is great. So there was still a gap. The social determinants of health often have very little to do with the health service. They're about public health, sure – exercise, smoking, obesity – but they're also about education and they're about housing. And if you could bring the different strands of government to focus on health inequalities and how you narrow them; the fact you get on a train on the Jubilee line at Westminster and go seven stops to Canning Town and your life expectancy reduces by one year at every stop. If you really want to do something about that, it has to be the Prime Minister leading it to coordinate the different government departments to bear down on it. And I think that's the one thing I'd have tried to do.

**HENNESSY**

So if I can give you a magic wand, that's the big reform you'd go for?

**JOHNSON**

I mean, that would take time. But if you gave me just one reform –

**HENNESSY**

Yes –

**JOHNSON**

– and I didn't have to worry about taking the Parliament with me or the country with me, I'd introduce a system of proportional representation. And I'd introduce a specific, AV-plus, as recommended in the Jenkins Report back in the late '90s.

**HENNESSY**

Roy Jenkins –

**JOHNSON**

Yeah, Roy Jenkins.

**HENNESSY**

That would remake our British politics.

**JOHNSON**

It would. But you'd still have a constituency link, but you'd have a proportional system. And, to me, the great success of a left-of-centre party in Europe, really – and, you know, it's sacrilege to say this in the Labour Party but I'm going to say it anyway – is the SNP in Scotland, under a system that is proportional and is not supposed to produce stable government. It's produced stable government, and a stable government left of centre, to the extent that, at the European elections, Labour was fifth in Scotland – *fifth*, for goodness sake.

**HENNESSY**

What trace would you like to leave on history?

**JOHNSON**

As a writer.

**HENNESSY**

Above all, a writer?

**JOHNSON**

I mean, we're all footprints in the sand in politics. In writing, my childhood memoir has now sold more than 500,000 copies –

**HENNESSY**

Yes –

**JOHNSON**

– and people are reading about my mother and those circumstances. There's no mark to my mother, there's not even a gravestone. Me and my sister, thanks to her fiancé, he bought a little rose bush in Kensal Rise cemetery, and there was a little plaque where we scattered her ashes. But we didn't realise you had to renew the subscription every five years or they ripped it up. So that went. There's no trace of my mother on this earth apart from that book. And if that leaves a trace in history, you know, if I'm thought of more as a writer than a politician, I'll be very pleased.

**HENNESSY**

You've done her proud, Alan. You really have.

**JOHNSON**

Thank you.

**HENNESSY**

Thank you very much.

**JOHNSON**

Thanks, Peter.

# Norman Lamont (Lord Lamont of Lerwick)

Series 7, Episode 3, first broadcast 12 August 2019

**Born** 8 May 1942; **Educated** Loretto School;
Fitzwilliam College, Cambridge

MP (Conservative) Kingston-upon-Thames 1972–97

Parliamentary Under-Secretary, Department of Energy,
1979–81; Minister of State, Department of Industry, 1981–83;
Minister of State, Department of Trade and Industry, 1983–85;
Minister of State, Ministry of Defence, 1985–86; Financial
Secretary to the Treasury, 1986–89; Chief Secretary to the
Treasury, 1989–90; Chancellor of the Exchequer, 1990–93

**Autobiography** *In Office*, 1999

### HENNESSY

With me today is Norman Lamont, Lord Lamont of Lerwick,
whose time as Chancellor of the Exchequer in John Major's government is remembered above all for one of the most vivid and
argued-about moments in British political and economic history
since the Second World War: when a serious sterling crisis produced Black Wednesday, 16 September 1992, which saw the pound
forced out of the European Exchange Rate Mechanism. A few years

later, in his book *Sovereign Britain*, Norman Lamont was brutally honest about what he called the 'collapse of government policy': 'There is no other way to describe it. It was certainly not planned. It was forced upon us, a humiliation for the government, for the Prime Minister and for myself.' Yet, for some, the enforced change of monetary policy laid down a golden pavement to a period of sustained recovery and economic growth. Today, Lord Lamont is one of the most eloquent advocates of our leaving the European Union. Norman, welcome.

### LAMONT

Thank you very much.

### HENNESSY

Tell me about childhood. You were born in Lerwick in the Shetland Islands. What kind of family was yours?

### LAMONT

Well, my father was *the* surgeon, the only surgeon in Shetland. He went to Shetland during the war in the Royal Army Medical Corps. He fell in love with the islands, fell in love with my mother, who was a local teacher – she taught French and German – and he decided to stay. And I lived in Shetland until I was, I think, about 11.

### HENNESSY

So you lived there from when you were born in 1942 to about 1951, '52?

### LAMONT

That's right. I went to the Lerwick Infants School and then the Lerwick Central School.

**HENNESSY**

Do you feel like a Norseman?

**LAMONT**

I certainly feel that Shetland is my home. I don't go there very often, but it is such a magical place and I still have a cousin there who I talk to. It remains in the memory as a very serene place, a very beautiful place, and I think of it as my ultimate home. I think I'd like to be buried there.

**HENNESSY**

Do you think it gives you, in a good sense, a slightly outsider's perspective on the United Kingdom? Because the northern isles are very distinctive – I mean, the Orkneys are very different from Shetland, of course, but there is something very, very distinctive about the northern isles.

**LAMONT**

I think that's right. I think it made one very conscious of Britain as an entity, not just Scotland, but *Britain* as an entity. And I always thought of myself as British, not just Scottish. I mean, I am Scottish and British, but I was very conscious of Britain as an entity and read about London as much as Edinburgh.

**HENNESSY**

Was it a wrench leaving Shetland to go to public school – Loretto, near Edinburgh – when you were, I think, ten, was it?

**LAMONT**

Well, I think for anyone aged ten to go away to school is quite a traumatic experience, but my schooldays weren't miserable in any way. And I used to travel to and from school by plane, went in these terribly old Dakotas – which, I remember, you'd go through an air pocket and you'd sort of fall a great distance and everybody on the plane would be sick and you were given brown paper bags to be sick in. That was how I went to school.

**HENNESSY**

Did you – the Norman Lamont we've come to know – emerge a bit at school, because you're quite a powerful debater, natural debater, your friends would say?

**LAMONT**

Debating was not a great thing at the school I was [at], but I did actually join the debating society and I was an active participant, and I remember taking part in a debate against the Royal High School in Edinburgh, who I remember completely massacred us. They were far more eloquent and far quicker-thinking than we were. But yes, that stirred my interest in debate. I was always very interested in history. I didn't actually do history A level, which I rather regret, but I did love history as a subject, which is, I think, where my interest in politics came from.

**HENNESSY**

Is there a moment when you realised you had quite a political charge inside yourself?

**LAMONT**

My mother was quite political. I was taken to political meetings. Political meetings in Shetland weren't that common, but I remember at the time of elections being taken. I think it was because my mother – well, maybe she couldn't get someone to look after me – but I remember coming and reading a book while someone went on and on about something. I think it was Sir David Maxwell Fyfe.

**HENNESSY**

Tell me about Cambridge. I think you get there in 1960, to Fitz-william College, and you rise through in a kind of gilded route, really: Chairman or President of the Conservative Association, also President of the Union. You were part of that legendary Conservative 'Cambridge mafia' – the list of names is glittering and far too long to read in this interview. But recapture the atmosphere there, because it was an interesting time for Conservatism.

**LAMONT**

I think it was at Cambridge that I first realised that I was interested in a political career. I mean, I could have gone in several directions. I might have been a journalist, I might have been a civil servant, but I knew I was interested in public affairs. And my generation at Cambridge were very political. Almost immediately when I came up, I met Kenneth Clarke, Michael Howard and John Gummer. They were all very keen on politics, and that further energised me and I got into my second year and my third year and they were thinking about standing for Parliament, I thought, well, I might stand for Parliament as well. But that was really how it evolved, and it was a very political time – CND, nuclear weapons. There were some very strong left-wing characters active in the Cambridge Union at the same time. They were very good debaters and very clever people. And so there was a very competitive political atmosphere there, and a lot of argument. And we had the Cuban crisis, where I remember people were really quite scared that we were on the verge of a nuclear war.

**HENNESSY**

The economics faculty, in which you were an undergraduate, was also quite left-wing wasn't it? – Nicholas Kaldor being one of the dominant figures. How did you, with your liberal capitalist instincts, I suppose one might describe them, fit in?

**LAMONT**

I started off reading English, and then I changed to reading economics. It may seem an odd combination, but I think English keeps one human and also provides one with a reading list for the rest of one's life. I changed to economics and did 'Part Two Economics.' I suppose my views then were just conventional Keynesian. Cambridge economics is very influenced by the great genius of Keynes. Kaldor was a brilliant lecturer and, I mean, I might not have liked his politics – not that it showed in his lectures – but he had an extraordinary, ingenious mind, and it was wonderful to listen to him. Mind you, one of the things that is interesting, if you take the great economists, many of them are brilliant prose writers. Alfred Marshall, Keynes, Pigou, and the same is true of Kaldor, Joan Robinson, who of course was sort of Marxist, but she writes so eloquently. It is a pleasure to read the prose of these people. They didn't just reduce it all to a lot of boring algebraic formulae.

**HENNESSY**

You go for the poetry of economics, not the plumbing.

**LAMONT**

The way of thinking –

**HENNESSY**

The way of thinking –

**LAMONT**

The philosophy –

**HENNESSY**

The way of thinking. You went to work, Norman, for Duncan Sandys, a very accomplished senior Conservative Cabinet Minister in the post-war years, who was legendary in Whitehall for being a nightmare to work with – very demanding of his staff. Did you find that was so?

**LAMONT**

No, it was a pleasure, I found, working for him. It was a project to do with nuclear disarmament. It may seem strange that Duncan – who was, you know, quite a hard man politically – but he very much believed in nuclear disarmament, worldwide nuclear disarmament. And what we were working on was the draft of a treaty that we were going to get other countries to sign, undertaking *not* to develop nuclear weapons in exchange for security guarantees.

**HENNESSY**

And you also went into the legendary Conservative Research Department, which was in its pomp in those days, wasn't it? It was a great influence, the Conservative Research Department.

**LAMONT**

Yes, the Conservative Research Department was – it was in Old Queen Street. It was full of very talented people. And you could hear the Guards' bands practising on Horse Guards as well, which was a pleasure.

**HENNESSY**

Who influenced you in the Research Department, amongst the big figures there?

**LAMONT**

Macleod used to come in quite a lot, I think he was the Chairman of the Research Department at the time. Enoch Powell came in a lot. And Enoch Powell was the most formidably clever man I've ever met in my life, I have to say. And he was always challenging and developing ideas.

**HENNESSY**

Then you go into the City for a while – Rothschild Bank, I think.

**LAMONT**

When I went to Rothschilds, I marvel at my own arrogance. I'm rather embarrassed by it, because I said to them, 'I'd like to have a job here, but I eventually intend to go into politics.' How I could be so presumptuous as to, a) be confident I'd get into politics and, b) that they should employ me while I went there temporarily. But I learnt a lot at Rothschilds. It's a wonderful firm, a family firm. I think I learnt a lot about the merits of private businesses as opposed to publicly quoted businesses.

**HENNESSY**

Your first opponent in the 1970 general election in Hull was John Prescott, who was running for the first time. Now, he was a phenomenon in the making. What did you make of the first encounters with JP?

**LAMONT**

Well, I liked John Prescott. He was a rather forbidding figure as an opponent. His sort of pamphlets began with the words, 'Now, Mr Lamont is a banker.'

**HENNESSY**

[*Laughs*] You come into Parliament in a by-election in 1972 for Kingston-upon-Thames, replacing John Boyd-Carpenter, I remember. But it's very interesting reading your maiden speech, Norman, because given where people associate you now in the spectrum of views – the big question of our era, the European question – your very first words in the House of Commons in your maiden speech in July 1972 were, 'I have to admit that for some years I've been strongly pro-European.' Admittedly, you go on instantly to describe how, institutionally, you mustn't rush things, that there has to be a natural evolution of institutions. You mustn't press the federal side of it all. But it's quite an interesting opening sentence for somebody who's ended up where you are.

**LAMONT**

Well, I *was* keen to join the European Economic Community. But I believed in it as an economic idea. Remember, this was the time when tariffs in the world were quite high, so actually there *was* a role and there was something useful for the EEC to do then in cutting tariffs and increasing the flow of trade. And I was strongly in favour of that. But I could see, particularly when I became a minister and engaged with Europe, I could see that the way Europe was going was towards becoming a federal organisation, an organisation very similar to a state called Europe. And personally, I didn't like this and I didn't think it would work. I wasn't sure it would work for other countries, but I didn't think it would work for Britain.

**HENNESSY**

Were you one of the first of the Conservative backbenchers to see the merits of Mrs Thatcher's challenge to Ted? Did you see great potential in her – 1975?

**LAMONT**

Well, I think I did. In the sense that I certainly was an enthusiastic supporter of her when she ran for the leadership. And I felt she had the right approach to economics. I felt the prices and incomes policy had helped to bring about the clash with the miners. I mean, the issue of the miners had to be dealt with, of course, but I felt the – creating this inflationary environment, passing laws on the price of this, the price of that, made clashes with certain interest groups almost inevitable.

**HENNESSY**

When she becomes Prime Minister, she appoints you to a variety of posts, and one of the most interesting ones you had, I think, as a junior minister, was having to deal with the nationalised industries, getting some of them ready for privatisation. Do you look back on that as a particularly fruitful period in your political career? Because it did change the nature of Britain's political economy cumulatively, didn't it, the privatisation programme, in which I have the feeling you probably believed 100 per cent?

**LAMONT**

I did believe 100 per cent. I remember when Margaret appointed me, she said, 'Your job is to work yourself out of a job' – i.e. don't have any industries left in the state sector by the time you finish. Well, of course that would be pretty impossible, but it was a good way of putting it. No, it was very stimulating. I enjoyed working with Norman Tebbit. I also met some marvellous people who were running these state industries, like Ian MacGregor who ran the steel industry and the coal industry. And there was a whole series of these very powerful businessmen who were determined to help us to privatise. I enjoyed working with them, and it was a very pioneering, innovative task to have to do.

**HENNESSY**

When you look at the whole privatisation experience, do you think it went a little bit too far in some of them? Do you think the public utilities should have gone into privatisation?

**LAMONT**

I have no problem with the privatisation of utilities provided they're properly regulated. I think the privatisation of the nuclear industry was pretty problematic, though, and I was not very enthusiastic about that.

**HENNESSY**

The civil nuclear, yes. Not many people will remember this, but you were involved in the Westland crisis of 1986, which I think is the nearest Mrs Thatcher came to being toppled until the end of her time in Number 10. Michael Heseltine walking out of the

Cabinet over government policy on rescuing the Westland heli-copter company in the West Country. And you were Minister of State, Minister for Defence Procurement, so you were right in the eye of that storm, weren't you?

**LAMONT**

To be honest, I felt a sort of personal conflict in it. In that, I mean, I like Michael Heseltine, I respect Michael Heseltine, I thought he was a good Secretary of State for Defence. I didn't actually agree with him on his policy on Westland – or I was sceptical about it – and against him, you had a very close friend of mine, Leon Brittan, in the Department of Trade and Industry. And I felt com-pletely conflicted by this. I also felt, rightly or wrongly, that Mrs Thatcher was treating Michael Heseltine a bit roughly. I mean, he was always complaining that he didn't get a hearing in Cabinet. I mean, some people dispute this. I wasn't there. But I went so far as to tell the Chief Whip that I thought Michael Heseltine was very unhappy about how he was being treated by Mrs Thatcher and they ought to be careful he didn't resign. And of course he *did* resign.

**HENNESSY**

So you had an inkling that he might walk out?

**LAMONT**

I did. He never said anything to me, but I just had an inkling this man is being driven to resign, because he was so angry at the way he was being treated, as he saw it.

**HENNESSY**

In the late '80s, you begin a long spell in the Treasury. I think you're still the only person who's held the three offices of Finan-cial Secretary to the Treasury, Chief Secretary and Chancellor, aren't you?

**LAMONT**

I think so, yes.

**HENNESSY**

Was that, for you, a coming home, given your interests and your background that far? Do you think the Treasury was your natural berth?

**LAMONT**

I was very pleased to go to the Treasury. I had a short period, as you've referred [to], in the Ministry of Defence, but I was not a natural person for the Ministry of Defence. And, to be honest, I didn't much like sort of spending all my life discussing, you know, what the kill ratio of a particular missile was. I found it very difficult. David Cameron once said to me he thought I was the nearest thing in the Conservative Party to a pacifist.

**HENNESSY**

Are you?

**LAMONT**

I'm not, no, I'm not. But I didn't really relish all this sort of talk about defence and strategies and so on. And I was very, very pleased to get out and go to the Treasury.

**HENNESSY**

You're Chief Secretary to the Treasury when Nigel Lawson resigns in 1989 over his disagreements with Professor Alan Walters, Mrs Thatcher's economic adviser. Were you tempted to go with him? Because you were quite close, weren't you?

**LAMONT**

I wasn't tempted to go with him – ironically, for two reasons. One, I didn't myself know very much about his relationship with Alan

Walters. I sympathised with him, but I didn't see it first-hand. But secondly, Nigel was also, I think, resigning partly over Mrs Thatcher's refusal to join the ERM. And –

**HENNESSY**

The Exchange Rate Mechanism –

**LAMONT**

– the Exchange Rate Mechanism. And I wasn't that sympathetic to joining the ERM myself, and I remember I was asked in the House of Commons by Giles Radice why I'd not resigned with Nigel Lawson, and the reply I gave was because I didn't agree with him about the ERM, which was rather ironic as I subsequently, in my own career, got entangled with the ERM. But I did try very hard to persuade Nigel not to resign. I thought Nigel was a brilliant Chancellor of the Exchequer. He was a great person to work for – stimulating, [he] delegated but gave one a clear strategic steer as well. I think he, you know, was a titan in British politics.

**HENNESSY**

Mrs Thatcher is finally persuaded about the European Exchange Rate Mechanism, that the UK should join, in October 1990 by Douglas Hurd as Foreign Secretary and John Major, who was Chancellor of the Exchequer at the time. You obviously had doubts from the beginning. And I think you also had doubts, if we were going to go in, that we went in at far too high a rate, at 2.95 Deutschmarks to the pound. Do you think you should have perhaps resigned over it? Because it became very fundamental to your – the tensions and the stresses and strains within the Major government.

**LAMONT**

Well, I didn't play any part in the decision to join the ERM, and I wasn't asked or told about it right up until the last minute. And

I remember meeting a very senior civil servant in the corridors. I said, 'What have we done this for?' And his reply was, 'It's politics.' And I remember, I just said, 'Well, I don't think I'd have done that.' But I had no participation in the decision. And I mean, as regards the rate at which we joined, I know nothing about how Mrs Thatcher was persuaded to join at that particular rate. To me, it is still a mystery how she was persuaded to join the ERM. I don't really – unless she just felt she couldn't afford to lose another Chancellor of the Exchequer, as she had lost Nigel Lawson.

#### HENNESSY

Why were your instincts so firmly against it? Because you believed in a low inflation economy, and shadowing the hard currency of Europe, the Deutschmark, was thought to be a good way of imposing discipline on us.

#### LAMONT

I wasn't totally against it. I was sort of ambivalent about it, neutral about it. When I said to Giles Radice, 'I don't agree with Nigel Lawson about the ERM,' I explained I believed you could run an economy *either* with a floating exchange rate system *or* a fixed exchange rate system. I personally preferred the flexibility of a floating exchange rate system, but it never occurred to me that it would prove impossible for Britain to remain in the ERM. And people sometimes say to me, 'Well, if your instincts were in favour of floating, why did you accept the job of Chancellor?' Well, I didn't sit down and think, 'Oh my goodness, is this going to turn into a disaster?' We'd lived with fixed exchange rates for a large period since the Second World War – not the ERM, but the Bretton Woods system. And, for that reason, I didn't think, just because we'd now joined the ERM, 'This won't work.' I thought that it'd probably work, like we worked with the Bretton Woods American-dominated, dollar-dominated, fixed exchange rate system.

**HENNESSY**

Mrs Thatcher falls very shortly after that, in November 1990, after Geoffrey Howe's resignation, the third of the great resignations of her premiership: Heseltine, Lawson, and then Howe. In the contest to succeed her, I think you had a disagreement with Nigel Lawson, your friend, because he wanted Michael Heseltine to succeed and you wanted John Major to succeed. Why did you go for John Major and not Michael Heseltine?

**LAMONT**

I had worked with Michael and I respected him. But I knew that Michael was very keen on the European Union and I think would have wanted us probably to join the single currency, would have supported a lot of integration. And I felt that John Major was probably *more* in sympathy – of course he was different – but more in sympathy with what Mrs Thatcher had done than Michael was. And I felt he was more likely to provide continuity with her policies, and I believe I was right.

**HENNESSY**

You became his campaign manager. Do you think you were somewhat – 'misled' is perhaps too strong a word – John Major has this great gift of appearing immensely sympathetic to other people's views. Do you think that you saw characteristics in him, policy beliefs, that weren't entirely there?

**LAMONT**

Possibly, but I think that's a bit harsh. I think I had observed John as Chancellor of the Exchequer – of course, if you're Chancellor of the Exchequer – and I'd seen him as Chief Secretary. If you're either Chief Secretary or Chancellor you have to sound pretty conservative – you are the only person who doesn't want to spend money, you're the only person who's worried about debt, the only person who's worried about borrowing. That was the context in which I had seen John Major, as opposed to Michael Heseltine, who was always wanting to spend more money, borrow more, intervene in industry. I think the context in which I saw John Major was one where he inevitably sounded perhaps more conservative than he really was.

**HENNESSY**

Very interesting. The general election of 1992 is a turn-up for the books, another Conservative majority, albeit much reduced – the sort of apogee of the Major years. And I think you let John Major know that you didn't want to stay for that long at the Treasury, didn't you, in the run-up to the election?

**LAMONT**

I did say that to him, yes.

**HENNESSY**

What was the reason for that? Did you want to go to the Foreign Office and do something different?

**LAMONT**

Well, I think I felt I'd made a number of changes and that, if we got out of the recession, that would be mission accomplished, so to speak. I sometimes got the impression he wasn't that comfortable with me. I did say what you've said, that I didn't want to remain Chancellor for very long. But we also were coming up to the first unified budget and I felt that would be a suitable point at which I could leave, having introduced a major administrative reform.

**HENNESSY**

Bringing the finance and the public spending together.

**LAMONT**

Yes.

**HENNESSY**

Yes. What were the roots of the discomfort between you and John Major?

**LAMONT**

Well, it was just – I think I'm more of a fiscal Conservative, more of a Conservative in economic matters than he was. I don't say that disrespectfully. He has very acute political antennae. I think I sometimes perhaps thought I was taking a longer view than he was taking. We're different personalities. But, you know, it wasn't an impossible partnership; I'm just saying I didn't think it was perhaps as comfortable as he would have liked it.

**HENNESSY**

It's very striking, reading your memoirs, that you found it very difficult to talk to him about your doubts about the Exchange Rate Mechanism, the European Exchange Rate Mechanism, that meetings would be scheduled and he'd want to talk about something else. Presumably that was a cause of tension.

**LAMONT**

Yes. That was quite late on, of course. That was the summer of '92. You've got to understand, however, that taking Britain into the Exchange Rate Mechanism was John Major's great achievement as Chancellor. So, understandably, he was rather reluctant to talk about ditching it as a policy. Whereas to me, I thought the policy – which I had accepted – had done some useful work, had helped to get inflation down, but I could see in the summer of '92 that policy was now too tight. And remaining in this I thought was going to prolong the recession and it would be better if either we got out or we suspended our membership, was what I wanted to do. And I twice tried to have meetings with him to discuss this, but he didn't want to. Initially, I thought he was prepared to, but it turned out he wasn't prepared to do it.

**HENNESSY**

Did you, as the summer deepened, have any feelings in your waters that there could be a great crash, a sterling crash?

**LAMONT**

No –

**HENNESSY**

You didn't –

**LAMONT**

I didn't. I was more worried about the recession not ending and our being driven into a depression. That was what I was really worried about. I didn't foresee what happened on the markets.

**HENNESSY**

Do you rerun in your head, Norman, now and again, the searing events of that Wednesday 16 September 1992? I remember it dawned very hot and warm, and you were up early, and you realised something big was happening. And the day unravelled in the most remarkable way. Do you rerun it as if it's an old movie in your head?

**LAMONT**

No, I don't think about it very much. I mean, I remember it perfectly vividly because it was an important day, but I don't agonise or think about it very much. I mean, people occasionally say to me rather absurd things like, 'What did it feel like?' Well, I didn't sort of sit around asking myself, 'What did it feel like?' As a politician, you're there to deal with crises and all I felt was, 'My goodness, what are we going to do about this?' Well, you know, we must do X, Y or Z. You're just getting on with things.

**HENNESSY**

Mind you, there are points of passion in your written account in your memoirs. For example, at the lunchtime when you want to see John Major to say, 'We really do need to get out, because the losses are so huge on the exchange markets and the Bank of England's intervening and nothing's happening in the way we want.' But you couldn't get to see him. He was seeing a group of backbenchers. And then you're also very passionate about John Major insisting that the big beasts, the other big beasts in the Cabinet, come in to share in the decision taking – Michael Heseltine, Douglas Hurd, Kenneth Clarke – to dip their hands in the blood. That is quite a searing read actually, in your memoirs. Do you still feel very strongly about all that? You are actually quite adamant in the way you've written it, that it should have been a Chancellor–Prime Minister decision, and taken quickly.

**LAMONT**

Well, I do think that. But you know, I'm not having a row with John Major all these years later. I couldn't understand why we couldn't have a meeting to discuss – you know, it was a very serious situation, we were losing money. By the way, one of the misperceptions people have is that I and the Bank of England were spending – within our own discretion – huge amounts of money to try and prop up sterling. This is not correct. We were not intervening very much in the markets at all on Black Wednesday. But once the pound had fallen outside its permitted bands, anyone could turn up in the Bank of England and demand to be paid at the official rate, so the reserves were being run down without us doing anything. It wasn't that we were trying to prop up – this is a myth that has somehow been perpetuated, that there we were stupidly trying to prop up the pound when it couldn't be propped up. But we were losing money because people were converting at the official rate. That made it urgent that we had a meeting. But the Prime Minister, I remember, was engaged with a lot of backbenchers, and then eventually we had this meeting at which there were other Cabinet ministers – Douglas Hurd, Kenneth Clarke, Michael Heseltine – present. Yes, I felt this was – well, I felt it was obvious what we had to do: we had to get out of the ERM. We were out, we'd lost our position and there was no point in arguing over it. But they were very reluctant, and I think maybe John was wise. He decided to make it a more collective decision.

**HENNESSY**

One of the most forlorn pictures of post-war British politics is you having to come out into the street outside the Treasury because Parliament isn't sitting – I think 7.30 in the evening – to announce that we were coming out. It's a terribly bleak moment for the country and for you, and it must be very difficult for you to look back at it with anything other than a bit of horror.

**LAMONT**

Well, I don't feel quite like that. The policy had been upset, but I was perfectly confident within myself that the economy was going to recover, that we would have an independent monetary policy. I knew instinctively where we would go. It was a great setback politically, but I didn't *feel* myself that it was going to have catastrophic economic consequences, and it did not, and I knew that from the word go.

**HENNESSY**

Do you look back and regret that you didn't resign that night? I know you thought about it, and John Major said he didn't want you to.

### LAMONT

No, I'm very glad I didn't resign. I mean, I did think about it and I consulted with colleagues. I didn't sort of selfishly sit there saying, 'I'm not going to resign.' I talked to a large number of Cabinet colleagues, and particularly my good friend Michael Howard. They all said, 'Look, if *you* go, what will happen is that everybody will then turn on the Prime Minister, because it was *his* policy, it was *he* who took us into the ERM, it was *his* whole idea. And if you go, he will be exposed, and you will just be the fall guy.' And John Major also wrote me a little note saying 'Do not resign.' And so I decided not to resign. The reason I'm glad I didn't resign was because I then was able to design a completely new policy for a new relationship with the Bank of England, the regime of inflation targeting, which may all sound rather narrow and trivial, but actually completely changed the way in which monetary policy was operated. It's the system under which the Bank of England operates today, and we took a big step by introducing a degree of openness and glasnost into the Bank of England. It was as near as you could get to making the Bank of England independent without actually doing so. I mean, I wanted to make the Bank of England independent, but I couldn't persuade John Major to do so.

### HENNESSY

That had to wait for Blair–Brown to come in, in '97.

### LAMONT

Yes. I mean, actually I went to see Blair and Brown and told them they should make the Bank of England independent.

### HENNESSY

That's very interesting. Did John Major actually say to you he wanted you to stay as Chancellor in September 1992, [so] as to be his 'lightning conductor'?

**LAMONT**

I can't remember [him saying] that to me, but he said that he thought the Chancellor was just being used as a sort of air-raid shelter for himself.

**HENNESSY**

Yes. When in the following May, '93, he asked you to resign, or to leave the Treasury, [and] he offered you the Department of the Environment, did you feel let down?

**LAMONT**

Well, I did. I mean, I don't want – you know, it doesn't give me any pleasure to go over all these feelings now. But what I felt, rightly or wrongly, I felt I'd done my best to implement his policy, which was one I had always been a little bit sceptical about. I didn't believe there had been anything incompetent in the way it had been handled, Black Wednesday. I know people used the word 'incompetence', but I don't believe there was any incompetence in the way it was handled. By the way, lots of other countries left the ERM. France had a great exchange rate crisis the following year. So, you know, the idea this was a British event and we were chucked out of something – the system collapsed, that was, that was what happened.

**HENNESSY**

Is it true that you and John Major haven't spoken since you resigned?

**LAMONT**

No, no, not at all true.

**HENNESSY**

I wonder where I got that from? – somewhere –

**LAMONT**

Well, no, there was a long period we didn't speak.

**HENNESSY**

Oh, there was a long period, but you're alright now?

**LAMONT**

Yes, well, as I have said to friends, grass grows over the battlefield. But no, I did at the time feel I'd done my best to implement his policy, and it's hardly my fault in a way that it – I mean, I assumed responsibility, but as I've said, it was very much the pressure of colleagues who wanted me to stay on. I also was, in '93 – I mean, this is one of the ironies of politics – but I introduced the toughest-ever budget I think there's probably been in '93, which put up a lot of taxes, was very tight on spending. It was extremely unpopular, and I still think it was the best thing I ever did.

**HENNESSY**

Very interesting. You've got rather a talent, Norman, if you don't mind me saying so, in your memoirs, for quotes. And there are two that struck me, perhaps in the aftermath of Black Wednes-day. One, you quote Virgil, 'In time even these things will appear amusing.' [*Lamont laughs*] And the other one is from Trotsky, of all people – a Conservative quoting Trotsky is quite a collector's item: 'History is the natural selection of accidents.' Do you think your use of Trotsky captures exactly the nature of the crash in 1992?

**LAMONT**

Well, I do. I think history is exactly that. History is a series of unpredicted events which look inevitable with hindsight, but actually very few people foresaw at the time.

**HENNESSY**

The following year, the Conservative Party conference is in

Bournemouth, 1994. And you steal the show at a fringe meeting by making a speech which got enormous coverage and had huge shock value then, in which you talk about life [as] perfectly possible outside the European Union. And I remember, in your memoir, you describe going to Maurice Saatchi's party afterwards and being cut by your former protégé, David Cameron, who'd been your special adviser at the Treasury. Now, that is a moment that, when the history of Britain in Europe is written – the *big* story – people will linger on that moment, won't they? Because you made the political weather for a little while.

**LAMONT**

Yes, well, one of the things that I experienced as Chancellor was coming face to face with the fact that a lot of European politicians believed in creating a federal Europe, a political Europe. I negotiated – it was one of the most important things and one of the most interesting things I did as Chancellor – I negotiated our opt-out from the single currency, making it clear that we would not join the single currency –

**HENNESSY**

This is Maastricht, yes –

**LAMONT**

This was at Maastricht, and that was one of the things I feel, you know, was one of the most important things in which I was involved. But it was that negotiation that convinced me that Europe – why else was the Euro being created? It was being created – not just for economic advantage – it was being created as a political instrument. The Euro was a symbol of the coming together of Europe and the Euro was designed to make it inevitable that you had a common budget, a common fiscal system, a common system of taxation. And I, from the whole time I'd been in politics, had been completely opposed to this. But as Chancellor I realised this was coming and then, when I left the government, I had the freedom to articulate these thoughts. And I first gave a paper to something called the Conservative Philosophy Group outlining all the options, and these were some of the things that are familiar today in the debate about Brexit, like the Norway solution or the Swiss solution. And I then repeated a lot of this in the speech in '94 that I made to the Conservative Party conference, where I was very careful in what I said, that I couldn't see anything that was unambiguously due to us from Europe. I mean, for example, the fact that we trade with Europe; I think we'll trade with Europe whether we're in or out of the EU. I pointed out, as I still do today, that the Swiss economy is more integrated with the European Union than *we* are, and Switzerland is not a member of the European Union. Economic integration does not depend just on political institutions at the superstructure level. And I felt it was important to articulate what I'd experienced as Chancellor, and so I did in '94. And it caused a degree of astonishment in some quarters. No one who'd held high office had said this. And so it had a big impact.

#### HENNESSY

There's one aspect of your time on the backbenches which is intriguing, really. In fact, I think it might have been a bit later; maybe you'd left the backbenches and gone to the House of Lords by this time. But you're regarded as a fairly 'small l' liberal politician in the British tradition of politics. It's your support for General Pinochet, when he was in Britain for medical treatment. And there was a warrant, I think, from a Spanish judge to have him tried for human rights abuses and so on. And you supported him very vociferously. Now, why was that, Norman?

#### LAMONT

Well, I don't like lynch mobs. And I felt that General Pinochet had sort of become a rather demonised figure. I happened to have been in Argentina when the pre-Pinochet government of Salvador

Allende came to power, and I remember seeing the refugees arriving in Buenos Aires fleeing from the Marxist President of Chile, Salvador Allende – people who were absolutely terrified for their livelihood. And, subsequently, Chile went into a period of chaos under Allende, and I understood very well why the military coup had happened. It had happened very much in response to calls from Parliament, calls from public opinion, and the army had taken over. I'm perfectly conscious that there were bad civil rights abuses under the military government.

**HENNESSY**

Really serious ones –

**LAMONT**

Yes, but we know exactly how many people were killed, because there was an examination post-Pinochet of that. And this was a complex situation which could easily have been a civil war in Chile. And I felt this was for the Chileans to judge. I thought it was ridiculous that a Spanish judge, a judge from a country that had not placed a single person on trial for any human rights abuses under Franco, should arrest a foreign head of a military government in another country. I felt that was totally inappropriate. I felt it was for the Chileans to deal with – I think it comes back to my strong belief in national sovereignty, really. And I felt that he should be sent back to Chile and the Chilean courts should judge – which is what subsequently happened.

**HENNESSY**

On perhaps one of the great causes, perhaps the greatest cause of your political life, Europe, you're optimistic about a post-Brexit Britain, aren't you?

**LAMONT**

Yes.

**HENNESSY**

In essence, why? What will it look like?

**LAMONT**

Well, my main reason for supporting Brexit is that we are getting out of a political project, not being part of this attempt to create a political union in Europe, which I think will end in disaster. You have a looming conflict between Italy and the rest of the EU. I mean, I think I'm fearful for the future of the European Union and I think, by being outside it, we will have a more tranquil, more stable existence. I don't believe that we're going to lose economically. I think trade goes where trade wants to go. And our trade, I would guess, will remain very much as it is, the present sort of level, in the future. But we will have the possibility of diversifying our trade with other countries in the world. But my main reason is political rather than economic.

**HENNESSY**

Looking back over the whole sweep of your political career, Norman, did you want to be Prime Minister?

**LAMONT**

No, I don't think I ever did.

**HENNESSY**

Why not?

**LAMONT**

Well, I was very, very interested in economics and public finance. My ambition initially was to be a Member of Parliament. I do think to be a Member of Parliament is a great thing. I love the Palace of Westminster, I love being there. And you know, even when I stopped being Chancellor of the Exchequer and became a backbencher, I loved going there every day. It was a great thing to be a Member of the House of Commons. I was very sad when I lost my seat in '97 because I liked the life of politics, I liked being there, I liked being able to do things, influence things, be part of the great current of events and trying to influence them. For me, I suppose I wanted to be a minister, but I was interested in economics, that was what I was interested in. I would not be any good as Prime Minister. I'm not interested in everything in politics. You have to be interested in everything. You have to have a range of human sympathy that I'm afraid I don't think I have. I have my own *narrow* interest. I would be hopeless as Prime Minister.

### HENNESSY

If by some quirk of fate you found yourself Prime Minister, what would you have done on day one?

### LAMONT

I think I'd have asked for a recount. [*Both laugh*]

### HENNESSY

What trace would you like to leave on history? How would you like to be remembered?

### LAMONT

Well, I'd like to be remembered as somebody who inherited the British economy at a very difficult moment and left it in better condition than it was when I first started. And I believe I did that. Also, [I'm] pleased that I was able to negotiate the opt-out from the single currency.

### HENNESSY

Yes. How do you think you *will* be remembered?

**LAMONT**

Well, I think I'll be remembered for Black Wednesday. I'll tell you what being at the centre of these events has made me: it has made me very sceptical about history. Because when I read the things that are written about things I know about – I mean, they're written admittedly in newspapers, but I think a lot of historians follow what's written in newspapers as well – I'm not convinced that history ever captures the accuracy of what really happened.

**HENNESSY**

I feel suitably chastened, you saying that. If I could grant you one last reform, what would it be? Wave a magic wand for you?

**LAMONT**

Well, I don't know about reform, but I think the great unresolved issue at the moment in public policy is care of the elderly and I'm part of a Lords committee looking into that, but I think that is something that needs to be tackled. It will need more resources. It needs some structural changes as well. It's imposing great costs on local government. It's a looming problem that's getting worse every day.

**HENNESSY**

Norman, thank you very much.

# Peter Hain (Lord Hain of Neath)

Series 7, Episode 4, first broadcast 19 August 2019

**Born** 16 February 1950; **Educated** Pretoria Boys
High School; Emanuel School; Queen Mary,
University of London; University of Sussex

MP (Labour) Neath 1991–2015

Parliamentary Under-Secretary, Wales, 1997–99; Minister of State,
Foreign & Commonwealth Office, 1999–2000; Minister of State,
Energy and Competitiveness in Europe, 2001–01; Minister of State,
Europe, 2001–02; Secretary of State for Wales, 2002–08; Leader of
the House of Commons and Lord Privy Seal, 2003–05; Secretary
of State for Northern Ireland, 2005–07; Secretary of State for Work
and Pensions, 2007–08; Secretary of State for Wales, 2009–10

**Autobiography** *Outside In*, 2012

**HENNESSY**

With me today is Peter Hain, Lord Hain of Neath, whose radical
formation as a boy and a young man took place in the intense
crucible of South African apartheid, before his family were exiled
to Britain in 1966. For all his later rise to senior positions in both
the Blair and Brown Cabinets, he has a vivid place in the national
collective memory as the young man who led the successful

opposition to the planned South African cricket tour of England in 1970. Peter, welcome.

**HAIN**

Thank you very much.

**HENNESSY**

Tell me about your formation and your childhood. You were born in 1950 in Nairobi, in what we then called 'Keenya' because it was still a British colony. Who were your parents and why were they in Kenya?

**HAIN**

My birth in Nairobi was an accident, in a way. My dad's first job on graduating from university in Johannesburg was to work as an architect in Nairobi, and I happened to arrive. My mum was pregnant with me, flying up in an old Dakota from Pretoria to Nairobi. And we spent a bit of time there. And then when I was a tiny toddler they drove all the way back down the length of Africa in a rickety old Lancia Aprilia car with the tyres constantly getting punctured, with the springs breaking, and it was a real adventure. And it was part of an extraordinary upbringing. They were, I think, for me – and not just for me – examples of fantastic parents, who were great fun, very disciplinarian, but also a joy to be with. I was enormously proud of them. And so it was an unusual upbringing, that on the one hand my dad could be teaching me how to play cricket, and then we faced an early morning raid from the Special Branch as young South African anti-apartheid activists, with no record of politics of that kind in their hinterland, on either side – my mum's side or my dad's side. [They] suddenly found themselves drawn into taking a stand against the evil of apartheid and showed enormous courage and great self-sacrifice, and I think were an example of people whose sense of duty propelled them increasingly to do the thing that

they thought was the right thing to do rather than for great ideological reasons.

**HENNESSY**

Now, they obviously shaped you and triggered your sense of injustice, acute sense of injustice, at apartheid. What had triggered
theirs?

**HAIN**

You know, I wrote a book a few years ago called *Ad & Wal* – nick-
names for Adelaine and Walter Hain – *Values, Duty, Sacrifice in
Apartheid South Africa*. And I tried to answer that question. And
I asked *them*, and they couldn't answer it themselves. Events –
they said they just felt that they needed to do things and support
people, and things got worse and worse for them. So, initially, the
police were raiding our house in the early 1960s – one of my earliest memories was being woken up finding Special Branch officers
in the bedroom I shared with my brother, aged about ten. A year
later, aged eleven, woken up in the early hours to be told that my
mum and dad had been jailed for supporting Nelson Mandela's
defiance campaign. They were released without charge after two
weeks because the police couldn't find incriminating evidence
against them, which actually was a draft leaflet that they'd been
in a black township to share with comrades, that my mum had
chewed up and spat out rather than reveal to the Special Branch
officers –

**HENNESSY**

– the comrades being the South African Liberal Party.

**HAIN**

They were members of the South African Liberal Party, which
at that time was the only legal non-racial party. The Progressive
Party of Helen Suzman believed in a qualified franchise – that's to

say, based on property. It was not universal, one person one vote. And although I have great admiration for Helen, my mum and dad's liberalism was very radical and very committed to universal franchise.

### HENNESSY

The early '60s was an extraordinary time because the British Prime Minister, Harold Macmillan, outraged the South African parliament with his 'Wind of Change' speech in Cape Town in 1960. And then there's the Sharpeville massacre very shortly afterwards – terrible carnage – when you were ten years old, I think. It is an extraordinary formation, Peter, compared to most radical British politicians, however strongly people feel injustice, to be living every hour of every day with what you were seeing and hearing.

### HAIN

None of my school friends with whom I played had anything like that experience. We were unique in Pretoria – the citadel, the capital of apartheid, especially at that time in the grim early '60s, where the police state was ubiquitous, and apartheid laws there went into every nook and cranny of society, from sport to sex. It was an extraordinary experience. So politics and radical politics was in my DNA, in a way. And it was life and death politics. People were literally dying. Friends were – were disappearing, being assassinated, and tortured, and so on. It was difficult on the one hand, and yet my mum and dad had this extraordinary ability to be abnormal compared with all their peers and relatives, but at the same time to be normal with their kids and their kids' friends – playing with us, officiating and marshalling at our bike races in our garden and things like this. They were a great model for how you *should* behave as parents.

### HENNESSY

There's an extraordinary, searing experience, which you vividly recall in your memoir, of a family friend – John Harris – who was involved in the bomb at Johannesburg railway station, being executed – a great family friend. At the age of 15, you had to do a reading next to his coffin – he'd only been executed a few hours earlier – because I think the authorities wouldn't let your father speak. Now, that is – is an *extraordinarily* searing experience for anybody of any age but, for a 15-year-old schoolboy, it must have been amazing.

**HAIN**

Yes it was. And it was not something I'd ever expected to do. I was quite a private, shy young boy, and people may find that surprising now. But the night before John Harris's execution, we realised that my dad, who was banned at the time, was denied permission to read the funeral address and officiate, in a way. There was nobody to do it. And I sort of offered. I didn't expect them to say, and his widow Anne to say, 'Yes, we'd like you to do it, that would be lovely, Peter.' But the whole experience with John Harris was fundamental to us and determined our future and helped propel us into exile.

**HENNESSY**

I think we should point out that you were not in favour of direct action that involved bombing and so on, but it was family friendship that was the basis of this.

**HAIN**

I always admire my mother and father for this as well. They completely opposed John Harris's decision to plant a bomb in Johannesburg railway station. Although he'd intended it out of desperation – there were many young white radicals, including liberals like him, who felt the same way – out of desperation that *all* the opposition had been closed down. Nelson Mandela was in prison. The high command of the ANC had been arrested. The ANC itself, the African National Congress, was illegal. John Harris felt he had to do something. And his chosen 'something' was to plant a bomb on Johannesburg railway station, to issue a 15-minute telephone warning explicitly to the police and to newspapers – and that was confirmed at his trial – to clear the concourse. He hadn't meant to kill anybody. But nevertheless he did, because they deliberately ignored his warning. It served their interests to actually have that bomb go off and kill an old lady, maim her young granddaughter and injure many others. My mum and dad completely opposed the violent strategy that the African Resistance Movement – of which John Harris became a member along with others of their friends, who tried to recruit them – because they thought it would play into the hands of the state. My dad, who'd served in the Italian campaign in the Second World War with the South African army, had a real detestation of violence. But they stood by his widow, Anne, and tiny boy, David, who came to stay with us. And that increased the pressure on the family because we were vilified. They took a stand. They disagreed with what John had done, but they didn't want to desert his family.

### HENNESSY

There's another family friend – I suppose you could call him that – Alan Paton, the great author of *Cry, the Beloved Country*. And you got to know him as a young man, and he said something to you which has stayed with you ever since, I think.

### HAIN

Yes, I met him at his house, the Long View – above Durban, outside Durban – when my mum and dad were driving around during the state of emergency. And he made a huge impression on me. And he said something to me which stuck – I was only ten at the time. He said, 'Don't be an all or nothing person, Peter. Be an all or *something* person.' And that has guided me in my politics ever since, to do something rather than to try everything and achieve little, if anything.

**HENNESSY**

The circumstances became so bleak that the family decided to come to Britain and make your family home in Putney.

**HAIN**

We steamed out of Cape Town in March 1966, and I remember looking at Robben Island – and Nelson Mandela was of course in there at that time – and that made a huge impression on me. And then we arrived in Southampton on a grey, drizzly April morning. What I didn't know was it was the day after the general election, when Labour had stormed to victory under Harold Wilson in a landslide, and there were Labour posters up on the window of the friend of my parents who was putting us up. And I remember seeing television for the first time. So this was an awakening. And then the following weekend my mum and dad went on a CND march, a Campaign for Nuclear Disarmament march, and my brother and I – 16 and 14 – went to see our team, Chelsea, play for the first time at Stamford Bridge.

**HENNESSY**

I think you were an engineer originally, you went to Imperial College and realised it wasn't for you. And you came under the spell of the magical Maurice Peston at Queen Mary College, in the East End of London, and did economics and found your niche.

**HAIN**

The LSE turned me down, as I think [I was] too much of a radical threat by then. And Maurice Peston and Trevor Smith enthusiastically welcomed me. And I had a wonderful three years, university degree there.

**HENNESSY**

You became a great public figure at a very young age because of protesting about the anticipated South African cricket tour of

England in 1970. Now, where did the idea come from that this was a way of getting at the apartheid regime, and that direct action involving the sacred green swards of the legendary English cricket grounds might be the way to do it?

### HAIN

It was non-violent direct action, and it was born out of the late 1960s ferment that I was sucked into as an 18-year-old, becoming increasingly interested in politics, reading voraciously, going to anti-Vietnam War demonstrations, reading about the sit-ins at Berkeley University in California and the LSE, and reading about non-violent direct action in the Gandhian tradition. And I was frustrated, first of all that white South African sports tours – and they were white South Africans, they were called 'South Africa' but they were *never* South Africa, they only became so after – after the transformation. As a sports-mad, young white South African, I knew how important sport was to the white apartheid elite. It was *so* critical to their whole morale. Apartheid was shunned across the world, but they were feted – the mighty Springboks were at Twickenham or the cricket team was at Lord's. And, over the years, the anti-apartheid movement had admirably protested outside Lord's or Twickenham, but to no effect. I came up with the idea of deploying non-violent direct action by running on the pitches and physically stopping the matches. And we started to do that, me and a few of my friends in the Young Liberals, in the summer of 1969. And it escalated to the point where the 'Stop the Seventy Tour' campaign was launched in September 1969 and, although it was my idea, I never expected to be the leader of it until others propelled me into that role. And I found myself suddenly, at age 19, being interviewed on every radio and television programme, on the front pages and the sports pages of the newspapers and becoming a notorious national figure – hated by the people on the right of politics and most sports fans, who didn't understand what we were doing wrecking their sport by running on the pitch at Twickenham and Murrayfield and Cardiff Arms Park and Swansea and so on and stopping the mighty Springboks who toured in '69, '70.

**HENNESSY**

You were different to student protesters weren't you, because you were a very earnest young man, you were very trim and tidy, had roll-neck sweaters – very polite, not hirsute at all.

**HAIN**

No, I wasn't.

**HENNESSY**

You were a very serious young man, weren't you?

**HAIN**

[*Laughing*] I suppose. I probably – I could be regarded as a bit of a boring young bloke as well.

**HENNESSY**

No, I wouldn't quite put it like that. [*Both laugh*]

**HAIN**

I mean, I'm afraid I was not into the late '60s sex, drugs and rock'n'roll scene. I was more interested in the radical politics. In fact, it absorbed my life. Yes, I suppose I was pretty earnest and dedicated. My dad particularly always said to me – and I had read Nelson Mandela's great aphorism about making a difference. The point, he said, to paraphrase, is not just to be there as a person, it's to make a difference. And I always tried to make a difference. Trade was going on, arms deals were going on – we were doing our best to fight that, but that's *really* difficult stuff, whereas here we could strike a blow against apartheid, which proved seminal in that, that year, South Africa, white South Africa, never toured in cricket and rugby again to Britain. And very shortly afterwards was kicked out by Australia and subsequently New Zealand after similar campaigns. White South Africa found herself isolated from world sport, which they craved. And so it was an enormously successful campaign, as Nelson Mandela pointed out when I first met him in 1991, and he said to me 'that campaign – the thing about it was we were on Robben Island in a news blackout then.' [He] didn't know about the man on the moon in 1969 and a lot of other world events, but their warders were such fanatical Spring-bok fans that they vented their fury at the demonstrations and the disruption on Mandela and his comrades, not realising they were communicating something absolutely precious: that there were thousands of people outside fighting for them.

**HENNESSY**

Why did your radicalism go down Young Liberal channels, because you've always had a socialistic element in your make-up, haven't you?

**HAIN**

Yes. When I formed my ideas in the sort of '68, '69, '70 period, I believed I was a libertarian socialist – not state control and eve-rything organised from the top, but from the bottom upwards, as it were: industrial democracy rather than nationalisation, to simplify it. And the Young Liberals, when I first got involved and joined in late '67, early '68, were very radical. They called themselves the 'Red Guards', after the – you know – the Mao '66 episode. And they had a very flamboyant leadership that was very good at catching the headlines, and they enthused me. And that's why I joined them and got involved and eventually became Young Liberal National Chairman in 1971.

**HENNESSY**

Your family came under direct attack from the South African

security forces with that letter bomb. It's extraordinary. Your sister Sally was opening this parcel, I think on the kitchen table, and then suddenly you realised it was a bomb. I mean, that's extraordinary, isn't it?

**HAIN**

Yes. It happened exactly that way. There was a pile of campaign material. My younger sister, Sally, in June 1972 – I was still living with my parents in Putney at their home – and suddenly, on the breakfast table, pulled out of a large envelope, was this contraption with terminals and wires constructed around a balsa wood base. And it turned out to be the kind of bomb that was assassinating anti-apartheid leaders worldwide – Ruth First, for example, a notable anti-apartheid leader whom I knew from London, was subsequently killed by exactly that kind of bomb. I was just very lucky that when Scotland Yard's IRA bomb squad came down – in the blink of an eyelid, it seemed, after we'd alerted the police – to make it safe, they said it would have blown not just me but the whole family and the house as well up. So I was very lucky indeed.

**HENNESSY**

Now, how did you get drawn into Labour politics? I think your friend Neil Kinnock had something to do with it.

**HAIN**

Yes. By the mid-1970s, I was becoming increasingly dissatisfied in the Young Liberals and the Liberal Party. I couldn't be a Young Liberal forever. I was, by 1977 when I decided to join the Labour Party, 27. And Neil Kinnock had been active in the anti-apartheid movement and had supported my appeal during my 1972 conspiracy trial. He'd been a Labour figure to support fundraising to help my defence. And so I went to him and said I wanted to join the Labour Party and could he advise me, because I was very well known then, and I wasn't sure whether I'd be well received.

Although I was very radical and I was a socialist and had been, as you pointed out, since my formative years, I was nevertheless from the Liberals, who were bitter rivals. And my entry was also encouraged by Tony Benn, whom I went to see privately. They were, of course, Benn and Kinnock, to end up bitter foes, but they were both really encouraging and supportive to me and it was the best decision that I made.

**HENNESSY**

You stand for Putney a couple of times, losing to David Mellor. What was it like cutting your teeth in electoral politics? Did you turn out to be good at it?

**HAIN**

You know, I never expected, when I joined the Labour Party – and never wanted, when I was in the Young Liberals – to be an MP. And I was asked, in Putney Labour Party – having been a member for a few years and campaigned very vigorously locally – to stand. And I got selected, much to my surprise. And then I found I really enjoyed it and *loved* the campaigning. Putney was notionally a marginal seat that we'd lost in 1979. And I fought it again also during the high noon of Thatcherism in 1987 – and lost again, despite running a magnificent campaign with hundreds of workers. And that's when my friends encouraged me, virtually instructed me, to seek a safe seat. And, by a remarkable series of coincidences that started with Michael Foot asking me to get involved in the selection for his own seat which he was vacating, retiring from –

**HENNESSY**

Ebbw Vale, yes –

**HAIN**

Yes. But as a result of that, I met trade unionists, and one of them rang me up – sitting in my office in the Union of Post Office

Workers, which I'd gone to work for as a research officer, having left university – rang me up and said, 'Peter, the selection in Neath is wide open. The MP surprisingly just announced the previous Friday evening that he's going to retire. You should go for it.' This is 1990.

#### HENNESSY

Did you know much about Wales? You've fallen in love with Wales big time ever since. You're very eloquent about Wales. You love it –

#### HAIN

I do, yes –

#### HENNESSY

But how much did you know then when you were selected as a candidate for Neath?

#### HAIN

I didn't really know Wales or its culture, to be perfectly frank, so it was a very fast learning curve. But I absolutely loved it. And somebody said to me, a bit of a wag said to me, 'Well, you may not be Welsh, Peter, but at least you're not bloody English.' [*Both laugh*] It wasn't said with venom, by the way, but just with a great deal of humour. And I just loved the culture and the valley politics and got involved, and actually was part of energising a local party that was just used to winning instead of campaigning for it. I treated it like a marginal seat, which actually – given that there were just six or seven months between me being selected and then suddenly a by-election appearing with the MP dying tragically – if I hadn't treated it as a marginal seat, down there every weekend from my job in London, campaigning and living in the constituency whenever I could and becoming known, I think I would have faced quite a difficulty in the subsequent by-election, particularly from Plaid Cymru, who ran a very aggressive campaign.

**HENNESSY**

Your relationship with Tony Blair, it's very interesting. You've never entirely been part of 'one of us', Blair Project, have you?

**HAIN**

No. I was never a Blairite. And they didn't pretend that I was. They were a bit suspicious of me. But I really liked Tony Blair as a person, and he was very generous towards me. He knew I was not of his particular New Labour politics, I was more radical and independently minded and occasionally caused waves and some irritation to him by saying things where I disagreed.

**HENNESSY**

About taxation, for example?

**HAIN**

Yes –

**HENNESSY**

Radical – radical views on higher taxes.

**HAIN**

Yes, indeed. I thought that the rich should pay more and middle Britain was being taxed too highly, and I said that in the Nye Bevan Lecture shortly after he'd appointed me Leader of the House of Commons as well as Secretary of State for Wales, because I'd been in the Cabinet then nearly a year. But Tony Blair was very good to work for. He was somebody who was very willing – although he ran a tight ship, a very Blairite kind of praetorian guard around his mission – if he trusted you, he'd delegate to you and let you get on with it, until you made a mistake. He was an easy person to work with. He was very visionary, very politically attuned. Tragically, over Iraq, [he] made a decision to invade which I supported as a Cabinet minister because I believed the intelligence, as we all did at the time. It was shown to be completely wrong and really, on that basis, we went to war on a lie, which I'll always regret. And it tarnished his own reputation, and I don't think the public ever forgave him for that. And yet, I was proud to be in that Labour government. I didn't think we were radical enough on some things; I thought Tony Blair neglected our base and our core traditional party members and values in that sense. And I think we paid a high price for it afterwards, and in a way paved the way to Corbynism – but that's another story. But we did amazing things: bringing devolution – constitutional innovation, the Freedom of Information Act, the Human Rights Act; doubling spending on the National Health Service; rescuing public services and railways that, frankly, were on their last legs when we took power in 1997; a statutory minimum wage. The list goes on and on. And I'm enormously proud of what we achieved and that I was able to be a minister in his government achieving it.

**HENNESSY**

I think one particular pleasure of your ministerial life, a singular pleasure really, is being made Minister for Africa in the Foreign Office. I think you relished every minute, didn't you?

**HAIN**

I did. I was –

**HENNESSY**

You were the last District Commissioner we sent – [*Hain laughs*]

**HAIN**

I was the only African-born British Minister for Africa that there's ever been. And Africa was a kind of third-order issue in the Foreign Office's sort of lexicon, for understandable reasons – you know, the Middle East and others were higher up. But I really prioritised Africa and loved it. And of course going back to South

Africa as Minister for Africa, and being feted at my old school and speaking at Pretoria Boys High – that's quite emotional even recalling it – to a mixed set of boys in the school assembly. When I was there, it was whites-only by law. Watching them play sport, mixed sport – that was not permitted. I was never allowed to play sport with or against anybody who wasn't white. So it was profoundly moving. And I decided also – and the old Alan Paton, Nelson Mandela, you know, 'Do something and make a difference,' which were my watchwords – I decided to focus on arms dealers flying in arms and getting paid in blood diamonds, to Angola and Sierra Leone, where we had British forces, and the Democratic Republic of Congo. Because I was receiving intelligence on my desk every day, virtually, saying we knew what they were doing, we were tracking their planes and all the rest of it, and we were doing nothing. I sort of had an argument with senior mandarins in the Foreign Office and with the secret intelligence service and with GCHQ, and said, 'Look, you know, we've got to do something. This is killing people.' In fact, these arms were being flown into Liberia, smuggled across the border and being used to shoot at our squaddies. And we were doing nothing. Now, there was a very good argument, which is you don't want to compromise your sources. British intelligence has a pretty long reach, and I got very close to it and worked closely with them and, you know, applaud and admired them. But I – anyway, a long battle, that took several months, I persuaded them to allow me to use the information and, via a planted question in Foreign Office Questions in early 2000, named these arms dealers for the first time, putting a lot of them out of business. They went absolutely ape about it and tried to sue me. Well, you can't, I'm using parliamentary privilege, which I was careful to do. And I particularly, I named Viktor Bout – a former KGB agent – as the merchant of death, because he was the primary arms runner. But that intervention led eventually to him being arrested and he's in jail. And there are books about him called *The Merchant of Death*, and I think a television programme the same.

So there was that, and then the other occasion where I'm proud I made a difference, though it left me uncomfortable as well, is I knew British policy had pretty well neglected Angola. I thought Angola was – had enormous potential to rejuvenate Africa. It's *immensely* rich in natural resources, from food to minerals. And there was this bitter civil war [with] the rebel UNITA army led by Jonas Savimbi, and we knew where he was but the Angolan army didn't. And, after a long battle, I persuaded both intelligence services and Foreign Office officials that I would pass the information to the Angolan army. They found him and they killed him. And as I *knew* would happen, the civil war ended. And Angola, many years later – because there was a corrupt governing elite at the time – is now beginning to show its real potential. So my watchword was making a difference, and I think those examples were ones where [I] did.

#### HENNESSY

Now we've talked briefly about Iraq – it's obviously left a deep scar on you, Peter, in the way that it has on many who were in that Cabinet [and] who went along with the decision on the basis of the intelligence as presented. But you had considerable pressure from your parents about that, and Nelson Mandela picked up the phone to you, didn't he? What did he say?

#### HAIN

By that stage, I had become close friends with Nelson Mandela. It was one of the privileges I had, to be greeted by him when I'd gone back as African Minister – 'Return of the prodigal son,' he told me and the waiting media. And he phoned me. Whereas he'd always been courteous and I never heard a bad thing said about anybody except Robert Mugabe, but he phoned me – and it was as if he was breathing fire on the phone – to say, 'You must tell Tony Blair, I've tried to get through to him, that this Iraq' – and this is on the eve of the invasion – 'this is going to *damage* Tony and damage you all. You're doing great work. He's doing fantastic work across the world and in Africa, but this is going to finish him.' And my mum and dad took the same view. My dad actually drafted a memorandum to me, which was uncannily prescient. And he was right, and Mandela was right, and I was wrong.

**HENNESSY**

Is that your greatest single regret in your political life?

**HAIN**

Yes, in geopolitical terms, undoubtedly. It was part of a collective Cabinet – unlike Robin Cook, my friend who resigned over it. No, I was wrong over it. My greatest regret, actually, was standing for the deputy leadership of the Labour Party in 2007. I'd been encouraged to do so, almost prompted to do so, by trade unionists and MPs and others. I did stand. I did badly. And people who said they supported me, actually encouraged me to stand, then went for other people. That's politics. But the worst thing about it was becoming embroiled in – in a thing to do with the failure to declare the donations that we'd received, some of them. £100,000 were properly declared in –

**HENNESSY**

In your campaign, yes –

**HAIN**

– in my campaign to be Deputy Leader. And I'd insisted they [be] properly declared. And somehow we didn't declare a great chunk of the other donations – not a penny went missing, not a penny came to me. But, as a result of that, the Electoral Commission unaccountably decided to – they're the regulators and they play an important role and it's important the rules are followed. And I went to them and I shopped myself. I said, 'I've discovered, to my horror some months later' – by now I was Secretary of State for Work and Pensions under Gordon Brown – 'that we hadn't declared all our donations.' I went to them and I said, 'We haven't declared them. These are the ones we haven't declared, but I don't know about the others.' And I uncovered – after painstaking work, which took weeks and weeks and weeks – lots of other unreported donations, and then they referred me to the police. And I had to resign. And the police investigated and referred it to the Director of Public Prosecutions, who found I wasn't responsible anyway under the law –

**HENNESSY**

And you were able to come back into office –

**HAIN**

And I was able to come back into office. But it really – they say all political careers end in failure. Well, mine didn't, as it happened, but it nearly did. And it left a really unpleasant taste, because I've been accused of lots of things, politically – for the views I held and things I did, like stopping the 1970 cricket tour – but never for sort of lack of integrity.

**HENNESSY**

When you've spoken about that episode in the past you've been quite interesting in describing yourself as still a bit of an outsider in Labour politics – insider/outsider is the theme of your memoir.

**HAIN**

The book, yes, yes.

**HENNESSY**

But this was an example of perhaps still being seen as an outsider, because you did much more poorly than anybody would have expected in that ballot.

**HAIN**

Yes, I think it was. And I suppose, coming from outside Britain and coming from outside British politics and yet becoming an insider: a member of the Privy Council; a Secretary of State; serving in the Cabinet for seven years, in the government as a whole for 12; being entrusted with some of the state's most precious secrets by the intelligence services, who'd kept an eye on me as a young anti-apartheid activist, by the way – the head of MI5 came to confess to me when I was looking into it as a Foreign Office minister. And yet I suppose I always saw, and see, British life in a different way from somebody like you, born in Britain. For a start, I'm not part of the class system –

**HENNESSY**

Yes –

**HAIN**

Everybody in Britain is born into the class system, whether –

**HENNESSY**

– branded on the tongue. And your – your tongue and accent are very distinctive, but they're not part of the class structure. [*Hain laughs*]

**HAIN**

They are not, no. So I suppose I viewed things as an outsider and perhaps in that election was seen as a bit of an outsider as well.

**HENNESSY**

I think, as an outside observer of your career, the most extraordinary moment – or certainly one of them, the most productive – is when you get Northern Ireland onto a new trajectory after the elections which produced a Sinn Fein–DUP executive: the St Andrews Agreement. Now, that's extraordinary, getting Ian Paisley to sit down with Adams and McGuinness and to actually pull off that deal. That was extraordinary at the time, but it still seems remarkably extraordinary looking back on it. Now, what was the key? Was your 'outsiderdom' a help there, because they knew you had form?

### HAIN

It was – in a different way to what I expected. And of course it happened after years of my predecessors as Secretary of State and of course Tony Blair's game-changing Good Friday Agreement, and all the work that had gone on. But I was – found myself in the position, dealing with the top dogs, being the DUP and Sinn Fein, Ian Paisley and Gerry Adams, Martin McGuinness. And Ian Paisley and I couldn't have been more different. I'm an 'on-the-left' radical; Ian Paisley was on the right. And we'd had disagreements on Northern Ireland as well over – over the years. And yet we became really close friends. And I – I remember having a – his 80th birthday. I invited him and the whole Paisley clan – you know, there were grandkids running around and under the banqueting table – to dinner to celebrate his 80th birthday.

### HENNESSY

In Hillsborough Castle?

### HAIN

At Hillsborough Castle, the official residence of the Secretary of State, where famous summits took place. And so building that relationship with him, getting to know him, understanding him, at the same time Gerry Adams and Martin McGuinness – they were both amongst the most professional negotiators I've ever come across. And managing to bring them together involved taking risks: threatening to introduce water charges, threatening to bring the political class down by withdrawing their salaries and the funding for their staff. They weren't doing their jobs, I said to the public in Northern Ireland and because –

**HENNESSY**

Because it's direct rule again, yes –

**HAIN**

– because it was direct rule and the Assembly was suspended. And so there were risks, because if you did bring the political class down – some of my predecessors were really worried about it – but I knew you had to take risks, because this was – you know, politics, I learnt, revolves around timing. Sometimes things come together at particular times, like the fall of the Berlin Wall in 1989 and the end of the Cold War. And by the way, I'd also experienced that in South Africa, the release of Mandela by de Klerk and that particular conjunction of forces. And I felt this was a moment for Tony Blair, as Prime Minister, Bertie Ahern as Taoiseach, the two of them really close, and Ian Paisley maybe fulfilling his destiny, and Adams and McGuinness, you know, getting into the latter stages of their political careers: this was the moment you did it or you didn't. If we'd missed that, I don't know that it'd have come round again. And it was the most fulfilling thing that I was able to help achieve.

**HENNESSY**

You've talked about your relationship with Tony Blair and his qualities. What about Gordon Brown? One of the most complicated and fascinating figures of recent British politics. You managed to get on with him pretty well, as well. You weren't part of the 'civil war'. The TB–GB civil war, were you?

**HAIN**

I wasn't. I was neither a Brownite nor a Blairite. And for that reason Gordon Brown, in some respects, was a bit wary of me. And his inner clique were, too. Because Gordon, unfortunately – though I think he's a giant of a figure and an immensely values-based person, of great stature and who'd been, by the way, our

Edinburgh organiser for the 'Stop the Seventy Tour' campaign back in 1969, '70 – is somebody, unlike Tony Blair, who was much more comfortable in his own skin and secure as an individual, Gordon Brown was a towering figure, an enormous brain, very well read, an ability to talk and understand the history of the Labour movement in Britain in a unique way, as he still does. And I enormously admired him and liked him as a person. But he didn't really delegate properly. And trust people. And when you're Prime Minister – and it was his own tragedy that, as Prime Minister, a job that he'd coveted for so long – it's such a big job, you've got to have people around you. And Tony Blair had the Alastair Campbells and the Sally Morgans and, above all, the Jonathan Powells – you could ring them up and you could say, 'What does Tony think about this idea?' And they'd either tell you straight away, as a Cabinet minister or a minister, or go away and find out and come straight back to you. Gordon Brown's inner circle was not like that at all. And yet I think his finest hour was rescuing Britain – and, in some cases, though people parodied it at the time, rescuing the world – from the global financial crisis by insisting that the G20 adopted a Keynesian demand management, public investment-led recovery to drag the world out of this private sector banking collapse and stop it plunging from recession into depression. And he did the same with the British economy.

**HENNESSY**

You've ended up, as so many Cabinet ministers do, in the Valhalla of Cabinet ministers: the House of Lords. And I get the impression you rather relish it. You come a lot, you talk a lot in a good way. And yet you've been frightfully rude about the House of Lords in the past. [*Hain laughs*] There was a time when you wanted to put a match to it. Have you changed your mind?

**HAIN**

I never wanted to put a match to it, but Ed Miliband – out of the blue

– asked me to go to the Lords. I said, 'Well, I don't agree with the place. I think it should be elected.' To which his reply was, 'That's why I want you there. As Prime Minister, I want to reform it.' So that's why I went, in a way. Of course, he didn't become Prime Minister. I think it should be at least 80 per cent elected, representing the whole of the country properly, and 20 per cent appointed. I *am* struck at the level of expertise there. The quality of the debate and the contributions are of a far higher nature [than] the House of Commons, having spent a quarter of a century as an MP. So, you know, I think it performs an admirable role. And yes, I have been active, particularly on my concern about the future of the Irish border on the Brexit crisis, and in using the Lords on two examples of parliamentary privilege: one to expose President Zuma of South Africa and the Gupta brothers, and the other to name Sir Philip Green.

**HENNESSY**

Did you ever want to be Prime Minister?

**HAIN**

You know, in standing for Deputy Leader, I'd hoped maybe to become Deputy Prime Minister. But I didn't seriously think that anybody from my background could do that job. And seeing it at close quarters, particularly under Tony Blair, and also the terrible pressures Gordon Brown went under during the financial crisis, I mean, it's a huge job, and I'm not sure I would have risen to that. But I am immensely privileged and grateful to have had the chance to contribute in government and to make a difference.

**HENNESSY**

If you had become Prime Minister, what would you have done on day one?

**HAIN**

I would have declared a climate change emergency and ordered the building of the Severn Barrage. Because I think climate change is such a gigantic threat to humankind. And I say the Severn Barrage because it is this vast natural energy generator through tidal power, which is lunar orientated, of course, so it's predictable, it can become base-load as well – equivalent to at least two nuclear power stations. It's a *vast* untapped resource.

**HENNESSY**

What trace do you think you'll leave on history?

**HAIN**

Well, I suppose two sons and seven grandchildren so far, and over 20 books. I hope people might remember me as somebody who took a stand on principle even when it was unpopular to do so, and tried to make a difference.

**HENNESSY**

If I could give you one last reform, wave a magic wand for you, what would it be?

**HAIN**

To establish a National Care Service to parallel the National Health Service. The chronic scandal, and it's almost criminal, of elderly care – and my wife, Elizabeth, and I have experienced this recently ourselves, personally – you know, just neglecting this, we can't continue to do so. And it cannot be resolved by private means alone. We've all got to pay more taxes and establish a proper National Care Service.

**HENNESSY**

Peter Hain, thank you very much indeed.

**HAIN**

Thank you.

# Picture Credits

Page xvi: Shirley Williams speaking at the launch of the Social and Liberal Democrats party in March 1988

Page 32: Jack Straw with Tony Blair at the Labour Party Conference in September 2004 (© Mike Goldwater/Alamy)

Page 58: Norman Tebbit with Prime Minister Margaret Thatcher at the reopening of the Grand Hotel in Brighton two years after it was bombed (© Simon Dack Archive/Alamy)

Page 84: Neil Kinnock addressing an anti-racism rally in Cardiff, July 1978 (© Robin Weaver/Alamy)

Page 106: John Major during the 1997 election campaign (© Mike Abrahams/Alamy)

Page 124: Roy Hattersley photographed on the terrace of the House of Commons (© Aardvark/Alamy)

Page 148: David Steel at the Liberal Party Conference in Brighton, September 1977 (© Keystone Pictures USA/Alamy)

Page 170: Margaret Beckett at a coal miners march in Hyde Park, February 1993 (© Doug Taylor/Alamy)

Page 194: David Owen speaking to crowds through a megaphone on the election trail in Sittingbourne, August 1987 (© Trinity Mirror/Mirrorpix/Alamy)

Page 220: Nigel Lawson, on stage with Margaret Thatcher and Kenneth Baker, receiving a standing ovation at the 1989 Conservative Party Conference in Blackpool (© Trinity Mirror/Mirrorpix/Alamy)

Page 246: Clare Short on the campaign trail before the Welsh devolution referendum of 1997 (© Jeff Morgan 15/Alamy)

Page 276: Michael Heseltine pictured touring Toxteth after riots in July 1981 (© Trinity Mirror/Mirrorpix/Alamy)

Page 310: Vince Cable speaking on Brexit in London, June 2017 (© Guy Corbishley/Alamy)

Page 340: Margaret Hodge at the Fabian Society New Year Conference in London, January 2017 (© WENN Rights Ltd/ Alamy)

Page 370: Kenneth Baker and Margaret Thatcher at the Conservative Party Conference in Bournemouth, 1990 (© Peter Jordan/Alamy)

Page 410: Tony Blair and his supporters during Labour's 1997 election campaign (© Ali Russell/Alamy)

Page 444: William Hague being introduced to Barack Obama by David Cameron in London, July 2008 (© Tom Stoddart/ Hulton Archive/Getty Images)

Page 472: Harriet Harman and Sadiq Khan at the Labour Party leadership election results, held at the Queen Elizabeth II Conference Centre in London, September 2015 (© WENN Rights Ltd/Alamy)

Page 498: Michael Howard and Margaret Thatcher at the opening of the Eurotunnel in Folkestone, 1994 (© Homer Sykes/Alamy)

Page 532: Paddy Ashdown photographed in June 1990 (© Peter Macdiarmid/Hulton Archive/Getty images)

Page 564: Sayeeda Warsi at the Hay Festival of Literature and the Arts, 2017 (© Keith Morris/Hay Ffotos/Alamy)

Page 596: David Blunkett arriving for his first day as an MP in 1987 with his guide dog, Paddy (© Stephen O'Connell/Alamy)

Page 624: Iain Duncan Smith speaking to assembled media outside the Houses of Parliament after Theresa May called a general election, April 2017 (© Jack Taylor/Getty Images)

Page 658: Chris Patten on the campaign trail for the 1992 general election in Bath (© Martin Beddall / Alamy Stock Photo)

Page 686: Alan Johnson with Lord Chancellor and Justice Secretary Jack Straw at the Labour Party Conference in

Brighton, 2009 (© Allstar Picture Library Ltd / Alamy Stock Photo)

Page 718: Norman Lamont and his treasury team preparing for the March 1993 budget (© Allstar Picture Library Ltd / Alamy Stock Photo)

Page 748: Peter Hain addressing Arms for South Africa protesters in Whitehall, July 1970 (© Trinity Mirror / Mirrorpix / Alamy Stock Photo)

# Index